SIXTY-EIGHTH ANNUAL ISSUE

THE MINISTERS MANUAL

(Doran's)

1993 EDITION

Edited by

JAMES W. COX

HarperSanFrancisco
A Division of HarperCollins*Publishers*

Editors of THE MINISTERS MANUAL

G. B. F. Hallock, D.D., 1926–1958
M. K. W. Heicher, Ph.D., 1943–1968
Charles L. Wallis, M.A., M.Div., 1969–1983
James W. Cox, M.Div., Ph.D.

Translations of the Bible referred to and quoted from in this book are indicated by their standard abbreviations, such as NRSV (New Revised Standard Version) and NIV (New International Version). In addition, some contributors have made their own translations and others have used a mixed text.

Other acknowledgments are on page 329.

THE MINISTERS MANUAL FOR 1993.
Copyright © 1992 by James W. Cox. All rights reserved. Printed in the United States of America. For information address HarperCollins Publishers, 10 East 53rd Street, New York, NY 10022.

Library of Congress Catalog Card Number
25–21658
ISSN 0738–5323

92 93 94 95 96 HAD 10 9 8 7 6 5 4 3 2

This edition is printed on acid-free paper that meets the American National Standards Institute Z39.48 Standard.

CONTENTS

PREFACE

The Ministers Manual is designed to be of help to ministers of many different communions. Materials offered here can suggest, challenge, and stimulate with fresh, creative ideas that enrich through a kind of cross-fertilization. It helps to get out of one's familiar environment occasionally and explore freely! Some pastors habitually choose their biblical texts and themes in a somewhat hit-or-miss fashion, depending on the sense of congregational need or personal preoccupation to decide what the sermon will be. Others regularly follow lectionaries and preach on the set lesson or lessons for the day. In either case, pastors will find in this volume help for what they consider their needs to be.

One sermon for each of the fifty-two Sundays is topically based and the other follows the Gospel selection in the lectionary. Sermon Suggestions, a weekly feature, is based (usually) on an Old Testament reading and an Epistle reading. These lectionary messages and brief outlines are according to the 1983 *Common Lectionary*. The lectionary for 1993 in Section I, however, is *The Common Lectionary (Revised, 1992)*. The changes do not affect substantially the lectionary messages based on the Gospel, but differences will be noted in a comparison of Old Testament and Epistle readings in the two lectionaries.

I am continually reminded that *The Ministers Manual* offers significant aids not only to pastors, but also to laypeople—for teaching, for devotional talks, and for personal inspiration. Letters from around the world, as well as casual conversation with ministers and others, indicate the wide use of this volume.

I continue to be grateful for the contributions of many individuals who provide me with materials from their own reading and ministry that go into *The Ministers Manual*. I wish to express gratitude also for the practical encouragement given by the trustees of the Southern Baptist Theological Seminary and President Roy Honeycutt and to thank publishers for permission to quote from their material. Alicia Gardner, office services supervisor, and Keitha Brasler, who typed the manuscript, also have my profound gratitude for their careful attention to the production of this volume. In addition, I am most appreciative of the faithful work of the editorial staff at Harper/San Francisco.

James W. Cox
The Southern Baptist Theological Seminary
2825 Lexington Road
Louisville, Kentucky 40280

SECTION I.
General Aids and Resources
Civil Year Calendars

1993

JANUARY	FEBRUARY	MARCH	APRIL

JANUARY

S	M	T	W	T	F	S
					1	2
3	4	5	6	7	8	9
10	11	12	13	14	15	16
17	18	19	20	21	22	23
24	25	26	27	28	29	30
31						

FEBRUARY

S	M	T	W	T	F	S
	1	2	3	4	5	6
7	8	9	10	11	12	13
14	15	16	17	18	19	20
21	22	23	24	25	26	27
28						

MARCH

S	M	T	W	T	F	S
	1	2	3	4	5	6
7	8	9	10	11	12	13
14	15	16	17	18	19	20
21	22	23	24	25	26	27
28	29	30	31			

APRIL

S	M	T	W	T	F	S
				1	2	3
4	5	6	7	8	9	10
11	12	13	14	15	16	17
18	19	20	21	22	23	24
25	26	27	28	29	30	

MAY

S	M	T	W	T	F	S
						1
2	3	4	5	6	7	8
9	10	11	12	13	14	15
16	17	18	19	20	21	22
23	24	25	26	27	28	29
30	31					

JUNE

S	M	T	W	T	F	S
		1	2	3	4	5
6	7	8	9	10	11	12
13	14	15	16	17	18	19
20	21	22	23	24	25	26
27	28	29	30			

JULY

S	M	T	W	T	F	S
				1	2	3
4	5	6	7	8	9	10
11	12	13	14	15	16	17
18	19	20	21	22	23	24
25	26	27	28	29	30	31

AUGUST

S	M	T	W	T	F	S
1	2	3	4	5	6	7
8	9	10	11	12	13	14
15	16	17	18	19	20	21
22	23	24	25	26	27	28
29	30	31				

SEPTEMBER

S	M	T	W	T	F	S
			1	2	3	4
5	6	7	8	9	10	11
12	13	14	15	16	17	18
19	20	21	22	23	24	25
26	27	28	29	30		

OCTOBER

S	M	T	W	T	F	S
					1	2
3	4	5	6	7	8	9
10	11	12	13	14	15	16
17	18	19	20	21	22	23
24	25	26	27	28	29	30
31						

NOVEMBER

S	M	T	W	T	F	S
	1	2	3	4	5	6
7	8	9	10	11	12	13
14	15	16	17	18	19	20
21	22	23	24	25	26	27
28	29	30				

DECEMBER

S	M	T	W	T	F	S
			1	2	3	4
5	6	7	8	9	10	11
12	13	14	15	16	17	18
19	20	21	22	23	24	25
26	27	28	29	30	31	

1994

JANUARY

S	M	T	W	T	F	S
						1
2	3	4	5	6	7	8
9	10	11	12	13	14	15
16	17	18	19	20	21	22
23	24	25	26	27	28	29
30	31					

FEBRUARY

S	M	T	W	T	F	S
		1	2	3	4	5
6	7	8	9	10	11	12
13	14	15	16	17	18	19
20	21	22	23	24	25	26
27	28					

MARCH

S	M	T	W	T	F	S
		1	2	3	4	5
6	7	8	9	10	11	12
13	14	15	16	17	18	19
20	21	22	23	24	25	26
27	28	29	30	31		

APRIL

S	M	T	W	T	F	S
					1	2
3	4	5	6	7	8	9
10	11	12	13	14	15	16
17	18	19	20	21	22	23
24	25	26	27	28	29	30

MAY

S	M	T	W	T	F	S
1	2	3	4	5	6	7
8	9	10	11	12	13	14
15	16	17	18	19	20	21
22	23	24	25	26	27	28
29	30	31				

JUNE

S	M	T	W	T	F	S
			1	2	3	4
5	6	7	8	9	10	11
12	13	14	15	16	17	18
19	20	21	22	23	24	25
26	27	28	29	30		

JULY

S	M	T	W	T	F	S
					1	2
3	4	5	6	7	8	9
10	11	12	13	14	15	16
17	18	19	20	21	22	23
24	25	26	27	28	29	30
31						

AUGUST

S	M	T	W	T	F	S
	1	2	3	4	5	6
7	8	9	10	11	12	13
14	15	16	17	18	19	20
21	22	23	24	25	26	27
28	29	30	31			

SEPTEMBER

S	M	T	W	T	F	S
				1	2	3
4	5	6	7	8	9	10
11	12	13	14	15	16	17
18	19	20	21	22	23	24
25	26	27	28	29	30	

OCTOBER

S	M	T	W	T	F	S
						1
2	3	4	5	6	7	8
9	10	11	12	13	14	15
16	17	18	19	20	21	22
23	24	25	26	27	28	29
30	31					

NOVEMBER

S	M	T	W	T	F	S
		1	2	3	4	5
6	7	8	9	10	11	12
13	14	15	16	17	18	19
20	21	22	23	24	25	26
27	28	29	30			

DECEMBER

S	M	T	W	T	F	S
				1	2	3
4	5	6	7	8	9	10
11	12	13	14	15	16	17
18	19	20	21	22	23	24
25	26	27	28	29	30	31

Church and Civic Calendar for 1993

1 New Year's Day
  The Name of Jesus
5 Twelfth Night
6 Epiphany
10 The Baptism of Jesus
17 Missionary Day
18 Confession of St. Peter
   Martin Luther King, Jr.
   Day
19 Robert E. Lee's Birthday
25 Conversion of St. Paul

1 National Freedom Day
2 Presentation of Jesus in
  Groundhog Daythe Temple
3 Four Chaplains Memorial
  Day
7 Race Relations Sunday
12 Lincoln's Birthday
14 St. Valentine's Day
14–21 Brotherhood Week
15 Susan B. Anthony Day
   Presidents' Day
22 Washington's Birthday
23 Shrove Tuesday
24 Ash Wednesday
28 First Sunday in Lent

5 World Day of Prayer
7 Second Sunday of Lent
  Purim
14 Third Sunday of Lent
17 St. Patrick's Day
21 Fourth Sunday of Lent
   Passion Sunday
25 The Anunciation
28 Fifth Sunday of Lent

4 Palm Sunday
  Passion Sunday (alternate)

Daylight Saving Time
Begins
4–10 Holy Week
6 Pesach
8 Maundy Thursday
9 Good Friday
11 Easter Sunday
14 Pan American Day
18 Easter (Orthodox)
25 St. Mark, Evangelist
30 Arbor Day

1 Law Day
  Loyalty Day
  May Day
  St. Philip and St. James,
  Apostles
4 National Teacher Day
2–9 National Family Week
9 Festival of the Christian
  Home
  Mother's Day
15 Armed Forces Day
16 Rural Life Sunday
20 Ascension Day
22 National Maritime Day
23 Victoria Day
26 Shavuoth
30 Pentecost (Whitsunday)
31 Memorial Day

6 Trinity Sunday
11 St. Barnabas, Apostle
13 Children's Day
14 Flag Day
20 Father's Day
24 Nativity of St. John the
   Baptist
29 St. Peter and St. Paul,
   Apostles

1 Canada Day (Canada)
4 Independence Day
22 St. Mary Magdalene
25 St. James the Elder,
   Apostle

AUGUST

4 Civic Holiday (Canada)
6 The Transfiguration
15 Mary, the Mother of Jesus
19 National Aviation Day
24 St. Bartholomew, Apostle

SEPTEMBER

5 Labor Sunday
6 Labor Day
12 Rally Day
17 Citizenship Day
16 Rosh Hashanah
21 St. Matthew, Apostle and
Evangelist
24 American Indian Day
25 Yom Kippur
26 Senior Citizens Day
28 Frances Willard Day
29 St. Michael and All Angels
30 Sukkoth

OCTOBER

3 World Communion
Sunday
4 Child Health Day
8 Simchat Torah
10 Laity Sunday
Thanksgiving Day
(Canada)
11 Columbus Day
15 World Poetry Day
18 St. Luke, Evangelist
24 United Nations Day
28 St. Simon and St. Jude,
Apostles
31 Reformation Day

Halloween
National UNICEF Day

NOVEMBER

1 All Saints' Day
2 Election Day All Souls' Day
5 World Community Day
11 Armistice Day
Remembrance Day
(Canada)
Veterans' Day
12 Elizabeth Cady Stanton
Day
14 Stewardship Sunday
21 Bible Sunday
Thanksgiving Sunday
25 Thanksgiving Day
28 First Sunday of Advent
30 St. Andrew, Apostle

DECEMBER

5 Second Sunday of Advent
9 Hanukkah
10 Human Rights Day
12 Third Sunday of Advent
15 Bill of Rights Day
17 Wright Brothers Day
19 Fourth Sunday of Advent
21 St. Thomas, Apostle
24 Christmas Eve
25 Christmas Day
26 St. Stephen, Deacon and
Martyr
Boxing Day (Canada)
27 St. John, Apostle and
Evangelist
28 The Holy Innocents,
Martyrs
31 New Year's Eve
Watch Night

The Common Lectionary for 1993

The following Scripture lessons are commended for use in public worship by various Protestant churches and the Roman Catholic church and include first, second, Gospel readings, and Psalms, according to Cycle A from January 3 to November 25 and according to Cycle B from November 28 to December 26. (Copyright 1992 Consultation on Common Texts.)

January 3: Jer. 31:7–14 (alt.); Sir. 24:1–12 (alt.); Ps. 147:12–20 (alt.); Wisd. of Sol. 10:15–21 (alt. resp.); Eph. 1:3–14; John 1:(1–9), 10–18.

EPIPHANY SEASON

January 10: Isa. 60:1–6; Ps. 72:1–7, 10–14; Eph. 3:1–12; Matt. 2:1–12 or Isa.

42:1–9; Ps. 29; Acts 10:34–43; Matt. 3:13–17.

January 17: Isa. 49:1–7; Ps. 40:1–11; 1 Cor. 1:1–9; John 1:29–42.

January 24: Isa. 9:1–4; Ps. 27:1, 4–9; 1 Cor. 1:10–18; Matt. 4:12–23.

January 31: Mic. 6:1–8; Ps. 15; 1 Cor. 1:18–31; Matt. 5:1–12.

February 7: Isa. 58:1–9a (9b–12); Ps. 112:1–9 (10); 1 Cor. 2:1–12 (13–16); Matt. 5:13–20.

February 14: Deut. 30:15–20 (alt.); Sir. 15:15–20 (alt.); Ps. 119:1–8; 1 Cor. 3:1–9; Matt. 5:21–37.

February 21 (Transfiguration): Exod. 24:12–18; Ps. 2 (alt.); Ps. 99; 2 Pet. 1:16–21; Matt. 17:1–9.

LENT

February 24 (Ash Wednesday): Jl 2:1–2, 12–17 (alt.); Isa. 58:1–12 (alt.); Ps. 51:1–17; 2 Cor. 5:20b–6:10; Matt. 6:1–6, 16–21.

February 28: Gen. 2:15–17; 3:1–7; Ps. 32; Rom. 5:12–19; Matt. 4:1–11.

March 7: Gen. 12:1–4a; Ps. 121; Rom. 4: 1–5, 13–17; John 3:1–17 (alt.); Matt. 17:1–9 (alt.).

March 14: Exod. 17:1–7; Ps. 95; Rom. 5: 1–11; John 4:5–42.

March 21: 1 Sam. 16:1–13; Ps. 23; Eph. 5:8–14; John 9:1–41.

March 28: Ezek. 37:1–14; Ps. 130; Rom. 8:6–11; John 11:1–45.

April 4 (Palm/Passion Sunday): Matt. 21:1–11 (Palms); Ps. 118:1–2, 19–29 (Palms); Isa. 50:4–9a; Ps. 31:9–16; Phil. 2:5–11; Matt. 26:14–27:66 (alt.); Matt. 27:11–54 (alt.).

April 5 (Monday): Isa. 42:1–9; Ps. 36:5–11; Heb. 9:11–15; John 12:1–11.

April 6 (Tuesday): Isa. 49:1–7; Ps. 71:1–14; 1 Cor. 1:18–31; John 12:20–36.

April 7 (Wednesday): Isa. 50:4–9a; Ps. 70; Heb. 12:1–3; John 13:21–32.

April 8 (Thursday): Exod. 12:1–4 (5–10), 11–14; Ps. 116:1–2, 12–19; 1 Cor. 11:23–26; John 13:1–17, 31b–35.

April 9 (Good Friday): Isa. 52:13–53:12; Ps. 22; Heb. 10:16–25 (alt.); Heb. 4:14–16, 5:7–9; John 18:1–19:42.

April 10 (Saturday): Job 14:1–14 (alt.); Lam. 3:1–9, 19–24 (alt.); Ps. 31:1–4,

15–16; 1 Pet. 4:1–8; Matt. 27:57–66 (alt.); John 19:38–42 (alt.).

SEASON OF EASTER

(Easter Vigil): Gen. 1:1–2:4a; Ps. 136:1–9, 23–26; Gen. 7:1–5, 11–18; 8:6–18; 9:8–13; Ps. 46; Gen. 22:1–18; Ps. 16; Exod. 14:10–31, 15:20–21; Exod. 15:1b–13, 17–18 (resp.); Isa. 55:1–11; Isa. 12:2–6 (resp.); Bar. 3:9–15, 32–4:4 (alt.); Prov. 8:1–8, 19–21; 9:4–6 (alt.); Ps. 19; Ezek. 36:24–28; Pss. 42 and 43; Ezek. 37:1–14; Ps. 143; Zeph. 3:14–20; Ps. 98; Rom. 6:3–11; Ps. 114; Matt. 28:1–10.

April 11 (Easter): Acts 10:34–43 (alt.); Jer. 31:1–6 (alt.); Ps. 118:1–2, 14–24; Col. 3:1–4 (alt.); Acts 10:34–43 (alt.); John 20:1–18 (alt.); Matt. 28:1–10 (alt.).

(Easter Evening): Isa. 25:6–9; Ps. 114; 1 Cor. 5:6b–8; Luke 24:13–49.

April 18: Acts 2:14a, 22–32; Ps. 16; 1 Pet. 1:3–9; John 20:19–31.

April 25: Acts 2:14a, 36–41; Ps. 116:1–4, 12–19; 1 Pet. 1:17–23; Luke 24:13–35.

May 2: Acts 2:42–47; Ps. 23; 1 Pet. 2:19–25; John 10:1–10.

May 9: Acts 7:55–60; Ps. 31:1–5, 15–16; 1 Pet. 2:2–10; John 14:1–14.

May 16: Acts 17:22–31; Ps. 66:8–20; 1 Pet. 3:13–22; John 14:15–21.

May 20 (Ascension): Acts 1:1–11; Ps. 47; Eph. 1:15–23; Luke 24:44–53.

May 23: Acts 1:6–14; Ps. 68:1–10, 32–35; 1 Pet. 4:12–14; 5:6–11; John 17:1–11.

SEASON OF PENTECOST

May 30 (Pentecost): Acts 2:1–21 (alt.); Num. 11:24–30 (alt.); Ps. 104:24–34, 35b; 1 Cor. 12:3b–13 (alt.); Acts 2:1–21 (alt.); John 20:19–23 (alt.); John 7:37–39 (alt.).

June 6 (Trinity): Gen. 1:1–2:4a; Ps. 8; 2 Cor. 13:11–13; Matt. 28:16–20.

June 13: Gen. 18:1–15 (21:1–7)+; Ps. 116:1–2, 12–19+; Rom. 5:1–8; Matt. 9:35–10:8 (9–23).

June 20: Gen. 21:8–21+; Ps. 86:1–10, 16–17+; Rom. 6:1b–11; Matt. 10:24–39.

June 27: Gen. 22:1–14+; Ps. 13+; Rom. 6:12–23; Matt. 10:40–42.

July 4: Gen. 24:34–38, 42–49, 58–67+; Ps. 45:10–17+; Song 2:8–18 (alt. resp.)+; Rom. 7:15–25a; Matt. 11:16–19, 25–30.

July 11: Gen. 25:19–34+; Ps. 119:105–112+; Rom. 8:1–11; Matt. 13:1–9, 18–23.

July 18: Gen. 28:10–19a+; Ps. 139:1–12, 23–24+; Rom. 8:12–25; Matt. 13:24–30, 36–43.

July 25: Gen. 29:15–28+; Ps. 105:1–11, 45b+ (alt.); Ps. 128+; Rom. 8:26–39; Matt. 13:31–33, 44–52.

August 1: Gen. 32:22–31+; Ps. 17:1–7, 15+; Rom. 9:1–5; Matt. 14:3–21.

August 8: Gen. 37:1–4, 12–28+; Ps. 105:1–6, 16–22, 45b+; Rom. 10:5–15; Matt. 14:22–33.

August 15: Gen. 45:1–15+; Ps. 133+; Rom. 11:1–2a, 29–32; Matt. 15:(10–20), 21–28.

August 22: Exod. 1:8–2:10+; Ps. 124+; Rom. 12:1–8; Matt. 16:13–20.

August 29: Exod. 3:1–15+; Ps. 105:1–6, 23–26, 45c+; Rom. 12:9–21; Matt. 16:21–28.

September 5: Exod. 12:1–14+; Ps. 149+; Rom. 13:8–14; Matt. 18:15–20.

September 12: Exod. 14:19–31+; Ps. 114 (alt.)+; Exod. 15:1b–11, 20–21 (alt. resp.)+; Rom. 14:1–12; Matt. 18:21–35.

September 19: Exod. 16:2–15+; Ps. 105:1–6, 37–45+; Phil. 1:21–30; Matt. 20:1–16.

September 26: Exod. 17:1–7+; Ps. 78:1–4, 12–16+; Phil. 2:1–13; Matt. 21:23–32.

October 3: Exod. 20:1–4, 7–9, 12–20+; Ps. 19+; Phil. 3:4b–14; Matt. 21:33–46.

October 10: Exod. 32:1–14+; Ps. 106:1–6, 19–23+; Phil. 4:1–9; Matt. 22:1–14.

October 17: Exod. 33:12–23+; Ps. 99+; 1 Thess. 1:1–10; Matt. 22:15–22.

October 24: Deut. 34:1–12+; Ps. 90:1–6, 13–17+; 1 Thess. 2:1–8; Matt. 22:34–46.

October 31: Jos. 3:7–17+; Ps. 107:1–7, 33–37+; 1 Thess. 2:9–13; Matt. 23:1–12.

November 1 (All Saints' Day): Rev. 7:9–17; Ps. 34:1–10, 22; 1 John 3:1–13; Matt. 5:1–12.

November 7. Jos. 24:1–3a, 14–25+; Ps. 78:1–7+; 1 Thess. 4:13–18; Matt. 25:1–13.

November 14: Judg. 4:1–7+; Ps. 123+; 1 Thess. 5:1–11; Matt. 25:14–30.

November 21 (Christ the King): Ezek. 34:11–16, 20–24; Ps. 100; Eph. 1:15–23; Matt. 25:31–46.

November 25 (Thanksgiving Day): Deut. 8:7–18; Ps. 65; 2 Cor. 9:6–15; Luke 17:11–19.

ADVENT

November 28: Isa. 64:1–9; Ps. 80:1–7, 17–19; 1 Cor. 1:3–9; Mark 13:24–37.

December 5: Isa. 40:1–11; Ps. 85:1–2, 8–13; 2 Pet. 3:8–15a; Mark 1:1–8.

December 12: Isa. 61:1–4, 8–11; Ps. 126 (alt.); Luke 1:46b–55 (alt. resp.); 1 Thess. 5:16–24; John 1:6–8, 19–28.

December 19: 2 Sam. 7:1–11, 16; Luke 1:47–55 (alt. resp.); Ps. 89:1–4, 19–26 (alt.); Rom. 16:25–27; Luke 1:26–38.

CHRISTMAS SEASON

December 25: Isa. 9:2–7; Ps. 96; Tit. 2:11–14; Luke 2:1–14 (15–20); Isa. 62:6–12; Ps. 97; Tit. 3:4–7; Luke 2:(1–7), 8–20); Isa. 52:7–10; Ps. 98; Heb. 1:1–4 (5–12); John 1:1–14.

December 26: Isa. 61:10–62:3; Ps. 148; Gal. 4:4–7; Luke 2:22–40.

Four-Year Church Calendar

	1993	1994	1995	1996
Ash Wednesday	February 24	February 16	March 1	February 21
Palm Sunday	April 4	March 27	April 9	March 31
Good Friday	April 9	April 1	April 14	April 5

Easter	April 11	April 5	April 16	April 7
Ascension Day	May 20	May 12	May 25	May 16
Pentecost	May 30	May 22	June 4	May 26
Trinity Sunday	June 6	May 29	June 11	June 2
Thanksgiving	November 25	November 24	November 23	November 28
Advent Sunday	November 28	November 27	December 3	December 1

Forty-Year Easter Calendar

1993 April 11	2002 March 31	2012 April 8	2022 April 17
1994 April 3	2003 April 20	2013 March 31	2023 April 9
1995 April 16	2004 April 11	2014 April 20	2024 March 31
1996 April 7	2005 March 27	2015 April 5	2025 April 20
1997 March 30	2006 April 16	2016 March 27	2026 April 5
1998 April 12	2007 April 8	2017 April 16	2027 March 28
1999 April 4	2008 March 23	2018 April 1	2028 April 16
2000 April 23	2009 April 12	2019 April 21	2029 April 1
2001 April 15	2010 April 4	2020 April 12	2030 April 21
	2011 April 24	2021 April 4	2031 April 13
			2032 March 28

Traditional Wedding Anniversary Identifications

1 Paper	7 Wool	13 Lace	35 Coral
2 Cotton	8 Bronze	14 Ivory	40 Ruby
3 Leather	9 Pottery	15 Crystal	45 Sapphire
4 Linen	10 Tin	20 China	50 Gold
5 Wood	11 Steel	25 Silver	55 Emerald
6 Iron	12 Silk	30 Pearl	60 Diamond

Colors Appropriate for Days and Seasons

White. Symbolizes purity, perfection, and joy and identifies festivals marking events, except Good Friday, in the life of Jesus: Christmas, Epiphany, Easter, Eastertide, Ascension Day; also Trinity Sunday, All Saints' Day, weddings, funerals. Gold may also be used.

Red. Symbolizes the Holy Spirit, martyrdom, and the love of God: Good Friday, Pentecost, and Sundays following.

Violet. Symbolizes penitence: Advent, Lent.

Green. Symbolizes mission to the world, hope, regeneration, nurture, and growth: Epiphany season, Kingdomtide, Rural Life Sunday, Labor Sunday, Thanksgiving Sunday.

Blue. Advent, in some churches.

Flowers in Season Appropriate for Church Use

January. Carnation or snowdrop.
February. Violet or primrose.
March. Jonquil or daffodil.
April. Lily, sweet pea, or daisy.
May. Lily of the valley or hawthorn.
June. Rose or honeysuckle.

July. Larkspur or water lily.
August. Gladiolus or poppy.
September. Aster or morning glory.
October. Calendula or cosmos.
November. Chrysanthemum.
December. Narcissus, holly, or poinsettia.

Historical, Cultural, and Religious Anniversaries in 1993

Compiled by Kenneth M. Cox

1983 (10 years). *February 22:* U.S. government offers to buy all the homes and businesses of Times Beach, Missouri, (pop. 2,400) because of hazardous soil contamination with dioxin. *April 12:* Harold Washington is sworn in as Chicago's first black mayor. *June 13:* Unmanned spacecraft *Pioneer 10* becomes the first man-made vehicle to leave the solar system. *August 21* Benigno Aquino, political enemy of Philippine President Ferdinand Marcos, is assassinated as he returns to Manila from the U.S. *September 1:* Soviet fighter pilot shoots down a South Korean commercial jetliner, killing 269 people. *November 2:* President Reagan signs legislation honoring Martin Luther King, Jr., with a federal holiday to commemorate his birthday.

1968 (25 years). *January 2:* Tet offensive begins as Vietcong and North Vietnamese forces attack numerous South Vietnamese cities. *January 23:* U.S. Navy intelligence ship USS *Pueblo* is seized by North Koreans, who hold the crew in captivity for eleven months. *March 16:* U.S. troops kill hundreds of men, women, and children in massacre at My Lai village in South Vietnam. *March 31:* President Johnson announces that he will not seek reelection. *April 4:* Martin Luther King, Jr., is assassinated outside his Memphis motel room. *May 2:* Houston surgeon Denton Cooley performs the first successful U.S. heart transplant. *June 5:* Sen. Robert F. Kennedy is assassinated in a hotel kitchen following a celebration of his victory in the California Democratic presidential primary. *July 1:* U.S., U.S.S.R., the United Kingdom, and fifty-eight other nations sign a nuclear nonproliferation treaty at the U.N. *August 20:* Soviet troops occupy Czechoslovakia. *Debut:* Uniform Monday Holiday Law.

1953 (40 years). *March 5:* Soviet leader Josef Stalin dies at seventy-three, after a quarter century of ruling the Soviet Union. *May 29:* Edmund Hillary ascends Mount Everest for the first time. *June 19:* Julius and Ethel Rosenberg are executed

for transmitting U.S. atomic secrets to the Soviets. *Debuts:* American Stock Exchange; Church of Scientology; IBM computer; *Playboy; TV Guide.*

1943 (50 years). *January 27:* At the Casablanca conference during World War II, President Roosevelt, British Prime Minister Churchill and French General de Gaulle demand the unconditional surrender of Germany, Italy, and Japan. *February 8:* Allied forces take Guadalcanal in the Solomon Islands. *June 4:* Juan Peron takes power in Argentina. *June 14:* U.S. Supreme Court invalidates a West Virginia law requiring schoolchildren to salute the flag under threat of expulsion. *July 25:* Italian premier Benito Mussolini resigns along with his cabinet. *Debuts:* American Broadcasting Company; Jefferson Memorial; Pentagon; term *antibiotic;* United Nations.

1918 (75 years). *January 8:* President Wilson outlines his fourteen points for peace in a message to Congress. *January 18:* The Union of Soviet Socialist Republics is officially proclaimed. *February 5:* Church and state are officially separated in Russia. *March 3:* Russian Bolshevik government signs the Treaty of Brest-Litovsk with Germany. *April 21:* German flying ace Baron Manfred von Richtofen, the "Red Baron," is shot down after scoring eighty Allied kills. *November 11:* Armistice signed between Germany and the Allies ends hostilities on the western front. *Debuts:* Automatic pop-up toaster; International Church of the Four-Square Gospel; Raggedy Ann doll; Ripley's "Believe It or Not!"; U.S. airmail stamps.

1893 (100 years). *August 30:* Louisiana politician Huey Long born (died September 10, 1935). *June 20:* Lizzie Borden acquitted of murdering her parents with an ax. *September 16:* Settlers rush to stake claims in northern Oklahoma Territory as the federal government officially opens the land. *Debuts:* Automobile carburetor; Cream of Wheat; Ferris wheel; Juicy Fruit chewing gum.

1868 (125 years). *February 21:* U.S. House of Representatives votes to impeach President Andrew Johnson for "high crimes and misdemeanors." *July 28:* Fourteenth Amendment to the Constitution is ratified. *Debut:* Memorial Day.

1843 (150 years). *Debuts: The Economist;* typewriter.

1818 (175 years). *July 30:* Novelist Emily Bronte born (died 1848). *October 20:* U.S.–Canadian border established at the forty-ninth parallel. *Debuts:* Brooks Brothers; hymn "Silent Night."

1783 (200 years). *January 21:* France's Louis XVI goes to the guillotine. *February 1:* France declares war on Britain and Holland, and Spain a month later. *February 25:* President Washington holds the first U.S. cabinet meeting, with his secretaries of state, treasury, and war and his attorney general and postmaster general.

April 22: President Washington issues a Proclamation of Neutrality in the British-French War. *October 16:* Marie Antoinette is executed in Paris. *November 10:* Worship of God is abolished in Paris, and a "cult of reason" is founded.

1693 (300 years). The Amish sect has its beginnings in schism from Mennonite church in Switzerland, led by Swiss Mennonite bishop Jacob Amman.

1643 (350 years). *May 14:* France's Louis XIII dies, succeeded by his four-year-old son, who begins a seventy-two-year reign as Louis XIV. *August or September:* English-American religious enthusiast Anne Marbury Hutchinson, scorned by Massachusetts Puritans, is killed by Indians. *September 25:* Assembly of Westminster institutes Presbyterianism in England. *Debut:* Barometer.

Anniversaries of Hymn Writers and Hymn-Tune Composers in 1993

Compiled by Hugh T. McElrath

25 years (1968). *Death* of Ferdinand Q. Blanchard (b. 1876), author of "Word of God, across the ages"; Leo Sowerby (b. 1895), composer of PERRY ("The people who in darkness walked"), ROSEDALE ("Come, risen Lord"); Healey Willan (b. 1880), composer of ST. BASIL ("Eternal, unchanging, we sing to thy praise").

50 years (1943). *Birth* of Mark Blankenship, author of "As we gather round the table," "In the family of God," "In the presence of the Lord," and others; composer of JUDSON, JACKSON, NORTH PHOENIX, KNEEL, and others; Gracia Grindal, author of "A light from heaven shone around," "The desert shall rejoice," and others; Granton Douglas Hay, author of "The Christ who died but rose again," "A lamp for our feet has been given," and others; Ken Medema, author/composer of "Come, let us reason" COME, LET US REASON and many others; McNeil Robinson II, composer of HAMPTON ("While shepherds watched their flocks"). *Death* of William Charter Piggot (b. 1872), author of "For those we love within the veil"; Geoffrey Turton Shaw (b. 1879),

composer of LANGHAM ("Father eternal, ruler of creation"), LIME STREET ("Brightest and best of the sons of the morning"); GILLAM ("Sunset and evening star"), DYM-CHURCH ("O worship the Lord in the beauty of holiness").

75 years (1918). *Birth* of Gene Bartlett (d. 1988), author/composer of "Tell the good news" RHEA, "Set my soul afire" SCALES, and others; R. T. Brooks, author of "Thanks to God whose word was spoken." *Death* of Henry Montagu Butler (b. 1833), author of "Lift up your hearts! we lift them to the Lord"; William Boyd Carpenter (b. 1841), author of "Before thy throne, O God, we kneel"; J. Wilbur Chapman (b. 1859), author of "Jesus! What a friend for sinners," "One day," and others; Charles C. Converse (b. 1832), author of "What a friend we have in Jesus"; Joseph H. Gilmore (b. 1834), author of "He leadeth me! O blessed thought"; Annie S. Hawks (b. 1835), author of "I need Thee every hour"; Henry Scott Holland (b. 1847), author of "Judge eternal, throned in splendor"; Charles Hubert Hastings Parry (b. 1848), composer of RUSTINGTON ("God whose giving knows no ending"), REPTON ("How clear is our vocation, Lord"), JERUSALEM ("And did those feet in ancient time"), and others; Alfred Scott Scott-Gatty (b. 1847), composer of WELWYN ("Lord God of hosts, whose purpose, never swerving"); Narayan Vaman Tilak (b. 1862), author of "One who is all unfit to count" and others.

100 years (1893). *Death* of Phillips Brooks (b. 1835), author of "O little town of Bethlehem"; John David Chambers (b. 1805), author of "All hail, adored Trinity"; John Ellerton (b. 1826), author of "Behold us, Lord, a little space," "The day Thou gavest, Lord, is ended," "Savior, again to thy dear name we raise," and others; George J. Elvey (b. 1816), composer of DIADEMATA ("Crown him with many crowns"), ST. GEORGE'S WINDSOR ("Come, ye thankful people, come"), and others; William Owen (b. 1814), composer of BRYN CALFARIA ("Unto Thee, our praise be given," "God, our Lord, a king remaining"); Charles Steggell (b. 1826), composer of CHRISTCHURCH ("Let all the world rejoice"); John Addington Symonds (b. 1926), author of "These things shall be! a nobler race."

125 years (1868). *Birth* of Laura Scherer Copenhaver (d. 1940), author of "Heralds of Christ, who bear the king's commands"; James Nichol Grieve (d. 1954), author of "Keep me, O God of grace"; William Vaughan Jenkins (d. 1920), author of "O God of love, to Thee we bow"; C. Austin Miles (d. 1946), author/ composer of "In the garden" GARDEN; William R. Newell (d. 1956), author of "At Calvary"; Henry Hallam Tweedy (d. 1953), author of "Eternal God, whose power upholds." *Death* of William B. Bradbury (b. 1816), composer of HE LEADETH ME ("He leadeth me, o blessed thought"), BRADBURY ("Savior, like a shepherd lead us"), ALETTA ("Holy Bible, book divine"), WOODWORTH ("Just as I am"), CHINA ("Jesus loves me"), SOLID ROCK ("My home is built"), and many others; Robert Campbell (b. 1814), translator of "At the Lamb's high feast we sing," "Hail the joyful day's return," "Come,

pure hearts, in joyful measure," and others; Henry Hart Milman (b. 1791), author of "Ride on, ride on in majesty."

150 years (1843). *Birth* of Ernest Edward Dugmore (d. 1925), author of "Almighty Father of all things that be"; Ralph E. Hudson (d. 1901), composer of HUDSON ("At the cross"), BLESSED NAME ("O for a thousand tongues to sing"), SATISFIED ("All my life I had a longing"), and author of "I'll live for Him"; F. W. H. Myers (d. 1901), author of "Hark, what a sound, and too divine for hearing." *Death* of Alexander Viets Griswold (b. 1766), author of "Holy Father, great creator"; John Kent (b. 1766), author of " 'Tis the church triumphant singing"; Francis Scott Key (b. 1779), author of "The star-spangled banner"; Henry Ware, Jr. (b. 1794), author of "Happy the home when God is there"; Samuel Webbe (b. 1770), composer of CONSOLATOR ("Come, ye disconsolate").

175 years (1818). *Birth* of Eliza Sibbald Alderson (d. 1889), author of "And now, beloved Lord, thy soul resigning"; Cecil Frances Alexander (d. 1895), author of "Jesus calls us," "All things bright and beautiful," "There is a green hill far away," "Once in royal David's city," and others; George Duffield, Jr. (d. 1888), author of "Stand up, stand up for Jesus"; Henri Friedrich Hemy (d. 1888), composer of ST. CATHERINE ("Faith of our fathers"); Edward John Hopkins (d. 1901), composer of ELLERS ("Savior, again to thy dear name we raise"); Thomas Toke Lynch (d. 1871), author of "Gracious Spirit, dwell with me"; John Mason Neale (d. 1866), author of "Good King Wenceslaus," "Art thou weary, heavy laden," and translator of "All glory, laud, and honor," "Jerusalem, the golden," "The day of resurrection," "Come, ye faithful, raise the strain" and many others; Silas J. Vail (d. 1884), composer of CLOSE TO THEE ("Thou, my everlasting portion"); Elizabeth Prentiss (d. 1878), author of "More love to thee, O Christ."

200 years (1793). *Birth* of John Clare (d. 1864), author of "A stranger once did bless the earth"; Henry Francis Lyte (d. 1847), author of "Praise, my soul, the king of heaven," "God of mercy, God of love," "Abide with me, fast falls the eventide," and others.

225 years (1768). *Birth* of Benjamin Carr (d. 1831), arranger of MADRID ("Come, Christians, join to sing"). *Death* of Joseph Grigg (b. 172?), author of "Jesus, and shall it ever be"; Joseph Hart (b. 1712), author of "Come, Holy Spirit, come," "Come, ye sinners, poor and needy"; John Wainwright (b. 1723), composer of YORKSHIRE ("Christians, rise, salute the happy morn").

250 years (1743). *Birth* of Anna Laetitia Barbauld (d. 1825), author of "Praise to God, immortal praise."

275 years (1718). *Birth* of John Cennick (d. 1755), author of parts of "Lo, he comes with clouds descending," "Children of the heavenly King," "Be present at our table, Lord," and others.

300 years (1693). Publication of *Neuver mehrtes Meiningisches Gesangbuch,* source of MUNICH ("O word of God incarnate").

375 years (1618). *Birth* of Johann Franck (d. 1677), author of "Jesus, priceless treasure," "Deck thyself, my soul with gladness," and others.

400 years (1593). *Birth* of George Herbert (d. 1632/33), author of "Let all the world in every corner sing," "King of glory, King of peace," "Come, my way, my truth, my life," "Teach me, my God and King," and others.

Quotable Quotations

1. Wisdom consists of the anticipation of consequences. — Norman Cousins

2. You can do more than pray, after you have prayed, but you cannot do more than pray until you have prayed. — John Bunyan

3. A good laugh is sunshine in a house. — William Makepeace Thackeray

4. Except for theology, there is no art that can be placed in comparison with music. — Martin Luther

5. God finds his complete life in and through us as we find ours in and through him and through each other in love and joy and cooperation. — Rufus Jones

6. It is hard to believe that a man is telling the truth when you know that you would lie if you were in his place. — H. L. Mencken

7. The past always looks better than it was. It's only pleasant because it isn't here. — Finley Peter Dunne

8. Myths are public dreams, dreams are private myths. — Joseph Campbell

9. It is easier to fight for one's principles than to live up to them. — Alfred Adler

10. Man has lost the capacity to foresee and to forestall. He will end by destroying the earth. — Albert Schweitzer

11. Marriage is not just spiritual communion and passionate embraces; marriage is also three meals a day and remembering to carry out the trash. — Joyce Brothers

12. To find God is but the beginning of wisdom, because then for all our days we have to learn his purpose with us and to live our lives with him. — H. G. Wells

13. Winners got scars too. — Johnny Cash

14. Love is the hardest lesson in Christianity; but, for that reason, it should be most our care to learn it. — William Penn

15. Anxiety is the interest paid on trouble before it is due. — Dean Inge

16. There is nothing that makes us love a man so much as praying for him. — William Law

17. Sufferings are but as little chips of the cross. — Joseph Church

18. Better is the sin which humbles us, than that duty which makes me proud. — Thomas Watson

19. The penalty of success is to be bored by the people who used to snub you. — Lady Nancy Astor

20. The best way to keep children home is to make the home atmosphere pleasant — and let the air out of the tires. — Dorothy Parker

21. Money brings some happiness. But after a certain point, it just brings more money. — Neil Simon

22. For most people unbelief in one thing is based on blind belief in another. — G. C. Lichtenberg

23. Morality is the herd instinct in the individual.—Friedrich Nietzsche

24. The only time people dislike gossip is when you gossip about them.—Will Rogers

25. A church exists by mission as fire exists by burning.—Emil Brunner

26. How many crimes are committed merely because their authors could not endure being wrong!—Albert Camus

27. The devil's most devilish when respectable.—Elizabeth Barrett

28. Noise proves nothing. Often a hen who has merely laid an egg cackles as if she laid an asteroid.—Mark Twain

29. The louder he talked of his honor, the faster we counted our spoons.—Ralph Waldo Emerson

30. Life is what happens to us while we are making other plans.—William Gaddis, Jr.

31. Injustice is relatively easy to bear; it is justice that hurts.—H. L. Mencken

32. Don't wait for the last judgment—it takes place every day.—Albert Camus

33. The test of a vocation is the love of the drudgery it involves.—Logan Pearsall Smith

34. Guilt is what civilizes.—Philip Lopate

35. We treat God as the police treat a man when he has been arrested; whatever he does will be used in evidence against him.—C. S. Lewis

36. It is the cunning slight of the devil to divide us that he may destroy us.—D. L. Moody

37. Nearly all our disasters come of a few fools having the "courage of their convictions."—Coventry Patmore

38. I do benefits for all religions—I'd hate to blow the hereafter on a technicality.—Bob Hope

39. There ain't much fun in medicine, but there's a good deal of medicine in fun.—Josh Billings

40. Silence is one of the hardest arguments to refute.—Josh Billings

41. Christ's performances outstrip his promises.—Nehemiah Rogers

42. In taking revenge, a man is but even with his enemy; but in passing it over, he is superior.—Francis Bacon

43. To say we love God and at the same time exercise cruelty toward the least creatures, is a contradiction in itself.—John Woolman

44. A fashion is nothing but an induced epidemic.—George Bernard Shaw

45. Do give books—religious or otherwise—for Christmas. They're never fattening, seldom sinful, and permanently personal.—Lenore Hershey

46. You don't have to travel around the world to understand that the sky is blue everywhere.—Goethe

47. Never go to bed mad. Stay up and fight.—Phyllis Diller

48. Living well is the best revenge.—George Herbert

49. The gospel is a declaration, not a debate.—James S. Stewart

50. Temptations are never so dangerous as when they come to us in a religious garb.—D. L. Moody

51. Real true faith is man's weakness leaning on God's strength.—D. L. Moody

52. When you say a situation or a person is hopeless, you are slamming the door in the face of God.—Charles L. Allen

53. When a friend dies, part of yourself dies, too.—St. John Irvine

54. The greatest pleasure I have known is to do a good action by stealth and to have it found out by accident.—Charles Lamb

55. One on God's side is a majority.—Wendell Phillips

56. Old age is always fifteen years older than I am.—Bernard Baruch

57. The natural man has only two primal passions: to get and to beget.—Sir William Osler

58. I confess that I cannot understand how we can plot, lie, cheat, and commit murder abroad and remain humane, honorable, trustworthy, and trusted at home.—Archibald Cox

59. Advice from friends is like the weather: some of it is good; some of it is bad.—Arnold Lobel

60. It's what you learn after you know it all that counts.—John Wooden

61. People in general are equally horrified at hearing the Christian religion

doubted and at seeing it practiced.—Samuel Butler

62. Most people have some sort of religion—at least they know what church they're staying away from.—John Erskine

63. Most people enjoy the inferiority of their best friends.—Lord Chesterfield

64. It is as absurd to argue men, as to torture them, into believing.—John Henry Newman

65. The church is not a gallery for the exhibition of eminent Christians but a school for the education of imperfect ones.—Henry Ward Beecher

66. Habit is overcome by habit.—Thomas à Kempis

67. We can't form our children on our own concepts; we must take them and love them as God gives them to us.—Goethe

68. Earth, with her thousand voices, praises God.—Samuel Taylor Coleridge

69. The service we render others is really the rent we pay for our room on the earth.—Sir Wilfred Grenfell

70. The years teach much which the days never know.—Ralph Waldo Emerson

71. The biggest seller is cookbooks and the second is diet books—how not to eat what you've just learned how to cook.—Andy Rooney

72. Courage is not simply one of the virtues but the form of every virtue at the testing point.—C. S. Lewis

73. Those who cannot remember the past are condemned to repeat it.—George Santayana

74. It may make a difference to all eternity whether we do right or wrong today.—James Freeman Clarke

75. Conscience warns us before it reproaches us.—Comtesse Diane

76. Cruelty isn't softened by tears, it feeds on them.—Publilius Syrus

77. A living experience of God is the crowning knowledge attainable to a human mind.—Walter Rauschenbusch

78. Believe those who are seeking the truth; doubt those who find it.—André Gide

79. Love thy neighbor, even when he plays the trombone.—Jewish proverb

80. Marriage is a great institution, and no family should be without it.—Channing Pollock

81. To be like Christ is to be a Christian.—William Penn

82. I think somehow we learn who we really are and then live with that decision.—Eleanor Roosevelt

83. The world is equally shocked at hearing Christianity criticized and seeing it practiced.—D. Elton Trueblood

84. Love's secret is to be always doing things for God and not to mind because they are such little ones.—Frederick William Faber

85. We forge the chains of our slavery with the strength of our freedom.—Peter Kreeft

86. God hides nothing. His very work from the beginning is revelation—a casting aside of veil after veil, a showing unto men of truth after truth.—George MacDonald

87. Be glad of life because it gives you the chance to love and to work and to play and to look up at the stars.—Henry Van Dyke

88. Affliction may be lasting, but it is not everlasting.—Thomas Watson

89. The devil can cite Scripture for his purpose.—Shakespeare

90. The harder you work, the luckier you get.—Gary Player

91. If you want your children to turn out well, spend twice as much time with them and half as much money.—Abigail Van Buren

92. Poetry is man's rebellion against being what he is.—James Branch Cabell

93. Man's hostility to God proves indisputably that he belongs to him. Where there is the possibility of hate, there and there alone is the possibility of love.—Paul Tillich

94. Happiness is a sort of atmosphere you can live in sometimes when you're lucky. Joy is a light that fills you with hope and faith and love.—Adela Rogers St. Johns

95. God dwells as glorious in a saint when he is in the dark as when he is in light, for darkness is his secret place, and his pavilion round about him are dark waters.—William Erbery

96. The significance of a man is not in what he attains but rather in what he longs to attain.—Kahlil Gibran

97. How good bad music and bad reason sound when we march against an enemy.—Friedrich Wilhelm Nietzsche

98. Tyranny is always better organized than freedom.—Charles Pierre Peguy

99. I never did anything worth doing by accident, nor did any of my inventions come by accident; they came by plain work.—Thomas Edison

Questions of Life and Religion

These questions may be useful to prime homiletic pumps, as discussion starters, or for study and youth groups.

1. Is it possible or desirable to ask, "What would Jesus do?" in decision making today?

2. How can we be sure that God accepts us?

3. Can another person or other persons help someone gain access to God?

4. Why would Jesus compare lust and anger with adultery and murder?

5. Was Luther right when he said that afflictions were his best teachers?

6. How can we establish a family altar for prayer in this busy, modern world?

7. What is the role of angels as the Bible describes their work?

8. Is anger appropriate in a Christian?

9. What are the practical values of church attendance?

10. What is the meaning of baptism?

11. What is the meaning of what we variously call the Lord's Supper, Communion, or the Eucharist?

12. Do some people find it naturally easier to be skeptical than others?

13. What are some simple, basic guidelines for understanding the Bible?

14. Is it necessary to be born again to be a Christian?

15. Why do we speak of "the precious blood" of our Lord Jesus Christ in relation to our "redemption"?

16. Does every Christian believer receive a divine "call"?

17. Is capital punishment ever right?

18. What is the difference between certainty and certitude in Christian belief?

19. How is Christian character formed?

20. Are children essential to make a home complete?

21. How are we to think of Jesus Christ in his relation to God?

22. Do miracles prove Jesus' divine Sonship?

23. What is the complete teaching of the New Testament on divorce?

24. Who is responsible for the evil in the world?

25. What is faith?

26. Why do we call God Father?

27. Is fault-finding necessary or useful?

28. How does "the fear of God" fit into our total understanding of God?

29. Do religious festivals play a vital role in the practice of our faith?

30. When are we in or when are we out of fellowship with God?

31. What is justification by faith?

32. How can we be sure that God has forgiven our sin?

33. Why is it difficult to forgive?

34. Are we ever truly free?

35. By what standards should we decide our giving to the church?

36. How does God use our gifts (abilities) in his service?

37. In what sense is the Bible the Word of God?

38. What is "the gospel"?

39. How does God guide us?

40. What is happiness?

41. Does God heal people today?

42. How does the Bible picture heaven?

43. Does God hide himself?

44. What does the Holy Spirit do in the lives of Christian believers?

45. What would an ideal Christian home look like?

46. How should humility work in one's life?

47. Is idleness a sin?

48. In what ways do we worship idols today?

49. What does it mean to be created in the image of God?

50. What do we mean by the inspiration of the Scriptures?

51. How does intercessory prayer promote the work of God?

52. Which should Christians practice toward people they differ with—tolerance or acceptance?

53. Does God seek our commitment by threat or by invitation?

54. How does Jesus compare with the leaders of other world religions?

55. How do the Jewish people figure into God's plan?

56. Can we experience joy even when everything seems to go wrong?

57. In what ways do we experience judgment here and now?

58. How can we affirm God's justice in view of life's obvious inequalities?

59. What is justification by faith?

60. In what ways does kindness express our Christian faith?

61. What is the kingdom of God?

62. Is knowledge an enemy of faith?

63. Can we predict the events of the earth's "last days"?

64. Does "law" play a positive role in Christian experience?

65. What meaning can "the laying on of hands upon the newly baptized" have?

66. What qualities should leaders in the church possess?

67. Are there many ways to lie?

68. How far does Christian liberty permit us to go?

69. What is the purpose of life?

70. How can one grow into Christlikeness?

71. What is the cure for loneliness?

72. How does one experientially recognize the lordship of Christ?

73. What does the word *love* mean in its several dimensions?

74. Can family loyalty be in conflict with loyalty to Christ?

75. What can we say for marriage versus "living together"?

76. When has one attained spiritual maturity?

77. What gives life meaning?

78. How can one learn the art of Christian meditation?

79. Does memory play a role in Christian character building?

80. What are the differing beliefs and attitudes of Christians and Jews regarding the Messiah?

81. Who are Christ's ministers?

82. What was the purpose of our Lord's miracles?

83. What is the mission of the church?

84. Can we make a case for Christian modesty?

85. Does contemporary television undermine moral values?

86. Are there special values in mothers raising their own children?

87. How much of our religion must we leave to the realm of mystery?

88. What is our duty to our nation?

89. Can nature reveal God?

90. Who needs to be born again?

91. Does obedience to God come naturally for believers?

92. What makes an offering acceptable to God?

93. What can make old age meaningful?

94. How can God be both one and three?

95. What are some of the subtle ways in which people oppress one another?

96. Do pain and suffering serve useful purposes?

97. How can we learn patience?

98. Is peace possible?

99. Does God answer all our prayers?

100. Why praise God?

Biblical Benedictions and Blessings

The Lord watch between me and thee, when we are absent from one another.—Gen. 31:49.

The Lord bless thee, and keep thee; the Lord make his face to shine upon thee, and be gracious unto thee; the Lord lift up his countenance upon thee, and give thee peace.—Num. 6:24–26.

The Lord our God be with us, as he was with our fathers; let him not leave us, nor forsake us; that he may incline our hearts unto him, to walk in all his ways, and to keep his commandments, and his statutes, and his judgments, which he commanded our fathers.—1 Kings 8:57–58.

Let the words of my mouth, and the meditation of my heart, be acceptable in thy sight, O Lord, my strength, and my redeemer.—Ps. 19:14.

Now the God of patience and consolation grant you to be likeminded one toward another according to Christ Jesus; that ye may with one mind and one mouth glorify God, even the Father of our Lord Jesus Christ. Now the God of hope fill you with all joy and peace in believing, that ye may abound in hope, through the power of the Holy Ghost. Now the God of peace be with you.—Rom. 15:5–6, 13, 33.

Now to him that is of power to establish you according to my gospel and the preaching of Jesus Christ, according to the revelation of the mystery, which was kept secret since the world began, but now is manifest, and by the scriptures of the prophets, according to the commandment of the everlasting God, made known to all nations for the obedience of faith: to God only wise, be glory through Jesus Christ for ever.—Rom. 16:25–27.

Grace be unto you, and peace, from God our Father, and from the Lord Jesus Christ.—1 Cor. 1:3.

The grace of the Lord Jesus Christ and the love of God, and the communion of the Holy Ghost, be with you all.—2 Cor. 13:14.

Peace be to the brethren, and love with faith, from God the Father and the Lord Jesus Christ. Grace be with all them that love our Lord Jesus Christ in sincerity.—Eph. 6:23–24.

And the peace of God, which passeth all understanding, shall keep your hearts and minds through Christ Jesus. Finally, brethren, whatsoever things are true,

whatsoever things are honest, whatsoever things are just; whatsoever things are pure, whatsoever things are lovely, whatsoever things are of good report; if there be any virtue, and if there be any praise, think on these things. Those things, which ye have both learned and received, and heard, and seen in me, do; and the God of peace shall be with you.—Phil. 4:7–9.

Wherefore also we pray always for you, that our God would count you worthy of this calling, and fulfill all the good pleasure of his goodness, and the work of faith with power; that the name of our Lord Jesus Christ may be glorified in you, and ye in him, according to the grace of our God and the Lord Jesus Christ.—2 Thess. 1:11–12.

Now the Lord of peace himself give you peace always by all means. The Lord be with you all. The grace of our Lord Jesus Christ be with you all.—2 Thess. 3:16–18.

Grace, mercy, and peace, from God our Father and Jesus Christ our Lord.—1 Tim. 1:2.

Now the God of peace, that brought again from the dead our Lord Jesus, that great shepherd of the sheep, through the blood of the everlasting covenant, make you perfect in every good work to do his will, working in you that which is well-pleasing in his sight, through Jesus Christ, to whom be glory for ever and ever.—Heb. 13:20–21.

The God of all grace, who hath called us unto his eternal glory by Christ Jesus, after that ye have suffered a while, make you perfect, establish, strengthen, settle you. To him be glory and dominion for ever and ever. Greet ye one another with a kiss of charity. Peace be with you all that are in Christ Jesus.—1 Pet. 5:10–11, 14.

Grace be with you, mercy, and peace, from God the Father, and from the Lord

Jesus Christ, the Son of the Father, in truth and love.—2 John 3.

Now unto him that is able to keep you from falling, and to present you faultless before the presence of his glory with exceeding joy, to the only wise God our Savior, be glory and majesty, dominion and power, both now and ever.—Jude 24–25.

Grace be unto you, and peace, from him which was, and which is to come; and from the seven Spirits which are before his throne; and from Jesus Christ, who is the faithful witness, and the first begotten of the dead, and the prince of the kings of the earth. Unto him that loved us, and washed us from our sins in his own blood, and hath made us kings and priests unto God and his Father; to him be glory and dominion for ever and ever.—Rev. 1:4–6.

SECTION II.
Sermons and Homiletic and Worship Aids for Fifty-two Sundays

SUNDAY: JANUARY THIRD

SERVICE OF WORSHIP

Sermon: The End Is Far from the Beginning

TEXT: 1 Cor. 13:11

What a remarkable journey life has been for many of us. How much some of us have seen; how much some of us have lived. There is so much to remember: love found and lost and found again; hopes that led us on; faith that fanned our efforts into being. How we worked; how we endured hurts which darkened our days and made us wonder and ask what life was all about. And then those moments of sweet reward: the day we knew that we had found our niche, sacrifices we made which left us rich. And so at last we have come to this day.

Now how far is today from the beginning? It is very far, isn't it? It is far when we let our minds sweep back over the years, and a thousand memories well up. Everything lives again. And now consider how far we have come. Yes, the end is far from the beginning. Some of us have come from farm to city, from simple living to a complex existence, from humble circumstances to places of affluence and influence.

Of course, we are thinking not so much of material circumstances as of our spiritual pilgrimage. How far have we come? In what direction have we moved? What forces have played upon us

through the years? What forces have pulled us away from the simple faith of our childhood days or driven us closer to God?

Thus we come to the inevitable question: How far is the end from the beginning in our own spiritual life?

I. When we think of our faith, how far is the end from the beginning? We know what our faith was when we were children. It was a simple trust. It accepted all things; it believed all things. But it had no wings. There were no horizons. There was no venturesomeness in that childhood faith.

(a) "But now that I am a man"—how is it now? Have we lost even that simple faith? Is it something which asserts itself only when life roughs us up? Or is it not even that much? Are we satisfied to live as best we can, just keeping from being crushed and content to shake off the blows?

(b) Or is our faith now infinitely more than it ever was when we were young? Is our faith something rebellious, defying circumstances? Does it inevitably turn us toward the light, unearthing one hope after another, always catching the gleam of something that is ahead of us? Is our faith something adventurous, at times making us do things which our common sense tells us not to do? There is something in our faith which makes one do "crazy" things, trust the sort of world we

17

have never had, believe in the sort of things we have wished for but have never seen. Well, how far has faith come since that yesterday long ago?

II. When we think of prayer, how far is the end from the beginning? "When I was a child, I prayed as a child." Prayers, then, were simple words. Our prayers moved in a simple world. They touched everything: father, mother, teacher—dolls, toys and puppy dogs . . . It was a world free from doubts, but there was no agony in those prayers. Those prayers had no Gethsemane—no struggle with God, no seeking to hold him, no pushing him away.

"But now that I am a man"—how is it now? Can I no longer pray? Is there now nothing within me except a deep silence, and the silence is never disturbed, not even by the echo of some voice beyond? Now that I am a man, do I say that prayer is really not important? I have tried it, but the world didn't change. Nothing ever came of prayer. Perhaps I never said to myself that I stopped at the wrong time—stopped too soon.

(b) Or now that I am a man, does prayer take me anywhere? Does it go with me when I climb that high mountain and success might make me dizzy? Or will it go with me when I go to my Calvary—as sooner or later I must—and bitterness might sweep through my soul? Will it be with me when I have no other armor to protect myself and no other weapon with which to slay some evil giant? There are times when a man must reach heaven—how will he do it? There are times when a man trembles and is afraid to go on, but he must go on—and how will he walk? Has prayer come to do that? How far have we come since the beginning?

III. When we think of Christ, how far is the end from the beginning? "When I was a child I thought as a child"—I saw him as a divine loveliness framed by my childish mind. But now that I am a man, what does he mean to me?

(a) Does he mean more to me now than he ever did? In times when life drains me of all strength, can I lean on him? In moments when I have no wisdom, do I find

understanding in his presence? Do I walk with him; do I talk with him? Have I come to the place where I know that I can do nothing without him? Does he mean that to me now?

(b) Does he mean even more than that? I know the world is in bitter agony. The world has been asking questions: Where is wisdom? Where is hope? Where is salvation? The world has not only been asking, the world has been crying for an answer. Do I now believe that Christ is the answer—the answer to all things: justice, righteousness, my own fulfillment, my own peace of mind, the heaven I would stretch over the heads of those I love, peace for all the world? Yes, I believe Christ is the answer to all this.

IV. So the end is far from the beginning. Now that you look back over the years, do you feel that you have lost something? What have you lost? Or do you feel that you have found something? What have you found? Some narrow ambition, something you cannot take with you? What forces have played upon you? Some selfish drive? Or some inexpressible desire to be and become and to believe? When you were a child, you spake as a child, you felt as a child, you thought as a child, but now that you are no longer a child—in all those things that matter most—how far is the end from the beginning?—Arnold H. Lowe

Illustrations

DISCOVERING AND REDISCOVERING. The discovery of the world in childhood is an approach toward God through wonder at his works. The adventure of the adult is the experience of God in action inspired and guided by him. The necessary progressive detachment from the world means closer fellowship with God. All through our lives we are learning to know him, first through study, then through action, and then through adoration: three adventures which are but one. There is always a new God to discover and a familiar God to rediscover, always a forward march.

The other day I met an old friend, an industrialist who has been wise enough to lay down his too heavy burden before he is too old, and who now gets great pleasure from everything he undertakes.

"Good day! How are you?" I asked him.

"Fine! I have realized that life begins with birth (*naissance*), continues with knowledge (*connaissance*), and ends in gratitude (*reconnaissance*)."—Paul Tournier

PRACTICE IN LEARNING.   When you start emotional re-education, your neocortex is like a rider who has ridden his horse up and down the same straight road to work for ten years. Until now, he could trust the horse to take him to and from work with little or no direct control. But recently the rider moved to another part of town. Instead of a straight road to work, he now has to make one right turn on the way out and a left turn on the way back.

From the very first day after the move, the rider (the neocortex) remembers and makes the correct turns without mistakes. But the horse (the limbic system) doesn't. Instead, it has a strong urge to go straight down the road, just as it has for the past ten years. The horse will require time and lots of practice in being guided around the correct turns before it learns to make them without being directed.

How long will it take before the horse learns to make the correct turns automatically? No one can say beforehand. Every horse differs in its ability to learn. Every rider differs in ability and willingness to teach his horse. The rider who gives his horse the most practice will teach his horse to make the correct turns without direction in the shortest time possible.—Maxie C. Maultaby, Jr.

Sermon Suggestions

WHEN   GOD'S   GOODNESS   PREVAILS. TEXT: Jer. 31:7–14. (1) The patience of human hope is rewarded, verses 7–9. (2) The proof of divine faithfulness is enjoyed, verses 10–14.

GOD'S SPECIAL BLESSING.   TEXT: Eph. 1:3–6, 15–18. (1) God has blessed us in Jesus Christ, verses 3–4a. (2) The purpose of this blessing, verses 4b–6. (3) The extent of this blessing, verses 15–18.

Worship Aids

CALL TO WORSHIP.   "It is written, As I live, saith the Lord, every knee shall bow to me, and every tongue shall confess to God. So then every one of us shall give account of himself to God" (Rom. 14:11–19).

INVOCATION.   Abide with us this morning, Father. Let your Spirit shine in us and your truth fill our hearts and minds as we worship here in this place. Then shall we be mightier than the accidents of life. Then shall we have the presence and power to handle the circumstances that surround us. Then will we be able to rise above our weaknesses. Today, teach us to walk as true children of God, followers of Christ who, having met here in his name, are energized to face the world in his power.—Henry Fields

OFFERTORY SENTENCE.   "The silver is mine, and the gold is mine, saith the Lord of hosts" (Hag. 2:8).

OFFERTORY PRAYER.   Lord, others have labored, and we have entered into the fruits of their labor; we give now that others may enjoy our bounty, materially and spiritually, that our sharing may point   to   God   and   make   the difference.—E. Lee Phillips

PRAYER.   O Father, you have not left yourself without witness in this world. You are constantly speaking to us, but so often it seems we have a hearing problem. Or, is it a willing problem? We do not will to hear you?

Your Word is in us, in the very fact of our incompleteness without you; your Word surrounds us in the beauty of the flowers at the altar, in the holiness of this place, in the song of the mocking bird that awakened us this morning; your Word is above us, breaking in upon us through the voice of the prophet, the apostle, and supremely through Jesus of Nazareth—your Word becoming flesh and dwelling among us.

Your Word is present, too, in all of our relationships. We pray that we may listen deeply to one another that we may hear it. We praise you that in the relationships of the family we are privileged to enter into the mystery of life and love. We cannot scale all of the heights or fathom all of the depths of this relationship, but we know that it is of your doing, and it is marvelous in our eyes. Into this new week we pray that we may go our way holding hands to face together the high purpose to which you call us, whether as parent or child.

Your fatherly intention toward us and all peoples is present, too, in your Word spoken to nations and between nations. We pray for the family of humankind in all of its joys and all of its hurts. For those who face death for their desire for freedom of themselves and others, we pray. "How long, O Lord, how long will the elders in our society sentence the youth to die for they know not what!" May those who die, face death with the confidence that "truth though crushed to earth shall rise again."

For your Word which has created the church and this household of faith we praise you. As your children, as brothers and sisters, we pray for one another. For the ill among us, we pray. Grant to them a faith, a love, a trust to be open to receive your healing grace. Where there are physical infirmities that must be lived with, we pray a wholeness of mind and spirit that transcends the brokenness of body.

We pray through him who is among us as your eternal Word teaching us and people everywhere to pray and live.—John M. Thompson

LECTIONARY MESSAGE

Topic: The Incarnate Word

Text: John 1:1–18

There is more to Jesus Christ than meets the eye. When the writer of the Fourth Gospel undertook to set forth the life and work of Jesus, he went back to the very beginning of all things. Even at that point, if we can call it a point, this one whom he called the Son of God, the Word of God, was there with God.

I. People have explained or characterized Jesus in many ways—and some of these attempts are commendable and intended to praise him. He was, in such views, a good man, a peerless prophet, a master teacher. These things could be said of other people, even though Jesus was superior to all of them. Still, Jesus cannot be explained by even the finest and most highly developed human qualities. He is to be explained only in terms of God. We have to go back as far as the human imagination can reach, even to begin to explain and understand Jesus. Therefore John put this Word of God—called Jesus in his earthly appearance—with God at the beginning of all things that exist. Further, John said, "All things came into being through him, and without him not one thing came into being" (v. 3, NRSV).

II. John said that "the Word was God," that is, *divine*. This Word came to expression in human history, in the person of Jesus Christ. He was the perfect picture or embodiment of what God is and is like. Jesus said to his disciple Philip, "Whoever has seen me has seen the Father" (John 14:9, NRSV). His purpose was and is to bring life and light into the world, and he has always been doing that, even before he was manifested in human flesh. The light that was in the Word shone in the world's darkness—moral and spiritual darkness—and the darkness could not put out that light. In all ages of human history darkness has waged war with the light of the divine Word, but the darkness has never won a final victory. Like the coming of morning after the long night, light has pushed back the shadows of human evil again and again.

III. This light-bringing Word, however, was not some mere impersonal force or influence working in and on human history. The Word was God coming in person to deal with other persons on person-to-person terms. His own people as a whole rejected him, just as the world as a whole has rejected him. Yet some have accepted him, discovered God in a fullness in him, and lived remarkable lives in companionship with him. To those "he gave power to become children of God" (v. 12).

IV. What gives us hope and encouragement in spite of the world's sin and our own sin is that in this creative Word of God we can find resources for living lives that are adequate and useful to God and others, even if these lives are not always victorious and overflowing with happiness. God's grace toward us knows no end. What we discover for the first time in Jesus Christ—mercy, forgiveness, status as God's children—is proven to us over and over again as we trust him in every reversal and crisis of life. As we trace the steps of Jesus among people of all kinds, we see that the love that seeks out the least and the lost is the love of the Father.—James W. Cox

SUNDAY: JANUARY TENTH

SERVICE OF WORSHIP

Sermon: Wedding at Cana

TEXT: John 2:1–12

There is a scene in Hamlet in which Hamlet is poking fun at an old man who is always full of advice but also always ready to agree with the last thing anybody says to him—a "yes" man. Hamlet says, "Do you see yonder cloud that's almost in the shape of a camel?" The old man replies, "Yes, 'tis like a camel indeed." Hamlet says, "Methinks it is like a weasel." "It is backed like a weasel." "Or, like a whale." "Very like a whale."

I. Preaching on John's stories is a little like that conversation. John's miracle stories are so easily linked to a whole host of symbolic meanings that one hardly knows where to stop. Take the present one, for example; on one level, it is simple a straightforward miracle story. At another, it is chock-full of potential hidden meanings. First, the straight story.

(a) Jesus and his disciples went to a wedding in Cana, the little town fifteen to twenty miles from Capernaum. Maybe Jesus was related to the bride or the groom—we'll never know. We only know that Mary told Jesus about the problem, and after hesitating a bit, Jesus miraculously provided more than enough wine for the party. He changed the water used for purifying the guests of uncleanness into wine, approximately 180 gallons, which the host of the feast thought was the best they'd had throughout the whole feast.

(b) That's the basic story, but there are some puzzling details. For example, 2:1 says this happened "on the third day." On the third day from what? There are no points of reference in the first chapter, and so some commentators think that this may be intended to remind the reader of the Resurrection. But what does changing water into wine have to do with Christ being raised from the dead?

(c) You see the point—once you start looking for symbolism in the miracles, it's hard to know where to stop or when to say that the cloud doesn't look like a whale or a camel at all. I think the key to this story is in verse 11, which says that the disciples believed in Christ because this miracle "manifested his glory"—it showed clearly Jesus' true, real nature.

II. We'll focus, then, on what this miracle tells us about Christ's identity. Let's pretend we are the disciples: What do we see about Jesus from this miracle?

(a) It shows him as the patient revealer: a teacher who brings his students along, bit by bit, as they can understand. In the first chapter, Jesus had impressed the disciples with his knowledge of them but had promised them greater things to come: "You will see the heavens opened, and the angels of God ascending and descending upon the Son of man"; yet he does something much less spectacular in this story, providing wine for a wedding feast. Jesus knew that they could not accept or understand his teaching about God all at once, so he began with something they could comprehend. The wedding party needed wine, and Christ could provide it. Later, he would reveal more heavenly truths to them.

(b) The miracle also shows Christ as a zealous reformer. The jars held water for Jewish rites of purification. Why would that be necessary at a wedding? The reason is that strictly observant Jews would cleanse themselves before eating, so that if they had touched a Gentile their food would not be contaminated.

Jesus made these jars, which symbolized the division between Jew and non-Jew, into something better. The prophets had foreseen the time when all nations would receive the invitation to worship God. The wedding feast of the last days would be a time when God would invite all people to be included. Jesus was saying, by his actions, that the time had come, a time for new ways and new customs, a time of openness and brotherhood between all peoples instead of the divisions the jars represented.

Jesus was an energetic reformer. In the next episode he took on the Temple; later in the Gospel he transformed the celebration of Hanukkah through healing a blind man and changed the Passover meal through institution of the Lord's Supper. Like the recycling plants that can take old glass or paper and make something fresh and new from it, so Christ can take our lives—all the sin and junk we've lived with all our lives—and make us over again. He can make us new, start us fresh—and that is quite a gift.

(c) Finally, the miracle shows Jesus to be an abundant provider. Feasts, particularly wedding feasts, were special times in the lives of poor Palestinian people, probably the only times some of them ever really ate their fill. Small wonder, then, that the prophets spoke of God's ideal kingdom as if it were one long banquet.

Only Jesus knows how to satisfy the world abundantly. Doctors can heal the body, but only Christ can heal the conscience of sin. You can satisfy your hunger at McDonalds, but only Jesus is the Bread of Life that brings salvation.

The miracle at Cana—the first one in John's Gospel—tells us some important things about Christ. He is a patient revealer, showing us the truth about God only as we can take it. He is a zealous reformer, changing those parts of our lives which need reform. He is an abundant provider, giving us all we need to be truly satisfied in this life and the next. We, like the disciples, can see his glory in this story and put our faith in him.—Richard Vinson

Illustrations

THE BOTTOM LINE.			We are thus led by the evangelist to read this story on a symbolic level and not merely on a story level. The trouble is that there are so many symbolic allusions in it. For example, contemporaries of the Gospel in the Greco-Roman world would be quite familiar with the manifestation of the god Dionysus in worship and even in miracles involving wine. Whether that background is relevant here or not is uncertain. There may also be in the mention of the ablution of jars an allusion to the inadequacy of Jewish ritual to cope with real human need. But the most plausible area of symbolism—in addition to the reference to the Passion—is that of the messianic setting in which the identity of Jesus as Messiah is implied. The occasion is a wedding feast, which, as the parables in Matt. 22:1–14 show, was a messianic occasion. The great abundance of wine provided recalls the imagery of Amos 9:13–14. Most of all, the remark of the steward in verse 10, "You have kept the best wine till now," invites the conclusion that the Messiah is now here.—George W. MacRae

MINISTER OF JOY.			Jesus was perfectly at home at a wedding feast. He was no severe, austere killjoy. He loved to share in the happy rejoicing of a wedding feast. There are certain religious people who shed a gloom wherever they go. There are certain people who are suspicious of all joy and happiness. To them religion is the thing of the black clothes, the low-ered voice, the expulsion of social fellow-ship. They descend like a gloom wher-ever they go. It was said of Alice Freeman Palmer, the great teacher, by one of her scholars: "She made me feel as if I was bathed in sunshine."—William Barclay

THE PROPER MASTER. Mary agreed and instructed the servants to carry out any orders her son might give. What Je-sus would do would be done because it agreed with the purpose of God and not simply because it pleased his mother.

In this lies the secret of happiness and purpose in life: to find the proper Mas-ter. Thus, it is necessary to cut through all family ties, all national traditions, all personal preferences, and all warm friendships until the supreme object of loyalty and affection is discovered. When that tremendous discovery is made, love, patriotism, ambition, and fellowship have a new, more realistic wealth of meaning. Even at the age of twelve Jesus knew that his life would be lived under orders from the heavenly Father (Luke 2:48–49), and in that relationship lay its significance and usefulness.

The missionary program of Christian-ity has gone forward because there were parents and children with spiritual matu-rity. They have seen that the will of God may carry an individual far from home and country, to places where wealth and cultural refinements do not exist. But they make the sacrifice, because they know that to reject the call of God is a greater sacrifice.—James W. Cox

Sermon Suggestions

THE LORD'S SERVANT. TEXT: Isa. 42:1–9. The Lord's servant was to be Is-rael, the nation. The highest fulfillment, however, is in Jesus Christ. (1) His task—ultimate justice, verses 1–4. (2) His power—the life-giving Creator Spirit, verses 5–9.

THE GOSPEL IN A NUTSHELL TEXT: Acts 10:34–43. (1) Jesus' message: Peace in all directions, verses 34–38. (2) Jesus'

manifestation: resurrection by the power of God, verses 39–41. (3) Jesus' mandate: proclamation of God's judgment and grace, verses 42–43.

Worship Aids

CALL TO WORSHIP. "It is a good thing to give thanks unto the Lord, and to sing praises unto thy name, O most High" (Ps. 92:1).

INVOCATION. Lord, God, Omnipotent, open us to your majesty and power as we pause to worship. Lift us from our tem-poral thinking into eternal perspectives that we may grasp more perfectly the purposes of God.—E. Lee Phillips

OFFERTORY SENTENCE. "For ye know the grace of our Lord Jesus Christ, that though he was rich, yet for your sakes he became poor, that ye through his poverty might be rich" (2 Cor. 8:9).

OFFERTORY PRAYER. Lord, we who have enough and to spare now give for those who have less and ever want for more. Lead us to be wise stewards in our bounty and to learn the "essentialness" of the way of Christ.—E. Lee Phillips

PRAYER. Abiding God, Lord of all un-derstanding, with our schedule it is let-down time. Decorations are put away, gift exchanges have been made, the kids are back in school, forgotten charges are arriving in the mail.

There is a strange penetrating sadness about it all. But on your schedule it is a time of glorious appearing. Magi bearing gifts behold the Christ child. Your man-ifestation of promise come true, of love made tangible, of hope fully realized, brings light and life to us even this hour. We rejoice that the best gift of all is for all, that your Word made flesh is our Sav-ior and Lord.

So as we worship this day, may the schedule of our world fade dim and the appearance of our Christ shine forth in gladness and joy.

O Christ, brightness of the Father's glory, flesh image of his Person, as the wise men brought gifts to you, so we bring our gifts, too. Accept the gift of our hands; open them and use them to touch and serve others. Accept the gift of our minds; illuminate them and through them think your thoughts of goodwill and redemption for all. Accept the gift of our hearts, soften them and pulse your love through them for the longing and unlovely of this world. Accept the gift of our lives; enable them and through them bring in your kingdom and fulfill your will.

O Holy Spirit, Light Divine, Breath of God, Comforter we pray in you for others; for your guidance in countries struggling for peace, justice, and a clean start; for your healing and strength for those who suffer, and hope and courage for their families.

We pray your tender peace and quiet grace for those finding it almost too much to face another year; for those grown old, alone, and who have no one to remember them; for those who have lost a loved one; for those torn and hurt by relationships betrayed and broken.

Spirit of the Living God, be alive and manifested in our church, we pray. Empower us to proclaim the good news boldly, to make disciples, to teach diligently, to serve humbly and faithfully, remembering you are with us always. So be it and thanks be to God.—William M. Johnson

LECTIONARY MESSAGE

Topic: Doing All That God Requires

TEXT: Matt. 3:13–17

When we look at the crisis experiences of Jesus, we may be inclined to believe that these experiences belong to him alone, that we should not compare our own with his. It is true that they had special meaning, messianic meaning; however, he was the incarnate Son of God, and this means that from a human point of view what happened to him in these crises may significantly parallel what goes on in your life and mine.

When Jesus came to be baptized by John, he said, "It is proper in this way to fulfill all righteousness" (v. 15, NRSV). In other words, Jesus was ready to do "all that God requires." This was not only Jesus' obligation; it is also ours. What, then, does it imply?

I. Doing all that God requires presupposes a divine plan. God has a plan for every human life. Augustine said, "You have made us for yourself, O God, and restless are our hearts until they rest in you." This does not mean, as some suppose, that all our actions are predetermined in such a way that we have no freedom. It means that the gracious, loving Creator wills for us to live under the conditions of our human existence in such a way that we reach our full potential. We see this dramatically in the life of Jesus Christ. The New Testament writers believed his "goings-forth" to be "from of old, from everlasting." John says, "He was in the beginning with God" (John 1:2, NRSV). But God has a plan for your life and mine also, and while such a life may not make a great impression on anyone, it may be what God requires of us— and no more than he requires. This is a truly awesome thought. We are here on this earth one time, and we have this one opportunity to bring God's plan for us to completion.

II. Furthermore, doing all that God requires awaits critical disclosure. We do not know what the journey will be like before we begin it, what extraordinary challenges will come to us along the way. Even Jesus said that he did not know the day and the hour of God's momentous inbreak into history in the final coming of the Son of man. But he was awaiting the Father's unfolding purpose and the special requirements that would be made clear at the proper time. The early years were a preparation and rehearsal for all that he was to do later.

Everything hangs together for the carrying out of God's plan. Even Simon Peter's denial of his Lord was so redeemed by God's grace that Simon was a better person despite his sin. Simon's great moment came later, and his earlier impatience and disobedience did not keep him from fulfilling his destiny.

III. Doing all that God requires means humble obedience to God's perceived will.

The Letter to the Hebrews tells us that Jesus learned obedience through the things that he suffered. There were choices to be made all along the way, some of them painful because of what they embraced, some of them painful because of what he had to give for them. Albert Schweitzer found God's plan to require him to give up certain attractive vocations for which he was fully prepared and that he would enjoy, in order to follow a different calling that was less attractive and that would impose suffer-

ing that he could have avoided. Eduard Schweizer writes, "In the Old Testament and above all in the Judaism of the last two centuries before Jesus, doing God's will consisted mainly of humble acceptance by the righteous man of the suffering imposed on him by God." Indeed, the word the Father spoke to Jesus at the baptism recalled the words in Isaiah concerning the Suffering Servant (Isa. 42:1).

Carrying out God's plan for our individual life, doing all that God requires, may entail hardship, but it will always offer the possibility of joy that no other way can promise.—James W. Cox

SUNDAY: JANUARY SEVENTEENTH

SERVICE OF WORSHIP

Sermon: Creating Art for the Master
Text: Psalm 149

It is a well-known fact that down through the centuries humanity has celebrated the cause of Christ through the arts. During the Middle Ages, Europe had one of its greatest moments of artistic fervor. The Renaissance brought into being perhaps the greatest of all artistic revivals. Through the Middle Ages all the way down to our contemporary age, people have tried to convey their innermost religious feelings through various media: music, paintings, sculpture, theater, poetry, and novels. Some have been more successful than others in stirring that which is most sacred in one's heart. Yet, both the performing and the visual arts have contributed vastly to the evangelism of the Western world. The paintings of Raphael and Michelangelo spoke much more deeply to an illiterate world about the love of God than any Latin chanted by a priest.

It has been the poet's artistic verses of a hymn which have contributed so heavily to the worship of God in Christ. Poets have always been able to sum up the very feelings that are at the core of our being. It was in his memoirs, entitled *Confieso Que He Vivido: Memorias,* that Pablo Neruda wrote, "Poetry is a deep inner

calling in man; from it came liturgy, the psalms, and also the content of religions." Neruda knew that the inner presence that one has of God can be expressed through the words of the poet, and those words easily make the transformation into the hymns we sing.

I. In Psalm 149 we see how the writer of this rather vigorous psalm of praise was describing something of what might be called today a war dance. The Hebrews wanted to give thanks for past accomplishment. They also wanted to be assured of God's abiding presence as they faced any approaching battles. We know that God is a jealous God, so his kingdom has no room for a rival, whether enemies or evil or death.[1] By performing this dance, they were in effect saying that they were loyal to their God, Yahweh, and expected his loyalty in return.

(a) The people were called together to "sing to the Lord a new song." Through a common art form of their day, they were expressing thanks to God for his help. This was an expression of gratitude to God for their military victory. They praised God with a very sacred dance, all

---

[1] Alton H. McEachern, "Psalms," *Layman's Bible Book Commentary,* vol. 8 (Nashville, TN: Broadman Press, 1981), 166.

the while making melody with the tambourine and harp.[2] The faithful Hebrews sang praises to glorify God after their triumph. They were singing for joy. They praised God with their united voices and with a sword dance. Israel's victory represented to all who would come into contact with them a sense of vengeance, chastisement, and the execution of judgment on their enemies. Their enemies were seen as God's foes as well.[3]

(b) Seen in the context of its times, this psalm is understandable. The really sad thing is that we have made so little progress in learning to love our enemies and make them our friends. We still seek vengeance and sing songs like "Onward, Christian Soldiers," which claim that God is always on our side, despite Jesus' teachings.

II. Most of us will never write a beautiful poem, though, or compose an eternal melody or paint a picture of such delight and magnificence that it will last into the next millenium. Our lives, however, can be the art form, when properly created, that will have the same results as the frescoes of the Sistine chapel.

(a) We live our lives so as to influence the world around us. Some of the influence is for the better. Some is not. When we have long passed from this world and the only thing remaining is what we actually left behind, the response from the world about our lives undoubtedly will be, "It's pretty, but is it art?" The art that spans eternity is not the audacious and ludicrous projects that are thrown together. If we could imagine Adam's thoughts when he drew that first picture in the dirt, we would realize that the art that will last for generations is the same art that touches the human spirit with its simplicity. Our lives must be lived in such a way that they can be looked upon as an art form in themselves.

(b) Despite his sense of humor, for which we undoubtedly remember Mark Twain, despite his flair for fun that could be seen in his writings, he pretty much

felt at the end that the world was pitiful and useless and that the human race was contemptible. It is common for ministers to divide people into groups of good and bad. But then one runs upon two different kinds of good people: those who end with the cynicism Mark Twain describes and those who crown life's close with radiance and zest.[4]

III. Our lives must take on a unique art form, even if it is one of animation. Cartoons used to spawn toys. Things have started to run just backwards in recent years. Toys have cartoons developed for them. Saturday mornings are just one big commercial for the latest fad of toys. There is one set of plastic action figures that have become the stars of their own cartoon shows. They're called the Transformers. The figures include automobiles, trucks, and cassette tapes, just to name a few. But these common everyday figures become very powerful and uncommon robots as they are twisted and transformed with the imagination of children.

The figures can have their forms changed at will. If the child wants to play with a car, then that is the shape that the figure can assume. But if a robot is needed, the figure can be transformed at will.

(a) So often we are like the Transformers. God has touched our lives and has transformed us into something artistically beautiful. Even though we want to serve him, even though we want to be Christ-like, we tend to do it when it best suits our needs. We don't mind being identified with Christ if it is in our best interest. Like Peter, we can say, "I don't know him!" if we think it is to our advantage.

(b) We must realize that it is God who changes us, who transforms us. We are not transformed by our will, but by his. We are changed by his power for our sake and for service for him and his children. He does not transform us against

[2]Ibid.
[3]Ibid.

[4]Harry Emerson Fosdick, *On Being Fit to Live With* (New York: Harper & Brothers, 1946), 159.

our will. As we allow him to come into our lives, he fashions us into something beautiful and will continue to change us into his image.

(c) God offers to change our death into life, our fears into faith, and our despair into hope. Will we allow God to transform us? Can we become something artistically beautiful, something that stirs another person's being, just by the presence of God in our lives?—Bobby J. Touchton

Illustrations

BEYOND FACTS.   The painters and the poets and the musicians know that there is an order of reality in which intellectual assurance plays no part and the reason is unimportant. It is not measurable by the machinery of our minds, but it is real. "All great poetry," Keats says, "should produce the instantaneous conviction, this is true." The function of art, Tolstoy said, is to make that understood which in the form of an argument would be incomprehensible. There is a field where all wonderful perfections of microscope and telescope fail, all exquisite niceties of weights and measures, as well as that which is behind them, the keen and driving power of the mind. No facts however indubitably detected, no effort of reason however magnificently maintained, can prove that Bach's music is beautiful.— Edith Hamilton, cited by Gerald Kennedy

FREEDOM THROUGH THE ARTS.   A report of the Julliard School of Music indicated that this school regarded it as its responsibility, among other duties, to help the student to "make his own judgments; to learn that art is not concerned with conformity; to equip the student to deal with the novel without ridicule or fear of its strangeness, yet without being impressed by sheer novelty, and with the ability to probe the depths of the unfamiliar."[1] The report expressed this

hope:"If the student truly absorbs the concept of free inquiry in the field of music . . . he will bring something of this approach not only to other fields of knowledge but to the conduct of his daily life."[2]—James W. Cox

Sermon Suggestions

PREPARATION FOR SERVICE.   TEXT: Isa. 49:1–7. (1) The Lord's prevenient call, verses 1–3. (2) The Servant's anguished ambivalence, verse 4. (3) The Lord's redeeming reversal, verses 5–7.

WHERE GOD'S GRACE BLESSES US. TEXT: 1 Cor. 1:1–9. (1) We are spiritually enriched for service to Christ. (2) We are assured that divine resources are available as long as we live.

Worship Aids

CALL TO WORSHIP.   "Because of God's great mercy to us I appeal to you: Offer yourselves as a living sacrifice to God, dedicated to his service and pleasing to him. This is the true worship that you should offer" (Rom. 12:1, TEV).

INVOCATION.   Lord, we boldly approach your throne for you beckon us and desire our fellowship. Give us a wider vision of life and a deeper understanding of your purposes. Align us through this service with your designs and give our hearts to sing your praise all through the week.—E. Lee Phillips

OFFERTORY SENTENCE.   "Give unto the Lord the glory due unto his name: bring an offering, and come before him; worship the Lord in the beauty of holiness" (1 Chron. 16:29).

OFFERTORY PRAYER.   Holy God, let deep needs be met through these gifts and the one true God honored.—E. Lee Phillips

PRAYER.   Eternal Father, walk with us in the plain paths where the day-by-day

---

[1]Jacques Barzun, *Music in American Life* (Gloucester, MA: Peter Smith, 1958), 59.

[2]Ibid.

routine settles down to a test of private perseverance, unheralded by any praise or the promise of some big reward. If the heavenly vision grows dim and our hearts become weary in well-doing, lay your hand upon us and steady our steps that we may press onward, even in darkness, toward the light ahead. If we are alone and the tasks of life seem more than we can do, or when done are not welcomed by the world, reveal your presence by our side that we may labor on with your help. Turn us this morning from dreams of far glory and unrealized hopes that we may work in the commonplace circumstances of this mortal world. Disclose to us the miracle of your grace in unexpected places as we fulfill our purposes in this life.

Father, in this world of hurry and worry, still us for a moment that we may get our bearings and meet the needs which you reveal to us day by day and which we so often do not see because we are blinded by our own ambitions and desires. Make us aware of the child who needs our guidance and help to make it to adulthood. Open our eyes to the falterings of the elderly, the struggles of the poor, the closed opportunities of the minorities, the struggle for bread of the uprooted, the cries of anguish from the depressed, the calls for support from the ones broken by life's burdens, the wail for direction from those who are lost. Show us the need to share sacred time with those who are lonely, those who are confined, those who are rejected by fellow humans. Create in us a spirit of generosity which sees opportunities to invest in others not only our wealth, but ourselves, that life may be made easier and more manageable for all sorts of folks we meet. Above all, may we truly be the instruments through which Christ becomes real in a redeeming way for men and women, boys and girls as we move through life seeking in conscious ways to proclaim him by what we are, what we do, and what we say. So grant that in this hour we may be empowered by his Spirit to meet the world in his love.—Henry Fields

LECTIONARY MESSAGE

Topic: What John Saw in Jesus
TEXT: John 1:29–34

The world will be forever indebted to John the Baptist for helping people to see the mission of Jesus Christ clearly and without prejudice or jealousy.

According to the Fourth Gospel, John did not know the real significance of Jesus until Jesus' baptism. But at that time John's eyes were opened to what he could scarcely have dreamed of before. Even today, there are people who have met Jesus of Nazareth in the pages of the New Testament and have heard others speak of him in conversation or in sermons but who have never realized his true meaning for their individual life or for the world.

After John's eyes were opened, Jesus was for John more than he had ever imagined. What did John the Baptist then see in Jesus?

I. *Jesus' significance.* Jesus fulfilled the role of the Servant of the Lord in Isaiah. The other three Gospels quote the words spoken from heaven that include a phrase from Isaiah 42, "in you I am well pleased." This implies that Jesus was the ideal fulfillment of all that was said of that Servant of the Lord, since any such phrase is a link to a larger context. John called Jesus the Lamb that God had provided, which was his way of linking Jesus with the Servant of the Lord, as described in Isaiah 53: "like a lamb that is led to the slaughter."

Specifically, John saw in Jesus the One who would remove the sin of the world. Joseph was told, "You are to name him Jesus, for he will save his people from their sins" (Matt. 1:21). What the patriarchs like Abraham could not do; what Moses the Lawgiver could not do; what the prophets could not do; what the priests and the entire sacrificial system could not do; this Jesus was to do—to deal effectively with the sin problem. Your sin and mine meets its match in the sacrificial love and work of Jesus Christ. His ethical teaching is incomparably beautiful, and the doing of his teaching is the world's best hope for the achievement of all the high goals of human society. We can begin to carry out his teaching, however, only when we are truly captured by his saving love.

II. *Jesus' enduement.* John saw in Jesus another aspect of his servanthood: Jesus was empowered by the Spirit of God to do what God had called him to do. "I have put my Spirit upon him; he will bring forth justice to the nations" (Isa. 42:1b). As described in Isaiah, God's Servant would work gently and patiently until he had accomplished what God sent him to do. This was precisely the spirit and style of Jesus—he gathered to God the outcasts and rejects, as well as many who were in the upper strata of society. His was not the way of threat and bombast but of love and grace and undergirding. Such is the way of the working of God's Spirit: "Not by might, nor by power, but by my Spirit, says the Lord of hosts" (Zech. 4:6b).

Clearly, the descent of the Spirit on Jesus at his baptism was not Jesus' first taste of the Spirit, but it was a special filling or equipping for what he was to do throughout his ministry. So it is with Jesus' followers. The Spirit of God touches the lives of believers at many times in many ways; however, a special time of dedication to a special calling may bring one into a deeper relationship to God that will make possible service that would otherwise be impossible or insignificant.

III. *Jesus' continuing mission.* John saw that what happened to Jesus at his baptism was just the beginning for something momentous. Jesus was to proliferate what he came to do, through others that *he* would fill with the Spirit, for he was the one who would baptize with the Spirit (v. 33). Our baptism, like that of Jesus, is not the climax of our experience with God: we have a continuing mission. In fact, we could say that what happens ideally in believer's baptism is laypeople's ordination for service. For other believers, we could say something similar for confirmation. Receiving of the Holy Spirit in such special contexts is not for private enjoyment or for the gaining of a personal sense of security. It is designed for the blessing of others—to pass on in gratitude and grace what one has received.—James W. Cox

SUNDAY: JANUARY TWENTY-FOURTH

SERVICE OF WORSHIP

Sermon: A Time for Rainbows

TEXT: Gen. 8:15–22; 9:8–16

If ever there has been a time for rainbows, that time is now. Rainbows are not just pretty, frivolous outcomes of rain showers. They are visual signs that God has given us another chance.

The story of the rainbow in Genesis pictures Noah coming out of a time of catastrophe. The Flood had covered the known world of Noah. It had drowned his acquaintances and his plans but not his hope! Noah's hope was not in anything that could be covered by the water; rather, his hope was in the Creator of the water.

The word *rainbow* here in Genesis is the same word for a warrior's bow. The symbolism is that God had hung up his bow in the clouds. It was as if God had said, "I'm not angry anymore. I'm through fighting. See, I am hanging up my bow." God's mercy is the bow over every act of judgment. This bow in the sky is a sign of hope.

We can endure a word of judgment, but we live by hope. We can put up with hardship, but we thrive on hope. We can live with deprivation, but we cannot live without hope. A young man and woman come to love each other and get married. They may not have much cash, but they are high on hope. When my wife and I were married, she had three words placed on the outside of my wedding ring: "Nothing but Hope." This is what the story of Noah and the rainbow says, too: "Nothing but hope."

I. We live in hope because God's Creation is dependable (8:22). Noah had lived through drastic changes in the world, but he still realized the natural rhythm still existed. As the *Good News Bible* puts it, "As long as the world exists, there will be a time for planting and a time for harvest. There will always be cold and heat, summer and winter, day and night."

Some of you have experienced enormous changes. You have seen two world wars and other conflicts. You have lived during the development of the atomic bomb. You lived through the turbulent sixties when it seemed that society was being torn apart. Many of you have had those disruptive experiences in your own lives. You have faced death, pain, children running away, and loss of jobs.

This is why it is comforting to hear Noah speak of the dependability of God's Creation. Yes, the Flood had come, but it was gone now. Now it was time to get back into rhythm. These predictable changes in the earth and in our lives give us a soothing feeling. God, and no one or nothing else, is the source of all security and stability. That is cause for hope.

II. Hope sustains us even when our world seems to fall apart. The world as Noah had known it was gone. His task after the Flood was to reconstruct his own life and rebuild his world.

In a sense, all major losses in our lives amount to the loss of our worlds. Some have built their own seemingly secure worlds with family, position, or the status of a bank account. The problem with all of those is their impermanence. A dream house can burn to the ground. The ideal mate can suddenly die. The perfect job can turn sour rather quickly. What we think of as our world can simply turn into chaos in the proverbial blink of an eye.

Duke McCall, president of the Baptist World Alliance, told of an experience after his wife died. A friend expressed his sorrow by saying, "I'm so sorry you lost your wife." Dr. McCall responded, "I didn't lose my wife. I know where she is. I'm the one who is lost." In a crisis like that, we are sustained by our hope in the Lord who hangs his rainbow in the sky and says, "I care about you."

III. We live in hope primarily because of God's promise (9:8–16). The rainbow was the sign of a covenant, an agreement, between God and Noah and his descendants. God came to Noah and pledged his care. Verses 14 through 16 put it this way: "Whenever I cover the sky with clouds and the rainbow appears, I will remember my promise to you and to all the animals that a flood will never again destroy all living beings. When the rainbow appears in the clouds, I will see it and remember the everlasting covenant between me and all living beings on earth" (GNB).[1]

God's promise of his love and care sustains us even though we do not always deserve it. You do not read very far in this story before you see Noah getting drunk and making a fool out of himself. God could have said, "If that's the way you are going to act, I'll withdraw my promise of care." He could have done that, but he did not. In fact, he intensified the promise. Many years after Noah, Jesus came along and brought a new covenant. It reaffirmed everything said to Noah but went deeper.

This is a time for rainbows. Our world needs them, and you and I individually need them. There's nothing but hope.—Don M. Aycock

Illustrations

TRYING TOO HARD. "Please leave something for God to do!" I once exclaimed to a man who was overcome with worries about how to avoid doing anything wrong. All this effort expended on oneself never leads to anything but fresh failure. In a talk I once heard, the lecturer called it trying to reach heaven by pulling on one's own hair. I am reminded of a child who cut his finger with a bread knife. The bread was hard, and so the child made such an effort that the knife went too far.—Paul Tournier

BOLD HOPE. The day will come when my physical body will be dead. I tell you what I should like to have you do. I should like for my physical body to be disposed of quickly and simply and then for my friends to come together in a room like this, to praise God and to rejoice. I hope there will not be a single tear. Is this not what you ask for yourself? Is this not what you would like when death comes to those whom you love most? The Christian way of facing the end is not the way of sorrow.

Older than the Apostles' Creed, older than the Nicene Creed, is perhaps the most profound conviction in the whole of our faith. And this is it. "I am persuaded that neither death nor life can separate us from the love of God in Jesus Christ our Lord." Of this I am persuaded, and by this I can live.—Elton Trueblood

Sermon Suggestions

GOD'S ACTION.   TEXT: Isa. 9:1–4. (1) Brings clarity out of confusion, verse 2. (2) Brings joy out of sadness, verse 3. (3) Brings freedom out of bondage, verse 4.

PERSONALITY CULT RELIGION.   TEXT: 1 Cor. 1:10–17. (1) It is divisive. (2) It creates rivals for Christ. (3) It empties Christ's cross of its power.

Worship Aids

CALL TO WORSHIP.   "Let us draw near with a true heart in full assurance of faith, having our hearts sprinkled from an evil conscience, and our bodies washed with pure water. Let us hold fast the profession of our faith without wavering (for he is faithful that promised); and let us consider one another to provoke unto love and to good works" (Heb. 10:22–24).

INVOCATION.   O Lord, where have we missed the way, when have we failed to do what we should have done, why have we done the opposite of what we affirm? Holy God, help us to face ourselves this day and in the presence of our Savior

and these believers find the truth that will make us whole.—E. Lee Phillips

OFFERTORY SENTENCE.   "The Lord is good to all: and his tender mercies are over all his works" (Ps. 145:9).

OFFERTORY PRAYER.   Lord, be merciful to us as we give that we not withhold what ought to be shared nor shirk the causes of the kingdom which Christ calls us to support.—E. Lee Phillips

PRAYER.   God, forgive us for supposing that we can put words in your mouth, but perhaps, you are asking of each of us:

Having eyes do you see?
Having ears do you hear?
And do you remember?

Through your Word so poignantly spoken are you reminding us that the tragedy of the disciples in seeing, but not seeing, in hearing, but not hearing, in seeing and hearing, but forgetting, can also be our tragedy?

O Father, "forgive us, when we drift from love's high moment to forgetfulness." Your amazing love and grace in the gift of life itself should keep us alert to miracles of your love and grace in everyday and everywhere. All things do become new when we really see them. To see them is to see them in their originality.

In your coming in Christ, we become new, because he opens our eyes to see ourself in all of our originality—a child of yours created and re-created by grace. Life is a miracle of your grace; our life is a miracle of your grace; all of life is a miracle of your grace. Why should we ever doubt that we do live in an open universe?

Ask and you shall receive—
Seek and you shall find—
Knock and it shall be opened unto you.

Through your strong Word proclaimed among us, save us from that familiarity that handles the mysteries of life casually—from that cynicism that shrugs at the incredible with indifference and from that callousness that keeps us from discerning the movings of your Spirit in the happenings and relationship of our everyday.

Grant, O Father, that this church may be a spiritual laboratory where, through daring faith, the fullness of your life is discovered in Jesus Christ and is released into the world for the wholeness of persons and the healing of the nations.— John M. Thompson

LECTIONARY MESSAGE

Topic: When the Kingdom Draws Near
TEXT: Matt. 4:12–23
Who has the right to rule over Creation and expect conformity to his will? Certainly the one who brought it into being. We human beings are a part of God's Creation, and God has every right to require us to conform to his purposes: He is Lord.

The old catechism asks, "What is the chief end of man?" and the proper answer is "To glorify God and enjoy him forever."

What we are talking about here is the kingdom of heaven, or as we read in the other synoptic Gospels, *the kingdom of God*. The kingdom of heaven or of God, means the rule of God in our lives. Of course, God has always been the Ruler, and his will has been carried out by human beings more or less as long as people have been aware of their Creator. But at this point in Jesus' life, the kingdom of God drew near in a climactic way, and there began a dramatic unfolding of its significance that would reach its final fulfillment in the coming age.

When the kingdom draws near, we see the following.
I. *Ancient Scripture is fulfilled.*
(a) Here and there in the Old Testament light broke through, pointing to a new day. Isaiah, especially, looked past the narrow nationalism of his contemporaries and saw the triumph of the God of the ends of the earth. "The people who sat in darkness have seen a great light" (v. 16a).

(b) Matthew, especially, among the evangelists was careful to show the connection between various Old Testament references to the Messiah and Jesus of Nazareth. While some may question the appropriateness of certain linkings, it appears that Matthew was in general quite correct in his attempts to show that the Messiah to whom the Old Testament looked forward was indeed Jesus.

(c) Throughout the history of God's people, there have been outstanding manifestations of God's kingdom at certain junctures. People have witnessed happenings that they did not hesitate to call miracles. D. S. Cairns noted that this seemed to be the case at some new frontier, where the gospel was being preached perhaps for the first time. The kingdom does keep breaking through, and Scripture does keep finding new fulfillments, as, for example, on the day of Pentecost.

II. *Repentance is the fitting response.*
(a) When God moves in, nothing can ever be the same again. Even the slightest awareness of God leads to some reaction or response. How much greater, then, is the result of a dramatic inbreak of the kingdom, like that which came in the person of Jesus Christ. Simeon said to Mary of the infant Jesus, "This child is destined for the falling and the rising of many in Israel" (Luke 2:34). Who knows when that "near end" of the kingdom will touch his or her life, with its demands and its opportunities?

(b) Never does the kingdom of God come near without opening new doors and charting new paths. Repentance is not necessarily accompanied by a weeping and gnashing of teeth: It can be mainly and simply a cool decision to change one's way, to follow the path that God will show.

III. *Proclaimers are needed.* Four men mentioned in our text demonstrated what can happen when Christ calls us, that is, how repentance leads to service. In truth, when a vital change takes place in a life, service to God and humanity will follow in one form or another.

(a) Christ calls us when we are about our usual occupations. He seeks us out where we are, sometimes where we are hiding in a flurry of activity designed to keep him at bay. The average church member would be surprised to learn what a wide variety of occupations students for the ministry were called from. Peter and Andrew, James and John were in the fishing business when Jesus called them to discipleship and to the task of fishing for people.

(b) Christ's call to us is decisive and may be costly. For the four men it meant giving up their nets and many other customary activities and certain creature comforts. But who can measure the re-

wards of living and serving in the presence of Jesus Christ? The compensations can always outweigh the costs.

IV. *Dramatic events follow.* We might think that Matthew speaks in hyperbole when he reports that Jesus went about "curing every disease and every sickness among the people" (v. 23b). If we were caught up in God's working, however, we might be tempted to use even bolder language to describe what God does when he has his way, who is "able to accomplish abundantly far more than all we can ask or imagine" (Eph. 3:20, NRSV).—James W. Cox

SUNDAY: JANUARY THIRTY-FIRST

SERVICE OF WORSHIP

Sermon: Happiness Is . . .
TEXT: Matt. 5:3–12

We Americans have been obsessed with the idea of happiness since Thomas Jefferson paraphrased John Locke. Jefferson wrote in the Declaration of Independence that the rights of man are "life, liberty, and the pursuit of happiness." We certainly pursue it as if this will-o'-the-wisp were our birthright.

There is nothing wrong with our being happy. In fact Jesus' Sermon on the Mount is the Master's manifesto of authentic happiness. Writing on the Beatitudes, Billy Graham called them "The Secret of Happiness," and Leonard Griffith entitled them "The Pathway to Happiness."

However, let me sound a warning here. There is a sharp contrast between the world's idea of happiness and Jesus' teaching. The world sees the source of happiness as success, money, power, and pride. They expect to achieve it by being aggressive and looking out for number one. Jesus' approach is revolutionary according to society's standards. In the Beatitudes we encounter a series of Jesus' "hard sayings."

Each Beatitude begins with the Greek word *makarios*. It can be translated "bless-

ed," "happy," "O how happy," "to be congratulated." George Buttrick translated *makarios* as "bravo joy." This inward joy is not simply based on circumstances, happenstance. It is deep and abiding—often defying outward conditions of life.

I. *Contrasts with the world's idea of happiness.* Jesus taught that kingdom persons are characterized by *poverty* of spirit. "Blessed are the poor in spirit" (literally beggars), verse 3. Happy are those who realize their spiritual poverty and rely on God's grace. This is the opposite of spiritual pride. "Nothing in my hand I bring; simply to thy cross I cling."

Sorrow is also pronounced blessed. Fortunate are those who have a godly sorrow for their sin (v. 4). They shall know the "comfort" of forgiveness and a new beginning.

Meek is perhaps the hardest beatitude to understand (v. 5). We think of someone who is meek as being mousey, henpecked, a Casper Milquetoast kind of person. However, here the word describes one who leads a God-controlled life. These are the majestic meek. God's gentlepeople. The French Bible translates the word meek as "debonair" (*les debonnaires*).

II. *Characteristics of Christian happiness.* *Hunger* and *thirst* for righteousness is a sign of spiritual wealth—as appetite is characteristic of physical health. Jesus promised that those who hunger for God will be "satisfied" (v. 6).

Mercy is also an indication of Christian happiness. Those who show mercy also receive it. Which of us is not in need of divine mercy and grace? How grand to be merciful in our dealings with others (v. 7).

Purity of heart, mind, and motives characterizes the Christian life as well. Believers are to be unpolluted by the world and its unworthy standards of right and wrong. Jesus said that those who are pure in attitude and life will "see God" (v. 8).

Peacemakers, not simply peacekeepers, are to be congratulated. It is easy to start a rumor, plant a suspicion or doubt. It is easy to start a war—there have been more than a hundred armed conflicts since the close of World War II. However, making peace is hard. President Jimmy Carter worked at peacemaking. Those who make peace will be called "the children of God," Jesus said. They are like their heavenly Father (v. 9).

III. *The Consequences of Living by the Beatitudes (vv. 10–12).* I would expect people who live by these high standards to be welcomed with open arms. Surely they enrich life and make the world a better place in which to live.

However, Jesus warned us that kingdom persons will be misunderstood by the world. They march to the beat of a different drummer and may expect to be despised, not applauded; persecuted, not honored. People who take the Sermon on the Mount seriously usually disturb those with lesser standards. However, they win God's favor, becoming like salt and light—change agents.

Happiness may be defined in many ways: reading a bedtime story to a toddler; watching the surf or the change of colors on a mountain range; the satisfaction of a job well done; a friend's smile, handshake, embrace; quality time spent together. Make your own list.

Happiness is elusive. If we deliberately go after it we are apt to miss it. Jesus said, "He who saves his life will lose it, and he who loses his life shall find (save) it" (Matt. 10:39). Authentic happiness is a by-product that frequently takes us by surprise.

Christian happiness most often comes from usefulness. It is when we lose our lives in the service of others that we most often find it. Albert Schweitzer said that only those who have learned to serve are happy.

Right relationships with God and others insure happiness and joy. I saw spiritual revival come to a church when estranged sisters became reconciled. Jesus knew this inner peace even within the shadow of his cross. The night of his betrayal he said to the disciples, "These things have I spoken to you that my joy may be in you, and that your joy may be full" (John 15:11). Here is real happiness. Jesus embodied, it, setting us an example.—Alton H. McEachern

Illustrations

DEFINITION OF HAPPINESS. But what is happiness? We ought to define our terms in the very first sentence lest misunderstandings arise from the very beginning. But we are going to evade the challenge and leave the definition of human happiness to metaphysicians and college sophomores, because happiness is not a thing that can be defined by mathematical formulas. Happiness is no apple that you can peel and eat. Happiness is a quality and an attribute of the good life. The more you try to define it the less you know about it. It is as ineluctable as electricity, as evanescent as melody, as indefinable as health, as variable as speed, time, matter, and the other fictions on which life itself is built. Happiness knows no standards and no limits. If we want to know what happiness is we must seek it, therefore, not as if it were a pot of gold at the end of the rainbow, but among human beings who are living richly and fully, the good life.—W. Béran Wolfe

"IN SPITE OF." Life has no traffic with all or none; it deals rather in "more or less." The neurotic becomes happy, which means in the long run overcoming his neurosis, when he is able to accept this "more or less" dialectic and distill his happiness out of the flux. He then learns that to be a man is to be imperfection impregnated by perfection, and that happiness comes only when one can creatively accept this human situation. He learns to affirm himself. He learns not to deride himself for his hates but to understand them and assimilate them as far as possible in his loves; he accepts his fears as the reverse side of his hopes, his lustful desires as the imperfection of his social tendencies, and his temptations to take refuge in falsehood as part of his understanding of truth. He recognizes himself as no simple pattern of clay but a dynamic personality. Nothing in himself will be perfect. Yet his very imperfections will imply some perfection which continually impregnates him and permits him thus to partake in the goodness of creation. One affirms oneself by moving from the "yes" of enthusiastic approval through the "no" of realization of one's imperfections to the "in spite of" which is the human situation. There is vast relief in this coming to terms with the strange creature which is oneself.—Rollo May

Sermon Suggestions

RELIGION'S BOTTOM LINE.   TEXT: Mic. 6:1–8, especially verse 8. (1) Obey the law—"do justice." (2) Follow the spirit of the law—"love kindness." (3) Live up to the requirements of a personal commitment—"walk humbly with your God."

CHRIST   CRUCIFIED.   TEXT: 1   Cor. 1:18–31. (1) He is a rebuke to the pride of human achievements. (2) He is the hope of the world's "nobodies."

Worship Aids

CALL TO WORSHIP.   "Thou wilt show me the path of life; in thy presence is fullness of joy; at thy right hand there are pleasures forevermore" (Ps. 16:11).

INVOCATION.   Help us to experience what we know to be true, O God, that genuine happiness and true joy can be found in your way and will. Save us from the deceptions that sometimes overtake us and lead us astray.

OFFERTORY SENTENCE.   "Each one, as a good manager of God's different gifts, must use for the good of others the special gift he has received from God" (1 Pet. 4:10, TEV).

OFFERTORY   PRAYER.   Spread   your power through our giving, Lord, that what we intend and you purpose may be fused in perfect harmony to meet the needs of the strongest, the weakest, and the neediest, as only Jesus can do.—E. Lee Phillips

PRAYER.   Merciful God, you know who we are, and we know all that you ask: that we act justly and love loyalty and that we walk wisely before you.

You know wherein we have failed you, and you know the hidden life of your righteousness within our own, the trees of integrity planted and watered in you.

Forgive us our dead branches, all in us that is leafless, gnarled, and bare. Prune as love requires. Protect and cherish all that is of you, lest we be cynical of ourselves, lest we not believe in your goodness, lest we lose heart.

Merciful God, teach us to love you, miserable sinners though we be, broken-winged birds, less than whole.—Peter Fribley

LECTIONARY MESSAGE

Topic: Who Is Truly Happy?
TEXT: Matt. 5:1–12

The words that Jesus spoke on the mountain are words of salvation. This salvation is for those who hear and take seriously what Jesus says.

The setting suggests a picture of a teacher surrounded by pupils or even, to some scholars, a royal setting: Jesus sits as a king, and his subjects surround him.

I. *The people addressed.* Jesus pronounces blessings on the masses, "the crowds"—though the crowds are represented by the "disciples" who came to him.

(a) Jesus did not address an elite group. His audience was made up of the *am ha'arets,* the "people of the land." Not the scribes and priests and rulers, but the ordinary people received the blessing. Christianity has always been, first of all, a grass-roots movement. The Apostle Paul, writing to Christians at Corinth a generation later, said, "Consider your own calling, brothers and sisters: not many of you were wise by human standards, not many were powerful, not many were of noble birth" (1 Cor. 1:26, NRSV). We must remember that there are always exceptions (Nicodemus, Joseph of Aramathea, Lydia, and others) in every generation of Christian history. God does love the up-and-out as well as the down-and-out!

(b) The type of people Jesus spoke to *then* ought to be an encouragement to the many seekers after a word from God today—the poor, the oppressed, the suffering, the confused. There is even hope for the exploiters, the oppressors, if they realize their need and take seriously what Jesus says.

II. *The message given.*

(a) Jesus gave a message of salvation. When he declared the people blessed, he, in a sense, congratulated them as recipients of salvation, something that belonged to them then and there, something to rejoice in at the present moment.

As we look at the separate Beatitudes, we see in ascending order the attitudes and actions of one who experiences salvation—all the way from a deep sense of spiritual need (poverty of spirit) to the ultimate consequences of faithful Christian living—facing persecution!

At the same time, Jesus gave a message of promise and hope. As Eduard Schweizer puts it, "All eight Beatitudes are permeated by God's 'Yes' that becomes reality in each Beatitude because of Jesus' presence, although the visible fulfillment of the promise rests solely in God's hands and will not be realized until the coming of his Kingdom."

The church's message today is a message of good news, of acceptance. You are accepted, whoever you are; accepted by the God who forgives, changes, strengthens, and calls to service through Jesus Christ. You today are so blessed by the same God and his Christ.

III. *The speaker.* Is all of this true? Well, it depends on who it is that speaks. No earthly ruler could guarantee it, nor any philosopher. The one who speaks is Jesus Christ, the Son of God. As the Epistle to the Hebrews says, "In these last days [God] has spoken to us by a Son" (1:2a, NRSV). The way it sounded to those who listened to Jesus that day was like this: "The crowds were astounded at his teaching, for he taught them as one having authority, and not as their scribes" (Matt. 7:28b–29, NRSV).

Is all of this true for us today? The way to find out whether the one who speaks is worthy of our trust and obedience is to give him a chance to prove himself to us. He welcomes our even tentative movements to follow him. He said, "My teaching is not mine but his who sent me. Anyone who resolves to do the will of God will know whether the teaching is from God or whether I am speaking on my own" (John 7:16–17, NRSV).—James W. Cox

SUNDAY: FEBRUARY SEVENTH

SERVICE OF WORSHIP

Sermon: Prayer, Hearing, and Action

TEXT: Isa. 6:1–8

Albert Day's *Autobiography of Prayer* relates a humorous incident in a drifting lifeboat in which one of the stronger crew members was overcome by fear. He dropped his oar and declared that he was going to pray. A seasoned sailor shouted, "Let the *little* fellow pray. You stick to the oars!" Our nervous jokes about prayer often raise the real questions we are asking. Is prayer an alternative to action? Is prayer reserved for the weak and the infirm or for the helpless moments in life when we have in desperation exhausted all other resources? Is prayer the last resort in dealing with the crisis situation—the emergency measure after all hope is lost? Is prayer a substitute for rowing the boat? Are prayer and action mutually exclusive alternatives? Does prayer imply dependence while action asserts independence? When you come to the crisis in life which leaves you feeling powerless and totally without recourse, do you turn to prayer?

For the activist among us, the hardest moment in life is the dead end which allows absolutely no alternatives and no solutions. The question today is the place of prayer in our lives. Among the platitudes in the vocabulary of the Christian Pharisee is the offer of prayer instead of action. James is critical of the faith which is lacking in work and finds an interesting model in the Christian who prefers to offer words, "Go in peace; keep warm and eat your fill," in the place of food and clothing. Just as the Christian needs an expanded vision of faith which incorporates faithful action, we need a larger image of prayer which finds its way to our feet.

I. Prayer is hearing the Word of God. With the death of King Uzziah, the last and only hope and the final alternative to a political repair of Judah's crumbling foundations was buried. The year 742 B.C. was a turning point in the tide of fortune for Israel and Judah. The era of peace and prosperity was ending with the expansion of Assyria. Isaiah was in a state of despair.

When all else fails, shall we pray? Isaiah certainly did not go to the Temple to volunteer for Uzziah's throne. This encounter with God is slightly different from the usual. Isaiah comes with no agenda except his grief, no petition with which to direct the ways of God, no words framed in careful prose to capture the great ideas of a great mind. There prayer is listening. The vision of God and song of the seraphs turns a side of prayer you may not have discovered. If prayer is only speaking petitions to God, you leave no room for hearing. The sense of God's holiness which confronted Isaiah is an experience of speechless awe. Rudolf Otto called it "mysterium tremendum." If indeed God is Creator and Lord, we should not be surprised to find God beyond our rational comprehension. The divine presence is never trivial or chummy. Pop Christianity may "have a little talk with Jesus," but it does not know the God for whom Christ cleared the Temple commerce. Isaiah would not recognize the God we confuse with the warm fuzzies. The hearing of the Word of God is beyond your usual senses. If you have never heard voices exactly as Isaiah describes, do not feel neglected. But if you have never experienced the reverent awe of Isaiah, you have prayed to a lesser god.

II. Prayer moves toward mission. The Word of God is a call to action: "Whom shall I send?" The word of prayer responds in commitment, "Here am I; send me!" The crushed prophet found his feet on his knees. He found the renewal of hope in the grace of forgiveness. Prayer opened the door to action. Work needs to be done, and covenants need to be established. Isaiah came to the Temple in despair and left with a mission, and I think that this is the norm rather than the exception. Prayer opens avenues of service and alternatives for action beyond imagination. Thus, you should not pray unless you are willing to go. Prayer is not the lever by which we move God. It is the link by which we are moved by God.

In the late eighteenth century, William Carey sat in his cobbler's shop meditating on the world. He was moved by the absence of the church in India. As he prayed daily for the world, he was compelled to become the response to his petition to God. In 1792 he asked his fellow Baptists to "expect great things from God; attempt great things for God." He not only became the first missionary to India, he launched the Christian world into the nineteenth-century missions movement. The globe representing the world for which he prayed was changed forever.—Larry Dipboye

Illustrations

HOW HEALTH COMES.   As light increases, we see ourselves to be worse than we thought. We are amazed at our former blindness as we see issuing forth from the depths of our heart a whole swarm of shameful feelings, like filthy reptiles crawling from a hidden cave. We never could have believed that we had harbored such things, and we stand aghast as we watch them gradually appear. But we must neither be amazed nor disheartened. We are not worse than we were; on the contrary, we are better. But while our faults diminish, the light by which we see them waxes brighter, and we are filled with horror. Bear in mind, for your comfort, that we only perceive our malady when the cure begins.—François Fénelon

BETTER PEOPLE, A BETTER WORLD.   Our world is never better unless someone in it is better. We assume that gadgets improve our world, as for instance a jet plane. We say, "It is better than a railroad train." But would Hiroshima agree with us? A jet plane can carry serum to a plague-stricken city or bombs to obliterate it, a doctor to a man crucially ill or a gangster to his gangland slayings. What or who determines the choice? The man, of course. So the world is not better unless someone in it is better. When shall we quit gaping at the work of our own hands? Our inventions have no final power. They are things. They have no will of their own. Each is a helpless "could be": They could serve our true life or destroy it. Radio warns of the approach of a tornado or offers a silly jingle to persuade us to buy what we don't need. A computer can't mend a broken heart. Is it not clear that the world is better only when someone is better?—George A. Buttrick

Sermon Suggestions

WHEN GOD FAILS TO NOTICE.   TEXT: Isa. 58:3–9a. (1) Religious rites and ceremonies have their place, such as the ancient fast. (2) But these performances become a mockery when they are a cloak for injustice in the workplace and for lack of compassion for the poor. (3) Attention to the spirit and object of religion will catch the attention of God and bring healing and answers to prayer.

THE MYSTERY OF GOD.   TEXT: 1 Cor. 2:1–11. (1) What it is: the redemption in Christ. (2) How it is known: by revelation through God's Spirit. (3) Who can know it: not those who rule this age but those who love God.

Worship Aids

CALL TO WORSHIP.   "Seek the Lord and his strength, seek his face continually" (1 Chron. 16:11).

INVOCATION.   Lord, we are weak in so many ways, and we need to be strengthened with your might in our inner being, so that we can do those things that in our better moments our hearts yearn to do.

OFFERTORY SENTENCE.   "Upon the first day of the week let every one of you lay by him in store, as God hath prospered him" (1 Cor. 16:2).

OFFERTORY PRAYER.   Lord, God, accept these tithes and offerings we bring with considerable sacrifice and much prayer through the Spirit and the Son.—E. Lee Phillips

PRAYER.   O you who are the great God and the great King above all gods, how can we appear before you except that you draw near to us. You draw near in the greatest way that you can in the fullness of your love and grace in the person of Jesus of Nazareth. In him you invite us—you plead with us—to come home, to receive our true estate as your children, your sons and daughters. We praise you for him who has heard this high calling and has come among us as your servant on this occasion proclaiming your amazing grace.

"Once we were no people, but now we are your people; once we had not received mercy, but now we have received mercy that we may declare the wonderful deeds of him who called us out of darkness into your marvelous light."

In our new estate as brothers and sisters, our lives are so intimately bound together that no one lives or dies unto himself or herself. Your fatherly love calls us as your children to pray and live for one another. As members of the Body of Christ we are being called, as he was, to give our life for the life of the world. This is a high calling! Who is ready for it? In our sense of weakness and inadequacy, may we know the strong Word of your grace that prepares us for anything. With the ill, the bereaved, the lonely, the estranged, the homeless, may we celebrate your grace mediated through the cross to heal, to make whole, to comfort, to strengthen, to set free, to reconcile.

As we reach out to the other, whoever the other may be, we pray for the healing of the nations that your strong Word, mighty to save, will deliver humankind from the peril of this hour that all peoples may know life, not death.—John Thompson

LECTIONARY MESSAGE

Topic: An Influence for Good
TEXT: Matt. 5:13–16

Did you ever wonder if you amount to anything in this world? Many persons and circumstances tell you in so many words that you do not count for much, if anything. Of course, some who love us assure us that life's negative messages are not correct, that we really do add something to life and the world.

To be sure, our little cheering section could be exaggerating what we mean to the world, but there is one whom we can trust to be right. He does not exaggerate. He speaks the truth.

I. Through Jesus Christ, God has declared that all of us who believe are in a position of positive influence.

(a) Like salt, the people of God have a preservative value. This is true of real Christianity as a whole, though Christians are never perfect. It is true also of believers individually, though we fall short of the glory of God. What is good in hu-

man nature, in human society, as far as that goes, is affirmed and enhanced by the presence of Christians in their midst. What is bad is retarded by what Christians are and do.

Like salt, the people of God add flavor to the world in which we live. Faith in God gives hope and joy and purpose. A spurious or counterfeit faith can cast a pall over God's good world. When such is the case, people reject the phony faith and tread it under foot. A character in a novel asked why there are so many delightful sinners and so many hangdog Christians.

(b) Like light, God's people function to show people the way—to show each other the way, to show outsiders the way. The Scriptures picture this world as enveloped in darkness, the darkness of ignorance and sin. Christians radiate light when they reflect Jesus Christ, the Light of the World.

Like light, God's people make things flourish; they are a positive, creative force. They are, in their own individual ways, the teachers, the encouragers, the healers.

II. It is clear, however, that our influence can be negative, definitely not like salt or light.

(a) Our influence over others can be eroded—unwittingly. Character does not collapse overnight. Of course, some indiscretion may come to light suddenly, unexpectedly. A process of disintegration, however, has gone on for a long time before—a gradual process. Neglect of the normal disciplines of the inner life makes us vulnerable to "the fiery darts of the evil one"! Our "saltiness" slips away; our light fades. Sadly, this can happen in such a way that others may notice and suffer from it before we are really sharply aware of what has happened.

(b) Or, our influence over others can be hidden—deliberately. Fear can cause it: Anxious about making a mistake, we, like the man in Jesus' parable, might hide something precious to us, put our light under a bushel basket. Jesus was willing to expose himself to criticism for associating with the wrong kind of people rather than fail to reach people who desperately needed God. Yet in an awkward attempt to be super Christians we may become less than Christian.

III. Our influence, however, is under our control.

(a) We could almost say that our influence is inevitable: We cannot be zeroes; we will positively or negatively have an impact on the lives of others. In this sense, at least, no one lives to himself, and no one dies to himself. Robinson Crusoe was no zero!

(b) Yet, being or becoming a positive influence involves struggle. One does not coast into the kind of personhood that Jesus congratulated and blessed. Personal problems touch the life of everyone. Jesus' disciples, the primary recipients of his blessing, knew temptation. Those same disciples suffered hardship and persecution, even death, as they struggled on to *become in fact* what they *actually were* in promise.

(c) To be and to become a positive influence is—and who would dispute it—a worthy goal for each and all of us who are called Christians. We are precisely in a position to bless and lift the lives of people around us, beginning with the members of our own family. And who knows how many beyond those nearest to us will be touched by what Jesus has declared us to be and will cause us to become? So will we glorify our heavenly Father.—James W. Cox

SUNDAY: FEBRUARY FOURTEENTH

SERVICE OF WORSHIP

Sermon: Who Are the Sons of God?

TEXT: Matt. 5:9

If we walk along the River Nile in Egypt and along the Appian Way outside of Rome, we pass the tombs of the great ones of those mighty empires. Back in those ancient days we read of Ramses in Egypt, Nimrod in Babylonia, Sargon in Assyria, and Caesar in Rome, all of whom were called sons of God! But, mark you, not because they were "peacemakers" but because they rode in chariots and came marching home triumphantly after waging successful war. Yonder in that day, too, there was a goddess, Venus, who was worshiped because she fired men's souls to jealousies and made them fight. There was another god, Saturn, who was the giver of harvests, who was beneficent, whose worship ceased because he never made war. Because he did not fight he could not be regarded as divine.

In the midst of that kind of sentiment, Jesus came and uttered his word: "Blessed are the peacemakers for they shall be called the sons of God." If anyone should come today and set himself against any known and workable natural law such as the law of gravitation, he would not be considered more of a fool than was Jesus when he declared, against the opinion of his day, that the men who are really godlike are not the war-makers but peacemakers.

There was nothing in all his teaching that so aroused people to opposition as his declaration that the peacemakers should be called sons of God. Men urged him to be something other than he was. If he, they said, was a son of God, he had to achieve the status by some other method than the one he was pursuing. But what he preached he put into practice, by his death. Since then it has dawned on occasional disciples that his way was right. The light dawned just about the time he died. Were I an artist I should paint four scenes of that dawning light.

I. The first picture would be that of the Roman centurion at the cross.

(a) Here was a man who was placed in charge of the Crucifixion. He stood "over against the cross." He could have touched Jesus with his hand at any time along that sorrowful way and perhaps helped to nail him on the cross. That cross was not high in the air as we have seen it depicted. Its base was not far from the ground, so that when the centurion stood in front of it his eyes were almost on a level with the face of Jesus. He could note the expression on the dying man's face; he could see the look in his eyes; and when Jesus expired, the one exclamation which escaped his lips was "This man spoke the truth. He was the Son of God."

(b) At whose shrine had this soldier worshiped, save at the shrine of Jupiter! When before in the history of the world did a Roman soldier condescend to speak of a convicted and crucified man as Son of God? And yet somehow the dying Jesus infused a conception into the mind of this soldier which contradicted all the notions of greatness which the world had upheld to that hour.

II. The second picture would be that of the watching crowd, walking before the cross and smiting their breasts and wagging their heads. They jeered, "He called himself the Son of God, and yet he can't come down from the cross." What they meant was that he no wise excelled in war. They, too, believed that the only people worthy of the name of the Son of God were warriors. But it is easy to detect that they, too, began to suspect that peacemaking could also be a sign of divinity.

III. Our third picture is that of two men who previously had been splendid cowards. They were both honorable men. With one, Jesus had had a conversation on the slopes of Olivet—there when soft midnight zephyrs were blowing. It was Nicodemus, a ruler of the Jews. The other was Joseph of Arimathea, a counselor of the Jews. Likely either one of these, and surely both of them together, could have saved Jesus from his grievous fate. But they deemed it not safe, just as other people since that time have failed to come to the rescue of a good man or cause for precisely the same reason.

Then these men witnessed him die! Ah, that was different! Thereafter they were changed men. Instead of slinking off into the darkness they became bold as lions. Fear was banished; one ran to Pilate to ask for the body of Jesus, the other to bring costly spices to honor the man the populace sought to disgrace. I can imagine a host of citizens laughing at both for tenderly taking this man from the cross and bearing him to the tomb. But to this ridicule they were indifferent. They had seen a sight they had never seen before. When that happens to any man, he will go on boldly doing what he thinks ought to be done.

IV. But now see a picture of what happened a generation or two later. The man who became the champion of this thing for which Jesus died—Paul—was dead. He had had a stormy career. They brought him into Rome, put him in prison, and finally beheaded him. Vespasian was emperor in Rome, and his son Titus lived with him. The Roman senate set out to honor these two. Why? Because they had gone over to this little country of Palestine and devastated it. The holy city of Jerusalem was obliterated, a million Jews were killed, vast numbers were sold as slaves into Egypt, and many were doomed to servitude in Rome.

(a) Here marched the victors: Roman soldiers with their flashing armor. Here were the spoils of war—the golden candlesticks of the Temple, the golden vine with its stock of gold, its clusters of rubies, emeralds, diamonds, and sapphires; in the triumph, too, were the treasure boxes of the Temple. In that procession was a line of prisoners, and in front of them danced the women, scattering flowers and perfumes, and the priests offered honors to these "sons of God" who had wrought such havoc. Up the Capitoline hill these "sons of God" rode in their gilded chariots while the populace shouted, "Vespasian and Titus, the divine ones, have triumphed."

(b) But Paul had had a different idea of "triumph." Of course, he had been put to death by conquering ones such as these we have described, but not long before the end he had exclaimed, "He has triumphed in his cross." Paul, too, beheld a procession. It was headed by those who sang, "Peace and goodwill to men." In that procession marched those who had won victories—folks like the widow of Nain, and Mary and Martha, from whose souls Jesus had dispelled sorrow; lepers who were healed of disease and shame; publicans and harlots out of whom had gone sin; prisoners who had been released from the prison house; a great host who had come up out of great tribulation—all these were offering their tribute to the Son of God. But this conqueror was not seated on a gilded throne, he was hanging from a wooden cross. And as the procession swept along, the multitude took up the cry, "He is worthy to receive glory and power and honor and dominion, for he was slain and hath redeemed us." God speed the day when that procession will sweep into its train the votaries of Jupiter and Mars who plague and lay waste our land today.

V. I do not know when that day will come. But one thing is sure: When men will glimpse what Jesus saw, they will regard war as he regarded it and as it really is—a business only for the devil. I know that the establishment of peace is a perplexing problem. For this reason precisely it is the part of wisdom to turn for an answer to the one whose death seemed folly but whose realism is able to bring peace to our quarreling and tormented world.—Frederick Keller Stamm

Illustrations

A THIRD ALTERNATIVE.   Ghandi once said that if he were ever given the choice of kill or be killed, he expected he would choose to kill. He then said that our choices are not that limited. There is a third alternative, the way of aggressive goodwill. Do you know where he learned that? In the Christian's Bible. He found it in the Sermon on the Mount. It is the ethic of the second mile that Jesus talked about and his first followers honored.—Robert W. Moore

SURVIVING THE FUTURE.   How is the Sermon on the Mount a way to survive the future? It gives us six practical steps of peacemaking:

Take imaginative, surprising, empathetic initiative.

Go talk to your brother.

Go two miles to make peace.

Feed the hungry, aid the poor.

Don't call your brother fool; respect him.

Pray for your enemies.

The Sermon on the Mount is a promise of participation in God's love, in God's kingdom, in God's deliverance, now as we repent and become peacemakers, and eternally in fellowship with him. Peacemakers are blessed, for they are sons of God. This helps us face the reality of our fears.—Glen H. Stassen

Sermon Suggestions

CHOICES.   TEXT: Deut. 30:15–20. (1) The biblical story of Moses' call to covenant renewal, Deut. 29:1–30:20. (2) The abiding truth: God has always been calling people to make vital choices that have immediate and lasting consequences. (3) The present application: Our obligatory choices today range widely—beginning with accepting Jesus Christ as Lord, with all future choices implied in that decision.

WHEN A CHURCH QUARRELS.   TEXT: 1 Cor. 3:1–9. (1) The problem: church dissension. (2) The solution: (a) Recognition of spiritual immaturity. (b) Recognition of differing vital roles of leadership for the church fellowship. (c) Recognition of the transcending purpose and role of God in growing the church.

Worship Aids

CALL TO WORSHIP.   "Seek the Lord and his strength, seek his face continually" (1 Chron. 16:11).

INVOCATION.   Loving Lord, let us worship with rapt attention, joyous abandon, profound thought, and receptive hearts, lest we miss the best God has for us and leave without finding the God who is always seeking us.—E. Lee Phillips

OFFERTORY SENTENCE.   "No man can serve two masters: for either he will hate the one, and love the other; or else he will hold to the one, and despise the other. Ye cannot serve God and mammon" (Matt. 6:24).

Lord, let us give with a loving attitude and a cheerful spirit because we have discovered giving in Jesus name is what matters most to us.—E. Lee Phillips

PRAYER. This is the day which you have made. Thank you, God! May we receive it in all its uniqueness. It is unlike any other day that we have ever lived. May we appreciate its freshness. No matter what yesterday may have been, the creative power of your Spirit is with us making all things new. May we have the discernment to see what new thing you are doing in our day and the willingness to be an instrument in the coming of your kingdom.

We thank you for the Church and for the churches. We praise you for this congregation that calls us to worship, to learn, to mission.

Help us together to perceive more sensitivity to what it means to be members of the Body of Christ. We all have not the same office, but your Spirit equips us for ministry according to our gifts. How great that we can complement one another and that the fullness of your love can be manifest in and through our life together!

We would pray for each other; may your love reach out through us to touch the life of each member of our church family. May those who are shaken because life has been so difficult, gain poise to handle creatively whatever life holds for them. Where the ache of loneliness persists, may you minister the balm of Gilead—the sense of your presence. May those walking through the valley have the faith to say, I will not fear, for Thou are with me. Free those who are ill, from fear and anxiety, that they may be open and trusting to receive the health of your healing grace.

Not only for our family and families would we pray, but for the human family in all the pain and agony of its brokenness. You are calling us to be what we already are by creation and redemption—community. Grant us wisdom, grant us courage for the living of these days, through him who is the consummation of the wisdom of the ages and the arbiter of all our alienation and who is present teaching us to pray and live with all peoples.—John Thompson

LECTIONARY MESSAGE

Topic: A Better Goodness

TEXT: Matt. 5:17–26

One can easily get a wrong impression of Jesus. He seemed to some to be easy on sin. Why would he hobnob with "drunkards and winebibbers" if he did not approve of their way of life? Why was he involved in disputes with the religious leaders about Sabbath-breaking if he was without fault? Yet, after "the days of his flesh," it was said of him that "he was without sin."

What was going on there? What did Jesus say for himself, for his attitude toward the rules and regulations by which the people of his time were supposed to live and which certain self-righteous people claimed to obey in detail?

Jesus proclaimed a better kind of goodness, a righteousness that was superior to that of the professionally religious people of his time.

I. *For Jesus, goodness is a matter of fulfillment.*

(a) What mental picture do many people have of God as he is found in the Old Testament? They see him as hard, unfeeling, arbitrary, even cruel. He is the "Lord of hosts" (that is, armies) and the commander and inspiration of holy wars. Even people who are moved and blessed by the psalms are shocked when they read of the psalmist praying concerning an enemy, "May his children be fatherless, and his wife a widow! / May his children wander about and beg; / may they be driven out of the ruins they inhabit!" (Ps. 109:9–10, RSV).

(b) We have to face the truth that even the best of people who lived before Jesus Christ came needed to receive much more of God's revelation than they were able to process in their generations. Yet God used their partial understandings and their limited faith to further his eternal purpose. One noted preacher affirmed the many basic truths that wind their way through the pages of the Old Testament, truths that come to expression in varying ways at different stages of the history of God's people. He designated this phenomenon "abiding truths in changing categories." From Jesus' point of view, it was a matter of fulfillment. What went before pointed to the fulfillment that was taking place in his own time: " it was said to the men of old. ... But I say to you ..." (vv. 21–22, RSV).

(c) The Apostle Paul looked beyond the inadequacies of legalism and wrote, "The whole law is fulfilled in one word, 'You shall love your neighbor as yourself' " (Gal. 5:14, RSV).

II. *For Jesus, goodness focuses on persons.*

(a) As majestic as the Law was and as much as Jesus appreciated it, he said in response to those who would put the Law above people, "The sabbath was made for humankind, and not humankind for the sabbath" (Mark 2:27, NRSV). As admirable as were many of those who strictly observed all religious requirements set forth in the Law, Jesus spent his time and energy on those who had deep spiritual needs and knew it.

(b) The Scriptures declare that our attitude toward persons indicates the presence or absence of spiritual life. "We know that we have passed from death to life because we love one another" (1 John 3:14, NRSV). Jesus' description of the last judgment, likewise, tells us that the quality of our faith turns on one thing—our service to the very least of human beings (Matt. 25:31–46).

III. *For Jesus, goodness is more demanding than merely obeying rules.*

(a) A set of rules can become a mechanical convenience, complete with loopholes. Some of Jesus' contemporaries were publicly committed to obey the Jewish Law, but many of those same people were clever and devious in getting around some of the most demanding and valid laws, thinking all the while that they had fulfilled the laws' requirements. What teaching of Jesus has not been challenged or twisted by someone who did not wish to live by it?

(b) Jesus' ethic of love is far more demanding than the "righteousness of the scribes and Pharisees." Genuine love of God and humankind may expose us to some risky decisions that an appeal to law cannot resolve. Situation ethics can be morally sloppy, self-serving, and sentimental. Some circumstances, however, offer no chart or compass except that provided by the love incarnate in Jesus Christ, who "is the end of the law so that there may be righteousness for everyone who believes" (Rom. 10:4, NRSV).—James W. Cox

SUNDAY: FEBRUARY TWENTY-FIRST

SERVICE OF WORSHIP

Sermon: Beating the Blues

TEXT: Prov. 17:22

If it's true that at Christmas, and as recently as Epiphany, people were on tiptoes with expectation, by mid-February they are simply standing around, flatfoot, wondering if there is some purposeful direction for their feet to go. Yes, February is the time for the blues. The climate alone is enough to cool the cockles of the warmest heart. As opposed to June, life in February seems to throw more stones, and it's harder than usual to pick them up and build an altar! This is the time of year when children complain, "Why are all the vitamins in the spinach and not in the ice cream?" This is the time of year when their fathers and mothers recall G. B. Shaw's definition of love as "a gross exaggeration of the difference between one person and everybody else." Yes, it was at this time of year that a dilapidated old New Yorker crept out of the cold and into the warmth of a greasy spoon, there to be met by a big ugly waiter with a filthy apron.

"OK, Mac, what's yours?"

"Two fried eggs and a few kind words!"

Soon the big ugly waiter returned, slapped the eggs down on the table, and started off.

"Hey, friend, you forgot the few kind words."

"Oh yeah ... don't eat dem eggs."

So what to do, when hope looks more like a candle about to burn out than a beacon blazing across the sky? What to do to beat the blues?

We could always pray for an encounter with God, an experience so overwhelming that it caused Moses to take off his shoes, Elijah to cover his face, Isaiah to fall apart and break into confession, and Peter to drop to his knees. But that might be to tempt the Lord; you can't, after all, order an encounter. Besides, even for prophets and saints such encounters are rare, which is probably for the best: "Go, go, go said the bird, / Humankind cannot bear very much reality" (T. S. Eliot, *Four Quartets*).

I. What all of us can do, even in cities like New York, is to appreciate daily what the hymn "O Worship the King" calls "the earth with its store of wonders untold." Living on the shores of the Hudson, I spend a fair amount of time observing gulls. Some of the time, mostly when they are in the water fighting and hollering at each other, they only succeed in deepening my depression, reminding me of certain meetings I attend and also of the origin of the expression "birdbrained." But they have only to take off into the air and start gliding, diving, hovering, and I find myself talking to their Creator and mine: "O God, if only we humans could be who we are so effortlessly."

"Thy bountiful care, what tongue can recite; it breathes in the air, it shines in the light." "The world," said Chesterton, "does not lack for wonders, only for a sense of wonder." Even human beings—nay, especially human beings—for all their gaucheries and downright wickedness, are wondrous. Of course, if your desire is to control them, human beings will appear smaller than they really are. But if you simply wonder at them—their sensibilities, subtleties, and surprises—human beings will appear bigger than

life. I never cease wondering at the courage that persists amid the fury of disease and pain. I never cease wondering at the way the human spirit in this city survives insult and injury. My mind boggles at the amount of time, energy, imagination it took to build the place. I never cease wondering at New York.

Aristotle was right: We should approach the world first with wonder, only later with doubt. If you are in the throes of the blues, see if you haven't gotten the order reversed. If you are approaching the world first with doubt, your sense of wonder could well be atrophying. "The world does not lack for wonders, only for a sense of wonder." Sören Kierkegaard said much the same: "The greatest miracles in the world take place there where people say, 'I don't see anything so miraculous about that.'"

So for those of you trying to beat the blues, I have a very simple wish: Between now and next Sunday, have a "wonderfull" week.

II. If wonder can do wonders against the blues, so, too, can anger. Of course, depression and boredom are both linked to anger, but to anger that is repressed. Repressed anger is lethal. A discerning friend of mine once remarked, "A thought-murder a day keeps the psychiatrist away." She was drawing the all-important line between feelings and behavior, insisting that while all behavior is not valid, all feelings are. Her words reminded me of St. Paul's: "Be angry but do not sin" (Eph. 4:26). Actually if we're never angry we probably are sinning; for just as the world does not lack for wonders, so it is hardly short of things to be mad about. Jesus never tolerated the intolerable and neither should we. Anger is not only a good counter to depression; given the madness and massive immoralities in which we are presently immersed, only a moral passion akin to Christ's can save our sanity.

Some years ago, an overly polite father, who had never been able to get close to his son, one day reported that he and his son had ended up rolling all over the floor in a fight. He was horrified, but I rather rejoiced. To be sure, that's not the best way for a father to get in touch with his son. But contact is contact; politeness can be a barrier more devastating than a blow.

Some people are afraid of being angry at their friends for fear of losing them. Well, isn't it better to be hated for what we are than loved for what we are not? And is not a true friend one who risks his friendship for the sake of his friend?

Henry Thoreau is remembered as a man who never trimmed the truth. Like Jesus, he never tolerated hypocrisy. Jesus said, "Woe to you, scribes and Pharisees, hypocrites" (Matt. 23:25). Thoreau said, "For every virtuous person, there are 999 patrons of virtue." Jesus said, "Not all who say, 'Lord, Lord,' shall enter the kingdom of heaven" (Matt. 7:21). Thoreau wrote of the New Testament, "Most people favor it outwardly, defend it with bigotry, and hardly ever read it."

Unheeded and unpopular in his time, Thoreau is today honored because he put something of substance into the mainstream of American history that sustains us over a hundred years later. Like Jesus he never repressed his anger, but he did keep it focused. Like Jesus, too, he was willing to risk his friendships for the sake of his friends.

So, all of you trying to beat the blues: Have not only a wonder-full week; have a feisty one, too. "Be angry but do not sin."

III. Most of all, start loving someone. You know how it is when psychologically you are on dead center, when you cannot move. In such moments it's important to do something, if only to clean a room. But when you're really depressed, you've got to try to do something for someone else. Visit someone in the hospital, write a fan letter to someone about whose good deed or words you read in the morning paper, take someone to the movies, contribute to some country's relief.

Of course it won't save the world, but that's not your business. Ultimately, we are not called upon to save the world. Ultimately, we are called on to do what's right, only penultimately to be effective. An how we get that order reversed! Imagine Socrates, as they handed him the hemlock, saying, "Hold everything. Is Plato going to write me up?" Imagine Nathan Hale stopping execution proceedings to inquire, "Are the thirteen colonies going to win? Is every kid in the new country going to memorize the last words I am now about to utter?"

I know how easy it is to get depressed, especially when the world appears ready to go down the drain and there seems to be so little any of us can do about it. Half the time when I stand up to plead for a disarmed planet, I feel like Rocinante, a tired hack of a horse being ridden by a quixotic idea. But then, who but God knows how effective any of us is going to be in anything we do? What we do know is that love is a necessity as well as a command; that love is like the loaves and fishes—there is never enough until we start sharing; and that of Jesus, our Lord and Savior, it is fair to say that "all the armies that ever marched, all the navies that ever sailed, all the kings that ever reigned, and all the parliaments that ever sat have not so affected humanity as has that one solitary loving life."

That thought is enough to snap me right out of it, to make me want to say all over again, "Bless the Lord, all his works, in all places of his dominion. Bless the Lord, O my soul."

Dear Christians, go out and have a wonder-full, feisty, and loving week. And may God bless you.—William Sloane Coffin

Illustrations

AT LONG LAST!   Into a liquid is dropped one drop of a second, and there is no result: another, and another, many others, one by one, apparently in vain. And then one more, precisely like the rest, and of a sudden, not as the outcome of that last alone, but as the culmination of the whole seemingly useless process, everything is changed! And day by day doggedly we pray and hope and toil and believe. And what is there to show for it? Not much, to outward seeming, it may be. And yet is far more going on than our eyes see! And one day may one other prayer, one other ordinary act of common faith, one more looking toward Jesus Christ bring the long process to its culmination, and we waken satisfied, because in his likeness—at last! Sudden or slow, dramatic or invisible, "it will come"—it will come! After all, says Samuel Rutherford, the end is sure: A long, steep road, a tired footsore traveler, and a warm welcome home, that is the worst that there can be.—Arthur John Gossip

THE WAY UP.   Self-pitiers of the world, stop it! You are using a method of control that works only on the stupid and weak and that makes a first-class sap out of you also. There are better ways of getting what you want out of life—for example, standing up for yourself, not worrying about how many people love you, accepting things as they are if you can't change them, not building events out of proportion or believing you must have your way at all times and will die if you are frustrated. Make those changes in your life, and I guarantee you that there will be far less self-pity in your life and far less depression as well.—Paul A. Hauck

Sermon Suggestions

THE LORD'S SUMMIT WITH MOSES. TEXT: Exod. 24:12–18. (1) The glory of the Lord in the giving of the Law. (2) The glory of the Lord in the grace and truth of Jesus Christ (John 1:14–18).

THE TRUTH OF JESUS CHRIST.   TEXT: 2 Pet. 1:16–21. (1) It is attested by eyewitnesses. (2) It is confirmed in the Scriptures. (3) It is to be interpreted by the intention of God.

Worship Aids

CALL TO WORSHIP.   "Cast thy burden upon the Lord, and he shall sustain thee" (Ps. 55:22).

INVOCATION.   Beginning at this very moment we would do as your Word tells us—roll our burden upon you. When we are weak or our strength is gone, you

can, you will help us. So lift us up, for we rest our entire weight upon your might.

OFFERTORY SENTENCE.   "Bless the Lord, O my soul, and forget not all his benefits" (Ps. 103:2).

OFFERTORY PRAYER.   Lord, sometimes we do not know how to give as we ought and at other times we do not give as well as we know. Help us now to give as the Scripture teaches and as our resources will allow.—E. Lee Phillips

PRAYER.   It is not easy for us, stepping onto the stage before you, dear God, and being just with you. For we have spent your week enslaved to our relentless schedule, accompanied by mindless talk and the dulling noise of commerce, scurrying about in maddening haste, abounding in busy self-importance. But now, gathered in your holy place, surrounded by our family of faith, in our private and collective silence; all the props and defenses of our talk and activity are hushed away. And we come into your presence awkward and ill prepared. We played too much to the world and lost our time and place with you.

Revealing and receiving God, who is showing us who you are in Jesus Christ our Lord, come into our hurting place this hour, hear our deepest sigh, our groan beyond words, yes, even the Spirit interceding on our behalf. May the breath of glad surprise breathe new joy and wholeness into our forlorn and broken spirits. Generous God of us all, be in us a fresh moving and redeeming of your Holy Spirit . . . come, Lord Jesus . . .

Creator and Lord of all seasons, the sharp coldness of this Sunday morning reminds us it is still winter. Epiphany giving way to the holy season reminds us, too, that the cold and hardness of humanity's heart greets our Lord as he begins his lonely journey to the cross. The stark barrenness of his rejection and death will come before his glorious Resurrection and new life. So as we live into these days of his Passion and pilgrimage, may we gird our lives with strong resolve to walk close to him and find ourselves, serving along side him among the hurts and needs of persons around us.

Inclusive God of us all, in this time of barriers and walls being struck down, may there be in our hearts and lives openness and response to the call of the gospel for unity and oneness in Christ for us all. May it pulse and live in our very being. Patient and understanding Father, you who are always more willing to receive than we are to come, thank you for these moments with you. May our silence and talk, our rest and walk this week, bring in your kingdom and honor your will. So be it in Christ.—William M. Johnson

LECTIONARY MESSAGE

Topic: "Listen to Him!"
TEXT: Matt. 17:1–9

I. This is a remarkable story, one of the most significant stories in the Gospels. Each of the synoptic Gospels reports this event that we could call a manifestation of the glory of God in Jesus Christ. We do not find it as such in the Gospel of John; however, the glory of God shines forth throughout the Gospel, breaking forth from obscurity in incident after incident.

Still, the glory of God, as it is manifested to us, even as it was to the disciples, is not an obvious blessing. Sometimes it comes as an imagined threat. When the disciples saw it they were "overcome by fear."

II. We are afraid in the hour of crisis, even if God is present. It may be that under the circumstances God himself is our greatest source of fear. We may not understand what he is doing, or if we do understand, we may not like what he is doing or is about to do. God may be calling us to face suffering of some kind. The situation may be utterly baffling, and yet we have to seek meaning in what is happening. Or we may be called to serve in ways and places that demand more of us than we feel able to give.

III. Is there a way out or through? The disciples must have missed the transforming significance of what the voice from heaven had just said: "Listen to him!" Only after the Resurrection did they really understand what this meant.

(a) Christ stands right at the center of the answer to our need. To listen to him is to let God in Christ deal with every fear that we face. To quell our fears, we have the reassuring presence of our Lord. The disciples had that going for them. When they lay on the ground shaking with terror, "Jesus came and touched them, saying, 'Get up and do not be afraid.'" We can always count on his presence, even today, even when we doubt. Jacob of old said of a remarkable experience that transformed his future, "Surely the Lord is in this place—and I did not know it" (Gen. 28:16, NRSV).

(b) Related to this is the power of the Resurrection. Jesus said, "Because I live, you also will live" (John 14:19, NRSV). Before the transfiguration experience, the disciples had heard much from Jesus about suffering—his and theirs. It was a grim prospect! But they could face it because he touched them and, as it were, raised them up: He said, "Get up and do not be afraid." We, too, can face suffering, knowing that the power of God can transform it.

Moreover, to experience meaning in a universe that seems to be "full of sound and fury, signifying nothing," we eventually see that we are caught up in the purpose of God unfolding in Jesus Christ. In him, life makes sense. In him, there is hope of a final, glorious fulfillment: "And all who have this hope in him purify themselves, just as he is pure" (1 John 3:3, NRSV).

(d) Listening to Jesus Christ, we all, ministers and laity alike, hear the call of God to serve the present age, despite wars, crime, disasters, and tragedies of every sort. Because of the transfiguration experience, Jesus was confirmed not only as the successor to Moses and Elijah but also as the one in whom all the divine promises of the past came to fulfillment. The vision with its dazzling and dramatic accompaniments prepared Jesus and his disciples for the sufferings and divine surprises that would follow, prepared them for everything to which God would call them. Listening to Jesus Christ can prepare the timid and fearful souls among us for the great things to which God calls us.

IV. If we do not listen to Jesus Christ, we will be driven by every wind and tossed about, with no sure moorings in this world. He alone has the words of eternal life, that is, life touched and transformed by the God who raises the dead.

V. What practical things can we do to help make such things real in our own life? We can pray, and if we pray aright, the dull black and white image of Jesus Christ in our minds will be transfigured into an image of him in bright living color. We can read the Bible with Jesus Christ, and his obscure image on its pages will step forth a living reality. Then we can go forth, descending our mountain of discovery in faith, as he calls us and goes before us.—James W. Cox

SUNDAY: FEBRUARY TWENTY-EIGHTH

SERVICE OF WORSHIP

Sermon: The Final Proof of Faith

Texts Matt. 7:16–20; John 14:8–11

The most convincing proof of our Christian convictions lies in the manner in which we live our faith. All the arguments in the world will not convince others of what we believe. However persuasively we state the case for honesty or virtue, if by so much as an iota we deviate from that honesty or violate that virtue, the argument breaks down.

The proof of our faith is not in some mathematical formula; it is in the texture of our lives. If men seek proof of what we say, they will not look for it in our words but in our integrity, in our courage and compassion. They will not search for it in the logic with which we interpret our creeds but in the sincerity with which we follow Christ.

I. The proof of our faith is in the touch of our lives. God is not found at the end of an argument but in the touch of mercy. Every day we touch people with our lives. What do we do to them?

(a) How often Christ *touched* someone. Each time he touched a life, there was a consequence—something happened. See how pivotal our lives are? A touch of our heart, and a life is influenced. It shatters every notion that we are isolated creatures going our way, untouched and untouching. We are not like ships which pass each other in the night, recognizing each other's presence only by faintly flickering lights. We are dynamic organisms which grow into each other, live upon each other, plague or bless each other, bedevil or heal each other. We always do something to each other. We touch others, and so, for better or worse, they will never be the same.

We look at our friends and say, "Our thoughts have played upon their minds." More than our thoughts have played upon their minds. Our souls, our faith, flow through their days. Because of our faith, Christ will mean more or Christ will mean less.

II. The proof of our faith lies in the measure in which we let our hearts feel for others. Christ is not found in a syllogism but in the spiritual concern with which our hearts are burdened.

(a) There is no hope for us unless once again we become compassionate. There is no escape from our dilemma until we look again at our Lord and see how deeply, at times how poignantly, he felt the least tremor of agony in a human soul. He looked upon a city and wept. When we look at our city, with its ugliness, its dark corners, do we weep? He looked upon a despondent, suffering soul and quickly he responded. When we see the tragedies about us, do we respond? How can people believe in our Christ when we look upon suffering but do not suffer?

(b) There is nothing more persuasive than an understanding heart. Without it there is neither love nor forgiveness.

Without it there is neither hope nor trust. When we see the storm of rebellion brewing in the lives of our children, we are quick to excuse or quick to condemn, but where is the understanding heart? When someone bruises us with foolish actions and bitter words, we are quick to retaliate or quick to complain, but where is the understanding heart and where then the proof of our faith?

III. The proof of our faith is in the stability with which we live through the alternating circumstances which confront us. We must learn from the physical universe that in every moving object there is a point of stability; in every moving circumstance there is a point of rest.

(a) But stability is something else, and faith is a matter of stability. Life moves through changing circumstances. Some barely brush us, so that we are hardly aware of them. Some tear us up by our very roots and leave us stranded as though a tornado had ripped through our souls. During all these alternating circumstances we have moods. There are tears; there is laughter; the heart is light, or the heart is heavy.

(b) But deeper than our moods is our faith. Moods change. They ride upon the winds of fortune and misfortune. But faith is stable. It is the soul's point of rest. There is faith in the goodness of God when we look at the blessings which have been showered upon us. There is the same faith in the goodness of God when the shadows fall and we see no blessings. Through all the changing circumstances of life, the heart is steady. Through all the changing scenes of life, faith is stable.

IV. We prove our faith when we reveal all of God. How difficult it was for the disciples to see God. He eluded them at every turn. Their minds could not leap that high or reach that far. God, they were told, was gracious and forgiving, endless in his power and plenteous in mercy. But they could never see him that way. Then Jesus stepped into their difficulty and said, "He that hath seen me hath seen the Father." Then they knew, and then they understood. They had looked at him and seen all of God.

(a) Men hear us say that God is a master architect who devised the universe, flawless in its operation. But as they look at us do they also know that he is a God of compassion? Men hear us say that God is a God of justice. They hear us say that he is the God of the Ten Commandments. But as they look at us do they also know that he is the God of the cross?

(b) How often the Apostle Paul must have thought back to another day when he pleaded his case before King Agrippa. He had made his defense with the art of the orator and thinker that he was. He pictured his background; he spoke of his conversion; he revealed the fire which burned in his soul; and when his last word had been uttered and his strength spent, Agrippa said, "Almost thou persuadest me to be a Christian." Now lingering in prison, Paul must have remembered Agrippa, and he must have asked himself over and over again, Why almost? Why not utterly? Where had he failed? What had he not done?

V. We are Christians. We believe in our Lord. We have our faith. Thousands have looked upon us; many have walked with us. And now that they have seen us, how many have said and are still saying, "Almost?" How many have seen us and followed Christ?—Arnold H. Lowe

Illustrations

THE CANDLE OF THE LORD.   "The spirit of man is the candle of the Lord" (Prov. 20:27). The essential connection between the life of God and the life of man is the great truth of the world, and that is the truth which Solomon sets forth in the striking words which I have chosen for my text this morning. The picture which the words suggest is very simple. An unlighted candle is standing in the darkness, and someone comes to light it. A blazing bit of paper holds the fire at first, but it is vague and fitful. It flares and wavers and at any moment may go out. But the vague, uncertain, flaring blaze touches the candle, and the candle catches fire, and at once you have a steady flame. It burns straight and clear and constant. The candle gives the fire a manifestation-point for all the room which is illuminated by it. The candle is glorified by the fire, and the fire is manifested by the candle. The two bear witness that they were made for one another by the way in which they fulfill each other's life. That fulfillment comes by the way in which the inferior substance renders obedience to its superior. The candle obeys the fire. The docile wax acknowledges that the subtle flame is its master, and it yields to his power; and so, like very faithful servant of a noble master, it at once gives its master's nobility the chance to utter itself, and its own substance is clothed with a glory which is not its own.—Phillips Brooks

EXAMPLE.   Returning from a visit with Fénelon, the archbishop of Cambrai, Lord Chesterfield said, "If I had stayed another day in his presence, I am afraid I would have become a Christian, his spirit was so pure, so attractive and beautiful."—Charles L. Wallis

Sermon Suggestions

AS IT ALL BEGAN.   TEXT: Gen. 2:4b–9, 15–17, 25–3:7. (1) God created humankind in a condition of delight and innocence. (2) God's purpose for humankind included responsibility to care for the ambient Creation and moral responsibility. (3) An alien power offered false promises to Adam and Eve that marred their relationship with their God. (4) This fiasco required the work of the same God to reverse the results of "man's first disobedience" and to fulfill God's original intent (see Rom. 5:15).

YOU—OLD AND NEW.   TEXT: Rom. 5:12–19. (1) In Adam we are marked by sin and death. (2) In Jesus Christ we are gifted with grace and life.

Worship Aids

CALL TO WORSHIP.   "Rejoice, inasmuch as ye are partakers of Christ's sufferings; that, when his glory shall be revealed, ye may be glad also with exceeding joy" (1 Pet. 4:13).

INVOCATION.   Holy God, allow that this day we may partake of the divine nature so that all our humanness may be purified and all our desires transformed by the love of God, lest we come to worship and miss the God who can alone make us free.—E. Lee Phillips

OFFERTORY SENTENCE.   "Thou art worthy, O Lord, to receive glory and honor and power; for thou hast created all things, and for they pleasure they are and were created" (Rev. 4:11).

OFFERTORY PRAYER.   Gracious Father, Creator, Redeemer, grant that the gift of our very selves, as well as our material substance, may glorify and honor you. In your mercy, receive what we bring.

PRAYER.   O God, we confess that we have been slow to hear your voice in the cry of human need; too often we have been unmoved by human misery, even our own; our understanding has been self-serving, and we have kept busy, a condition we clearly prefer; we have been cozy with the pharaohs of this world, endlessly patient with their empty promises, and too loathe to work and pray for their destruction; and the strange, bright world of your peace and justice frightens us.

We have not trusted in your promises; we have not disciplined our bodies and spirits to serve you, and we have not eaten and drunk the goodness you provide. Dabbling in many things, we have not willed one thing with all our heart; risking little, we have succeeded; and at the end of the day things ranged against you loom too large and you too small.

Have mercy upon us, O God, and turn our hearts from evil and resignation and from that good which is less than your purpose; drive away our demons and to our guardian angels open our eyes; cause us to see what you see and to hear what you hear and, like Moses, to receive your commission for your people in bondage by name and by fire.—Peter Fribley

LECTIONARY MESSAGE

Topic: Tried and Triumphant

TEXT: Matt. 4:1–11

The story of temptation begins in the Bible with Eve and Adam. Of course both were involved. The brief reference in Gen. 3:6 reveals that Eve's temptation involved three powerful impulses: (1) sensuous appetites—to satisfy the body; (2) appreciation of the beautiful—in God's Creation; (3) godlike knowledge—good from evil. She yielded, and so did Adam. Is it possible to overcome temptation? There is, in Matt. 4:1–11, a resounding yes—presuming that you want to. There is a surprising similarity in the three powerful impulses and the three temptations to which Jesus was subjected.

I. He was tried by material needs. Simply speaking, after forty days of fasting he was hungry. Simply speaking, there is nothing basically wrong about satisfying your hunger. Simply speaking, said the tempter, here is an easy way to satisfy your hunger.

Hunger represents many material needs. Later in his ministry he would say, "Foxes have holes, birds have nests, but I have nowhere to rest my head." He said this to a prospective follower.

"If you are God's Son . . ." And the presumption in the Greek grammatical construction is that you are God's Son. Realize your ministry in this manner. Perform a miracle to satisfy your own needs. Use your great ability to create a material kingdom.

Not so . . . there is more to man than matter. You cannot ultimately satisfy him by ministering solely to his material needs.

II. He was tried by spiritual ambitions. Simply speaking, he was only starting out—he needed a gimmick. Simply speaking, this was a sure way to draw a crowd. Simply speaking, he could prove that he was God's Son.

Clearly the temptation is representative of many performer/priests. The lists runs from snake-handlers to television manipulators. It is difficult to sort out spiritual ambitions from any other kind.

"If you are God's Son . . ." And the presumption is that you are God's Son. Show off your faith—you are depending on him for bread—press your relationship with your father.

Not so . . . I will not presume on that relationship. Nor will I deal on the surface of man's superstitions. I will not work a miracle to mystify.

III. He was tried by political goals. Simply speaking, he was in a hurry to win the world. Simply speaking, he wanted to succeed. Simply speaking, it appears that everything belongs to the devil.

The temptation is suspiciously representative of much current civil religion: Let's make an alliance and win! There is no conditional clause, "If you are God's Son . . ." God's Son wouldn't act like that.

Not so . . . I am a person of integrity. I will not compromise my clarity to achieve a purpose. . . . You cannot serve God and Mammon.

The temptation experience came after the spiritual triumph in his baptism. The Spirit was with him in the wilderness. And if there is any question about the reality of the temptations, I refer you to Heb. 4:15 or to Gen. 3:6. His triumph was expressed in his understanding of Scripture, as revealing the will of God. The devil left him—Luke adds, "for a season" (4:13). This was not the last of his temptations.—J. Estill Jones

SUNDAY: MARCH SEVENTH

SERVICE OF WORSHIP

Sermon: Life and Death

TEXT: Psalm 90

In this country we are preoccupied with our physical existence. By the development of medical knowledge and science we have prolonged it. By our civilized arts of living we have refined it, and by our scientific advancement we have made it more comfortable. Death brings that existence to an end. Hence, we are inclined to think of death as the worst thing that can happen to anybody, and we do everything we can to act as though it did not exist. We cloak it with flowers; we screen it behind sentimental music; and we almost never speak about it.

I propose to speak about it not in the full splendor of New Testament faith but against the somber background of Old Testament thought. Granted, of course, that what I say is by no means all there is to be said; nevertheless, it is the foundation on which a real faith in life after death must rest. At the moment I am concerned not so much with what comes after death as I am in the coming of death itself.

I. There are three facts about death that are like the piers of a bridge, and the first is this: Death is not like a disease that comes to some but not to all; death comes to everybody. It is like birth; it happens to everyone. It has no favorites.

(a) The man who wrote the ninetieth psalm took a rather grim view of life, to be sure, but at least he was realistic about death. He wrote, We are like grass. In the morning, with the dew on it, it is fresh and green and alive. But during the day the reaper comes and mows it, and when you see it in the evening it is faded and withered, dead. We are like that, all of us. He made it very clear that there were no exceptions and no exemptions; we are all like grass.

(b) That fact leads us to the solemn observation that death is a normal part of man's natural experience. In itself it is not evil; it may, to be sure, often be attended by evil circumstances. But death itself is not evil, any more than birth is evil. In itself death is not tragic; it may, to be sure, be accompanied by tragic circumstances when it comes prematurely to one too young to die. Some of you know all too well that it is often attended by a sadness too deep for words when people who have loved each other for many years are separated. But the fact of death in itself is not sad.

II. The second fact about death is this: Death puts an end to our physical existence, this existence which we have to varying degrees enjoyed. The psalmist, I am afraid, did not enjoy his very much, because he lived in hard times, and he talked about life as a span of toil and trouble. And even though people lived to be seventy or eighty years old, their trouble increased the longer they lived. But most of us, if we had the choice between our physical existence and the cessation of it, would choose to go on with it. Death when it comes is the end of it.

(a) In other words, to put it into journalistic language, we all have a deadline to meet. We do not have all the time in the world. Some people have more than others, but not one has very much. The psalmist's response to that fact, to the fact that death puts and actual end to our physical existence, was a prayer which we might well add to our treasury of prayers—"O teach us so to count our days that we may take it to heart," or in the prayer book version, "So teach us to number our days that we may apply our hearts unto wisdom."

(b) The fact that life is so short makes it seem to some people futile. Perhaps you know people like that. When they are faced with the fact that they haven't much time, and that in that time they may not be able to accomplish very much, they let down all the tension and think that the best thing they can do while they are here is to make the most of it and have as good a time as they can. That is one response to the brevity of life, certainly not a very noble one.

(c) Most people, I think, when they really confront the fact of the brevity of their lives and the fact that the time is short, are most likely to take the psalmist's way and be convinced of the seriousness of life. The shorter life is, the more serious it is.

We haven't all the time in the world, and one of the things that we who are likely to be rather casual about life and carefree in the spending of our time ought to realize quite solemnly is that we have only one chance. We shall never have another. We may have other opportunities on the other side of death; we know nothing about those, and it is better not to speculate about them. We know what the conditions of physical existence are, and we know that the time will come when that will end, and we shall never have another chance like the one we have now. We don't want to go through life abnormally tense and anxious, but neither do we want to go through life listless and limp and carefree, when the time is short and the chance we have now is the only chance we will ever have to live here.

So our prayer is the same prayer that the psalmist prayed, "O God, teach us to count our days," and we might add, "We know that we have only one chance. O God, help us not to miss it."

III. One more thing we should consider before we leave this theme. This is the third and far more subtle fact about death, far more difficult to put into words. There are things that do not die. There are things in our ordinary experience right around us that outlast us.

(a) It is something like an old house. You live in it; you are perfectly aware of the fact that other families have lived in it. They have come and gone. It has outlived them all. It will outlive you. But in the very fact of its durability you feel it embracing you; it gives you a kind of security and safety that makes you strong and confident to go through life and to face its brevity and its transiency with good spirit. Like a child, you have a place to come home to, and you are safe. When you think of things like that, they lead you on to greater things which outlast and outlive you.

(b) The psalmist felt that way about God. He was conscious of a tremendous distance between himself and God. There was the distance of time. His life was so brief; God's life had no beginning and no ending. God did not die, and he did. Men come and go; God goes on forever. There was also the distance of quality. God was not evil, and he was. It made him tremble when he thought about it. Yet in that very distance the psalmist found his dwelling place. "Lord, thou hast been our dwelling place in all generations." It was as though the God who

was here to make the hills and the sea and the dry land before any men appeared and who will be here long after their going was, in a way, like the family home: embracing, surrounding, protecting, giving a kind of security and a safety that people otherwise would not have. The psalmist had a short life and not an altogether sweet one, but he had a place to come home to.

IV. What I wish to put into your minds, that it may stay there through the years, is this: Whereas a near, friendly God may give you comfort and help when you need it, the God of the cosmos is not like you, brief in time and years; not like you, subject to sin and evil and mistake, but everlastingly good and eternal, gives you a home and the security that only a home can give. It is the majesty of God that is our final defense against the fear of death, for in spite of the fact that death comes to all of us, that life is so short and because it is so short is therefore so serious, nevertheless it is safe because God is so great. He is our dwelling place from generation to generation, and we have no fear either in life or in death. — Theodore Parker Ferris

Illustrations

INTENSITY.   One of the most colorful personalities in this city thirty years ago was Dr. Hans Zinsser. He wrote several widely read books so that many of us who did not know him personally knew him through his books. In the last one he tells how on his last return from a trip abroad he realized before he left the ship that he had a disease that was incurable. He diagnosed it himself but in order to be sure he went to one of his friends, a Boston doctor, who confirmed the diagnosis. He describes himself and his doctor friend standing in the doctor's office looking out the window onto the Charles River basin. He said they stood there in silence for a few minutes, and in those few minutes something happened to him. "Everything," he writes about himself, "that went on about him or within him from that moment on struck upon his heart and mind with a new and powerful resonance." Because he knew that he didn't have much time, life became more intense. All the experiences that he enjoyed in the past he enjoyed more. He went back and reread all the books that he loved and delighted in them more than he had the first time he read them. Everything that shone at all for him shone with a new splendor because the time was short. He didn't have all the time in the world to waste, to fritter away. He had only a few weeks, perhaps only a few days. Every day was precious, every moment was something to be counted and treasured, and he said life began to glow with an intensity that he had never before known in all his life.—Theodore Parker Ferris

A CLOUD OF WITNESSES. Where then do we find and how do we experience closeness with the dead? In the communion of Christ. Whenever this unconditional love of God in Christ comes close to us, there the dead, whom we love, are also close to us. The closer we come to Christ, the deeper we come into communion with the dead. Christ, however, is present in the gospel, in the Eucharist, and in the communion of the brothers and sisters. When, in the worship service of the Latin American base communities, the names of the dead, of the disappeared, and of the martyrs are called, then the whole congregation shouts, *"Presente!"* They are present in the communion of Christ.—Jürgen Moltmann

Sermon Suggestions

THE PATH TO GREATNESS. TEXT: Gen. 12:1–4a (4b–8). (1) By listening to God. (2) By obeying God. (3) By being a blessing to all (see Mark 10:35–45).

WHAT COUNTS IN RELIGION. TEXT: Rom. 4:1–5 (6–12), 13–17. (1) Not externals, as with Abraham. (2) Not externals, as with Paul's contemporaries. (3) Not externals, in our present circumstances. (4) Though externals are important as signs and seals of faith, it is God's unearned kindness (grace) that brings forgiveness and acceptance.

Worship Aids

CALL TO WORSHIP. "I sought the Lord, and he heard me, and delivered me from all my fears" (Ps. 34:4).

INVOCATION. O Lord, we would know you better, we would sit at your feet and drink of your Word and be led of your Spirit. Involve us in the things of this earth that matter and part us from the trivial and cheap. Lead us to always know the difference, for we worship and pray in the name of Jesus.—E. Lee Phillips

OFFERTORY SENTENCE. "Truly, truly I tell you, unless a grain of wheat falls into the earth and dies, it remains a single grain; but if it dies, it bears rich fruit. He who loves his life loses it, and he who cares not for his life in this world will preserve it for eternal life" (John 12:24–25, Moffatt).

OFFERTORY PRAYER. Lord, let cheerfulness be integral to our giving that gladness may abound in our hearts. May the edification of many result from these gifts through the pain and great joy of Christ our King.—E. Lee Phillips

PRAYER. O Lord, most holy, who has found us wanting and yet has not forsaken us, deliver us in these days of Lent from all the littleness of heart, shallowness of mind, and smugness of spirit that would keep us from entering into the full dimensions of your love purpose revealed in the life teachings and Passion of Jesus. Search us deeply that in fellowship with him we may be cleansed from all insincerities: pious poses, cheap securities, careless devotions, thoughtless prayers. As in these days with Jesus we "set our face steadfastly toward Jerusalem," may it be in such commitment that no confrontation will turn us from doing your will. In our looking unto him—the pioneer and validation of our faith—may we discover our drooping hands being lifted and our sagging knees being straightened.

We praise you for your Word. May we

be responsive to its challenge to be peacemakers in this time and place.

As persons and as your church may we face boldly the rigors of your love as Jesus did in seeking a common security for all humankind. May we hear your call to the higher patriotism that we may love all persons as brothers and sisters and love this world as you love it.

For your love and grace that we have experienced as persons, as a church, as a nation, as a world we are grateful. May your healing grace be ministered to those among us who have special need—to any who are broken in body, mind, spirit, or heart through him who is your Word of grace declared from the beginning and is present among us now as the living Lord.—John M. Thompson

LECTIONARY MESSAGE

Topic: Heavenly Matters
TEXT: John 3:1–17

We don't know a great deal about him, but all that we know is good. Later in the ministry, Nicodemus defended Jesus before his fellow Pharisees (John 7:50). He assisted Joseph of Arimathea in anointing the body of Jesus for his burial (John 19:39). Here he came by night (why we do not know) complimenting Jesus for his miracle-working ministry. Jesus responded by removing the subject immediately to heavenly matters.

I. *Heavenly matters concern earthly persons.* Let us not suppose that there is no traffic between heaven and earth. The relationship is quite close, described as something of Jacob's ladder in the person of Jesus himself (John 1:51). Here a Jewish rabbi is approached by a Jewish ruler. Nicodemus was highly reputable among the Jews. So was Jesus. These two earthly persons began to talk about miracles, and Jesus abruptly shifted the conversation to a different sort of miracle.

They yet talked of earthly matters, of birth. That's down-to-earth. Of course, birth is something of a miracle, as all parents can attest. And what person among us has not described the bundle of life as a gift from heaven? When Jesus spoke of a new birth, however, his visitor became very earthy: How can it be? How can a person be born again?

II. *Heavenly matters concern spiritual truth.* How smoothly he made the transition—"born of water and the Spirit"! Water and spirit, flesh and spirit—is all Creation spirit? And all of this having to do with birth, with being. These are essentials. The kingdom of God is composed of such persons, of such realities, of such essentials. "Don't be surprised," he said, "new birth is necessary for even understanding spiritual truth."

The Spirit is free, unbounded by earthly ties of time and place. Like the wind, it blows and goes where it likes. The same word in Greek is translated first "spirit" then "wind." You hear it, but you don't know where it comes from or where it is going. This spirit of freedom characterizes the person who is born of the Spirit. But that calls for a new birth, a birth from above.

III. *Heavenly matters concern imponderables.* There is a difference between physical birth and the new birth. And if the one is miraculous, how about the other? In a friendly rebuke Jesus reminded Nicodemus that as "the teacher of Israel" he ought to know these things. Yet they are beyond the ken of earthly intellect. Who can explain the wind? Who can know the Spirit? And if you do not understand earthly things, how can you understand heavenly matters?

This understanding comes only through the new birth. It is framed in the revelation of God's Son. He is God's witness. He has been there. He has been here. He understands, and he reveals all of this as a matter of faith. Revelation may defy reason and thereby be an imponderable. Faith also may defy reason and thereby be an imponderable. Faith, like understanding, is concerned with both earthly and heavenly matters.

IV. *Heavenly matters concern god's love.* Here is an imponderable. Or at least it is incredible. Paul struggled with it (Rom. 5:6–8). In the death of Christ, God commended his love to us. So, while by earthly understanding it is incredible, love is one of those heavenly matters that become credible through faith. Faith accepts that challenge.

Such love is impossible. God loved the world so much as to give his only Son for it. And because God did it, the impossible is yet possible. Such love is unlimited. Nicodemus could scarcely imagine God loving all his own people, the Jews. To stretch that imagination to include the world describes it as unlimited. Yet, as Jesus knew and as Nicodemus came to know, that love is limited by its object, by the faith of the person loved. But these are heavenly matters.—J. Estill Jones

SUNDAY: MARCH FOURTEENTH

SERVICE OF WORSHIP

Sermon: The House of Prayer, the House of Growth

TEXT: Matt. 21:12–14

In the context of our Gospel, I would like to reflect with you upon the reduction of life, upon the house of prayer, upon the moment of healing.

I. When we listen to our Gospel this morning, we ask of ourselves, What do we give the church and why? "And Jesus went into the Temple of God and cast out all them that sold doves and sheep and oxen." Scholars in our generation, who have access to a whole avalanche of secondary materials and historical manuscripts that surround our text, tell us that, in all likelihood, Jesus was not distressed over those who sold souvenirs, or what we would call souvenirs, in the Temple because the faithful came from all over the nation to the Temple in Jerusalem on their annual pilgrimage. They wanted a trinket to take back with them to remind them of that occasion. I don't think our Lord was distressed about that, then or now, nor was he, scholars tell us, distressed with the money changers, because one had to pay an annual tax as one made one's pilgrimage to the Temple, and people did not always have the right coinage. It was a convenience for the faithful to have the money changers there. Probably, say they, these tables were knocked over as Jesus attempted to drive the sheep and the oxen from the Temple of God, because there was something involved in purchasing an animal of sacrifice. There was some kind of spiritual transfer from the awe that was inspired by the Temple of God to a truncated spiritual experience wherein one would give the sheep to the priest and be not troubled. But the greater purposes of the Temple serve the quest for faith, hope, loyalty, and love, the things that you and I struggle with in our sacred journey.

Dag Hammarskjold writes, "It is not the repeated mistakes, the long succession of petty betrayals—though, God knows, they would give cause enough for anxiety and self-contempt—but the huge elementary mistake, is the betrayal of that within me which is greater than I—a complacent adjustment to alien demands."

Business as usual. Do not change your life here in the Temple of God or stand there, awestruck, wondering why God has created you. Buy a sheep, send it on its way, have your business, your sacred obligation done with dispatch, and no change. If that be the temptation of that era, we ask of ourselves, how would we define this church, this temple of God? How would you define it? What happens here? "And Jesus said unto them, 'It is written, my house shall be called a house of prayer.' "

II. Jorge Luis Borges, that Argentine poet and student of literature, writes in his journal, "I remember Fragment 91 of Heraclitus: 'You will not go down twice to the same river,' I admire his dialectic skill because the facility with which we accept the first meaning ('The river is different') clandestinely imposes the second one ('I am different'). . . ."

We know readily we will not go down to the same river, but what we forget is that we do not take the person down to the river. We are in flux. And Jesus spoke to that. The Temple of God existed for men and women who knew that life is a fluid, ever-changing process. He said, "This, as it is written, is a house of prayer." This is a house of change. This is a house of growth.

In 1957, Elizabeth Kubler-Ross completed her psychiatric training in Switzerland and came to the University of Chicago, where she, with other clinicians, dealt recurrently with the dying in the hospitals of that city. Tormented by our cultural inability to deal appropriately with the dying, in 1969 she wrote the book that so many of us have read and quoted, *On Death and Dying,* wherein she stipulated five stages that most people go through when informed by the physician that their life will soon end. The first is the experience of denial. Someone must have mixed up the blood samples. Not me. The second is anger. Why me? Look at me. Look at the other people who I know have misspent their lives. Why me? The next stage is bargaining. Oh fine, I'll be more attentive. I'll be in church. I'll change my ways. Next is depression. Separation from everyone and everything that has been familiar and of value. Lastly is the experience of acceptance.

Two and one-half years ago, Scott Peck came to Boston. In the course of his public deliberation he said, "What we did not know in 1969 when Kubler-Ross wrote that useful volume was that the whole process of growth and human change follows those five steps." We encounter the Lord God in his temple. We encounter his presence, his Word. They do make demands upon me. My first reaction is denial. Mahatma Ghandi said, "If you would change the world, do not waste your time organizing rallies and giving speeches, but prepare yourself for a mountain of suffering." Jesus said to Peter, "I must go to Jerusalem." I must go face my detractors. The overwhelming likelihood is that I will be put on trial and put to death. Peter took hold of him and said, "I will not permit it." I will not permit this suffering. Denial and anger.

Some weeks ago we reflected upon our Gospel and the man who comes down out of the tombs and says, "I know who you are, Jesus of Nazareth. Why have you come to torment me?" Anger. I know who you are. Confrontation. The Lord's Christ. Do we not sometimes feel that way in the spirit of Augustine? "Oh Lord, arise and save me, but not yet!" Or, we bargain with God. It is easy to buy the sheep. But we have our burdens, our own cross, our own depressions. We say, with our Lord, in our heart of hearts, My God, my God, why hast thou forsaken me? Why am I alone? Why am I so depressed? In that moment of acceptance, that blessed moment of God's presence, that acceptance of his presence and his power, we say, "Into thy hands I commend my spirit. Into thy hands I commend my life."

III. How then can we be healed? How can we be transformed? How can we be born again? How can we be liberated? Use the lexicon of your life. We know the question. We know the yearning. "And the blind and the lame came to Jesus in the Temple, and he healed them." Why the blind and the lame? Because they were desperate people. Jesus was confronted during his entire ministry with desperate people who came to him and, in their desperation, had let go of their defenses and what was Jesus could flow into them.

Alfred Margulies, of Harvard's medical school, a year ago wrote that volume, *The Empathic Imagination,* in which he struggled with the whole issue of empathy. How does he, how do his colleagues, dedicated men and women, break through all of those defenses, that encrustation of personal and cultural history, to touch and heal and change a person? How? He said the first thing he is aware of is that we have to discover wonder. Then, in the spirit of the *mysterium tremendum,* the awe, if you will, we have to take that interior journey to discover our interior landscapes. How easy it is for us to look at our broken world and to describe all the circumstances of a tormented humanity and yet forget somehow that the major responsibility that God has consigned to me is that interior battle?

Jesus in the Temple reminded those who would hear him, "My house is a house of prayer." My house is a house of change. My house is a house of growth and hope. We ask of ourselves, can we in this Lenten season open yourselves to the Lord's Christ, in the spirit of the lame and the blind and the desperate?

Simone Weil, in her volume *Gravity and Grace,* says, "God loves us for us, not so that we will love him. God loves us so we will love ourselves." That is the power that is in the Temple. Jesus is there in the Temple of God's power and promise, and those who are desperate know it. They come to him immediately.

When you and I can open ourselves to God's love, then I can love myself; you can love yourself; we can be changed and healed.—Spencer M. Rice

Illustrations

RELEARNING PRAYER. We have to learn how to pray again. It is learned only in quiet and composure. Prayer means first of all the assurance of the presence of God, or as those of old well said, "coming before God," "standing before his face." That is not so simple. It requires an effort of the will—and more than that. "I will arise and go to my Father." That resolution requires the courage to let God tell you the truth, the humiliating knowledge that you can no longer help yourself. Only he really seeks God, for whom all other doors are bolted. God himself meets us only when we are at the end of our knowledge and power.—Emil Brunner

HE HAS A SECRET. The praying man becomes a divinely "subversive agent," the spy of God in the City of Mansoul. He cannot bring the great day of the Lord, any more than he can create light. But he can reflect light. Outwardly he may seem no different from other men. He passes a friend in the street and says, "Hello, Jim"; he goes daily to the office and answers letters; he laughs and weeps as life brings happiness or sorrow; he dies at last as all men die. But he has a secret: he knows that the kingdom of light is just beyond the walls, and daily he receives its messages. So people find light in him and hardly guess its source. Then they say, "Perhaps there is something more than enlightened self-interest. Perhaps the clue is in Jesus." A worldly woman, having paid a social call on Alice Meynell, said afterward to a friend, "I feel somehow as if I must go to church and pray."—George A. Buttrick

Sermon Suggestions

MASSAH AND MERIBAH. TEXT: Exod. 17:3–7. (1) When things go wrong in our lives, we are tempted to give in to increasingly destructive complaint. (2) A further evidence of our lack of faith is our demand for a sign or a miracle. (3) Spiritual survival may require sheer faith in God's goodness and a refusal to put God to the test (see Matt. 4:3–7.)

PEACE WITH GOD. TEXT: Rom. 5:1–11. (1) The initiative comes from God's side. (2) We respond in faith, and our estrangement is overcome. (3) God's intention in this process is that we ultimately share his glory.

Worship Aids

CALL TO WORSHIP. "When thou saidst, Seek ye my face, my heart said unto thee, Thy face, Lord, will I seek" (Ps. 27:8).

INVOCATION. When others turn away from us for one reason or another, help us to turn to thee, O Lord. Grant us to be able to confront in ourselves those things that alienate others, and may we never turn to thee for refuge when we need most thy gracious judgment and redeeming discipline. Yet, when we must stand against neighbors or principalities and powers for thee, give us wisdom and courage to do what is right.

OFFERTORY SENTENCE. "It is in God's power to provide you richly with every good gift: thus you will have ample means in yourselves to meet each and every situation, with enough and to spare for every good cause" (2 Cor. 9:8, NEB).

OFFERTORY PRAYER.   Lord, God, who can turn small hopes into great treasures and see into every living heart, take the meager gifts we bring and multiply them into great usefulness for the salvation of many.—E. Lee Phillips

PRAYER.   Our thoughts and impressions run far and deep as we gather in this place of worship this morning, Father. We come to thank you that we are not as other men are, underfed. The fruits of the field are ours, and the harvest is truly plenteous. Our barns are glutted with the bounties of your hand. Hunger keeps its distance, and starvation to us is a stranger. While our Christian brothers in other lands faint and die and malnutrition takes its toll, gluttony is our temptation. Forgive us, Father, when we allow our abundance of plenty to eat to make us selfish and cause us to forget that fellow human beings are starving for just a little of the bread which we take for granted.

Then we thank you, Father, that we are not as other men, empty of hand. Things clutter up our lives. Our hands cannot hold the abundance of things which are ours. Indeed, possessions choke our souls and in too many instances rot our spirits. Yet while our fellow human brothers across the world suffer from a lack of worldly goods, we cast away our overflow, making our trash heaps wealthier than most men's homes. Forgive us, Father, for glutting life with things we do not need while others suffer from lack of life's bare necessities.

Again we thank you, Father, that we are not as other men and women—ill clothed. The latest fashions are ours, and we cling to the style of the moment. Our garments overflow our closets. Yet abroad in the world are those who have no coats to protect them from winter's chill nor garments to shade them from summer's heat. Some do not even possess the meager necessities to adequately cover their naked bodies. Forgive us, Father, for our unawareness of such need and our failure to do what we can to help clothe the naked of the world.

We do thank you, O God, that we are not as other men are—ill housed. Our roofs protect us from the cruel hand of nature. The walls of our abodes retain the warmth which cheers our souls and comforts our bodies. We defy the elements. Help us to remember our brothers and sisters who live in caves and whose weary feet know no resting place. Protect them, Father, from the natural world that would destroy them and forgive us wherein we have failed to meet the challenge to aid these fellow humans in distress. Forbid, Father, that this service be a mockery to you, that we pray and praise you with our lips while our hearts are far from you—far distant because we are smug and complacent about the needs of fellow Christians and others who live in poverty and need which by your grace living in us could be alleviated. So meet us with challenge and stir us to act in your name that others in the world may know the love and power of the Christ we have met and serve.—Henry Fields

LECTIONARY MESSAGE

Topic: Only a Woman
TEXT: John 4:5–26 (27–42)
That's the way she would be described—only a woman. In those dark days of male ascendancy what difference did a woman make? That's the way she would have been described a few years ago. The male-dominated culture would hardly have noticed her until the feminist movement began to make men sit up and take notice. But long before the modern feminist movement Jesus had recognized the worth of women.

I. *Only a woman—drawing water.* There must have been many women at Jacob's well that day. This was woman's work—going to the well, filling the water jar or skin, and taking it back home. This woman had experience. She knew that the well was deep and a drawing instrument was necessary to get water.

She had come a long way (v. 15) to get water and knew that she would have to return on the next day and the next and the next. She was tired of the ordeal. But so were countless others. What's so special about her?

II. *Only a woman—talking with Jesus.* Men rarely talked with women in public—except to proposition them. His disciples returned (v. 27) and were surprised. Even she was surprised. You talk with me, a woman and a Samaritan woman at that? Of course Jesus talked with other women, but a Samaritan woman?

They talked about water: Jesus asked for a drink. Then he offered to give her water. This conversation about water included both physical H^2O and spiritual water. This was her area of interest, her area of expertise. If she were an authority on anything, it was water—unless it was husbands. Soon the conversation zeroed in on the woman's spiritual needs.

III. *Only a woman—searched by the Spirit.* The relationship between water and the spirit is close in the New Testament. It was relatively easy for Jesus to shift the conversation. She was shocked at his imperative. "Go, call your husband." He ought to be here when we talk about spiritual matters. It was a springboard to search out and minister to the woman's needs.

Whether the reference in the five husbands is to the gods of the Samaritan people or is to be taken literally, the interest of the woman was spiritual. She betrayed no guilt at the number of husbands but instead recognized Jesus as a prophet. She then posed the question of the Samaritan nation: Where are we to worship? Jesus replied that worship was confined neither to Mount Gerizim nor to Mount Zion. God is spirit. His worship must be in spirit and in truth.

IV. *Only a woman—found by God.* The significant statement was "God is spirit." In her quest she confessed her belief that Messiah would come and answer her questions. Where is he?

Jesus responded immediately, "I am he." Jesus found her—she did not find Jesus. Jesus initiated the conversation. He looked for her and found her.

V. *Only a woman—a convincing witness.* She left her water pot when the disciples came and went to her own people. "Come, see a man," she invited. And then in explanation of the invitation, declared, "He told me everything I ever did." They came to Jesus, and they believed on Jesus, first because of the woman's testimony and later because of their own experience with Jesus.

Many believed because of her, but she directed them to Jesus. Was she "only a woman" again? Or would she ever be "only a woman"?—J. Estill Jones

SUNDAY: MARCH TWENTY-FIRST

SERVICE OF WORSHIP

Sermon: Mission Accomplished!

TEXT: John 19:28-30

The end of life approaches. Death is a friend to one who hangs on a cross. The final breath should sound something like a sigh of relief, a literal expiration. But something is out of order here. The final word in John, the last breath, has the ring of victory. It is like the Latin *finis* at the end of a book or "The End" at the conclusion of a movie. Yet this is more than the closing of a chapter. This is the pivot on which history turns, the completion of a mission. For John, unlike the other Gospels, Jesus is always in complete control. The characteristic word for crucifixion, "lifted up," has all of the flavor of one who rises above the crass and cruel level of his time and place. For John, the cross of Christ, which on the surface is an execution, rises to a higher level. It becomes a promotion, a glorification! Thus, the final word is far from a whimper of defeat. The last word of the ministry of our Lord is the declaration "Mission accomplished!" The purpose for which he came is fulfilled. Have your ever been able to say that about anything in this life?

I. Fulfillment seems to be the impossible quest. One of my most difficult adjustments in moving from the school world into the real world was the shocking discovery that life is not divided into semesters. Something about the ritual of registration, attendance, final examination, and evaluation become a comfortable cycle which does not exist off campus. I was frustrated for several years before I realized that I would have to organize my own life. No artificial structure exists to set boundaries and to declare "the end" on most of our tasks. Thus, people typically move through life with many loose ends and much unfinished business. The perfectionist thrust into the real world is a formula for high anxiety. If your ducks are all in a row, perhaps you should look again. They are probably made of wood. If they were real, they would be fluttering around the yard like the rest of your high ideals. If report cards came out tomorrow, most of us would get a grade of "incomplete" on some of our most important commitments. Life is full of loose ends rather than neatly tied bows. Is that bad?

The mission of Christ was not so different. One of the frustrations of early Christians was the unfinished business of the kingdom of God. The disciples wanted to tie up all of the loose ends of history, to establish the kingdom with Israel. They could cite evidence of the kingdom, the blind see, the lame walk, and the dead are raised; but blindness, lameness, and death continued. Jesus was the incarnate patience of God. When the Christ passed on the tempter's simple formula to own the kingdoms of this world, he brushed aside all shortcuts to glory. This was no "ala-kazam, hocus-pocus" Christ. He was willing to walk toward the kingdom step-by-step, mission-by-mission. Finally, the hope of the kingdom became a mission in progress rather than a mission accomplished.

II. Fulfillment is a quality of God. Isa. 55:11 is both a declaration and a promise. Like the rain and snow that do not

return to heaven until they have accomplished their life-giving task, the Word of God "shall not return to me empty, but it shall accomplish that which I purpose." The Fourth Gospel begins with the Word, which was from the beginning, become flesh to live among us. The apex is the completed mission of the Word of God, the return to the Father. "It is finished!" is the climax of the drama, for here the Word has completed the circle.

Follow the word *finished* through John. From the first, Jesus is obsessed with the will of his Father (4:34): "My food is to do the will of him who sent me and *to complete* his work." Jesus compares his ministry with John on the level of a mission assignment (5:36): "The works that the Father has given me *to complete,* the very works that I am doing, testify on my behalf that the Father has sent me." The priestly prayer of Jesus in the final hours before his arrest reflects a sense of accomplishment (17:4), "I glorified you on earth by *finishing* the work that you gave me to do"; and intercedes for the disciples (17:23), "that they may become *perfectly* one." Jesus prayed for their fulfillment. The last word from the cross was a familiar word for the mission of Christ which became a prayer for the fulfillment of the disciples' mission.

Life in Christ is a steadfast move toward the finish line but not just to termination. Christ calls us toward completion, fulfillment, but not on our terms of success. Two realities underlie the finished mission of the Christ. It led to the cross, and it left a trillion loose ends floating in the sea of history. If the Son of God was only responsible for one link in the chain of history, how do you expect to tie all of the loose ends of this imperfect world in the scope of your life and calling?

The perfection of God is tempered by patience. "It is finished." "It" is not everything, but it is enough for now, and you are called to active waiting. All of us are pieces of the puzzle of an incomplete world. Anything that we finish here is fragmentary. Even for the Christ, "It is finished" is not an end but a beginning. The end of a mission is the advent of a new epoch moving toward the time when "thy kingdom come. Thy will be done on earth as it is in heaven."—Larry Dipboye

Illustrations

ASSURANCE. This seventh word has been referred to as "a proclamation of victory." I hardly think so. Victory is postponed until Easter. It is rather a proclamation of assurance. Jesus has rallied from the despair of "My God, my God, why hast thou forsaken me?" and from the distress of "I thirst." The final word is spoken from strength rather than from weakness, from confidence rather than bewilderment, from peace rather than turmoil. He has done all he could on earth for God: "It is finished." Now he gives himself over to the care of God, to the Father with whom he had always been in contact. It is good to know that our Lord died in confident trust.—James T. Cleland

WHAT COUNTS. A young man once fell in love with a girl and saw the starlight in her eyes when he proposed. I saw that once long ago myself, and many of you did. He bought a ring to give her, but he was poor, and it wasn't a very big diamond. He said to her apologetically, "It is not a very big stone." But she replied, "It is as big as we make it."—Gerald Kennedy

Sermon Suggestions

GOD'S CHOICE OF A LEADER. TEXT: 1 Sam. 16:1–13. (1) It comes in time of need. (2) It may involve risks. (3) It assuredly follows criteria that defy common human judgments.

LIVING AS CHILDREN OF LIGHT. TEXT: Eph. 5:8–14. (1) Requires our earnest search for what is "good and right and true." (2) Requires rejection of what is obviously wrong.

Worship Aids

CALL TO WORSHIP. "The Spirit and the bride say, Come. And let him that heareth say, Come. And let him that is athirst come. And whosoever will, let him take the water of life freely" (Rev. 22:17).

INVOCATION. We accept your invitation, Spirit of God. We thirst. As we worship, lead us to that river of water of life that makes glad the city of God.

OFFERTORY SENTENCE. "He that findeth his life shall lose it, and he that loseth his life for my sake shall find it" (Matt. 10:39).

OFFERTORY PRAYER. In your Word, O God, you have told us that our life does not consist in the abundance of the things we possess. Yet we act the part of fools and miss life that is real. Change us, Lord, and grant that we may find that abundant life in you that even death cannot take away.

PRAYER. As you did call Abraham at the dawn of recorded history, so you are calling us out of our history, O God. With the dispatch that Abraham answered, may we respond, "He went out not knowing where he was going."

Your call is always a call to walk by faith—not by sight. Your call is to the open road, to go out not knowing where we are going—to live with expectancy; to embrace the untried, the not-yet; to perceive the new thing you are doing in our day. Your call is to the windswept frontiers of existence—to venture and adventure, to live on the growing edge. You are calling us to the road less traveled, for narrow is the gate and disciplined is the way that leads to life.

How we want a faith for security, but you call us to a faith for insecurity. We want to tent on the old campground, but you are calling us with the dawn of each new day to break camp and move on. Your call is always to the unknown, to some land of your promise. With Abraham of old, we, too, are pilgrims looking for that city whose builder and maker you are.

As you do call us again and again, may we hear your call loud and clear in the Word spoken in this hour. You are calling us to a renewed sense of mission—to "enlarge the place of our habitation," to embrace the inclusiveness of your love, to proclaim your salvation to those near as well as those afar. We pray for such commitment as to grasp with both hands—with all our mind and heart and person—the new day of opportunity that has dawned upon us.

How we thank you for Abraham and all those heroes and heroines of the faith who have modeled for us the pilgrim life! How we thank you for him who in these last days so responded to your call to faith that he chose your will even when it meant his own Crucifixion.

Let us now run with perseverance the course that is set before us, looking unto Jesus, the pioneer and validator of our faith, who for the joy that was set before him endured the cross, despising the shame, and is now seated at your right hand, loving us, praying for us, cheering us on.—John Thompson

LECTIONARY MESSAGE

Topic: Can a Blind Person See?
TEXT: John 9:1–41

You've seen them, haven't you? Tap, tap, tapping their way down a crowded street, being careful not to brush up against a building or stumble off the curb. But surely you've never been so foolish as to ask the question, "Can a blind person see?" Of course, a blind person can't see!

But you know the story in this ninth chapter of the Gospel according to John. It begins, "And as he [Jesus] passed by . . ." Ah, that's just it: Jesus never did simply pass by. Things were always different when he passed by: The grass was greener, the smiles were more tender. The disciples spotted the man, born blind. They asked the wrong question: "Rabbi, who sinned, this man, or his parents, that he should be born blind?" Not a word about what we can do to help.

The story continues with the right answer to the wrong question: That's not the point. "But that the works of God should be manifest in him we must work. . . ." And he, spitting on the ground and making clay from the spittle,

healed the man—even though it was the Sabbath. A series of dialogues comprises the rest of the chapter. They revolved around the question, Can a blind person see? Of course not! Oh . . . ?

I. *Blind but seeing.* There are some things a blind person *can* see! His other senses are more highly developed, and he can "see" with his ears, his nose, and his tongue. Most amazing is the ability to see with the fingers and read the Braille writing.

But beyond that . . . This blind person could see that he was blind. That's ever so important when a person refuses to admit vision impairment. He had insight enough to see that he needed help. When Jesus healed his eyes, he knew what had happened to him. He could see that. He knew that Jesus was special, although Jesus did not reappear until late in the story.

As the conversation continued with the religious leaders denying the miracle and denying Jesus and excommunicating the seeing/blind person, he could see that what they were doing was wrong. Can a blind person see? Of course a blind person can see.

II. *Seeing but blind.* There are some persons with normal 20/20 eyesight who are blind. These, for example, ignored the man's previous blindness and current sighted state. They knew that it was the Sabbath and were blinded by it. They were more concerned that Jesus had spit on the ground, thus disturbing the dirt (the equivalent of plowing on the Sabbath!), than with the man's condition. They knew that healing of a blind person was impossible, and they were blinded by it. They knew that God had spoken to Moses and were blinded by it: "We know that God spoke to Moses, but as for this man [Jesus] we don't know whence he is." Moses said, "Remember the Sabbath day to keep it holy."

The story ends with a face-to-face meeting between the blind person who could see and Jesus—after the religious leaders had cast him out of the synagogue. Progressively, he had come to the point of confession: "Do you believe on the Son of God?" "Who is he, Lord, that

I may believe on him?" "He it is that speaketh with thee." "Lord, I believe."

The religious leaders knew that the man's confession was right, and they were blinded by it. Jesus brought sight to the blind. Can a blind person see? Of course. Only a blind person can see—one who sees the helplessness of his own condition.—J. Estill Jones

SUNDAY: MARCH TWENTY-EIGHT

SERVICE OF WORSHIP

Sermon: Wait and See

TEXTS: Ezek. 17:22–24; Matt. 13:31–32

I. Our text for this morning is one of those passages in the Bible that preach the message of hope. It's a parable of biblical hope. When he told that parable, the audience got the punch line immediately. There's a punch line in this parable. It's like a joke. Like all punch lines, it comes at the end. It's the last line. "Birds of the air come and make nests in its branches." That's the punch line.

(a) That phrase appeared in stories about giant cedars and referred to great powers. That's what the cedar was a symbol of, the great political powers of this world. They were called giant cedars, "in whose branches birds come and make their nests." So when you heard about birds making their nests, you thought of these great empires, like Rome.

(b) That's what Jesus' audience undoubtedly thought of immediately: Rome, who was oppressing them. A giant cedar of a kingdom, one of the great kingdoms of all time, in comparison to which the kingdom of God, as it was then manifest among them, was just a small handful of believers. It was like a mustard seed and hidden somewhere: buried, tiny, insignificant.

(c) In the Old Testament lesson for this morning out of the Book of Ezekiel, Ezekiel predicted that one day Israel was going to be a great cedar, like all the other nations round about her. One day, he said, God is going to take a sprig from the tallest cedar and plant it on the mountain, presumably in Jerusalem. That is to say that someday Israel is going to be great like all the nations of the world.

But to show you how radical Jesus' message is, he doesn't talk about taking a sprig from a cedar. He doesn't talk about a cedar at all. He talks about an unimpressive, lackluster bush, sort of a weed. You've all seen the mustard plant. It's unimpressive, which is the way the kingdom of God looks right now compared to the great empires and institutions of this world. But just wait and see, because you never know. In fact, this may be the year.

(d) We are to live with that kind of hope. It is what characterizes the Christian. I want to outline what that would look like and to do it with alliteration. It's not often that I do this, outline a sermon in three points, and certainly not often with alliteration—have each point start with the same letter, the letter *P*. Here they are: patience, persistence, and perspicacity. I had to work to get that third one in there, but it's a wonderful word, and it works wonderfully to describe what hope is able to do.

II. *Perspicacity* means keenness of vision. Better yet, it means discriminating vision, not fooled by appearances, not attracted to what everybody else is attracted to, but able to see what other people don't see. Evaluating, for instance, the events of one's life or the events of history with a discriminating eye, with a vision that is able to see a mustard seed in this world as well as a giant cedar.

(a) People with perspicacity rarely use absolutes in describing events—such as, "This is the worst thing that could ever happen."

(b) They rarely say that. Or, "I don't think I'll get over this." And they never say, "This is the end. We'll never recover from this." Nor do they say, "I'll never be happy again." Nor do they say, "He'll always be the same. He'll never change."

(c) Absolute claims about your life, or absolute claims about history are the sign of the lack of hope. To believe in God means that there is always possibility. There are very few things, therefore, that can be predicted in this world with any certainty at all. People with perspicacity know that, so they always have hope. They have this keenness of vision, this discriminating vision that enables them to see mustard seeds when everybody else can see only the cedars.

(d) Perspicacity. It's the keenness of insight that refuses to be taken in by predictions, because it knows who controls the future, and therefore it knows there will always be a new season. So maybe this will be the year.

III. Which leads to the second characteristic, patience. Patience is the evidence that you know who's in charge, and so you can wait for God to act. It's called "waiting on the Lord," and it's the hardest thing for some of us to do, for religious people as well as secular people.

(a) In fact, I think there are some religious people for whom it is especially hard, the Protestant type, who believe we must always be up and doing if we're going to be religious. They are always trying to save themselves or someone else or save the world. None of which we can do. We can't save ourselves. We can't save anybody else. We can't save the world. God does that. That's God's business. The hardest thing for us to grasp is that we have to let God do that.

(b) Which is why Jesus has all of these farmer parables. You notice that? They're all over the place. Here in the thirteenth chapter of Matthew they are literally back-to-back. The parable of the sower, the parable of the wheat and the tares, the parable of the mustard seed. One after another. They all say one thing: Be patient. It's as if he is hammering it home. Be patient, be patient, be patient. There is only so much that you can do.

(c) That's not a counsel for quietism, nor a do-nothingism. We are supposed to do something. We are supposed to improve ourselves. We are supposed to adopt spiritual disciplines so that we can continue to perfect ourselves. We are supposed to love our neighbors. But we will do all of that better and without the despair that accompanies the impatient if we remember there is only so much that we can do. We're like a farmer sowing a seed. That's all we can do. For the rest, we have to wait for God.

IV. And it's also why we should be persistent. That's the third characteristic. Be persistent in good works, because you never know. God may use what you do in a mighty way. You can't control that. God controls that. Someday the timing may be just right. That's how these things happen, you know. Small deeds become big events when the timing is right.

(a) That's what hope does. It gives you persistence. You don't stop after seven innings if you're behind. You don't stop after seven innings if you look at what you are up against and it looks like something terrible, some giant cedar, and you feel like you're just some small mustard seed. You don't give up. You keep going clear to the end, because anything can happen. That's the perspective of hope. Because God is in charge, anything can happen, if you are persistent.

(b) This parable, I think, is here to get you thinking. How are you going to live in a world in which a kingdom is hidden? How are you going to live in a world in which most people don't believe it's even here? How are you going to live in a world for which you pray, "Thy kingdom come, they will be done on earth as it is in heaven"?

One day that's going to happen, in God's time. In the meantime, how do you live?—Mark Trotter

Illustrations

VICTORY NOT YET. Life resembles a poem the last line of which has not been written. Yet the meaning of the whole depends upon it. We know what it is to participate in God's cumulative victory over the chaos of existence. Yet the victory is not yet won. We know that God works creatively and redemptively to overcome all that estranges us from him. Yet we continually cry, How long, O Lord, how long.—Daniel Day Williams

TAKE TIME.   Never be in a hurry to believe; never try to conquer doubts against time. Time is one of the grand elements in thought as truly as in motion. If you cannot open a doubt today, keep it till tomorrow; do not be afraid to keep it for whole years. One of the greatest talents in religious discovery is the finding how to hang up questions and let them hang without being at all anxious about them. Turn a free glance on them now and then as they hang, move freely about them, and see them, first on one side, and then on another, and by and by when you turn some corner of thought, you will be delighted and astonished to see how quietly and easily they open their secret and let you in.—Horace Bushnell

Sermon Suggestions

"CAN THESE BONES LIVE?"   TEXT: Ezek. 37:1-14. (1) Then: A narration and explanation of the text, showing the hope of Israel in God for the revival of the kingdom. (2) Always: An exposition of the conviction that God is in command of life's most unpromising circumstances. (3) Now: Just as—and because—God raised Jesus Christ from the dead, God can revive his erring people today, giving them vitality, influence, and hope.

TWO WAYS TO LIVE.   TEXT: Rom. 8:6–11. (1) We may live according to the flesh or according to the Spirit. (2) When we choose the one or the other, we at the same time choose the consequences. (3) If we choose the way of the Spirit, we can expect the God of Christ's Resurrection to empower us to please God.

Worship Aids

CALL TO WORSHIP.   "The Lord is nigh unto them that are of a broken heart, and saveth such as be of a contrite spirit" (Ps. 34:18).

INVOCATION.   When we need you, you are there, O Lord, even when you seem far away. At this very moment you are present to dry our tears, quiet our anxious hearts, and show us a better way, and we thank you. So let us worship you.

OFFERTORY SENTENCE.   "God, who supplies seed for the sower and bread to eat, will also supply you with all the seed you need and will make it grow and produce a rich harvest from your generosity" (2 Cor. 9:10).

OFFERTORY PRAYER.   Lord, let what we bring reflect what we believe that what we intend may be multiplied by your power for the redemption of many.—E. Lee Phillips

PRAYER.   Almighty God, Creator of the good earth, grand designer of heaven and sea, breath of life to humankind, you are the Lord of all birth, life, death, and resurrection. Thanks be to God, Maker and Father of us all.

God of generous wealth and pure beauty, springtime is bursting forth with new life and glorious color. We pause, and our spirits smile, and we give thanks for the smell of turned soil, lush green grass beneath our feet, weightless clouds dancing in the azure sky, bright sunlight warming our tender skin, the many faces of flowers beaming their rainbow of splendid colors; for birds singing freely in the budding trees, children running carefree in the park, head up as parent flies a kite in the playful wind, and hearts turning to new hope and fresh start. This is our Father's world, and it is spring time . . . and behold, it is good. And in awe and gratitude, we whisper our thanks again.

God of compassion and cleansing, baptism and deliverance, we confess our sin . . . as we have been led in song, we wish to be made clean. Bathe us all over, O God, with your costly grace and suffered forgiveness. Today, let baptism make real again the death of old self and way and the birth to new life and self in Christ. And thank you for receiving us back . . . anew . . . again.

God of all knowing and ever presence, we pray as the Body of Christ for those suffering heavily today: the ones in our presence now grieving the loss of a mate or loved one and those bearing silently overwhelming burdens. O God, empower and move us to be faithful persons of light and redemption to a dark and lost world.

God in Christ, Lord of Lent, as we walk on with you to the cross, tune our hearts to thee, and grant to us a pure heart that we may see thee, a humble heart that we may know thee, a quiet heart that we may hear thee, an open heart that we may love thee, an obedient heart that we may follow thee, a loving heart that we may serve thee.

God of forever and now, we offer our worship and prayer in the name of Jesus Christ, our Savior and Lord.—William M. Johnson

LECTIONARY MESSAGE

Topic: From Despair to Hope
TEXT: John 11:1–16 (17–45)

The story of Lazarus—sickness and death and resurrection—is recorded only in the Gospel according to John. It is filled with symbolism and meaning, sometimes below the surface. It is a story of despair and hope and beyond hope. It is a story of the home and of love. It shares in ancient lamentation customs but breathes with the presence of Jesus. Two statements from Jesus and two statements from the sisters, Martha and Mary, tell the story.

I. *He is sick—he is sleeping.* Jesus and his disciples had crossed the Jordan into Peraea. Opposition of the religious leaders threatened his ministry. There he received the message that Lazarus, his friend and brother of Martha and Mary, was sick. The sisters called on him for help, reminding Jesus, "he whom thou lovest." And Jesus stayed where he was for two more days. Some friend!

God was at work, and God's glory was assured. This sickness did not have death as its purpose or end, as final as death seems. We forget that death is not the end of the world but only the beginning of life. Anxiety yields to despair. Worry yields to hopelessness. Let us not be heartless. Though Jesus was in command of the situation, what about Martha and Mary, watching their brother become weaker and die?

To the concern of the disciples Jesus responded, "Our friend Lazarus has fallen asleep." How we grasp at straws—if he is sleeping, he will recover.

II. *He is dead—Let us go.* Jesus spoke plainly. His disciples had moved from despair to false hope and now back to despair. Jesus was not there when his friends needed him. And now he declares that he is glad he was not there. All of this became an appeal to faith. Surely this faith might have been challenged in some less frightening manner.

It was Thomas who voiced the feeling of the disciples: "Let us go also that we may die with him"—a note of despair or of cynicism? How final death is! And this came from Thomas who after the Resurrection of Jesus refused to believe "except I place my hand in his side." There is work to be done. The glory of God is at hand. Faith must be challenged—despite the dangers lurking in Judaea. "Let us go."

III. *If you had been here—I am here.* Four days Lazarus had been in the tomb. Already his spirit had escaped the confines of the burial wrappings. The grieving process must have been at its height—Jewish friends had come from Jerusalem. Martha heard that Jesus was finally coming and went to meet him. What was her attitude? Rebuke, disappointment, despair, hope?

"If you had been here, my brother would not have died." This was her rebuke, her despair, but with a bit of hope she confessed, "Yet God will give you anything you ask." "Your brother will rise again." "I know that he will rise at the last day"—but what about right now? "I am [not only 'was' or 'will be'] the Resurrection and the life"—I am here. You wonder where God is in struggle and sorrow? He's right there—believe it.

IV. *If you had been here—Where is he?* At Martha's summons Mary went to meet Jesus . . . in despair or hope. She copied her sister's greetings, "If you had been here. . . ." Jesus groaned in his spirit and wept openly ... in despair or hope. "Where is he?" he asked. To the place of greatest need—God is here!

And he came to the tomb and raised Lazarus from the dead and raised hope from despair. And faith arose from the hope, and love was overwhelming. There is hope for us in the Resurrection of Jesus. There is hope in the presence of the Holy Spirit. There is hope in the providential care of the Father. So we, too, move from despair to hope.—J. Estill Jones

SUNDAY: APRIL FOURTH

SERVICE OF WORSHIP

Sermon: Godly Sorrow and Worldly Sorrow

Text: 2 Cor. 7:5–13

I. Paul speaks in these verses of two contrasting kinds of sorrow: godly sorrow versus worldly sorrow.[1]

The background for these verses is in 2 Corinthians 2. A brother in the Corinthian church has publicly attacked Paul. He has probably said untrue things in order to undermine Paul's position with the people. Paul has written a letter asking them to discipline this brother. After a painfully long wait, Paul hears that this brother has been disciplined by the church. In turn Paul now urges the church to temper their discipline so that it not be too severe: "For such a one this punishment by the majority is enough; so you should rather turn and comfort, or he may be overwhelmed by excessive sorrow" (2:6–7).

Now later in chapter 7 Paul is thanking the church for their support of him manifested in their discipline of this brother, and he returns to the theme of church discipline. Discipline is always for the purpose of forgiveness and restoration—whether in church or school or family. Inclusion not exclusion is the goal. The church is at the same time a community of morals and mercy. As a community of morals, discipline is necessary for those who flaunt their violation of the values of the community. But because the church is also a community of mercy, grace always our first and last word, discipline is always for the purpose of restoration—the reinclusion of the offending member.

Paul now returns to this theme, speaking not only for the brother but now also to the church which had responded to Paul's letter of complaint and disciplined the brother. His letter had grieved them, but their grief had moved them to proper action: "As it is, I rejoice, not because you were grieved, but because you were grieved into repenting; for you felt a godly grief. . . . For godly grief produces a repentance that leads to salvation and brings no regret, but worldly grief produces death" (7:8–10).

Here is an important and intriguing contrast: godly sorrow (*kata theon lupe*) versus worldly sorrow (*tou kosmou lupe*). Godly sorrow leads to salvation, repentance, healing, and life. Worldly sorrow leads to death, despair, and destruction.

II. Godly sorrow is the spiritual sadness that realizes one has wounded another and thereby wounded the divine love, the dearest love in the world. This excruciating pain of the soul feels that one, to use the words of James Denny, "has fallen away from the grace and friendship of God." To feel such sadness is to really grieve, grieve not in a self-consumed, narcissistic, and despairing way, but with a "healing, hopeful sorrow."[2] To grieve in such a way is to know you can change, that your change will make a difference, and that such change will be met with the welcoming mercy of God. Therein it is hopeful.

In contrast we see worldly sorrow. There are two forms of such sorrow. The first is a kind of insincere sorrow that is

---

[1]Denny, 255.

[2]Ibid., 256.

expressed only to coerce a quick forgiveness. Such sorrow does not feel the pain or know the damage that one's actions have caused and so issues a flip apology designed to quickly fix things as if nothing has happened, no injury incurred. Such an apology expects forgiveness, as if saying, "I'm sorry" entitles you to forgiveness. We are witnessing a wave of such insincere, worldly sorrow today from preachers to politicians, from judges to generals.

Wise parents learn early on to distinguish worldly and godly sorrow in their children's voices. Children learn that tears may work better than anything else in getting what they want: sympathy or forgiveness or, better yet, getting their tormenting brother or sister in trouble. Wise parents discern the difference between deep, true tears and insincere tears used as a ploy.

But insincere sorrow is not the kind of worldly sorrow Paul is focusing on here. What he has in mind is an oppressive sorrow that ladens a person with guilt so that it leaves a person in paralyzing despair. The first kind of worldly sorrow is practiced by the person with no conscience; this kind of sorrow is the plight of the person with a tyrannical conscience, an inner judging voice that never lets them off the hook. It is the kind of conscience more severe than God ever is because God's righteousness is always wrapped in mercy.

Sometimes the church or parents or culture imposes such a tyrannical conscience on children. Oft times they prey on people with such tender consciences, knowing guilt is the best method of control. Such worldly sorrow, however, leads to death.

That is why Paul is clear to remind the Corinthians now that discipline has been administered to forgive and comfort the brother lest he be overwhelmed with excessive sorrow. Such excessive sorrow is the worldly sorrow that despairs of forgiveness or restoration and gives up. It does not lead to repentance, healing, and life because it despairs of the possibility of grace.

Many times we practice overkill on our fallen folk, dropping atom bombs of condemnation on the mud huts of their guilt. Why does the church shoot its wounded? Only because we lose sight of our Lord who lived by the deep mercy of God who offered "grace greater than our sin." Paul exclaimed, Sin abounds but grace abounds all the more! (Rom. 5:20)—something he never knew until he met the risen Lord.

Remember our Lord of whom it was said, "He will not break a bruised reed or quench a smoldering wick" (Matt. 12:20). Our churches and our world are filled with bruised reeds and smoldering wicks, people overcome with a worldly sorrow leading them to despair and death. It is compassion not condemnation, mercy not criticism that will lead them to the grace of God. And our Lord, righteous and merciful, gentle, patient, and kind will not break the bruised reed or quench the smoldering wick. He will not lay on us a worldly sorrow that leads to death but will lure us by grace to a repentance that leads to life. Often our religion breaks bruised hearts, but Jesus comes with grace welcome as rain to parched souls.

III. The contrast of godly sorrow and worldly sorrow find their counterparts, their types, in two of Jesus' disciples, Peter and Judas.[3] Peter's godly sorrow led to repentance and life, to an encounter with the risen Lord at the Sea of Tiberius where Peter was restored by grace and called by grace to be a disciple again, to be Peter again. And Judas' worldly sorrow led to despair and death.

Judas betrayed Jesus, leading the soldiers to capture him, betraying him with a kiss. "Hail, Master!" he said and kissed him. And Jesus said, "Friend, why are you here?" (Matt. 26:49–50).

The great sadness of this story is that Judas didn't wait, couldn't wait for Easter, until Jesus rose and appeared to him. So overcome with worldly sorrow, despairing of any hope of forgiveness and

[3]Peter and Judas as types of these two sorrows was mentioned by H. C. G. Moule, 7.4.

restoration, he killed himself (Matt. 27:5).

The resurrection appearance that didn't happen. Can you imagine how wonderful it would have been? Grace enough for Peter, grace enough for Judas. Grace enough for denial and enough for betrayal, too.

Judas no doubt would have been alone, too ashamed to have made his way back to the rest of the disciples. And this Stranger would have come up behind him and said, "Friend, why are you here?" And Judas would have turned and said, "Master." And Jesus would have said, "Judas, you, too, are forgiven. You belong with us. Come on, let's go rejoin the rest." How wonderful that would have been.

And this time it would have been Jesus who gave the kiss, not the kiss of death but the kiss of life and, to use the words of the psalmist, with "lips moist with grace," grace greater than all our sins.[4]

Why did Judas despair of such grace? Why do any of us? We cannot know. It is hid in the mystery of the human mind and held in the mercy of a loving God. This missed opportunity of grace, however, is powerful to turn our minds to Paul's contrast between worldly and godly sorrow. And it should compel us, the church, to be such a people of grace that we not heap worldly sorrow on our bruised reeds of souls lest they despair to see the Savior's kind face.—H. Stephen Shoemaker

Illustrations

DOING JUDAS JUSTICE OR MERCY? Yes, I think we must think tenderly of Judas, not emphasizing the greed of the man, not supposing him dreadfully wicked; but seeing him as a hot-blooded patriot, whose nationalism Jesus wanted to sublimate into a love of the kingdom of the men of all nations; seeing him as one who let Christ down without meaning to, be-

cause he would not understand. Perhaps that is the explanation of a good many of our sins. Most of us do not deliberately plot to hurt that holy love of which Jesus is the personification and Incarnation. Our instincts get out of hand though, and our selfishness grows up in the dark, and our pride seems such a precious thing to keep. We say hot, bitter, cruel, impatient words, and do unconsidered, thoughtless things. Thus we all betray him.

O break, O break, hard heart of mine;
Thy weak self-love and guilty pride
His Pilate and His Judas are;
Jesus my Lord is crucified.

But if we will turn, even now, to him, seeking the mercy which he offers and the love which can restore, then those eyes will shine upon us in utter forgiveness; that hand will be stretched out to raise us from the dust; that divine voice will say to us the word that was said to Judas: "Friend!"—Leslie D. Weatherhead

DIVINE SUPPORT. It is clear that God is pleased to grant his support to the weak rather than to the strong, to those who are conscious of their weakness, of their failures, of their faults and of their powerlessness to overcome them, rather than to those who are self-satisfied and proud of their victories over themselves and of their social success and their faith. God offers his support to the sick, to those who are in affliction, to all the despised, the despairing, to little David rather than to Goliath the giant, to the adulterous woman rather than to her virtuous accusers, to the humble members of the church of Corinth rather than to the clever arguers of the Areopagus.—Paul Tournier

Sermon Suggestions

ONE WHO SPEAKS FOR GOD. TEXT: Isa. 50:4–9a. (1) Must listen to and be taught by God. (2) Must be prepared for rejection by those one seeks to help. (3) Can expect the continuing help and ultimate vindication of God.

[4]This image comes from Frederick Buechner, *Peculiar Treasures* (San Francisco: Harper & Row, 1979), 83.

SOLVING CHURCH DISPUTES. TEXT: Phil. 2:5–11. Christ Jesus offers the paradigm. (1) Christ had legitimate position. (2) For the sake of God's purpose and the good of others he gave up what he could rightfully claim. (3) As a result, God gave him a name and a position that outshone his pristine glory.

Worship Aids

CALL TO WORSHIP. "Whosoever exalteth himself shall be abased, and he that humbleth himself shall be exalted" (Luke 14:11).

INVOCATION. In the spirit of Jesus, who entered Jerusalem in peace and humility and yet who conquered the hearts of millions across the ages, enable us to trust your way and power to accomplish your purposes and follow in the hallowed path that Jesus traveled before us. May this service of worship lead us to a new devotion to his way, your way, the way of the cross, but the way of glory.

OFFERTORY SENTENCE. "He that taketh not his cross, and followeth after me, is not worthy of me" (Matt. 10:38).

OFFERTORY PRAYER. Lord, let us give as though it were all we could give, as though it were our last and best gift, for we can never forget Jesus gave that way for us!—E. Lee Phillips

PRAYER. O Father, as we begin this historic week so filled with the drama that has brought life and immortality to light, keep us from that casualness that would cause us to think that we can pass through these days as innocent bystanders. Make us sensitive to the fickleness in our own lives as we are to the vacillating ways of a Pilate, the betraying ways of Judas, or denying ways of a Peter.

In the events of this week, we sense that the agony of this world is your agony and that you are dying a thousand deaths that we may be reconciled to you as our Maker, Father; to our true self, as your son, your daughter; to one another, as sister, brother. Called to be instruments of reconciliation, may we not turn from the agony of love when it comes to us in the shape of a cross. May we be so in tune with your love purpose that we may be courageous to pray in our Gethsemane, "Not my will but yours be done."

Grant to those among us who are sick in mind, body, or spirit, the healing of your grace; to those who are lonely, bereft of loved one or friend, the consciousness of your abiding presence; to the stranger within our gates, a sense of at-homeness with your people.

In the affairs of the world, we pray with the Hebrew poet that "mercy and truth shall meet and that justice and peace will kiss." We pray for the peace of Jerusalem—that land we think of as holy because of your advent into history there, but made so unholy today with the brokenness of hostilities and bloodshed. May those who seek its peace through justice and equanimity faithfully and courageously persevere.

We pray for the leaders of our nation and the leaders of all nations that we may seek that spirit of unity which celebrates the human family. Grant them such wisdom to know and understand that your purpose is effected not through might, nor by power, but by your Spirit. May your Spirit so brood over the chaos of these times, bring a just order for all, that *shalom* may prevail.

May the highest aspiration for your church be confirmed in and through us, that indeed "the kingdoms of this world may become the kingdom of our Lord and his Christ" who is present among us as your eternal Word.—John Thompson

LECTIONARY MESSAGE

Topic: From Question to Confession
TEXT: Matt. 27:11–54
A great New Testament scholar came to the story recorded here and wept unashamedly before his class. He could not read the story apart from tears. It is the story of great love and great sacrifice. More, it is the story of Gentiles—from the Roman governor's question to the Roman centurion's confession. More, it is the story of the pilgrimage of many a

person—from "Who is he?" to "The Son of God."

I. *The governor's question.* Note the perspective from which it was asked. The governor was in the position of judge. The governor had certain preconceived ideas of what a king was like. He himself was subject to the Roman emperor. He sensed that a king was in a position of authority. He knew something of the power of a king, what with legionnaires all around him. He may even have identified a king with his sovereignty—his rule or the extent of his kingdom.

And so he asked, "Are you the king of the Jews?" Jesus did not have much to say at his trial but to this question he replied, "You say it." A second question is often ignored. To many accusations Pilate replied with a question: "Don't you hear how many things they witness against you?" Silence from Jesus. A third question was directed to the crowd: "Whom shall I release to you, Barabbas or Jesus?" The crowd answered readily, "Barabbas." Again the governor asked, "What then shall I do with Jesus?" The answer: "Crucify him!" Again the governor asked, "Why what evil has he done?" And the crowd merely called for his crucifixion. Perhaps as much in response to his wife's protest as to the crowd, he washed his hands before them. But all the soaps and perfumes of the Near East could not cleanse his hands—nor could all the waters of the Jordan, nor could all the washings of baptism. He sought to place the blame on the Jews—"I am innocent!" But he wasn't—any more than we are.

Perhaps the original question was asked out of curiosity: "Are you the king of the Jews?" Much like the window-shopper's reply: "May I help you?" "No, I'm just looking." It was noninvolving: Are you somebody's king? You certainly are not mine.

The church never tired of telling the story. Early preachers never omitted the account of Jesus' suffering and death. Little wonder that there is so much agreement in the New Testament accounts: his mocking by the crowds, Simon pressed into service, the accusation written, "This is Jesus, the king of the Jews." Was Pilate answering his own question? Then there was the cry of dereliction, "My God, my God . . . ," and all of this was followed by a natural uproar in Jerusalem: the veil of the temple torn, the earthquake, the opening of the tombs. A friend insists that the sermon that does not deal with the cross is not a Christian sermon.

II. *The centurion's confession.* Another Roman witnessed the Crucifixion. The Roman centurion joins a noble band of centurions cited in the New Testament. All of them are complimented by the writers. This one, unnamed, had been a witness to all of these things. His confession is clear, "Truly this man was God's Son."

His confession was born of observation. He had observed Jesus dying. He had observed nature's reaction. No political pressure forced his confession. No peer pressure encouraged it. It was based on his experience of Jesus' presence. And perhaps there were others "with him watching" who joined in the confession.

It is the pilgrimage of many a person—from "Who is he?" to "The Son of God!"—J. Estill Jones

SUNDAY: APRIL ELEVENTH

SERVICE OF WORSHIP

Sermon: Death—But Life!
    TEXT: Rom. 6:23
    My dear brothers and sisters, did you hear it? Death—but life! When in these days we wish each other "good Easter" or "happy Easter," we will want to remember that a great deal is at stake: death—but life.

Let us underline the *but!* Death and life are not just two words, concepts, or ideas. They describe a journey, a history embodied in our Lord Jesus Christ on Easter morning when he rose from the dead. Then and there, in him, it was accomplished once for all, but then and there also for us. Hence his Easter story is our history as well. Death—but life, eternal life! This is why "we know that we have passed out of death into life."

This is what happened in the Easter story, in Jesus Christ. Now let us ponder the various moments of this event one by one.

I. The wages of sin is death. There seems to be no choice but to begin with this beginning of the Easter story.

(a) Death is called here "the wages of sin." It could also be called the pay, the salary, the compensation paid by sin to those who are in its service and work for it. Strange, isn't it? Sin fulfills here the function of the paymaster in the armed services or of the employer or his cashier in a business enterprise who pays the employees and workers. Here is what is your due, what you have earned through your efforts. Is it the correct amount? Take a good look! Absolutely correct, isn't it? This is what you deserve, and you've got it: death, not more, not less, and nothing else.

But what kind of paymaster or employer is this sin with such a tremendous payoff? Sin is not confined to the evil things we do. It is the evil within us, the evil which we are. Shall we call it our pride or our laziness, or shall we call it the deceit of our life? Let us call it for once the great defiance which turns us again and again into the enemies of God and of our fellowmen, even of our own selves.

(b) What is death, the wages paid by sin? Here again we must think beyond the first caption that may come to mind when we hear the word *death*. Not only shall we die one day. Death is much greater and much more dangerous than that. It is the great no, the shadow that hangs over our human life and accompanies all its movements. Death means that this no has been pronounced over us. Death means that we inescapably wither and wilt, returning to dust and ashes. This is death as paid by sin.

(c) This is truly our history. One might also say that the history of the world is but one great demonstration of the fact that the wages of sin is death. But let us shelve for a moment the history of the world. It is anyhow best understood when it is seen through the history of our own lives. And here it is crystal clear; the wages of sin is death. But now mark this! Because Jesus Christ was willing to make our history his own; because he took our sin upon himself as though he himself had committed it; because he volunteered in our behalf to pocket the wages of sin—therefore he suffered, was crucified, died, and was buried; therefore the Easter story begins with Jesus Christ lying dead in the tomb. This he willed and this he did. All of us lay there. The wages of our sin were paid on Easter morning. Our death occurred on the cross. The no, meant to strike us mightily, struck the one who was without sin and did not deserve death. It was executed in his flesh to the bitter end.

II. But the free gift of God is eternal life. We have been talking about the dismal beginning of the Easter story. Here is now its glorious outcome; here is the joyous onward; here is the one-way street along which Christ's history proceeded and whereon we, thanks to him, advance, too. On this road sin and death, its wages, lie no longer ahead of us, but behind us.

(a) Eternal life was the destination of Christ's journey. It is the destination of our journey as well, since the Easter story happened for us. No backing out, dear brothers and sisters! Eternal life is man's life when God has spoken his yes upon it, once for all, unconditionally and unreservedly, not to be changed anymore. Eternal life is man's life lived with God, in his bright light, nourished and sustained by his own life. Eternal life is man's life committed to the service of God and thereby to the service of the neighbor, a life which certainly also serves him best who is allowed to live it.

(b) Eternal life is the free gift of God. It is not the wages, the salary, this compensation, as death is the wages of sin. Eternal life is not our due from God. It is nothing we have earned. It is not a payment for services well done. God is a very distinguished gentleman whose privilege and enjoyment it is to give freely and to be merciful. Hence he grants eternal life. Hence human life experienced as eternal life is his undeserved and free gift, his gift of grace.

(c) Remember, this was the outcome of the Easter story, the history of Jesus Christ, just as death as the wages of sin was its beginning. With Christ's Resurrection from the dead, God's free gift, eternal life, entered the world. He, the dear Son; he, the faithful and obedient servant; he who was willing to make our sin his own and to die our death in replacement of us; he, Jesus Christ, was raised from the dead and recalled from the tomb by the Father. He was robed in eternal life. But now remember also, dear brothers and sisters, that God so acted in Jesus Christ in order that we, truly all of us, without exception, may share in this free gift of life eternal. His story now becomes ours, just as before ours became his. This was accomplished when the Easter story reached its climax. There all of us, mankind itself, were made free for eternal life. The Lord is risen! He is risen indeed! In him and with him we, too, are risen indeed.

III. Granted all this, what remains there for us to be done? Only one thing: to perceive, to accept, and to take to heart that this is so. God's free gift is eternal life in Jesus Christ our Lord. Do you know whom we would resemble were we not to perceive and accept this truth? We would resemble a fool who is likely to say these days: spring is not here yet; the cherry trees are not yet in bloom, it is still raining; the cold weather prevails and, who knows, there may even be some more snow. Would such not be the words of a fool?

Sin and death are conquered; God's free gift prevails, his gift of eternal life for us all. Shall we not very humbly pay heed to this message? Death—but life! "Wake up, sleeper, and rise from the dead, that Jesus Christ may be your light!" He, Jesus Christ, who made our history his own and, in a marvelous turnabout, made his wondrous history our

own! He in whom the kingdom of the devil is already destroyed! In whom the kingdom of God and of his peace has already come, to us, to you and me, to us all, on the earth and in the whole world! Amen.—Karl Barth

Illustrations

UNWORTHY, BUT LOVED. The most difficult part of the resurrection message for me to believe is that God in Christ did all this for us long before we did anything worthy of this kind of love. Christ died, rose again, and comes to us now not because we are worthy of God but simply because God loves us as we are. God is seeking us out as Jesus picked out his disciples and friends and then sought them out after his Resurrection to bring them back to life. The greater our need, the greater God's effort to seek us who are like the prodigal, the elder brother and the straying sheep. The Resurrection reveals the loving and seeking God who would find us and help us achieve the deepest and most lasting desires of our being. What greater gift could we receive? We need simply to cease running away and receive the grace upon grace that the risen Lord holds in his hands for us.—Morton Kelsey

THE LIFE OF GOD. Eternal life is the life of God himself, and into that life we, too, may enter when we accept what Jesus Christ has done for us, and what he tells us about God.

We shall never enter into the full ideas of eternal life until we rid ourselves of the almost instinctive assumption that eternal life means primarily life which goes on for ever. Long ago the Greeks saw that such a life would be by no means necessarily a blessing.

They told the story of Aurora, the goddess of dawn, who fell in love with Tithonus, the mortal youth. Zeus offered her any gift she might choose for her mortal lover. She asked that Tithonus might never die; but she forgot to ask that he might remain for ever young. So Tithonus lived forever, growing older and older and more and more decrepit till life became a terrible and intolerable curse.

Life is only of value when it is nothing less than the life of God—and that is the meaning of eternal life.—William Barclay.

Sermon Suggestions

GOOD NEWS FOR ALL.   TEXT: Acts 10:34–43, NRSV. (1) None are special favorites of God, verses 34–35. (2) God gave Jesus Christ to be "Lord of all," verse 36. (3) Therefore, "everyone who believes in him receives forgiveness of sins through his name," verse 43.

THE NEW LIFE.   TEXT: Col. 3:1–4, NRSV. (1) Our redeemed status: "raised with Christ." (2) Our consequent obligation: "seek the things that are above." (3) Our assured destiny: "with him in glory."

Worship Aids

CALL TO WORSHIP.   "Thine eyes shall see the king in his beauty" (Isa. 33:17a).

INVOCATION.   Lord, over whom no other holds power, in whom all things needful are possible, whose will cannot be vanquished and whose purposes are everlasting; roll away every stone in our lives that keeps us from you and lead us by the holy light in the loving eyes of Jesus Christ, our living Lord.—E. Lee Phillips

OFFERTORY   SENTENCE.   "He that spared not his own Son, but delivered him up for us all, how shall he not with him freely give us all things" (Rom. 8:32).

OFFERTORY PRAYER.   Lord, let us say with our giving what we believe in our hearts, that what we do and how we do it may proclaim a Savior, a salvation, and a triumphant Resurrection.—E. Lee Phillips

PRAYER.   What a day! This is the day which you have made, O God, giving significance to all our days. May we come with such faith and expectancy as to receive it in all of its glory and power. Life is going somewhere, and even nails and a cross cannot stop it. As you turned the despair of the disciples into hope, so give us faith to believe that every good which has seemed to be overcome by evil and every love which has seemed to be buried by hate and every relationship that has been eclipsed by estrangement shall rise again to new life.

Forgive us when, in our doubts and our fears, we live on the wrong side of Easter. For all of us, let this be a day of rejoicing and great gladness—a day when we fully understand that although with men the saving of man is impossible, with you all things are possible. Let this be a day when you surprise us with the insight that in our weakness you can make perfect your strength and through the foolishness of the cross you reveal your wisdom and power. Whatever the present circumstance of our life, may we comprehend that to refuse to hope is to have made the decision to die. If there are those among us still wrapped by the grave clothes of doubt, of fear, of cynicism, we pray that we may be released to live life in the new age heralded by the good news of that first Easter morning: "Christ is risen." We praise you, O Father, that by the Resurrection we assuredly know that all your promises find their yes in Christ.

Knowing a love that even death cannot vanquish, we rejoice in a fellowship not limited by time or space—the communion of saints. Sharing such communion, we realize that no one lives or dies unto himself—we are all bound in one bundle of life.

O Father, may we here, and all who are the Church everywhere, pursue with renewed commitment your love purpose made known in the life, ministry, Passion, and living again of Christ. Bless family and friends with whom we are privileged to celebrate most intimately the goodness of life. Bless the ill according to their need and those who keep faithful vigil in their behalf. May those bereft of loved one or friend know the assurance that "life is ever lord of death and love can never lose its own." For those with civil authority over us, we pray the enlightenment of the truth which though "crushed to earth shall rise again."

Thanks be to you, for you give us the victory through our Lord Jesus Christ, who is present among us as your eternal Word.—John M. Thompson

LECTIONARY MESSAGE

Topic: They Have Taken Away My Lord

Text: John 20:1–18

On a Saturday before an Easter Sunday several years ago I saw it on a church bulletin board. The church was located on a busy corner, and most of the traffic was exposed to the sign. I never found out whether it was the announcement of the Easter Sunday morning sermon title or a mere Scripture verse for public disclosure. It was somewhat shocking to the Easter spirit: "They have taken away my Lord."

I've often thought about it since that time. I wonder if it would do for a Sunday morning sermon. It is a cry of disappointment. Out of the depths of sorrow, Mary voiced the tragic realization. As if it were not enough for them to have crucified him, now they have removed his body from the tomb. It is a cry of despair. She had come early to visit the tomb and perhaps to anoint the body. Now I'll never see him again. It is also a current, a modern cry: "They have taken away my Lord." And that makes it a likely sermon title.

I. *Why have they taken him away?* Why did they? Why did they ask that he be executed? At least three answers come to mind.

(a) He's too good for them. They were continually shamed by his words and his behavior. He paid attention to women and little children and publicans and prostitutes. He gently healed the suffering. They couldn't stand to have him around.

(b) He's meddlesome. He called them hypocrites. He knew their objectives. He took their law seriously.

(c) He's unbelievable. No one can be that pure, that strong, that wise. They had tried to trip him, to no avail. They didn't want him around—so they took him away.

II. *Where have they taken him?* They took him to the cemetery, but he wouldn't stay there. Prayer is frequently made in the cemetery by folks who won't pray anywhere else. It's a godly place, fit for respect and reverence and rest. Leave him there.

They took him to the wedding, but he won't stay there. Cana of Galilee was not the last wedding where he has been present. Brides and grooms and parents and friends think about God in the church, but after the wedding he is no longer a welcome guest. You can't leave him there.

They take him to kindergarten, but he won't stay there. When the child begins to grow up his parents are less concerned about the Lord and so is the child. But you can't leave him there.

They take him to the hospital. There's a good place for him—with the sick. They think about the Lord and ask his healing. But then when they begin to recover, he won't stay at the hospital.

They take him to church—on Sunday morning—and they would like to leave him there so he won't interfere during the week.

III. *How have they managed it?*

(a) By leaving him out of their daily life. As the followers of Zoroaster in the ancient world were required once a year to extinguish all fires and journey to the Temple of the Sun to find light again, so the Christian must return to the source of his light from time to time, from day to day. Remembering the celebration of Communion—worshiping in the fellowship of the saints, ministering to human need.

(b) By refusing to hearken in obedience. How often an appearance after the Resurrection is coupled with the word *Go.* He can be effectively removed by continuing disobedience, and the separation is clear to both parties.

(c) By laughing at his immediacy. Ah, he's safely hidden away in a corner of heaven. He doesn't care what I say or do. The world is much too big for him to be interested in me.

It is not possible—they cannot
   Take my Lord away;
He lives, you see, within my heart
   And this is Easter Day.
Though men may turn their backs to
   him
And mock at every turn—
They only take themselves away
When his great love they spurn.

He's there—in comfort: Believe me. He's there—in challenge to believe: Try me. He's there—in commission: Follow me!—J. Estill Jones

SUNDAY: APRIL EIGHTEENTH

SERVICE OF WORSHIP

Sermon: On Being Raised with Christ
   TEXT: Col. 3:1
   "If ye then be risen with Christ, seek those things which are above, where Christ sitteth on the right hand of God."
   You have heard that sentence every single year of your life if you have been at one of the Communion services on Easter Day. I often wonder what it means to you when you hear it. I was only a little boy when I heard it for the first time. I was at the first Easter service at six o'clock in the morning, with my mother and father. At that time, it didn't mean anything to me.
   But strangely enough, even though the words didn't mean anything to me, I remembered them. These first words of Scripture that were read in the service stayed in my mind.
   Later I began to ask two questions about them. The first is, How can I be risen with Christ while I am still alive? Christ rose from the dead, How can I be raised with him if I am not yet dead? The second question was, What are the things we are supposed to seek, and how can I ever hope to find them if they are so far above me as the heavens? "Seek those things which are *above,* where Christ sitteth on the right hand of God." How can I be risen with Christ while I am still alive, and what are the things that I am supposed to seek?
   I. The answer to both questions begins with the understanding that St. Paul is using words figuratively, not literally.

This is an old story to many of you; you do the same thing all the time. When you see someone who does a difficult thing and does it well, you say, He *rose* to the occasion. You are not suggesting that his feet left the ground. You are not making any reference to the level of his position, high or low. When a person is running on one cylinder, when he is limp, you sometimes say that he is more *dead* than alive. You are not implying that he is dead and buried, that he is a corpse walking about. You are simply using language in a figurative sense to say that he is dead on his feet.
   This is a very elementary lesson and you might think that everyone had learned it by now, but they have not. I meet people again and again, people just as intelligent as you, who have not learned it, and when they come across passages like these in the Bible, they are absolutely misled because they have not learned that simple fact. Once you do learn it, you can see how you can be risen with Christ while you are still alive.
   (a) You can think of other experiences which point to the fact that there are people who raise other people to a different level. This is one of the most exciting things in human experience. Going back to the eighteenth century, there was Edmund Burke, British orator, writer, and statesman. Someone once wrote about him, "If one stood under a doorway to escape a passing shower with Edmund Burke, one went away with one's shoulders thrown back, with heart uplifted to face the realities and battles of life." You have known people like that.

Come to our own century, there was Alfred North Whitehead, one of the most extraordinary men of our time. Someone said that his life was written in three volumes: the first, Cambridge, England; the second, London; and the third, Cambridge, Massachusetts. All of us who live here praise God that his life did not end before the third volume was written. He came here to teach philosophy at Harvard. He was already an old man, but that third chapter of his life was one of the richest ones. A man, once a student of his, wrote that instead of allowing a student twenty minutes for a conference, he often gave him a whole afternoon or a whole evening. And then he added this revealing line: "From that inspiration a man comes back with a changed tone." Whitehead was a man completely in the context of our human life who could raise other human beings to a higher level.

(b) Now you may ask, It is all very well to see Christ in other people, but do we never see the Christ directly? I do. My experience may not be like yours, and there is no reason why it should be, and you must not feel guilty if it isn't because we are all different and we all respond to different things in different ways. I see Christ most vividly, the risen Christ, at the end of the Good Friday service, even more than I do on Easter. Easter says what I already know and tells what has already been done. When you come to the end of the Three Hours and have gone through the shame and the pain, the humiliation and the sin, the suffering and the death, when you have gone all through that, there he stands in his regal simplicity, alone; beside him everything else fades away, and he claims the allegiance and love of the whole world.

When that happens, for the time being at least, you have been raised to another level of existence. At least for the time being the clouds of life that can be so thick and so frightening are below you instead of around you or on top of you, and you come away with "a changed tone."

II. That experience suggests the answer to the second question. Seek those things which are above—what things? Certainly not heavenly things as opposed to earthly things. Through the ages people have been misled about that. In the letter St. Paul goes on to say, "Set your affection on things above, not on things on the earth." Certainly, St. Paul could not have meant that I am to shun every material thing, everything in which the beauty and goodness of God is made manifest.

What it means to me is that once you have been raised to a new level, your aim is different. In place of the word *seek*, the word *aim* may help you to see more clearly what it means. Your aim is different. You do not aim at the same things you aimed at before, or you do not aim at the same things in the same way.

(a) For example, you do not aim at money as you did before. It is not because money is inherently evil, because it isn't; but you do not aim at it as an end in itself. When it becomes an end, it swallows you up, as it has swallowed up thousands of American human beings now who would do anything for a dollar. You aim at money, but you aim at it in a different way. You aim at it as a means to an end, the means to do things for yourself and for your family and for other people.

(b) You do not aim at happiness as you did before. That may sound strange to you because happiness is a good thing, and we want everyone to be happy if he can be; but we cannot be happy all the time in life, and the sooner we find it out, the better. Albert Camus in one of his journals suggested how the aim shifts. When he was only twenty-three, he said, "What I want now is not happiness but awareness." At my best, I want that. I cannot be happy all the time, and I don't expect to be, but I would like to be more aware of more things and of more people, be more sensitive to what is going on around me, than I was before I had been raised to that new level of existence.

(c) You do not aim at pleasing everyone the way you may have done before. This is one of the temptations that comes to every person in a position like mine; to every political leader, to everyone who is at the head of any institution. It is the beguiling temptation to please everyone. Once you have been raised up to the new level, you do not aim at that. You aim at the courage to be yourself, not the self that *you* would like to be, but the self that you think *God* wants you to be, and you aim to be yourself without deliberately hurting anyone else. You would rather *be hurt* than hurt.

(d)Also, more and more as you live on this level you do not aim as you once did to be free of life's handicaps. There are times when you would like to shake them all off, all your physical liabilities, all the things which make life difficult for you, all the inconveniences in your work, all the opposition that you have to face, all the decisions you have to make. But you change your aim. You do not aim to be free of life's handicaps; you aim to handle them well, to meet them as well as you can when they come.

III. One thing you must remember. The first verb in the sentence is passive. The correct translation is, If you have *been* raised with Christ. You cannot do it yourself. It is something that is done to you. All you can do is to put yourself in a position to be exposed to the lifting power. The second verb is active: *seek.* That is something that you do; you must work on it. The tone will be changed, raised to a higher pitch; but to keep it from dropping, you will have to keep working on it.—Theodore Parker Ferris

Illustrations

THE REAL NEW AGE.   We get no description of the risen Christ, and we get no clue to the experience of the witnesses. All we have is a bundle of bright apocalyptic images, a few confessions of faith, and some indirect mention of the corporate life of Christian communities. But we can preach what we are given. Easter is still a confession of faith: Jesus is Lord! And still we can stare wide-eyed at the durable shape of our common life; we preach, we forgive, we break bread. Perhaps when we put a confession of faith together with common ministry, we too can exclaim, "Risen! Christ is risen

indeed!" and realize that we are living in the hidden but very real new age of God's favor.—David G. Buttrick

THE LAST WORD.   "He's alive!" cries the Roman centurion in Charles Rann Kennedy's play *The Terrible Meek.* "I can't kill him. All the empires can't kill him."

Christ is ever rising again. Day by day men seek to bury him under the debris of history or embalm him in creed and phrase and definition or immure him within the walls of churches and institutions or smother him under a load of the cares and riches and pleasures of this life or stab him to death with the daggers of their sins. But always he rises, phoenix-like, from the ashes of the fires of selfishness and carelessness in which we allow his power over our lives to be destroyed. Ever and again he is lifted up out of the common things of life, a vindication of his life and a triumph over the powers that did him to death, and all men are drawn to him as irresistibly as the earth is held in its orbit around the sun. The empty tomb opens before the world, telling us it is God who still has the last word, not ourselves; that on Easter Day life looks forward, onward, upward, God-ward.—Elmer S. Freeman

Sermon Suggestions

THIS JESUS.   TEXT: Acts 2:14a, 22–32. (1) His "deeds of power, wonders, and signs." (2) The treatment people gave to him. (3) God's exaltation of him.

ULTIMATE HOPE.   TEXT: 1 Peter 1:3–9. (1) Our living hope. (2) Our divine security. (3) Our temporal testing. (4) Our resolute joy. (5) Our ultimate salvation.

Worship Aids

CALL TO WORSHIP.   "Blessed are they that have not seen and yet have believed" (John 20:29b).

INVOCATION.   Keep after us, Lord, get through to us, stir us up, lead us where we need to go, and help us to catch a vision of it all through this service of divine worship.—E. Lee Phillips

OFFERTORY SENTENCE.   "And he said to them, 'Go into all the world, and give the good news to everyone'" (Mark 16:15, N.T. in Basic English).

OFFERTORY PRAYER.   Lord, move in the gifts we bring this day that the gospel might be spread and lives transformed in the Redeemer's name.—E. Lee Phillips

PRAYER.   Hear, O Lord, our prayers for persons of a troubled spirit, volatile mixtures of panic and hope; persons about to explode: that the fires of their anger, abated, fuel good works and not destroy; that they find a place to stand; that they unwind, know good days, be able to laugh; that out of their heat come light, out of the civil war of their divided heart come peace.

We also pray for those who love them of a troubled spirit: that they be able to endure; that they find a pace they can hold; that they be resourceful, cunning even; grant them a double portion of your spirit, the manner of the sixth day, inasmuch as they must believe for two.

Show us how to revive these dead, like Elijah, who stretched three times upon the son of the widow of Zarepath, crying, "Yahweh, my God, may the soul of this child, I beg you, come into him again," show us how to revive these dead.

Hear, O Lord, their piteous cries for help, the heaviness of our hearts ascending as incense before thy throne.—Peter Fribley

LECTIONARY MESSAGE

Topic: That You May Believe
TEXT: John 20:19–31

Have you ever wondered why the four Gospels are different? Have you ever asked, "Why did this Gospel contain this story?" This Gospel states the reason for the selection of various sayings and events. It is clear in verse 31: "these are written, that you may believe...." Included in the larger context are two post-Resurrection appearances. They are familiar stories. They occurred a week apart—the first on Resurrection Sunday and the second eight days later.

I. *From fear to faith.*

(a) "On that day" sets the stage for action. Peter and another disciple and Mary Magdalene had visited the tomb early and had found Jesus' body gone. Mary had seen the Lord and had told the disciples. Now the disciples had gathered at evening, scared.

"Fear knocked at the door / Faith answered / There was no one there." Someone said it.

(b) The disciples gathered and shut the doors because they were frightened. Their fears were at least threefold.

(1) Fear of the religious establishment. They knew what they had done to Jesus, and they feared for their own safety. If they had been able to execute Jesus, for all his popularity, they would not hesitate to seize the disciples.

(2) Fear of being alone. Jesus was not with them. For many months, perhaps three years, they had followed him up and down the dusty roads, into homes and onto mountainsides. They had come to depend on him for leadership and for strength. Now he was not there—whether or not he had been raised from the dead.

(3) Fear of being together. Despite the presence of Jesus, occasional disagreements had developed. "Who is the greatest?" for example. Judas had betrayed his Lord and the fellowship. Peter had denied his Lord and the fellowship. Who else is capable of betrayal or denial?

(c) Then Jesus appeared, and they were glad when they saw the Lord. He was there in the midst of them—a victor over death. His Resurrection vindicated his ministry. Neither the Jews nor death could hold him. His presence proved reassuring. They were not alone. He was with them, teaching, assuring. His first word was "Peace be unto you." Regardless of conflicting ambitions and understanding, Jesus was there to referee. Their loyalty to him and love for him made disagreement less likely. How quickly in his presence they moved from fear to faith.

II. *Blindness and denial.* "But Thomas was not with them when Jesus came." Now Thomas had been outspoken on previous occasions. When Sunday evening services were more popular we theorized that "he wasn't in church on Sunday night." The other disciples enthusiastically reported, "We have seen the Lord." Mary had previously reported, "I have seen the Lord."

Thomas had not seen the Lord. He was absent from the fellowship. He suffered from self-imposed blindness. Had he enjoyed fellowship with the others on Resurrection Sunday he would have shared both their fear and their faith. As it was he knew only fear. Perhaps he was afraid to be with the group that night. There is strength in fellowship. It's easier to believe when you are with other believers.

The others had seen the Lord. Theirs was not a secondhand report of the Resurrection. They had talked with him. Thomas identified seeing with believing. So it was relatively easy for Thomas to move beyond blindness to denial. His statement, "Except I shall see . . . ," sounds almost insolent. Did he expect a personal appearance for his own sake? Did he think Jesus owed him special treatment? He would deny any report that fell short of a personal appearance: "I will not believe."

III. *Sight and confession.* Eight days later—perhaps on the next Sunday—Thomas was with the disciples when Jesus came. Jesus challenged his faithlessness. "Here, Thomas, place your fingers in the nail holes and your hand in my side . . . and be not faithless, but believing." Thomas no longer needed physical proofs gained by feeling. He had seen Jesus. He heard the challenge: Believe.

With his sight came his confession: "My Lord and my God." But sight, said Jesus, is not necessary for faith. Jesus blessed those who believed yet had not seen. We have seen Jesus in the flesh; yet we have believed. We gladly accept Jesus' blessing. Now these stories have been written that you may believe.—J. Estill Jones

SUNDAY: APRIL TWENTY-FIFTH

SERVICE OF WORSHIP

Sermon: Reasons to Rejoice
TEXT: 1 Pet. 1:3–9

Dr. Alexander Whyte of Edinburgh was famous for his pulpit prayers. He always found something to thank God for, even in bad times. One dark, stormy morning a member of his congregation thought to himself, "The preacher will have nothing to thank God for on a wretched morning like this." But Whyte began his prayer, "We thank thee, O God, that it is not always like this."

Thanksgiving and rejoicing come naturally to a people of faith. Thanksgiving and rejoicing are at the very heart of a growing relationship with God. When we live a life of dependence upon God, we learn to rejoice in whatever circumstances we find ourselves.

In his letter written to Christians scattered across Asia Minor, Peter says life should be filled with rejoicing. Even in the midst of trials, we can rejoice. He calls these individuals in 1 Peter 1:1 "pilgrims" or "sojourners," indicating their temporary residency status and their spiritual situation. They were living their lives away from the support of the Jerusalem Christians.

In a real sense, they were spiritual sojourners also. So are we. This world really isn't our home; we are just passing through on our way to our eternal home. And we need to learn how to rejoice, even in the midst of trial.

Let's look at 1 Peter 1:3–9 and consider "reasons to rejoice." We'll see that God's people can rejoice because of their new life in Christ, because of their living hope, because of their inheritance, and because of their security in the power of God.

I. God's people can rejoice because of their new life in Christ. Verse 6 says, "In this you greatly rejoice" (NIV). In what? Verse 3 says God has "begotten us again." This phrase refers to the new life we have experienced through entering into a personal relationship with Jesus Christ. The God of Creation has made something new out of something old—he has breathed new life into our empty spiritual condition. Because Jesus lives in our life, we have joy and meaning, and we don't have to face life with griping and complaining. That is a reason to rejoice!

Verse 3 says the means by which we have been begotten again is through the resurrected Jesus Christ. Peter says only through Jesus Christ can we have this new life. Jesus said, "I am the way, the truth, and the life, no man comes to the Father but by me." We know people who think all they have to do is live a good life, come to church now and then, maybe even drop something into the offering plate, and they'll be all right. We know better than that, and we can rejoice because we have new life in Christ.

Not only do we have new life in Jesus Christ, but we also have a living hope.

II. God's people can rejoice because of their living hope. Peter says in verse 3 God has "begotten us again unto a lively hope." Our hope is not empty or in vain because Jesus was raised from the grave and is alive. Our hope is grounded in Jesus and in his Resurrection power.

People around us put hope in every kind of material thing. They put hope in the stock market or in their bank account or in a job or in a person. The stock market plummets, an emergency wipes out their bank account or that person fails them or their company abruptly dismisses them, and they no longer have a job. Where is their hope? The only hope that is alive is that which we put into a living Lord Jesus Christ. Peter says we have reason to rejoice because our hope is alive.

Oscar Hammerstein, the composer of Rogers and Hammerstein fame, once said, "I just can't write anything without hope in it." When we have Jesus Christ in our life, our hope is not dead but is alive because Jesus Christ lives! And for that we can rejoice! Peter gives a third reason to rejoice.

III. God's people can rejoice because of their inheritance. Speaking in verse 4 Peter uses four words or phrases to describe in detail this new inheritance that our new birth brings. First, it is "incorruptible." Our inheritance will never perish or die. Earthly inheritances are eroded by time or devalued by inflation or lost or used unwisely. Our heavenly inheritance will never perish.

He says also our inheritance is "undefiled." This word means that our inheritance will never spoil nor be stained. Our life on earth is surrounded by contamination. The air we breathe is polluted, the lakes we fish in are filled with rubbish, and our rivers are dumps for sewage. Peter reminds us our place in heaven is undefiled.

Peter says our inheritance does not fade away. Time wilts flowers or yellows clippings we place in our scrapbook. Leaves fall from trees, blossoms drop from flowers, but our place in heaven will never wilt or fade away.

Finally, this inheritance is "reserved" for us. We have a mansion with our name on it, waiting for us. Our salvation secures our place in heaven.

IV. God's people can rejoice because of their security in the power of God. Verse 5 says we "are kept by the power of God." Even though outward circumstances may hammer away at us and even though trials abound, God is keeping us by his power.

This word kept can be translated "being guarded." It is the picture of the sentry stationed at the front of the city gates who marches and keeps watch around the clock guarding our lives. The word suggests continuous action. The guard is neither challenged nor goes to sleep. We are constantly being shielded by God's power.

This was good news to Peter's readers. These new Christians were trying to live out their lives in the face of persecution and harassment. They may have felt insecure and endangered. Peter encouraged them by saying that God was protecting them and undergirding them. When facing the pressures of life, we need to remember that "underneath are the everlasting arms" (Deut. 33:27) and that we are kept by the power of God.

Our tendency in life is to complain about our circumstances, to gripe about our situation. Peter reminds us that we have good reasons to rejoice and that our lives must be filled with thanksgiving and rejoicing, even in the midst of trials.—David Chancey

Illustrations

GRACE.   In the arid lands that were the birthplace of monotheistic religion, the desert was a primary symbol of trial and temptation. And water, especially freshly flowing "living water, became a prominent image of God's grace. Just as fresh water could transform wastelands into gardens, the living water of God's Spirit could cause love to grow within the most parched and willful souls. In the psalms, the soul thirsts for God "as a deer yearns for running waters," "like a dry and weary land." And in Isaiah, God promises grace: "Let the desert rejoice. . . . For waters shall break forth in the thirsty ground. . . . The wasteland will be turned into an Eden. . . . You will become like a watered garden."—Gerald G. May

LIFE IN "CHRIST-CONTROL."   My automobile has the device called cruise control. On the highway I get the speed up to the legal limit. Then I push the cruise control button. With that I do not worry about the speed. Neither do I worry about the hills and valleys on the highway. When the car comes to a hill or mountain, the flow of gasoline increases automatically so that the car moves along at an even pace, regardless of the terrain. In like fashion as a Christian I can move at an even pace along life's highway, whether the road leads through the even plains or over rugged mountains. When the going gets tough, I have strength for every challenge because of the One putting power in me. Regardless of what is happening around me, I know joy and peace within.

Why is this possible? Because somewhere along my Christian pilgrimage I put my life in Christ-control.—Herschel H. Hobbs

Sermon Suggestions

THE AUTHORITY OF THE CRUCIFIED JESUS. TEXT: Acts 2:14a, 36–41. (1) It is an authority conferred by God. (2) This authority makes possible a new relation to God—forgiveness of sins and experience of the Holy Spirit. (3) This authority requires commitment and amendment of life.

"THE TIME OF YOUR EXILE."   TEXT: 1 Pet. 1:17–23, NRSV. (1) A time to live in "reverent fear." (2) A time to remember the price of our salvation. (3) A time to love one another in keeping with the nature and purpose of our experience of God.

Worship Aids

CALL TO WORSHIP.   "And Jesus came and spake unto them, saying, All power is given unto me in heaven and in earth. Go ye therefore and teach all nations, baptizing them in the name of the Father and of the Son and of the Holy Ghost: teaching them to observe all things whatsoever I have commanded you, and, lo, I am with you always, even unto the end of the world" (Matt. 28:18–20).

INVOCATION.   As we have accepted your command given long ago to your disciples, O Lord, so help us to rejoice in your promised presence. May this service of worship remind us that where two or three are gathered together in your name, there you are present. Grant, then, that we may honor you, express our love to you in prayer and song, and commit ourselves anew to the spreading of the good news everywhere.

OFFERTORY SENTENCE.   "Give, and it shall be given unto you; good measure, pressed down, and shaken together, and running over, shall men give into your bosom. For with the same measure that ye mete withal it shall be measured to you again" (Luke 6:38).

OFFERTORY PRAYER. Thank you, God, for blessings received. May every gift we enjoy be offered up to you as our stewardship, for your direction and glory, though it be for food, clothes, shelter, and even fun, as well as for the support of the needy, the seeking of the lost, and the many good works of your people.

PRAYER. We praise you, O God, for your mighty deeds for our salvation. Your strong grace delivered the children of Israel from their bondage in Egypt and now in these last days you come in the person of your only Son, Jesus of Nazareth, declaring a grace in him sufficient, yea, more than sufficient, to deliver us from the bondage of all our sin.

For Christ's gift of the church to keep alive the story and to mediate the grace of your might, we are indeed grateful. We praise you for the blessed fellowship of your church in this time and place and the opportunities for worship, learning, and ministry that it offers.

Praise be to you—Father, Son, and Holy Spirit.—John Thompson

LECTIONARY MESSAGE

Topic: Known to Them
TEXT: Luke 24:13–35

One of the most interesting of the post-Resurrection narratives is that set on the way to Emmaus. Two believers walked along, overwhelmed by the experience of the Crucifixion and the report of the Resurrection. Jesus joined them but they did not know him. Their eyes were restrained from recognizing him. In the developing story the reader expects recognition at several places. Only later do they come to know him.

How do we realize the presence of Christ? In what experience is his presence most clearly known? Must we go to the Temple, Isaiah style, to see the Lord

God? Is the vision clearer on the Isle of Patmos, subject to persecution?

I. *Not in conversation.* In the story of the Emmaus journey, there appeared to be a great deal of conversation. It's natural to talk when with a good friend on a long walk. We have a way of emphasizing the power of the fellowship for realizing the presence of Christ. But this recognition did not come in conversation though it was a conversation between believers.

Though about Jesus himself, the conversation did not open their eyes. One would suppose this thrust of the conversation would certainly make Jesus recognizable, but they were too deeply involved in disappointment and hopelessness. Though in the presence of Jesus himself their conversation did not produce a vision of the Lord. This was the surprise: Jesus was there with them, and they did not know him.

II. *Not in reminiscence.* We sometimes think that we can recreate a past experience by reminiscing. Though in accurate remembering the events of the past several days, the presence of Christ was hidden from them. They remembered his ministry and his betrayal and his death, but they did not recognize him. Though in thoughtful recitation of their hope, yet they did not know the person walking with them. "We hoped that it was he who should redeem Israel." But now he's dead and it's all over. Is there yet hope?

Though there were reports of angels and an empty tomb, they reminisced in vain. Were their faith and hope so restrained as to blind their eyes? Did they not believe the reports? It would seem that the vision would become clearer the longer they reminisced. But for all their remembering they did not know Jesus.

III. *Not in study of the bible.* Though Jesus himself led them from Moses through the prophets in their allusions to God's redemption and his redeemer, they did not know him. Surely they should have seen through the interpretation of familiar scriptures. Though centered in references to Jesus, these passages did not open their eyes to their traveling companion. What will it take for them to know him?

Though their study was under the most excellent of Bible scholars, they could not know that Jesus was their teacher. As many times as he had opened the Scriptures to them, their eyes were so blinded by despair that they did not perceive his presence.

IV. *Only in "the breaking of the bread."* Their journey finished, Jesus made as if he would continue. They insisted that he stay because the hour was late, because of the pleasure of his company. And when they sat down to eat, he took the bread and blessed it, and breaking it, he gave to

them. "And their eyes were opened." In the closeness of breaking the bread, in experience symbolizing his body, they saw him. In fond remembering of that last supper in which they shared his body in the bread, in that remembering they recognized him. In renewing the new covenant, described so eloquently by Jeremiah, they knew him.

In conversation, in reminiscing, in study of the Bible, they missed him. The breaking of the bread brought it all into focus, and they saw him.—J. Estill Jones

SUNDAY: MAY SECOND

SERVICE OF WORSHIP

Sermon: The Victory of Faith
TEXT: 1 John 5:1–5

No doubt, we learn quite early in life that loving can be—to put it mildly—a painful process. We're no sooner on our feet when we've discovered love to be problematic and loaded with potential for personal peril!

When it's ripe, few things taste sweeter than love. And when it sours, few things are as bitter, leaving a bad taste in our mouths. The rose called "love" has a stem filled with thorns. Like the twin masks of Greek drama, love wears two faces: one a smile and the other a frown!

I. No wonder our love for others tends to be conditional and to that extent cautious! We love while gazing over our shoulders. The past experiences with love influence our present expressions of love. We attempt to minimize our losses by assuring that we'll get at least as much as we give. Love often becomes conditional because that's in essence how we gain and keep some control.

(a) We all have a love-hate relationship with the world, don't we? We love the beauty of a golden sunset in autumn. We hate the barrenness of the trees in winter's cold. We love the fields of flowers, the flight of geese, the taste of good food. We hate weeds and wasps, floods and

fierce summer storms. We love the delightful and hate the distasteful!

Christians, too, are caught in the horns of this dilemma. In fact, we are prone to even greater vacillation, because we have been called to be "in the world, but not of the world." The "world" represents the realm of our greatest temptations. It's here that we find ourselves torn between deep devotion to our Lord and the hardfisted desires of the world. And more often than not, our love of God gets lost in the sinful shuffle.

II. But don't make the mistake of assuming that it's merely the material matters that seduce the saints. The world offers power, prestige, and position as well. It honors those who succeed, even if by selfish gain. The world admires ambition and rewards only the winners. It tells us that true security will be found only in those things the eye can see. And it warns us to avoid giving any impression of personal weakness.

(a) And there's an even more virulent form of this same temptation. I sometimes wonder if the world and its evil prince don't make it a point to tempt Christians to hate. That's right—I said hate! After all, that's the one action that without doubt is so characteristic of this world. And it's subtle, too.

I suppose when we hear the word *hate* we have images of hooded men bombing black churches, gangs of teenagers with handguns, or mobs of people driven mad with the burning of the American flag. But Satan's temptation is far more subtle.

His is the temptation to trample all over the feelings of another. The blatant disregard for the manner in which our harsh and unrelenting criticism can wound, and eventually weaken, the faith of a brother or sister. The tendency to treat others as though they were nothing more than a means to our ends. And then there are other forms of temptation: backbiting, malicious gossip, prejudice cloaking itself as piety.

(b) Sometimes we're tempted to bash other Christians who don't believe as we do. Soon we create categories in which we can then claim to have effectively separated the "wheat from the weeds." Labels become the way we distinguish between disciples we'll love and those we stand ready to reject. Before long we've managed to create a community of like-minded people—enabling us to avoid the risks of real Christ-like love! And good old Satan stands in the background smirking.

He might suggest that we begin by loving only those who will love us in return. Then, he might add, make sure to exclude those who aren't of a like mind. Finally, why not define your faith so narrowly that no one will be able to disagree and then remain in your "fellowship"?

(c) The truth is that the world, life, and love are all but completely predictable! So we feel the need to secure ourselves against the shifting sands of this world. But if we're not careful we'll give in to the demon of self-interest, succumbing to a false sense of security. I'm talking about that form of self-centeredness which seems to have taken a stranglehold on contemporary society—and I fear, on many of God's faithful as well!

III. In this morning's epistle lesson we hear John speak of three terms essential to true Christian discipleship. No one can be divorced from the others. They're held together, as if by the hand of God. I'm referring to "love, faith, and the covenant commandments."

(a) I suppose you could call these three terms the "trinity of true Christian char-

acter!" For John—and hopefully for us as well—they define the dimensions of a disciplined discipleship. If the commandments represent the substance of our faith, then love represents the form of our faith. In other words, for John, faith involves commitment as well as content!

To be alive in the Spirit of the risen Christ is to give feet to our faith! It's nothing less than love translated into the language of a limitless compassion and godly concern for the least, the lost, and the lonely of this world.

(b) John seeks to convince us that the church exists for one reason only: to make real the love of God in this crazy, mixed-up world of ours. In and through the church, we can discover the courage to be embraced by Christ's love. And then Christ's love empowers us to love others as deeply, as devotedly, and as deliberately as he first loved and loves us. As the Apostle Paul once wrote, "I can do all things through him who strengthens me."

IV. The love of God made manifest in the cross of Christ is the very same love which made his Resurrection a reality. And only that love has already conquered the chaos and confusion of life in this world. And this is the only love capable of creating new life!

(a) Only God's love, poured out into the life of the Christian, assures us that we, too, shall one day conquer. Because to be in Christ is to be in him who has already conquered through a divine love that knows no limits. "Take courage," Jesus said, "I have already conquered the world!" Only Christ-like love is constant and consistent and persistent. And only his love will ultimately conquer all.

(b) The Apostle Paul has written, "If I have prophetic powers and understand all mysteries and all knowledge and if I have all faith, so as to remove mountains, but have not love, I am nothing!" And elsewhere John has written, "Perfect love casts out fear." I'm certain he meant "fear" in every form we've ever known it to take.

(c) We should have learned by now that the persistence of Christ-like love has the power to prevail in this world. We should also know that Christ's kingdom shall never be conquered. After two thousand years of abuse, apathy, and ambition, the church stands as the visible witness to the endurance of Christ's love and the certainty of his coming victory!

V. "This is the victory that overcomes the world, our faith." And the victory of faith can only be found in the love of God for creature and Creation. A love made manifest in Jesus Christ. A love which the Lord promises to plant in the lives of all his faithful. A constant and consistent love—unshaken by the shifting sands of culture and society. The only love capable of conquering the world's calamity and confusion.

(a) John put it this way: "By this we know that we love the children of God, when we love God and obey his commandments. For the love of God is this, that we obey his commandments." And, of course, God's commandments are quite clear, aren't they? We're to give priority to God and secondly to our neighbor.

(b) God's commandments "are not burdensome" because they are born of a deeply rich and rewarding divine love. And they give birth to a similar love in the life of the believer. This is the only love with the power to free us from all fear and to finally liberate Creation from its longing for security. "For whatever is born of God conquers the world!"—Albert J. D. Walsh

Illustrations

FAITH'S FINAL SECURITY.   When we get into that rich experience of possessing God and being possessed by him we can say about any so-called catastrophe what Rupert Brooke said about war:

War knows no power. Safe shall be my going,
Secretly armed against all death's endeavor;
Safe though all safety's lost; safe where men fall;
And if these poor limbs die, safest of all.

Yes, and we shall have won our little victory and in our own small way be able to say with the Master, "I have overcome the world." "This is the victory that overcometh the world, even our faith."—Leslie D. Weatherhead

LIFE BEGINS—WHERE?   Following the funeral services for a beloved lady, one of her nephews handed me her personal journal. Tucked away in the pages of handwritten script was this entry: "Life doesn't begin at twenty or at forty but at Calvary!"—Albert J. D. Walsh

Sermon Suggestions

A GLIMPSE OF FIRST-CENTURY CHRISTIANITY.   TEXT: Acts 2:42–47. (1) Disciplined worship, verses 42 and 46. (2) Reckless generosity, verses 44–45; 5:4. (3) Notable response, verses 43 and 47.

TAKING IT ON THE CHIN.   TEXT: 1 Pet. 2:19–25. (1) Enduring unjust suffering is difficult. (2) Yet such suffering has God's approval. (3) In fact, there is something Christ-like and even redemptive in it.

Worship Aids

CALL TO WORSHIP.   "He shall call upon me, and I will answer him: I will be with him in trouble; I will deliver him and honor him" (Ps. 91:15).

INVOCATION.   Lord, let this hour be all it can be for us as children of God, worshiping God, praising God, calling the name of God, desirous of the things of God, seeking the will of God, that we might be faithful in every way to our maker and our God.—E. Lee Phillips

OFFERTORY   SENTENCE.   "Remember that the person who plants few seeds will have a small crop; the one who plants many seeds will have a large crop" (2 Cor. 9:6, TEV).

OFFERTORY PRAYER.   Gracious God, as we plant the seeds of our devotion, in the form of tithes and offerings, may what we give grow and prosper. To that end, we pray for wisdom in the management of the church's stewardship and fervent prayer to be raised on behalf of those causes strengthened and supported by our gifts.

PRAYER.   Here we are, Father, a mixed lot, coming from various needs and struggles, needing most to find light by which to walk through the darkness surrounding us. Some are mired in the bog of self-pity because life has dealt them a rough hand for the moment and the expectations of former times seem to wane before their very eyes. This morning they need to be granted a new lease on life, one girded with vision of what can yet be, one saturated with courage to continue. Let their need be met as we worship here in your presence, we pray.

Some come to this place today bearing burdens too heavy to carry in their own strength. A helping hand from a fellow pilgrim would lighten their load and assurance that inner strength is present would mightily encourage them as they make their journey along. Give them the courage to trust others to help with their load, to share their need and kindle the inner fires which fire the furnace of inner strength for them. Let their need be met as we worship here in your presence, we pray.

Some come to this place this morning knowing that life on this earth is limited in terms of time and the abilities to function fully. For some there is fear of the unknown, for others there is a sadness at the thought of leaving a place of familiarity which has been enjoyed throughout their lives. Still others sink into remorsefulness because of the limited time left to walk the familiar pathways of earth life. Let each hear and understand and be comforted by your Word of presence. Let them hear you say again that you are with every one of us, even unto the end of the age. Let their need be met as we worship here this morning, we pray.

Some come in gladness, alert and alive to every note of the music of the spheres. Let their song be heard abroad. Let their joy be caught as a delightful gift. Let gladness fill all our hearts and minds and souls as we worship here before you this morning, we pray.

Especially there are those who need this morning to hear a word of salvation from sins, Father. Lost and wandering in the darkness, they need to know that there is light and hope and life given from a Father of love. Let conviction come this morning. Let repentance answer and bring salvation to the hearts and lives of all who need to encounter the Christ of life today. May their need be met as we worship here.—Henry Fields

LECTIONARY MESSAGE

Topic: Life in Abundance
TEXT: John 10:1–10

Who would not like to escape the narrow confines of prejudice and intolerance, of sectionalism and sectarianism and live the abundant life? Who would not like to move from the darkness of legalism and lovelessness into the light of grace? This is the offer of Jesus, made in solemn tones which identified himself with the Father God: "I AM."

I. *Life in the fold.* The fold in the Near East is a simple pen for huddling purposes. It is a means of protection. The shepherd himself spends the night where the sheep are safely gathered—perhaps securing the fold with his own body. It protects against homelessness. A stranger in the city at night, passing by lighted homes, finds a door opened in the darkness. It's a means of identification . . . that's my door!

It protects against night dangers. He is the light. He is the door. Thus the narrow gate becomes a guard against thieves and robbers. It protects against false shepherds. There are many false guides—leading to everything but life. Many take advantage of the sheep and use them for their own purposes. This fold is the new society, the church— protective, inclusive, therapeutic.

II. *Life in the following.* Life abundant is not fulfilled in the fold. The sheep belong, and the shepherd belongs, but they belong to one another. The shepherd leads the sheep out of the fold. Indeed there is just a hint that he "puts them out." He does not leave them alone, however. He leads them in pastures green, by waters still. He leads them so as to attract other sheep, homeless, to the fold and to the flock.

He goes before them, risking the dangers, already familiar in his ministry. He directs them in the paths of righteousness. They know his voice. At best they respond only to his voice; they will not follow strangers whose voices they do not know. That there are competing voices the presence of thieves and robbers indicates: "His own sheep" follow.

III. *Life in freedom.* The fold has a shepherd. The fold has a door. Perhaps they are one and the same. Jesus' use of the "I AM" appears to be an identification with Yahweh whose absoluteness is described in Exod. 3:14. There is a series of such identifications in this Gospel: I AM the door, I AM the Good Shepherd, I AM the Bread of Life. But this simply insures the freedom of the sheep: They shall go in and go out.

Life has its entrances and its exits. It is strange that freedom should be so sought by the world of men. The world promises but cannot deliver. The very pursuit of freedom enslaves. Yet the Christian is the freest of persons even though the slave of all. The door to the fold opens into the arena of activity—where the action is. And we bask in that freedom.

IV. *Life in faith.* Yet this life abundant is not without its cost. You see, sheep are not shepherded and protected and pampered and promised freedom just because they are sweet, woolly, little lambs. They become wool factories or even mutton chops. This is their life. If you suppose the door offers only protection, you're dead already—and quite protected.

Here is access to God—not a god manipulating, maneuvering, frightening, bribing, or laying down the law, but the God like Jesus. Jesus opened a way through the veil, into the very presence of God. There is security in faith, and faith thrives on freedom. Faith works, sticks its neck out, takes a risk, follows, obeys, is not static—and the sheep move in and out freely. This is life in abundance.—J. Estill Jones

SUNDAY: MAY NINTH

SERVICE OF WORSHIP

Sermon: A Supernatural Use for Our Suffering

TEXT: John 14:15–21

I. This morning I would like to reflect with you, in the context of this our Gospel lesson, upon identity, upon discovery, upon Easter.

(a) Jesus said to his disciples, "If you love me, you will keep my commandments." In your mind, what is the great commandment that Jesus poses to his disciples then and now? The writer of our Gospel, St. John, thrice quotes Jesus as saying, "I give you a new commandment, that you love one another."

(b) I suggest to you this morning that Jesus, speaking to disciples of all ages, calls us to follow him in our efforts to love one another, because following Jesus we all know is an unfolding process. You and I are different every day. Our knowledge of God is different every day. Our knowledge of our world, of our friends, of our expectations and failures, is different every day. It is a growth process.

II. Some five years ago, standing in this pulpit for one of our Lenten lectures, Scott Peck repeated that citation from his volume *The Road Less Traveled,* "The path to sainthood goes through adulthood. There are no quick and easy shortcuts. . . . An identity must be established before it can be transcended. One must find one's self before one can lose it." This is, for many, a difficult teaching: that one must establish an identity in order to follow the Lord's Christ.

(a) We might ask ourselves, if we need find and secure an identity to follow this

Jesus, the Christ, how? How are we to discover that identity? "The Father will give you another counselor to be with you forever, even the Spirit of truth."

(b) There is, in some measure, a contest in our lives between the exercise of the ego and the exercise of the soul. Ego is that magnificent attribute of life which one might think of as the executive function of personality. Those of you who are managers know the importance of that quality of life, that ability to see and solve problems with ease and accuracy. Yet there is something overbearing about the ego. It attempts to measure every matter of life, to direct and control, if not balanced by one's spiritual existence. We all have antennae. We pick up vast radiations from the world around us, human feelings and reactions, sensory perceptions of every kind. In the spirit of the English philosophers of three hundred years ago, "precepts are not concepts." We pick up a mountain of information, and the ego must sort and focus and concentrate on one thing at a time. You and I could not cross the street, read a book, write a check, or speak to a friend were we not endowed with this capacity to narrow the great intake with which we as humans are blessed.

III. Jesus said to his disciples, "Take up your cross and follow me. He who would save his life will lose it, and he who will lose it will find it." We need to have that identity in order to say, "Take up your identity and follow me. Take up your life and follow me."

(a) Prayer opens the soul for the content of our identity, honoring the executive function of personality and those majestic tools of mind. We discipline ourselves to open our lives in prayer, in meditation, to the visitation of God's Spirit. "The Father will give you another counselor, even the Spirit of truth."

We seek confidence and peace in Easter. Jesus said, "I will not leave you desolate. I will come to you. You will see me. Because I live, you will live also."

(b) Simone Weil in *Gravity and Grace* says, "The extreme greatness of Christianity lies in the fact that it does not seek a supernatural remedy for suffering, but a supernatural use for suffering." That is the core of Christianity. When you and I attempt to find our identity under God, to wrench open our lives and our souls in times of prayer and meditation, to allow the Spirit of God to come into our lives, then we allow the supernatural Spirit to use that which you and I have forged in the everyday.

IV. We are the children of God, and we come to this Christ, this Christ who lived, this Christ who died, this Christ who rose again. We come to this Easter Christ; we come to him and hear him say again, "I will not leave you desolate. Because I live, you will live also."—Spencer M. Rice

Illustrations

CREATIVE ADVENTURE. I always remember the remark of one of our boys when he had broken his leg while skiing. He had told us towards the end of the day that he was going to go quickly up to make one last descent. Mechanical ski-lifts (fine routines!) did not yet exist. But since he did not reappear we went to look for him. It was I who found him, and as I bent over him he said in a rather solemn tone of voice, "At last, something has happened to me!" I was quite surprised. He had felt overprotected, and I had not realized it. He felt that his life was too ordinary to answer his need for creative adventure.—Paul Tournier

WITHOUT FEAR. Eric Erickson in his *Ages of Man* writes, "Healthy children will not fear life if their elders have integrity enough not to fear death."—Spencer M. Rice

Sermon Suggestions

LIKE CHRIST, LIKE CHRISTIAN. TEXT: Acts 7:55–60. (1) Then: Stephen, in the spirit and pattern of his Lord and Savior, gave up his life with a prayer for his persecutors. (2) Always: Christian history is replete with stories of believers who have won their persecutors to faith by forgiving love. (3) Now: There are opportunities in our everyday experience to let creative Christian love overcome hostility and injustice and win the perpetrators to faith (see Rom. 12:17–21).

A GLORIOUS MIXTURE OF IMAGES. TEXT: 1 Pet. 2:2–10, NRSV. Christians are (1) like newborn infants; (2) like living stones; (3) a special people with a priestly function in the world.

Worship Aids

CALL TO WORSHIP. "Man doth not live by bread only, but by every word that proceedeth out of the mouth of the Lord doth man live" (Eut. 8:3b).

INVOCATION. Lord, let the Word get to us, let the Spirit deal with us, let the Savior encounter us as never before; for this we pray and nothing more.—E. Lee Phillips

OFFERTORY SENTENCE. "No servant can be the slave of two masters; for either he will hate the first and love the second, or he will be devoted to the first and think nothing of the second. You cannot serve God and money" (Matt. 6:24, NEB).

OFFERTORY PRAYER. Save us, O God, from slavery to material things, things we have and things we passionately desire. May our freedom in Christ give us perspective and balance as we choose and use the good gifts of this mortal life. And so may we serve you and one another.

PRAYER.
We pray for families on the ropes,
    kids living on the edge
    of self-destructive behavior,
        falling, falling,
        feeling bereft,
        feeling angry, confused,
            guilty, sad,
            and scared, scared,
            beneath all the hardness,
            scared;

We pray for kids
    who are disowned,
        hurled out before they can fly,
        hurled like birds in a storm,

falling prey to prowling things,
falling prey
    to all that feeds
    on all that moves,
    vulnerable, in the grass;

From the spitting eyes of cynics
    and the talons of the heartless,
        from all who expect them to fail,
        want them to,
        tell them they will,
        from all who know all about
        such no-good kids,
        had their brother,
        had their sister,
        had their dad,
        know the whole family,
        know they're all no good,
        from all such wisdom
    protect them, O Lord;
    shield them
        as a mother rabbit would shield her
            young,
            lest they be swept away,
            lest they be borne aloft
            with talons in their backs,
            lest, written off,
            they write off life,
            curse it,
            not its deformities,
            not its meanness,
            but life;

We pray for kids
    who are disowned;
Protect them, O Lord,
    shield them,
        as a mother rabbit would shield her
            young,
            lest they be swept away.
                                    —Peter Fribley

LECTIONARY MESSAGE

Topic: In Confusion Consider
TEXT: John 14:1–14
Hardly a Christian funeral occurs without the use of some of these verses. We have so limited the application of these truths that we fail to see how apt they are to life as we live it. It will help us to understand the "troubled" if we link it as did the author to the conversation with

Peter at the end of the preceding chapter. For that matter, the entire thirteenth chapter is a source of troubling.

And Jesus encourages his followers not to be troubled. How shall we handle troubling thoughts and circumstances? In confusion, consider:

I. *Believing.* "Seeing is believing" was Philip's philosophy. It is shared by many contemporaries. "Show us the Father," he said. Can you believe that Jesus revealed God as he was and is? Sometimes, when bad things happen to good people, it is difficult to identify Jesus with God. Believing is resting in God's love, and that is a great leap of faith. Look at the frequency of the verb in these verses: "Believe in God," "Believe in me," "Believe that I am in the Father," "Believe me for the very works' sake," "He that believeth on me."

Robert Browning penned his faith in "Death in the Desert":

I say the acknowledgement of God in
  Christ
Accepted by thy reason, solves for thee
All questions in the earth and out of it.
In confusion, consider believing.

Also consider:

II. *Absolutes.* As elsewhere in this Gospel, Jesus refers to himself with "I AM." He thus relates closely with God. "I AM the way," he said and certainly referred to God's way. An early name for the Christian life-style was simply The Way. "I AM the truth," he said and surely identified with God's truth, the truth of God's love. How sad that there should be so much misunderstanding.

"I AM the life," he said and clearly described his own life-style: This is the life. It is God's life, the way and the truth of vicarious suffering.

In confusion, consider absolutes. Further, consider:

III. *Experience.* "Have I been so long with you, Philip?" His experience with the disciples included his miracles and his continuing message. His experience with the Father was reflected in his ministry—revealed in his ministry. "I do not speak for myself, but for him." "I do not work for myself, but for him."

Always it is reassuring to remember our experience with Jesus. In confusion, consider experience. Still further, consider:

IV. *Asking.* The prayer promise is wide. We have learned that we can talk with God about anything "whatsoever." "Anything—I will do it." Of course the simple phrase "in my name" is all important. "Anything" in line with his will. "Anything" in line with his love. "Anything" in line with his life.

To ask in his name is not only to recognize his character but to commit oneself to that way of life. To ask in his name is not only to "ask" but to "give." To ask in his name is not only to "want" but to "need."

In confusion, consider asking.—J. Estill Jones

SUNDAY: MAY SIXTEENTH

SERVICE OF WORSHIP

Sermon: If I Had One Wish ...

TEXTS: 1 Kings 3:3–15; James 1:1–8

For what would you wish if you could have one wish and the guarantee that it would come true? Some would wish for world peace, no doubt, or maybe some other worldwide benefit, such as a continuous supply of food for all. Others would wish for more personal benefits such as big money. Still others, in a desperate frame of mind, would wish for some satisfaction to an immediate frustration, such as seeing an overbearing employer out on the streets without work and no hope of it in the future.

I. We have heard read the story of a young king—King Solomon—who was about twenty years old at the time. As we join the story, he is a new king—perhaps still mourning the death of his father, King David, and probably—also—insecure in his position.

(a) As David's youngest son, he had not been the heir apparent to the throne, but he was the choice of many persons influential with David, not the least of which were Bathsheba and Nathan. So Solomon became king but not with unanimous support, and, as a result, several men dangerous to the reign of Solomon had to be eliminated.

All of this fresh in the mind of the young king, he also was clearly inexperienced with the weighty decisions required of a king. But he had this going for him: "Solomon loved the Lord, walking in the statutes of David his father."

(b) This was a high compliment to Solomon, of course, but the writer saw one problem with Solomon in spite of his other pious attributes and his great promise.

The thing with Solomon was that Solomon worshiped "at the high places." In the minds of many of his subjects, the "high places" brought to mind paganism because pagans had this hang-up about being as elevated as possible while trying to appease their gods, and—furthermore—the truly pious persons of God regarded Jerusalem as the only really appropriate place for public worship. The writer of 1 Kings obviously had the expectation that the royalty among the people of God should abide by such a basic worship practice. But Solomon sacrificed and burnt incense at Gibeon, *the* great high place (v. 4). Of course, he was the king. If he were going to do it, he had to do it at the best possible high place.

II. So here he was, six miles northwest of Jerusalem, involved in worship. He had gone there for the purpose of worship and likely also to seek prayerfully in worship God's guidance in this overpowering task of leading the people of God.

(a) Not in the sanctuary, mind you, but at the place where Solomon slept. God appeared to Solomon in a dream, which was a very commonly expected method of divine communication. In the dream, God speaks to Solomon, and Solomon doesn't know of any way God could speak more clearly or more directly than in a dream, so he is at peace about how God is speaking to him.

(b) God says to the young king, "Ask what I shall give you." God's statement to Solomon somehow reminds us of Jesus' teaching on prayer: "Ask, and it will be given you. Seek, and you will find. Knock, and it will be opened to you." And as powerful and true as is that teaching by our Lord, the statement by God to Solomon is more direct and somehow more vivid in our imaginations. "Ask what I shall give you."

(c) Solomon had a ready response. He had carried this burden with him to worship and away again on more than one occasion. Who knows but what Solomon went to worship that day for the express purpose of seeing if God might help him with his struggle. But it hadn't happened that day, and that is not unusual, is it? Sometimes our pain is so great that even when we come to worship seeking an answer, seeking a way to have our load lightened somehow, we have been known to leave still weighed down. So it was with Solomon. And because of this, Solomon knew exactly what he wanted to ask of God under these fascinating circumstances. Speaking to God in his dream, Solomon says, "Give me the wisdom I need to rule your people with justice and to know the difference between good and evil." Wisdom. The young king wants wisdom: wisdom to rule with justice, wisdom to know the difference between good and evil, right and wrong. Solomon wishes for wisdom to make just decisions in behalf of God and among the people of God; to do so, he had to know the difference between right and wrong.

III. The writer of the Book of James actually urges us to ask of God in prayer the blessing of wisdom. Wisdom enough to know the difference between right and wrong, good and evil, is essential in order for God's people to make day-to-day decisions. Even when we know, much of our decision making can still be overwhelming, but without knowing (and I'm not suggesting that we can necessarily have certainty on every issue), it is impossible for us to honor God.

(a) Christians and others are hungry to know—to have some assurance that decisions they make are right decisions, decisions which can bring the best in typically complex circumstances, and decisions which, being ethical, bring honor to God. If I had one wish, would I wish for wisdom to know clearly what is right and what is wrong in God's sight? Would you?

(b) We live in times when the distinction between right and wrong somehow seems to be more blurred than it used to be. Alternatives in few issues are so clearly black and white; there is more and more gray all the time. Further, deciding and doing what is right isn't always the avenue of joy or the path of least resistance. Often the right choice is the most difficult to make and the most difficult to live with. And the need to make momentous decisions can come to us in a day's time, at a moment's notice. Suddenly there is the decision to be made about whether or not a loved one should be sustained on life support systems. Suddenly a woman must decide about abortion as a way of dealing with an unwanted pregnancy which, the doctor has said, may very well threaten her life. Suddenly one of us is in the position of deciding whether or not what we have heard about the sanctity of a marriage covenant and what we have lived to this point in a relationship is right. Suddenly a church has to decide how inclusive it really is and to what degree Christ-like acceptance and love will be demonstrated.

(c) God heard Solomon making his wish. And God was pleased. God told Solomon that because he had wished for something quite unselfish (not riches or a long life), God would grant his wish. God promised Solomon "a wise and discerning mind." He would have the ability with God's ongoing help to accomplish that which would bring honor to God and which would point the persons over which he ruled in the right direction. So wise would the young king become that nobody before or after him would equal him in his moral wisdom. The story is that God was so pleased with Solomon's unselfish wish that Solomon would be the recipient of those benefits which most of us might have "spent" our one wish trying for: wealth and honor. Solomon was

also promised a long reign provided he continued with the same attitude which had brought him to God in search of wisdom at the beginning of this episode. The point is, in the long haul choosing for God, deciding to do what pleases God—regardless of the consequences—is the right thing to do.

IV. From Gibeon, Solomon returned to Jerusalem and the Temple there. He stood before the Ark of the Covenant (where the presence of the living God was thought to dwell). And he worshiped again; that worship led to celebration. The king "made a feast for all his servants." Who wouldn't have done the same after the assurance he'd received from God; God was going to be with him, and he knew that whatever else might befall him he was where he should be.

In the midst of what pulls us and what presses us and what occupies our attention; in a world of lax morals and amorality and arrogance and closemindedness and closed communities—let us wish with the young king of old for wisdom to know the difference between right and wrong and, with that blessed gift, the God-given courage to act for the right. The way is clearer for us than it was for Solomon because we now have seen God at work in Jesus Christ our Lord, but we still seek clarity and courage from the God whom we worship.—David Albert Farmer

Illustrations

GOD'S WAYS.   Is history a sarcasm, and are its ambiguities a fatal flaw? Often we shall wonder and fear. We are on a tiny swinging ball, perchance the only personal ball in the whole cosmos. Why should our hope be hope? We remember a conversation in a Hardy novel:

"Did you say the stars were worlds, Tess?"

"Yes."

"All like ours?"

"I don't know; but I think so. They sometimes seem to be like apples on our stubbard tree. Most of them splendid and sound—a few blighted."

"Which do we live on—a splendid one or a blighted one?"

"A blighted one."

Then we remember Christ. His was no blighted life and no blighted death. If all history be "static," the "old, old story" is clear and lovely music. We could not despair, had we not first hoped. We must choose now to believe either the static or the music. The static is static: We know that it is rattle and raucousness. The music is music. We could never have imagined such redemption. But then, God's ways are not our ways. "God so loved the world that he gave his only begotten Son, that whosoever believeth . . ." We can believe. It is grand and heartbreaking and heart-mending belief. Then we will believe and bow before the Mystery, so awe-struck in power, so tumultuous in judgment, so lowly in love.—George A. Buttrick

THE PATIENCE AND WISDOM OF GOD.   It is to be noted that the wisdom of God characterizes his whole activity as reliable and liberating, as something in which we can have confidence, just because his wisdom consists in and finally evinces itself as his firmness and self-consistency, the satisfaction of his *decentia* or *convenientia divina*. When God is apprehended as the One who under all circumstances is intelligence and reason in this way, purposing and deciding and speaking and acting on this basis, the knowledge of God means that we can have confidence in him, that we can be free, that all the uncertainty and darkness of the capricious and irrational is ended.—Karl Barth

Sermon Suggestions

A CHRISTIAN APOLOGETIC.   TEXT: Acts 17:22–31. (1) All people, even in their idolatries and materialisms, and especially there, are reaching out for God, whether they know it or not. (2) God has reached out toward us all, to meet us at the end of our rope, particularly in his revelation and salvation in Jesus Christ. (3) Some, perhaps most, "seekers" walk away pondering and postponing decision, while some find in Jesus Christ the answer to their quest and ultimately to their questions.

HOW TO STAND UP FOR JESUS CHRIST. TEXT: 1 Pet. 3:13–22. (1) Make a special place in your heart for him. (2) Be ready to give account of your faith in him. (3) Live a life consistent with your professed faith. (4) Be willing to suffer for him, if it is God's will.

Worship Aids

CALL TO WORSHIP.   "Let us not be weary in well doing; for in due season we shall reap, if we faint not" (Gal. 6:9).

INVOCATION.   O Lord our Shepherd, who hast set before us green valleys and steep mountains and gone with us every step of the way; bless us as we enter this bright plain of worship and bring us triumphantly to the other side, renewed in strength, emboldened in spirit, and refreshed for the journey ahead.—E. Lee Phillips

OFFERTORY SENTENCE.   "What God the Father considers to be pure and genuine religion is this: to take care of orphans and widows in their suffering and to keep oneself from being corrupted by the world" (James 1:27, TEV).

OFFERTORY PRAYER.   Our Father, as our religion is being tested every day in practical circumstances, as well as here at the altar of our stewardship, grant us wisdom, love, and grace to become and to be what befits us as Christians.

PRAYER.   O Lord, we pray for the family of the Body of Christ the church: for young parents who want their children to know Jesus; for teenagers who want someone they can talk to; for persons negotiating the narrows of middle age; for the elderly, reaping the harvest of their faith and wanting a community that shall outlive their dwindling circle of old friends, as a candle wants air. Bless our church family, and attune us all to God's plenty in the great banquet of gifts among us, gifts of youth and age, of health and illness, of eagerness and frailty.—Peter Fribley

LECTIONARY MESSAGE

Topic: Love and Obey
TEXT: John 14:15–21

"Trust and obey, for there's no other way / To be happy in Jesus, but to trust and obey."

The words to the familiar gospel song might as well be "love and obey." For just as trust is best expressed in obedience, so is love best expressed in obedience.

"If you love me . . ." you will obey. Jesus was realistic. He did not take the love of his disciples for granted. He did not presume on their loving obedience. The conditional construction indicates a condition undetermined but with prospect of determination. As yet they had not suffered the sorrow of crucifixion nor the pains of persecution. Then they may determine their love for him. But if their love is conditioned, their obedience is not. If you love me, you will obey.

This is a covenant between parents and children. This is a covenant between master and disciples. And the love involved is quality love. It is not of the "puppy" variety nor of the emotion-exhausting variety. It is the sort of self-giving love that is the Father's love for the world. Obedience springs out of that love. We do not obey because we are afraid to disobey. We do not obey because we hope to earn his love. He loves and we love—and because we love, we obey—"*if* you love."

"I will pray. . . ." What a promise from Jesus! Our experience with him indicates that he will keep his promises: "He has never broken any promise spoken." His promise specifically is that he will give a Comforter, but generally his intercessory prayer is wider than that.

Imagine his praying for you. You need a friend. Be assured that Jesus is praying—how shall we say it—is representing your need before the Father. You need forgiveness. What better intercessor than one who has experienced temptation himself! You need courage to face danger. He understands, and he promises to pray for you. You need strength to overcome temptation—strength to serve. He will pray for you. This is his promise. Out of that love pact, can you do less than obey?

"God will give you another Comforter." The word is transliterated from the Greek as *Paraclete*. Literally it is one who calls alongside. Like an athletic coach who stands on the sideline and calls encouragement and counsel to a team member, this Paraclete ministers to our need—alongside. Here is no temporary gift—but "that he may be with you forever." He will help you translate love into obedience.

He is the Spirit of truth. Jesus said of himself, "I am the truth." His Spirit continually challenges our loyalty to the truth. Here is no relative rumor but an absolute principle. He will not leave us as orphans but promises his presence. It is not as if he calls us to love and obey an absentee lord but to continue in the same relationship.

Love and obey. The promise continues. You will know Jesus and the Father better in the close fellowship of love and obedience. And there is the assurance of loving and being loved that obedience offers. Obedience provides a fresh manifestation of Jesus. In obedience we relive his ministry. In obedience we redie his Crucifixion. In obedience we realize his Resurrection.—J. Estill Jones

SUNDAY: MAY TWENTY-THIRD

SERVICE OF WORSHIP

Sermon: Out of the Depths
TEXT: Ps. 130:1–2

Even if you don't know very much about the Bible, I believe you can identify with Psalm 130. Psalms are poems; actually they're intensely emotional writings that arise out of the agony and the ecstasy of human experience. Psalm 130 arises out of agony.

I. I am impressed that this psalm is a cry that ascends to God out of the depths of misery. Surely there is loudness here—the cry is strong and powerful—at least at the beginning of misery, before it wears us down.

(a) When total disaster surrounds us, words are no longer available nor even useful. Rational thought vanishes. Only a wail of despair can reach our lips, when we're alone and no one can hear us. In our solitude, when the magnitude of our woe overwhelms us, our cry escapes, not just from our lips but from deep within, beginning softly and rising to a crescendo of grief.

(b) After the cry from out of the depths for mercy, there is a reference to sins. The person who wrote this psalm was afflicted with guilt. He couldn't get his sins out of his mind. Did you find or, if you are in anguish now, do you find that your thoughts in time of anguish tend to drift toward your sins?

II. From my own experience and from conversations with others, I have noticed that when life is going very smoothly, we don't think much about our sins. But when life begins to unravel, we wonder what we have done wrong that deserves such punishment. I say punishment because when agony takes over in our lives we feel as if we are being punished.

(a) Now, it is true that often we can trace our agony directly to what we have done. Some horrible physical illnesses, for example, are the result of sinful conduct. Some family and marriage problems, too, that can drive people into despair are caused in some degree by their sinful behavior.

(b) Most people seem to have a mechanism that leads them to conclude that if things are going smoothly in their lives and they are prospering, apparently God is pleased with them. Even people who are not very religious establish that connection. When circumstances are suddenly reversed and disaster sets in, people draw the opposite conclusion: "What have I done wrong?"

III. Psalm 130 continues with a glorious announcement that sin need not be viewed as a barrier between the sufferer and God. When we are overwhelmed by guilt and in despair, we should not feel that it is hopeless to turn to God. The psalmist declares, "If you, O Lord, kept a record of sin, O Lord, who could stand? But with you there is forgiveness; therefore you are feared" (vv. 3–4). This is a marvelous hope-giving vision of the merciful nature of God. He will pay attention to a cry for mercy, for he is merciful.

(a) The people of the Old Testament know that God was a forgiving God who did not treat his people as their sins deserved. But Psalm 130, which declares, "With you there is forgiveness; therefore you are feared," was written many centuries before God displayed his full forgiving grace by sending his one and only Son, Jesus Christ, into the world to pay for human sin. Today we can appreciate God's forgiveness even more than the psalmist, for we know what God actually went through to accomplish his forgiving work.

(b) There is nothing easy or simple about being forgiven, however. Some people expect God to wink at sin and forgive it as a matter of course. That is his business, his job, his specialty, they reason. But the only way God could forgive was to arrange that sin be taken care of through the gift of the Son of his love. And now that Christ has come and been victorious over sin and death, we can say, with a certainty the writer of Psalm 130 could not even know, that there is forgiveness with God.

(c) Did you notice the writer of Psalm 130 said that, because there is forgiveness with God, "therefore [he is] feared"? This is not a fear that makes people cringe in a corner or curl up into the fetal position; it is the awe we feel when we observe something grand.

IV. God will not hold the anguished sinner's sins against him. As we read further, we notice that the anguished psalmist expresses great anticipation: "I wait for the Lord, my soul waits, and in his word I put my hope. My soul waits for the Lord more than watchmen wait for the morning. . . ."

(a) With these words, we encounter the great advantage that can accompany agony. How is it possible for agony to bear any advantage? This will probably sound strange to you when I explain it, unless you are one who has gone through great distress and has met God there. The fact is, though, that the richest spiritual experiences come to us in our agony. The psalmist is referring to such an experience when he tells how he waits for the Lord.

(b) Here is a person in the depths of agony whose trouble is so comprehensive and intensive that the only thing he can do is cry out to the Lord. Then, in the midst of agony, he suddenly realizes what God has done for him. He is saved. His sins have been taken away. There is no barrier between him and God. God loves him. As he puts it, "O Israel, put your hope in the Lord, for with the Lord is unfailing love and with him is full redemption." So in his misery the psalmist sees the love of God as he never saw it before.

V. Psalm 130 describes a very special experience that involves agony relieved by the knowledge of God's full forgiveness and the peace that goes with that knowledge. No one asks for such an experience. But when God gives it, it is precious. When there is nowhere else to turn and you turn to God, you discover the wonder of faith. When there is no one else to lean on and you lean on God, when everything else fails and you wait for God, you discover the wonder of faith.

(a) For us, everything depends on Christ. Christ is our Savior—he has made forgiveness possible. Christ is the one who sends his Holy Spirit, whom he calls the Great Comforter. Christ is the one who comes to care for us in our despair. The writer of Psalm 130 could speak only about God, which is good in itself, but now God has appeared to us in Jesus Christ. Now we can lean on Christ. Now we can trust him, for he has accomplished salvation for us. And we discover that the deeper we delve, the sweeter the grace of Jesus Christ becomes. He is a glorious Savior. As we have noticed, Psalm 130 ends on this glorious note: "He himself will redeem Israel from all their sins."

(b) If you cry out to God and confess your sins, he will save you. Have you been reading this message and wondering with every passing moment if there might be something here that could lift you out of your despair? I point you to Jesus. Call out to him. Cry out to him. If you cannot utter a word anymore because you are too weak, speak in your mind to Christ. Ask him to forgive your sins, even if your sins have brought you to this sad state. He will forgive you, and he will save you.—Joel Nederhood

Illustrations

THE HIDDENNESS OF GOD. The psalms of lament lead us finally to the deepest dimension of the witness for the Bible: faith's acknowledgement that the God who reveals himself in history remains hidden. He does not become the prisoner of men's thoughts or the captive of their schemes, nor is his purpose easily discernible in the unfolding drama of human history. Living in the space between promise and fulfillment, men of faith are torn between the no and the yes. In the New Testament we find that the very place where God's victory is manifest—the cross—is the place where the shadows are deepest. Jesus appropriately takes the laments of the Psalter into his own suffering with us. To be sure, the darkness is illumined by the dawn of Easter morning; but the darkness remains as a trial for faith.—Bernhard W. Anderson

MERCY AND HOLINESS. The belief in the forgiveness of sins is an entirely serious matter; the grace of God cancels sins, but not its seriousness. Indeed, the claim of the holy God upon man's obedience, far from being reduced by his grace, only becomes weightier than ever. And in this the poet sees God's true intentions: "And so must all men fear thee, / And by thy grace must live." This thought of the psalmist, that forgiveness leads to the fear of God, reaches the heights of the New Testament realization of the kindness of God which leads man to repentance (Rom. 2:4; cf. Luke 5:8). It expresses the paradoxical tension inherent in the fact that man simultaneously believes in the mercy of God, on which he utterly depends, and in the holiness of God, to which he is wholly subject.—Artur Weiser

Sermon Suggestions

ON THE WAY TO THE ESCHATON.   TEXT: Acts 1:6–14. (1) *The incident:* In the exchange between Jesus and his apostles, Jesus charged his disciples with the task of bearing witness to him, without preoccupation with God's secret timetable for the consummation of all things. (2) *The application:* Those who speak for Jesus Christ should be concerned to (a) leave the future in God's hands; (b) look to God for power to represent him in this world and in the present times; (c) commit themselves to carry out the task of witness to the remotest parts of earth; (d) begin in simple prayer and devotion with the people closest at hand.

IF YOU THINK ALL MUST BE ROSY. TEXT: 1 Pet. 4:12–14. (1) Persecutions are always possible. (2) Nevertheless, rejoicing is possible also, if we recognize our solidarity with the Christ who suffered.

Worship Aids

CALL TO WORSHIP.   "Cast thy burden upon the Lord, and he shall sustain thee" (Ps. 55:22a).

INVOCATION.   Lord, we bring to this place many concerns, cares, and burdens, but we come in faith, though sometimes doubting, expecting strength of grace to see us through. To this end, speak to our hearts through Scripture, song, and

sermon, and we shall be able to praise you.

OFFERTORY SENTENCE.   "My God shall supply all your need according to his riches in glory by Christ Jesus" (Phil. 4:19).

OFFERTORY PRAYER.   O God, tame our desires to fit our needs and stir up our desires to suit the needs of your kingdom. Let our offerings help bring this prayer to fulfillment.

PRAYER.   Father, thank you for today. With what love you love us that we should have this beautiful world in which to live; with what love you love us that grace should abound to heal us and make us whole even in the face of the most threatening and shattering of circumstance; with what love you love us that with patience and understanding and mercy you should fashion us to an eternal glory: "Eye has not seen, nor ear heard, neither has entered into the mind of man what you prepare for those who love you."
Forgive us the lack of love and imagination that on the domestic front we continue to fight fire with fire—violence with violence—and then deplore the ineffective results. Open our minds and hearts to receive more fully your love—that love that looks for ways of being constructive, even to dying on a cross.
For all with urgent needs, we pray. For those with anxious minds and hearts among us, we pray the Master's "peace be still!"—the gift of your shalom without which nothing else matters. For national and international leaders, who may or may not know you, struggling with the meaning of your Word for all peoples, we pray.—John M. Thompson

LECTIONARY MESSAGE

Topic: That They May Be One
TEXT: John 17:1–11
This is the Lord's Prayer. It is true that we usually refer to Matt. 6:9–13 as the

Lord's Prayer. Technically that is the model prayer that Jesus taught his disciples. This entire chapter may properly be described as the Lord's Prayer. It is the last recorded prayer of Jesus before his experience in the Garden of Gethsemane. It is a prayer for his disciples. It is prayer of preparation for the events that were to follow—preparation both for the disciples and their Lord.

I. *This is eternal life*. The authority over all flesh that the Father granted the Son allowed him to give his followers eternal life. In this Gospel, that eternal life is considered to have already begun with faith and experiences only a minor interruption at death. This life is the knowledge of God and of his Christ. The relationship is ever so close. God glorified the Son, and the Son glorified God. At this point in his ministry he could say that he had accomplished his task.

This eternal life is the relationship between God the Father and the Son and the Son's disciples. The closer the relationship, the more binding the relationship, the greater chance that the prayer might be answered: that they may be one.

II. *They have kept thy word*. Here again the closeness of the relationship is the key. Even as Jesus kept the Father's word, so they learned from him and have kept his word. Indeed it was a part of Jesus' teaching that there was no truth apart from God. They knew that God was the source of Jesus' words.

Although they may not have understood the relationships of the Trinity any better than we, they do not appear to have confused the Father and the Son.

III. *They believed that you sent me*. This was a leap of faith for a monotheistic Jew—especially to go beyond the sense of prophetic mission. Having taken that leap of faith, they became the object of prayer, Jesus' prayer. He prayed for them (and for us) in a way that he did not pray for the world.

You have given them to me. Jesus exercised good stewardship of God's gifts. Among those gifts were his disciples. Yet the unity of Father and Son meant that they yet belonged to both, the Father and the Son. Jesus saw them share in his ministry, and he was glorified in them. It is as Paul wrote to the church at Colossae of the gospel's mystery: "Christ in you, the hope of glory" (Col. 1:27). With the deed accomplished he could approach the Father again.

IV. *Holy father, keep them*. The petition is twofold:

(a) Keep them in thy name. The very nature of God the Father offers assurance to the believer. The Son shares in the Father's name.

(b) That they may be one—even as we are one with different functions, but one purpose; with different manifestations, but one revelation; with different ministries, but one Lord; with different opportunities, but one love . . . that they may be one.

The tragedy of unanswered prayer was never clearer. Our religious life is characterized by diversity, which is healthy. But we have allowed our diversity to defeat any struggle toward unity. Somehow we must achieve unity in diversity . . . that we may be one.—J. Estill Jones

SUNDAY: MAY THIRTIETH

SERVICE OF WORSHIP

Sermon: The Undoing of Babel (Pentecost)

TEXTS: Acts 2:1–8; Gen. 11:1–9

I. An amazing revolution began with the new people of God born in Christ. The walls of hostility between peoples of the world began to crack. To be sure, the walls did not fall, but the foundations were moved, and demolition was begun. God has never excluded anyone; but elitism, racism, nationalism, and various forms of social bigotry are parasites which attach themselves to the children of God like fleas on a dog. I do not for a moment believe that God is responsible for chaos and conflict, but consider the backdrop of Babel. Babel is an example of ancient etiology—a story to explain a common landmark or fact. The tower of Babel answers the question "Why is the world confused by a variety of languages?" Hatred of Babylon and curiosity about the Persian ziggurats were a part of the unwritten agenda along with the essential fact of human sinfulness. Every parent knows to be as concerned about a quiet conspiracy as for open conflict in the play of children. Why are people more likely to unite in a war than in a cause of peace? Babel does not stand against international peace so much as it notes our human tendency to rally around the wrong causes. Karl Barth observed that the sin was neither in the search for unity nor the ambition to bridge the gap to heaven. It was in the motive: "let us make a name for ourselves"—the denial of a need for God, a rejection of grace. The fundamental evil of this world, exposed in the story of Babel, is the narrow mentality which allows people to exclude one another. The clearest sign of healing of God's humanity is a reign of peace grounded in the power of God.

II. With no direct connection, Christian Pentecost was the undoing of Babel. Pentecost had been the traditional Jewish celebration of the giving of the Law, building the people of God around basic principles of life. The Jewish festival took on a new meaning. The same Spirit of God whom Luke had reported (3:22, 4:1) descending on Jesus at his baptism and filling Jesus at his temptation, filled the church at Pentecost. The miracle was a moment of world peace in miniature. The linguistic diversity of the world which continues to stand as a reminder of human arrogance and international chaos—Babel—disappeared for a moment. Rather than a conspiracy to replace God, the unity here was the bonding power of the Spirit of God. The glue which caused the children of Abraham to stick together was the covenant—a tie with God which bonded the multitude of individuals into community. The bond which would bring the new people of God together was the Spirit of God. The Spirit was evident in the removal of the language barriers to the new people of God.

(a) In a National Public Radio discussion of the global economy the necessity of learning other languages was the subject of concern. The speaker recalled an old joke: "Someone who speaks two languages is called 'bilingual'; three languages, 'trilingual'; and one language, 'American.'" The angry moves to legislate English as the official and only language of some communities is not only a resentment of the invasion of diversity into our little kingdoms. The arrogance of Babel is not the unity of language but the attempt to possess the high place, the assumption that I live at the center, thus, understanding is everyone else's problem.

(1) A basic step toward understanding the Bible is exposure to the Hebrew and Greek languages of origin. Even if the seminary student never develops any significant degree of linguistic expertise, the study of language exposes a biblical culture which will not permit an easy assumption that the Bible is "American" or Southern. If you would hear the Word of God, listen in the language and culture to which the Word first came.

(2) The first step in becoming a missionary is to develop an understanding of the people with whom you minister. That usually means language school, but it also involves learning another culture. On a trip through South America, I became acquainted with a missionary in Peru, Elbert Smithen, who had his first exposure to the Spanish language growing up in a south Texas community. I doubt that Elbert had an inkling of the ultimate use he would put to his knowledge of Spanish when he was learning to communicate with Mexican-Americans. M. Theron Rankin identified missionaries, "who, in the name of Christ, will lose themselves and bury their lives among the people to whom they go; missionaries who live and serve along with the people, who speak their language, who acquire the capacities for sympathy for their miseries and

human hungers, and who learn to love them personally and individually."

(b) The gift and the opportunity to learn another language is not available to all of us, but we should not resist the opportunity which diversity brings to our children. It may well be the beginning of a new Pentecost.

III. What is the miracle here? Is it the strange sound of the wind, the appearance of tongues as of fire, the strange behavior and speech of the disciples? The miracle we tend to overlook may well be the central meaning of this event. When the Spirit of God moves among a people, a new level of understanding sets the course toward a new level of unity. It had to begin with a coming together of the church. Somebody has to cross a barrier to begin the peace. If this peace is allowed to go unchecked, it is as likely to break out into the world community now as then. Paul was not there, but he seemed to know what it was about: "The fruit of the Spirit is love, joy, peace, patience, kindness, generosity, faithfulness, gentleness, and self-control." Every manifestation of the Spirit of God is a step toward forming the fragmented lost persons of Creation into the one people of God.—Larry Dipboye

Illustrations

IDOLATRY.   Ministers, doctors, psychologists, counselors, teachers, writers, artists, actors, politicians, newspaper men, and movie producers—all of us, knowingly or unknowingly, participate in the collective guilt of our time: We produce idolatry instead of faith. We exploit the crises of our fellowmen, the breakdown of their egocentricity, their suffering and their opportunity for further development, for our own egocentric or idolatrous goals. We loudly proclaim our philosophy, our art, our policy as the general remedy, and by doing so we—silently—offer ourselves as idols. For most of us, to be a success means to be idolized.—Fritz Kunkel

THE MEANING OF LOVE.   Love is the only way to grasp another human being

in the innermost core of his personality. No one can become fully aware of the very essence of another human being unless he loves him. By the spiritual act of love he is enabled to see the essential traits and features in the beloved person; and even more, he sees that which is potential in him; which is not yet actualized but yet ought to be actualized. Furthermore, by his love, the loving person enables the beloved person to actualize these potentialities. By making him aware of what he can be and of what he should become, he makes these potentialities come true.—Victor E. Frankl

Sermon Suggestions

THE COMING OF THE SPIRIT.   TEXT: Acts 2:1–21. (1) Removes barriers to understanding. (2) Removes barriers to our common salvation in the Lord Jesus Christ.

"FOR THE GOOD OF ALL."   TEXT: 1 Cor. 12:3b–13, TEV. (1) The variety of spiritual gifts. (2) The one source of all gifts. (3) The purpose of the several gifts, verse 7.

Worship Aids

CALL TO WORSHIP.   "There is no difference between the Jew and the Greek: for the same Lord over all is rich unto all that call upon him. For whosoever shall call upon the name of the Lord shall be saved" (Rom. 10:12–13).

INVOCATION.   Gracious Lord, open our hearts wide today, wider than ever before, to each other in this congregation and to the people outside this house of worship. We ask this in the name of the one who has poured out his Spirit upon all flesh.

OFFERTORY SENTENCE.   "You shall receive power when the Holy Spirit has come upon you; and you shall be my witnesses in Jerusalem and in all Judea and Samaria and to the end of the earth" (Acts 1:8, RSV).

OFFERTORY PRAYER. Lord Jesus Christ, let your Spirit bless and direct these offerings, so that each of us participating may truly be your witnesses throughout the world.

PRAYER. Keep us, O God, from taking for granted that which has been bought with so great a price. We give thanks and praise you for the Church and for the churches that have called us out and nurtured us in the faith, and for this congregation—its life and ministry in which we are privileged to share. We are grateful for those models of the faith—in patriarch, in prophet, in Messiah, in parent, in Sunday school teacher, in minister, in youth counselor, in friend, in companion, who have awakened us to life and called us to eternal life. For those loving, thoughtful, forgiving persons who have supported and encouraged us when we have stumbled and fallen, we give thanks—these spiritual mentors who have counseled us along the way when life has been threatened with chaos—how patiently and wisely they brought order to our thinking and encouragement to our spirit. What we owe to these, your angels of mercy, who have been there at every turning—ministering your persevering love and amazing grace!

With the gift of this heritage, we pray that we may be faithful to the goal in Christ Jesus. In him you keep loving us. You are never through with us. You keep challenging us to steeper heights and to greater depths. Whatever the year or the years may bring we continue to grow in the grace and knowledge of our Lord and Savior Jesus Christ.

We pray for your healing grace to minister wholeness to our brokenness whatever that brokenness may be. You are always waiting to give but many times we are not ready to receive. We pray for an increase of faith and love and trust, that we may be open to the fullness of your grace and truth in Christ. Whatever our circumstance, we pray that we may be victor rather than victim through him who is our living Lord and is among us.—John M. Thompson

LECTIONARY MESSAGE

Topic: Streams of Living Grace
TEXT: John 7:37–39

On the last day of the Feast of Tabernacles, Jesus promised the resources yet to come on the day of Pentecost, fifty days away. He promised a spiritual power that would refresh every believer and, through believers, the world, with constant grace.

I. The eighth day of the Feast of Tabernacles was a commemoration of leaving the tents in the wilderness to enter the Promised Land, of leaving the dryness of the desert to enjoy the springs and streams of God's abundance. The day was celebrated by the people's leaving their temporary tents and returning to their homes.

The commemoration of the water from the rock in the desert was expressed each of the other seven days of the feast by drawing water from the pool of Siloam in a gold pitcher and carrying it to the Temple. On the eighth day, this carrying of water was discontinued.

Also on the eighth day, there was a holy convocation. It was on this day that Jesus promised that believers would themselves become carriers of relief, giving new streams of life for the welfare of others. Only believers received this promise—only Jesus could give it.

The apostle explains, for later readers, that the Holy Spirit, then still to be given, was the subject of Jesus' prophecy.

II. This last feast day, when water was no longer carried from the pool to the Temple, was the occasion for Jesus to reveal the true source of constant spiritual refreshing. He at this point could only promise the Holy Spirit. As he told later on (16:7), "If I go not away, the Comforter will not come, but I will send him to you when I depart." What is emphasized here is that the true source of spiritual blessing is a smitten Jesus. Jesus could not depart until he had fulfilled his redemptive purpose and had been crucified. Therefore, there is no source of the healing, refreshing streams of spiritual grace except the crucified, smitten, and resurrected Christ. As the Holy Spirit for a time could indwell only the Lord himself, later he would indwell and act through all believers.

Just as the water from the smitten rock in the desert, which had given life to the desert travelers, was no longer necessary when they entered the Promised Land, so now Jesus is telling the disciples that the real refreshing streams of life are soon to be theirs, directly from him who would ever dwell within them.

It is a blessing for us to observe here the continuity of God's communication to his people, as Jesus uses the symbols of the Feast of Tabernacles to promise the great and glorious event of the future Feast of Weeks, known as Pentecost.

III. Believers in Jesus Christ have become the city of God, and like every great city in the world, they shall become great because of the mighty stream beside which they are built. The promise that Jesus quoted from Isa. 12:3, that with joy we should draw water out of the wells of salvation, and as he promised in John 6:35 that "he that believeth on me shall never thirst," and in 4:14, "Whosoever

drinketh of the water that I shall give him shall never thirst; but the water that I shall give him shall be in him a well of water springing up into everlasting life," all together make us realize that our greatness is from him and will diminish and dry up without him.

The water of which he speaks is his Holy Spirit, for it is the Spirit that gives life and that will "make glad the city of God" (Ps. 46:4). This life-giving Spirit is for the blessing of the world's people. Why should the rivers that flow with life-giving water from the believers remain dammed up so that they become stale? We must see to it that they flow out over the land—our land of promise—to reach the sea, the sea of humanity they were meant to bless and redeem, as the mighty Amazon gives life to ships even a hundred miles out to sea.

The glory of Pentecost for the Christian is that the need is filled from a never-dying source and that the Holy Spirit is released to glorify him and through him his world.—John R. Rodman

SUNDAY: JUNE SIXTH

SERVICE OF WORSHIP

Sermon: The Greatness of God
Text: Ps. 95:3

Our inherited idea of deity, it is commonly insisted today, goes back to old Hebrew conceptions born in an ancient land were men still thought the earth flat, with Sheol, the place of the dead, a little way below and the heavens a few miles above. If in our modern world, the complainants say, God is to be credible and intelligible, we must grasp a new and more adequate conception of him, starting from different premises and scaled to different dimensions.

This demand for a more worthy and adequate conception of God has struck many people as news and shocking news at that. As a matter of fact, achieving a worthier idea of God has always been the problem of religion. Only a dead religion

can escape it. Every living religion grows and, growing, seeks more adequate conceptions of the Eternal. Indeed, the glory of the Hebrew-Christian tradition lies in having done that—its history can be told in terms of that. Moreover, so far from condescending to the ancient Hebrews, we shall be fortunate if we handle our problem in this realm as courageously and fruitfully as they handled theirs. "The Lord is a great God," said the psalmist. That sounds as though even then they were reaching out for a larger idea of God. Of course they were!

Repeatedly in the Hebrew-Christian tradition, to which we belong, we have faced this issue, where we had either to grasp a deeper conception of God or else give up God altogether, and we have never given him up yet. Neither will we surrender God now. We will grasp a worthier idea of him. That thing is happening with us which has happened ever since our thought of God started with stories of Sinai and the Garden of Eden. Some people stand looking back and saying, God is gone! But the rest of us are standing in reverence before a vaster universe and are saying, The Lord is a great God.

If this is the story of the development of the idea of God in our own tradition so that that tradition can say about itself what Paul said about himself, "When I was a child, I spake as a child, I understood as a child, I thought as a child; but when I became a man, I put away childish things," let us try to help ourselves in dealing with this present confusion about God.

I. In the first place, we should not be upset by religion's "growing pains."

(a) To be sure, the discomfort is irritating. In particular, mankind is incorrigibly lazy, would like to stop progressing, and especially would always prefer to stop thinking. The hardest work in the world is thinking, and especially getting larger thoughts. It would be comfortable, then, if we could say about God, that is the final thought of him; that finishes our concept of deity, and we shall never have to think about it again. But, after all, is there any one of us who would choose that? Just where would we stop in this long story of man's developing conception of the Eternal? With Sinai? With the geographically limited god? With the god of the old astronomy? We know we are unpayably indebted to those forefathers of ours who went through the discomfort of expanding religious experience and thought, and came forth with a guerdon and reward to show for it, "a great God."

(b) As we look back upon our forefathers, thankful for the contribution which they have made to our idea of God, so will our children look back on this generation and estimate our worth in part by what we do now, when once more religion reaches out for a more adequate conception of the Eternal.

To be sure, this process is confusing and always has been. They called Socrates an atheist. But he was no atheist. He had so splendid an idea of God, as Plato interprets him, that centuries after his martyrdom his name was often coupled with Christ's by the Christian fathers of the church, and his sayings were quoted as though from the Bible itself.

Many people do not know that the early Christians were themselves called atheists. Of course, what that meant was that they denied the current ideas of the pagan gods, but in fact they were working out an idea of God, in terms of spirit and love, to which the future belonged.

Multitudes of people think Voltaire an atheist. Voltaire did not come within reaching distance of being an atheist. What he denied was current ideas of God. Voltaire was one of the greatest humanitarians of history. He had in him many things both lovely and unlovely, but he cared about people, especially people whom other people had wronged, and the only God he could believe in was a God who loved people.

We need not be upset by religion's "growing pains." This generation will not give up God.

II. In the second place, we should recognize frankly that to our limited and partial minds the real God is incomprehensible.

(a) The immediate result of the fact that the real God is always to us incomprehensible is that we must think of him in terms of symbolism. Whenever anybody thinks of anything universal he has to think in symbolic terms.

Sometimes I think it would be worthwhile to preach a series of sermons on symbols, because we use them constantly and so many people do not know what they are doing when they do use them.

All life is full of symbols. A handshake is a symbol, a lifted hat is a symbol, a kiss is a symbol, the country's flag is a symbol. What is that keepsake in your pocketbook? It is a little thing, but it reminds you; it has associations; it makes you think of somebody. What is that wedding ring upon your finger? What is the cross in the chancel? That is Christianity's keepsake. That is Christianity's wedding ring. That is Christianity's flag.

(b) When, now, we think of the great God, we have to use symbols. We take some element within our experience and lift it up as far as we can reach and use it to help us think about him. We call him a rock and a fortress and a high tower. We call him father and mother and husband and friend. We call him Ancient of Days and the Hound of Heaven. Men call him the eternal lotus flower and the Rose of Sharon and the bright and morning star. And Christians say they see the light of the knowledge of the glory of God in the face of Jesus Christ. These are all symbols of the great God.

Recognizing that all our thoughts of God are inadequate, sometimes even childish, seeing that we cannot with our partial thought grasp the full compass of the Eternal, we are tempted to give up God altogether. But this is the wrong approach. It is far truer to think of God in terms of an inadequate symbol than not to think of him at all. The great God is; our partial ideas of him are partly true.

III. Nevertheless, we should not leave the matter there. What we have said about symbolic thinking concerning God seems to me true and important, but it is not the end of the matter, and if one takes it for the end one leaves God too vague to do business with. Let us, therefore, say this further thing: God is very great, but he has a near end where he literally touches us. How important are the consequences from that fact—God has a near end!

(a) Recently I visited once more my island off the coast of Maine and fell in love again with the sea. Now, I do not know the whole sea. It is very great. I never sailed the tropic ocean where the Orinoco and the Amazon pour out their floods through primeval woods. I never watched the Antarctic sea where today pioneers press their perilous journeys over the polar ice pack. Wide areas of the sea are to me unknown, but I know the sea. It has a near end. I washes my island. I can sit beside it and bathe in it and sail over it and be sung to sleep by the music of it.

So is God. He is so great that in his vastness we can think of him only in symbolic terms, but he has a near end. Indeed, the nub of the whole inquiry about the nature of deity lies in the answer to this question: Where do we think in our experience we touch the near end of God? Do we think that only matter is the near end of him and that all the God there is is simply physical, or do we think that in spiritual life at its best we have touched the near end of deity and that, when we start with that and think out through that as far as we can go, we are thinking most truly about him?

(b) To believe in the Christian God is to believe that in spiritual life at its best we have touched the hither side of God. Whatever more he may be, he is that. Ask the New Testament what God is, and the New Testament says, "God is love." Say to the New Testament, then, Where do we reach him? and it answers, "He that abideth in love abideth in God, and God abideth in him." That is God's near end.

Of course, this is what the "divinity of Jesus" means. Many people are troubled because they cannot believe that all of the great God was in Jesus. Of course, all of the great God was not in Jesus. The omnipresence of the great God was not in Jesus. The omnipotence of the great God, swinging the eternal stars, was not in Jesus. No intelligent theology ever meant by the "divinity of Jesus" what some people think is implied in it, but this it does mean, that in the spiritual life and character of Christ we touch the near end of God. There God reaches us. There he washes our island.

IV. Go out, then, into this generation so confused about God. If they say to us, We need a larger idea of him, let us answer, Yes. But say this other thing also: God has a near end; in everything that we call beautiful or good or true he touches us; there we do business with him. "Know ye not that ye are a temple of God, and that the Spirit of God dwelleth in you?"—Harry Emerson Fosdick

Illustrations

GOD INEXPRESSIBLE.   My God, my God. Thou art a direct God, may I not say a literal God, a God that wouldest be understood literally, and according to the plain sense of all that thou sayest? But thou art also a figurative, a metaphorical God too; a God in whose words there is such a height of figures, such voyages, such peregrinations to fetch remote and precious metaphors, such extensions, such spreadings, such Curtains of Allegories, such third Heavens of Hyperboles, such harmonious elocutions. O, what words but thine can express the inexpressible texture, and composition of thy word.—John Donne (1572–1631)

THE BOTTOM LINE OF FAITH.   Luther had experiences which he describes as attacks of utter despair (*Anfechtung*), as the frightful threat of a complete meaninglessness. He felt these moments as satanic attacks in which everything was menaced: his Christian faith, the confidence of his work, the Reformation, the forgiveness of sins. Everything broke down in the extreme moments of this despair, nothing was left of the courage to be. Luther in these moments, and in the descriptions he gives of them, anticipated the descriptions of them by modern existentialism. But for him this was not the last word. The last word was the first commandment, the statement that God is God. It reminded him of the unconditional element in humane experience of which one can be aware even in the abyss of meaninglessness. And this awareness saved him.—Paul Tillich

Sermon Suggestions

TAKING THE LORD TO HEART.   TEXT: Deut. 4:32–40. (1) God's electing love, verses 32–38. (2) The appropriate and promising response, verses 33–40.

THREE-THINKING BELIEVERS.   TEXT: 2 Cor. 13:5–14, especially verse 13. (1) Christian experience begins in our experience of the grace (kindness) of Jesus Christ. (2) This experience points to its source in God, who is unbounded love. (3) From that perception we savor our communion through the Spirit with God and with our fellow believers.

Worship Aids

CALL TO WORSHIP.   "The Lord reigneth: let the earth rejoice" (Ps. 97:1a).

INVOCATION.   We rejoice today, O Lord, for we know that you are in control. We do not understand all of your ways, but we know you and trust you. Let that faith pervade all that we do during this time of prayer and praise.

OFFERTORY SENTENCE.   "The earth is the Lord's and the fullness thereof; the world, and they that dwell therein" (Ps. 24:1).

OFFERTORY PRAYER.   It is all yours, O Lord, all that we are and have. Take this portion of our material possessions and glorify your name through a multiplying witness to your love.

PRAYER.   Great is your faithfulness, O God our Father, We, the sometimes faithful, come in confession this morning admitting that we are fickle when we know that you are ever faithful. We know that we practice duplicity even though as followers we have given our lives to being authentic. We live amid divided loyalties even as we seek your wholeness. We even come halfhearted into your presence to worship and invoke your presence when we should be invoking our own. So often we emotionally and even physically saunter into your presence with our hands in our pockets when you are calling for all that we are and have to stand before you.

Deliver us from our pretense and call us to a commitment that eagerly seeks your face, listens to your counsel, and goes out to do your will. Let us hear the deep in you calling to the deep in us that we may plumb the depths of what you would have us be. Remind us of your love freely given that we might be free to attain the highest possibilities you have for us. Assure us that we are acceptable to you even as we are, when we face our sins, lay them before you in honest confession and receive your grace and forgiveness.—Henry Fields

LECTIONARY MESSAGE

Topic: The Strong and Blessed Name
TEXT: Matt. 28:16–20

I. Here Jesus instructs his disciples that the Trinity is the authority for Christian baptism, as its realm of fellowship and power is the partnership into which they are to baptize the nations.

The unity of the three persons of the Trinity is implied in the use of the singular form of *name*—"into the name. . . ." The name is not of one, but of three; it is not plural, the *names* of the Father, the son, and the Holy Spirit; it is not three different names, as the name of the Father, the name of the son, and the name of the Holy Spirit; but it is the one name for our God, Savior, and Lord.

The preposition is also interesting. It is not "*in* the name of," but "*into* the name of." The one being baptized is forever leaving one way of life and forever entering a wholly different one.

We ought to ask, in teaching or studying any tenet of Christian faith, what the *facts* were that led the early Christians to accept the doctrine. They spoke of events, not of theories. Jesus is, in this text, speaking of a fact he knew.

The whole New Testament is resonant with the historic events that had "final and absolute significance" (J. S. Stewart, *A Faith to Proclaim,* p. 13). These are the acts of God—acts of his presence, his healing, and his redeeming love. The story of the early church's preaching was the story of all that Jesus was, what he did, and what he said. The believers and their life of faith were created by the fact of the Trinity, not vice versa.

II. The Gospels reiterate the word *hapax,* the emphasis being on the once-for-all fact of God's becoming flesh and spirit, the eternal truth of his being now and forever visible to and viable for the believers. The uniqueness of the act is the focus for Paul in Romans, for Peter in his epistles, for Jude, and for the writer to the Hebrews. The great declaration of Christianity is the kerygma, the message that God has changed eternity for the world by once becoming human, shedding his blood for all persons, and giving his Spirit freely to every believer. No longer do we look for redemption—it is here! The kingdom of God is on earth in every faithful heart! The purpose of the universe is fulfilled and has come to pass, as Heb. 10:10 says, "by that will we are sanctified through the offering of the body of Jesus Christ once for all."

The completeness and continuity are bound up in the finality of Jesus' bringing God for all to see and love. The *hapax,* once, has the sense of totality, being derived from *hapas,* literally meaning "for absolutely all." We need no other.

III. The baptism of which Jesus speaks is a seal on the accomplished fact of salvation, but equally significantly it is the door to a saved life. For the believer, redeemed once for all, has still to live in the flesh. He or she will be beset by a full selection of the ills and evils of human life, as the arena in which he or she works out the victory of Christ that is within. The saved believer must believe every hour of every day, in sickness and in health, in good times and bad—bearing about, for constant comfort, consolation, and fortitude, the last words of our text: "Lo, I am with you all the days until the close of the current age."

Jesus has thus transferred to us, through the Holy Spirit, "all the power" shared with him, the Son, by the Father. Indeed, the power and glory of the Trinity are ours forever in all life's vicissitudes.—John R. Rodman

SUNDAY: JUNE THIRTEENTH

SERVICE OF WORSHIP

Sermon: When Jesus Follows You
TEXT: Matt. 9:18–19, 23–26

It takes courage to follow Jesus. When we hear him say to those who sat scattered along the hillside, "Blessed are ye, when men shall revile you, and persecute you, and shall say all manner of evil against you falsely, for my sake," we know that it took courage. When we read that as they followed him they were afraid, we know that it took courage, for fear is the inseparable twin of courage. Those of us who have tried to walk in his footsteps know what courage it takes when some fear grips our hearts, when we sense how far the road with him can lead, how high the Christian adventure can lift us, how much acceptance and how much surrender it may mean.

There is an incident in the New Testament which turns our thinking clear around. It is full of the human pathos which sooner or later touches all of us. A brokenhearted father had come to tell Jesus about the death of his child, and having told him, turned straight toward his home. Then Jesus followed. We need no interpreter to tell us the deeper meaning of this small-town drama. All the history and all the pageantry of our souls are in it. What happened so long ago has happened to every one of us. There have been times, have there not, when we poured out our hearts, said all there was to say, and went our way. Then suddenly we sensed that we were not alone. He followed us. The soul knows its crisis, when our world falls apart and every certainty seems to vanish. There are no words in such moments. Prayers are stifled. Fortunate are the man and the woman who know that in that hour they need not walk alone. After all, Christianity is a faith for crisis. It does not matter whether it is a crisis of joy or a crisis of sorrow.

I. So let us ask ourselves some questions which reach deep. Have we the courage to ask Jesus to follow us to the place where we live?

(a) Our home is our world. It is the only world we really know. Everything we are is reflected there: our integrity, our vulgarity, the shadowy nature of our weakness, the iridescent light of our virtue. Now have we the courage to leave the door ajar, so that he may enter, too? Would we dare to ask him to be near during those moments of intimate relationships when we say things the world

must never hear or know? Would we wish him to follow our thoughts, no matter where they lead? Our dreams, no matter with what they play? Our hopes, no matter what they encircle?

(b) What is it that makes a home? They are simple things: thoughtfulness, the heart's quick sensing of someone's wants; trust, which has neither fathom nor horizon; patience, this long waiting for children to grow up and become men and women; an unselfish concern for others; and, in the end, the healing of wounds. Marriage was meant to be beautiful—not without seeking, not without probing into each other's souls—but beautiful. Now will you have the courage to ask him to follow you from the altar down the long road? Now will you have the courage to let faith in Christ mean something to you?

II. Let us ask another question. Have we the courage to ask Jesus to follow us to the moment in which are tested?

(a) There are times when we are like men sinking into the quicksand. We do not want to yield to our weakness; we do not want to be what we are not; but we feel ourselves alone and helpless. We are in the grip of something not ourselves. The heart is divided; the mind is befogged. In that one moment, sometimes blazing with the fury of greed, sometimes burning in the heat of passion, we see the old standards by which we were reared grow hazy. We begin to rationalize. We justify our actions; we seek to persuade ourselves that we have found a better wisdom and a new morality; we live as though there were no future, as though there were nothing but this one throbbing sound. What poor, foolish gamblers we are! If only then we could remember that there is a tomorrow, and tomorrow it will be remorse and loneliness and penitence.

(b) There are other times of testing when we must follow our course, when we must stand against our own kind, when we must set ourselves against our own families and follow a voice that cannot be silenced. We cannot be deaf to that voice; we cannot turn from that sense of duty in ourselves. There is only one road, and we must walk on that road. But there is that other voice whispering of the price we shall have to pay, telling of the cross we shall have to bear. If in that moment we waver, we will never be ourselves, and we will never build a better world.

III. Let us ask one more question of ourselves. Have we the courage to ask him to follow us to the place of our fears?

(a) There are those bitter days when our minds are torn by conflicts. We are afraid. Fear dominates everything we do. Fear dominates everything we do. We do not trust ourselves, for we know we shall fail. We do not trust our friends, for we are persuaded that they cannot help us. We fear tomorrow, for it may overwhelm us. Truly our souls are sick. Panic takes hold upon us, and we run from door to door, from psychiatrist to psychiatrist, seeking relief. Have we then the courage to ask Jesus to follow us to the place of our need?

(b) What is it we do when the heart is troubled? We ask, but there is no answer. We hope, but the winds of chance carry our dreams away. We look for fulfillment, but there is never any end, and we must walk on and on, plodding along the way. We grow bitter about life. But it might have been different had we but asked Jesus to follow us. How many answers we would have found, how many dreams might have come to earth, and how much fulfillment we might have seen!

(c) If only we had the courage to ask him to follow us, what faith could do then! How faith would become articulate; how it would meet every problem with which the mind and heart are burdened. With what assurance we would meet our difficulties. With what serenity we could speak to ourselves, and with what dignity we could bear our troubles.

IV. Yes, it takes courage to follow Jesus. It is the heroic strain in us which makes us say, "Where he leads me, I will follow." But it takes more courage to ask him to follow us. The road before us may be long—the night may fall upon our way—we may be afraid. Then we hear footsteps. We look back and see the shadow of his figure following after us. Now it is as though there were a lantern in our hands. We know that all will be well, for he will be with us wherever our need is. And who indeed can ask more of his Lord than that?—Arnold H. Lowe

Illustrations

LIVING AT A NEW ADDRESS. We may understand very little about the meaning of Jesus Christ, but at least this much we know: A human life has been lived on this earth which no longer centers in or revolves about its own self but gives itself away for the sake of others. If we live in this atmosphere even slightly, then a desire that would ruin the life of my wife or my children can never be right under any circumstances. Or how could I hoard money or possessions until I had completely dispossessed and destroyed others? Or how could I still let myself be so enslaved to good food or drink that nothing else could compete? Such things go on no longer, not because we have become so different, but because the atmosphere that surrounds us is changed.—Eduard Schweizer

WHEN LOVE LIFTS. John A. Redhead told of a priest during the Middle Ages who announced to his congregation that he would preach a sermon on the love of God. At the appointed time the cathedral was filled with eager listeners. It was late in the afternoon and the sinking sun, shining through the stained-glass windows, flooded the nave with magnificent colors. When the time for the sermon arrived, the priest did not go to the pulpit. Instead, he went very slowly to the candelabra, selected a lighted candle, then went up to the marble crucifix beside the high altar. Without uttering a single word he held the candle to the wounds in the feet of the Christ, then to the wounds in the hands and side. Deliberately, he climbed higher, held the light on the throne-crowned brow. The old priest had finished his sermon on the love of God. The word had already been spoken—the word of God's love revealed through

Christ's redemptive suffering.—Gaston Foote

Sermon Suggestions

CHALLENGING THE PLEASURE PRINCIPLE. TEXT: Gen. 25:19–34. (1) Then: The story of Esau's selling of his birthright. (2) Always: Immediate satisfaction may bring long-term suffering as a consequence. Biblical and other examples. (3) Now: Therefore (a) be willing to postpone your pleasures; (b) find legitimate ways to gratify your needs; (c) give positive reinforcement to your decisions through the available disciplines of the Christian life.

THE PROOF OF GOD'S LOVE. TEXT: Rom. 5:6–11. (1) It is not to be found in nature—which is "red in tooth and claw." (2) It is not to be found in a trouble-free, prosperous life—which is "the exception rather than the rule." (3) It is to be found in the cross of Christ—which contradicts all norms for demonstrating either "the power of God" or "the wisdom of God."

CALL TO WORSHIP. "I was glad when they said unto me, Let us go into the house of the Lord" (Ps. 122:1).

INVOCATION. Our Father, we have much to make us glad as we come to this place. Grant that what we give and receive here will make glad those who are not present but to whom we may be individually and collectively a blessing.

OFFERTORY SENTENCE. "And he said to them all, If any man will come after me, let him deny himself and take up his cross daily and follow me" (Luke 9:23).

OFFERTORY PRAYER. O God, you are calling us to walk a way that is not always easy, yet the presence of the crucified Christ gives us courage, touches our hearts, and opens our purses. Help us to see our important roles as we extend his love through what we do and what we give.

PRAYER. Walk with us, O God, in the plain paths where the day-by-day routine settles down to a test of private perseverance, unheralded by the accolade of praise or bright reward. If the heavenly vision grows dim, and our hearts are weary in well-doing, lay thy hand upon us and steady our steps that we may press onward, even in darkness, toward the light ahead. If we are alone, and the task seems more than we can do, or if done, not at all welcomed by the world, reveal thy presence at our side that we may labor with thy help. Turn us from the dreams of far glory to work in the commonplace circumstances of this mortal world and disclose to us the miracle of thy grace in unexpected places. Even so may thy will be done on earth as it is in heaven, through Jesus Christ our Lord.—Samuel H. Miller

LECTIONARY MESSAGE

Topic: June 13: The Moral Mandate for Christian Service
TEXT: Matt. 9:35–10:8

I. After showing his disciples all the crowds and their distressed conditions, Jesus shows his compassion for them by asking the disciples to pray the Lord of the harvest to send laborers into his harvest. He then grants the disciples a share of his infinite power—"all power in heaven and in earth" (28:18)—over evil spirits and over all manner of sickness and disease. The grant of power is for a purpose—they are to seek out "the lost sheep of the house of Israel." These "lost sheep" would be the 'am ha'ares, the "people of the land," people who, because of their work, might be ceremonially unclean and therefore spurned by the religious elite. They are to find them and spread among them the kind of miraculous healings that Jesus himself had been doing wherever he could go. Just as he did, they were to "heal the sick, cleanse the lepers, raise the dead, and cast out devils."

But why *should* they do all that? They had been with him and seen his blessed work, but—they had lives to live, families to care for, other work to do. Why should they surrender all for such service? Because, Jesus explained, "Freely ye have received, freely give."

II. "Freely ye have received!" Many people today would respond, "Oh, yeah? I've worked for everything I ever got!" But consider how freely you have received.

What about life itself? You didn't breathe the breath of the sweet-scented fields and gardens without first receiving life freely. How about receiving it back, when some illness threatened to take it from you? And the food to sustain it—who grew and marketed and prepared that? And the joys of arts, athletics, companionship—how could you say you had only what your work and effort had earned for you?

What about clothing and a home? Of course you were cared for in your infancy and youth. Can you say you have not freely received? Even now, could you build the house and provide the water, the power, the heat and light? You could not weave the cloth of all kinds and fashion it so well for yourself—you do receive freely an inestimable value of the work and effort of others.

What about your education, your learning? You have freely received (perhaps more than you wanted at the time) of the skills and the understanding, the language, and the numerical, business, scientific, psychological, and social knowledge that enable you to develop your life as you choose.

Consider also your salvation. It has never cost you anything except what you are better off without. Jesus freely died for you and gave you the fullness of eternal life.

III. "Freely give!" Once you understand that "justice" and "equality" and "fairness" have been far outdistanced by the grace and liberality of all that has been provided for you, you can no longer assert your independence and your right to ignore the needs of those around you. As you are a Christian, Christ says, "Freely you have received, freely give." If some "sacrifice" is involved, you may reject it on the ground that you've "got to live!" Is that the answer of a redeemed person? "I've got to live!" *Do* you? Think of the couple who, in serious dangers every day of their mission lives, when exhorted to leave the threats and the perils behind and come home to safety and "normal lives," responded, "We can die if need be, but we must do what God requires."

If fairness, justice, and security are what we prize, we are not the people Jesus took us for.—John R. Rodman

SUNDAY: JUNE TWENTIETH

SERVICE OF WORSHIP

Sermon: The Drama of Conversion

TEXT: Acts 9:1–22

The conversion of Saul is not the annual trek of the town drunk to the altar in the spring revival meeting. It is pure drama. Through the power of God, Christian enemy number one becomes apostle number thirteen. That is conversion! I assisted in a revival meeting during my last semester at Baylor University. Staying in the parsonage, experiencing the church in a village setting and a preview of life in pastoral ministry was excellent seminary preparation. A layman in the church had a big dinner for the revival team and church leaders. I happened to be seated across from our host. As we ate, he began to tell of the crass immorality of his life before he found Christ. I assumed that the confessional came from the spiritual high of our services until he came to the focus of his story: "Son, it took as much grace to save you as it did to save me." I still do not believe that my host intended to be insulting.

I. Human nature causes us to measure our lives by those around us and often leads to an unhealthy church game—"My conversion is more dramatic than yours."

My friend was slightly intimidated by my youthful piety. Little did he know that I was equally intimidated by his worldly experience. How would I ever convince people of their need of conversion with such a boring background. My repertoire of sin did not contain one felony. The man was right. At best (or worst), I was a petty sinner rescued from a puddle, while the truly great preachers had been in the pit.

II. Agonizing insecurities surface in the conversion of Saul. Is this the model for salvation? The story must be important to be told three times in Acts. Jewish apologist Hyam Maccoby argues that Paul rather than Jesus is the founder of Christianity and that the Damascus road conversion is the inaugural event. Here began the departure from Judaism. Saul is not a nice guy. He appears (7:58) just in time to tend the coats of the mob stoning Stephen to death. Then he is pictured (8:3) ravaging the church, "dragging off both men and women" and (9:1) "breathing threats and murder against the disciples of the Lord." Yet Paul's account of his own conversion sounds a note of integrity. Saul was "convinced that I ought to do many things against the name of Jesus" (26:9). Perhaps this upstart rabbi was not vicious so much as he was misdirected. Saul comes across as a consistent extremist. Moderation is not in his vocabulary. Whatever he does, whether persecution of the church or proclamation of the gospel, is done to the limit. Saul is radical to the core, and Paul is really a continuation of the same man, with one notable exception—the energy of his commitment has been totally redirected.

III. The Christian rebirth is always a continuation of the same person. The language of rebirth coupled with a new name seems to imply a total rejection of the former self and can be quite attractive to folks who do not like themselves. But the man and the memory are still intact. The word is redemption. God works with the person created at birth and developed through life. Christian conversion, the rebirth, is indeed a change in direction and destiny. The focus of commitment in life makes all of the difference. Saul demonstrates that even religion can be monstrous.

If Saul is an example of the power of God to redirect life toward the redemptive purpose of the kingdom, he is not only a model but a measure of conversion. When any religious experience becomes the legal standard by which authentic salvation is determined, we fall into the same distortion of faith which characterized Saul the persecutor. The fact remains, only Saul is Saul. We walk with God down similar paths, but no two people walk the same steps. To box and package any conversion experience denies our uniqueness before God and reduces our relationship with God to a cheap commodity. The personal quality of salvation is essential to the person you are. For good or ill, the world is fresh out of Sauls.

Jesus was in the home of Simon the Pharisee when a woman of the streets came into the picture. Simon was critical of the tolerance of Jesus for her lavish acts of bathing and anointing his feet. Through a parable, Jesus defined a distinction in individual experience which brings our picture into focus. The depth of love for God is in direct proportion to the degree of one's sense of forgiveness and grace. Being good, or at least thinking oneself good, has a demonic element more venomous than unpretentious immorality. Self-righteous Simon, like self-righteous Saul, loses all sense of his need of God, and the next worst step is to play the censorious role of a god to others.

Thirty years later I have not forgotten a layman's idea about God's grace. It was not his immoral experience that I needed, but the need of God. May God save us from our own goodness.—Larry Dipboye

Illustrations

DISHARMONY WITHIN.   If the truth be told, none of us has a good conscience. Whether we are aware of it or not, there is a fateful disharmony deep within our nature. "How can I get rid of my sins," cried Luther, "and get right with him who is of purer eyes than to behold iniquity?" And the answer became the watchword of the Reformation. Centuries later G. K. Chesterton explained why he took the reverse trail and became a Roman Catholic. He put it in six words: "To get rid of my sins. . . ." John Whale, recalling these two instances and commenting on them, observed, "If you know any history, if you know your own heart, you will not dismiss these moving words as morbid eccentricity." Indeed you will not!—Elam Davies

CONVERSIONS. Do not circumscribe God's power by saying it must come to you in a particular way. Many of us have envied the definiteness of another's religious experience. I believe God wants to come to you just as definitely, but he may want to do it in a different way.

A Lutheran minister I know traveled seventeen hundred miles to seek a conversion like his Methodist mother-in-law had. He admired her and her experience greatly. But he was reminded that God is not necessarily a Methodist! God gave him a rather quiet conversion, but a real one—I saw him twenty-five years later, still going strong.

Another man told me that at the time of his conversion from unbelief to faith in God, a blinding white light shone around him. But after that God seemed to lead him in quiet ways, sometimes not showing him until the last minute which way to go, and then with just the gentlest feeling to clarify the decision. The initiative lies with God all the time. All we have to do is to be open.—Sam Shoemaker

Sermon Suggestions

WAKING UP TO GOD. TEXT: Gen. 28:10–17. (1) We may go along in this life unseeing and unknowing, as far as God is concerned. (2) Then some unexpected events interrupts our practical atheism, and God becomes real. (3) Therefore, we should take this tide at its flood and go with it, or we, by exposing ourselves to the most favorable conditions, enter sooner into the most rewarding fellowship with God.

WHOSE SLAVE ARE YOU? TEXT: Rom. 5:12–19, NRSV.. (1) We as believers in Christ reject sin as a way of life. (2) One way or the other we are slaves—either of sin or of righteousness. (3) Becoming instruments of righteousness is possible because (a) we have been brought from death to life; (b) we are not under law but under grace; (c) our religion is a religion of the heart, more a matter of wanting to serve God than of having to serve him.

Worship Aids

CALL TO WORSHIP. "He was in the world, and the world was made through him, yet the world knew him not. He came to his own home, and his own people received him not. But to all who received him, who believed in his name, he gave power to become children of God" (John 1:10–12, RSV).

INVOCATION. O Lord, from whom earth is but one of many planets but of whom Christ Jesus is the unique savior of sinners; steal into our worship today with unusual insights and strong leadings. Make us as never before people of God, who worship in harmony and love.—E. Lee Phillips

OFFERTORY SENTENCE. "Now as you excel in everything—in faith, in utterance, in knowledge, in all earnestness, and in your love for us—see that you excel in this gracious work also" (2 Cor. 8:7, RSV).

OFFERTORY SENTENCE. Lord, bless these gifts our hands bring and these hymns our voices sing and these prayers our hearts pray and fill them with heavenly purposes for earthly good in God's own will and way.—E. Lee Phillips

PRAYER. Except for your mercy, O Father, none of us would be here this morning. In your love and mercy, you have followed us into the far country of our own willfulness and called us back home. We thank you that in the Father's house, in your house, there is bread enough and to spare. You hand to us a cup of grace that is not only full but running over. As the Divine Host you prepare a table for us not only in the presence of our friends but in the presence of our enemies—those enemies within—the doubts, the fears, the insecurities that would make cowards of us all. Even in the presence of these you provide sustenance—bread that is bread indeed and drink that is drink indeed that we may be strong and live.

For your Word in Christ that makes us wise unto salvation—that ministers wholeness—that mediates health, we are grateful. Thank you for your Word of grace that calls us to renewed commitment to be your church in this time and place.

We pray for ourselves that we may be faithful channels of your grace living for the sake of others in all of our relationships. We pray for each other, for we are members one of another. We pray for any weak among us who are wrestling with decisions that are difficult but right. We pray for the strong that they may be sensitive to and supportive of those needing encouragement. We pray for those physically ill or infirm, that they may experience a wholeness that even transcends health of body. We pray for those sick of soul that oneness—that atonement—that reconciliation which will enable them to homeness with you, with themselves, with all others.

With every week unraveling another skein of the web of subterfuge with which we have entangled ourselves in trying to seek advantage over others, we are not so sure that we are the "good guys" we have posed as being before the world. O merciful God, deliver us from the conceit by which we have but deceived ourselves. We all stand in the need of your grace; the ground is level at the foot of the cross. We pray for leadership that rules in fear of you—with awe and reverence for the true, with the wisdom to lead others, with a commitment to justice for all.

And now, O God, grant us wisdom, grant us courage, so that we may live as we have prayed, that we fail not man or you.—John M. Thompson

LECTIONARY MESSAGE

Topic: Avoiding Persecution by Conquering It
TEXT: Matt. 10:24–33

In this chapter, Jesus has been talking to his disciples about coming dangers, "discrimination," trials in men's councils, betrayal even by family members, and wholesale persecution of the kind that was aimed at Christian leaders by early communist dictators, who closed churches, killed priests and worshipers, and burned Bibles and prayer books.

Now he utters some principles of Christian life, some survival truths to help conquer fear and to maintain the courage Christians need to sustain morality today.

I. Christ teaches a true measure of human values. We cannot determine the correctness of the course of our lives until we determine the goal toward which we are traveling. If we do not place the value on life itself, we cannot evaluate any of its component elements.

(a) The disciples are reminded that Jesus shares their persecutions, as did the prophets before them (5:10–12). "They" have called the master of the house "Beelzebub." The servants can expect to receive what the master did, but they should have no fear on that account—the teacher and the student, the master and the servant, shall receive what they both seek, in the coming revelation to all the world of the lordship of Jesus and his representation of the Father in redeeming believers.

(b) The goal of all our living is to know that our souls are redeemed. The purpose of life is to live beyond it, whether still in it or after it ends. The power of God is as the Lord of life, the Creator of what shall not end, the One who can redeem both soul and body in heaven. The "fear of the Lord," the respect of him and confidence in his power, is what will remove our fear.

(c) People are important individually, as Jesus shows in comparing them to sparrows—sparrows whose falling is known to their heavenly Father. When he says, "Ye are of more value than many sparrows," he is saying in a telling understatement that the ruler of the universe attends to each one of his children in all his or her moments, moments of either triumph or defeat, or of ordinary work and care.

II. The purpose and goal of life being clear, we can then evaluate the course by which we shall reach it. Jesus sums it all up in his promise to confess before God all those who confess him before men. This is one of the secrets that are to be made public. Each one is required to open up his or her life to men and women nearby. If this involves judgment, then judgment must be administered by oneself so he or she may face the world fearlessly, claiming the redemption of Christ and confessing him, thus to be owned to by him.

(a) Then the course of life must be to live a constant confession, first in the family, where the identity with Christ will renew unselfishness, honesty, active help and encouragement, and the other fruits of the Spirit (Gal. 5:22, 23).

(b) The confession will be open in the school or workplace. Can we reinstate the idea, as a practical course, that belonging to Christ and confessing him involves turning one's back on some of the practices, minor or major, of dishonesty, deceit, and animosity that are common to school and business today?

(c) Can it also mean rejecting some of the harmful personal habits that will in the end victimize their practitioners but also be costly to society? If God "numbers the very hairs of our head" (I do *not* accept that as hyperbole), can *we* do less than eliminate what destroys our lives?

III. We must remember—"Whosoever shall deny me before men, him will I also deny before my Father which is in heaven."—John R. Rodman

SUNDAY: JUNE TWENTY-SEVENTH

SERVICE OF WORSHIP

Sermon: Becoming

TEXT: Luke 7:36–50

Lloyd Douglas, in his book *The Big Fisherman*, describes in language all too frank the reaction we sometimes have to Jesus. The story involves the life of Peter, the apostle, and his efforts to reject Jesus as an imposter form the plot around which the early part of the novel revolves. Listen to Douglas's description of Peter's attitude about Jesus.

Simon had found himself wishing that the Carpenter would be soon exposed as an ordinary man who had nothing much to work with but a winning voice, a confident manner, and the ability to make people listen to him—and trust Him.

How often have we met the words of Jesus with the very same attitude. Wishing that in fact Jesus were nothing more than an ordinary man whose words were not the Words of God and thus not a pattern for our life. Wishing that his example of life was nothing more than what he would call "filled with charisma" to the point that others would follow him.

But, alas, in our confrontations with him and his Word we soon find that he is no ordinary man who had nothing more than a winning voice, a confident manner, and the ability to make people trust him.

Our scripture text today is one of those places we might wish contained the words of an ordinary man. That way we would not have to concern ourselves with its troubling words or the power of its message.

In this passage, Jesus teaches us a fundamental element of the gospel message—what a person can become is more important than who he is, because the gospel penetrates to the deepest levels of human need. The most basic lesson of this incident from the life of Christ is that potential kingdom worth is far more important than worldly status. In other words, what a person can become is more this issue of Christian concern than who that person is upon meeting Jesus.

I. Other than Jesus, there are two main characters in this story. And it is from the examples of these two different people that Jesus teaches us this important lesson.

(a) The first is Simon, the Pharisee. He had reached the zenith of Judaism as a Pharisee. His knowledge of the Law would certainly go unquestioned. As a Pharisee, he likely had considerable social prominence in his community. The appearance of the story that Jesus tells leads one to believe that he was a man of wealth—a fine house with servants providing the meal would likely indicate that. And no doubt he was intelligent— Jesus asks him a question about forgiveness, and immediately he knew the answer.

And so our first character was much like we ourselves would like to be. He was a well-educated, socially prominent, Bible believing, upper-middle-class individual—what appears to be the ultimate goal of some of our religious approaches to God.

(b) The second character is a lowly woman, whose name we do not even know. In his ever cautious way, Luke simply introduces her as an "immoral woman"—a woman who was a sinner. Had Luke been as blunt as we are prone to be, he would likely have said "there was a woman who was a harlot—a streetwalker." Unlike Simon, she was probably uneducated, knew little of the Scriptures, and was certainly not socially prominent, at least for the right reasons.

Thus in contrast to Simon, our second character hardly rates a mention. She was poor, he was rich; she was an outcast, he was a part of the religious "in crowd"; she felt unworthy, he was very confident of his self-worth. In other words, she was filled with all the things that we often think would disqualify one from being a part of the kingdom of God.

II. The response of Jesus to these two characters teaches us that what a person can become is more important than who he is. That is, potential worth is far more important than worldly status.

(a) Jesus was not impressed with Simon, in spite of who Simon thought he was. Simon had provided Jesus with a fine meal, an invitation to a prominent household. But his motivation for inviting Jesus was not to see if he could serve Jesus but to see if Jesus had some flaw that would make it obvious that he was nothing more than an imposter.

The scene turns to Jesus, and with a touch of anger in his voice and perhaps his eyebrows raised just a little he says to Simon, "Simon, I have something to say to you."

Then in a voice dripping with the attitude of "I dare you to reprimand me," Simon says to Jesus, "Say it, teacher."

Jesus then makes it clear that Simon's meal was of no value to him. You see, Simon desperately needed to change— even though he considered himself so great. And Jesus saw his unwillingness to admit that, much less make such changes.

(b) But this lowly woman, who comes to Jesus, impresses him as a source in whom he can find real joy for the kingdom.

She had so little to commend her, except that she recognized her need to make changes in her life. We cannot even comprehend the personal risk she took just to be there. And once there, she offered him a gift of sacrifice, beyond her means to give.

To this poor woman Jesus said, "Your sins, though many, are forgiven."

III. What was the difference in these two which caused Jesus to have such a vastly different attitude toward them? Simon was proud of who he was. The woman was interested in what she could become! And what you can become is always more important than who you are. The reason that this was true is because of the nature of the gospel to reach to all level of human needs. And of course this means that our ability to serve Jesus is not based upon who we are but what we are willing to become.

(a) Look at the contrast in the service of these two.

(1) The lowly woman—a wretched, immoral woman—offers Jesus gifts of sacrifice. She brought an alabaster vial of perfume. She washed his feet with tears of regret about her life. And she dried them with her own hair, a woman's glory in that day. And what Jesus saw in her was a gift of sacrifice, of faith, of love. Her ability to serve Jesus was not stifled by the fact that she was coming from a life of sin. Rather it was enhanced by the fact that she was interested in what she could become.

(2) On the other hand, when we look at what Simon did—or, perhaps better, did not do—for Jesus a great contrast is obvious. Simon the Pharisee, a leader of Israel. Certainly one in whom we would expect to find great things. But his ability to offer acceptable service to Jesus was not enhanced by the fact that he was so religious.

Jesus says, "Simon, I came into your house, the house of a leader of Israel, and you did not even provide the common courtesies of life." You see, there was no water for his feet, no oil for his head, and no greeting of welcome for him. What Jesus saw in Simon was nothing more than a "sanctimonious fault finder" to use the words of A. B. Bruce.

Under his breath, Simon mutters, "IF he were a prophet, and I am sure he is not, he would never talk to this sinful woman, much less allow her to wash his feet." Instead of service, Simon's religious attitudes caused him to consider himself of more worth than this woman.

(b) It is crucial that we see the attitude Jesus expresses toward these two.

(1) To Simon, Jesus clearly points out the abject failure of religion that is characterized by a false piety, sanctimonious fault finding, and a general attitude of "I'm better than you are."

(2) To the woman, he says, "Go in peace, your sins are forgiven, your faith has made you whole." And this was in spite of the fact that she had come to him from such wretched circumstances.

The whole point is that one's position in life has nothing to do with whether or not we can come to Jesus, in faith, to find real meaning to life and to offer acceptable service to him. Even though Simon rejected her in the name of religion, Jesus found real joy in her interest in becoming.

(c) What was the difference? Was it okay for her to sin? Was her past life something which pleased Jesus? Was it wrong for Simon to be well educated, socially prominent, and a Bible believer? Not at all. Jesus was not happy about her past life, and there is nothing wrong with achievement in life.

The difference was that Simon was proud of who he was—was more interested in testing Jesus than changing his own attitudes and more interested in maintaining his piety than to risk helping this woman. And she, as wretched as she must have been, was ashamed of who she was; afraid of entering Simon's house; and afraid of standing before Jesus, who could read her heart; but excited about who she could become, once forgiven by Jesus.

Sometimes I think that we all wish that he had been an ordinary man. Then surely he would have known that the real hero of our story was Simon. For he was doing all the things that we seem to accept as standards of the faith: He was outwardly pious, religious, and sanctimonious. He had several real accomplishments under his spiritual belt.

And this woman was exactly the opposite. She was an immoral harlot—a sinner and certainly not worthy of our concern any more than she was worthy of Simon's concern.

Occasionally sanctimonious fault finding becomes a part of our lives. We get so wrapped up in our false piety, our religious attitudes that sinners come seeking our help only to find that we are too religious to be of much help.

In our quest for our church to grow—to reach beyond ourselves to those in need—who is our hero? Are we imitating Simon, who set such clear limits to those in need? Who is our hero? Are we imitating Simon, who set such clear limits to what he would do for God? Or do we imitate Jesus, who knew that what a person can become is far more important than who he is—because the gospel has power to reach to the very deepest levels of human need?

May Simon never be our hero!

And remember, these are not the words of an ordinary man!—Samuel W. Huxford

Illustrations

THE DIVINE ROMANCE.   It was the refusal of man to love the best that created the most difficult problem in the whole history of humanity, namely the problem of restoring man to the favor of Divine Love. In short, the problem was this: Man had sinned; but his sin was not merely a rebellion against another man but a revolt against the Infinite Love of God. Therefore his sin was infinite. But, it may be asked, since man is finite, how can he commit an infinite crime? The answer to that question is that an offense, an injury or a sin is always to be measured by the one sinned against. It would be, for example, a far greater offense to insult the mayor of a city than a citizen of that city, and it would be a greater offense to commit a crime against the governor of the state than against the mayor. In like manner, it would be a still greater offense to commit a felony against the President of the United States than against the governor of any state. In other words, sin is measured by the one sinned against. Man sinned against God. God is infinite. Therefore, man's offense is infinite.—Fulton J. Sheen

C. S. LEWIS'S CONVERSION.   You must picture me alone in that room in Magdalen, night after night, feeling, whenever my mind lifted even for a second from my work, the steady, unrelenting approach of him who I so earnestly desired not to meet. That which I greatly feared had at last come upon me. In the Trinity Term of 1929 I gave in and admitted that God was God and knelt and prayed: Perhaps, that night, the most dejected and reluctant convert in all England. I did not then see what is now the most shining and obvious thing: the Divine humility which will accept a convert even on such terms. The Prodigal Son at least walked home on his own feet. But who can duly adore that Love which will open the high gates to a prodigal who is brought in kicking, struggling, resentful, and darting his eyes in every direction for a chance of escape? The words *compelle intrare*, compel them to come in, have been so abused by wicked men that we shudder at them; but, properly understood, they plumb the depth of the Divine mercy. The hardness of God is kinder than the softness of men, and his compulsion is our liberation.—C. S. Lewis

Sermon Suggestions

WHY GOD STRUGGLES WITH US.   TEXT: Gen. 32:22–32. (1) Sometimes it brings a new awareness of God. (2) Sometimes it purges the inner life of old, festered moral impurities. (3) Always it is focused on the future, to prepare us for problems, duties, and opportunities that lie ahead.

THE DEEPER MEANING OF BAPTISM. TEXT: Rom. 6:3–11. (1) It means that you are united with Christ, that you share everything with him. (2) It means that you reject once and for all the kind of life you might live apart from Christ. (3) It means that your new life of faith is made alive to God by the very power that raised Christ from the dead.

Worship Aids

CALL TO WORSHIP.   "Clothe yourselves, all of you, with humility toward one another, for 'God opposes the proud, but gives grace to the humble' " (1 Pet. 5:5b, RSV).

INVOCATION.   Have mercy upon us, O Lord, and look with favor on our worship, for we are a sinful people and are often blinded by our temptations. Give us clarity of mind today and fortitude of purpose to do as God leads and live to love.—E. Lee Phillips

OFFERTORY SENTENCE. "And he said unto them, Take heed, and beware of covetousness: for a man's life consisteth not in the abundance of the things which he possesseth" (Luke 12:15).

OFFERTORY PRAYER. As we give this day, O Lord, teach us the quiet rewards of Christian stewardship and the joys of serving a caring God.—E. Lee Phillips

PRAYER. Gracious God, we give you thanks for summer's opportunities for time together: parents and adult children; children and grandparents; parents and children; simple things done together; news exchanged.

Be with families whose wells have run dry: who of such life feel spectators; be with families burdened with grief or brokenness or sickness or any sort of anxiety.

Help us, in good days and bad, to turn to the underground streams of hidden strength; to turn, in sober reflection, to the quiet waters of a new day; and, in all things, to turn in faith, hope, and love.

Through the merits of our blessed Savior, we pray.—Peter Fribley

LECTIONARY MESSAGE

Topic: Not Peace, But a Sword
TEXT: Matt. 10:34–42

I. Jesus has long borne the title Prince of Peace. Yet here, in his own words, is his denial that peace is his purpose. The conflict he brings involves family relationships, setting young against old; it involves life's work or vocation, building the cross into every transaction; it affects a person's entire life, life itself, all the pointless, purposeless pursuit of pure pleasure.

What is the sword that Jesus brings? It is the sword which will pierce not the body but the soul (Luke 2:35; Jer. 4:10), the sword of judgment between the eternal and the temporal; it is the sword which cannot be quiet or be put away (Jer. 47:6, 7) as long as its charge is unfulfilled. It is the sword of the Spirit, the Word of God (Eph. 6:17).

II. Jesus is telling us all that we cannot make peace with the world as we find it. Consider recently publicized scandals: Congressmen overdrawing personal bank accounts (even with their recently elevated salaries); prominent celebrities disclosing early lives as victims of sexual abuse (surely cause to set daughter against father and mother); the chief executive officer of a public program to house the needy taking a huge income; robbery and burglary and random murders permeating every city and suburb; and remaining practices of cruelty, unfairness, and victimization based on the accidental properties of race or color or national origin. Jesus is telling us all that the sword must be taken up, that peace must be broken, in a world like this.

III. Jesus has set the course and blazed the trail—we must follow him. Each of us may have peace with God through our Lord Jesus Christ, approaching the Father in family grace, as we cross the bridge of Christ's cross. Now, we must live "confessing him."

We must approach the question of what life is all about—the life that by saving, we lose, or by losing for Christ's sake, we save. It is well known that this life "consists not in the abundance of things possessed" (Luke 12:15). It is not well practiced as the truth. We have seen bumper stickers proclaiming, "He who dies with the most toys, wins." Sadly, it must be acknowledged that many of us live with that attitude and practice that philosophy, the hedonism long ago discredited by serious thinkers. Our hedonistic calculus cannot conclude that making peace with pain is the best that a Christian can do. In fact, the calculus itself, the very accounting of the balance of pleasure and pain, is so distracting, so consciousness-consuming as to defeat the living of a Christian life, the life of disturbance of the peace in a wicked world. The sword must be struck against extreme self-centeredness as well as against cruelty and hate. The only peace one can achieve in this live is to live it unselfconsciously doing the best in one's work, learning the most in one's study, helping the most people through one's confession, to find the peace that Jesus did bring. The selfless service of God is the secret to ending self-slavery.—John R. Rodman

SUNDAY: JULY FOURTH

SERVICE OF WORSHIP

Sermon: As Free—As the Servants of God

TEXTS: 1 Pet. 2:16; Luke 21:25–26; Rom. 15:4–13

If it's Peter himself who is saying here that you are not to make your freedom an excuse for doing anything that's wrong, it's because he has learned the hard way that Christian freedom always has its limitations: You are only as free as the servants of God; no less, no more.

I. What does it mean in the Bible to be free? Back of the word, of course, and back of a dozen kindred words, lies the thought of humanity's terrible wrestling with some kind of bondage.

(a) A dozen variants of the theme provide the subject matter of the Greek tragedies. For the Jew, the symbol of it was that faraway hateful slavery in Egypt. Every year at the Passover, as the story of the Exodus was handed down from father to son, God's mighty act of redemption kept repeating itself, buying a man back from under the lash of his taskmaster, striking off his shackles, bringing him up out of his exile and home again. He couldn't forget it or ever stop talking about it. It was the very pattern of his history, and it would go on being that forever. Without it life never had made or could make any sense!

(b) So he killed the thing he loved. It's the undying tragedy of man's existence. The privilege he had by God's gift, he tried to possess. Like an ancestral estate, it had come down to him from his fathers: What was to keep him from building a fence around it and posting some rules and living on the inside of his heritage with the Almighty? The New Testament tells what happened when God broke through. It wasn't easy to understand a man who paid no attention to the fence and went around outside as well as inside healing the brokenhearted, preaching deliverance to the captives, and setting at liberty them that were bruised. Certainly you couldn't call the Jews any of these things. They were the children of Abraham. Then get this fellow out of the way! He was an offense. They weren't safe with him around.

(c) And that's exactly how it is from beginning to end. Here is the secret of the only freedom the Bible knows anything about: It comes of an appalling insecurity! You destroy it when you try to acquire it; you lose it when all you want to do is to keep it! It doesn't mean that suddenly, in the twinkling of an eye, you are rid of anything on the day's agenda. You haven't been snatched away from the blood and the sweat and the tears, on the beaches, across the fields, and in the streets. There hasn't been any Shangri-la for anybody I know, where the tumult and the shouting die. There's nothing but the eternal faithfulness of a God who offers himself to you in Jesus Christ, up to the head of the nails! Then what kind of business would you suppose might be afoot if that's what it is that happens? Nothing but a skirmish somewhere off among the hills or a bit of a scuffle in a back alley?

II. When the Bible insists that whoever you are, whatever the past, you are this day set free, it means that for the first time in your life perhaps you are free to fight your way through all that, rid of everything that would narrow your life down to what it has been or hem it in with what you call its possibilities.

(a) Give the enemy what name you like beyond flesh and blood, speak of principalities and power; but know that the odds are no longer over there; they are over here, where you are. It's a battle that's been won, and that you never have to lose. The question is, do you realize that, and do you ever thank God for it?

(b) We sometimes talk about our literature of defeat and would like to have you understand that it's far too pessimistic. I submit that it isn't pessimistic enough. It's only half the picture. To be caught in a steel vise is bad; it's worse to be caught in a steel vise without having to be! We are sufficiently familiar in our day with men and women, not always on the stage or in some novel, who are desperately unhappy, laboring under some anxiety, weighed down by some sense of guilt, wanting to be what they are not and are afraid they never can become before death overtakes them; and we are asked on all sides to believe that they are typical of our generation—people held fast in the grim jaws of Fate.

III. But right here the Bible holds up its hand, like a traffic officer at the corner, and the light turns yellow, then red. In the lessons we are brought face-to-face with two very specific situations which seem to limit still further this already strangely limited freedom of ours, even to negate it. Let's look at them. The epistle is taken from the fifteenth chapter of Romans, the fourth through the thirteenth verses. The one point which Paul is driving home throughout the letter is that nothing can hamper us now, no law that has to be obeyed if we are to achieve some status before God, no rules that have to be followed if we want to share in this new order of things under the lordship of Christ: when suddenly here toward the end he seems to throw everything into reverse! Just when we are about ready to say that we have begun to understand something of the freedom that is ours in the gospel, he appears to reach out for it and take it all back.

(a) And to our surprise the Epistle to the Romans begins to dispute its own point of view. The freedom of God begins to provide us with chains. Listen! We who are strong are to bear the burdens of the weak. There it is, cramping our style. We are to be like-minded, one toward another, receiving one another as Christ also received us; not to please ourselves, because Christ did not please himself. What does that do, if it doesn't hedge us about? It reads like the denial, the utter impoverishment of the self. It reads in a word like the bankruptcy of freedom.

(b) But wait a minute. The burden that's being laid on us is the burden of love, and what if there were not freedom for you anywhere once you get out from under that? In his play *No Exit*, Sartre says that hell is—other people. And the New Testament goes on saying, "Ah, God pity us, but there is no other heaven!" It's the simplest fact of all and the hardest that what seems to hedge in these little selves of ours is the only thing that can enlarge them. The very lives around us which so often we feel to be closing in upon us are many a time the only offers of escape that are held out to us. And never think you won't be reminded of it, over and over again.

(c) To be free is to plunge into human life, "up to the elbows," without looking at the price tag or wondering about the payoff. To take inside what's outside, never mind how much it hurts; and to see fewer things out there and more faces. Something had happened to the inside of the poet who on an autumn evening "saw the ruddy moon lean over a hedge like a red-faced farmer," while all about "were the wistful stars with white faces, like town children." The moon and the stars were a farmer and the village teacher's brood!

IV. And there once more the Bible holds up its hand, and the traffic we've just got going again grinds to a full stop, this time in front of the Gospel that was read. It's a magnificent panorama: "And there shall be signs in the sun and in the moon and in the stars; and upon the earth distress of nations, with perplexity; the sea and the waves roaring"—to the Jew that was the symbol of primeval chaos—"men's hearts failing them for fear and for looking after those things which are coming on the earth: for the powers of heaven shall be shaken." No doubt the disciples thought Jesus was talking about his coming again at the end of the world.

(a) For me the more meaningful question is this: When it's a matter of believing, why try to stop with the Second Coming, when Christ comes again in every event that overtakes human life? In any case, to get back to the point, what we have here is something surely which negates everything that even looks like freedom. When all that's steady in your world reels round like a drunken man—and that does happen: there are times when you don't have to press the figure very far, if indeed it is a figure. When all that's solid enough to lean on dissolves, who on earth can be free? That cancels everything!

(b) Why then at the precise moment when this unbelievable tumult rises to its climax does Christ assert that by the right arm of God instead of canceling everything it establishes everything? "When these things begin to come to pass, then look up and lift up your heads; for your redemption draweth nigh!" You have run into that nevertheless of God which is the very ground of your freedom. Where else will you come upon it if not in the hour when you realize that all this which we name life is under the shattering, reshaping hand of God?

(c) How else can God protect us, asks Karl Barth, than by reminding us constantly of death and so just as constantly directing us toward life? How else can he protect us from the kind of faith which smugly hails the "breakdown of secular thought" as the one sure way to religious revival? How else can he protect us from beliefs that "you can put in your pocket"? From a religion that wants to buy all the "promises cheaply"? How else can he drive us out of the "petty trivialities . . . in which men are normally imprisoned" and so make us "free to apprehend what is certain and living and eternal"? "When these things begin to come to pass, then look up." Here is no negation of any man's freedom; this may well be the final affirmation of it: when he finds out for himself what it is he cannot lose.

V. Only then can the meaning of this text come whole—not one half of it, but both halves: "As free—as the servants of God." What is strangest of all is that Peter found it no hardship any longer to end the verse like that. He wasn't pulling out a sword now to hack his way into freedom or denying his Lord in order to

break his way into it. It didn't seem to be just a gift either: you couldn't "butter your toast with it." It had arrived down a long, hard road. But as he got ready to sign his letter, with martyrdom perhaps not too far off, there was a benediction on his lips. Shall we let him pronounce it on us, let it settle down on our hearts wherever it will? It isn't for people who are any longer in prison.—Paul Scherer

Illustrations

FREEDOM AND RESPONSIBILITY. Man is condemned to be free. Condemned, because he did not create himself, yet is nevertheless at liberty, and from the moment that he is thrown into this world he is responsible for everything he does.—Jean Paul Sartre

FREEDOM AND LOYALTY. What have been the great hours of our lives, rememberable to our dying day? They are the hours when we were carried out by ourselves by something that mastered us—the breath-taking sweep of great mountains, the spell of great music, inner dedication to a cause concerning which we said, Not my will, thine be done, or the love of some person to whom we pledged deathless fidelity, "to have and to hold from this day forward, for better for worse, for richer for poorer, in sickness and in health, to love and to cherish, till death us do part." It is our loyalties that make life worth living.—Harry Emerson Fosdick

Sermon Suggestions

THE WAYS OF GOD'S PROVIDENCE. TEXT: Exod. 1:6–14, 22–2:10. (1) God's providence faces overwhelming odds. (2) God's providence at last prevails with overwhelming results.

OUR INNER WARFARE. TEXT: Rom. 7:14–25a. (1) *Situation:* Every true believer, deep down, wants to do God's will. (2) *Complication:* Conflicting desires are also present and cause guilt, discouragement, and despair. (3) *Resolution:* Through Jesus Christ, God forgives sin, gives courage and hope, and at last delivers us from every trace of sin.

Worship Aids

CALL TO WORSHIP. "Peter began: 'I now see how true it is that God has no favorites, but that in every nation the man who is godfearing and does what is right is acceptable to him' hin/'" (Acts 10:34–35, NEB).

INVOCATION. Today, O God, grant that we may see that your grace is for everyone, regardless of race or nation and that we all are duty-bound in love to do what is right.We thank you for the coming of our Lord Jesus Christ to show us the way, to reveal to us the truth, and to impart to us the life that is abundant.

OFFERTORY SENTENCE. "Set your mind on God's kingdom and his justice before everything else, and all the rest will come to you as well" (Matt. 6:33, NEB).

OFFERTORY PRAYER. Forgive us, O Lord, for living our lives upside down, putting material considerations above spiritual foundations. Give us the faith to see that in your will can be found all that we need and more.

PRAYER. Almighty God, we remember our nation's failures: We remember our wars. Fiercely proud, we honor those who have defended our liberties, bearing the burden of battle. We, a nation of immigrants, cherish the good fortune that we are here.

Yet somewhere deep within we are troubled. Our native-born poor haunt us. Closed factories, closed chapters, closed dreams. The drawn and listless faces of our low-paid friends bespeak the human price of sterile policy. Our offers of arms make a mockery of those who are starving and beg for food; the brutality of our allies turns us pale; and somewhere deep within, in the inner recesses of our finest selves, we dimly know that because of us, in lands we scarce can name, people die.

Grant us, O God, the fairness loyally to own the best we have done but the grace to grieve, that through repentance we may grow and find a better way, and that the wretched of the earth may be blessed with fairness and take heart.—Peter Fribley

LECTIONARY MESSAGE

Topic: The Insufficiency of Wisdom and Knowledge

TEXT: Matt. 11:25–30

I. This day memorializes that day, July 4, 1776, when our forefathers felt strong enough to declare collective independence from the government of George III, king of Great Britain. That independence of political sovereignty was fully realized after a long and trying war and was established through representative consultations and formation of a constitution that has guided our nation from 1789 to this day.

Our nation's independence economically and socially has developed on a set of great principles and on an exceptionally great store of natural resources of water, forest, wildlife, and mineral deposits waiting to be developed by the industrial and scientific age. So great has been the contribution of basic science to our strength of invention and engineering that many have been led to apotheosize science at the expense of spiritual faith.

II. It is true that a large proportion of the life we enjoy is due to contributions of science. Medicine is one science whose wonders never cease, saving formerly hopelessly ill patients from formerly unconquerable diseases and injuries. We should be foolish indeed to think we could go back to a previous unscientific age and live without it.

Do we, therefore, have trouble-free cities and towns? Do we have a high degree of satisfaction among all our population? Are we free of disease, crime, poverty, ignorance, racial strife, unemployment, fear, and anxiety? We can only launch more scientific studies, but the problems increase faster than the solutions.

Great philosophies have come and gone, to be superseded by other more sophisticated explanations of and rules for right living in a complex world.

Both science and philosophy, full as they are of promise and much as is hoped for from them, are empty of satisfaction. The understanding of life is somehow bound up to knowledge of eternity. For time and its demands can be truly evaluated or appreciated only in terms of eternity.

The understanding of the kingdom of God encompasses time and eternity, interprets life in terms of eternal life, and guides the present in the light of Jesus' revelation of the future. We shall never be independent until we are dependent on Jesus Christ.

III. Somehow, the unsophisticated, unworldly-wise, fresh and open-minded people have an advantage in receiving Jesus' revelation. Jesus declares that his Father, the Lord of heaven and earth, has kept the truths Jesus proclaimed throughout his teaching and healing ministry hidden from the wise and understanding and revealed them unto children. The scribes and rabbis, the tradi-

tional keepers of Israel's storehouse of truth and wisdom, have so encumbered their minds that their spirits cannot be open.

The "babes" are saved by their ignorance. Thereby they escape the mental preoccupation with preconceived ideas on moral and religious subjects which set the scribes beyond Christ's influence.

Even in our great sciences, momentous discoveries are made by those whose experience is so limited that they do not know what cannot be done or what will not work. They proceed with steps that lead them into fresh, new understandings and insights. So spiritual insight, such that souls may be at peace and may rest amid turmoil and trepidation, comes to those who simply accept it as Jesus gives it. While the world seeks for happiness and pursues it relentlessly, Jesus gives to the soul and spirit a resting place that perpetually yields joy. He reveals that rest is not in a bed, is not a cessation of bodily movement, but is in a trusting spirit, full of God's truth through Jesus Christ.—John R. Rodman

SUNDAY: JULY ELEVENTH

SERVICE OF WORSHIP

Sermon: The Rolling Thunder

TEXTS: Psalm 29; Matt. 8:23–27

A description of a storm and the calm after the storm can be a description of our world and our lives. Caught in the midst of a storm—whether personal or political, whether of our own doing or seemingly out of our control, all too often we are buffeted by the storms of life, by the consequences of our actions, by events which seem to spiral us into an uncertain future and raise questions about whether we must struggle alone in life.

I. The psalm, interestingly, begins not with the storm or its aftermath but with our relationship with God. And that is important, is it not, for that is where all of life begins and where our response to the tumult of life begins.

(a) "Ascribe to the Lord, ascribe to the Lord glory and strength, ascribe to the Lord the glory due his name, worship the Lord in the splendor of his holiness."

The affirmation is that all begins and ends in God. It is to God that our glory and worship and praise belong. And certainly it is there that our walk with him must begin and be centered.

(b) The psalmist reminds us that at the center of our life, at the beginning must be our relationship with God.

Now I know that at any time in our life we can strike up a relationship with God. That's really what Jesus Christ offers to us—but if we find ourself in the midst of a storm, buffeted from all sides by wind, rain, lightening, and thunder, it is a bit more difficult to find God than if we are walking with him all the way.

In Genesis we read, "In the beginning—God." That's exactly how the

Bible begins—in the beginning, God. It is assumed that God is where you begin, and everything develops from there.

II. The psalmist then moves to the description of the storm. He likens the thunder to the voice of God. And he compares the rolling thunder to the power and majesty of God. Certainly we know that a thunderstorm can be powerful—in both positive and negative ways.

(a) That power is positive. In the power of a storm, the pressures of the atmosphere are released; in the power of a storm old trees are uprooted that new may take their place; in the power of a storm rain so badly needed by the earth and its inhabitants is given; in the power of the storm as trees are removed paths of sunlight open to replenish other plants and make paths and openings.

(b) The psalmist reminds us that God's power can be judgmental as well as a blessing.

He breaks the cedars of Lebanon—tall powerful trees which live for generations, yet can be felled by a mighty wind.

He strikes with flashes of lightening. The palm tree outside of our house was struck and killed. Lightening goes for the highest object—a reminder to consider how we view ourselves and our position in life and how much more vulnerable we become the higher we ascend.

The voice of the lord shakes the desert, it twists the oaks, it strips the forests bare.

God, whom we proclaim as a loving, forgiving God, is a God of judgment, a God who suffers and agonizes over us when we turn our backs on him, when we exalt ourselves instead of him, when we put other things or people or objects at the center of our lives.

III. And yet, in that last verse we read, "He twists the oaks and strips the forest bare, and in his temple, the people all cry—GLORY!" Here we find the pivotal line on which this whole psalm turns: "and the people cry—GLORY!"

(a) That glory is more powerful than the crash of thunder, the sweep of the wind, or the flood of the rains. For you see, this psalm, which is written in the midst of a storm, which is given to us for times like these when we seem to be in the midst of personal and global storms which create uncertainty and threaten our safety, the psalmist adds this rainbow arch over this psalm of the storm: "The Lord sits enthroned over the flood, the Lord is enthroned as king forever."

You will remember that the psalm began with God, and so in the midst of the storm, and after the storm it ends with God.

"The Lord gives strength to his people, the Lord blesses his people with peace."

(b) Now, how is that peace offered? Only through Jesus Christ our Lord. In John 14:27 we read, "Peace I leave with you, my peace I give to you. I do not give to you as the world gives. Do not let your hearts be troubled, and do not be afraid."

Does God speak to you in the midst of the storm? Do you see that into the storm of the world, God sent Jesus Christ? As Jesus Christ stilled the storm on the sea of Galilee, so too, as he who rides above the storm, he too can give us peace within ourselves—not eliminating the storms, for they are a part of God's Creation, but teaching us how to listen to the thunder and discern God's will and love for us, through the peace which is ours in Christ Jesus.

IV. How you listen to the thunder, how you respond to the gift of God in Jesus Christ is your decision. But the opportunity is yours to respond if you will allow Christ to become the center of your life and to offer you peace through knowing that in him we are the Lord's and nothing can happen to us that will separate us from his love in Christ.— Kenneth D. MacHarg

Illustrations

COURAGE FOR TODAY. Stout hearts are not easy to keep. All of us have problems: sickness, death, defeat, disillusionment, financial difficulties; until existence seems to be nothing but struggle. But it has never been placid and never will be. It is like a ship which puts down its anchors against the gale and the currents dragging us on the rocks. All is well so long as the anchors hold, but when one gives way as the tempest is at its height, hope begins to desert us. Mustering our courage, we put down another anchor somewhere else and again the ship drags. When we think we have the ship fast, a current unfelt when we anchored to the bottom of life comes against the bow of our boat. We thought we were turned toward the open sea where we would be safe, but when the treacherous current hits our craft, no mariner is able to cope with the disaster.—Preston Bradley

NEVERTHELESS.   It's a word that carries the tang of high adventure, reckless valor, and the faith that overcomes the world.

"If it be possible," prayed Jesus, "let this cup pass—nevertheless. . . ."

"We are creatures of blind fate," growls the cynic, "and it's silly to look for divine guidance." "Nevertheless," replies the voice of faith, "we are in our Father's care."

"You cannot change God's plans for you," shouts the cynic. "Your prayers are ridiculous." "Nevertheless," replies the confident voice, "I shall continue to ask in faith, believing."

"What's this nonsense about finding prosperity by giving one's hard-earned things away," sneers the cynic, "and winning battles by refusing to fight—and seeking a crown by bearing a cross?" "Nevertheless," answer the adventurers. "Nevertheless."

"You have fished the shoals all your life," shout the fishermen. "You know there's nothing out there in the dark water." "Nevertheless," says Simon, "at his word I will lower the net."—Lloyd C. Douglas

Sermon Suggestions

THE PEOPLE GOD HAS TO WORK WITH. TEXT: Exod. 2:11–22. (1) Where Moses was right: He identified with his people, wanted to help them and was ready to do something for them. (2) Where Moses was wrong: He resorted to violence to achieve his ends and did not wait for God to act. (3) Nevertheless, God was even

then preparing Moses for future leadership.

BECAUSE YOU ARE GOD'S CHILD.   TEXT: Rom. 8:9–17. (1) The Spirit of Christ dwells in you. (2) This Spirit works in you now to achieve righteousness. (3) This Spirit promises you future life in union with the risen Christ. (4) Meanwhile, when you, in the company of your fellow believers, cry "Abba! Father!" you receive confirmation that you are truly one of God's children, with all of the blessings that that includes.

Worship Aids

CALL TO WORSHIP.   "My heart is ready, ready, O God, for song and melody" (Ps. 57:7, Moffatt).

INVOCATION.   In this time of worship, O Lord, strengthen our hearts to do your will. Cleanse us of our sins by your forgiving grace, and help us to know fullness of joy in praising you.

OFFERTORY SENTENCE.   "If ye will obey my voice indeed and keep my covenant, then ye shall be a peculiar treasure unto me above all people: for all the earth is mine, and ye shall be unto me a kingdom of priests and a holy nation" (Exod. 19:5–6a).

OFFERTORY PRAYER.   Thank you, Lord, for the privilege that you give us to be of special service to you as we are of service to the world, to pray for that world and to share with that world the unsearchable riches of Jesus Christ the Savior.

PRAYER.   In these days, confronted with the contradictions of men and of nations, we do not find it easy to appear before you. Surely to pray now is to pray for your mercy. May we be careful how we pray lest our prayers deny the faith we have again confessed in this holy place. In our saner moments we realize we can have no audience with you except we bring our brother and sister with us, for you are the God and Father of us all. There is no more insightful word declared by prophet, priest, and Messiah than this. This is your Word declared from the beginning and now present in the Word becoming flesh in Jesus of Nazareth. We pray that your strong Word, mighty to save, will deliver humankind from the peril of this hour, that all peoples may know life not death. It is your Word which from the beginning brings order out of chaos and is our only hope in every generation.—John Thompson

LECTIONARY MESSAGE

Topic: The Grace of Hearing Ears

TEXT: Matt. 13:1–9, 18–23

I. The implication of verse 9 is that *some do not* have the necessary "ears" for hearing Jesus or that some with ears will receive sounds but will not perceive intelligently the import of those sounds. Many questions necessarily arose from Jesus' exhortation, as well as from the parable itself. The question dealt within the verses between the parable and its explanation is that of the purpose of parabolic preaching. Questions from this statement itself needed to be answered as part of Jesus' intention. Why, indeed, does he teach in parables, knowing that many will not see beneath the surface?

His exhortation is an indication that there is a hidden meaning to be found. What about those who think that the story is simply an entertainment or, at most, a helpful hint to farmers to be careful where they sow their precious seed? There must be many who have not gone beyond literalism in the hearing of stories, who never think to look for meanings or interpretations other than the obvious.

There used to be a saying about people's understanding of life that went something like this: "He who knows and knows that he knows is wise; follow him. He who knows and knows not that he knows is asleep; awaken him. He who knows not and knows that he knows not is ignorant; teach him. He who knows not and knows not that he knows not is a fool; shun him." This story is about the spiritually wise or asleep or ignorant and the spiritually foolish.

II. We cannot say that Jesus implied his indifference toward those whose indifference he could not overcome; we can conclude that he faced the fact of human nature that some will not see their need and will refuse help when it is proffered. Are we to think that God himself gave up on them and that they were reprobate eternally or that they themselves were somehow responsible for their condition? By his citation of Isa. 6:9, Jesus seems to intend a judgment against those who from long ago, by deliberate choice, have closed their own organs of spiritual perception against God's truth. They are a continual challenge to the gospel of Jesus' salvation, which is adequate for any and all but effective only for those who will hear and respond. David Dickson, a great preacher and teacher of the time of the Scottish covenants, writes, "There is an affected and voluntary blindnesse of minde, and hardnesse of heart, which men draw on by custome of sinning" (*Exposition of Matthew* [London: 1647], 195).

III. Jesus says, "Hear ye therefore the parable of the sower." Jesus knew also that there were many who would see that a deeper meaning lay beneath the surface of the words. They could be persuaded and stirred up to study, to understand, and to make use of what was spoken. To carry the analogy with the parable, they were soil that could be worked with, that could be cleared and weeded and nurtured to become, if not already, "good soil." They were those who "had ears to hear." They included, and still include, the disciples, for whom Jesus had a clear interpretation. They had enough faith to ask for help, knowing it was needed and that Jesus was willing and eager to impart it to them. To those who see the need and who ask, Jesus gives a full explanation. Dickson again says, "Whosoever get grace to turn from their sins, to repent and to believe in Jesus Christ, are not given over to a reprobate sense, but shal surely be saved; for while he saith, He will not grant them grace to hear and understand; that is, to believe and repent least they should be healed, he importeth, that if they did believe and repent, they behoved undoubtedly to be healed; the exercise of Faith and Repentance being infallibly markes of saving grace."—John R. Rodman.

SUNDAY: JULY EIGHTEENTH

SERVICE OF WORSHIP

Sermon: When Faith Falters

Text: Ps. 77:1–15

When someone tells me that he has never had a moment of probing religious doubt I find myself wondering whether he has ever known a moment of vital religious conviction. For if one fact stands out above all others in the history of religion, it is this: The price of a great faith is a great and continuous struggle to get it, to keep it, and to share it. I know of no exception to this rule among those whose religious faith has changed the course of history. That is why it is a serious mistake to think of faith as a placid lake under the bewitching beauty of the full moon. It is much more like the ocean in storm, the swift current of the full river where one must stay alert if he would stay alive. Faith is a fight as well as peace. Faith is a purpose making headway against a storm, adjusting itself to the swiftly rushing current of life and events. The cost of faith is high, but no higher than we should expect it to be when we consider what it means to us.

Those who want a placid faith in seven easy lessons will want to stay clear of the Seventy-seventh Psalm. For it is one of our most vivid pictures of a devout man fighting to steady a faltering faith. It can teach us so much about the meaning of faith that it deserves a close look.

I. The first and most common reason why faith falters is the one we see in the experience of the psalmist: the occurrence of some tragic event that contradicts or challenges the promises of faith.

(a) Paul's ancestral faith faltered before the steady witness of the early Christians, particularly the stoning of Stephen. He was forced to rethink it, and it simply did not stand up under the ordeal. The early church was puzzled by the Crucifixion of Christ. For half a century after this had happened it looked like a defeat, and

Christians were forced to do some of their steadiest thinking about it in order to fit it into the pattern of Christian victory.

(b) In our own lives, the death of a loved one or the defeat of our nation or cause can force our faith to falter. All such events raise doubts about the accuracy of traditional beliefs in the love and the goodness of God. I think it safe to say that faith is faltering all over the world today because of the tragic and unpredictable character of events.

(c) Wherever we turn in a breaking and broken world we find faith faltering and asking, "Hath God forgotten to be gracious? Is his lovingkindness clean gone forever? Will he be favorable no more?"

II. A second reason why faith falters is the discovery that traditional religious ideas no longer fit our new experiences. The very nature of life makes it almost inescapable.

(a) How true we find this to be in the simple process of growing up! There is no way we can begin life with so adequate a system of ideas that our experience does not change them. The wisdom of our parents, while helpful, is not infallible. It can steady us, but it cannot remove the elements of conflict and uncertainty from our life. Yet it is a jar when first we discover their inadequacy, discover that our parents are far from infallible and that we must make our own decisions and find our own way into the future.

(b) This is no new experience for our religious tradition. Two of the great heroes of early Christianity, Paul and Origen, went through the twilight period of faltering doubt on their way to a greater faith for themselves and for those who were to come after them. Each had been born and nurtured in one tradition and had found that that tradition was seriously challenged by the new Christian faith. It could not have been an easy

SUNDAY: JULY EIGHTEENTH 131

struggle for them to modify the old and accept the new, but both did it.

(c) Wherever we turn, then, in this matter of living, we find there is some evidence for the generalization that the heresy of yesterday is likely to be the orthodoxy of today and the outmoded good of tomorrow. This progression does not proceed smoothly, like an escalator. It goes by fits and starts, with doubt and faltering faith in evidence all along the way, especially at points of greatest growth.

III. When faith falters, what do we do? What can we do?

(a) Although our first and strongest temptation is to retreat from the challenge to an earlier and stronger position, we have no real alternative to moving steadily ahead through the clouds of lowering doubt, suffering, and hardship in search of an even greater faith than we have ever known. Paul could have bowed off the stage of history when he lost faith in Judaism. He could have returned to Tarsus and spent his life making tents and staying well within the limits of traditional thoughts and ways. Had he done so, we would have lost our best example of the sheer power of faith in God.

(b) It will be easier for us to gird up our energies for this move ahead if we recall for a moment our indebtedness to those experiences when faith faltered.

We owe the book of Job to a series of men over several generations whose faith in the providence of God faltered in the presence of evil in the world. We owe most of the Old Testament to men whose faith faltered not once but many times as they experienced or recalled the tragedies and defeats in Hebrew history. We owe the New Testament to men whose faith in ancestral ideas faltered before the challenge of Christian ideas and experiences. We owe the Reformation to men whose faith under severe challenge pushed beyond the inadequate systems of thought and institutions in which they had been reared to more adequate ones that they passed on to us.

IV. There come times—not one but many—for all when faith falters. It is as universal an experience, I suspect, as we

shall find in religion. There are times when we outgrow traditional ideas—not all of them at any one time, to be sure, but some of them are certain to be challenged by every great experience that hits us or our generation.

(a) It is always a disturbing experience to have our traditional faith challenged by new facts and experiences. Yet there is no escape from it—not even that offered by a kind of automatic dogmatism that seems to be coming into favor these days. We have been treated to a number of public instances in which people have taken refuge from doubt in the fortress of traditional authority in religion. They profess to find steadiness of soul in accepting the teachings of some one church or sect. They shout triumphantly, "This is it!"

(b) Institutions as well as people face times when they must turn from traditional policies and answers in order to meet the problems of the present more adequately. Every reader of Christian history can cite a dozen times when the church has had to do this. I have never known a time when the church, trying as she is to minister to a broken world, needed to have a greater sense of freedom and flexibility to move in new directions than now. Neither man nor any one church liveth unto itself alone any more. The leaders we need will know that it will take big keys, the biggest we have, to open the locked doors of a better future. The lock on the door of fear is great, but it can be opened with the key of trust. The lock on the door of greed is great, but it can be turned by the key of sharing. The lock on the door of hatred is great, but there is a key that fits—the key of love. All these keys can be in our hands if first they are in the hearts of Christian men and women the world over. And despite cynics, skeptics and fainthearted ones, we must use them now and be ready to move toward a better world than men have ever known.

V. Let us remember then when our faith falters in this business of living, as it will, that God's steadying hand is on our shoulder leading us on to even greater things.

And when you falter in the task, as falter you will repeatedly, and find yourself asking, "Will the Lord cast off forever? Is his lovingkindness clean gone forever? Hath God forgotten to be gracious?" remember then the necessity of moving straight ahead toward a greater faith, knowing you will be sustained by the God of the universe.

When our faith falters before some great task, some great locked door, some experiences of tragedy, and we ask, "Is God great enough for that?" then listen and we will hear the answer as given by those who have gone before us: "Yes, and greater than that!"—Harold A. Bosley

Illustrations

THROUGH PERPLEXITY TO FAITH. Although there come times when one is sure of God, there are also times of faltering and doubt. And our third difficulty is just there. Why should not God prove himself to us beyond question? There is no proof of any of life's greatest goods. No one can demonstrate the beauty of a spring day: It is self-evident or it does not exist for us. No one can convince us of the desirableness of a friend or of the height, depth, length, and breadth of a wife's love. These we know for ourselves. It is so of God. There is no proof that he is or that he loves. He comes to us along some one of his thousand paths and lays hold of us, and we respond.—Henry Sloan Coffin

A FIGHTING FAITH. In one of his books Thornton Wilder tells of an aged missionary bishop who was spending the last two years of his life in retirement in France. The pathos of those years is summed up in this line: "His was a fighting faith, and when he no longer had battles to fight, his faith withered away."—Harold A. Bosley

Sermon Suggestions

THE WAYS OF A DIVINE CALL. TEXT: Exod. 3:1–12. (1) God calls unexpectedly,

verses 1–5. (2) God is known in historical events, verse 6. (3) God cares for his people and works to help them, verses 7–10. (4) God confirms his call, verses 11–12.

A FUTURE WORTH WAITING FOR. TEXT: Rom. 8:18–25. (1) A future that takes present suffering for granted. (2) A future that makes present suffering worthwhile.

Worship Aids

CALL TO WORSHIP. "Honor thy father and thy mother: that thy days may be long upon the land which the Lord thy God giveth thee" (Exod. 20:12).

INVOCATION. Our Father in heaven, when many things are unsteady and insecure, plant our feet firmly on those values that abide. Grant to the fathers of our world a sense of responsibility to show forth the reliability of the one "with whom there is no variation or shadow due to change."

OFFERTORY SENTENCE. "Although the fig tree shall not blossom, neither shall fruit be in the vines; the labor of the olive shall fail, and the fields shall yield no meat; the flock shall be cut off from the fold, and there shall be no herd in the stalls: "Yet I will rejoice in the Lord, I will joy in the God of my salvation" (Hab. 3:17–18).

OFFERTORY PRAYER. Give us determination, O God, to be faithful in our stewardship, even when reverses come and we are tempted to turn away from our duties. And give us joy in such times, as we look to you, the God of our salvation.

PRAYER. Almighty God, evermore creating, we praise you for your creative genius which brought order out of chaos and fashioned this beautiful world for our home and created us in your image. Your image in us may very well be the gift of imagination and the ability to create. What a high calling to be cocreators with you!

O heavenly Parent, who out of the imagination and creativity of your great love has ordained the family for the welfare and happiness of humankind, we thank you for this nest for our incubation and for our fledgling years until we become strong enough to try our wings. What an imaginative design for the continuing of the human race!

On this day we praise you for those parents who have stirred up in us the gift of faith that we should be here this morning among your people praising your name, hungering for your Word, thirsting for your cup of grace, responding for your call in Christ to be and become.

For the family which has given us life, for the family of which we are a part today, for the family of faith to which we have been called through this church, for our solidarity with all humankind as your family, we give thanks and rejoice.

Through your Word on this occasion we have been reminded of the awesome responsibility of parenting. Forgive us when as parents we have attempted to turn our children into rubber stamps or carbon copies of ourselves through self-indulgence that paraded as love or through our own ignorance or insecurity of who we are as persons. But may we not live by our regrets but by your forgiving love and the gospel of beginning again. Your abounding grace is calling us to redeem the time.

As on this occasion we are moved to celebrate the meaning of life in its deeper dimensions, we do pray for ourselves and our families:

For our sisters and brothers in this family of faith who suffer any brokenness, we pray for an openness—a faith, a love, a trust—that the healing powers of your amazing grace may make whole. Where there is any estrangement among us, we pray for reconciliation that community may be celebrated. For those among us passing through the valley of the shadow of death, sensing the weakness of our own finiteness, may we experience the strength of your everlasting arms.

Grant unto us true family love, that we may belong more entirely to those whom you have given us, understanding each other, day by day, more instinctively; forbearing each other, day by day, more patiently; growing, day by day, more closely into oneness with each other.

We pray, too, for the human family—for families that today are the victims of hostility and war, displaced persons, without homeland or home, living daily with the tenuousness and uncertainties of existence as refugees. We pray for the leaders of nations and the community of nations, that with wisdom, imagination, and courage they may persevere in seeking understanding, justice, peace among all peoples.

Bless us now as together we pray the prayer that is most appropriately the prayer of your family . . .—John Thompson

LECTIONARY MESSAGE

Topic: Leave the Weeds
Text: Matt. 13:24–30, 36–43
No "proper" gardener wants weeds. Weeds compete with the good plants for sun, water, and nutriments. Weeds make harvesting difficult. Weeds are unsightly. Weeds always seem to grow faster. When left to themselves, they quickly go to seed and make more weeds. And yet there are times when weeds are best left alone. This parable is about such a time.

I. *The parable (v. 24–30).* A man sowed good seed in his field, and it grew. But his enemy came during the night and sowed weeds among his wheat. The specific weed was the darnel plant, a weed related to wheat which resembles it closely in its early growth stages. This is why the man's servants did not even recognize the weed until the fruit began to form (v. 26). They were ready and willing to pull up the weeds (v. 28). But the householder advised against it. They might uproot the wheat in the process (v. 29). The "punchline" occurs in verse 30a: Wheat and weeds are to be left to grow until harvest time. The final statement assures us that the weeds will get their just due at harvest time: They will be separated, bundled, and burned, and the wheat gathered into the granary (v. 30b).

II. *The interpretation (v. 36–40).* As so often with the parables of Jesus, the interpretation is given privately to the disciples and is in some tension with the parable itself. At least, in this instance, it focuses on only one aspect of the parable—the theme of judgment, which is only explicitly in the final verse of the parable (v. 30). The interpretation *does* make the dramatis personae unmistakable: Jesus is the householder; the enemy is the devil; the good seed are the kingdom children; the bad are the devil's. The harvest is the last judgment, and the angels the reapers. But who are the householder's servants? Presumably the disciples, Jesus' servants.

Given these details, we are ready to return to the parable. We now know the weeds are really bad. They are to be burned in the fires of the final assise. But where are they growing? The interpretation speaks of the field as the "world" (v. 38). Now no one would want to deny that the world is full of weeds. But the point of the parable is that the weeds are growing in the midst of the wheat. This would indicate that the weeds are sown in the midst of the children of the kingdom. Augustine so understood it. We have here a picture of the church, consisting of weeds growing together with the wheat.

What is the implication, then, of the master's direction that both be left to grow together until the final harvest?

Certainly that the ultimate judgment lies with God. But could it have an even more direct implication for the life of the church—that sometimes we spend too much effort trying to pull weeds from the congregational life and not enough in sowing seed?

Sometimes weeds are best left alone. Every good gardener knows that. For one, you had better know your plants well when you start pulling weeds. My son refuses to weed our flower bed because there are so many volunteers from previous years, and he can't tell the flowers from the weeds. When a church starts cleaning out its garden, it runs the risk of pulling flowers the householder would have used. And then there is the real danger of uprooting the good plants when yanking the weeds. That was the problem with the wheat and the darnel in Jesus' parable (v. 29). Overzealous weed-pulling in congregations can hurt the health of the whole body. And finally, when you take up all your time with the weeds, there is none left for new plantings. That happened to me this year. I spent so much time weeding, I never got around to planting my fall garden. It looked great for a time. Then the blight got it, and now there's nothing. My neighbor isn't fussy about weeds. He has lots of them—also lots of beans. He got his fall garden in. I wonder if it could be the same with a church? Jesus' parable would indicate that it is.—John Polhill

SUNDAY: JULY TWENTY-FIFTH

SERVICE OF WORSHIP

Sermon: When God Breaks Through
TEXT: John 8:39–59

It is written in one place of the crowd around Jesus. Then took they up stones to cast at him. . . . They were angry because they were afraid; afraid because Jesus was strange. He was outside their experience. He seemed to come from another world, where their traditions and their judgment were not at home. They could make nothing of his claims except blasphemy. They could make nothing of his conduct except devilry. He was beyond them quite, a kind of weird phantasm. And it sent vagrant chills up and down their spines. That's what happened. I'm certain of it. God was there but in a pattern that was queerer than queer: a poor carpenter "not yet fifty years old," with that in his voice which sounded like the sea, and a touch that was life itself. It made their flesh tingle, and they resented it; resented it with a red surge of anger, which drove the fear clean out of their marrow and left them ready on the instant with their clenched fists to put him out of the way. That's really what sent Jesus to the cross.

I. I want to start with that here. If God is anything, by reason of his very nature as God, he's incalculable! You can't extend to infinity the lines of your reason and arrive at him. You can't hold up the highest notion you have of him, stand on tiptoe with it, and say, "There! That's God!" He's other than you think; save as Christ has shown that he's disposed toward us as One that pitieth his children! He dwells in a light that's inaccessible and fully of glory, and the motions of his stately Spirit are in a world where your logic and mine rarely if ever made his kind of sense! We're just in a fog about him—let's say that to ourselves solemnly: All we know is Jesus; we've seen that much of his face. The rest is hidden, and none of it is subject to our judgments. I think sometimes if we had any, even the vaguest, conceit of his majesty, we shouldn't be expecting him to fit so neatly into the tight little categories of the human mind!

(a) Here are our sacred traditions, for instance: There's no guarantee anywhere that he isn't going to break through them. Take this one that's set so firmly in our American way of looking at life. What we call the privilege of property, "the immortality of the status quo," as Dr. Luccock puts it. He says it was phrased in its purest form some years ago when the president of a great railway spoke of "the Christian men to whom God in his infinite wisdom had given control of the vested interests of this country." You'll not find any cruder statement than that anywhere, no more blunt or honest attempt to identify the kingdom of heaven with the order which our hands have built. And it won't do. Nobody on this earth can blueprint the mind and purpose of God like that!

(b) I tell you, nothing is safe with a living God around! Not your job, not your health, not your home! Not even the church! If catastrophe, dismal and complete, smashes its way into all of them, injustice, bereavement, pain—don't look bewildered, as if the whole universe had gone crazy and there were no rhyme in any of it and no decency at all. This One with whom we have to do is not as we are. That's all. He doesn't think of us as we think of ourselves. He doesn't limit us by the horizons that we see. He doesn't deal with us as we suppose he should. He doesn't manage his business with the human soul along any of the lines we lay down. It's silly to doubt him because we can't understand him! I'd sooner doubt him if we could! He'd be no longer God!

II. How then, if he's like that—how shall we behave ourselves toward him? There, in the eighth chapter of John, Jesus gives this that I've been trying to say its practical point. He describes the sort of person who isn't going to miss that deathless Presence in the world just because it breaks through his own neat and diminutive ideas! "He that is of God," so it runs, "heareth God's words." He's every day on the lookout. He's listening for a Voice. He's waiting and straining to catch some syllable out of eternity.

(a) That kind of taut expectancy is stressed all through the New Testament. The men who set down their experiences here went out into the world sure of Christ but sure of nothing else under the sun. They didn't know where God was going to come ripping his way into life with the very next breath. For the soul of them they couldn't tell! The days were full of him. There was no natural order, called law, empty and staring and stupid. There was no routine. They were forever glancing behind them and in front of them and on every side—like people confident that something was going to happen, and it was going to be God, but nobody could possibly say what it was going to look like otherwise.

(b) And Jesus defines this man of God as one who keeps his saying. He's always on the right side of things, because he's been doing God's will in Christ; never will miss the step of this One whom he's been loving and serving his whole life through! "If a man keep my saying. . . ." It isn't at all a question, you see, as to whether or not Christ's sayings make sense. Maybe they don't. No matter.

When he says that any separate soul is worth more than the whole world in God's scales, that sounds ridiculous. But are you willing to say yes to it and start living by it for no other reason on earth than that he said it? When he says that love will work and hate won't, it's just a silly jumble to me: especially out there in business, where we're likely to be cheated out of everything we've got; and yonder among the nations, where loving anybody looks like suicide! But are you willing to take Christ's word for it, just because it is his word?

III. Then there's this other equipment, faith: simply a bare, defenseless confidence that in and under and over and around all things whatsoever is God: the love and wisdom and power and abiding presence of Christ! "Before Abraham was, I am." That was Jesus' way of putting it. Whatever happened or when, if you looked up you'd find his face there, and in it would be nothing but tenderness and the sure knowledge of victory! Victory for men and women beaten against a wall who can still leave their anxieties to him: all these things they never will understand, that harass their souls; certain that he's going to work it out in the end.

(a) People can leave their lives to God and stake all there is on his handling of them! Job did that, when calamity came rushing in on him. It stripped him of everything that made the months and the years tolerable, and through no fault of his own! But there beyond it was God, and the far-off desperate cry of Job's soul still lingers on the earth: "Though he slay me, yet will I trust him!"

(b) It happened some time ago to a man of whom I read. He had lost an uncommonly brilliant and promising son. The lad was killed in a railroad accident. And when the news came, in the first paroxysm of his grief, the father strode over to the pastor of his church. He didn't even ring the bell. He walked into the house, through the library, seized his minister roughly by the arm, and cried, the tears not yet dry on his cheeks, "Tell me, sir, where was God when my son was killed?" And in that terrible moment the other answered, "My friend, God was just where he was when his own son was killed!" Jesus could commit his life to those hands. Can't you and I commit ours and the lives of others? And even in the hour of darkness hold on in the dark!

IV. "Then took they up stones to cast at him. . . ." If there's any taut and waiting expectancy in your heart; if there's any steadiness in your feet, as you keep walking down the way of Christ's will; if there's any stubborn, ultimate confidence in your soul, as you stand there at your wits' end looking for God: you'll never be found on that wrong side of things when he breaks through—with fear in your marrow and anger on your face and stones in your hands and God yonder—to whom all things are subject. Who shall yet make them prosper and serve you! God in Jesus, holding out his last gallant bid for the love that should be in your eyes!—Paul Scherer

Illustrations

HE COMES TO US.   No doubt the psalmists already knew something of the grace of God who forgives us our sins and redeems us from corruption. "Praise the Lord, O my soul, and forget not all his benefits. For he forgiveth thy sins and healeth all thy diseases." Thus Psalm 103. But the Word has not yet become flesh; the Savior has not yet been born; the redemptive plan of God has not yet been fully disclosed. For only through him, Jesus, the Savior, do we know that God does not remain aloof from us in his eternity. He comes to us clothed in temporality in order to bestow upon us eternity. He the eternal God has become man in order to invest us creatures of time with eternity. Hence we do not advance inexorably and irredeemably toward death, as they suppose who do not know God. It is our faith that "whosoever believeth on me will live though he die."—Emil Brunner

HE IS HERE.   You'll go to your desk in the morning or you'll stay at home and cook the dinner or you'll take lunch with a friend: and you won't be thinking God yourself! You'll be treating him as if he weren't here! You'll be taking it for granted that he's all safely put away in some holy place, with nothing much to do, letting things take their course! I don't blame anybody for getting tired of that. But I've lived long enough to know it's our own fault! We go walking around alone on Monday and call it blue. Tuesday is just a tough day at the office. Wednesday and Thursday the market drops. Friday nothing happens, and Saturday we play golf. You wouldn't recognize your own brother, honestly you wouldn't, if you locked him out of the whole week like that! We've got to begin living life as it is, instinct with God; unless we're willing to have him seem like a stranger from one year's end to the other.—Paul Scherer

Sermon Suggestions

GOD TELLS WHO HE IS.   TEXT: Exod. 3:13–20, NRSV. When God says, "I am who I am," (1) it speaks of God's freedom; (2) it speaks of God's transcendence; (3) withal, it speaks of God's mystery and points forward to the statement in the Rev. 1:4 about the one "who is and who was and who is to come."

HELP IS ON THE WAY.   TEXT: Rom. 8:26–30. (1) To assist our prayers. (2) To control events in our lives. (3) To conform us to the image of God's Son.

Worship Aids

CALL TO WORSHIP.   "We all, with open face, beholding as in a glass the glory of the Lord, are changed into the same image from glory to glory, even as by the Spirit of the Lord" (2 Cor. 3:18).

INVOCATION.   Help us today to stop, look, and listen in this service of worship that we may see your glorious face, hear your incomparable Word, and be transformed by your Spirit, O Lord, we pray.

OFFERTORY SENTENCE.   "Walk in love, as Christ loved us and gave himself up

for us, a fragrant offering and sacrifice to God" (Eph. 5:2, RSV).

OFFERTORY PRAYER.   We realize, O Lord, that love makes many demands of us, some of them pleasant, some of them painful. Give us insight to understand that such love reflects your own self-giving and that we can find new joy as we enter into your spirit of giving.

PRAYER.   Creator God, we adore you for the music of all created things: earth to heaven and heaven to earth, the mustard seed to the crescent moon and evening star, the flower in the crannied wall to the Perseid meteor shower; all green and growing things; all that delights ear and eye; and, in every field and pond, Creation's choral evensong; a loon's antiphon.

Creator God, we thank you for singular graces: that we have been spared and have a measure of health; that there is somewhere on earth that we have roots, and that they sustain us wherever we are thrown; that we have a friend, someone whom to see is to be home; that we have where to lay our head and this and that to do; and a few created, material things, mostly plain but dear, and a comfort in the watches of the night.

Merciful God, we confess that we have broken the covenant with Noah and all flesh; that we are making of the earth a desert and calling it required, and of the desert a waste it never was; forests are felled, fossil fuel sought at fools' prices, and the poor are sold for a pair of shoes; the list goes on and on. For we are laying waste this lovely place, this gracious, green and provident place, whereon you have been pleased to plant us, and the confessional formula is apt: Forgive me, Father, for I have sinned.

Redeemer God, Lamb of God, save us from our folly and incline not our hearts to evil. From times of reflection and renewal send us forth with a clearer and a stronger faith. Set our hearts upon those disciplines that shall build upon this time, that it may not be lost but heard, read, marked, and inwardly digested. In little things grant us increase of faithfulness, and to great changes shut not our hearts.

Triune God, Creator, Son, and Holy Spirit, joyous celebrant of all that truly is: How dear is thy dwelling place, O Lord of hosts! Unto you be the glory, now and always.—Peter Fribley

LECTIONARY MESSAGE

Topic: Images of the Kingdom
Text: Matt. 13:44–52

Matthew 13 is a collection of Jesus' parables, all of which have the "kingdom of heaven" as their subject. The "kingdom of heaven" or "kingdom of God" refers to the reign or rule of God. Wherever God rules in people's lives, there his kingdom is present. Jesus' central message was that the kingdom has come in a special way, that god has drawn near and seeks to rule in human lives. For Matthew, to submit to God's rule is to experience both grace and demand. The four parabolic teachings of Matt. 13:44–52 illustrate this.

I. *Two parables of joy (vv. 44–46).* God's kingdom comes as a windfall, an unexpected joy, a priceless treasure. That is the central message of the twin parables of the hidden treasure and the pearl of great price. The images would have been familiar to Jesus' Palestinian audience. The uncovering of large sums of money and valuables buried in clay pots was not an uncommon occurrence in a land which had experienced frequent invasion from foreign armies. The picture is that of a common day laborer who would have owned no property of his own but discovered the treasure totally by accident, perhaps in a plowing job for which he had been hired. His reaction is one of joy and abandon in light of the unanticipated bonanza. He sells "everything he has" (v. 44) in order to purchase the field and claim the treasure. The merchant's windfall was not totally by chance. He was looking for pearls for his stock. It was still totally unexpected when he came across the priceless pearl. Pearls were particularly valued in the ancient world, and there are accounts of some worth tens of thousands of dollars. This was

such a pearl, as is indicated by *his* abandon. He sold all his goods, indeed all *he* had in order to claim this pearl beyond all price.

These twin parables have a double thrust. On the one hand is that of abandon. Membership in God's kingdom, laying hold of the treasure, demands complete allegiance, the forsaking of *all*. No other earthly claim can take precedence. On the other hand, there is the sheer joy of the newfound treasure. The kingdom becomes the supreme joy of one's life before which all other values pale in significance. It is *worth* the abandon.

II. *A parable of judgment (vv. 47–51).* The Matthean form of the parables often bears a note of judgment. That is the main point in the parable of the seinenet. A net is cast into the lake and brings forth fish of every kind. Some are inedible or unclean and are cast aside for destruction. Others are gathered together into vessels. Interestingly, the application, which links the parable explicitly to the final judgment, deals only with the torment to befall the unjust, not the coming joy for the just (vv. 49–50). The element of judgment, of God's just demand, is unmistakable.

The parable itself, much like that of the weeds among the wheat (13:24–30), depicts a world in which both good and evil coexist. Perhaps it serves as a reminder that the church is to exist *in the world* and not withdraw from it. The good fish are not found in their own isolated schools but intermingled with the bad. How else are they to have any influence on the bad?

III. *A simile of stewardship (v. 52).* Matt. 13:52 serves as a conclusion to all of Jesus' parables. Jesus likens the teacher of the kingdom message to a householder who brings forth both old and new from his treasure. Many interpreters see Matthew as having been a Jewish scribe converted to Christianity. If so, this verse could be seen as his autograph, a picture of how he saw his own task in passing on the truth of both old and new. From his Jewish background he had a firm grasp on the demands of God and the prospect of an inevitable final accounting before a just God. But in the gospel he had come to experience the *new* message of God's mercy and forgiveness. He has found the sheer joy of the pearl beyond price. Both the old and the new shine forth in this collection of parables.—John Polhill

SUNDAY: AUGUST FIRST

SERVICE OF WORSHIP

Sermon: A Portrait of Faith
TEXT: Luke 7:2–9

There is always a difference between the manner in which the theologians define faith and the way in which a biographer, such as Luke, looks at it. What he does is to draw a picture of it. He draws a picture of faith, hangs it on the wall where the spectators can see it, and then puts Jesus' terse comments under it.

It falls with a strange shock upon our ears today, to hear Luke announce that it was "a certain centurion," a captain in the Roman army, who gave such a splendid exhibition of faith as to surprise Jesus and make him exclaim, "I have not found so great faith, no, not in Israel." Think of it! A soldier—a heathen soldier—speaking with confidence and with such perfect faith to Jesus! We would naturally expect arrogance, conceit, tyranny, a sort of "top sergeant" air.

But that isn't what the Jewish elders conveyed to Jesus. The army captain's slave was sick and about to die, and when these emissaries approached Jesus they said, "He deserves to have this favor from you; for he is a lover of our nation; it was he who built our synagogue."

I. It was the first word of the conversation, and we see in this picture, drawn so carefully by the hand of an artist, the fact that faith can be expressed only in a man of nobility of character.

(a) One thing is sure, no man will ever come anywhere near having anyone put his trust in him unless, in his makeup, there is an unconscious persuasion that he is a person of nobleness of character. Long before this centurion had taken up his residence in Capernaum, there lived an Egyptian sage by the name of Ptah Hotep, who had set down a number of great sayings, among which was this one:

"Live in a house of friendliness, and men shall come and give gifts to you of themselves." In all probability this centurion knew nothing of this saying, but somehow in his own life he had come to learn its worth.

(b) It is probable, too, that he did not know that Jesus, to whom his friends were appearing, had uttered a word such as this: "Give, and it shall be given unto you; good measure, pressed down, and shaken together, and running over, shall men give into your bosom." He knew nothing of this utterance, but he had practiced it in his daily life.

II. Here was a man who had managed to gain the wholesome respect of three different classes.

(a) First, of his slave. When he fell ill, the centurion agonized over him to the extent of wanting to do something toward his recovery aside from wishing him well. The slave was something more to him than chattel. He was a human personality, with feelings such as the centurion possessed. For a long time some of us have been pleading for just this attitude to be shown toward the working classes, as constituting one of the ways of solving our economic and industrial difficulties. Let us read our history. Go back to the day when the cry went up to Pharaoh, "Let my people go," and to the day when King Rehoboam said to the people, "Whereas my father did lade you with a heavy yoke, I will add to your yoke: my father hath chastised you with whips, but I will chastise you with scorpions." History will repeat itself in any civilization unless that civilization is charged and sensitized with the spirit of justice.

(b) This centurion was just, also, toward the Jewish officials. In those days the Romans called the Jew a dog and the Jew hated the yoke of the Roman. They were ready to fly at each other's throat.

But the centurion's attitude disarmed the prejudice of the Jew and made him his friend. If goodness doesn't work, nothing will.

(c) But more than that, this centurion had gained the love of his neighbors. It was not only on review days that they saw him, when he was marching his hundred soldiers up and down the streets of Capernaum, not alone when he was on dress parade but as he was going about his ordinary duties of being a citizen. If the world can see the man whose material goods have placed him in a position of power and authority as a man of nobility of character, gentle in his manner toward his fellows and considerate of the lowly, men will bring gifts to him of themselves.

III. Turning the picture around and listening to the centurion injecting himself into the conversation, we discover that he had a loftier conception of who and what Jesus was than had the elders. "I am not worthy that thou shouldest enter under my roof, wherefore neither thought I myself worthy to come unto thee."

(a) And yet, with a thousand evidences about us of the power of big things, we scorn this quality of humility as a milk-and-water virtue and compare it with weakness. Let us note a contrast. Out of Hebrew folklore comes the story of the strong man, Samson. His strength resided in his long hair. To a treacherous wife he gave away his secret, and while he slept she sheared him of his hair. She roused him and taunted him: "The Philistines be upon thee, Samson. And he awoke out of his sleep and said, I will go out as at other times before and shake myself." And here's the tragedy! "He wist not that the Lord was departed from him." With sightless eyes he was forced to grind in the prison house.

(b) Here on the other hand was that great leader, Moses, going up into the mountain to speak to Jehovah. He came down from the mountain with a new light in his eyes, and the people saw his glorified countenance. But the record states, "Moses wist not that the skin of his face shone." Every man must have in himself a real element of greatness from which to stoop. It is impossible to stoop from nothing.

IV. One wonders why a good man's estimate of himself should fall below that formed of him by his neighbors.

(a) First of all, because he knows more about himself than do his neighbors. Most people would shrink from telling others the innermost secrets of their hearts. Consider the unholy thoughts which cross our minds and stain our souls; see the constant struggle we have with the little meannesses which insist on rising to the surface. Is there anyone entirely free from every unholy ambition? If one never recognizes these spiritual handicaps, he will never be humble, and never can it be said of him, "I have not found so great faith, no, not in Israel."

(b) Then, again, the better one becomes, the higher does his standard of goodness rise. The better his life, the loftier his ideal. Stand before all the knowledge in the world and compare that with the little you know! Searchers after truth stand in wonder and awe before the vastness and complexity of the universe and declare that they are only children picking up pebbles on the shore of knowledge.

Something like that is true when the good man stands before Jesus. It is difficult to reach up to him, and yet what amazing qualities of character we long for within ourselves. A man who congratulates himself on his personal worthiness is really unworthy.

V. Finally, the man of faith is the one who has the feeling of being God-sent. "I also," continued the centurion, "am a man set under authority." A surgeon once said, "If you want to see my religion come and see me operate." What sense of responsibility and duty, what strong feeling that he is the instrument in the hand of an infinite God to restore the sick to health!

(a) To have a passion for the good, a love for the true, a longing for the beautiful: what are these but aspects of the holy God? It's our business to bring all this to pass, but the final issue is not in our hands but in God's.

(b) "He is worthy for whom you should do this. . . . I am not worthy. . . . I too am a man under authority." Is it any wonder that under this portrait Jesus could write this brief comment, "I have not found so great faith, no, not in Israel"?—Frederick Keller Stamm

Illustrations

CHRIST WITHIN. When a man becomes a Christian the natural process is this: The living Christ enters into his soul. Development begins. The quickening life seizes upon the soul, assimilates surrounding elements, and begins to fashion it. According to the great Law of Conformity to Type this fashioning takes a specific form. It is that of the artist who fashions. And all through life this wonderful, mystical, glorious, yet perfectly definite process goes on "until Christ be formed" in it.—Henry Drummond

FORGIVENESS, HUMAN AND DIVINE. The story is told of John Selwyn, onetime bishop of Melanesia, that once he found it necessary to rebuke a native candidate for baptism. The man, but once removed from cannibalism, becoming enraged by the rebuke, struck the bishop a violent blow in the face. Selwyn might easily have felled him where he stood, for he was no weakling; an amateur boxer of repute, he had also rowed in the Cambridge boat. What passed through his mind we can only guess; was it sudden anger, fierce resentment, desire to give as good as and better than he had received? None of this did he express, if it was there at all. Folding his arms, he stood quietly waiting for the next blow or whatever else might follow. This was so utterly unexpected that the angry native paused, then turning away from the calm face that looked into his own wild one, he ran headlong, utterly discomfited, from the scene.

Years later when Selwyn had returned to England and gone back to a Cambridge college, this same native came to another missionary and asked to be baptized as a Christian believer. He was examined as to his faith and then asked what name he would like to take on being baptized. "Call me John Selwyn," he replied, "for it was he who first taught me what Christ is like."—John Trevor Davies

Sermon Suggestions

CHRIST—OUR PASSOVER.   TEXT: Exod. 12:1–14. (1) Then: the narrative of the Passover prior to the Exodus. (2) Always: the continuing significance of Passover, for Christians as well as for Jews—a celebration of (a) freedom; (b) redemption; (c) thanksgiving. (3) Now: every observance of the Lord's Supper gives the opportunity to focus again on the present significance of the closing days of Jesus' life, of his death, and of his Resurrection, with thanksgiving (*eucharistia*).

UTTER   CONFIDENCE.   TEXT: Rom. 8:31–39. (1) The basis of our confidence: God. (2) The gift that makes us brave: God's own Son. (3) The work that makes us right with God: the intercession of Christ for us. (4) The scope of our victory: every eventuality conceivable.

Worship Aids

CALL TO WORSHIP. "O give thanks unto the Lord: for he is good, because his mercy endureth for ever" (Ps. 118:1).

INVOCATION. Lord, we are here to give thanks to you, for your mercies have sustained us up to this very hour. We trust in your unfailing presence to go with us unto the days to come, and we open our hearts to you now, that you may teach us, comfort us, correct us, and guide us, that we may know that enduring mercy in its many dimensions.

OFFERTORY SENTENCE. "If a brother or sister be naked and destitute of daily food, and one of you say unto them, Depart in peace, be ye warmed and filled; notwithstanding ye give them not those things which are needful to the body; what doth it profit? Even so faith, if it hath not works, is dead, being alone" (James 2:15–17).

OFFERTORY PRAYER. Compassionate God, even in our works strengthen our faith and in our faith proliferate our good deeds. By your grace, may we turn our faces and our hearts more and more toward those persons and causes that need what we can do with our little or our much.

PRAYER. There is a wideness in your mercy, Father, which we do not fully understand. Yet we are thankful that you meet us in mercy and love rather than in justice and wrath. This morning we need a large portion of mercy in our various situations. Some here have walked roads which have brought disgrace to themselves and those whom they love. Spur of the moment indulgences have caused lifetime shadows to descend over them, and they will have to live with the results of their sins ever before them and the world. Extend to these sufferers who have failed to be all that they have the potential to be a large measure of mercy that they may not feel completely alone in their life walk. And lead us, their fellow human family members, to practice the art of mercy after the fashion of the merciful Christ.

Some have been made the victims of disturbing circumstances which have forever left their imprint and burden to warp lives and rob personalities. You know better than we human fellow pilgrims the struggle which these folks deal with daily. Let them be aware of your tender mercy and love as they deal with life as best they can. And lead us, their fellow human family members, to practice the art of understanding mercy toward them after the fashion of the merciful Christ.

Some gathered here today are carrying heavy loads for others which sometimes seem about to break their lives and spirits. Long have they struggled in the heat of the day, and we wonder how much longer they can endure. Give them the mercy of your strength and the endurance of your courage as they stagger on along their journey. And lead us, their fellow human family members, to practice the art of helping mercy toward them after the fashion of the merciful Christ.

Many gathered here this morning have experienced the wonder of your saving mercy as they have unloaded their sinful burdens and followed you into a new life. Let that happen for others this morning who need salvation from themselves and their killing sins. And lead us, their fellow human family members, to practice the art of forgiving, saving mercy toward them after the fashion of the merciful Christ.—Henry Fields

LECTIONARY MESSAGE

Topic: The Lord's Provision for All People

TEXT: Matt. 14:13–21

The miracles of feeding the multitudes have from the time of the earliest church fathers been given a eucharistic interpretation. Indeed, this application is to be found with the Gospel writers themselves. It is most evident in the sixth chapter of John where the feeding of the multitude is followed by Jesus' discourse on the Bread of Life. One must "eat [his] flesh and drink [his] blood" to have eternal life (John 6:53). The eucharistic emphasis is also to be found in Matthew's account of the feeding of the five thousand, although far more subtly than in John. In Matthew, Jesus' words of blessing are strongly reminiscent of the words of institution in the Lord's Supper: Taking bread, blessing it, breaking it, giving it to the disciples. The *wording* is identical (v. 19; cf. 26:26). Also, unlike Mark, his likely source, he does not mention the distribution of the fish—only of the bread, making the parallel to the Lord's Supper even more pronounced (v. 19; cf. Mark 6:41). The feeding miracles are, consequently, appropriate texts for a communion meditation. Several emphases are particularly suited to the occasion.

I. *The Lord's provision.* The feeding miracles belong to the category of the nature miracles. The most prominent emphasis in all of these is the divine providence. In a desert place, far from any source of provision, either human or natural, Jesus amply provides sustenance for a great multitude of people. It is a reminder of our dependence upon God for all our daily needs. Augustine so understood the feeding miracles, maintaining that only the timing was extraordinary, for Jesus performed in an instant the same miracle of growth that God performs yearly in the cycle of great harvests from a few seed. The Lord's Supper is the only sacrament of the church that involves our natural need for food and drink. It is an apt occasion for reminding us that God is our ultimate provider for both our physical and our spiritual needs.

II. *The deset place.* The feedings take place in a desert region (v. 15), which evokes images of Israel's wilderness experience. This connection is explicit in the Johannine account, where the crowds link Jesus' giving them bread to the manna in the wilderness (John 6:31). The Old Testament prophets often called Israel back to its wilderness days. It was a time of particular closeness to God, of absolute dependence upon his providence. Isolated in the wilderness, Israel was free from the influence of her neighbors, the ordinary distractions of life, and the temptations that come with these. The same was true for the crowds who experienced Jesus' feeding miracles. Alone with Jesus in the wilderness, totally

lacking in their own provision, they were totally attendant to him, totally dependent on him. So it is with the communion celebration of the church. It is a time to be alone with the Lord, free from life's ordinary distractions, to reaffirm our dependence on him.

III. *The inclusive feeding.* Matthew appends a note to his narrative of the feeding of the five thousand which is unique among the Gospel accounts. The number of five thousand, he says, was the number of *men* fed and did not even include the women and children who experienced the miracle (v. 21). In this manner the inclusive nature of the feeding is heightened. It involved a vast number and included all ages and sexes. The same emphasis is to be found in the parallel account of the feeding of the four thousand, which is set on gentile soil and is replete with symbolism pointing to the Gentiles (Matt. 15:32–39). It is Matthew's way of saying that the Lord's table is open to all people, Jew and Gentile, male and female. As the church gathers for the supper, it is a time for remembering its servant role of going into all the highways and byways of the world and inviting all people to the Lord's table.—John Polhill

SUNDAY: AUGUST EIGHTH

SERVICE OF WORSHIP

Sermon: Beyond Obedience

TEXT: Acts 12:18–23

For sixteen years our family included a mild-mannered terrier named Curly, a description not only of his hair but his pedigree. Curly was a great companion to our children. He was tolerant of almost everybody and everything. I often noted that he was an excellent "watchdog." He could patiently watch anyone, anywhere, do anything without exhibiting the slightest disapproval. His one big neurosis was fear of storms. He would bark defiantly at thunder, and when he could no longer hear, a flash of light was

sufficient to set off a protest. Carolyn gave old Curly a new image one day when she decided that he was barking at God. For years we had imagined the old dog to be a wimp, and all along he was really a theological rebel.

Following the thunder and lightning an old woman appears on the screen to denounce the imitation of butter with, "It's not nice to fool Mother Nature!" In all of us there is a rebel that fantasizes about standing up to the high and the mighty, perhaps even to the Almighty. The brief cameo appearance of King Herod Agrippa, grandson of Herod the Great, the last king of Israel, stands as a landmark warning to world rulers who are tempted to think too highly of themselves and to the foolish people who fashion their own gods.

Agrippa's popularity in the execution of James encouraged a repeat performance with Peter as the victim. Peter's freedom came from an authority higher then the king. An angel of God led Peter to safety, and after the apostle was safely removed to Caesarea, Luke reported the demise of Agrippa. Luke and Josephus agree on the occasion of the king's death. As the people hailed him as a god, the petty tyrant developed a severe abdominal pain. Luke, however, attributed Agrippa's abdominal pain to worms and the judgment of God: "An angel of the Lord struck him down, and he was eaten by worms and died." William Willimon views Luke's purpose with tongue in cheek: "The response of God to such silly presumption on the part of kings is swift, ruthless, pitiless, ugly desecration. Herod becomes food for worms. God is not nice to those who try to be God."

God does not typically strike down acts of sacrilege from either peasants or kings. Success and failure, life and death, are poor measures of the judgment of the God who sends his rain upon the evil and the good. The message here is about a church launched into world history by the authority of God revealed in Christ. The persistent theme is that no power or authority on earth can stand against the calling of God in Christ. Before the Sanhedrin's gag order, Peter declared, "We must obey God rather than any human authority." The calling of God is above all human powers both religious and secular.

I. Only God is God. If indeed levels and grades can be assigned, the worst evil is the arrogant assumption of the place and authority of God. The repugnance of idolatry in the Jewish mind was rooted not only in the first commandment but in the most basic principle of religion—only God is God. Original Sin in the Garden of Paradise goes far beyond tripping over a rule. The temptation is rivalry to the authority and knowledge of God. Daniel should be read in the light of events around 167 B.C. when it was written

rather than the Babylonian epoch in which it is set. Syrian ruler of Israel Antiochus IV Epiphanes declared himself to be "manifest God." He infuriated his Jewish subjects by prohibiting circumcision and Sabbath observance, burning the Torah, and sacrificing a pig on an altar to Zeus in the Jerusalem Temple. Daniel obeyed the higher authority of God over the king and prevailed. This apocalyptic theme is present is Acts. Agrippa is another in a long line of petty tyrants in Jewish history who, daring to play god, were stopped by their own mortality.

II. Blind obedience is idolatry. People play God when they assume the absolute knowledge and/or authority of God over Creation. Not only the instant threat of nuclear holocaust but the more subtle threat of environmental pollution raises questions about our stewardship of life and Creation. One does not have to be a king to assume the right to destroy. Political expressions of idolatry tend to have a larger impact on history, but playing god is common in families, businesses, and churches as well. Our memory of Adolf Hitler in the political sphere and Jim Jones in religion ought to chill our cry for a king to rule over us, but also remember that demagogues are raised by people. People of every age seem all too willing to submit body, mind, and soul to petty tyrants. The human will to abdicate responsibility for moral decision is as offensive as the human will to play god. Indeed, we enthrone our human gods and maintain their illusions of grandeur by our refusal to think or to stand against their will. The liberty with which we have been endowed by our Creator is more often relinquished without question than taken by force.

Dorothee Sölle wrote *Beyond Mere Obedience* out of her personal experience as a German, a Christian, and a woman. The Nazi Holocaust, the traditional subjection of women to men, and religious authoritarianism are realities of our age which call us to a higher obedience. Yes, to obey God is better than sacrifice; but, except for the Son, God's authority has no surrogate. Jesus called for people to look beyond the established orders to a world yet to be revealed. Until the final word of God is pronounced, the absolute will of God remains a mystery. No human entity ever has the absolute right of the Creator. The kingdom is a future waiting to be fulfilled.—Larry Dipboye

Illustrations

THE NEW LEGALISM. We find that Jesus and Paul proposed love as a substitute for law. John identified love with God himself. I fear that Christian scribes and Pharisees have substituted law for love. Oddly enough, in the long run it is a more facile and supple morality, more easily bent to "the complexities of modern society" and other such things. It puts back the ceiling which Jesus removed and restores the security which so many people find in doing what someone has told them is the right thing. In the community of cannibals who will take a strong stand against eating people?—John L. McKenzie

CHRIST THE CENTER. Just as a planet rushing through space is only a comet on its way to destruction until it is caught by some central sun and begins to revolve around that sun as its center and its life; so my life is an aimless comet burning itself out in its own self-will, till it finds the pull and attraction of Christ's love, halts its deadly way, and forever revolves around him, its central Sun and its life.—E. Stanley Jones

Sermon Suggestions

DON'T BE SURPRISED! TEXT: Exod. 14:19–31. (1) When God is for us we may be helped in our deepest trouble by blessings hoped for and by blessings hardly dreamed of. (2) When God so blesses, the appropriate response is fear, faith, and following of godly leadership.

IF YOU ONLY KNEW. TEXT: Rom. 9:1–5, NRSV. (1) Are you a person who has not accepted Jesus as the Christ? (2) Are you aware that there are people who have "great sorrow and unceasing an-

guish" in their hearts for you? (3) Can you believe that all God's gracious and special acts through the ages are potentially for you, just as they were intended first for Israel (Rom 1:16)?

Worship Aids

CALL TO WORSHIP. "Blessed are they that do his commandments, that they may have right to the tree of life and may enter in through the gates into the city" (Rev. 22:14).

INVOCATION. As we ascend your holy hill for worship, give us clean hands and a pure heart and a renewal of spirit for the doing of your gracious will.

OFFERTORY SENTENCE. "And he said unto them, Take heed and beware of covetousness; for a man's life consisteth not in the abundance of the things which he possesseth" (Luke 12:15).

OFFERTORY PRAYER. Almighty and most merciful God, we remember before you all poor and neglected persons whom it would be easy for us to forget: the homeless and the destitute, the old and the sick, and all who have none to care for them. Help us to heal those who are broken in body or spirit, and to turn their sorrow into joy. Grant this, Father, for the love of your Son, who for our sake became poor, Jesus Christ our Lord.—The Book of Common Prayer

PRAYER. O gracious God, you cause the rain to fall upon the earth, watering its furrows and giving it life. Send, we pray, the life-giving rains, that the earth may yield its increase and that we, with grateful hearts, may give you thanks. To the glory of your name.

God of Abraham, Isaac, and Jacob; God of Sarah and Hagar; God of the fat years and of the lean; God of Job: You test your people, that it may be known whose hearts truly praise you. Center our lives in your kingdom, that in the years that the rains do not come, the lean years, we may be found faithful and ever in love with you, persevering in your purposes with cleaned, glad, and joyful hearts.—Peter Fribley

LECTIONARY MESSAGE

Topic: Steps to Faith

TEXT: Matt. 14:22–33

Mark (6:45–52) and John (6:15–21) also relate the story of Jesus walking on the water. Like the preceding feeding of the five thousand, it is one of the "nature miracles" which emphasize the Lord's providence. Here Jesus is shown treading the deep, the watery chaos. For the little ship of the church, the story assures the Lord's presence, his taking it through the high seas that threaten its life.

Unique to Matthew is the account of Peter's attempt to join Jesus on the water. It is one of several unique Matthean traditions about Peter. All of them depict Peter in some role of leadership among the disciples. Here Peter serves as a paradigm of faith for every disciple. His experience highlights several characteristics which are essential to faith.

I. *Commitment.* All faith begins with commitment. By its very nature, faith is dependence upon, trust in, commitment to another. Peter shows this sort of trust in his initial response to Jesus' sudden apparition on the water. "Lord, command me to come to you on the water" (v. 28). It is a genuine commitment of faith. Peter trusts his Lord, even takes the initiative in requesting the Lord's command to come to him. Still, he waits for the invitation. Faith ventures nothing on its own.

II. *Courage.* Faith is courageous. Faith is a commitment of absolute trust in another's leadership, of following that leadership even into situations of threat and danger. Faith takes risks. Peter certainly shows that sort of courageous faith in Jesus in this scene. The waves are high, the boat is pitching in the billows. The sudden ghostly appearance of Jesus in the early morning mists has only heightened the fear and anxiety of the disciples. But Peter has faith in Jesus, a faith willing to run all risks. At the Lord's bidding for him to come, Peter is in the water and on his way. A disciple who is not willing to be courageous and take the risks will never rise above mediocrity.

III. *Concentration.* Peter's failure in faith was neither at the point of commitment nor of courage. It was his lack of concentration, of carry-through, that failed him. Once in the water, he became aware of the heaving waves about him. His attention was diverted away from Jesus and on the surging water, and he became frightened (v. 30). Everyone engaged in sports knows the importance of concentration. Eyes must be riveted to the target—the ball, the uprights, the hoop. To allow anything going on around you to divert your attention is to guarantee a miss. It is no different for faith. With faith, the goal is the one in whom you have placed your trust. When faith breaks its concentration on Jesus, one is left to one's own resources and to inevitable failure. Jesus' question to Peter aptly sums up the problem. "Why did you doubt?" (v. 31). The word translated "doubt" means literally to take one's stand in two directions at the same time. With faith, initial commitment, even uncommon courage are not enough. It takes undivided attention, total concentration on Jesus, who is himself both the object and the means to the goal.—John Polhill

SUNDAY: AUGUST FIFTEENTH

SERVICE OF WORSHIP

Sermon: God's Voice in the Valleys

TEXTS: 1 Kings 19:1–12; Rom. 11:1–6

There are valleys through which we all have to walk. The valleys are real, and to a great degree—to be expected. Therefore, we would do well to learn the truth that God speaks in the valleys. God's voice can be heard even in the valleys. Elijah learned this lesson and so should we.

I. Remember Elijah? We know of Elijah especially in his ministry during the reign of King Ahab in Israel. Ahab became very lax in his faithfulness to God. He had married Jezebel from Tyre; she was devout in her worship of the god Baal. Baal was the Canaanite storm and fertility god to whom Jezebel was devoted. Right in Israel, she openly worshiped this false god, erected a temple in his honor, and even supported a college to train his prophets.

(a) You may remember that there came a great drought in the land. Elijah went to Ahab to announce the end of the drought. Ahab called him a troublemaker of Israel, but Elijah—not being a shy man—accused Ahab of apostasy, turning his back on God. Elijah then challenged the prophets of Baal to a contest to determine whose god was the God. All of Israel was called out to witness this now famous event on Mount Carmel.

(b) Elijah was the only prophet of the living God pitted against some 450 prophets of Baal. The people decided that two altars be arranged—one for Baal and one for Yahweh, the God of Israel. Unkindled wood was placed on the altars, and over the wood—on each altar—was placed a sacrificial animal. Whichever god provided fire for his altar would be the winner—accepted as the God by all involved; at least that's what the people agreed to.

(c) The prophets of Baal went first. But, as you know, all their efforts were in vain. Their wood pile wasn't so much as warmed by the sun.

So Elijah prayed, and the fire of the Lord fell from heaven and consumed the sacrificial animal. Soon after this, so also came the rain which the people needed so desperately. Many people who witnessed this confessed God as their God in that very place, and was Elijah ever on a mountaintop—no pun intended. He was elated, overwhelmed with joy and enthusiasm. He had seen God working that day in a mighty way. Nothing could get Elijah down now . . . or could it?

II. The very next biblical scene that is set begins a strange turn of events. Elijah's mountaintop experience would quickly be challenged: "Then Jezebel sent a messenger to Elijah, saying, 'So may the gods do to me, and more also, if I do not make your life as one of them by tomorrow.' "

(a) Elijah knew that Jezebel was a woman who got what she wanted—whatever it took. Her threat was not an empty one. She fully intended to have him killed by the next day. So he and his personal attendant left, fleeing for life. At Beersheba, Elijah left his servant. He had to face what was ahead alone, at least without human companionship.

(b) From Beersheba, Elijah walked a whole day straight into the desert—rather aimlessly, I suppose—just going with no real destination in mind. He really didn't know where to go or what to do. He sat down under a shrub and said to God, "I've had enough. Take my life, God. It's all over for me anyway." And he went to sleep. Like so many of us, when the going gets tough he was ready to give it all up.

(c) Elijah hadn't made the first attempt to see that his needs for food and water were provided for. Caught up with his problems, he had launched out into the wilderness with nothing. But God ministered to Elijah in spite of himself. Through his messenger, God provided bread and water for him. Elijah ate a little bit and drank some, but soon he went back to sleep.

The angel of the Lord woke him up a second time and said, "Your journey isn't going to end here. Get up and eat some more. You've got a long way to go." Somehow Elijah responded. He ate and drank enough to get him on his way for a forty-day and forty-night trip to Mount Horeb.

III. Yet in spite of the possibility of hope and in spite of God's powerful working to sustain him, Elijah still hadn't come out of the valley emotionally and spiritually. Once he was at Horeb, he found a cave and simply went in there to feel sorry for himself. For all practical purposes, Elijah had given up on life, but God hadn't given up on him. How many times has the very same thing been true for us?

(a) He hadn't been in that cave very long when the voice of God spoke to him and said, "What are you doing here, Elijah?" Elijah answers, "You should know. I've been your man. Here I am—an Israelite—in the midst of a people who have forsaken your covenants. I'm the only one who has kept my commitment to you in the whole land. Why, these crazy Israelites have killed the other prophets. I'm the only one left, and the queen is after me now. I'm not going to be around much longer."

God said, "Elijah, I've got something more to say to you. I want you to listen for me and to me: Go out there and stand on the mountain and listen."

And behold the Lord passed by, and a great and strong wind rent the mountains and broke in pieces the rocks before the Lord, but the Lord was not in the wind; and after the wind an earthquake, but the Lord was not in the earthquake; and after the earthquake a fire, but the Lord was not in the fire; and after the fire a still, small voice.

(b) God's voice in the valleys. God doesn't say, "Your pain doesn't matter to me. I don't have the time to hear your complaining." No, God's still, small voice is the voice of assurance. It is both a reminder and a proof that God has not forsaken us in our times of great need. But God doesn't bowl us over with sounds like a storm. God speaks in a whisper—like the sound of stillness, in the quietest of quiets, after the storm.

(c) God may be ignored, but we cannot escape the reality of God and God's love. God asks Elijah another time, "Elijah, what are you doing here?" This time God wanted to know why Elijah wanted to stay in his valley. But Elijah gives the same answer. In essence, he said to God, "Serving you gets me no where, God. The people you ask me to minister to have killed off all the other prophets. Now their godless queen is after me. What's the use? They don't care about me and evidently you don't either."

(d) Elijah had been in the valley. No one would deny that—least of all, God.

God knew that Elijah was hurt and discouraged and frightened. But God wanted to help Elijah, and Elijah was refusing to be helped. Elijah heard God's loving voice even in the valley, but he ignored it. He wouldn't accept God's support and love. God did not promise him a trouble-free life or ministry. God did not promise Elijah deliverance from this dilemma, but God did promise him God's abiding presence. Still, all Elijah could feel was self-pity.

IV. The next time God's voice came to Elijah in his valley, there was a great difference. God had stopped asking questions and instead said, "Elijah, get up off your self-pity and get back to your business! If you are my man, then you will go and anoint a new king for Syria. Get on with it!"

(a) Elijah, by the way, did get over it, and he went back to doing what he was supposed to do, what God had called him to do. As it turned out, he wasn't the only one in Israel who was being faithful to God—even though that is what he had claimed. As a matter of fact, there were about seven thousand or so faithful souls.

(b) Can we ever get things distorted when we wallow in self-pity. Here's proof that even God gets tired of it. But the story insists—nonetheless—that God does speak to us lovingly and kindly when we have a valley to walk through.

(c) What are the standards for being called a person of God? It has nothing to do with what crises come or don't come into your life. It has nothing to do with how we think we measure up against other people. The standards are God's, and they have to do with God's grace—not what we would require of others. Imagine Elijah's audacity and the confusion he experienced in his valley. He was not the only faithful one in Israel—not even the only faithful prophet. We are not the only faithful ones who experience crisis either.

V. If you're in a valley today—and they are very real—how can you expect to hear God speaking to you in your need? Not in a booming way like some glad-handed well-wisher. Not in any earth-shattering way that will knock you off your feet and force you to hear God whether you want to or not. And not in a way that ignores the reality of your crisis. But in the midst of your need, God speaks loving words, healing words, words of encouragement, words of expectation—in a still, small voice—one which you may have to strain to hear.—David Albert Farmer

Illustrations

GOD DOES GUIDE US. To those who have no experience of this guidance, denial will seem easy. But it is perilous to deny anything on that ground alone. One is reminded of the little girl who thought that she had exhausted mathematics when she had learned the twelve-times table, and when her grandfather said, with a twinkle in his eye, "What's thirteen times thirteen?" she turned on him with undisguised scorn and said, "Don't be silly, Grandpa: there's no such thing."

Some people deny the reality of guidance simply because they've never experienced it, never ventured on the faith, never submitted to the discipline of it, never listened in. But it is real. As real as God and as free as his love.—W. E. Sangster

THE INNER VOICE. When I was deciding the question of my life's work I received a letter from a college president saying, "It is the will of the faculty, the will of the student body, the will of the townspeople, and we believe, the will of God that you should teach in this college." At the same time I received a letter from a trusted friend saying, "I believe it is the will of God that you should go into evangelistic work in America." Then a letter came from the board of missions saying, "It is our will to send you to India." Here was a perfect traffic jam of wills! These were all secondhand, and I felt that I had a right to firsthand knowledge in such a crisis. Not that I would despise the opinions of friends in spiritual guidance, for God often guides through them. But obviously here they could not be depended on. So I took the letter from the board, went to my room, spread it out and said, "Now, Father, my life is not my own and I must answer this. Lead me and I'll follow."

Very clearly the Inner Voice said, "It is India."

"All right," I replied, "that settles it—it is India."

I arose from my knees and wrote at once, saying I was ready. The Inner Voice did not fail me then. It has never failed me since.—E. Stanley Jones

Sermon Suggestions

THE POSSIBLE VIRTUE OF COMPLAINT. TEXT: Exod. 16:2–15. (1) Obedience to the will of God sometimes brings us into hazardous circumstances. (2) It is human, honest, and possibly helpful to complain —ultimately to God. (3) God's concern for us, even before we ask, is so generous that at last we must praise him for his embarrassingly gracious providence.

GOD IS DETERMINED. TEXT: Rom. 11:13–16, 29–32, especially verse 29. (1) God is determined to make his salvation available to all. (2) There have been problems: the election of Israel first; Israel's early rejection of the gospel. (3) Yet God is resourceful, and he will bring his purpose to fulfillment in his mercy shown to all—both Jews and Gentiles.

Worship Aids

CALL TO WORSHIP. "Trust in the Lord. Have faith, do not despair. Trust in the Lord" (Ps. 27:14, TEV).

INVOCATION. Lord, you have proven again and again your faithfulness in all circumstances. Up to this point you have helped us, and we look to you for renewed faith in your providence and presence as we meet for worship.

OFFERTORY SENTENCE. "Praise the Lord, all people on earth; praise his glory and might. Praise the Lord's glorious name; bring an offering and come into his Temple" (Ps. 96:7–8, TEV).

OFFERTORY PRAYER.   Let our very offerings praise you, O Lord. As they represent our love, we lift them up to you, and as they make possible the knowledge of you around the world, they will, we trust, continue and extend your praise.

PRAYER.   We thank you, God,

for people who are there when we
need them and all that sees us through,
all that talks us back from the brink,
    people with time,
    people with no agenda,
    people who listen to our story;
it could be anyone—a fellow worker,
    a teacher, a friend, it could be kin;
it could be the living or the dead,
it could be music,
    some stream of notes, some fall of
    fingers upon keys, some trumpet
    sound,
    some immortal melody, some human
    voice that has carved a channel in
    the geography of our heart to water
    all in its way, where otherwise
    would
    be witheredness and dryness and
    death
it could be books—the world of the
    promised kingdom within, those
    vases
    of loveliness and poignance and
    contentment, moments that are
    snatched Sabbaths;
it could be silence—the sound of
    coolness of shade on a summer
    day,
    the sound of acceptance;
it could be the devotional classics of
    our faith, well known or private,
    classics our very own;
it could be a place—some roll of the
    land, some row of trees, some skyline
    at morning, some house, some back
    door, where, time and again, our
    spirit returns to get its bearings,
    to know we are loved, to know who
    we are;
it could be memory—what someone
    used

to say, what we always used to do,
    the little things that are the only
    things that last;
it could be Scriptures—its stories,
    its wars, its loves, its betrayals,
    its parables, its miracles, its
    disasters, and always, always, the
    Psalms, always the choir of the
        Psalms;
it could be you, Creator,
it could be you, Spirit,
it could be you, Son,
it could be you, O blessed Trinity,
    no mere formula, but life,
    three rivers in one;
We thank you, God,
    for all that sees us through,
For we are all survivors, God,
    spilled here by some good fortune
    that we should live to see
    the light of day;
Open our hearts to your glory about
us,
    in the ripening grain
    and in the portals of heaven
    that are the eyes of the least,
    lest, spilled into life,
    our hearts alone should say no
    to their creator.
                                    —Peter Fribley

LECTIONARY MESSAGE

Topic: Tenacious Faith

TEXT: Matt. 15:21–28

The incident with the Canaanite woman is one of those many passages in the Gospel accounts of Jesus' ministry which look forward to the gentile mission of the early church. That is unmistakable here. Jesus is in the region of Tyre and Sidon, gentile territory. The woman is identified as a Canaanite, a non-Jew, and the epithet *dog* is applied to her, a term often employed by Jews to denote Gentiles. Even more, the preceding half of Matthew 15 deals with Jesus' rejection of the Jewish laws of clean and unclean, the very purity laws which so often served to separate Jews from "unclean" Gentiles who did not observe such rules. Jesus' rejection of these laws paved the way for acceptance of the Gentiles. In this passage which immediately follows, Jesus carries through on his principle and responds to a Gentile's request.

There is another lesson in the story. It is set by the woman. It is a lesson in faith—persistent, tenacious faith. The story is quite dramatic. The woman had every reason to give up. The disciples, even Jesus, seemed to rebuff her. Still, like the dogs in Jesus' saying, she clung to his heels and refused to relax her grip. In the end her faith prevailed.

I. *Hindrances to faith*. The disciples serve as the foil in the story. They represent implicitly the Jewish viewpoint. Why should Jesus give the time of day to this person? After all, she was a Gentile, a woman, a general nuisance with her persistent pleas. "Send her away. She's hampering our mission" (v. 23). One should not be too hard on the disciples. There are times most of us get so caught up in what *we* see as the Lord's business that we have no time for, perhaps even become annoyed with, the very ones most in need, those most open to faith.

II. *A challenge to faith*. But the surprise comes when Jesus *doesn't* rebuke the disciples. We expect that. Instead, he seems to take up where they left off and rebuff the woman in even harsher terms. "My ministry is to Israel—not you Gentiles" (v. 24). That was true. Jesus did limit his outreach primarily to the Jews. That was how he saw his mission—to God's chosen people, to Israel first. But he had a wider vision, that from that band of committed Jews the word of God's salvation would spread to the ends of the earth. *We* know that. But did this woman? Probably not. What she *did* know was that her daughter was desperately ill, and she had faith that Jesus could heal the child. So she clung on, falling at Jesus' feet and continuing her pleas (v. 25). And Jesus' challenge to her faith intensified. "The Bread of Life is for the Jews, the children, not for gentile dogs" (v. 26). The words must have hurt. Her hope was in Jesus, and now *he* seemed like the most prejudiced of Jews. Most would have placed their tail between their legs and limped away. Not this woman. She accepted the challenge and snapped back.

III. *The triumph of faith*. "But, master, even the puppies get the crumbs which fall from the table" (v. 27). The woman's faith was not only tenacious. It was also resourceful. She has the last word with Jesus in the exchange. And he *liked* being bested in the repartee. He granted her request. Her daughter was healed. Above all, he commended her *faith* (v. 28).

One should not be put off by Jesus' harsh words about dogs. In the first part of the chapter, Matthew has made it infinitely clear where Jesus stood on such things. For him there were no pure and impure, no gentile "dogs." But in this world where there is plenty of prejudice and rejection, obstacles to faith abound. The faith that Jesus commends, the faith this woman showed, is not so easily discouraged. It is a tenacious faith.—John Polhill

SUNDAY: AUGUST TWENTY-SECOND

SERVICE OF WORSHIP

Sermon: Taking No Offense in Jesus

TEXT: Luke 7:19–23

I. Has Jesus ever offended you? Today we who think we follow Jesus must be about the task of doing some honest soul-searching to see if Jesus offends us. Today we come like the disciples of John the Baptist and ask, "Are you the one sent from God? Or should we look for another?" The only answer we will be given is one which is truly a hard saying from Jesus. Jesus says to us, "Blessed are you who take no offense in me."

This is a difficult answer for us to grasp. "Blessed are you who take no offense in me." It is one that is surely hard on us. What does Jesus mean? Does he mean for us to take it as a warning that he and his work are not to be ignored? Yes. Is his answer an appeal for us to have faith in him? Yes. It is these things and more. It is an invitation to believe in him and not stumble because of him. It is a claim for us to commit to Jesus rather than be offended by him.

But let us be careful about how we might get offended this day. Our hearts might protest and be offended by the mere suggestion or slightest mention of the hint that we could be offended by Jesus. The possibility offends us as it were. Let us learn from that good man of strong faith John the Baptist. He sends his disciples to Jesus because his heart is in the midst of doubt, and he sits on the verge of committing himself to Jesus and his way. But he has held back. Possibly he has been offended by Jesus. Hence, Jesus' response to the disciples to send back to John, "Blessed are you who take no offense in me."

The words that Jesus uses here are very difficult to translate. When Jesus says for us not to take offense in him, he has in mind the twin images of stumbling because of him as well as falling away in disbelief. As difficult as the words are to translate, though, we can translate them in our hearts. Walter Brueggeman has Jesus saying, "Lucky are you, if you are not upset."

II. Why would Jesus upset us? Because that is the way it can be with Jesus in our lives. It can be an upsetting reality to have Jesus close to you and to allow yourself to get close to Jesus. Jesus is dangerous and loves us with the very love of God. Jesus is subversive and always turning the tables on us. He is a scandal to how we think he should act. Jesus never operates according to our own preferred ways of doing things.

Jesus offends our good manners. He is always more odd than we thought him previously to be. It seems we are always at odds with him. Jesus surprises us more often than not and never quite does things as we expected or anticipated. Our hearts do not always hear Jesus gladly. Sometimes our souls rise up and do not call him blessed. When Jesus gets close to us he upsets the balance. He turns us inside out. He turns our world upside down. Jesus exposes our darkness, and that is never a pretty sight. He beholds exactly who we are, and that is not a welcome prospect. Jesus uncovers our sin so that our hearts stand naked before the eyes of God. He shatters our hypocrisies, destroys our illusions, burns away our masks of deception, speaks the truth against our lies, and puts an end to our spiritual pretensions.

This kind of Jesus offends us. It is a spiritual reality that we can indeed be offended, outraged, put off by, and repelled by this Jesus. At best we just shake our heads in disbelief at Jesus. At our worst we fall by the wayside, wander off into the wilderness, choose emptiness, turn our backs on his love, walk out into the desert, and beat a fast retreat away from being a committed disciple.

Still Jesus comes to us, and still he says, "Blessed are you who take no offense in me." I. Howard Marshall says in his commentary on Luke's Gospel that this saying of Jesus "refers to the possibility of a person not accepting Jesus as 'the Coming One' because he stumbles at the kind of things done and left undone by Jesus and thinks that Jesus should have behaved differently." (I. Howard Marshall, *Commentary on Luke,* [Grand Rapids: Eerdmans, 1978], 292.) The man from Nazareth is truly, as Marcus Borg says, the "undomesticated Jesus."

III. Before we are offended too strongly by this Jesus, let us risk taking one more look at him. Let us get up close to Jesus, real close so that Jesus just might go deep down into our hearts. If we look at Jesus, we might be offended just as the people of his own day were.

Remember Jesus' response to military power: "Fear not them that kill the body, but fear those realities which can steal your soul." Remember Jesus' response to the political leaders: "Render unto Caesar what belongs to him, but never forget that your life belongs to God." Herod knew from the start the truth that Jesus' kingdom was not of his world. Remember Jesus' response to violence when he refused to lead the people in a revolt which they expected him to do on that fateful day we now call Palm Sunday. Remember Jesus' refusal to answer Pilate and thus passing the verdict once and for all on doing the dishonest, expedient thing. Remember Jesus' harsh word against the use of force: "Those that live by the sword die by the sword." Remember Jesus' parable to the rich and powerful that ends with the haunting words, "Fool! This night your soul is required of you." Remember Jesus' harsh indictment against hypocrisy in the guise of following God by saying that one day those who shout loudly, "Lord, Lord," will meet their downfall. Remember Jesus' response to the religious leaders of his day which caused them to take offense in him. Jesus lashed out against the Pharisees, the conservatives, and accused them of binding unbearable burdens on the backs of spiritually hungry people. Jesus taunted the Sadducees, the liberals, for their lack of genuine conviction and commitment to the message of God. Jesus said of both that they were blind guides. Remember Jesus' response to those who were smug in their self-righteousness: "You who are without sin cast the first stone." Remember Jesus' response to James and John when they wanted what they thought were their just spiritual desserts: "You do not have a clue what you are asking!" Remember Jesus' response to Peter about forgiveness: "I tell you, Peter, that you can never stop forgiving. Seventy times seven, I tell you, Peter." On and on we could go. Jesus does offend us. He offends us quite often and with unrelenting regularity.

IV. The bottom line is that Jesus will not be tamed by us. He will not be held by our hard hearts. He cannot be boxed in by our narrow vision. He refuses to fit our traditional molds and popular notions of who we think he is and how he ought to act. Jesus is larger than the narrow gates of our spirits and the small rooms of our souls. He sees more than our blind eyes can. We will never figure out who this Jesus really is. He is, quite simply, beyond our control. He is not our possession. He is not at our beck and call. Rather, he comes demanding our lives. Our lives, it seems, do not belong to us. Our lives belong to God. What an offensive thought!

The time to respond to this Jesus who might well offend us is right now. Our hearts come asking Jesus their questions this day: "Are you the one from God or should we look for another?" The response of Jesus will call to the eyes of our souls the truth of his life and ministry in our midst already: The blind see, the lame walk, the lepers are cleansed, the deaf hear, the dead are raised, and the spiritually hungry have the good news preached to them. It is toward this one that we are asked to turn in belief. It is this one who says, "Blessed are you who take no offense in me."

Like John the Baptist sent his disciples to Jesus, we send our hearts to Jesus. We may come wearing the tears of anguish on our face torn from hearts in the midst of the deep shadows of dark nights of our souls. If so, we come offering our tears and doubts to Jesus. We may come with slow and timid steps echoing the hint of the dawning of a new day to walk in faith. If so, we come bringing our caution and fear. At least we can come.

To be offended by Jesus will be to miss Jesus passing by our lives. To be offended by Jesus will mean that we will not be blessed. By our commitment to Jesus we will stand or fall.

Jesus speaks to each one this day: "Blessed are you who take no offense in me."—Rickey J. Ray

Illustrations

THE WORD AND THE SACRAMENTS. Throughout the Scriptures, God discloses himself in events, in mighty and compassionate acts in human affairs. In the call of a solitary patriarch to take his family and possessions upon a long and venturesome journey; in the mysterious moving of the conscience of a lawgiver to enact a loftier righteousness for his people in the advance of clans of tribesmen to take possession of a land and set up a more just and fraternal society; in the defeats of apostate monarchs, and in the summons by prophets to repentance and godlier life, above all, in the birth, life, teaching, cross, and Resurrection of Jesus of Nazareth, God acts. Responsive spirits recognize his presence, interpret his activity, communicate their interpretation to a community, the church, which conserves and abundantly utters the memory of God's goodness. That church transmits her evangel in symbolic rites, like the Passover and the Supper of the Lord, and proclaims it in her prophetic message. She becomes a messenger to the nations, a light to lighten the Gentiles.—Henry Sloane Coffin

VITAL EXPERIENCE.   To have had a vital and redemptive contact with Jesus is to know, beyond doubt or challenge, that it is along the lines of the pattern of the soul of Jesus that God's world plan is built. The man whose own life has suddenly leapt into meaning beneath the touch of Jesus, who has seen his own experience transformed from a chaos into a cosmos by some never-to-be-forgotten Damascus encounter, has a right to claim that he has found the clue to the riddle of life and destiny. In this sense, at least, Browning's bold words are true, that "the acknowledgement of God in Christ solves all questions in the earth and out of it." It is a root conviction of Christian experience that a man who is united to Christ by faith has not only found a personal Savior: He has come into touch with ultimate reality.—James S. Stewart

Sermon Suggestions

WHY PRAISE THE LORD?   TEXT: Psalm 95 (1) Because of his greatness, verses 1–5. (2) Because of his grace in Creation and redemption, verses 6–7a. (3) Because of the certainty of judgment that results when he is ignored, verses 7b–11.

THE DIMENSIONS OF GOD'S PROVIDENCE. TEXT: Rom. 11:33–36. (1) God is Father and Creator—all things are from him. (2) God is Redeemer as incarnate in Jesus Christ—all things are through him. (3) God is the object of worship in the Spirit—all things are to him.

Worship Aids

CALL TO WORSHIP.   "How beautiful upon the mountains are the feet of him that bringeth good tidings, that publish-

eth peace; that bringeth good tidings of good, that publisheth salvation; that saith unto Zion, thy God reigneth" (Isa. 52:7).

INVOCATION.   Today, O God, we thank you for pastors and lay people—ministers *all*, preachers *all*. Grant us to know the importance to all people everywhere of what we do here and what we proclaim to the ends of the earth.

OFFERTORY SENTENCE.   "Take ye from among you an offering unto the Lord: whosoever is of a willing heart, let him bring it" (Exod. 35:5).

OFFERTORY   PRAYER.   Lord,   if   our hearts are not willing, make them willing to share the glorious gospel of Christ wherever men and women, boys and girls, need your love and grace.

PRAYER.   Merciful God, we pray for the very old and all who care for them: children and grandchildren, brothers and sisters, the friends and townspeople who still know them; all church ministries of sympathy, witness, and service. Make us the blessing to them that we would that someone be to us when we are they, should we live so long.

We pray for the staff of nursing homes and doctors and nurses. Help us to learn from the very old: the wisdom that is theirs and, when much is gone, what is left. To treasure the little things, savor the morsel, delight in the small, to drink of the still water that runs deep.—Peter Fribley

LECTIONARY MESSAGE

Topic: You Are the Christ
TEXT: Matt. 16:13–20
During the 1970s it was not unusual to hear young persons say that they were trying to find themselves. They asked questions like, What is my purpose in life? What is life all about? And who am I? Was it that these questions did not interest earlier generations? I'm not sure of the answer to that question. Perhaps the social unrest of the sixties provided the environment where the questions were

more relevant and easier to ask. The strange thing is, they are important questions, ones that should be asked by all who are attempting to live rather than merely exist.

I. Is it possible that Jesus was asking just such an existential question when he queried his disciples in Caesarea Philippi? "Who do men say that the Son of man is?" Here is a crucial question for Jesus. Is Jesus, in the mystery of the Incarnation—the mystery that in Jesus we see full humanity and full divinity—seeking to understand his personhood and his mission? Is that why he identifies himself with humanity in this question (Son of man)? If we take the doctrine of the Incarnation seriously, we have to be careful about the foreknowledge we credit Jesus with having. In his full humanity, Jesus attempted to respond faithfully to his understanding of God and God's will for his life. Is this question a part of that inquiry?

The disciples responded, "Some say John the Baptist, others say Elijah, and others Jeremiah or one of the prophets." Then he asked, "But who do you say that I am?" And Simon Peter replied, "You are the Christ, the Son of the living God." And Jesus answered him, "Blessed are you, Simon Bar-Jona! For flesh and blood has not revealed this to you, but my Father who is in heaven."

II. Is it possible that Peter's reply was not only a revelatory moment for Peter but for Jesus as well? What Jesus had understood in his spiritual pilgrimage with God was now communicated to him through one of his disciples. Jesus' baptism marked a crucial moment of revelation for him. Jesus' authority as a teacher and his power to heal the sick and possessed helped to confirm his divine destiny. But Peter's confession at Caesarea Philippi showed that God had revealed Christ to another. That's how we know Christ, through the revelation of God.

Jesus continued, "And I tell you, you are Peter, and on this rock I will build my church, and the powers of death shall not prevail against it." Since the church is Christ's, even the gates of hell are not an obstacle. The church holds the keys of the kingdom of heaven and is charged with making God's kingdom an ever-present reality now upon the earth.

III. Finally, Jesus told his disciples to tell no one that he was the Christ—that revelation was not yet ready to be heard. But now the church has the responsibility to tell the whole world of God's Christ: Jesus is Lord.—Craig A. Loscalzo

SUNDAY: AUGUST TWENTY-NINTH

SERVICE OF WORSHIP

Sermon: Crumbs of Love
TEXT: Matt. 15:21–28

On this story of Jesus and the Canaanite woman the scholars try to take the rudeness out of Jesus' words by suggesting that he is joking with her. Professor Barclay correctly comments, "The tone and look with which a thing is said makes all the difference. A thing which seems hard can be said with a disarming smile. We can call a friend, "an old villain" or "a rascal" with a smile and tone which takes all the sting out of it and fills it with affection.

Jesus' harsh and biting words, "It is not good to take the children's bread and to cast it to the dogs," are watered down by some scholarship. Jesus could not have meant what he said. The commentaries rush to rescue Jesus from negative publicity by saying that surely these words were said in jest; a smile and an "elbow in the ribs" must have lightened the weight of these words.

It is a shame that our scholars do not trust their Jesus. Perhaps Jesus knew exactly what he was doing saying rough and hard things to this woman. Sometimes the truth is not gentle or kind. We ought at least to attempt to understand the story as it is before we start trying to change its thrust by putting it into the context of comedy. It is possible for this story to be good news as it is.

I. This is the only time in his ministry that Jesus goes outside the Jewish territory. He goes into the region of Tyre and Sidon. And there he is confronted with a plea for help. Human suffering and pain are everywhere. The woman's daughter is dying. The plea for help is implicit in the facts. Jesus is there confronted with this terrible question of whether or not there is a limit to God's power to help. Is God's grace, love, and power available to just everybody, or is there a limit to that love and mercy? Are some people excluded? Can pagans, Gentiles, Samaritans, and others receive and benefit from the mercy and grace of God for which they have not been preparing? The Jewish people had been waiting for God to come for ages. The Gentiles had not been longing or hoping for his coming. We have seen what happens to countries when democracy is installed and the people are not prepared by education and economic realities for democracy. It fails. Can the love of God be effective for those who have no history of living, worshiping, and waiting for the One Holy God.

This woman was likely a Gentile who worshiped a variety of gods. She did not honor just one sovereign God. The pagan world had lots of little gods who did not care about her and whom she did not have to love to obey. The pagan culture had only to learn how to appease, sacrifice, and manipulate the heavenly powers. This was a world of fertility gods, war gods, love goddesses, moon goddesses, and a host of little goddesses and demons. It was a jungle of passions and loyalties. How could Jesus give to that woman anything that would be received correctly? Was there a limit to God's grace?

We are fast discovering that it is only in those societies and cultures where there is One Creator Lord that there can be any absolute value to us as individuals. It is only when we have some vision of a new heaven and a new earth that we have some ethical standards. It is only when we are endowed by our Creator with rights that we may talk about equality of individuals, because apart from the dignity, worth, value of individuals given by God all other standards of evaluation are relative standards, conditional values, limited worth, which result from comparing me with others.

II. How could the Bread that was made to be given to those who had been following and worshiping God ever since Abraham be nourishing for one who had grown up on such a different religious diet. It is not right to take bread prepared for a salt-free diet and give it to one who needs salt. Jesus knew that this kingdom of God had been sent to the children of Israel, for those who had been hungering and thirsting for the Messiah for generations. The kingdom of God, he knew, is for those who have been waiting, waiting, watching, and hoping for years, like Simeon and Anna. It is the gift of God those who from the days of King David have been awaiting and hoping the coming of David's son. Is not the coming Messiah limited only to those who have been expecting a Messiah? The Son of David brings bread that nourishes only to those who have been singing "Come Thou Long Expected Jesus." Is this Bread of Life really for all people broken or is it limited only to those who have been waiting for it?

III. And Jesus says, Yes there is a limit to this bread. Jesus says, I cannot take this bread out of the mouths of those who have been waiting for it and give it away carelessly to one who just shows up at the table. Now, no matter how you ever try to say it, a limit always sounds harsh. When you say that the legal age for drinking is twenty-one, those twenty, nineteen, eighteen will not be happy. Those just below the limit think the limit is cruel and arbitrary. Every time a teacher says an A is for those who earn the average of ninety-five to one hundred, those who make an average of ninety-four think that limit is mean and legalistic. In a culture where one of our leading stockbroker firms tries to tell us that there are no boundaries, to say there are limits is to be pessimistic, defeatist, cruel, and not very loving. Jesus says to this woman's plea for help, "I cannot take that which has been sent to those who have been hungering and thirsting after

God's righteousness and just give it to everybody. There is a limit to God's grace, and limits always sound cruel and callous. The limit is that God's love can come only to those who are waiting for it.

IV. I don't really know what that woman felt when she heard Jesus' words. To be compared to a dog! I do know that in the story Matthew does not report any signs of indignation. She does not walk away like the rich young ruler. She simply says to Jesus that there are others who, like the family dogs, have been sitting, begging, waiting under the table for whatever crumbs might fall. She is bold enough to say that she has been waiting, hoping, watching, longing for the coming of the grace of God the way our dogs circle the floor under the table for whatever scraps and spills might come. There are others, she points out, besides just the children of Israel who have been hungering and thirsting for whatever crumbs of love and peace might fall to the floor. There are those who have been nourished and kept alive by finding a few crumbs of love and who are waiting under the table for more. If God's love is coming to those who wait for it, do not think that only those in the family are waiting, but there are others, yes, under the table like dogs who wait for a few crumbs.

Jesus is in awe of her faith: " 'O woman, great is your faith, be it to you as you want.' And her daughter was healed from that hour."

V. Jesus suggests that there are limits to God's grace and mercy. God cannot give forgiveness to those who have no sense of guilt and do not think they need redemption. God cannot give love to a person who does not want to be loved. God cannot give strength, comfort, encouragement, and peace to one who refuses to admit the need for strength, who will not admit a weakness. God cannot give hope to those who are satisfied with what they now have. God has no way to give faith to those who will trust no one but themselves.

There are limits to the power and love of God. God's kingdom cannot be established in every heart, and so it will not be built in all places. That will always sound unloving and ungracious of God. It will sound harsh and discriminatory, but we ought not to try to make it sound like a joke. Not even God can give bread to one who will not take it. Not even God will make a person drink of living water if she does not feel a thirst. Even God will not force reconciliation where no reconciliation is wanted. God will not make whole and better than new that which no one will confess is broken. It is always amazing how much pain and suffering people will endure without ever talking about it or acknowledging it. A saviour is worthless to those who have no need to be saved.

But there is also the good news that Christ has come in joy and gladness to all those who wait, long, know, watch, and are ready to be made whole by the love and power of God. Those who wait at the table as guests and those who wait under the table as dogs, God comes to all who are watching and waiting the coming of God's power to change and redeem us. — Rick Brand

Illustrations

OUR DUTY TO LOVE THOSE WE SEE. Purely human love is always about to fly after or fly away with the beloved's perfections. We say that a seducer steals a girl's heart, but one must say of all merely human love, even when it is most beautiful, that there is something thievish about it, that it even steals the beloved's perfections; whereas Christian love grants the beloved all his imperfections and weaknesses and in all his changes remains with him, loving the person it sees.

If this were not so, Christ would never have loved, for where could he have found the perfect man!—Sören Kierkegaard

ARE YOU SORRY?   Let me tell you a story. It comes from Bruce Marshall's novel *The World, the Flesh and Father Smith.* It is of a young priest trying to persuade a dying sailor to confess his sins so that he may receive absolution and the last rites of the church. But the old sailor has a courageous honesty. He's not sorry for all the Jezebels he knew in foreign ports. He had enjoyed them, and he wouldn't deny it. But the priest, despite his youth, was wise. He asked the sailor if he was sorry for not being sorry for having known all these women? The old sailor said, "Yes," and he was absolved.—James T. Cleland

Sermon Suggestions

FOR GOD'S PEOPLE OF EVERY AGE. TEXT: Exod. 19:1–9, NRSV. (1) God's people are recipients of special grace, verse 4. (2) God's people enter their destiny through loyal love, verse 5. (3) God's people render special service for God as "a priestly kingdom," verse 6.

CHRISTIAN CONDUCT. TEXT: Rom. 12:1–13. (1) Its source: the mercies of God, set forth in Rom. 3:21–8:39. (2) Its goal: personal transformation and obedience. (3) Its expression: cooperative service with people having "gifts that differ." (4) Its motivation: genuine love.

Worship Aids

CALL TO WORSHIP.   "By this shall all men know that ye are my disciples," said Jesus, "if ye have love one to another" (John 13:35).

INVOCATION.   Give us understanding hearts, O God, hearts shaped by the love of our Lord Jesus Christ, so that we may love one another, despite faults and failings. To that end, forgive our sins, and may we forgive one another as you for Christ's sake have forgiven us.

OFFERTORY SENTENCE.   "As we have therefore opportunity, let us do good unto all men, especially unto them who are of the household of faith" (Gal. 6:10).

OFFERTORY PRAYER.   Lord, there is no end to our opportunities to do good to people; we can never say that what we do is ever quite enough. Nevertheless, we of-

fer our stewardship to you and ask you to guide us as we render our Christian service in general and as we bring our offerings in particular.

PRAYER.   O creator of all that is, was, and shall be, we marvel that you have so created us in your image that we are not left to the loneliness of our finitude, but that we can communicate and relate to you as a child to his parent. Whatever our language, you hear us. There is a "deep speaking unto deep" that undergirds the elusive and broken words that we attempt to form with our lips.

From the beginning you have been speaking a life-giving Word. Your Word is spoken in nature—how beautiful that Word—but at times how awesome. Your Word was so spoken through the affairs of the people Israel to reveal your presence and purpose to all humankind. The story of their pilgrimage from slavery, through the trials of the wilderness, to the Promised Land haunts as the likely pilgrimage of every person. Even more presently your Word is here in the flesh and blood of Jesus and dwells among us in the meaning of his life, ministry, Passion, living again. In your coming in him and being with him to the end and beyond, we know assuredly that you are with us through all of life's vicissitudes and that no matter how great the fracture there is the grace that heals. And so in every dark night of the soul we find ourselves singing, "Emmanuel, God with us." May the indwelling gift of your Spirit to illumine and energize call to mind your Word from the beginning and quicken our minds and hearts and persons to do your will in the flesh and blood of our time and place.

In these moments, we have been confronted again that this is our vocation as the *ecclesia,* the "called out ones," to be the light of the world, the light in any dark corner, the salt of the earth, that savor that preserves and gives zest and meaning to life. That we may fulfill this high calling may we so feed on your Word that it becomes for us the Bread of Life and through us the Bread that is bread indeed for many.

For your Word of grace that makes all things new, we pray, not only for our personal relationships but for the healing of the nations. Deliver us from those who would provoke rather than reconcile—who incite fear rather than inspire brotherhood and sisterhood—who are more concerned to fill the coffers of the merchants of death than to mediate life through peace and through loving and life-giving policies. We pray for us and our fellow citizens that responsibly we may exercise the franchise to choose policy and leadership for these critical times.

To pray "Our Father" as we so often do, may we realize how intimately we are bound together in a common bundle of life. What an amazing network of production, finance, and commerce nurtures and sustains our daily lives! On this day we would pray for all of those to whom we are indebted for life-giving services, that we all too often take for granted. We pray, too, for those where there is any brokenness in health, in sorrow, in estrangement, in disappointment, in failure, to the end that the quickening of your Word of grace may make them whole. For those students—our children and grandchildren—who are entering into new opportunities of education, we pray a wise investment of this year. May those who are their teachers, professors, counselors see their vocation as a high calling, not only to impart knowledge, but to mediate life.

And now, O God, grant to each of us such responsiveness to your Word that the good work you have begun in us may be perfected to your glory, through him who teaches us to pray and live.—John Thompson

LECTIONARY MESSAGE

Topic: Radical Discipleship
Text: Matt. 16:21–28

I. *Peter misses the point.* Following Peter's declaration that Jesus was the Christ, Jesus prepared his disciples for the realities that would come. He foreshadowed the events that would take place in Jerusalem—the elders, chief priests, and scribes would seek and obtain Jesus'

death, but on the third day he would be raised. Peter was unwilling to believe his ears. "The Christ will not have to suffer such things," he thought. Jesus rebuked him by suggesting that, though he was sensitive to the revelation of God (cf. Matt. 16:13–20), his mind was still locked into the ways of humankind.

II. *The paradox of discipleship.* Jesus' response to Peter provoked a lesson to all the disciples about discipleship. Discipleship is a response to God's will and not to human prerogatives. Peter's misunderstanding of the nature of the Christ was due to his misconception about the character of discipleship. Those who decide to follow Jesus will learn what it means to deny self. Bearing a cross and denying self was a difficult idea for the disciples of the first century. Self-denial is immensely harder in our societal context, which caters to self-fulfillment and self-ingratiation. Neil Postman's *Amusing Ourselves to Death* characterizes a society bent on self. Real discipleship is losing oneself for the gospel. Paradox characterizes discipleship: "For whoever would save his or her life will lose it, and whoever loses his or her life for my sake will find it." These words are difficult for any generation of disciples.

III. *True disciples believe and act.* Truly following Christ is a matter of belief and behavior. Jesus said that the Father will repay all according to what they have *done.* Orthodoxy is not the only measure of discipleship. Jesus demands that one's discipleship involve more than words. "Practice what you preach," we say. James echoed Jesus' concern when he wrote that believers should be "doers of the word and not hearers only." Is today's church acting out the word in the world? Or is the church merely interested in self?

Many people are skeptical about the church today. George Barna points out in *The Frog in the Kettle* that contemporary people view the church as an antiquated and irrelevant institution. Is it possible that society's assessment of the church is a result of the church's arguments about right doctrine and lack of concern about right actions?

Today's text is a reminder that the measure of success for ministry is faithfulness to Christ. Human measures of success get in the way of Christ achieving his purpose through the church. Our faithfulness to the gospel is directly proportional to our willingness to deny ourselves in following Christ. If we are truly faithful, Christ will be glorified, and we will be on the way of losing ourselves for Christ's sake. Perhaps such a model of discipleship would convince the world that our message is good news indeed.—Craig A. Loscalzo

SUNDAY: SEPTEMBER FIFTH

SERVICE OF WORSHIP

Sermon: Anger—God's Gift to Us
TEXT: Eph. 4:26–27

I have come to the conclusion that anger is God's gift to us, that it is central in the repentance/forgiveness process, and that it must be understood and handled appropriately in order to experience the abundant life that Jesus came to give.

Anger is a response to anxiety which comes to us when we experience a threat to our personhood. That threat may be something as simple and straightforward as a knife or gun aimed at our body or as distant as a critical remark made in reference to our spouse or child. When the threat is perceived, anxiety is the result and in response to that anxiety, we will feel a need to express either fear or anger.

If anger is God's gift to us, how does it or should it function in the life of the Christian? If repentance is the hinge upon which we swing from sin to forgiveness, then the proper understanding and direction of anger is the hinge pin. Anger is the pin that keeps us properly directed between sin and forgiveness.

When you understand your anger, you will understand wherein you have been sinned against. Then you may properly express your anger in the direction of the one who has sinned against you. And most important, you will be able to see clearly how their sinning against you has caused or might cause you to sin against others. You can repent of your sin and turn from it. You will not find that at all difficult to do.

The concepts that I have alluded to here need biblical support and explanation. So let us turn to God's Word at this point.

I. Anger is not sinful (be angry and sin not).

(a) We have wondered about Jesus in the Temple. Let me make this quick and as painless as possible for you. Jesus was angry when he cleansed the Temple. There is no doubt in my mind that Jesus was angry! Just read what was going on in the house of God. Read what Jesus said about it. In Matt. 21:13 Jesus "said unto them, It is written, 'My house shall be called the house of prayer, but ye have made it a den of thieves.' "

(b) But look with me at another passage of Scripture. In Mark 3:5, we read, "And when he had looked round about on them with anger, being grieved for the hardness of their hearts, he saith unto the man, 'Stretch forth thine hand,' and he stretched it out; and his hand was restored whole as the other."

There is no other word which will translate the Greek word here: It was anger with which Jesus looked upon them.

(c) There is a place in Matt. 5:22 where Jesus says, "But I say unto you, that whosoever is angry with his brother without a cause shall be in danger of the judgment. . . ."

We might more properly read and understand what Jesus was saying if we read, "Whoever is constantly angry with his brother is in danger of the judgment."

We hide, suppress, and deny our anger at our brother, sister, children, and parents, until we find ourselves doing just what Jesus warned against: We are constantly angry with them. We are angry with them when we wish that we were not.

What is the answer to this situation?

II. Anger is to be expressed properly (don't let the sun . . .).

(a) The answer for this situation is to turn back to God's Word and to do what it tells us to do. Be angry and sin not and don't let the sun go down on your anger.

I have had a great deal of anger in my life for all of my life. Had it not been for Donna's willingness to allow me and encourage me to express my anger at the moment I felt it and had it not been for her willingness to express her anger at the moment she felt it, we might not have made it as a married couple.

(b) I hope that there are those of you here who will say, having heard this sermon, "I understood that all along." But I must say that this understanding of the central importance of anger, its understanding, recognition in our lives, its proper direction and its appropriate expression have struck me as completely new ideas.

Now let us move to the idea of the proper direction of anger.

III. Anger is to be properly directed (Matt. 18:15f.).

(a) In Matt. 18:15–18, Jesus has given us the key to the proper direction and expression of our anger. "Moreover, if thy brother trespass against thee, go and tell him his fault between thee and him alone; if he shall hear thee, thou hast gained thy brother. But if he will not hear thee, then take with thee one or two more, that in the mouth of two or three witnesses every word may be established. And if he shall neglect to hear them, tell it unto the church; but if he neglect to hear the church, let him be unto thee as a heathen man and a publican."

(b) When we get Jesus' perspective on anger and realize that we have an imperative statement from him on the subject, which is that we are to go to our brother or sister when they have sinned against us, then things look a bit differently to us.

I still well remember the time when a friend of mine had been trying to tell me that some of my behavior was below his

standard for a Christian. Finally, I made, what seemed to him, an inappropriate comment. He turned to me and angrily said, with his finger pointed in my face, "I rebuke that in the name of Jesus!" I felt as though my face had been slapped. But I got the message.

IV. There are some here who have suffered terribly at the hands of other persons. Perhaps you thought that the anger you have felt is wrong, sinful, and against God. No! It isn't. It is God's gift to you to help you discern between your sin and the sin that has been sinned against you.

(a) It is my conviction that until you get in touch with the anger that God gave you in those moments of having been sinned against, you will never become properly oriented toward God nor your fellowman. You will be stuck in the sin or repentance mode but never experiencing the peace of God.

(b) Perhaps you are aware of having carried a terrible burden of anger or of guilt for things that you have simply not done. I offer you the understanding of a God who wants more than anything for you to experience the abundant life.—H. Barry Carter

Illustrations

THINKING DIFFERENTLY.   An old man in India sat down in the shade of an ancient banyan tree whose roots disappeared far away in a swamp. Presently he discerned a commotion where the roots entered the water. Concentrating his attention, he saw that a scorpion had become helplessly entangled in the roots. Pulling himself to his feet, he made his way carefully along the tops of the roots to the place where the scorpion was trapped. He reached down to extricate it. But each time he touched the scorpion, it lashed his hand with its tail, stinging him painfully. Finally his hand was so swollen he could no longer close his fingers, so he withdrew to the shade of the tree to wait for the swelling to go down. As he arrived at the trunk, he saw a young man standing above him on the road laughing at him. "You're a fool," said the young man, "wasting your time trying to help a

scorpion that can only do you harm."
The old man replied, "Simply because it
is in the nature of the scorpion to sting,
should I change my nature, which is to
save?"—William Sloane Coffin

DISCIPLINE YOURSELF.   You may not
enjoy shutting your mouth when what
you really want to do is shoot it off, but
for your health and the health of others
it is better in the long run that you do so.
Blow up in haste and cool off at leisure is
the sad tale being learned by millions of
people throughout the world. Yet learning self-discipline, no matter how hard it
may be initially, is still much easier than
sitting it out in prison for fifty years. So
bite your lips or dig your fingernails into
your palms, because holding yourself
back will be easier on you than expressing cruel hostility will be.—Paul A.
Hauck

Sermon Suggestions

WHEN THE LORD DESCENDS.   TEXT:
Exod. 19:16–24. (1) Signs of God's presence and revelation may inspire fear and
trembling. (2) Yet God's ultimate purpose is to bless his people, as shown in his
revelation in Jesus Christ (John 1:16–18).

GUIDELINES FOR CHRISTIAN CITIZENS.
TEXT: Rom. 13:1–10. (1) God has instituted the principle of law and order. (2)
The Christian, like everyone else, is
obliged to recognize civil authority and
obey the laws of society. (3) However, by
being subject to a higher principle, the
Christian can fulfill the requirements of a
just society and of God at the same time.

Worship Aids

CALL TO WORSHIP.   "Show me thy
ways, O Lord; teach me thy paths" (Ps.
25:4).

INVOCATION.   We are here to learn, O
Lord, as well as to praise you. Teach us as
we worship—in songs and hymns, in the
reading of Scripture, in the sacrament of
word and table, and in fellowship with
one another—and as we are taught what

to be and to do, grant us the will to obey
and praise you in all things and everywhere.

OFFERTORY SENTENCE.   "Bless the
Lord, O my soul, and forget not all his
benefits" (Ps. 103:2).

OFFERTORY PRAYER.   As we look back,
O Lord, we remember: forgiveness of
sin, healing of disease, deliverance from
danger, and blessings too many to number. Receive these gifts, unworthy as they
may be, as tokens of gratitude for your
goodness and manifold mercies.

PRAYER.   A Prayer of Petition and
Thanks.
    Leader: God our Creator, we pray for
persons whose work is highly dangerous,
whose work is repetitive, monotonous,
and dull, whose work leaves them exhausted, for persons who are not equal to
their tasks, whose tasks do not use their
talents, for persons in whose work benefits are few, wages low, and the future
bleak.
    People: Hear our prayer, O Lord, and
let our cry come unto you.
    Leader: God of six days and of rest, we
pray for persons training for some difficult task, for persons retraining for some
new task, for widows and divorcees and
all who enter the job market scarred and
scared, for persons whose hands today
fall idle, for illegal aliens and all on the
run, for persons whose skills are meager,
for persons whose skills no one wants, for
all of us when we ask of work and life too
much for too little, when our memories
for life's kindnesses are too short, and for
life's meanness too long.
    People: Hear our prayer, O Lord, and
let our cry come unto you.
    Leader: God of planting and sowing, we
pray that when we succeed we not become hard, making our good fortune
other people's cross, nor, when we fail,
bitter, that we see beyond the quick
profit, that we see beyond the mirage of
what we can own, that we see the faces of
people, and the world of beloved places,
of beauty and of unfading right.

People: Hear our prayer, O Lord, and let our cry come unto you.

Leader: God of the harvest, we pray that, letting go of yesterday and tomorrow, we be free to receive today with open arms, that we cherish in the everyday the less that is more, that, inasmuch as we'll wear out whatever, or swear life has denied us its crowning decrepitude, we wear out for what is worth the candle, and for whom.

People: Hear our prayer, O Lord, and let our cry come unto you.

Leader: God of Creation, Lord of heaven and earth, we pray that we may be wise enough to invest in friends, in family, in beloved places, in the nameless numbers of vulnerable people whose disreputable company our Lord preferred, that we may be wise enough to invest in the coming kingdom of right, no boondoggle developed on sand, but a house erected on solid rock, title clear, held by Jesus, ne'er-do-well of Nazareth, and our Lord.

People: Hear our prayer, O Lord, and let our cry come unto you.

Leader: For people it is a joy to work with, a joy to work for, a joy to hire; for worthwhile work and things that go well; for work we love; for people who volunteer their time, do not weary of well-doing, but arise daily for others, for all who do not retire from discipleship; for all who give their work their best, and bring out our own.

People: We give you thanks, O Lord.

Leader: For all who labor for more just trade and the coming kingdom of fairness, for all who labor for the end of the manufacture of the weapons of death, for all who labor for the health of Creation.

People: We give you thanks, O Lord.

Leader: For musicians and poets, for dancers and painters and sculptors, for artisans in precious stones and metals, for writers and dramatists, for philosophers and chroniclers and novelists, for jugglers and acrobats and double-jointed contortionists, for athletes, actors and actresses, and all whose work is not practical, unless it be true that the crown of Creation is the Sabbath rest, unless it be

true that it is but lost labor that we rise up early and so late take rest, and eat the bread of carefulness, unless it be true that the lilies of the field are right, and Solomon in all his mortgaged glory wrong; which faith we do confess, and thus.

People: We give you thanks, O Lord. Amen. — Peter Fribley

LECTIONARY MESSAGE

Topic: Dealing with Conflict in the Church

TEXT: Matt. 18:15–20

I. *One-to-one reconciliation first.* If you have been around the church for any length of time you know that it is not immune to conflict. Wherever there are people, the potential for friction looms. Idealistically we would hope that the church would be one group in society where we could avoid pettiness and trivial problems that plague relationships. But the church, the *ecclesia,* is human, with all the frailties, weaknesses, and sinfulness that characterize the whole of humankind. The church has the potential of being different. Being redeemed and working out our own salvation implies that we are in process, not having yet arrived (Phil. 3:12–16). We have the potential of dealing with conflict creatively.

Jesus suggested that if someone wrongs us, the first step in handling the conflict is to go to that person, alone, and discuss the issue. Typically in the church, everyone knows about what has happened before we ever think about going to the person and attempting to deal with the problem. Jesus knew that problems between people are often a matter of a misunderstanding, a misperception, miscommunication. When we attempt to deal with the problem one-on-one we may quickly find that a potential conflict is nothing more than a misunderstanding of facts. The gospel is the opportunity for a second chance. Going to the person who has wronged you, going alone, going before you have made a public scene about it, offers the other person a second chance. If you can reconcile the issue, you have gained a brother or a sister in faith.

II. *Take witnesses next.* Jesus knew that one-on-one reconciliation is not always possible. Anger, frustration, jealousy, hardheadedness, the inability to think of meaningful solutions get in the way of reconciliation. (Remember, we may be the one who is angry and hardheaded though.) If that is the case, take one or two others with you so that there is the opportunity for unbiased negotiations. Also, the witnesses can later attest to what they saw and heard. This insures that anger and deceit is not getting in the way of authentic reconciliation.

III. *The church is the next step.* If you are unable to resolve your conflict, even with the help of others, the differences should be brought before the entire assembly. In years past, church discipline was abused, and people were wrongly castigated from the church assembly, which was turned into a "kangaroo court." Jesus is suggesting the authentic use of Christian love, compassion, and fellowship (*koinonia*) for resolving conflicts that cannot be settled on more personal levels.

IV. *Reconciliation is not always possible.* The tragic truth is conflict resolution is not always possible. Sometimes we are sinned against, and our best efforts at reconciliation are scoffed at and ridiculed. When this happens, relationship is breached—a painful reality to which Jesus admitted.

V. *The presence of Christ in the church.* But as a kind of postscript, Jesus holds out the hope that we in the church will recognize that when even two are together in his name, he is in the midst of the gathering. Is Jesus suggesting that his presence should be the motivation to reconcile at all cost (cf. 2 Cor. 5:19)? I wonder.—Craig A. Loscalzo

SUNDAY: SEPTEMBER TWELFTH

SERVICE OF WORSHIP

Sermon: Wrestling with God

TEXT: Gen. 32:22–30

In the quiet of the night beside the stream called Jabbok, Jacob was about to become embroiled in a wrestling match. It was no game—it would be for keeps. The prize was to be Jacob's own soul.

That night would prove to be a turning point in Jacob's life, for it was the night he would discover his own skills were insufficient, his own efforts inadequate. It was the night Jacob would discover his own weakness, in order that he might discover God's strength.

Perhaps today you are involved in struggles of your own. You may be struggling with family issues or with concerns about job or school. Maybe you are struggling with the difficulties of aging or changes in your life that seem so tough to handle. Perhaps, like Jacob, you are wrestling with God even now. In these verses you can discover God's strength for your struggle.

Three truths emerge from this passage which may shed light on your struggle.

I. When we wrestle with God, we do not emerge unscarred.

(a) There is always a price to be paid when we struggle with God. As Jacob settled in for a restless night, there suddenly appeared a mysterious figure who wrestled with him through the night. The prophet Hosea would describe the visitor as an angel; Jacob felt he had encountered God face-to-face. It was a divine messenger who wrestled with Jacob that night.

(b) As dawn approached, perhaps Jacob felt he had the edge—that he would triumph over this mysterious opponent. Then, at the moment of confidence, the divine visitor reached down and touched Jacob's hip, wrenching the bone out of its socket. In a moment, Jacob's power to continue wrestling is gone!

Jacob came face-to-face with his own powerlessness. Here was a foe he could not outsmart, could not outwit, could not manipulate. Suddenly Jacob was at the end of his own resources. He encountered his own weakness.

(c) If you and I are to be used by God, we must discover our own weakness. We must reach the point at which we recognize that God does not need our looks, our talents, our skills—that he is most interested in using our weakness, our helplessness. For it is only then that we will allow his power to work.

II. When we wrestle with God, we do not emerge unchanged.

(a) Jacob would never be the same man again. Indeed, things had already changed. Jacob could no longer wrestle; he could simply cling to his opponent. The self-reliant Jacob now held on, powerless to fight, begging for a blessing from this divine messenger. How ironic: The one who stole a blessing from his father now must beg for the blessing of God!

(b) In recognizing his own weakness and insufficiency, Jacob opened the door for a new chapter in his life. A time when he would no longer rely on his own wits for survival but could rely on God. God's power would be *his* power; God's victory would be *his* victory.

(c) It is impossible to have a true encounter with God and remain the same. There is a custom in certain villages in Italy. On New Year's Eve, as midnight approaches, the streets are almost empty. No cars, no pedestrians, even the police take cover. Then as midnight arrives, the windows of the houses fly open. To the sound of music, laughter and fireworks, each family throws into the streets old crockery, hated personal possessions— anything that reminds them of something bad about the past year. The idea is to start fresh for the new year.

Paul said that when we yield our lives to Christ, we become "new creatures in Christ; old things are passed away, behold, all things become new." Jacob recognized his own weakness and yielded himself to the power and strength found only in God. In the process, he became a new person: Israel, the one who prevails in God.

III. When we wrestle with God, we do not emerge unblessed.

(a) You remember the story of how Isaac, the father of Jacob and Esau, planned to bestow his blessing on the eldest son, Esau. At the encouragement and with the aid of his mother, Rebekah, Jacob puts on Esau's clothes, places an animal skin on his arms to simulate Esau's hairy arms, and deceives Isaac into giving his blessing to the younger son rather than the elder.

Now, wrestling with a divine messenger, Jacob clings desperately to his opponent, seeking a blessing from God. Centuries later, the prophet Hosea would describe Jacob's plea for God's blessing: "He wept and made supplication unto him." Not a demand, but a tearful pleading. No longer does Jacob seek to gain the advantage through trickery or deceit; out of a broken spirit, he begs for God's blessing.

(b) How often it is true that we are unable to receive God's best when we are strong; only by being reduced to a position of weakness and helplessness are we open to receive God's special blessing and power in our lives.

Rather than let the messenger go when God's presence was so close, Jacob was willing to risk his life to obtain the blessing. God's favor meant more than his own life—and this, at last, was Jacob's surrender to the will and purpose of God.

(c) As you struggle with God in your own life, will you surrender to his will? Are you willing to yield your will to his in order to receive God's blessing on your life? There is so much God wishes to do for us, if we are willing to stop fighting and start clinging.

It is in surrender to God that we find victory. It is in acknowledgment of my own weakness that I discover God's strength. It is in losing our lives for Christ's sake that we truly find life.— Michael Duduit

Illustrations

THE WAY.   An architect who made a beautiful city in an Arizona desert told me that the architecture of an area is determined by the lack of materials. Because they can't get those materials, they have to take others, and these determine the architecture. The lack produces the construction type—they make their lacks work. You can make your lacks work; you can make them drive you into new directions.

A lack of beauty drives many a woman into constructive usefulness, for if she had beauty she would be caught at that level and never get beyond it. But, lacking it, she decides to turn her energies into accomplishment—and does. Many a man lacking talents decides to make the most of what he has, offers them to God, has them heightened, and goes beyond other people more richly endowed.—E. Stanley Jones

OLD MAN TROUBLE.   An old, old legend tells of a time when the people of the earth made proud lament, each in his own behalf. Each was full of anger and envy because life had treated him unfairly compared with others. His troubles were too many, more than others had to bear, and they were heavier and harder too.

Each one saw his neighbor walking lightly under his load of care and difficulty, or so it seemed, and it made him unhappy. Every man was sure that if he could trade troubles with his fellow man—all save a few—life would be easier, and he would be more contented. At last something was done about it.

In order to rectify that unjust state of affairs, the gods arranged that on a given day each man should bring his burden to a certain place, cast it on a great pile of burdens, and be rid of it for good. There was one condition, to which no one objected—each man should select for himself another burden, one of the lighter loads he so enviously observed others carrying.

All the world was happy, so the legend goes—but not for long. As each man examined the burden he had chosen, he found it different, heavier, and harder to bear than his old one. Before long every man returned, asking that he be given back his own load again. He knew it, was

used to it, and was contented to bear it.—Joseph Fort Newton

Sermon Suggestions

GRACE FIRST AND LAST.   TEXT: Exod. 20:1–20. (1) God, under no obligation, freely chooses to redeem a people to call his own, verse 2. (2) Those people, under heavy obligation, express their gratitude and love in honoring God, verses 3–11, and in respecting the rights of other human beings, verses 12–17. (3) Such rules are not designed to make God's people afraid but to enable them to live morally productive lives, verses 18–20.

IS THAT ANY OF YOUR BUSINESS?   TEXT: Rom. 14:5–12, NRSV. (1) There must be an irreducible minimum for Christian behavior. (2) There are, however, some areas for legitimate differences of opinion, where it is easy to pass judgment. (3) The one fact to give us pause is this: "Each of us" (criticized and critic alike) "will be accountable to God," and God alone will be our final judge.

Worship Aids

CALL TO WORSHIP.   " 'I have set before you life and death, blessing and cursing.' saith the Lord, 'herefore choose life' " (Deut. 30:19b).

INVOCATION.   Lord, we are aware that each new day presents us with new choices that tend toward life and happiness or toward the opposite. Strengthen our moral courage today to go with you and find the abundant life that Jesus Christ came to give.

OFFERTORY SENTENCE.   "These words Moses spoke to all the community of Israelites: This is the command the Lord has given: Each of you set aside a contribution to the Lord. Let all who wish bring a contribution to the Lord" (Exod. 34:4b–51, NEB).

OFFERTORY PRAYER.   Bless now, O Lord, these offerings that we have set aside from our material means. May that blessing follow every gift and every prayer to the ends of the earth.

PRAYER. Shepherd of Israel, we pray for persons who live out their lives with a heavy physical or mental burden, and for those who love, cherish, and protect them. Mostly they are out of sight, but we glimpse them now and then. Downs syndrome persons, persons with autism. Persons who will never put two words together; persons tortured by the demons of the mind. We thank you for the joys and gifts that they bring, if we could but bridge the moat of our fears long enough to let them in.

Shepherd Lord, you healed the Gerasene demoniac and the paralytic by the pool and the man born blind. Leprosy you healed, but its effects you could not undo. We pray for these persons, irreparably ravaged, and for those who care for them and for those for whom no one cares and for ourselves.—Peter Fribley

LECTIONARY MESSAGE

Topic: Must I Always Forgive?
TEXT: Matt. 18:21–35

I. *Peter's question.* Peter's question echoes the questions we ask about forgiving others. It's a good question. It shows that Peter was beginning to understand what Jesus had been teaching. The question shows that he had grown beyond "an eye for an eye" legalistic understanding of relationships. He admits that when he is sinned against, he is supposed to forgive the offender. What Peter wants to know is how many times do I have to keep offering the other cheek and forgiving? And then he tacks on his second question: "As many as seven times?" Peter is looking for affirmation from Jesus. The rabbis said that a person could be forgiven three times. Peter thinks he'll impress Jesus by his generosity. Forgiving seven times is more than twice as much as the rabbis prescribe.

Can't you see Peter, sitting tall in the midst of the other disciples, gloating that

he's getting the idea? He reminds me of one of those kids in school that raises her hand for every question—and always has the right answer. After she's called on, the teacher says, "You're correct," and she turns around to the class and gives this big Cheshire-cat grin. Peter was waiting for Jesus to say, "You're correct." Jesus floored Peter when he said, "I do not say to you seven times, but seventy times seven!" And just like Peter, we shrink in our seats and mumble something like, "He's got to be kidding!"

II. *Our trouble with forgiveness.* Forgiveness and reconciliation are the business of Christians. But forgiveness is not something that comes naturally for most of us. Forgiveness is difficult because we seek fairness: "It's just not fair!" Forgiveness is difficult when we hold grudges. The infamous feud between the Hatfields and the McCoys went on because two families wouldn't let go of a grudge. Forgiveness is difficult because of jealousy. When someone who has wronged us is better off than we are, we decide that they don't need our forgiveness. Forgiveness is difficult because we don't fully understand what it means. A little girl broke her aunt's teacup. The aunt said, "That's all right dear, I didn't like that cup anyway." That's not forgiveness. Real forgiveness is the aunt saying, "That was the most valuable cup I own. I don't own another one like it. You should have been more careful. And I love you and forgive you." Forgiveness is not easy.

III. *In response to Peter's question, Jesus tells a story.* The principle of the parable is hard to miss. Real forgiveness comes from the heart as we realize how forgiven we are. To be unforgiving shows that one has not accepted God's principle of forgiveness. God's forgiveness of us and our forgiveness of others is directly linked. God is always ready to forgive; however, I wonder if God can enter an unforgiving heart? "Must I always forgive?" That's the question today's text provokes. Jesus' answer seems clear. It's time to forgive.—Craig A. Loscalzo

SUNDAY: SEPTEMBER NINETEENTH

SERVICE OF WORSHIP

Sermon: Oh, We Mean Well!

TEXT: Luke 14:25–35

While we need to restudy and relearn all of Jesus' teachings, this one seems especially urgent for the Christian church these days.

As Luke reconstructs events, Jesus and his disciples were journeying toward Jerusalem. This was to be their final and fateful journey together to the big city. He knew that once he was there a showdown with religious and civil authorities was all but inevitable, and he had dark premonitions as to the outcome.

As we get the picture, Jesus had two types of followers as he journeyed toward Jerusalem. Far and away the larger number was "the multitude" who halfway believed him to be the Messiah and wanted to be on hand for the grand opening of the kingdom he was bringing. It was, according to tradition, to be a day of glory and triumph—with rewards and rejoicing for all.

Jesus' disciples constituted the rest of his companions. By disciples we should probably understand not alone the Twelve but many more who followed him faithfully. These seemed only dimly to perceive that this was no ordinary trek to the holy city: This was it—the long awaited day when God through his Son was to announce, inaugurate, and unveil to all his kingdom.

Of course he had tried to bring both multitude and disciples down to earth before but without much success. It must have been as frustrating to him as to any teacher to know that he was saying one thing while they were hearing another. But frustrating or no, he called a halt to the journey long enough to have another try at confronting them with the stark realities beckoning him and all who followed him to Jerusalem.

He wanted to be sure they understood the seriousness of what they were doing. He wanted people generally and his disciples particularly to appreciate the revolutionary nature of the kingdom he was inaugurating. He wanted them to glimpse the hard personal price each one might be called on to pay for it, for he was certain that dark days lay ahead.

I. With good cause, one New Testament scholar gives these parables the title: "Warnings against precipitancy and half-heartedness in following Christ." Jesus makes four points in his brief discourse—and they are as relevant to discipleship today as ever they were.

(a) First, a choice is required and a cross must be borne. We continue to be shocked by his firm demand, "If any one comes to me and does not hate his own father and mother and wife and children and brothers and sisters, yes, and even his own life, he cannot be my disciple." *Hate* is a strong word, and as used here it simply does not mean what we usually mean by it. It means choice against these relationships, choice to leave them and follow him no matter what the cost. Such a choice is bound to be a heavy cross, but it must be daily assumed by all who would follow him and be loyal to him to the end. A choice is required and a cross must be borne.

(b) A second warning is couched in the parables of counting the cost of building a temple before you ever start and the wisdom of a king who evaluates his strength before he gets in a war. Jesus is saying, in effect, count the cost of following me, count it with great care. If you doubt whether you have what it takes, don't go any further; turn away; go home—go anywhere but with me to Jerusalem.

(c) A third emphasis warns them to renounce all possessions as well as all earthly relationships. Jesus knew how hard it was to love God and mammon, so hard that it could not be done. He did not try it himself and he warned his disciples to make as clean a break as possible with any entangling alliances with the world. It is as hard as ever for a man who is deeply concerned about his property to be deeply concerned about his soul.

(d) A final warning to the well-wishers and would-be disciples is to keep their convictions strong and creative, not to lose their enthusiasm for the kingdom nor let their loyalty to it run down. He urged those who wanted to follow him to do so with the full awareness of what they were doing—then they would be like salt that was really salty. But if their convictions faltered, if their loyalty waned, if their enthusiasm petered out, then they would be quite worthless.

These parables are indeed a warning "against precipitancy and half-heartedness in following Christ." Good intentions and well-wishing have their proper place, but they are not enough for any of the serious work of Christian discipleship then or now.

II. The best of intentions is not enough for either the Great Commandment or the Great Commission of our Lord.

The Great Commandment, he said, is to love God and man utterly. This, obviously, goes far beyond anything that would qualify as "good intentions." This means decision, commitment, consecration—or it means nothing at all.

(a) To love God is to know him as our Creator, to own him as our Father. It is to be always sensitive to his presence in his world, to be aware of him and to rejoice in him. It is to thrill to his presence in the unfolded and unfolding world in which we live. It is to be driven to our knees "when I consider thy heavens, the work of thy fingers, the moon and the stars which thou hast ordained," there to ask in hushed wonder, "What is man that thou art mindful of him? And the son of man that thou visitest him?" To love him means to find the strength and purpose of our life in him, to worship him with all our soul, and to follow where he leads with all the energies of our life.

(b) To love man utterly runs as far beyond good intentions as does the love of God. It means to own all men as fellow creatures of God, made in his image even as we are. It is to learn to look at other people with trust and understanding and, as they fail, with compassion and forgiveness. It is to refuse to be blocked away from anyone by hate, prejudice, or fear and to try by every means at our disposal to build a creative relationship with him.

Love of man is not the syrupy sentimentalism it sometimes seems. It means entering into the arena of public action and commitment in behalf of causes in which we believe and of persons whose rights are endangered. We are finding this out as we seek to remove the stain of segregation from every part of our church thought and life. It cannot be done speedily. It cannot be done easily. But it can and must and will be done when we realize that good intentions are not enough and move firmly and fairly beyond them into the realm of church law, church policy and program, and fellowship within the local church.

To love man is to take his problems as our problems, to lose ourselves in them with understanding and compassion, and to share as much as we are able in the effort to solve them.

III. Good intentions are not enough to carry out the Great Commission of our Lord, to go to the ends of the earth with the gospel.

(a) David Livingstone, one of the most virile Christian leaders of all time, had as his motto "Fear God, and work hard." He learned it in his austere home in Scotland and practiced it all his life.

Livingstone belongs to that select company of souls who not only know that good intentions are not enough but know also that their most strenuous efforts will not complete the really big jobs. Even so, they tackle them with all the energy they have and for all of the days God gives them to live. Then they hand them over to others, confident both in what they have done and in the fact that the work will continue. All great men of action are men of great faith in God, in themselves, and in what he will yet bring to pass.

(b) Like any other religious leader, Paul was led by great dreams and powerful insights, but he was not content to contemplate them, nor was he exhausted by them. When summing up his life effort for a young preacher called Timothy, he did not say, "I have had a great vision; I have had a wonderful dream."

Not Paul! He said, "I have fought a good fight, I have finished my course, I have kept the faith." And there we have it: the life work of Paul—a positive, declarative statement of faith born of a positive, declarative life of Christian discipleship. That is the way Paul summed up his Christian witness. How would we sum up ours?—Harold A. Bosley

Illustrations

THE LITTLE THINGS.   It is folly to think that because I am only one and can do very little, and that what I do counts for little, I need not do anything. As if a soldier should say that, since he is only one man, he might as well knock off and go to the movies. It would mean that the battle would be lost.

All of us are ready to do some big spectacular thing—to go into the spotlight. But it is the tireless doing of obscure, unknown things, the endless hidden fidelities and goodnesses, that really count. That things are as well with us as they are is due to quiet, anonymous loyalties.—Joseph Fort Newton

FIVE MINUTES LONGER.   When the Duke of Wellington met his Waterloo it was a victory that determined the future course of history. The man whose battle strategy put an end to the grandiose schemes of the Little Corsican is quoted as saying more than once that British soldiers were no braver than Frenchmen, but they could be brave five minutes longer.—Frederick Brown Harvis

Sermon Suggestions

ON BEING QUICK TO TURN ASIDE. TEXT: Exod. 32:1–14, NRSV. Why are we quick to turn aside from God's way? (1) There may be a crisis of leadership. (2) There may be the pull of old habits. (3) There may be the promise of an easier religion. (4) There is surely a forgetting that the true God is a God of both judgment and of grace.

IF HEAVEN IS BETTER, WHAT ARE WE DOING HERE?   TEXT: Phil. 1:21–27. (1) The

dilemma: the desire to depart this life to be with Christ, which is far better, or to remain here amid life's burdens. (2) The drawback: to depart prematurely would leave God's plan for us unfulfilled and our part of his work undone. (3) The decision: to be with Christ here in this life as we do his work, living his life, and to accept death, when it comes, as gain.

Worship Aids

CALL TO WORSHIP.   "If we walk in the light, as he is in the light, we have fellowship with one another, and the blood of Jesus Christ his Son cleanseth us from all sin" (1 John 1:7).

INVOCATION.   Almighty and most merciful Father, we have erred and strayed from thy ways like lost sheep; we have followed too much the devices and desires of our own hearts; we have offended against thy holy laws; we have left undone those things which we ought to have done; and we have done those things which we ought not to have done. But thou, O Lord, have mercy upon us, spare thou those who confess their faults, restore thou those who are penitent, according to thy promises declared unto mankind in Christ Jesus our Lord; and grant, O most merciful Father, for his sake, that we may hereafter live a godly, righteous, and sober life, to the glory of thy holy Name. Amen.—*The Book of Common Prayer*

OFFERTORY SENTENCE.   "Every one of us shall give account of himself to God" (Rom. 14:12).

OFFERTORY PRAYER.   We have accepted our responsibility to you, O God. Now help us to rejoice and be glad in it as we lay before you our thoughts, our deeds, and our tithes and offerings.

PRAYER.   "Have you not known? Have you not heard, the Lord is the everlasting God, the Creator of the ends of the earth?" In these difficult times help us to center down, to be still and know that you are God. "Whom have we in heaven but you? And there is none we desire upon earth other than you. Our flesh and our heart fail; but you are the strength of our heart and our portion forever." "Great is thy faithfulness."

We praise you for this opportunity to meditate upon your Law, to celebrate together your Word of grace.

From the beginning and in all kinds of times, your Word is a word of grace or none should live. With the newness of every day we are made consciousness of the grace-fullness of your Creation from the Garden of Eden to the freshness of this morning hour.

In times past you did not forget your people in their bondage in Egypt but called a shepherd carefully schooled in the rigors of the wilderness to lead them out and through forty years of wandering. However the story of their deliverance may be told, it is the story of your grace.

The fullness of your grace is present in the person, the life, the ministry, the Passion, the living again of Jesus of Nazareth. And it is your grace in him as the Messiah that delivers us from the bondage of our Egypts. That the church has been faithful to this story of your grace and shares it with us, we praise you and give you thanks.

We pray for ourselves as a church family that we may all know the grace of your healing, the wholeness of your love. Where there is any estrangement among us or in families of which we are a part, we pray for the courage and strength to love, that forgiveness and reconciliation may be celebrated. If we cannot be instruments of your peace here, how can we be instruments of your peace anywhere? How can we honestly pray for the peace of the world and forestall peace among ourselves?

We pray for the brokenness of the world. Your Word has created a cosmos, but living apart from your Word, how quickly man renders it a chaos. But you so love the world that you give your only Son. You send your Son not to condemn the world but that the world through him might live.—John Thompson

LECTIONARY MESSAGE

Topic: The Parable of the Generous Householder

Text: Matt. 20:1–16

People want to know what God is really like. Today's text provides a glimpse of a picture of God. Often called the parable of the laborers in the vineyard, I like to call it the parable of the generous householder. Here's why: At six o'clock in the morning the householder went to look for workers to work the vineyard. He told them he would pay them a day's wages for their work.

At nine o'clock, the householder returned and hired additional workers telling them, "You go to the vineyard and work, and whatever is right, I will pay you." He didn't guarantee them a day's wage, but they believed he would be fair with them, so they went to work in his vineyard. At noon, at three o'clock in the afternoon, and again at five o'clock, just one hour before quitting time, he hired still more laborers.

Evening came, and the householder said to his steward, "Call the laborers and pay them their wages, beginning with the last up to the first." When those hired at five o'clock in the afternoon came up, each of them received a full day's wage. The generosity of the householder shocked them. When those who were hired at six o'clock in the morning came, they thought they, too, would receive more, but they received a day's wage—the same amount as those who only worked an hour. They were furious: "It's just not fair!" That's what I'd say. But you have to be careful with these parables of Jesus; he always hooks us into siding with the wrong folks. As he speaks to them, he seems to be speaking directly to us.

The parable reminds us that we don't find God; God searches for us and finds us. The Bible reminds us again and again that we know God, understand God, experience God as the One made know to us through the pages of Scripture (Luke 24:13–35). God comes looking for us in the hedges and the highways, in the places where we try our best to hide from him, in our jealousy and selfishness, in our loneliness and despair, he comes looking for us. As we desperately wait in line, hoping to get a break at a new job, hoping to get a break at life, he taps us on the shoulder and says, "How would you like to work in my vineyard?"

The householder shows compassion and generosity to those who only had time to work for an hour. What good would it do for a person to go home with only an hour's wage? God's blessing and generosity toward us are not dependent on how much work we do. That's a real problem for modern people who are deceived by the lie "you get what you deserve." God gives us blessings as a sign of God's grace; we do not earn God's love, it is free.

The hidden secret of the parable is that God always surprises us with great joy. God's grace comes to us when we least expect it, as surprise. The last will be first and the first last is a real surprise. It's a surprise of grace. That's what I call good news.—Craig A. Loscalzo

SUNDAY: SEPTEMBER TWENTY-SIXTH

SERVICE OF WORSHIP

Sermon: The Inescapable Presence of God

TEXTS: Psalm 139; Matt. 28:20; Rom 8:39

The Bible is altogether persuaded that try as you will, go where you may, you can never escape from God.

Men and women do try to flee from God, for his presence often makes us exceedingly uncomfortable. There are times when all of us would like nothing better than to escape the troublesome presence of God when he makes us ashamed of ourselves and disturbs the easy devices and desires of our own hearts. Furthermore, life holds no more terrible experience than to feel that we have been abandoned by God. Not that we want to escape from him, but that he has forsaken us; this is what tears some people all to pieces, the consequence of having lost the faith of the 139th Psalm. And at the last how many there are who approach life's end with the conviction that whatever has been their relationship to God in this life, death is the final escape from God: seeing nothing ahead but dissolution for the body and oblivion for the soul. You see, it does make a difference, our persuasion as to his presence. There are some forks in life's road past which we all must journey. What difference does it make which road we choose to follow?

I. One fork where the ways of life divide is the point at which all of us must decide who will be the Master of our lives, the Captain of our souls. That decision will be determined by whether we believe that all life is held in God's hands, whether we believe that though we journey from here to Timbuktu we are still in God's keeping. His controlling touch still upon all the consequences of our behavior, or whether we believe that we can take life out of God's hands and make the consequences whatever we want. You do not have to look far to see that people often believe they can escape from God by ignoring him, by seizing the reins and driving off in pursuit of their own desires. And God lets us go, to the end of the tether; sometimes the tether stretches to incredible lengths. But it is never long enough to avoid our being overtaken by him, for he makes his presence felt first in the stirrings of conscience, and where conscience is either ignored or dead we are reminded by his judgment. Paul tried to get away, but God overtook him on the Damascus road.

(a) We are made so that we cannot shuffle God off so easily as we think. We can face God with contrite heart and accept his forgiveness. We can bury sin within ourselves and then support life by all kinds of defense mechanisms to handle our guilt (God's heavy hand). What we cannot do is run away from judgment. It may not catch us until the day of judgment, but somewhere God overtakes us. And why not! We live in a moral universe. None of us is privileged.

(b) We live in a moral universe where events happen "on account of God," and from this there is no escape. "If I make my bed in Sheol," said the psalmist. Earlier translators called it "hell." Whatever the original biblical meaning of the word, for two generations we have been watching the world make its bed in hell—and behold, God is here in terrifying judgment! We make our bed in the hell of a crushing armaments race that obliterates all the best endeavors and aspirations of human souls. We make our bed in the hell of staggering injustices to the colored races and colonial peoples of the earth, and now we reap the harvest of race conflict and communism. We make our bed in the hell of trying to operate government and organize the world without reference to divine support and moral justice. But by seizing control of our own destinies, calling ourselves captains of our souls, we have not got rid of God. Not by principalities and powers can we elude the Creator and Sustainer of the world, nor by making our bed in hell and disclaiming the moral sanctions. Behold, God is here in terrible judgment.

(c) But the opposite is also true. Just as God is ever present in judgment, he is also ever with us in support of the best that we attempt. And the number is legion of people who have been able to stand in some difficult and steep place because they trusted—and found—that God was standing with them.

II. At another fork where the ways divide we face a choice that calls to question our faith concerning the ever-present love of God. What will you do in the day of adversity, when some overwhelming disaster engulfs your soul? Then it is no academic matter whether or not you have drifted beyond God's reach.

(a) And what about the life that suffers no crushing blow but simply drags on from one day to the next with no apparent meaning, no aspiration to lift it up, no joy, no adventure. "Tomorrow and tomorrow and tomorrow, creeps on this petty pace" until the person cries in despair, "What does it all mean? Why is my life such a futility?" With all of these people we stand at the fork in the road. In such moments we turn for assurance to the passages of Scripture which speak of inescapable Presence. We can give no final or real answer to their question "Why?" But through Christ we can give them assurances that God does not leave us to drift away into the night of doubt and sorrow or defeat. If I say surely this darkness shall cover me, behold even this night shall be light about me.

(b) No darkness is too great for him. The greatest darkness in all the earth, the darkness of Calvary, was not too great for God. Jesus cried, too, in that darkness, "My God, my God, why!" But he trusted God beyond the darkness. Looking at Jesus and knowing that he suffered there for us, seeing in him the limitless love of God, people have lost the fear of darkness. It was for our sakes that God sent Christ into the world and if God loved him and stayed with him through his Calvary on account of us will he not also accompany us through whatever Gethsemane and Calvary life compels us to endure? If God be for us, he will. Jesus' last words were "It is finished," and "Father, into thy hands I commend my spirit." If there is someone listening now in gross darkness, feeling he has escaped from God's love, the word of our gospel is to you as it was to Jesus: Holding fast to love, whatever your misgivings, you are holding fast to God.

III. But what about the last fork in the road from which we do not return? Faith indeed measures the difference here. But if God be with us through all the other divides in the road, if he stays with us in every darkness of soul along the way to the very end, don't you think he goes with us even beyond the end?

(a) The psalmist thought so. In a groping way, long before the Hebrews had grown to any articulated faith in eternal life, he believed, "When I awake, I am still with thee." Paul was sure of it: "I am persuaded that not even death shall separate us from the love of God." And Jesus comes to us to tell us that God loves us not for a lifetime but for eternity. "He that believeth in me shall never die." And this faith can be the redemption of life from fear and despair. Believing that the last turning of the road leads not to endless oblivion but to greater life can change every aspect of life here and now, endowing our years with greater dimensions, new meaning, and holy purpose. These can encompass, surround, and sustain every circumstance into which we fall.

(b) The inescapable presence of God! When you stand at the last divide, where the ways of life part forever, if you have walked with Christ across the hills and valleys of this pilgrimage, a Voice will come from down one of the roads saying, "Come, it is I, your Lord and Savior."—Robert E. Luccock

Illustrations

PRESENCE OF GOD.   In one of his novels, Georges Bernanos writes of a priest who "with an absolute certitude knew" that "the joy he suddenly felt was a presence," and concludes, "The feeling of this mysterious presence was so vivid that he turned his head abruptly, as if to meet the glance of a friend." In similar language the Hebrew traditions stated long ago, "Yahweh used to speak to Moses face-to-face, as a man speaks to his friend" (Exod. 33:11).—Samuel Terrien

GOD THROUGH US.   A man had lost a son in a tragic accident; grief had brought him near to his wit's end. He was on the verge either of suicide or ruin by alcohol, but the minister kept seeking him in the blackest hours, going to his home when some inner sense sounded the warning of great need, finding it "necessary" to go to New York at the same time the man journeyed there on business, and keeping just close enough to him so he knew he was watching him, but not invading the man's private life. The man confessed later that this minister, who represented God to him, had pulled him back from the pit. Through him he was sure of a God who goes where we go and suffers what we suffer.—Robert E. Luccock

Sermon Suggestions

HOW MUCH OF GOD CAN YOU SEE? TEXT: Exod. 33:12–23. (1) God permits us to enter into dialogue with him. (2) God's presence goes with us wherever we are. (3) Yet the hiddenness, in various degrees, of God's person and plans is always to be reckoned with.

HUMILITY AND HOW IT HAPPENS. TEXT: Phil. 2:1–13. (1) An exhortation toward it, verses 1–4. (2) An example of it, verses 5–11. (3) The power to achieve it, verses 12–13.

Worship Aids

CALL TO WORSHIP.   "For God so loved the world, that he gave his only begotten Son, that whosoever believeth in him should not perish but have everlasting life" (John 3:16).

INVOCATION.   Almighty Father, whose chosen dwelling is the heart that longs for your presence and humbly seeks your love, deepen within us the sense of shame and sorrow for the wrongs we have done and for the good we have left undone. Strengthen every desire to amend our lives according to your will. Give us light to guide us and souls attuned to hear your Word that we may always do those things which are pleasing in your sight.—Henry Fields

OFFERTORY SENTENCE.   "I will freely sacrifice unto thee: I will praise thy name, O Lord; for it is good" (Ps. 54:6).

OFFERTORY PRAYER.   Here are our gifts, Father, laid on your altar. Use them, we pray, that your truth may not falter.—Henry Fields

PRAYER.   That you are calling us in Christ to be and become, we praise you, O Father. Through your great love we have been adopted and are your children, but it does not yet appear what we shall be. The whole Creation is standing on tiptoe to see the fulfillment of your sons and daughters that you have ordained in Christ. We thank you for those who have responded to your call this morning to be your church in this time and place. We thank you for all of those who have been faithful to the gospel—parents, Sunday school teachers, ministers, friends, mates—that we have all been brought to the knowledge and experience of your saving grace in Christ.

Once we were no people, but now we are your people; once we had not received mercy, but now we have received mercy that we may declare the wonderful deeds of him who called us out of darkness into your marvelous light. Praise be to you—Father, Son, and Holy Spirit.—John M. Thompson

LECTIONARY MESSAGE

Topic: Faith is Obedience
TEXT: Matt. 21:28–32

Faith seems to have an elusive quality. Just when you think you have it in your grasp, it slips away again. We need to be reminded constantly what faith is, how it works in our lives, and how we express it in relation to God. Matthew's parable of the two sons should help us in this endeavor.

The parable of the two sons is the first in a trilogy of true-faith parables in which Matthew exegetes for us his understanding of faith. For this gospel writer faith is holding firm to the covenant of God. It is obedient faith. In the case of our parable, Matthew makes it quite clear that this faith leads one to go out and work in the vineyard not just talk about it. Faith is obedience.

I. *Two sons.* Jesus, the master at using the simple, the familiar, the contemporary to tease the mind into action, tells the story of a father who asks his two sons to go work in the vineyard. At the very beginning one should point out that the response of both sons is imperfect. One says no and then on second thought decides to go, and the other says yes but for some strange reason never enters the fields. Neither response would bring a great deal of satisfaction to the father. But given a choice one has to say the first response is preferable to the last. A key

word to that response is the word *repent.* This certainly holds some implications for the interpretation of this parable.

II. *Two Israels.* Unlike some of the parables, the meaning of this story is crystal clear. The two sons in the parable represent two groups in Israel. The common folk of the land had rejected the earlier call of God the Father. Stoning the prophets, they gave a resounding No! and turned aside to their own crude way of life. But under the impact of the preaching of John the Baptist they repented. At the same time another Israel, the religious leaders—the Pharisees, the pastors, the rabbis—had given a fervent Yes, sir! This Israel lived a more respectable life, said the right things, and followed the Law but never went out into the vineyard to work.

"Which of the two did what his father wanted?" Matthew's implications are clear. Jesus saw two Israels: believing and unbelieving Israel. Faith was still active in the *am ha-arez,* the despised people of the land. What a strange turn of events. The the tax collectors and the whores, the religious pariahs, are going into the kingdom of God ahead of the publicly devout. John had brought a demand for righteous living, and when they responded they found the will of God. The religious leaders had expressed a zeal for God, while those responding to John the Baptist had chosen to do the ethical will of God, and the two were different.

Repentance and doing highlighted the difference between those who went into the fields and those who did not. Israel's leaders lived their lives in theological correctness but made obedience to the ethical will of God secondary. Matthew is repeating the clarion call of Paul, only the obedience of faith brings salvation.

The story is also filled with hope. If the harlots and the tax collectors can experience a dramatic change in their lives, then why not the priests. Jesus' ministry emphasized over and over that the arms of divine mercy are still open. With the hope is also an urgent evangelistic challenge.

III. *Two Americas.* Just as there were two Israels, there are two Americas.

There are those who say yes and never go into the vineyard. The parable surely sounds a warning to those who assume that talking and thinking about the will of God is sufficient. Matthew speaks loudly. Faith is obedience! Repentance and doing are essential! There is a sec-ond America: those who have found through faith the way of righteousness and the enabling gift of the Spirit which accompanies them into the vineyard of God. Their faith is available to all who call upon the name of the Lord.—John Dever

SUNDAY: OCTOBER THIRD

SERVICE OF WORSHIP

Sermon: Overcome Evil with Good
TEXT: Rom. 12:14–21

Who was it who said, We become like the things we hate? It is a frightening prospect! When our animosities and angers gain supremacy, we are radically changed. When hatred and bitterness consume us, we grow vengeful and mean.

We are a people in need of what the Apostle Paul called a more excellent way. Paul then detailed that way under the name of love. "Love," wrote the apostle, "is patient and kind; love is not jealous or boastful; it is not arrogant or rude. Love does not insist on its own way; it is not irritable or resentful; it does not rejoice at wrong, but rejoices in the right."

I. In his New Testament letter to Christians at Rome, Paul made a specific application of love's way in a message about personal relationships. His summary statement was this: "Do not be overcome by evil, but overcome evil with good." Do not become like the things you hate; turn matters around (Paul was teaching) and let love and goodness reign supreme. In the spirit of Jesus he was bold to say, "Bless those who persecute you; bless and do not curse them."

(a) Paul offered a series of exhortations at this point in his Letter to the Romans. "Repay no one evil for evil," he said, "but take thought for what is noble in the sight of all." Then he wrote, "never avenge yourselves, but leave it to the wrath of God." His last statement was the one I just quoted, "Do not be overcome by evil, but overcome evil with good." Paul's concern was for the triumph of love and goodness. He was warning his listeners that evil wins when we respond in kind. He anticipated the words of Martin Luther King, Jr., who said, "Darkness cannot drive out darkness; only light can do that."

(b) Affirming and asserting the good becomes our challenge. It is a challenge only met as we live close to the source of goodness which for us is and always will be Jesus Christ. Well-intentioned efforts, unsupported by the grace and help of God in Christ, are inadequate at best. The needed ingredient for your good resolve and mine is the power of Christ's goodness at work in us. We have to begin by placing ourselves close to him, perhaps adopting as our own the prayer hymn which says, "More like the Master I would live and grow; more of his love to others I would show; more zeal to labor, more courage to be true. More consecration for work he bids me do." Finding ourselves thus in harmony with Jesus Christ it becomes possible to affirm and assert goodness in the face of evil and wrong.

II. Christ-based goodness has an imperishable quality to it. Such good "has no fear," as playwright Christopher Fry says in his drama *A Sleep of Prisoners*. A character in that play named Meadows extols "the power that blesses" by saying, "Good is itself, whatever comes. It grows, and makes, and bravely Persuades, beyond all tilt of wrong; Stronger than anger, wiser than strategy, Enough to subdue cities and men if we believe it with a long courage of truth."

(a) I would add, if we receive it from the person of Christ. Goodness in the ultimate, lasting, and imperishable sense is not self-generated; it is God-given. It is a gift of grace, connecting with our own innate capacity to be loving, caring, and serving people.

A simple litany passed along by one of our members describes this behavior. The litany goes like this: "Returning good for good is manlike. Returning evil for good is devil-like. Returning good for evil is Christ-like." To be among the overcomers, those committed to overcoming evil with good, is the place Christ would have us be.

(b) Out of Christian history comes an astonishing story of such an overcomer. His name was Telemachus, a monk who lived in Asia Minor around A.D. 400. Telemachus was deeply disturbed by the brutality and violence of the popular gladiatorial games of the Roman Empire. The Christian emperor Honorius was among those who watched these matches with regularity. Telemachus, burdened by such displays, one day took it upon himself to attend; as the fighting was at fever pitch, he jumped into the arena, between the gladiators. "In the name of our Master, stop fighting," he cried. The warriors stopped, confused. But the spectators became furious. Turning into a mob, they advanced upon Telemachus with sticks and stones until he was beaten to death. Then a spirit of revulsion swept over the crowd. Emperor Honorius abruptly left the Colosseum and the games were over. Shortly afterwards, Honorius passed an edict banning all future gladiatorial games. That one person, Telemachus, stood up to the evil of them, and their violence was halted.

III. Admittedly, one persons's effort may seem futile against entrenched evil. But that does not mean a person should refrain from acting. Many individuals together have an even better chance to make a significant difference—which is why we need each other and the community of the church. One brick at a time, one step at a time, initiated by many of us can equal a power for good far greater than the evil we may be up against in any given situation.

(a) "Overcome evil with good." This admonition is a way of pointing us to the more excellent way of love. The love of Christ constrains us to act in no other way than as peacemakers: those who embrace good over evil, those who lock out hatred, those who would make the enemy a friend.

(b) Let our prayer on this day be one of asking God to fill us with divine goodness that we may be among the overcomers— the instruments of God's peace in a world of turmoil and need.—John H. Townsend

Illustrations

CREATIVE COMPARISON. A conceited young fellow wants to paint the portrait of his mother. With ill-prepared canvas and with much conceit he makes a portrait that he thinks to be wonderfully like her. He is very proud of it. He sets it on the table of his studio. Conceive that someone, an artist rare or one following the photographer's art, shall have, with exquisite pains, really brought out the likeness of the mother so that everyone who sees it thinks at first that it is she herself. He says not a word but goes and puts it by the side of the other and leaves. The young man comes back. He is so happy. He thinks he is Titian or his grandson, and he pictures in his mind what he will become when he gets a little more cultivation. On going into his studio he looks—and throws the picture he has painted under the table. There has not been a word said to him, but there was the exquisite likeness of his mother put beside his, and his looked so hateful that he would not have anything to do with it.

By the side of a bad deed put a beautiful deed. By the side of a wrong put the characteristic right. Leave them alone. They will fight with each other, and the beautiful and the good will overcome the evil. Overcome evil with good.—Henry Ward Beecher

SHORTSIGHTED REFORMERS. The ardent young reformers often seem to think that whatever is must be wrong. They feel impelled to turn everything inside out and end for end before we can make any social headway. One often feels like asking them, "How much wheat have you produced in the last year?" If they were entirely frank, they might feel compelled to say, "Oh, we are not raising wheat. We are not dirt farmers. But look how we lashed those tares!"—Charles R. Brown

Sermon Suggestions

CHANGING LEADERSHIP. TEXT: Num. 27:12–23. (1) It was the will of God, verses 12–16. (2) It was for the good of the people, verse 17. (3) It was done in proper order, verses 18–21. (4) It was done with fitting magnanimity, verses 22–23.

OUR TRUE HOME—WHY WE LOVE IT. TEXT: Phil. 3:12–21, especially verses 20–21. (1) As Christians, "we are a colony of heaven," verse 20 (Moffatt). (2) We live in expectation of a Savior, the Lord Jesus Christ. (3) We are assured of a new and glorious state of existence made possible by the power of God.

Worship Aids

CALL TO WORSHIP. "Know therefore that the Lord thy God, he is God, the faithful God, which keepeth covenant and mercy with them that love him and keep his commandments to a thousand generations" (Deut. 7:9).

INVOCATION. O Lord, in this our day continue your mercy toward us and through us to the coming generations, as we seek to love you and keep your commandments. May your presence among us, leading us onward, assure us of your faithfulness in covenant with us.

OFFERTORY SENTENCE. "God is able to make all grace abound toward you; that ye, always having all sufficiency in all things, may abound to every good work" (2 Cor. 9:8).

OFFERTORY PRAYER. Gifts at their best denote love from giver to receiver, Father. May these gifts tell a magnificent story of the love of these believers here gathered.—Henry Fields

PRAYER. Gracious Lord, in Jesus you taught us that you are among us as one who serves, and in your Son Jesus, you whom the stars obey set aside your crown and took up a towel and washed the disciples' feet.

Teach us to set aside our crowns—our crowns of fear and our crowns of pride; our crowns of knowledge and uncentered busyness; our crowning arguments; even our crowns of knowing just what is needed; and of despair; that we may take up a towel and do what we can, and be all we can be; trusting in your promise and leaving it there—leaving the outcome to the clarity and mystery of your love.

And in all things make us your glad disciples, in harmony with you: your life and ministry, your death, your new life.—Peter Fribley

LECTIONARY MESSAGE

Topic: The Patience of God
TEXT: Matt. 21:33–43
The parable of the wicked vinedresser sets the longsuffering patience of God over against the incredible resistance of humankind. The parable's portrayal of God as the householder with seemingly unending patience is so overstated it even borders on making God look foolish. But such is salvation history. God's love has continually persevered. Is there no end to this tolerance? Is there no limit to God's grace? What does the parable tell us?

There are several levels of meaning to the story of the depraved tenants. Jesus' immediate audience saw the parallel between the householder and God, and the wicked tenants and Israel. But twentieth-century interpreters must move beyond the immediate context to see the modern parallel between the tenants and contemporary perverters who trample on the grace of God.

I. *God's trust and patience.* Jesus' story is about God. The verbs in verse 33: *planted, set, dug, built, let,* and *went* all point to the active, caring, loving, attitude of God toward his vineyard. God carefully orchestrated and cultivated the formation of a people of God for salvation and then went away entrusting the responsibility to his people, the tenants, to till, cultivate, and harvest. He expected his vineyard to produce fruit.

There is a phenomenal amount of trust placed in the tenants. God doesn't stand over them to guide, cajole, and warn over and over at the least provocation like we sometimes do with our subordinates (and our children!). God entrusts his work to those human beings made in his image, not angels or spirits. In his absence they are in complete charge.

When ready to claim his harvest, the master (God) sends representatives, not once, but twice. His patience seems unending. The first group was beaten, stoned, or killed. The second group met the same fate. But the owner was still patient. Finally thinking it inconceivable that his own son would be rejected, he sent him. "They will honor my son," he says. Frederick Bruner observes, "The Lord's confidence in the mission of the son gives the measure of the crime that disappointed it."

The wicked tenants failed their final opportunity. The ultimate test, the final messenger, the son, was cast out and killed. An ordinary landlord would have attacked these insolent, rebellious, greedy tenants, but God sent his Son! This beautifully exhibits the essential character of God. God is love! God is patient!

II. *Humankind's responsibility.* The tenants were provided with everything they needed to make their task achievable. They were given the freedom to do the task as they wished. Faith in the master seems to be the ingredient that was missing. This was an opportunity for growth! They blew it. On a personal level, our response to responsibility often determines our success or failure.

If faith was the missing ingredient, greed and murderous instinct were certainly central ingredients. The behavior of these tenants was so consistent, it seemed basic to their nature . . . the perfect example of humanity's rebellious response to God's love. The people of God resisting God's love!

III. *God's judgment.* God's judgment and humanity's accountability are sure. The patience of God does have a limit. When the son is rejected, the wicked tenants have gone too far. The vineyard will be taken away and given to those who will honor the owner. The lesson is quite clear. Faith demands responsible behavior or all opportunity for service and the joy of tending God's vineyard will be taken away and given to another. God's love demands God's judgment.—John Dever

SUNDAY: OCTOBER TENTH

SERVICE OF WORSHIP

Sermon: A Creative Minority

TEXT: Gen. 18:32 (ARV)

I. This story of Abraham takes us into a world as strange to our ways of thinking as Swift's island of Lilliput. It is the story of a man bargaining with God. In the story the city of Sodom was to be destroyed by an angry God. Abraham, with a heart of compassion, does not want it destroyed. The mind of Abraham, as depicted here, expresses a growing understanding of the nature of God, a stage in the emergence of ethical monotheism out of primitive magic. Abraham asks the penetrating theological question, "Shall not the judge of all the earth do right?"

(a) So Abraham starts to bargain with God, "How many good men would be needed to save the city?" Would fifty do it? Yes. Then, adroitly, he drops down. How about forty? Thirty? Twenty? Then the last venture: "Do not get angry, but— suppose there were only ten good men found in Sodom? Would ten be enough?"

Abraham wins. He wins the answer from God: "I will not destroy it for the sake of the ten."

(b) Ten men would have saved Sodom. That is a sharp, imaginative picture of a timeless and timely truth, that the saving force in any group, community, or civilization is a creative minority.

That was a center of Jesus' teaching, that the redemptive force in the world is a minority factor, such as yeast or leaven. Today we are in a burning city. To some it seems to be a doomed world. If it is to be saved at all, it will be saved by a comparatively few.

II. The hope of a secure and livable world lies in a minority of disciplined and dedicated minds and hearts, set not on the preservation of any status quo nor of the sanctified stupidities of the past but on the building of an order in which the possibilities of life may be realized.

(a) Three things can be said confidently. For one thing, there must be a deepening and widening of a sense of responsibility. One funeral must be held promptly. It is long overdue. For one of the prominent figures of history has died, the "innocent bystander." He is no more. No one is an innocent bystander. The area of responsibility has widened; the sense of responsibility must be deepened.

(b) In the second place, a task for a saving minority is to keep the mind over the emotions. St. Paul wrote, "I keep my body under." We may add, "I keep my emotions under my mind, as driving power to be directed by the mind." The line of least resistance is to let the emotions run amuck. The brain must muscle in to some major conflicts in our day, to make clear, for instance, the need of showing to the world a demonstration of democracy in our own land, a democracy not only in rhetoric but in deed, not only in patriotic songs but in economic and political justice.

(c) In the third place, the mind must tighten its hold on the truth that one life counts. Turn to almost any one of the hundreds of books published in the past few years on some aspect of the international situation. In the last chapter there often will be found, in varying language, this conclusion: that the final resource is in the power of public opinion. That is where we come in. Each of us has an influence on some area of public opinion; call it only a backyard, if you will. But it is real. Multiply those areas, and the forces of change for the better are at work. History has its word of validation and encouragement for every land.

III. A truly saving minority for our Sodom will include people whose belief in God is a power. It was a very small minority which saved the Hebrew nation: its prophets, Amos, Hosea, Micah, Isaiah, Jeremiah; its singers in the Psalms; its group of the pious who looked for the redemption of Israel. Their faith in God was the means through which the high heritage of Israel was passed on to the world. One word from the Psalms pictures vividly what faith in God gives— "God is a sun and a shield." God gives defense and illumination to one life and to two billion lives, linked together. Both are desperately needed.

(a) There is cosmic backing for our dearest values and hopes, and in the struggle for a kingdom of God, of righteousness, joy, and peace, faith in the God and Father of our Lord Jesus Christ brings illumination to the path ahead, as well as fortification. If we have the mind of Christ, his evaluations, it will throw light on means as well as ends.

(b) In Robert Nathan's little fantasy *Mr. Whittle and the Morning Star,* Mr. Whittle believes that the world is coming to an end. He has a conversation with God. Mr. Whittle says with impatience, "If it has to be, it has to be. It's the waiting around I don't like. Only, why don't you get it over with?"

"Don't rush me," God replies. "I am trying to think of a way out."

Does it sound like blasphemy? Perhaps. But in a real way it sounds like the New Testament. "We are workers together with God." Through the minds of his children, through your mind and mine, your will and mine, God is seeking to find "a way out."—Halford E. Luccock

Illustrations

THE HOPE OF THE WORLD. Wherever a true idea is born and a creative minority rallies around it, there is the beginning of victory. That is encouraging, and it is true. It is not, however, a truth to go to sleep on. We Christians were intended to be that minority. We were to be the salt of the earth, said Jesus. We were to be the light of the world. We were to be the leaven in the lump of the race. There is no possibility of misunderstanding his meaning, my friends. When a man becomes a real Christian he is supposed to move over into that small, creative, sacrificial minority seized upon by visions of a better world and standing for them until they shall permeate mankind with their truth. That does make being a Christian serious business! That is more than believing in a creed. That is more than partaking of the sacraments. That is more than the comfort of worship or the use of beauty as a road to God. That is joining the real church in the original Greek meaning of the word *church*, *ecclesia*—called out—a minority selected from the majority to be leaven.—Harry Emerson Fosdick

THE LITTLE TASK. Always keep your eyes open for the little task, because it is the little task that is important to Jesus Christ. The future of the kingdom of God does not depend on the enthusiasm of this or that powerful person; those great ones are necessary, too, but it is equally necessary to have a great number of little people who will do a little thing in the service of Christ.

The great flowing rivers represent only a small part of all the water that is necessary to nourish and sustain the earth. Beside the flowing river there is the water in the earth—the subterranean water—and there are the little streams which continually enter the river and feed it and prevent it from sinking into the earth. Without these other waters—the silent hidden subterranean waters and the trickling streams—the great river could no longer flow. Thus it is with the little tasks to be fulfilled by us all.—Albert Schweitzer

Sermon Suggestions

THE SECRET OF GREATNESS. TEXT: Deut. 34:1–12. (1) The Deuteronomic vignette of Moses' greatness. (2) The explanation of Moses' greatness: Moses was empowered by God. (3) The lessons to be learned: (a) we can hardly aspire to another's greatness; (b) nevertheless, all of us in our individual availability to God, to God's power, and to God's will can achieve greatness as God defines greatness (see Matt. 20:20–28).

SOMETHING TO THINK ABOUT. TEXT: Phil. 4:1–9. (1) Intelligent prayer ushers us into the incomprehensible peace of God, verses 6–7. (2) Filling the heart and mind with excellent and praise-worthy thoughts will sustain our experience of the peace of God, verses 8–9.

Worship Aids

CALL TO WORSHIP. "Whatsoever ye do in word or deed, do all in the name of the Lord Jesus, giving thanks to God and the Father by him" (Col. 3:17).

INVOCATION. Father, we know that we belong to you and that we experience your peace when we abide in your presence. We come to worship you as best we know how. We have understood from your Word that you are never far from us. But sometimes we are far from you, Father. We allow the tumult of the world and preoccupation with too many tasks to build distances from you on our side of the equation of life. Still our souls and rein in our wandering minds that we may come to that point of peace and there gain insight and power and determination truly to do your will, even as did those disciples whom Jesus taught to pray: (Lord's Prayer).

OFFERTORY SENTENCE. "And the king shall answer and say unto them, Verily I say unto you, Inasmuch as ye have done it unto one of the least of these my brethren, ye have done it unto me" (Matt. 25:40).

OFFERTORY PRAYER. Father, help us to become unobstructed channels through which your love flows to others as our gifts are used for the glory of your kingdom throughout the world.—Henry Fields

PRAYER. Father, on this special day we come into your presence knowing that you are never far from us. Yet here in this sacred place we long to find you more fully that you may lift us up into a new faith in you and a new vision of what you are about with us. For the dark hours come when questions arise concerning you, and doubts throng in.

O God, from whose great reservoir of goodness these streams flow, make us more certain about you, until today we, too, shall say, "The Lord is the strength of my life; of whom shall I be afraid?"

In this faith lift us to a new courage. You see our daily need for fortitude and valor. Save us from soft optimism. Don't let sentimentality beguile us. Save us from saying "Peace, peace" when there is no peace, and may we never try to heal deep diseases with easy words. Give us honesty to face hard facts, and yet, with it all, give us courage, we pray.

You see our varied needs, Father. Meet us in the solitariness of our own souls and with your still, small voice deal with us one by one. For our sins, grant us the grace of sincere penitence and cleanse us with your pardon. Comfort us in our grief with your steadfastness, that the storms of sorrow may not beat us down. In our anxiety clarify our vision and direct our steps. Oh, how we pray that you will unsnarl some tangled life in this company today and bring us all to a keen awareness of your presence and calling.—Henry Fields

LECTIONARY MESSAGE

Topic: The Parable of the Wedding Banquet
TEXT: Matt. 22:1–14

The kingdom of heaven is not just a first-century concern, for who among us has not at least for short periods of time wondered what life with God would be like. The parables concerning the kingdom of God speak as forcefully to the twentieth-century seeker as to those who heard the words of Jesus in the first century. The parable of the wedding banquet is about the kingdom of God.

I. *The message is delivered.* The invitation to the banquet moves from a general request for preparation to a specific date for the wedding feast. The invitation is not an order to report, but those invited were expected to respond immediately— the table was set, the meal was ready.

The messenger has an important role in the story and has an equally important task in the continued giving of the invitation to the kingdom of God. Proclaiming the joy of the event, the messenger is to invite, make the offer attractive, and to portray the sense of wonder that awaits those who accept the invitation. No gifts are expected. Come as you are. Wedding garments will be supplied.

Far too often we decorate the invitation with added expectations. Before you come into the kingdom of God you must do this and stop doing that. Get your life straight; do an about face. But God acts in a different way. The simple invitation to come is given. Once you have entered into the joy of the kingdom, then obedient faith will be expected. But for the present, just come.

II. *The message is rejected.* In our more sympathetic moments we can understand the reluctance to respond to the invitation. We, too, have full agendas, and one more task or one more party is more than we can handle. We just have to say no! Luke in his account of the parable details the excuses given. One bought a field, another a yoke of oxen, and still another had married a wife. These everyday concerns are important. But are they more important than the call to eternity?

The road to hell is not always paved by what we usually designate as sin, but with misplaced priorities. Those responding to the banquet invitation were saying,

"Some other time. I have no use for you in what I plan today." We can turn down the invitation for a variety of reasons: ambition, prejudice, business, family, etc. All seem real at the moment. William Barclay says, "A man can be so busy making a living that he fails to make a life."

III. *A new invitation is given.* The messengers are sent out again. This time they were to go into the crowded cities and bring everyone they saw, both good and bad, to the banquet. Surely they will rejoice at the opportunity. The message is clear. When those who have been charged with being the bearers of the Christian tradition fail, then God will turn to others who rejoice in their newfound Christianity. Calvin put it rather bluntly. "If he did not spare the natural branches, the same vengeance awaits us today if we do not respond to his call."

IV. *The king appears.* The parable ends in a clarion call to accountability. The king appears, greets his guests, but finds one without a wedding garment and has him cast out. The penalty seems harsh. Was not everyone invited to come as they are? Yes, but once they entered they were expected to put on a new garment. Calvin says that once we enter the kingdom we are expected to practice the new life. Luther says we must put on the wedding garment of faith. We can come as we are, but we can't stay as we are. The faith of obedience that Matthew proclaims throughout his Gospel is given added emphasis.

V. *Conclusion.* Even with all its somberness, the parable of the wedding banquet is still an image of joy. The joy of discipleship is found in the festive image of the wedding. Those who came and put on the wedding garment shared in the festive occasion. The joy of entering the kingdom of God is real.—John Dever

SUNDAY: OCTOBER SEVENTEENTH

SERVICE OF WORSHIP

Sermon: The Community of Love
TEXT: John 13:31–38

I. There's a science fiction story about invaders from outer space—actually, there are a million sci-fi stories that start out that way! But this one is a little out of the ordinary. Instead of shooting up the place with their freeze rays, in this story the invaders set up devices all over the globe that render all guns, bombs, tanks, planes, and other implements of war inoperable, along with all electrical devices. When the invaders place their demands, all they want is for all the nations of the earth to stop fighting with each other. From that point on, earth will have to be a community of love.

It's too simple, of course. We won't solve the problems of our planet by waiting to be invaded by friendly aliens. That's a childish excuse, like protesting that you aren't responsible for picking up your room until someone makes you do it. No, if we want to make a community of love, we must do it ourselves. We must reach down into our hearts and draw upon all the love there and really start loving each other. We can build the community of love if we try, can't we?

Actually, history is littered with our attempts to do just that. We humans just don't seem able to sustain the effort to keep it going. The Shakers were a community of Christians in the 1800s who lived simply and peaceably among themselves; they celebrated the presence of Christ among them in song and dance and hoped that they could bring the whole world into their way of thinking. Now they are just an interesting group in America's past.

II. It's no surprise, actually. Look at the episode we read today. Jesus had been with these people for three years, teaching, doing miracles, showing them the inner nature of god in everything he did. Judas, one of his twelve disciples, in the hour when Jesus needed him the most, was so controlled by the forces of darkness that he betrayed Jesus to his enemies. He had lived with the light of the world for three years but was still overcome by evil. Peter, the strongest personality among the disciples, claims to be willing to lay down his life for Christ. If Jesus is going to die, then so will Peter, defending his Lord. What happens? Peter loses his nerve and fails. The rest of the Twelve simply scatter; none speaks for Jesus at this trial; none even buries Jesus.

Think about that for a minute. Jesus was the greatest teacher that ever lived. He poured himself into these people for three years of intensive study. He showed God and God's will more clearly to the world than they had ever seen it before. Yet the community of the Twelve began to dissolve even before Jesus died. No wonder we can't build the community of love on our own.

It takes a power greater than ours to do it. An invasion of sorts, not of Martians, but of God's power in Christ. When Judas left the room to start the process of betrayal that would lead to Jesus' death, Jesus did not despair; in fact, he acted like he was relieved that things were underway. "Now is the Son of man glorified, and in him God is glorified." God's glory is his inner nature—who he really is. Jesus has been claiming all along to show that glory in his teaching and his miracles. If you look and listen to Jesus, you see God. Now he claims that his death will show the same thing.

III. That's one of the most amazing things about the Gospel of John. Crucifixion, remember, was the worst form of capital punishment the Romans could think up, and they reserved it for the worst of criminals, those who needed to be public examples. Matthew, Mark, and Luke all say in one way or another that Jesus didn't deserve it. He was an innocent man, and the Crucifixion was a tragedy that never should have happened. In John, however, the cross is interpreted as Jesus' greatest moment of triumph, and the point at which he revealed God most clearly. The cross, the symbol of death at its most horrible, becomes a symbol of hope and life.

And a symbol of the new community, too. After Jesus tells them that he will die and by his death show God's glory, he gives them the new commandment. "A new commandment I give to you, that you love one another, even as I have loved you. . . . By this shall all know you to be my disciples, if you have love among each other." A new commandment: not new in the sense that God was urging his people to love each other for the first time, because that is part of the Old Testament. It is new because it is the foundation for the church, this new community of love that Jesus is beginning. They will be famous for their love for each other, and that will mark them as Christ's disciples.

IV. Hold on here—aren't we forgetting how the story begins? Judas goes out to hand Jesus over to his enemies, Jesus tells Peter that he will betray him three times, and we know that all of this and more will come true. This is no community of love—it is scarcely a community at all, because it is already disintegrating.

The key is, though, that we are describing the church before the cross and Resurrection. After Jesus changed the cross into the door to God's power, an amazing transformation occurred in the disciples, too. Peter, who wanted to lay down his life for Christ but who could not keep his nerve, preached for Jesus in the city of Rome during the time of Nero and was crucified for his faith. We don't know for certain what happened to the rest of the Twelve, but tradition has it that they all lost their lives defending the gospel. And they and their followers were so obviously filled with God's power that within three hundred years the very empire which crucified Jesus became Christian.

Quite a contrast, isn't it, to compare the disciples on either side of Easter. The question for us to answer is which group we are most like. How closely do we resemble the community of love which Jesus commissioned us to be? Do people know we are Christ's followers because of the way we love each other? The cross is the only door to the power that will make us into that community of love—we can never do it on our own. Let us meditate on the cross as the power that can help us to love one another. — Richard Vinson

Illustrations

TOO BLIND TO SEE.   After a decade of teaching in a respected theological seminary, I returned to the work of a pastor. When the initial excitement of that venture had subsided, I settled down to the frightfully busy routine of sermon building, meetings, membership recruitment, pastoral evangelism, and endless visitation. One busy day, I made the rounds of four hospitals to visit ailing church members. As I walked down the hallway to make my final visit, I found myself weary and full of self-pity. Did I leave the seminary classroom, I mused, to become a hospital chaplain? Then, in one of those moments rare to me, a light burst in my brain and a voice seemed to say, "I was sick, and you visited me." Nothing so chastens a person as a reminder like that! Christ had been before me in every sick person that day, but I saw him only in that last person I visited. — Nolan P. Howington

LEARNING TO LOVE.   Sir Gordon Guggisberg was a man outside the church. A Canadian of Swiss descent, he was intelligent, strikingly handsome, and played cricket extremely well. As a brigadier general he served his country through the First World War with unique dedication and loyalty. After the war he became governor of the gold coast of Africa. Sir Gordon felt no need of religion. On his shaving mirror he placed a card bearing the motto, "For God, for King, for Country." He said, "God meant nothing to me, the king meant a little, the country everything." One day a gallant Christian said earnestly to the governor, "you love your country because you have served it all your life; you have taken every opportunity of seeing the king; but you have never sought or even wished to know God." Himself a forthright man, Sir Gordon admired this forthright approach, and when he asked how one could know God, his friend replied, "Some of us be-

lieve that Jesus of Nazareth knew more of God than any other man, so we put aside some time each morning to study his thought of God and to let his Father speak to us." Guggisberg replied, "Damn it! I'll try it. It's worth it if it's true." Six months later he was a convinced Christian, and through the succeeding years he gave his life to the service of the Africans whom he came to love. He founded a system of higher education for his people and became the most progressive governor in all Africa. He died a poor man because he had given all his possessions to help his people. — Harold B. Walker, as retold by A. Leonard Griffith.

Sermon Suggestions

THE STORY OF RUTH, PART I.   TEXT: Ruth 1:1–19a. (1) After the death of her husband and two sons, Naomi prepares to return from Moab to her homeland alone. (2) Despite Naomi's protests, Ruth declares her intention to go with her and avows her undying devotion to Naomi and to Naomi's God. (3) Naomi yields to Ruth's determination, and they both go to Bethlehem.

WORDS–AND DEEDS.   TEXT: 1 Thess. 1:1–10. (1) The words of the gospel are of decisive importance. (2) Only the incarnation of words in deeds, however, brings the words to their ultimate significance.

Worship Aids

CALL TO WORSHIP.   "Love must be completely sincere. Hate what is evil, hold on to what is good" (Rom. 12:9, TEV).

INVOCATION.   Keep on teaching us, O Lord, how to love with the love of Christ. To that end, help us cling to what we have been shown to be good and reject all that would poison the wellsprings of concern and care for others.

OFFERTORY SENTENCE.   "Where your treasure is, there will your heart be also" (Matt. 6:21).

OFFERTORY PRAYER. This very moment is a testing time, Father, that shows where our truest affections and loyalties lie. May we be found faithful—if not today, surely in the days to come.

PRAYER. As we observe the orderliness of your Creation, witness the changing of the seasons, behold the waxing and waning of life, we come to you, Father, seeking to put our priorities in order and to submit our minds and our memories to you. Help us to remember all that is pleasing to you and to forget what is better forgotten.

We remember the great dreams of youth when we were unhampered by barriers of wealth-seeking, limited opportunities, and stymied efforts, and we wanted to go forth unselfishly to do great things in the world. O Father, may those memories summon us again to what is heroic and brave and true as we continue our walk down the roadway of the days and years.

We remember, too, Father, when love was young and hope was living and faith was strong and unhindered by clouding issues. We remember the great and hallowed experiences of earlier days which made an everlasting impression on our hearts and minds. Give us the courage to recall those enriching experiences of life that we may recapture a lost vision and reclaim a misplaced purpose for our lives as we venture into the tomorrows before us.

We remember the powerful souls, men and women, we have known, strong and radiant spirits whose paths crossed ours. In this hour remind us of the inspiration which we received from them, the challenge we accepted as we learned from them and the pathway on which they set our lives, which leads toward noble living and service in Christ's name. Give us the grace ever to follow their high challenge as they walked after the Savior of all of life.

We remember those times of sorrow and loss when life caved in and we felt utterly alone. And we recall how through the fog of that sorrow and loneliness you came to us in all gentleness to restore our souls. We also remember times of unanswered prayer and how later we learned that no answer was best. We remember how failures which caused pain were turned into stepping stones and by your grace became points of real achievement.

And now, remembering, may the spirit of Christ once again captivate our souls, saving us from our sins, swinging us from selfishness to service and calling us unto you.—Henry Fields

LECTIONARY MESSAGE

Topic: Paying Taxes to Caesar
TEXT: Matt. 22:15–22

How should a Christian relate to the state? The question seems rather simple and straightforward, but the answer has perplexed the followers of Christ for centuries. Some have embraced the state as a sacred agent of God and awarded it their total, unreserved allegiance. Others have withdrawn totally from any political involvement with the government. Most have found their response somewhere on the spectrum between these extremes. What does Jesus say? Today's passage has provided the basic sociopolitical answer for most ethicists and theologians. "Give to Caesar what is Caesar's and to God what is God's." But what does it mean?

The final week of Jesus' life was enmeshed in controversy. From the cleansing of the Temple to the Crucifixion, the days were filled with altercation, disputes, and confrontations. Matthew summarizes part of this period in a set of four controversy stories (Matt. 22:15–46). The first of these deals with the sociopolitical question of paying taxes to Caesar (Matt. 22:15–22). Jesus' reply reverberated in the memory of the early church (Rom. 13:7 and 1 Pet. 2:13) and later gave direction to Christian political ethics.

I. "What is your opinion?" Controversy often produces strange allies. The Herodians (friends of the Romans) and the Pharisees (staunch supporters of the Jewish religious structure) had nothing in common but their hatred for Jesus. In their eyes, he was a threat to Rome and Judaism. So in a brief moment of alliance they came to Jesus with a well-constructed plan to either discredit him with the people or charge him with treason.

After a few flattering remarks, they pose their question. "Tell us then, what is your opinion? Is it right to pay taxes to Caesar or not?"

Most agree that they were referring to the hated poll tax, a small tax levied on women aged twelve to sixty-five and men aged fourteen to sixty-five. A yes would be to forfeit his popular support, and a no would invite an immediate arrest.

II. "Show me the coin." Jesus' response was not exactly what they expected. "Show me the coin used for paying the tax." They showed him a silver denarius. "Whose portrait is this? And whose inscription?" " 'Caesar's,' they replied." And so it was. It had the picture of Tiberius Caesar on one side and his mother, Livia, on the other. The letters struck on the coin read, "Tiberius Caesar majestic son of the divine Augustus."

III. "Give to Caesar what is Caesar's." Jesus' final sentence establishes a guiding principle for the Christian's relationship to the state. It is not a law, but it establishes a truth of limited responsibility to political power. "Give to Caesar what is

Caesar's. . . . " Every citizen has duties to the state. When we enjoy the benefits of Caesar, then we are obligated to pay taxes and give reasonable support to the government. There are limitations.

IV. "Give to God what is God's." The second part of Jesus' pronouncement is crucial. "Give to God what is God's." Human beings are made in the image of God and therefore are God's. There are limitations to the claims the state can make on God's people. The state may be God's agent for justice and protection, but it becomes demonic when it demands total allegiance. Caesar cannot claim our conscience, nor our worship. These belong to God.

When Americans proclaim, "America! Love it or leave it" they are implying unconditional obedience or absolute uncritical allegiance. This is dangerously close to identifying our nation with the sovereignty of God. The Caesar/God formula prohibits this.

Jesus makes it quite clear that there are those who give the state too little and there are those who give the state too much. Our task is to continually ask ourselves what does it mean for us to "give to Caesar what is Caesar's and to God what is God's."—John Dever

SUNDAY: OCTOBER TWENTY-FOURTH

SERVICE OF WORSHIP

Sermon: The Bush Still Burns

TEXTS: Exod. 3:1–12; also, 1 Cor. 12:4–11

"And the bush was blazing, yet it was not consumed."

I. I've often wondered at these words. My mind has vividly imagined this moment in the life of a renegade shepherd named Moses. Images of fire and fascination. The mysterious and the majestic breaking into the mundane world of labor and love and longing. The almighty God, disclosed in this realm of human dreams and desires, dreads and daily struggles.

"And the bush was blazing, yet it was not consumed."

I imagine Moses—staff in hand—leans his back against a boulder and turns his eyes toward home. His thoughts are filled with confusion. The prince has become a poor shepherd. And the shepherd is suddenly thinking about those who will one day be his sheep. Slaves in Egypt. The people he loves. The people he longs for. The people he's powerless to liberate. His heart burns—and the blaze begins to consume what little hope he ever had.

"And the bush was blazing, yet it was not consumed."

A flicker of bright light catches the corner of his eye. "He looks, and the bush is blazing!" What madness is this? Some hallucination brought on by the hot sun? A brush fire along the side of the mountain?

Surely nothing unusual. Nothing alarming. Nothing important enough to drag the shepherd from the sheep.

Then again—close the eyes—rub! Open—close, rub—open!

It can't be! But—it is!

Staring, startled, stunned into silence for just a breath—a wild beating of that hopeless heart. It can't be! But it is!

"And the bush was blazing, yet it was not consumed!"

Then Moses said, "I must turn aside and look at this great sight and see why the bush is not burned up."

Fear and trembling. Being in the presence of something sacred. Drawn into the drama of a God who won't let go. A God whose grace can burn away—yet not consume.

Moses said, "I must turn aside." That small word *must* embodies the power of the mysterious and the majestic. The presence of God Almighty pulls us away from shallow concerns and places before us the challenges of sacred compassions.

"I have observed the misery of my people who are in Egypt; I have heard their cry on account of their taskmasters. Indeed, I know their sufferings, and I have come down to deliver them from the Egyptians."

II. God pulls us—like Moses—away from the world, for a moment of majesty and mystery, a moment for fire and fascination. A moment to bring us to our knees—back to our senses—back to our saintly calling.

God sends us forth—like Moses—burns his words, his will, his ways into our minds and hearts. God ignites the fires of faith within the church. The fire that will blaze but not consume. The fire that makes compassion compulsory.

And like Moses, the church will glow with a glory that's not her own but a reflection of that greater light—from her Redeemer. The fires of faith burn within her life, and she cries out with the prophet Jeremiah, "If I say, 'I will not

mention God or speak any more in God's name,' then within me there is something like a burning fire shut up in my bones. I am weary with holding it in, and I cannot."

And we should not! Even at the risk of being burned, we can only stand before this blessing and rejoice in the call of our Redeemer. Time and again we can "turn aside and see this great sight"—God gracing the world through the ministry of the church, through the fires of faith!

"And the bush was blazing, yet it was not consumed!"

III. And the bush still burns. All along the frontiers of our individual and corporate ministries God ignites the brush fires of faith.

We see the glory of God every day in those small, yet sacred, moments when suddenly God's burning grace catches our eye and, perhaps, our hearts, and we gave in wonder. Then we remember, don't we? We remember that our Redeemer is always there, just behind the tears and tragedy and triumph. But there nonetheless!

Igniting those fires of faith in some place or even in someone yet unknown. But sooner or later God's fire will flare up where we least expect it—when we least expect it: in the corner bed of some intensive care unit, in the room of some rejected and lonely soul, in the home of a cheerful believer, in a song of joy on a Sunday morning.

Then and there the bush will burn, and we, too, will "turn aside and see this great sight!" And when we do, our hearts will begin to burn with a new hope, our devotions will be fired by a new dream, and our lives will be purged of those things that make for despair and resignation.

"The bush was blazing, yet it was not consumed."

IV. The bush still burns and will never be consumed but will one day be consummated. Until that great day, she burns, burns with the light of God's love, burns with the glory of God's grace, burns with the bounty of God's blessings, burns with the fires of God's forgiveness! The bush will burn until such time as her light is no longer needed in this world. And that day will come. We have God's own promise in the words of John: "I saw no temple in the city, for its temple is the Lord God the Almighty and the Lamb. And the city has no need of sun or moon to shine on it, for the glory of God is its light, and its lamp is the Lamb."

But until that day you and I will watch and wait and be lost in a holy wonder—as the bush still burns!—Albert J. D. Walsh

Illustrations

THE FIRE ON THE ALTAR.   Every man of faith has two altars in his life: the altar in the church and the altar in the heart. The altar in the church is suggested for us in the word of the sixth chapter of Leviticus in the words "Fire shall be kept burning on the altar; it shall never go out." And the altar of the heart is suggested by the words found in 2 Timothy, chapter 1: "Stir into flame the gift . . . which is with you." There is a fire in the midst of the people of God, and there is the fire in the recesses of the heart. All of it is the fire of God.—Raymond Bryan Brown

HEARTS AFLAME.   Blaise Pascal, after a long search, found God in November of 1654. He tried, almost in vain, to find words to express what had happened. Finally, he settled for the word *fire!* The burst of energy capsulated in that single expression has been sufficient to propel his story around the world. We do not need a careful description of his religious experience. The single, energetic word *fire* telegraphs the essence of what happened and suggests the flow of energy that followed.

John Wesley went to Aldersgate Street—you know the story—the fire of God came down upon him on a May evening in 1738. Before the little Bible study group dismissed, John stood to his feet and said there was something he must share. "About a quarter before nine," he said, "my heart was strangely warmed."—Donald E. Demaray

Sermon Suggestions

THE STORY OF RUTH, PART II: A PROMISING ENCOUNTER.   TEXT: Ruth 2:1–13. (1) Trusting providence, Ruth gleans a field in the barley harvest. (2) Arriving at his part of the harvest field, Boaz notices Ruth and inquires about her. (3) Boaz, having heard beforehand of Ruth's devotion to Naomi, blesses Ruth, and Ruth hopes for his continuing favor.

"GOD WHO TESTS OUR HEARTS."   TEXT: 1 Thess. 2:1–8, NRSV. In sharing "the gospel of God" (1) are our methods and motives honorable? (2) are we caring and gentle? (3) are we personally involved and self-giving?

Worship Aids

CALL TO WORSHIP.   "I will call to mind the deeds of the Lord; I will remember your wonders of old" (Ps. 77:11, NRSV).

INVOCATION.   We would be pleased today, O Lord, with one of your smaller miracles, the healing someone's aching heart, the clarifying of someone's confused mind, or the gift of courage for someone's burden of overwhelming cares. If you worked your amazing wonders then, surely now you will do "exceeding abundantly above all that we ask or think."

OFFERTORY SENTENCE.   "Keep your life free from love of money and be content with what you have; for he has said, 'I will never fail you nor forsake you' " (Heb. 13:5, RSV).

OFFERTORY PRAYER.   Lord, give us the faith to believe in your mission and ministry; the courage to act on your behalf in the world of human need and lostness, and the willingness to make sacrificial gifts of our possessions, that there may be means available to send where you want to send those who have heard you calling them to go in your name.—Henry Fields

PRAYER. We do not think about it often enough, Father, this truth that we are your creatures made in your image. Sometimes that image is hard to discern. Thank you for your grace, which enables us to become more of what we were made to be.

We come to confess to you that it is our sins which mar your image in us. We are not worthy of your love and grace. But we are thankful that you do not deal with us as we deserve. Forgive us, Father, we pray. Forgive our pride and self-righteousness. Forgive our greed and selfishness. Forgive our waste of time and energy. Forgive us for neglecting those who need us and those for whom we have a special and family responsibility. Forgive us we pray for Jesus sake.

Today speak clearly to us. Reveal to us some truth that will enable us to be fortified in the doing of your will. Pray show us your will just for today. We do not ask strength for some far away future. Just give us strength for today, and in all that we do help, us to serve you better.

We pray for one another. For the anxious and the troubled, we ask your peace of mind. For the physically and mentally ill, we ask your health. For the lonely and the neglected, we ask your encouraging presence. We give ourselves to being the channels through which you move that others may be lifted and guided in your ways.

Now in these moments we worship and listen and wait, that we may encounter the Holy Spirit and experience through him your presence and truth.

LECTIONARY MESSAGE

Topic: The Greatest Commandment
TEXT: Matt. 22:34–46

Very early in my theological pilgrimage I learned a triangular theology. One should love God, love self, and love neighbor. What seemed like a simple formula for Christian living has been called into question more than once. Secularization, individualism, and humanism have all taken their toll. Secularization pushes God to the fringe of our living. Individualism destroys community and meaningful relations with neighbors. Humanism elevates human possibilities through scientific technology to the level of God. The first-century story of the greatest commandment seems to offer some hope for my twentieth-century dilemma.

I. *Love of God.* "Teacher, which is the greatest commandment in the Law? Jesus replied, 'Love the Lord your God with all your heart and with your soul and with your mind.' " This first part of the answer is in essence the first point of my triangular theology—and of course the most important point. Throughout his ministry Jesus made it quite clear that God is the main reality of all life. When God gets moved to the fringes, life gets all messed up.

It is interesting to note that we are to love (agape) the "Lord your God." This is the Lord of Israel who has made himself known in history, the God who through his actions has made claims to our love. John captures this when he says, "We love him because he first loved us" (1 John 4:19).

Jesus states emphatically that he has not come to destroy the Law, but here and in the Beatitudes he moves us beyond the Law to attitude as the basis of our relationship—an attitude of love. He moves us toward a direction to face. And since nobody has or ever will accomplish this commandment fully, grace is implied in, between, and through these lines of Scripture. Love is commanded. Grace is given. These become the basis of our relationship with the Lord our God.

II. *Love of self.* "And the second is like it: 'Love your neighbor as yourself.' " For years I thought that people loved themselves too much, but just the opposite is true. We do not love ourselves enough. Deep down we do not like what we are, where we are, and who we are. We need to come to love ourselves for God's sake. Bernard of Clairvaux discovered this in the twelfth century. He noted four stages toward spiritual maturity: Love of self for self's sake; love of God for self's sake; love of God for God's sake; love self for God's sake.

It is imperative that we come to a healthy love for ourselves before we can authentically love others. The basis for this self-love is in our relationship with God. Through Christ we have been forgiven and acceptance of that forgiveness sets us free—free to be authentic selves. Our highest challenge is to come to love ourselves for God's sake. Out of this love comes love for neighbor.

III. *Love of neighbor.* The triangle is not complete unless the love for neighbor is added. Jesus, the master teacher, was concerned for people. The New Testament is full of examples: the healing of the blind man, eating with Zacchaeus, weeping over Jerusalem, showing mercy for the multitudes. We are to love our neighbor, and the story of the Good Samaritan makes it clear that our neighbor is anyone who needs our help. Love of neighbor can be expressed in individual acts or in social action. Helping to destroy oppressive social structures is also an expression of agape.

IV. *How?* the encounter with the Pharisees is extended to the question of "Whose Son is the Christ?" (vv. 41–46). The essence of this passage is that Jesus is more than a Son of David, he is the very Son of God. It is through this Son of God that one learns to love God, love self, and love neighbor.—John Dever

SUNDAY: OCTOBER THIRTY-FIRST

SERVICE OF WORSHIP

Sermon: The Hobgoblin Circuit
Text: 2 Tim. 1:7

Over the years I have preached Advent sermons, Christmas sermons, Lenten sermons, Easter sermons, Pentecost sermons. This is my very first Halloween sermon.

I. By the eighties it has surely become obvious that this scientific culture in which we are supposed to live rational lives freed from any intrusions of the supernatural—and therefore cleared of all superstitious practices—has never existed. We are rapidly becoming one of the most superstitious generations in our history.

(a) Let's have a look at the "Hobgoblin circuit" in the United States. I'm thinking of the enormous network of superstition and the occult that covers the country— the ubiquitous horoscopes that are to be found in almost all newspapers; the Ouija boards; the tarot cards; the proliferation of crystal-gazers and fortune tellers; the passion for astrology; the thousands of little superstitions spawned by lotto and the gambling craze; the growing cults of satanism and witchcraft. Such things are no longer to be dismissed as either trivial pursuits that are not to be taken seriously or as clandestine activities of little groups of cranks and weirdos.

(b) What should a Christian think about this hobgoblin circuit, and what are the churches doing about it? Protestants and Roman Catholics, Fundamentalists and liberals—all have been inclined to ignore it, either because this kind of thing has no place in their religious life or because they are scared of it and believe it to be dangerous, if not forbidden, territory for a believer. As for the secularists, there is no need to fuss: all religion belongs in the hobgoblin circuit, and their "Brave New World" will eventually contain no trace of the supernatural. They are still under the illusion that the diminution of the influence of religion leads to elimination of superstitions. I would argue that history shows that, on the contrary, when religion wanes in any country it is not replaced by popular rationalist philosophy that leads to a universal happiness and peace. In the course of this century the vacuum left by the waning of religion in Western countries has been filled by an army of superstitious cults and beliefs. Perfect secularism by no means casts out fear.

II. It is time to turn to our sourcebook and listen for the Word of God. What has the Bible to say about the hobgoblin circuit? Three convictions about the hobgoblin circuit grip my mind and heart, and I offer them to you in the Spirit of Christ who has given us, says St. Paul, not a spirit of fear but "of power, love, and a sound mind."

(a) The first is that, while the Bible is based throughout on the reality of God who speaks to us from a dimension beyond the reach of our investigation and often breaks through to us in ways that we cannot understand, the Bible is not really a spooky book. Neither Old nor New Testaments show much interest in the activities of goblins and hobgoblins or in communication with the dead. Throughout the emphasis is on our moral obligations here and now as servants of the holy God of love. Paul warned the young churches against wasting their time with questions about ghosts and devils and the more spectacular of what he called "the gifts of the Spirit." With all his readiness to accept—even to expect—miracles, he was a great advocate of what he called "the sound mind." First things first.

(b) The second conviction I want to pass on may not be so acceptable to those who keep their religion "decently and in order." For I'm speaking now of what seems to me perfectly clear from Scripture: there is a supernatural dimension with which we have to do, and in it there are not only the spirit of "the just made perfect" but malevolent powers as well.

Both Old and New Testaments, although being reticent about angels, devils, and all that, express resounding warnings against trafficking with mediums and spirits of the departed, and the other customs derived from the idolatrous religions around them. Although I would not want to condemn any modern Christian who takes the hobgoblin light-heartedly and reads horoscopes for fun, I believe that the Christian faith condemns territory that is "dangerous for our spiritual health."

(c) Why? Because—and this is the third conviction to which I have come—all such dabbling supposes that we live in a world without knowing who is in control, for thus we are condemned to live in fear. The Christian gospel declares that Christ faced down all hostile cosmic powers at Calvary and defeated them as he rose from the dead. When this gospel was first heard in the ancient world, a great weight of anxiety and fear was lifted from the shoulders of those who accepted Christ and were baptized into the fellowship of his church.

III. Paul sums it up in the words of our text, which we could well inscribe in our hearts: "God hath not given us the spirit of fear [or its poor relation "depression"] but of love [which in its perfection "casts out all fear"] and of a sound mind [which we need desperately as we wade into the mysteries of the hobgoblin]. We need not be assertive and dogmatic or afraid to change our minds. What we want to know in the depths of our heart and the surface of our minds is that this sometimes terrifying world is not in the hands of astrologers, mediums, or the devil but of the God and Father of Jesus Christ our Lord.—David H. C. Read

Illustrations

THE QUESTION OF GOD'S POWER.   An idol is anything we substitute for the true God. We expect our idols to fill our lives with meaning, to make us happy, to supply us with whatever we need. We look to the idols to protect us from our doubts about our worth, from our feelings of guilt and emptiness, from our fears of weakness, suffering, and death. But the idols cannot deliver what we demand of them. Entrusting ourselves to idols leads not to fulfillment but to self-destruction and quite frequently to the destruction of others as well. Every idol is like the sorcerer in the legend of the sorcerer's apprentice. The power given to us by the idol quickly overpowers us and makes us its slave.

The idols of power are within us and around us. They compete for our allegiance. Knowledge is power, we are told. Money is power, others say. Power comes from the barrel of a gun, according to a revolutionary saying. These are only a few of the more common confessions of where ultimate power is sought and found in our time. The true God also exercises power. As the Apostle Paul writes, "The kingdom of God does not consist in talk but in power" (1 Cor. 4:20). But the power of the kingdom of God is different from the power of the idols. Christ is "the power of God" (1 Cor. 1:24); the gospel is "the power of God for salvation" (Rom. 1:16). When one entrusts oneself to the true God whose power is radically different from all other powers, one is thrust into the struggle between God and the gods. Where faith in the God of the gospel dawns in human life, the twilight of all our powerful gods begins.—Daniel L. Migliore

ARE WE PART OF THE PROBLEM OR OF THE ANSWER? One full moonlight night in Palestine I stood on the summit of Mount Tabor and, looking fifteen miles across the plain to the dim shadow of Mount Gilboa, thought of the ancient days when Saul was king of Israel and when, perhaps on such a night, he slipped away from his army and sought the witch of Endor in her cave, there on Little Hermon far below me. Note this: In the twenty-eighth chapter of 1 Samuel we read, "Now Saul had cleared the mediums and wizards out of the country." So he recognized witchcraft as a public evil and had issued an edict against it—all witches and wizards, begone! But four verses afterward we read this: "Saul said to his courtiers, 'Find me a witch, that I may go and consult her.' " That is one of the most human passages in the Bible—a man recognizing a public evil as evil, but when the pinch came, becoming himself part of the problem. All witches begone! but four verses afterward, Seek me a witch!—Harry Emerson Fosdick

Sermon Suggestions

THE STORY OF RUTH, PART III: A HAPPY OUTCOME. TEXT: Ruth 4:7–17. (1) Boaz has a rival who can make a claim to Elimelech's property and household. (2) The rival renounces his claim, and Boaz marries Ruth. (3) Ruth, the foreigner, thus becomes the ancestress of Jesus (Matt. 1:4–6; Luke 3:32).

PROFILE FOR PREACHERS. TEXT: 1 Thess. 2:9–13, 17–20. (1) Adaptability, verse 9. (2) Integrity, verse 10. (3) Empathy, verses 11–12. (4) Fidelity, verse 13. (5) Affection, verses 17–19.

Worship Aids

CALL TO WORSHIP. "Be not conformed to this world; but be ye transformed by the renewing of your mind, that ye may prove what is that good and acceptable and perfect will of God" (Rom. 12:2).

INVOCATION. Yours is the power to turn the shadow of our night into morning, Father. So here in this sacred place as we gather to worship we ask that you satisfy us with your mercy that we may rejoice and be glad all the day. In this hour lift the light of your countenance upon us, calm every troubled thought and guide our feet into the ways of peace. Grant us serenity in the midst of our hurried, harried lives even as you perfect your strength in the midst of our weakness.—Henry Fields

OFFERTORY SENTENCE. "Let your light so shine before men that they may see your good works and glorify your Father which is in heaven" (Matt. 5:16).

OFFERTORY PRAYER. Open our eyes, O God, that we see not only the beauty but also the ugliness of the world, not only the good but the evil, and then take away our discouragement and give us that fortitude of spirit that will send us with Jesus as he went out into the night when he was betrayed to take up his cross for the good of mankind.—Theodore Parker Ferris

PRAYER. In this sacred hour we gather as a congregation, Father, to open our hearts to you and express our gratitude for all your loving kindness to us through the days of our lives. Remembering how you have met us in our deepest need and led us through our darkest night, we come to acknowledge our endless dependence on you. We confess that we have not always loved you with all our heart, soul, strength, and mind. We have allowed little concerns of this earthly walk to become so important that we have sought to follow our desires and wants rather than sought to know and do your will. We have concentrated so intently on schemes to get our way that we have forgotten your ways. We have allowed desire to lead us where we had no business going and have neglected the paths along which we knew you would have us walk. Father, forgive our blindness and our willingness to be drawn away from the highest that we know. Renew a right spirit with us. Bring us face to face with our sins and their frightening impact on us as well as on others. Lead us by your Spirit to repentance, that point of turning, so that we may be made whole again and set free from the shackles which our sins place around us. Indeed today, Father, renew a right spirit with us that we may be released to continue the building of your kingdom.

Oh, come close to us, Father, we pray. Teach us the greatness of your presence. Bless those who fight their battles of life on beds of pain. Sustain the spirit of those who know that they are close to heaven's door and so soon will take that step which crosses eternity's threshold. Quicken the spirits of those who must make the decisions which will affect many people. Break the hardness of the hearts of those who harbor hate and malice and forget love and brotherhood because they have turned from you. Indeed, today let unrighteousness be destroyed in the heart of every man and woman, that the kingdom of this world may truly become the kingdom of Christ, where he shall reign in love and power forever and ever. Amen.—Henry Fields

LECTIONARY MESSAGE

Topic: Practicing What You Preach
TEXT: Matt. 23:1–12

Religious leaders are frequently put on the spot. They necessarily give a great deal of counsel concerning behavior: sometimes requested, often ignored. Because of this position they may live in a fishbowl. They are encouraged from time to time to "practice what you preach." Of course it is only fair and reasonable to expect them (us) to do this. Jesus introduced a series of seven woes, spoken in denunciation of the Pharisees and scribes, with a harsh description of their behavior. This description serves as an exhortation to current ministry.

I. *Say it and do it (vv. 1–3)*. The scribes and Pharisees chose positions of maximum exposure. They sat in pompous places. They called Moses as witness. They posed against the background of a magnificent heritage. They were recognized religious leaders. The "Moses seat" in the synagogue was a place of prominence, honored by all.

They told the people what to do. They told them how to be religious. This was their task. This was their responsibility. They spoke the truth, based on God's revelation to Moses. Jesus had confidence in their teaching. He encouraged the multitudes and his disciples to do what they said.

They did not themselves obey the Law. Jesus condemned them for not doing what they told others to do. His words were terse and true: "They say and do not." It would have been better if they had said nothing. It would have been best for them if they had obeyed their own counsel. Here is advice for us: Say it and do it.

II. *Be right and be loving (v. 4)*. They took the Law seriously—for the other fellow. They made religion heavy and harsh. The Law as they interpreted it was a burden to be borne, and it was not light. Legalism is like that. It does not provide wings for light flight. It wears and bears down on the shoulders.

The Pharisees and scribes "laid it on." Not all of the requirements of the Law were designed to be a burden. When these teachers interpreted the Law, however, it was burdensome. The emphasis is on their willful heaping the statutes on the shoulders of the people.

The larger tragedy was that they did not so much as lift a finger to help them bear the burden—no sympathy, no kind words, no comfort, no loving. Here is advice for us: Be right and be loving.

III. *Watch out for your motive (vv. 5–7).* Admittedly they worked "to be seen of men." Jesus was harsh in his judgment: "all their works" he said. They dressed for that purpose. They even enlarged the decorative fringes so there could be no mistake about their piety. They socialized for that purpose—to be seen of men.

They wanted to be noticed—chief place at feasts and chief place in the synagogues. They wanted to be noticed, and they got what they were after. But that's all they got (Matt. 6:2, 5, 16). Here is advice for us: Watch out for your motive.

IV. *Be humble and be a minister (vv. 8–12).* He spoke directly to his followers: Don't pretend to be a teacher; don't pretend to be a spiritual father; don't pretend to be a master. "He that is greatest among you shall be your servant."

And the longing of the masses is the cry of the poet Edgar A. Guest: "I'd rather see a sermon / than hear one any day. / I'd rather one should walk with me / than merely tell the way. . . ." —J. Estill Jones

SUNDAY: NOVEMBER SEVENTH

SERVICE OF WORSHIP

Sermon: Dealing with the Eternal

TEXT: 2 Sam. 6:9

Let us look at one of the most difficult stories in the Old Testament and see if God is not speaking some word to us through it. After David had been made king and captured Jerusalem, he must bring the Ark up to the holy city. The Ark was a chest in which the Law God gave to Moses was kept. So David and his men placed the sacred chest on a cart drawn by oxen, and accompanied by a host of people singing and dancing, they started on the journey from the house of Abinadab to Jerusalem. It was a joyous occasion, a sort of triumphal procession. But at one place on the journey the oxen stumbled, and it looked as if the Ark would fall off the cart. A man named Uzzah, standing alongside, put out his hand to steady it and almost immediately he fell dead. The tragedy made a great impression upon people, and they said he must have been stricken by the Lord for putting his hand on the holy object.

To me this story is saying that there are some things which are not to be manipulated or interfered with by human beings. There are some things in life which are for us to adjust to and not for us to arrange to suit our wishes. Surely we are being told that not every reality is amendable to our desires and that, if a generation assumes it has the right to arrange everything to its convenience, that generation will die. There are eternal truths which cannot be amended.

I. In three crucial areas we must come to terms with this truth. The first is morality. I believe in the moral law. I believe that God has established this as unchangeable and as unmanipulatable as the law of gravity. I believe that the only choice we have is to discover what the law is and live by it or to ignore it and die by it.

(a) All my life I have been hearing about a "new morality." Every generation seems to assume that the moral principles of their fathers are old-fashioned and outgrown. Every new point of view assumes that some things formerly thought wrong are no longer wrong and that we can act as if we live in a new moral climate. It is certainly true that some of the interpretations of morality and some of the customs we have established are outgrown and could be discarded. But I do not believe there is any such thing as a new morality, and so far as morals are concerned, the same kind of behavior which brought the downfall of Greece or Rome will bring the downfall of America or Russia.

(b) We are constantly under the demand to rethink our sex attitudes and our sex customs. Nothing seems more old-fashioned to the modern generation than the way their fathers and mothers courted and married. Some of the Victorian attitudes toward marriage fifty years ago are always good for hilarity and amusement. It is true, of course, that some of those things seem stilted, stuffy, and should be outgrown.

But essentially we cannot change anything about this terrible, wonderful gift God has given us. It is still true that rules operate, and if we follow them, sex becomes fulfillment and joy. If we ignore those laws, sex turns into lust and degradation. It is still true that no man can use a woman as a means to an end, nor can a woman use a man as a pawn to fulfill an ambition. The relationship between man and woman is something holy and unchangeable. When we forget this, all of our sophistication and smartness become a mere cover for failure and defeat.

(c) The family is deeply affected by its environment. Modern families live a different kind of life than our fathers knew. But the essential thing about the family has not changed, and what children learn from their parents and their homes is still the fundamental determinant of their future. Mothers may think they can turn their children over to housekeepers and have their own careers outside the home, but that does not work any better today than it did a thousand years ago. There are unchanging laws which govern the home and the family, and if in the name of being new and up to date we ignore those laws and break them, the only result is broken homes and delinquency.

(d) We obey the laws of righteousness in our society to save us from the jungle. Civilization depends upon justice and equity. Amos lived eight hundred years before Christ, and in unforgettable lines he described the demands of the moral law. He pronounced retribution on those who bought the poor for silver and the needy for a pair of shoes. The moral law demands, he said, that "justice roll down like waters and righteousness like an ever-flowing stream." There is nothing new in that, and there is nothing changeable about it either.

II. The second realm where we must not interfere is freedom. Here there is a sense in which it is all or nothing, and the moment we begin to manipulate or limit, we have destroyed it.

(a) Take, for example, censorship. Someone is always coming along with the very best of intentions to keep what they regard as the indecent from other people.

Censorship seems to be so reasonable if it is being practiced by good people. But the difficulty is, if it works for one side, it will work for the other. Supposing a Hitler comes to power and decides that some things are not good for the people to read. Suppose the tyrant wants to keep truth from the citizens of the nation. When the principle of censorship has been established, then there is no legitimate reason why, if used by one side, it cannot be used by the other. I am quite willing to accept censorship if I can be the censor, but I begin to ask questions about it if someone with whom I thoroughly disagree wants to do the censoring.

I have come to the conclusion finally that censorship is wrong and that it raises more questions than it solves. We have to raise the tastes of all men so that the filthy and the obscene will have no appeal. Freedom to read must be respected, and except in a very few extreme cases, we must insist on men's right to choose for themselves.

(b) Or look at this principle in terms of ideas. Are there some ideas that are positively dangerous? Possibly. Are there some ideas that are disgusting? Of course. But who is to decide and who shall have the final word? Jesus said that the truth would make us free, and the only way men find truth is to be at liberty to investigate every idea.

Justice Oliver Wendell Holmes, Jr., in the Abrams case in 1919, wrote these words: "But when men have realized that time has upset many fighting faiths, they may come to believe even more than they believe the very foundations of their own conduct that the ultimate good desired is better reached by free trade in ideas—that the best test of truth is the power of the thought to get itself accepted in the competition of the market, and that truth is the only ground upon which their wishes safely can be carried out. That at any rate is the theory of our Constitution. It is an experiment, as all life is an experiment. Every year if not every day we have to wager our salvation upon some prophecy based upon imperfect knowledge." Words not to be forgotten!

(c) The freedom of man is an idea that cannot be limited. South Africa established its apartheid policy and determined to keep the black man in virtual slavery. I thought when I visited that unhappy land years ago that they are merely postponing a terrible day of judgment because all men will be free. In America we are discovering that the revolution of civil rights has been held off for a hundred years but that now it has arrived. The history of slavery is clear enough. You cannot demand freedom for yourself and deny it to your brother. The moment we censor it or limit it, we have destroyed it. Freedom is of a piece, and it can never be divided.

III. Now the third thing to be said is that we must apply this principle to God. God is not someone to use, and it is for men to discover his will and yield themselves to it without compromise.

(a) Let us understand that we cannot manipulate God. There are some pseudo-Christian sects of our time which promise certain rewards if we learn how to use God for our benefit. There are some groups within Christianity itself which are guilty of this blasphemy. Indeed, to some extent our American religion falls into the trap of teaching people that God is one of those resources we can use for profit. We try to package him and market him.

(b) Consider our attitude toward worship. We come to the conclusion that worship is merely a feeling we may build up by certain techniques. We conclude that to worship is to make ourselves feel better, and we use the church and God as means of quieting our fears and increasing our happiness. Our hymns are too often subjective and become sentimental. The great hymns of the church are always objective and center our attention on God and his majesty. We develop

lighting systems which can go up and down with great artistry to give us a sense of being in an unreal world far from all the harsh glare of life. Believe me, our fathers were nearer to truth with their plain meetinghouses, their hard benches, and their willingness to listen to a man expound on what God expected from them.

(c) Much of our religion has become so informal that it smacks of a political rally. I have heard prayers that disdain the use of the more formal King James *thou* and talk to God as if he were the man next door. Woe unto us when we lose our sense of the holiness of the Almighty and minimize the awesome and indeed terrifying experience of coming into his presence.

(d) God is to be found, and God is to be obeyed. He gave his laws to Moses in the Ten Commandments, and today we wonder if they are not unnecessarily severe and negative. We would prefer something more positive. But the Jew understood that God commands and man obeys. Through all these centuries it has been proved true that to accept the commandments is to live and to deny them is to die. Nothing in our modern life has changed the reality of these judgments, which are true and righteous altogether.

IV. In the closing part of the Gospel of St. Mark there is a verse which at first sounds out of place. It occurs in the story of the appearances of the resurrected Christ to the disciples. "And he said to them, 'Go into all the world and preach the gospel to the whole Creation. He who believes and is baptized will be saved; but he who does not believe will be condemned" (16:15–16). Is this not unnecessarily harsh coming from the resurrected Christ? The King James Version has it that those who do not believe will be damned. This hard word needs to be spoken to this generation. He does not adjust himself to suit the desires of even his well-meaning followers, and the sooner we understand this truth, the better for us. Let us not forget that God made us in his image but that we did not make him in our image. To try to move him into a better position will only bring the disaster upon us which came to Uz-zah when he tried to interfere with the Ark.—Gerald Kennedy

Illustrations

DEALING WITH THE ETERNAL.   There came to my desk a paper from one of our theological seminaries. Included in it was a tribute to a retiring professor written by an alumnus. The tribute said that this man had presented "a reasonable deity who was acceptable and understandable to scientist and saint." I said to myself that God must be very pleased that somebody made him acceptable to some people. I shuddered that anyone would think that this is the task of a theologian. We need great poets, it is true, who can "justify the ways of God to men" as Milton once put it. But actually what we need more than anything else is for men to declare what God's will is and to warn us that a refusal to do it is death. A president of the University of New Hampshire, traveling through the mountains of his state in October, was heard to murmur, "I hope I'll never get used to it." May we never get used to the greatness of the moral law, the glory of freedom, and the majesty of God. May we have grace enough to know that these are not to be maneuvered but accepted.—Gerald Kennedy

THE GOOD FIGHT.   Faith can be described as battle against evil. The fight goes on from morning till night, day by day, year by year, until we may rest in peace where the evil one has no access. The only way to do battle is constantly to remember that I belong to God, I am the possession of the Lord Jesus Christ, I belong to the world of light and no longer to the reign of darkness. The devil cannot be fought directly. We can overcome him only by opposing his rule with the name of Christ. For he does not fear us, he only fears Christ. Our own will and our own strength are insufficient to destroy him. But in the confrontation with Christ he must yield. Hence we need not be afraid of him. "If God is for us, who may be against us?" Clothed in the whole armor of God, as the Letter to the Ephesians puts it, we are able to quench all the flaming darts of the evil one. Fear is forbidden, but we must know him and exercise ourselves instantly to notice his approach in the manner of soldiers in the trenches who smell poison gas. Gas masks must be put on even before the onset of the attack. We must immediately protect ourselves with the Word of Christ—and the enemy will not prevail against us.—Emil Brunner

Sermon Suggestions

WHAT GOD WANTS.   TEXT: Amos 5:18–24. (1) We may not know what we are asking for when we long for God's day of justice: it could work against us. (2) Our religious practices, in which we take pride and imagine ourselves secure, may actually blind us to our sinfulness and need. (3) What God wants from us is justice and righteousness, for "the enemy" may be "us."

WORDS WITH WHICH TO ENCOURAGE ONE ANOTHER.   TEXT: 1 Thess. 4:13–18. (1) Words about the cross and Resurrection. (2) Words about the return of the Lord Jesus Christ. (3) Words about the destiny both of those dead in Christ and of those alive at his coming.

Worship Aids

CALL TO WORSHIP.   "As it is written, Eye hath not seen, nor ear heard, neither have entered into the heart of man, the things which God hath prepared for them that love him" (1 Cor. 2:9).

INVOCATION.   O God, who hast taught us to trust in thee as our loving Father, open our hearts and share that most daring faith which thou hast revealed to thy servants in all ages, till the littleness of our knowledge is lost in the greatness of thy love.—Theodore Parker Ferris

OFFERTORY SENTENCE.   "Lay up for yourselves treasures in heaven, where neither moth nor rust doth corrupt, and where thieves do not break through nor steal" (Matt. 6:20).

OFFERTORY PRAYER. Let the love of God, my heavenly Father, the grace of Jesus Christ, my Lord, and the joy of the sanctifying Spirit, sealing up the promise of God as my security, and writing his law and gospel in my heart, be my heritage and joy, and I shall never envy the most prosperous sinner their portion in this life but shall live and die in the thankful praise of God of my salvation, who is essential, infinite, joyful love.—Richard Baxter (1615–91)

PRAYER. Forever God, before the beginning, you were, and in the beginning you called forth heaven and earth. With precision and good measure, each day you gave shape to Creation and filled the new earth with life. And you formed us in your holy image and called us very good.

Master Builder, the gladness and pleasure of your handiwork surround us with beauty and wonder. You are worthy, O Lord, to receive glory and honor and praise. And in the fullness of time, you gave us your Son, Jesus, who is your holy work of redemption and eternal life. We honor him with our soul's glory, joy, and crown. And now, by the person and work of your Holy Spirit, we breathe your presence, walk in your graciousness, and enter your sanctuary to worship thee as Creator and Lord of all. Forever God, Lord of the end, we live and serve in the sure and certain hope that you are Omega, our forever.

God and Lord of all nations, we pray for persons in places still divided by walls of race, class, pride, prejudice. May the labor of our hearts and hands be the tearing down of all barriers that separate your children and our human family.

We voice prayers of gratitude for veterans who have given much that we might live in freedom and without walls. In response, empower us to work for peace and goodwill for all the world. We pray for our church and our call to be your healing body in a broken world. We pray for personal call in our lives to be

laborers in the harvest. Teach us in Christ, to work with love, remembering that good work is love made visible. In Christ, your love made visible to us, we pray.—William M. Johnson

LECTIONARY MESSAGE

Topic: A Parable of Preparation
TEXT: Matt. 25:1–13

"The kingdom of heaven is like this," he said. The parable of the ten virgins is familiar. Ten maidens took their lamps to meet the bridegroom, a part of the ancient ritual. Five of them were foolish and took no extra oil. Five of them were wise and took extra oil. The bridegroom was late, the maidens slept. At midnight the bridegroom was announced. Immediately the maidens began to trim their lamps. The lamps of the foolish girls were sputtering, and they asked for oil from the wise ones.

The wise maidens were yet wise: We cannot let you have any of our oil; then we would run out. The foolish ones went to buy oil. While they were gone, the bridegroom arrived, was welcomed, went in to the marriage feast, and closed the door. Then the five foolish maidens came and were refused admittance. The word of the Lord is current: "Watch therefore, for you know not the day or the hour."

Now how is the kingdom of heaven like that? The subject of the kingdom of heaven must always be prepared for any development.

I. *Here is the basis of wisdom (vv. 2–4).* The distinction between the wise and the foolish is simple and sharp. The wise are prepared. The foolish are not prepared. There do not appear to be any other differences. All were together until the lack of preparation on the part of the foolish forced their separation.

Why? Perhaps the foolish were so caught up in the fun of the moment. Perhaps they did not take their opportunity seriously. Perhaps they thought they could get by. Perhaps they presumed on the bridegroom's good nature. And perhaps the wise were so caught up in the happiness of the couple. Who can tell?

II. *Here is the coming of the crisis (vv. 5–10).* It's coming for all of us. It may be a wedding at midnight, though probably not. It may be a sick family member. It may be a misunderstanding church member. It may be the betrayal of confidence by a friend.

We can be sure that the crisis is coming. It may be our own death. Five were prepared; five were unprepared.

III. *Here is judgment on the foolish (vv. 11–13).* They shut themselves out. They were not present when the bridegroom arrived. Despite their impassioned cries, "Lord, Lord, open to us," his answer was abrupt: "I don't know you."

The point of comparison is preparation and the lack of it. The kingdom of heaven is not the end of a broad comfortable path for strolling. This path leads to destruction. "Narrow is the gate and straitened the way" (Matt. 7:13–14). Be prepared!

On a lonely mountain road, painted in luminous paint on the rock alongside— "Prepare to meet thy God." It's the word of Amos directed to modern travelers. There are situations where judgment is final. Be prepared!—J. Estill Jones

SUNDAY: NOVEMBER FOURTEENTH

SERVICE OF WORSHIP

Sermon: The Faith Question

TEXT: John 1:45–51

As we move through the first chapter of John's Gospel, we see the circle of discipleship widening. First, there was John the Baptist pointing to Jesus and saying, "Behold, the Lamb of God!" (v. 36). Then Andrew and his friend came, heard, and followed. Andrew ran and corralled his brother, Simon. Moving north the next day toward Galilee, Jesus found Philip. And Philip, excited and breathless, ran to tell his friend Nathanael.

Reluctantly, Nathanael came and saw more than he intended. Suddenly, Nathanael encountered Jesus firsthand. He was moved because Jesus knew him through and through. Only someone very special could have known his name even though they had never met. Nathanael was impressed by Jesus' knowledge of him. He exclaimed, "Rabbi, you are the Son of God! You are the king of Israel!" (v. 49).

But all this was background. These words merely form the framework for the question Jesus would ask. This query is a question of belief. Jesus asked Nathanael, "Because I said to you, I saw you under the fig tree, do you believe?" (v. 50).

I. This question was a faith question: Why do you believe? These words were not only addressed to some first-century would-be disciple, they were addressed to all of us who walk across the stage. "Tell me honestly," Jesus said, "why do you believe?"

(a) Nathanael believed because before him stood One that knew his name before they had ever been introduced. He was impressed because Jesus knew his past history. Here was someone who could read the signs in the heavens and maybe even in a person's heart. Anybody would believe someone who knew so much.

(b) But Jesus was not impressed with the confession of Nathanael. He knew this man had a long way to go: Do you believe because I said I saw you under a fig tree? Then Jesus followed his question with a promise, "Truly, truly, I say to you, you will see heaven opened, and the angels of God ascending and descending upon the Son of man" (v. 51). Nathanael, there is another kind of faith. Another way of seeing. There is a faith that you know little about. Elementary, first-grade faith must have a sign, a proof, something nailed down and proven. There is a test-tube faith that can be measured and analyzed. But there is another kind of faith. This deeper kind of faith is also seeing. But this seeing is so strange and different that it takes a lifetime to know. Jesus told Nathanael there was a seeing that he had yet to discover.

II. What can we learn about this second kind of faith? What can we learn about this through-a-glass-darkly kind of faith that Paul talked of?

(a) In such a faith relationship we begin to know by experience—to see. But this is a different kind of sight. Here we find a deep, gut-level kind of knowing that no one can take from us. John called this seeing as strange as watching angels ascend and descend upon the Son of man.

(b) Here is one way I have encountered this second kind of faith. On the back wall of a church building where I once served hung an oil painting. I wondered about that painting, and one day someone explained the picture and its history. I was told that a young graduate student and his wife had come to our town. While they were there, they had lost a little girl. When the baby got sick, that church had reached out. They prayed. They visited. They took food. They had loved and cared for this young couple. When the baby died, they had walked with the broken couple through their terrible grief. There were days when the young man and his wife wondered if they would make it. Somehow they had found the grace to go on. The young man finally had finished his degree and moved to another place.

But before he left, he had wanted to leave something behind for the people who had helped him and his wife. He had painted a picture: a beautiful oil painting. It was a pleasant scene with woods and a natural setting. The person who told me the story asked me to look closely at the picture. Can you see it, he asked? I was puzzled. Keep looking, he said. I kept looking, and suddenly the picture began to change. At the heart of that pleasant scene of trees and sky and waterfall, I could make out the shape of a cross and a man on the cross. Jesus was at the center of it all.

III. We find Nathanael's name mentioned only once more in the Gospel accounts. His name appears again in the twentieth chapter of John. He was with Peter and the other disciples. Jesus had been crucified. They were still devastated. So Simon Peter led them all back to what they had known before Jesus came into their lives. They returned to fishing nets, water, boats, and seines. They fished all night and caught nothing. Toward morning with the fog heavy on the lake they heard a voice they had heard before. They knew who it was.

I have wondered often about that story. As they moved toward shore, did Nathanael remember a promise made years before? A faith that found the strength to go on, people coming back from the dead—resurrections? I wonder if Nathanael remembered, that misty morning, the promise of Jesus: "You will see heaven opened, and the angels of God ascending and descending upon the Son of man" (v.51). Did he remember? I wonder, things being as they are, if we will remember, too.—Roger Lovette

Illustrations

SPASMS OF FAITH. Faith and love are apt to be spasmodic in the best minds. Men live on the brink of mysteries and harmonies into which they never enter, and with their hand on the doorlatch they die outside.—Ralph Waldo Emerson

THE KINDS OF BELIEVING. Martin Luther said there are two kinds of believing. One kind of belief is to believe things about God. He said there are some things that we can affirm about God that we can also say about the Turks, the devil, or hell. These are facts: encyclopedia knowledge. This is belief. Luther then talked of another kind of faith. Not only do we believe in God, but we begin to put our trust in him. We bet our lives on the truth that there is a God. We even begin to give him our money because we really do believe this business. We surrender to him. We follow him. We believe that he is with us, and nothing can separate us from his love.—Roger Lovette

Sermon Suggestions

CAN WE BE SAVED?   TEXT: Zeph. 1:7, 12–18. (1) The situation for both believers and unbelievers seems hopeless in the day of God's judgment and justice. (2) Yet there is hope (see Zeph. 2:3).

WISE WORDS ON LAST THINGS.   TEXT: 1 Thess. 5:1–11. (1) You do not need a timetable, for the day of the Lord will come unexpectedly. (2) We should be prepared, alert, and confident because of God's purpose for us. (3) We should help one another to be ready.

Worship Aids

CALL TO WORSHIP.   "O magnify the Lord with me, and let us exalt his name together" (Ps. 34:3).

INVOCATION.   Our Father God, because we are thy children, we are here, homeward bound, looking homeward because the feeling has been stirred within us in the first moment of worship that we belong to thee and that thou dost belong to us. We shall always be aweary and alien until we are in thine own heart of hearts, reconciled by the love thou hast given to the world in our Elder Brother. Father, we thank thee for this hour. Let us open all the doors of gratitude that the good angels of thy mercy and guidance may come in. We will give thee all the glory of this blessing through endless ages as we respond in our prayer unto thee.—Frank W. Gunsaulus

OFFERTORY SENTENCE.   "Freely ye have received, freely give" (Matt. 10:8b).

OFFERTORY PRAYER.   Lord, we have received faith, hope, and love because there were those who gave freely not only of their spiritual resources, but also of their financial means to get the message out. Now let us and help us to share all that we have received with your blessing.

PRAYER.   Our Father, we look back on the years that are gone, and shame and sorrow come upon us, for the harm we have done to others rises up in our memory to accuse us. Some we have seared with the fire of our lust, and some we have scorched by the heat of our anger. In some we helped to quench the glow of young ideals by our selfish pride and craft, and in some we have nipped the opening bloom of faith by the frost of our unbelief.

We might have followed thy blessed footsteps, O Christ, binding up the bruised hearts of our brothers and building the wayward passions of the young to firmer manhood. Instead, there are poor hearts now broken and darkened because they encountered us on the way, and some perhaps remember us only as the beginning of their misery or sin.

O God, we know that all our prayers can never bring back the past, and no tears can wash out the red marks with which we have scarred some life that stands before our memory with accusing eyes. Grant that at least a humble and pure life may grow out of our late contrition, that in the brief days still left to us we may comfort and heal where we have scorned and crushed. Change us by the power of thy saving grace from sources of evil into forces for good, that with all our strength we may fight the wrongs we have aided and aid the right we have clogged. Grant us this boon, that for every harm we have done, we may do some brace act of salvation, and that for every soul that has stumbled or fallen through us, we may bring to thee some other weak or despairing one, whose strength has been renewed by our love, that so the face of thy Christ may smile upon us and the light within us may shine undimmed.—Walter Rauschenbusch

LECTIONARY MESSAGE

Topic: A Parable of Responsibility

TEXT: Matt. 25:14–30

When I was a child in the 1930s I regularly took a nickel to Sunday school. I did not receive an allowance. I was given a nickel, and I gave it to God. When I began delivering papers and making some money, I was able to increase my gift from my own earnings. When I went to college I was flat broke. I worked for the princely sum of fifteen cents an hour on the campus, typing, tutoring, teaching. All of this was applied to tuition, room, and board. I saw no money.

My sister had finished college the spring before I entered and worked at a bank in Oklahoma City. She understood my plight and regularly gave me a dollar a week that I might have something to give to the church in Shawnee, and I gave it to the church. It was given to me to give. I was responsible for its use.

Stories abound of people using something for God. Moses and his staff, Deborah and her needle, and a lad with a lunch. This parable was directed to the nation Israel and to the new Israel and to individual subjects of God's kingdom. The kingdom of heaven is like this.

I. *What we have God gives.* What they had in the parable their master gave them. They were bond slaves. He trusted them with his goods—the kingdom of heaven is like that. He gave to them according to their ability—the kingdom of heaven is like that. He did not serve as a policeman over them—the kingdom of heaven is like that. He expected them to produce dividends—the kingdom of heaven is like that. He returned and there was a reckoning—the kingdom of heaven is like that. He rewarded their faithfulness—the kingdom of heaven is like that. But there was another servant.

II. *What we have we are free to use.* The servants were freed by their master's absence. The third servant's reply is a reflection on his master. It is insolence and presumption on man's part to question the terms on which God has created him. It is not our business to sit in judgment on God. It is our business to do the best in the situation where we are. A servant's highest reward is to be allowed to go on serving. If one person refuses to serve, someone else will. God's work goes on. What we have, we are free to use. We may use it, abuse it, lose it.

III. *We are judged by our faithfulness.* We are not judged by our prettiness, our smartness, or our size. To the first two servants he had said, "Well done, thou good and *faithful* servant." To the third servant he had said, "Thou wicked and *slothful* servant." The opposite of faithful is slothful. A sloth is characterized by slowness, laziness, indifference. The third servant revealed a defiant attitude. He expressed himself insolently. He knew that he had been unfaithful.

IV. *We are rewarded by a more significant task.* "The windows of heaven will be opened"—there is the promise of Malachi. But more comes from heaven than monetary gifts. There are more excellent gifts from God. You do a good job on something, and you are offered a bigger job. The reward for such responsible service is opportunity for further and larger service.

But there was another servant.

"For unto every one that hath shall be given, and he shall have abundance: but from him that hath not, even that which he had shall be taken away." What did they "have" that he did not "have"?—J. Estill Jones

SUNDAY: NOVEMBER TWENTY-FIRST

SERVICE OF WORSHIP

Sermon: The Mantle of Charity
TEXT: Gen. 9:20–23

I do not recall having heard or read a sermon based on this Old Testament incident. I readily agree with the fastidious that this is not a decorous scene to look upon. Drunkenness never is pleasant to behold.

The one factor in this sorry scene which lifts it out of grossness and invests it with decency is the deed of Noah's sons in taking a garment and walking backward with averted eyes and covering the naked body of their father as he lay sprawled out in a drunken stupor.

On the whole, the mantle of charity is not often in evidence in the Old Testament. That literature is starkly realistic. If we had been writing about Abraham, Jacob, and David, we would have glossed over certain wrongdoings of which they were guilty or omitted them altogether. But the chroniclers of the Old Testament told the truth about their heroes, shocking though it sometimes was.

In this frank portrayal of human frailties the New Testament differs from the Old. Not that the New glosses over wrongdoing; not at all. The deadly wages of sin are set down, and the dire consequences of evil traced "in characters indelible and known." Still, as a rule, the climate of the New Testament is gentler and more favorable to justice tempered with mercy than the Old. But of this more later on.

I. Like the quality of mercy, the ministry of the mantle of charity is twice blest. It blesses him who gives and him who takes. In truth, the mantling of charity about the human frailties of others is itself a mark of mercy—is love in action.

(a) Imagine what would happen if human beings spoke in public their opinions and criticism of one another which they speak guardedly in private or the uncharitable thoughts they cherish but do not put in words. Imagine the consequences! Families would disintegrate, churches become discordant and in turmoil, communities belligerent and embroiled in strife. Why, life would be unendurable. It is the understanding heart, the tempered spirit, the guarded tongue, the love that "thinketh no evil," which holds the family together, unifies the church, and saves the community and the state from dissolution.

(b) Take a close-up view of our heroes, not for the purpose of *debunking*—how I dislike this word, but it is in the dictionaries and its meaning familiar to us all. Some of our heroes had feet of clay, and all of them being human had faults and weaknesses.

Look at Martin Luther. He sometimes threw wild words around carelessly. He was obstinate and not always easy to work with. The one big splotch on his escutcheon is his failure to side with the poor and the disinherited in the Peasants' War, choosing rather to stand with the powerful, the nobles, and on the side of the highly placed. Yet we throw the mantle of charity over Luther's mistakes. His virtues and his accomplishments far outnumber and outweigh his weaknesses.

And there is Lincoln! He was not a demigod. He had his weaknesses, frailties. They were known to his friends. They were better known to himself. And who cares to recall them save to show the great human being Lincoln was.

(c) There was once a famous American statesman whose political life was embattled, and he missed the grand price—the presidency. In his latter years, in conversation with a young newspaperman who had come to interview him, he took the reporter to a window overlooking a wooded park. "See the trees," he said, "how beautiful they look from here, but if you examine them closely you will find ugly knots, broken branches,and dead limbs. So it is with men in public life. Better look at them from a distance and credit them for what good they have done and forget their faults and frailties." There is something in this; the mantle of charity is in the word picture that statesman painted.

II. Not only is it necessary to walk backward and spread the mantle of charity over individuals, we are obliged to do likewise with movements, organizations, crafts and the world of business, professions, and vocations in general.

(a) The political world is nearly always in disruption, and presidential campaigns, nightmares four months long. Yet, this is democracy at work. It is not working as smoothly and as righteously as we could wish, but it is working, and what is more, we work with it and vote as we choose. Over the excesses, puerilities, banalities, and sometimes hypocrisies, we throw the mantle of charity, remembering that out of such strange and uncouth methods we have discovered and put in office a Jackson, a Lincoln, and a Cleveland. Fisher Ames, one of the founding fathers of our republic, was right: "A democracy is like a raft;hard to steer, and your feet are always wet."

(b) Coming closer home, behold my own beloved brotherhood, the Disciples of Christ! Born of prayer for the unity of the churches, we are split among ourselves three ways. It would be easy to throw up our hands in despair and cry, "A plague on all three houses." But we do well to remember that the note of unity which our pulpits sounded almost alone for a century has brought forth results. Now with few exceptions that note of unity is being sounded clear and strong by the major denominations. We have much to praise in our movement for the unity of the divided house of God, and over the divisions and controversies among our brethren we throw the mantle of charity, saying humbly betimes, "To know all is to forgive all."

III. It is time we turn to the New Testament, where the climate is especially favorable to the mantle of charity and where it is so often in beneficent use. One is embarrassed by the wealth of teaching, incident, and illustration on the side of compassion, forgiveness, mercy without stint, which he finds in this Christian literature. Only a few instances out of many are cited here, incidents so notable, so tender, so full of compassion as should move the dullest heart.

(a) The enemies of Jesus brought a woman taken in adultery into his presence, saying "Master, in the Law Moses commanded us to stone such persons. What therefore dost thou say?" The episode was a brazen act on the part of her accusers. He stooped and silently wrote in the dust. They continued to ask him, "What are you going to do with this woman?" He raised himself up and said: "Let him that is without sin among you be the first to cast a stone at her." Hearing this unexpected reply, the accusers went away, one by one, beginning with the oldest. Jesus and the woman were left alone. He raised himself up and said to her, "Has no one condemned thee?" She answered, "No one, Lord." Then said Jesus, "Neither do I condemn thee. Go thy way

and sin no more." Was ever the mantle of charity more gently draped over an erring human being?

(b) There is the case of Peter, who, in an hour of crisis both for his Master and himself, denied that he was a follower of Jesus, denied that he even so much as knew him, and accompanied the denials with rude oaths. On the seashore the Christ came to Simon Peter and gave him the opportunity to confess him thrice, in the memorable words, "Thou knowest I love thee." And on the day of Pentecost it was none other than Simon Peter who was the spokesman, the preacher of the first Christian sermon ever delivered. Nor is there likelihood that any of his fellow Christians took him aside after that notable service he rendered that day to say in envy or downright meanness, "See here, Peter, don't you remember that you are the one who on a certain fateful night denied your Lord three times?" No, so far as we know, nothing happened like that. His fellow Christians threw the mantle of charity about that shabby episode and never referred to it again.

(c) Then there was Judas, who betrayed his Lord. John, in after years, remembered that at the Last Supper, Jesus dipped the bread in the sop and gave it to him who had already bargained to sell his Master to the enemies. By that gesture it was as though Jesus said to Judas, "You see I love you, Judas. Now can you do this thing to me? Judas, I love you." Was not this unprecedented courtesy a mantling of the would-be betrayer with a love that was reluctant to let him go on with the wicked bargain? For one, I think so. And at the bitter end, with the shouts of derision and jeers of those who willed that he should die upon the cross, Jesus prayed, "Father forgive them for they know not what they do." Was ever so ineffable a mantle of charity divine flung over the madding mob that clamored for his blood?

IV. The mantle of charity! What a theme! Who can do justice to it? It occurs to me that I have said but a little of the much that could be said on so vast and neglected a subject. But I hope I have said enough perchance to soften the hard heart that is stubbornly set against justice, compassion, mercy, and forgiveness.— Edgar DeWitt Jones

Illustrations

NONE WITHOUT FAULT. Diogenes is pictured going about with a lantern looking for an honest man. He could have found that kind of a man without a lantern had he looked in the right places. But Diogenes, with his lantern, could not have found a faultless person; no more can we, although we may turn a powerful, dazzling searchlight on humanity.— Edgar DeWitt Jones

THE EVIL IN US. The fact cannot be altered that in his person, even if it is that of the most outstanding Christian brother, I will encounter at some point and in some form the "evil" in which he (like myself) unfortunately has a part. Shall I then reckon it to him (*logizesthai*)? Shall I take it down in writing against him? Shall I always hold it against him? Shall I nail him to it so that in part at least I always interpret him in the light of it, shaping my attitude accordingly and always regarding him as in some degree a bad man? I can do this, and there is no little inclination to do so. But love cannot and does not do it, not only because it is self-giving, but because as such it is a reflection of the love of God, which has to do with men who are wholly bad but according to 2 Cor. 5:19 does not impute or reckon their trespasses to them. The man who loves does not compile a dossier about his neighbor. There is, however, a third possibility—the most dreadful of all. This consists in the blatant perversity of actually "rejoicing" that even the most upright of our neighbors continually put themselves in the wrong in relation to us and others, not to speak of God. There is a refined satisfaction which I can procure for myself by making perhaps a show of the deepest sympathy, by actually experiencing it in the guise and feeling of the greatest readiness to forgive, but by seeing that I am set by contrast in a much better light myself, that I am equipped and incited to a much more worthy representation of that which is good, and that I am thus confirmed and strengthened and exalted and assured in my own excellence.—Karl Barth

Sermon Suggestions

WHAT GOD THE GOOD SHEPHERD WANTS FOR HIS PEOPLE. TEXT: Ezek. 34:11–16, 20–24. (1) Then: Israel was scattered, but God in caring concern and love purposed to gather, to feed, and to heal and strengthen his people and to bring them under his authority. At the same time he would judge their oppressors. (2) Always: God is bound to his people in an everlasting covenant and in all circumstances seeks their good. (3) Now: (a) In the worst conditions we can expect God to be working for our good. (b) This may involve God's wrath against oppressive persons and institutions, even against the evil of his own people. (c) God's ultimate purpose, however, is justice and blessing (see John 10:27–30).

CHRIST THE KING. TEXT: 1 Cor. 15:20–28. (1) By the power of God, Christ conquered death in his Resurrection. (2) By the will of God, all will be made alive in Christ. (3) In the purpose of God, Christ the Son will surrender all sovereignty to the Father, "so that God may be all in all" (v. 28, NRSV).

Worship Aids

CALL TO WORSHIP. "All the law is filled in one word, even in this: Thou shalt love thy neighbor as thyself" (Gal. 5:14).

INVOCATION. Giver of earthly beauty and bounty, we come with gratitude into your presence this thanksgiving season. In this sacred hour remind us anew that because we have freely received the treasures of your love and care, that we are called to freely give love and care and the goods of life to those who have needs which they cannot meet in their own strength and power and skill. In this hour stir our hearts and lives to caring service such as Jesus gave.—Henry Fields

OFFERTORY SENTENCE. "If I give away all I have, and if I deliver my body to be burned, but have not love, I gain nothing" (1 Cor. 13:3, RSV).

OFFERTORY PRAYER. O Holy One of Israel, you are the faithful steward of all creation. From eternity to eternity you lovingly tend all that you have made. Like a faithful gardener, you stoop over your creatures—to order and reorder, to prune, bandage, and feed.

In Jesus Christ you sent one to redress the vineyard that yielded wild grapes—the human heart. In Jesus Christ, the faithful steward, you came to make our hearts new—by teaching and healing, by joyous story and luminous presence.

We thank you that you call us to be stewards—in treating as a trust all that we have; in the gardener's faithfulness in little things; in hearing the cry of a hurt Creation and in the joyful retelling of your story.

Where we have been good stewards, claim us as your own. Where we have been unfaithful stewards—through misuse and neglect, through pride and greed and all our woundedness, call us back to your hope and your tasks.—Peter Fribley

PRAYER. Whom have we in heaven but you? And there is nothing on earth we desire besides you. Our flesh and our heart may fail, but you are the strength of our heart and our portion forever.

As we contemplate your presence among us, your being, your fatherliness, your motherliness, your love that perseveres in the face of any estrangement, your light that no darkness can ever put out, your beneficent ways to all persons, what joy abounds! Praise be to you, O God, in whom we live and move and have our being.

What opportunities await us as we have awakened to the light of this new day. Alert us to the possibilities of this day, of this hour, of this moment, for today is the day of salvation and now is the timely time. How pregnant this moment is with life! May the birthing of new life in us be the experience of our every breath.

Some people would give anything to share this opportunity of worship! May we not treat it routinely. It is our life. For man or woman or young person or child shall not live by bread alone but by your every word. May we grasp this opportunity with both hands—with all our being—with all our mind, heart, and strength. If we seek you with all our heart, we shall surely find you. Blessed are the pure in heart, those with a single eye, those who concentrate, for they shall see you. This is the vision we need. May we wait for you as those who wait for the morning—in great expectation. We know that we shall not be disappointed. Thank you, God!

What resourcefulness is ours—but what potential goes untapped. This is our sin—the unfulfilled potential of our lives. Time marches on, and we sleep through a revolution—the coming of your kingdom. Teach each one of us to pray: Thy kingdom come, thy will be done, beginning with me.

We praise you for our life together in this time and place.

With what intimacies our lives are bound into one bundle. No man is an island; we are all part of the main. No person lives or dies unto herself or himself. May our uniqueness as persons be not a stumbling block—an occasion for estrangement—but an invitation to glory in your creative love. With this love and appreciation of our self and of the otherness of every other, we would pray for one another.

May we who daily experience companionship be sensitive to the needs of the alone. Some of us are anxious over those whose health is precarious. Grant us the wise trust to commit them to your healing grace and keeping in Christ, Those crying out in anguish of soul in bereavement of loved one or friend, grant the hope of a love that never ends.

We pray for the unity of the Spirit in the bonds of peace. In word and deed may the church be faithful to the gospel of reconciliation—your gift in Christ and for the healing of all brokenness and the healing of the nations.

Once we were no people, but now we are your people. Once we had not received mercy, but now we have received mercy that we may declare the wonderful deeds of him who called us out of darkness into your marvelous light. And now, O Father, with all your good gifts grant us the faith to live as we have prayed, through him who is our faith and teaches us when we pray, to pray together, Our Father. . . .—John Thompson

LECTIONARY MESSAGE

Topic: A Parable of Judgment
Text: Matt. 25:31–46

It's almost a tale of unconscious goodness or unconscious badness. In any event the behavior is so far removed from the pretense condemned in chapter 23 as to be refreshing. It is even refreshing to hear of the "goats" professing their ignorance of the Lord's presence with his people.

This is the last of Jesus' parables in Matthew. It follows parables on preparation and responsibility. But how do you prepare for the judgment? What is the basis of judgment? What you do? What you don't do?

I. *Judgment is a necessary part of a moral government.* It promises a goal out there. Jesus spoke frequently of rewards. Paul wrote, "If in this life only we have hope we are of all men most miserable" (1 Cor. 15:19). Rewards are not confined to this life. The parable describes the future, "When the Son of man shall come in all his glory. . . ."

It recognizes the difference between good and evil—the ultimate difference when all the bills are in. Note the immediate division: The sheep and the goats were distinguishable. Before their deeds or lack of them were mentioned they were different, recognizably (by their master) so.

It thrives on sincerity and truth. Neither group was conscious of having done or not done anything out of character. Their actions were quite normal—an expression of who they were. All of this is true "from the foundation of the world." It is a part of the moral fiber of the universe.

II. *The true basis of judgment is what you are.* Here God's judgment is less limited than human judgment. This is true because God knows what you are. You do or don't do naturally on the basis of what you are. There is no pretense here: Neither group knew that it was the king who was so involved with his people.

Yet it is what you do because of what you are. One of the characteristics of the true saint is that the saint forgets self in service of God and humanity. The righteous had ministered to the needs of many because they were filled with love and it overflowed to human need. The unrighteous were not filled with love, hence no overflow. These were not "real good people" or "real bad people," popularly speaking. They would not have chosen the best seats or prayed the longest prayers.

III. *God is interested in what you are.* A story by William Hale White about Mrs. Joll is significant. She was crude and tactless, but she came to the aid of a stranger in distress. The novelist writes that "she had the one thing needful—the one thing which, if there ever is to be a judgment day, will put her on the right hand, when all sorts of scientific people, religious people, students of poetry, people with exquisite emotions will go to the left and be doomed everlastingly" (George Buttrick, *Interpreters Bible*, vol. 7, pp. 563–64).

But the supposition is that she was judged on the basis of her unconscious goodness and others were judged on the basis of their unconscious neglect—as in the parable. A key phrase in the parable is "inasmuch as." This is the way we serve the Lord. This is the way we minister. Of course if the goats had seen the Lord's presence in the midst of his people, they would have worshiped and they would have ministered. The sheep did it anyhow. God is interested in that.—J. Estill Jones

SUNDAY: NOVEMBER TWENTY-EIGHTH

SERVICE OF WORSHIP

Sermon: How Christ Comes; In the Sign of the Sacraments

TEXT: Num. 16:38

"They shall be a sign." The writer is talking about certain material objects which were to be used in the worship of the Temple. It is the word sign that I am plucking from the text this morning, and the word *hallowed* or *holy* which is attached to a beaten-out sheet of metal. We are going to think about how a material object—whether it's metal, earth, paper, cloth, water, bread, wine—can become holy, an instrument to bring us closer to God.

I. For three Sundays of Advent I am speaking about how Christ comes to us, and today we are concentrating on the sacraments. A sacrament has been defined as "an outward and visible sign of an inward and invisible grace." A sacrament links heaven and earth.

(a) Anything can thus be sacramental for the believer. But each of us can think of something material that has special spiritual meaning of us—a memento, a wedding ring, a Bible that belonged to someone dear to us, a particular church or spire, a corner of the countryside that has this quality of the holy. These are the special signs through which God comes near. In them the spiritual comes to a bright focus, and God is more real and near.

(b) Jesus, trained as he was in the signs of his ancestral religion, wanted to leave his disciples special signs by which he could continue to come to them and their successors, renewing their loyalty, drawing them closer to him and to one another. "What is a sacrament?" asks the shorter catechism and answers, "A sacrament is a holy ordinance instituted by Christ, wherein, by sensible signs, Christ and the benefits of the new covenant are represented, sealed, and applied to believers." It goes on to state that "the sacraments of the New Testament are Baptism and the Lord's Supper."

II. You will be relieved to know that I am not about to launch into a discourse on the theological meaning of the sacraments. I want to say two simple things about baptism and the Lord's Supper which may shed light upon their meaning and encourage us on the Christian way.

(a) Baptism is the sacrament of belonging. In the very first days of the church those who heard the gospel and responded declared their faith, received instruction, and were admitted to the company of believers by this sacrament. Normally they descended into a river or pool of water as a sign that they were united with Christ in his death and burial, then emerged as a sign of their union with him in his Resurrection. They now belonged to the family of Christ. For the rest of their lives they carried with them the invisible sign of belonging. Their baptism meant that they belonged to the Lord and the company of his disciples.

When talking to children here about their own baptism, I sometimes tell a little story. It dates back to the time when a king reigned in Britain, and one day I found myself at Balmoral castle in the Scottish Highlands where the royal family has its vacation every year. Out in the garden a little dog was frisking around, and naturally I joined in the game. When I got him in my arms I noted that, like most dogs, he had a little medallion hanging from his collar, and I was curious enough to examine what it said. In the middle was his name—"Bobs." Then around about, where the name and address of the owner is usually to be found, were the simple words "I belong to the King." You can guess what I tell the children—and now I am telling you. All who are baptized Christians have this invisible sign imprinted on them: "I belong to King Jesus." This is why we pray at every baptism here that we may be reminded of our own baptism. To belong to Christ, to belong to his church, means a continual obligation to live as his true disciple. It is the living sign of the new life to which we have been called, the grace that is given us to keep going to the end.

(b) The Lord's Supper is the sign of uniting. It is a sacrament of our uniting with Christ and his church and therefore a means by which we are strengthened for the ongoing discipleship. Baptism is once and for all the sign of the One to whom we belong. The Holy Communion is constantly repeated. If baptism is our setting out on that journey, this is our ration for the road. We can't keep going unless we are constantly renewed in our union with him and with our fellow-Christians. Again, the sacrament speaks of the nearness of the crucified and risen Lord. This is how Christ comes to us—his advent in our baptism is followed by his constant coming with the bread and wine.

We may not be capable of understanding in our minds how Christ comes, but we are all able to stretch out our hands, take, eat, and drink. There are times when this may be all we are able to express of our desire to receive him. Words fail us. Our minds fail us. But we can still take and eat and then, maybe, the inward eyes will be opened "and we recognize him."—David H. C. Read

Illustrations

WHAT THE LORD DOES FOR ME IN MY CONVERSION AND BAPTISM. (1) He brings me into union with the Lord Jesus Christ in his death and Resurrection. (2) He washes away all my sin, granting to me full remission and forgiveness. (3) He clothes me with the new nature of the Lord Jesus Christ. (4) He gives to me the Holy Spirit, through whom I become a son of God. (5) He incorporates me into the Body of Christ, the universal church.—Stephen F. Winward

THE MEANING OF COMMUNION. I love the words of Queen Elizabeth, in the sixteenth century. In the midst of dreadful squabbles about the presence of Christ in the sacrament she was asked her opinion and replied, "Twas God the Word that spake it, He took the bread and brake it;

And what the word did make it; That I believe and take it."—David H. C. Read

Sermon Suggestions

WHEN GOD HIDES HIS FACE. TEXT: Isa. 63:16–64:8. (1) We may become callous and hard-hearted (63:17, 19; 64:5b–7). (2) Still, we may, as did the prophet, yearn for a reprise of better days and a renewal of faith and obedience (64:1–5a). (3) Thank God, our Lord, our Father still lives, and we can hope that he will remake us (64:8).

"KEEP AWAKE!" TEXT: Mark 13:32–37. (1) Because the Son of man will return unexpectedly. (2) Because we, his servants, have ongoing responsibilities. (3) Because we can expect to give account of our faithfulness.

Worship Aids

CALL TO WORSHIP. "When Christ, who is our life, shall appear, then shall ye also appear with him in glory" (Col. 3:4).

INVOCATION. That you are the God who comes and keeps coming in your love that never gives up, we are grateful. For this privilege to celebrate your coming, we worship and adore you. May your Word strangely come alive in songs and anthems, through its reading and preaching, through its dramatization in the sacrament. May your Spirit quicken mind and heart that not only in this season but in every season we may practice hospitality to the Highest—the fullness of your grace and truth in the Babe of Bethlehem, in Jesus of Nazareth, in the Christ of the cross, in our living Lord. Praise be to you—Father, Son, and Holy Spirit.—John Thompson

OFFERTORY SENTENCE. "The silver is mine, and the gold is mine, saith the Lord of hosts" (Hag. 2:8).

OFFERTORY PRAYER. Help us, Father, to make thankful offering of our substance and our lives that the day of the Lord may be prepared for your coming into the hearts of men and women. May days of joy and peace descend upon us all as we give as you gave when Christ Jesus came to Bethlehem.—Henry Fields

PRAYER. Prepare our hearts, O Father, for the coming of the Lord, Christ Jesus. May the wind of the Spirit blow away the dust and dead leaves which we have allowed to accumulate in our spirits. May the fires of the Spirit purge and refine and warm our hearts. Let the doors of our souls be open to bid him welcome as he comes once again to us in this Advent season. Grant unto us some of the virtues and graces, some of the flowers of the Spirit, that the rooms of our lives may be decorated for his coming. Help us to spread the table of joy and thanksgiving and break the alabaster box of sacrifice in honor of his presence. Fulfill his promise, Father, that you will come to our homes and hearts and with him abide with us.

In this Advent season, take from our souls the strain and stress that so often accompanies our activities this time of the year. Let none of the little human duties cause us to miss the wonder of his presence with us. Let wonder awake in our eyes like the wonder that sparkles in the eyes of a child. Tune our ears to the music of the spheres. Sensitize our souls to the touch of your Spirit and grant to us the childlike trust that rejoices in your presence.

Father, bring new hope to the world with the coming of Christmas. Help men and nations to let all enmities and hatreds, all evil plans and passions be lost in the limbo of yesterday. Let all men and women, leaders and followers, greet and rejoice in a new day of peace on earth and goodwill toward all men. To that end let us direct our lives and hearts beginning today as we celebrate the preparation of Advent.—Henry Fields

LECTIONARY MESSAGE

Topic: Living on the Alert
TEXT: Mark 13:32–37

The Advent season is a time of patient waiting and preparation for the coming of our Lord. It's the same year after year. The birth narratives in Matthew and Luke, the Christmas stories and carols, the activities that surround the season, the joy of giving and receiving—all these combine to prepare us for his coming.

But what "coming" is it for which we prepare and wait? Is it the Lord's long awaited Second Coming that will usher in the final consummation of the ages? Is it our death, at which time we will enter into his presence forever? The Lord's coming may very well be these, and for these we certainly need to be prepared, but it can also be something else. Our Advent waiting and preparation marks the deep belief that God can and does divinely intervene into the routine events of human life. Advent says that God may come to us at any time, in any experience, and that when he comes our lives are never the same again.

Jesus told his listening audience, and later Mark told his reading audience, that God's inbreaking into our lives may come at any time. And so we are to be ready— living on the alert.

I. For some the moving hand of God will come during our darkest moments. The eternal may indeed come to us in the hour of our greatest need, when our souls hurt, when temptation raises itself to prominence, when loneliness and depression seem to take control of our better senses. Since such experiences as these often come quite unexpectedly, preparation for them must come in the more calm moments that precede them. Jesus' warning that we "take heed and watch" is a word about the hurtful effects that come when we are unprepared for the unexpected. Sorrow and loss can come to us without a moment's notice. And what then? If no prior preparation has been made, no reservoir of faith built up, what are we to do? It is too late then to be ready. Readiness is what we do now as we prepare, as we wait, as we watch.

II. Our greatest danger to watchfulness is the illusion of well-being. When things are progressing smoothly, we tend to think life will always be this way. As the commonplace inoculates us against a world of reality, we become unprepared for the hour of surprise. When the householder in this parable leaves, he gives to his servants useful and meaningful tasks—and then commands that they be watchful lest upon his return he find them sleeping. Such slothfulness could not be tolerated. As we sleep, life's purposes can pass by us unnoticed. We can become blind to the evil that exists around us, can take lightly the message of Christ as our salvation and as the alternative to the world's destruction, and can become insensitive to God and to one another. We must not, as the saying goes, "let down our guard." We must be watchful.

III. The words Jesus spoke to his followers so long ago, he says again to us. "And what I say to you, I say to all: watch." For the earliest disciples, the call to watchfulness was a word of hope (though hope deferred). The early read-

ers of Mark's Gospel, facing certain religious persecution and the temptation to compromise that goes with it, needed to hear this word of hope. Be watchful. Be hopeful. You cannot know at what hour, maybe very soon, that the Master may come. The reward of your faith is near at hand. That message is ours, too. Because there is so much at stake, we cannot afford to cease our vigil. We, too, are to be ready, persistent in our faith, unyielding in our convictions, unwilling to compromise our loyalty to Christ.

Most any life-style is sufficient for the ordinary days, but not for the hour when the Master comes! Perfunctory religion is not capable of preparing us for the day of the Lord. This Advent season is once again our chance to be reminded that the Lord is coming—and we are to be on the alert!—Lee McGlone

SUNDAY: DECEMBER FIFTH

SERVICE OF WORSHIP

Sermon: How Christ Comes; In the Words of the Bible

TEXT: Luke 24:27

If you claim to be a disciple of Christ, let me ask you a blunt question: What part does the Bible play in your communion with him? If you're like me, you may be tempted to answer simply, Not enough. We all know the theory. We've all heard often enough how important it is to read what is written in this book. Many of us try to follow some plan of daily Scripture reading. All this adds up to a conviction that this is a unique and indispensable way through which Christ comes to us today. We meet him in the words of the Bible. Do you find it so in practice?

I. The picture Luke gives us is plain. "And beginning at Moses and all the prophets, he expounded unto them in all the Scriptures the things concerning himself." It is through the words of the entire Bible that Christ comes to us.

(a) How are we to find him there? In Fundamentalist circles the solution of-

fered is to emphasize certain verses in the Old Testament which are interpreted as foretelling the life, death, and Resurrection of Jesus. The point is not that those who hear in these words an echo of the miraculous birth of Jesus are wrong but that this kind of search for isolated verses to prove that the Old Testament forecast in detail all that the New Testament tells us about Jesus is not the best way to find Christ in the Old Testament.

The more liberal churches tend to ignore the question altogether. In many Protestant churches, if the Old Testament was heard at all, the reading was confined to a few very well known passages. It became the custom to have only one Scripture reading, which was usually from the Gospels. The Old Testament became a kind of poor relation kept in the cellar and apologized for. The result has been an epidemic of biblical illiteracy from which all of us are still suffering.

(b) I went through all the stages. As a child I remember hearing and reading about Jesus and being entranced by some of the more dramatic and colorful Old Testament stories. As an adolescent I was mightily influenced by supercilious scholars and persuasive agnostics who delighted in talking about the primitive nature of these biblical books with their myths and legends. Then I went through an ultra-evangelical stage when I did read the Bible for myself but was always guided by those who tried to ignore its human aspect and concentrated on every passage that could be twisted to yield the dogma to which they were bound. It was not until seminary days that I began to glimpse that tremendous world of the Bible with its vast variety of human experience shot through with the presence of the living God and to meet again the Christ who is the climax of the story, the Christ who began to show me "in all the Scriptures the things concerning himself."

II. Why do we have to turn to a book to learn about Jesus? Doesn't he come to us through our family tradition, through the lives of his followers today, through the worship of his church, and through the sacraments we were thinking about last Sunday?

(a) Why do we need these words carefully preserved over the years? The answer is that the content of the Bible is the anchor that prevents the church from drifting away from the authentic knowledge of Jesus and prevents us from creating a new Jesus "after the imagination of our hearts." The church of Christ would almost certainly have disappeared like the hundreds of other religious movements that were alive in the first century A.D. if it had not been anchored to the recorded facts of his life, death, and Resurrection as attested in the Gospels, to the facts of the foundation of the church as recorded in the Acts and the Epistles, and to the unique story of the people of God from which he came, as recorded in the Old Testament.

(b) This is why we declare that the Scriptures of the Old and New Testaments are "the unique and authoritative witness to Jesus Christ in the church universal." The ordination question goes on: "and God's Word to you." We need the book to be constantly reminded of who he is, this Christ who comes to us. And

we need this book because, by the power of the Holy Spirit, it can actually become "God's Word to us."

III. If you are among those who want to know Christ better, then you are right to have that nagging feeling that you ought to be doing more active reading of the Bible. What better time than this, when we are about to celebrate the coming of Christ into our world, to discover in the Bible how he may come to you with fresh power and penetration. We would never say so, but isn't it true that we often behave as if we already knew all these is to be known about Jesus Christ? So how do we begin?

(a) Briefly, try beginning with a Gospel and read it right through as you would any other book. Get a Bible that is uncluttered with numbered verses, italics, footnotes, and other impediments. Forget that it seems to be stuffed with vaguely familiar quotations. Let Jesus step from the printed page and make his impression on you as if it were the first time you had heard of him.

(b) Then I suggest going on to the book of the Acts to discover what happened to the first followers of Jesus, how they maintained contact with him as a living Presence, how they began to continue his ministry as the new Body of Christ on earth, how they challenged the pagan world, how they spread the gospel into the most unlikely places.

(c) Next, I suggest the reading of a few Epistles where you find some of the apostles, chiefly Paul, reflecting on the meaning of Christ's coming, asking why he was put to death, affirming their experience of his being still alive, and offering some pointed instructions about how Christians should behave—at home, at work, to people in need, to the government, to one another. Here we learn that the first Christians were as assorted a group of human beings as we are.

(d) The next step should be a visit to the more unfamiliar territory of the Old Testament. Remember that this is where Jesus lived. Try the psalms, many of which he had by heart. Read Deuteronomy, which seems to have been his favorite book, and let the vigor of the Law of

Moses make its impression. You will be reminded of Jesus at every turn as you go on to read the extraordinary story of his people and find yourself drawn into the conversation of the living God with his people.

(e) The next step would be into the world of the prophets, those lonely figures with their ears open to the Word of God and senses tingling with the need to draw their people back to him. Begin with the shorter books like Amos or Hosea and leave the complications of Ezekiel for the time being. Jesus knew the prophets. When he told these two disciples about "the things concerning himself," I don't think he was simply saying that an occasional verse seemed to describe what was to happen to him but that in these books we learn the great themes of God's glory and compassion, of suffering and redemption, of struggle and victory—all of which became incarnate in him.

(f) Lastly, you could dip into the apocalyptic books, like Daniel and the Revelation, which unfortunately seem to be the first choice for the fanatics of the airwaves today. If you have any poetry in your soul, you may find in these books the Christ who comes to us as Victor, Ruler of the Universe, and Lord of all history. Let him come; let him come without stopping to ask the meaning of every cryptic name or symbol.

IV. May your experience—and mine—be that of the great Augustine who as a young man living it up in the jet set of the Roman Empire, but inwardly in a turmoil of mind and spirit, heard one day a voice saying, "Take and read." A Bible was near. He took and read. Christ came, and his life was totally transformed. Remember that after we have done all we can to understand the Bible it is the Holy Spirit who comes as the great Interpreter so that the words of the book become "God's Word to us"—and his Word is Christ.—David H. C. Read

Illustrations

THE WHOLE WORD OF GOD.   In Israel's history there is no message that does not

point beyond itself, that does not express its character as the Word of the divine partner at work in it. Every such message strives toward its consummation in the message of the history of Jesus Christ. Already containing this message within itself, Israel's history is to this extent already Gospel.

Theology would not respond to the whole Word of God if it wished only to hear and to speak of the Word become flesh. It would totally miss the truth of this Word if it proclaimed simply and solely the history of Jesus Christ, the Savior of the world. As if the reconciliation of the world with God were made at the expense of, or in abstraction from, the promises given to Israel! If theology wishes to hear and repeat what God has said, it must remain attentive to what *happened* in Israel's history.—Karl Barth

AUGUSTINE'S CONVERSION.   I was saying these things and weeping in the most bitter contrition of my heart, when suddenly I heard the voice of a boy or a girl—I know not which—coming from the neighboring house, chanting over and over again, "Pick it up, read it; pick it up, read it." Immediately I ceased weeping and began most earnestly to think whether it was usual for children in some kind of game to sing such a song, but I could not remember ever having heard the like. So, damming the torrent of my tears, I got to my feet, for I could not but think that this was a divine command to open the Bible and read the first passage I should light upon.

So I quickly returned to the bench where Alypius was sitting, for there I had put down the apostle's book when I had left there. I snatched it up, opened it, and in silence read the paragraph on which my eyes first fell: "Not in rioting and drunkenness, not in chambering and wantonness, not in strife and envying, but put on the Lord Jesus Christ, and make no provision for the flesh to fulfill the lusts thereof." I wanted to read no further, nor did I need to. For instantly, as the sentence ended, there was infused in my heart something like the light of full certainty and all the gloom of doubt vanished away.—Augustine

Sermon Suggestions

SOME WONDERFUL TRUTHS ABOUT GOD. TEXT: Isa. 40:1–11. (1) God's ultimate purpose is to bring good to his people, verses 1 and 2. (2) God's glory is revealed through his triumphant deliverance of his people from oppression and perils along the way, verses 3–5. (3) In contrast to the passing things of earth, God's purpose and word will endure forever, verses 6–11.

"WHILE YOU ARE WAITING."   TEXT: 2 Pet. 3:8–15a. (1) Get God's perspective on the delayed day of the Lord. (2) But be prepared for that day to come unexpectedly. (3) Consequently, seek this twofold experience: (a) peace of soul, and (b) purity of life.

Worship Aids

CALL TO WORSHIP.   "Behold the days come, saith the Lord God, that I will send a famine in the land, not a famine of bread, nor a thirst for water, but of hearing the words of the Lord" (Amos 8:11).

INVOCATION.   Thank you, Father, that we have a place like this to which we can come and worship you. As we come this morning may we bring a sense of destiny that we have been born to the kingdom for such a time as this. Open our oft times clouded eyes that we may see clearly where Christ is trying to lead us, that we may indeed minister of your name and grace to the lost, the lonely, the ill, the bereft, the discouraged, the disillusioned, and the cynical. Kindle a sense of joy in us that we are a part of a lifting community that makes a difference in the lives of people. Fortify us with your strength and power that we may invest our energies in the eternal matters of life.—Henry Fields

OFFERTORY SENTENCE.   " 'Why spend money on what does not satisfy? Why spend your wages and still be hungry? Listen to me,' says the Lord, 'and do what I say, and you will enjoy the best food of all' " (Isa. 55:2, TEV).

OFFERTORY PRAYER.   We thank you, Lord, for the privilege of investing life and money in what brings true satisfaction to ourselves and blessing to others. May your word so expressed in what we are and in what we do not return to you empty but accomplish what you intend.

PRAYER.   O God, this day we thank you for your Book.
For those who wrote it, for those
  who lived close to you, so that
  you could speak to them and so
  give them a message for their
  day and for ours;
    We thank you, O God.
For those who translated it into our
  own languages, often at the cost
  of blood and sweat and agony and
  in the tongue we know;
    We thank you, O God.
For scholars whose devoted and
  consecrated study and toil has
  opened the meaning of your Book
  to others;
    We thank you, O God.
For those who print it and publish
  it, and for the great Bible
  Societies who work makes it
  possible for the poorest of
  people all over the world to
  possess your word;
    We thank you, O God.
For its thrilling stories of high
  and gallant adventure;
For its poetry which lingers for
  ever in the memory of men;
For its teaching about how to live
  and how to act and how to
  speak;
For its record of the thoughts of
  men about you and about our
  blessed Lord;
For its comfort in sorrow, for its
  guidance in perplexity, for its
  hope in despair;
Above all else for its picture of
  Jesus:
    We thank you, O God.

Make us at all times
  Constant in reading it;
  Glad to listen to it;
  Eager to study it;
  Retentive to remember it;
  Resolute to obey it.
And so grant that in searching the Scriptures we may find life for ourselves and for others; through Jesus Christ our Lord.

—William Barclay

LECTIONARY MESSAGE

Topic: A Voice Crying in the Wilderness

TEXT: Mark 1:1–8

"The beginning of the Gospel of Jesus Christ, the Son of God." Thus begins the account of Jesus' life and message we call the Gospel of Mark. There are no Christmas stories here, no angels, no miraculous birth, no wise men, no Mary and Joseph—only the stark "the beginning of the Gospel of Jesus Christ." The fullness of time had come. The curtain was drawn, and God stepped personally into the human scene. A new day had dawned, and it all began with a lone voice, filled with deep emotion, crying in the wilderness.

I. Four hundred years of prophetic silence was about to come to an end. But the new Word from God would not come in the accepted arenas of public debate, not in political maneuvering, not in the circles of wealth nor religious influence. It would come from an obscure, rugged, religious zealot we know as John the Baptist and his preaching in the wilderness. What a sight he was! Dressed in camel's hair, eating locusts and drinking wild honey, he surely was an unforgettable character. But even more unforgettable than his appearance was the message he proclaimed.

II. To people who believed they were God's elect, who had all their religious questions answered in the Law, who for hundreds of years had found comfort in their unique relation to God, to these people John said, "You must repent of your sins." Thus began the Gospel in Mark's account. Thus it begins for us today. It is a shocking word, though absolutely true, that life with God begins in repentance. What John called for and what Jesus later called for in his first sermon was more than simple remorse. One can be sorry for our sin, even do penance, and yet remain unforgiven. Repentance is getting honest with God. It is tearing down the barriers of deceit, removing our long-held dependence on self-sufficiency, and placing all of life into the hands of God—to do with as God pleases. Repentance is no easy thing.

III. The voice in the wilderness apparently was heard and heeded by many. People came from all parts of Judea. Yet the voice had no desire to call attention to himself. His role was to prepare the way for one that was greater than he. Here John discovered his life's intention, his niche. As with John, the greatest significance and joy of every believer is in pointing to Another. To baptize with water was one thing—and a good thing. But the Greater was soon to come who would baptize with the Holy Spirit. The gift of God's own Self, the personal experience of divinity in our humanity, the grace-gift that causes all other goodnesses to pale in comparison—this One would come to disclose even more fully the love of God. John said, "Be ready to listen to him."

That voice crying in the wilderness is longing to be heard over and again. Listen and you may hear it this Advent season. It is the cry that calls us beyond the superficial observance of a religious holiday and forces us to hear the word from heaven say, "Repent, for the kingdom of God is at hand."—Lee McGlone

SUNDAY: DECEMBER TWELFTH

SERVICE OF WORSHIP

Sermon: How Christ Comes; Unexpectedly

TEXT: "The kingdom of God is within you" (Luke 17:21, KJV); "The kingdom of God is among you" (Luke 17:21, NEB).

On the last two Sundays I spoke here about how Christ comes to us in the sacraments of his church and through the content of the Bible which we possess. Some of you may have wondered, "Is this the only way in which Christ finds men, women, and children today? Is he like a foreign diplomat in some lands, strictly limited in his movements, confined to a certain area? Is my experience of Christ to be limited to the expected places and expected times, such as around eleven o'clock on a Sunday morning in church? Does Christ never come near when I'm out on the ocean under the stars or gazing at the soaring Andes on the cliff-edge at Machu Picchu or listening to a segment of "Masterpiece Theater" or seeing the newborn baby in a hospital ward or standing by the deathbed of one we love—or, for that matter, when we are packed like sardines on a subway car?"

I. We began our service this morning by singing, "Come, thou long-expected Jesus." Yes, he was long expected, but sometimes this kind of expectation blinds us to the unexpectedness of God. Those long ago who expected the arrival of a conquering king to overthrow their enemies or a messiah descending from heaven with clouds and forks of lightning or a messiah who would be born and raised within the precincts of the Temple were not ready for the unexpected—the Advent of the Son of God in a stable from the womb of a girl whom nobody knew except a handful of her family and friends. From the hearts of the shepherds and the wise men, on the lips of Mary and Elizabeth, the magnificats that arose at the first Christmas were their way of saying, "Come, thou unexpected Jesus."

(a) Listen to the words of Jesus about the coming of the kingdom, the rule of God, the Way, the Truth, and the Life that was incarnate in him. "You cannot tell by observation when the kingdom of God comes. There will be no saying, 'Look, here it is!'; for in fact the kingdom of God is among you."

(b) That is how this text reads in the New English Bible. But all who were raised on the King James Version expect to hear "The kingdom of God is *within* you." I have printed both versions because they can both be justified. They each have a word to say to us about the unexpected coming of Christ to us in our daily life in the modern world.

II. "The kingdom of God is among you." Who are the "you" he is speaking about? Is it a group of his disciples wherever they happen to get together? Yes; he does mean that as we know from the promise "Where two or three are gathered together in my name, there am I in the midst of them."

(a) But you will find that he also comes to us when we meet in his name in sudden, unexpected ways. Last week on one of those calendar-packed days, I was called to conduct a funeral in a little chapel on the west side. When I entered the chapel, after talking with the sister, I found that no one else was to be present. They had no family or close friends here. Let me tell you that as I conducted a short service, I was unexpectedly and acutely aware of the presence of Christ. He was there. He knew that one who had just died. He knew the sorrowing sister better than anyone else. And he was reminding me of the infinite value of every one of his human family. I was ashamed that in any way his presence could have been unexpected by me.

(b) Yet this promise of his presence spreads beyond the family of his church and our services and ceremonies. In recent years we have become more than ever aware of the literal meaning of the words Jesus spoke about caring for the hungry, the thirsty, those without clothes, the sick, and the prisoners. "Anything you did for one of these my brethren, however humble, you did for me." "You did for me." That bundle of breathing rags lying on the grating on the sidewalk, that sick and cantankerous friend whom you would rather not visit, those prisoners who have no one even to send them a Christmas card—do we really believe that in them we are meeting Christ?

(c) There are more than a few today who are beginning to meet Christ as they respond to their instinct to help the helpless and care about those who are shunned by our society. The kingdom of God is among us just where such help is being offered, whether in the name of Christ or not. He is there—not just here in the chancel of our church, and it may be that among those who are alienated by the organized churches some are unexpectedly finding him in the experience of doing the very work that he did in caring for the physical needs of the needy.

III. Then what about that other sanctuary, the sanctuary of our souls? "Neither shall they say, Lo here! or lo there! for, behold, the kingdom of God is within you." This is, after all, where Christ must come to you and me if he is to come at all. Too often we externalize the Christ we need, seeking him with our minds alone, as if he were some proposition to be proved or some obscure figure to be revered, while every Gospel tells us, especially the fourth, that he is right here within the believing heart.

(a) It is in that mysterious center that is the real you that we find the kingdom. The prophets of Israel were able to shout to a despondent people, like Zephaniah in a time of crisis, "The Lord thy God in the midst of the mighty: He will save, he will rejoice over thee with joy" because he had this inner vision, this quiet confidence in his soul that the Lord is king. Believers in every age have been able to see Christ coming in the most unexpected places because he had first come to reign in the very center of their souls.

(b) In our baptism we have the sign that Christ is within us. In the Holy Communion we have the sign that we are really one with him. The trouble is that we are often too distracted or too bound up in the externals of our religion—or is it too busy—to realize that he is there? We don't hear the voice that keeps saying: "Be still and know that I am God." A church can become so absorbed in its programs—doing, doing, doing—that we forget the Christ within who is concerned with our being, being united with him and growing in his likeness.

IV. "I am among you," says Christ, "in unexpected places." "I am within you," says Christ, and this may be the most unexpected place of all.—David H. C. Read

Illustrations

"A GREAT PRESENCE." As I lay on the trundle bed on the night of March 3, 1877, I could not go to sleep. We had just had family prayers, and Father was reading and Mother was knitting. My younger brother had fallen asleep beside me; but I was in distress over my sins. In my desperation I lifted my eyes upward and began to talk in a whisper to the Savior. I said to him, "Lord Jesus, I do not know what to do. I have prayed, but I get no relief. I have read the Bible, but my sins are still a burden on my soul. I have listened to preaching, but find no help. I do not know what to do except to turn it all over to you; and if I am lost, I will go down trusting you." Then something happened. It seemed that a great Presence filled the room and said to me almost in audible words, "My boy, I have been waiting for you to do what you have just done. You can count on me to save you. I will not fail you." My pillow was presently wet with tears of joy that Christ Jesus was now my personal Savior. I looked up to the old family clock on the mantel, and it was five minutes to eight o'clock on the evening of March 3, 1877, the day before Rutherford B. Hayes was inaugurated as President of the United States.—John R. Sampey

A CONTINUING FRIENDSHIP. When Jesus is present, all is well and nothing seems difficult; but when Jesus is not present, everything is hard.

When Jesus speaks not inwardly to us, all other comfort is nothing worth; but if

Jesus speak but one word, we feel great consolation.

Did not Mary rise immediately from the place where she wept when Martha said to her, "The Master is come and calleth for thee"?

Happy hour! when Jesus calleth from tears to spiritual joy.

How dry and hard art thou without Jesus! How foolish and vain, if thou desire anything out of Jesus!

Is not this a greater loss than if thou shouldst lose the whole world?—Thomas á Kempis

Sermon Suggestions

WHEN GOD'S SPIRIT IS UPON HIS SERVANT. TEXT: Isa. 61:1–4, 8–11. (1) He will bring good news and comfort to the oppressed. (2) He will bring stability and purpose to those thus encouraged. (3) He will reward them abundantly.

THE WILL OF GOD FOR US. TEXT: 1 Thess. 5:16–24, NRSV. (1) What we must do: (a) rejoice always; (b) pray without giving up in discouragement; (c) look behind and beyond our troubles for blessings, and give thanks. (2) What God will do: faithfully perform what he has set out to do with and for us—keep us holy and special.

Worship Aids

CALL TO WORSHIP. "You know what hour it is, how it is full time now for you to wake from sleep. For salvation is nearer to us now than when we first believed" (Rom. 13:11, RSV).

INVOCATION. May this service of worship be a time of divine surprises. Grant that unexpected blessings alert us to your presence and to our opportunities as your servant people.

OFFERTORY SENTENCE. "The rendering of this service not only supplies the wants of the saints but also overflows in many thanksgivings to God" (2 Cor. 9:12, RSV).

OFFERTORY PRAYER. Father, as we plan and work and buy in order to bring joy at Christmas to those we especially love, grant that we may remember also others for whom no special plans will be made and who have no money to buy gifts to brighten the eyes of little children. Show us how to enjoy the holiday season in ways that will overflow "in many thanksgivings" to you.

PRAYER. You have made yourself known to us, Father, as a God of light and love and truth and strength. At this Advent season we pause and remember how you came in Jesus Christ to reveal to us the deepest and highest aspects of your nature and love. Sometimes it is hard for us to understand how you have called us to follow Christ and become colleagues in your work in the world. We ask your blessings upon us as we gather together. May we find renewed strength in your presence and multiplied strength in one another. Today, in this sacred place, let your Holy Spirit bind us together in singleness of purpose and devotion to the enterprises of the Lord.

We cannot stay long in your presence, Father, without feeling the need to ask forgiveness for our sins and failures. Most of us do not blatantly and overtly go out to do some sin in the world, yet we so often fall into sins because we let down our guard or leave undone those things which we know are in keeping with your will. So we humbly come this morning seeking forgiveness, Father. Forgive us for being silent as individuals and as a congregation when our voice would have made a difference in the direction of a life entrusted to us. Forgive us for becoming so wrapped up in programs and schedules that we overlook the many opportunities which parade before us daily. Forgive us for looking the other way to avoid involvement when our involvement in a situation and life might glorify the Lord. Forgive us for being more concerned with buildings and budgets than with people and lostness all about us. Forgive us for claiming kinship with Christ but denying him the lordship he seeks that we might become disciples with power and love in the world in his name. Forgive us for worshiping the child of Bethlehem and not introducing him to the children within the shadow of the church steeple. This morning meet us with renewed insight and determination, that we may go from this place of worship and make a difference in the world because we have met in Jesus name.—Henry Fields

LECTIONARY MESSAGE

Topic: A Witness to Christ
TEXT: John 1:6–8, 19–28

All Christians operate within a sphere of influence, an arena of testimony, through which we touch the lives of others. The very nature of our faith is such that we desire to make a positive difference in our world by pointing others to the answers we have found in Christ. Today's text provides an example of one who found his purpose in life as a witness to Christ. His name was John. He came "for testimony, to bear witness."

I. His witness began as he clearly identified his role. "Who are you?" he was asked. Surely, for any Christian, there is no more probing question. It forces some severe introspection that, while necessary to our spiritual growth, may be quite discomforting. "I am not the Christ and not Elijah and not the prophet. I am the voice, the voice crying in the wilderness," he said. The good news here is that John recognized his calling and that he was contented to be what God wanted him to be. Anything other than his response would have made difficult the completion of his task. Every calling is a high calling in God's kingdom. Our significance in that kingdom will never be complete until we can answer the question, Who are you?

II. His witness had content. He was surely "the voice crying in the wilder-

ness," but he wasn't crying out just anything. His message was clear and to the point. Quoting Isaiah, he declared that his intention was to "make straight the way of the Lord." He was to turn the consciousness of the people godward, to ready the minds of many for a new thing about to happen, to herald the good news of God's entry into history. In doing so, John fulfilled the prophetic task of speaking forth the message of God. Such a task if no less significant for us. As the moral conscience of a nation that seems to have lost its morality, the church stands in that same prophetic role. Our task is to declare the word of God to our day and to authenticate it through lives marked by integrity.

III. His witness pointed to the promise of godly grace. "If you are not the Christ nor Elijah nor the prophet," said his adversaries, "then why are you out here baptizing and calling people to repent?" That is a good question. After all, John's preaching was hard and demanding. It denounced people for their sinfulness and spoke of God's judgment. If he was not someone who could remedy the condition of the people, why make such an issue? And John answered, "My baptism is of water." At its best, his work was an image of something far greater that was yet to come: "Among you stands one whom you do not know, even he who comes after me, the thong of whose sandal I am not worthy to untie." John pointed beyond himself to the Christ. In Christ there was the remedy needed for our human predicament. In Christ, there was godly grace.

The witness you and I bear to the world is basically, as it was with John, a pointing to Christ. Through hymn and prayer, through sermon and anthem, through word and deed our highest calling and greatest joy is to point to Christ. Who are we? We are witnesses to Christ!—Lee McGlone

SUNDAY: DECEMBER NINETEENTH

SERVICE OF WORSHIP

Sermon: A Carpenter's Christmas

TEXT: Matt. 1:18–25

At Christmastime we customarily focus our thoughts on Mary and the baby Jesus. The Madonna and child even appear regularly on our postage stamps! The Gospel of Luke with its stories of the Annunciation and Mary's visit to Elizabeth (1:26–56) is the center of this focus on Jesus and Mary. We think warm thoughts about the mother and child, but what about Joseph?

Unlike Luke, the Gospel of Matthew turns the spotlight a little more upon Joseph in its story of the birth of Jesus. Luther's famous remark offers some perspective, as we consider Joseph's role in this sacred drama: "The greatest miracle of Christmas was not that Mary conceived but that Joseph believed!"

I. *Joseph's dilemma (vv. 18–19).* According to the Law of Moses, Mary's out-of-wedlock pregnancy should be punished by putting her to death (Lev. 20:10). Betrothed women were frequently treated by the Law as if they were already married (Deut. 23:23–24). So a betrothed couple could only be separated by a divorce (v. 19).

Joseph was a "just" (Greek: *dikaios*) man, which not only primarily means that he was "righteous" but also secondarily implies that he was "good" and "kind." He thus decides to follow the middle course. Although he believes that, given the circumstances, he cannot take Mary as his wife, he does not want to divorce her publicly and risk her death. Instead, he plans to "divorce her quietly" (v. 19).

II. *God's direction (vv. 20–23).* In several places Matthew describes God's message coming to people in dreams (2:12, 13, 19; 27:19). Joseph's dream not only instructs him to take Mary as his wife but names the baby (vv. 20–21). Jesus' name is given with an emphasis upon his mission as Savior for Israel (in contrast, see Luke 1:31–33). Matthew's account of the angel's announcement of Jesus' name reminds us of the description of Joshua (the Hebrew equivalent of the Greek name *Jesus*) in Sirach (Ecclesiasticus) 46:1, "He became, *in accordance with his name,* a great savior of God's elect."

Matthew then (vv. 22–23) points to Jesus' birth as fulfilling the prophecy of Isa. 7:14. Isaiah's' name *Emmanuel* is an important theme in Matthew's Gospel (cf. "I am with you always" in 28:20). Much of our Christian understanding of the Incarnation turns upon this theme of the presence of God in Jesus Christ.

III. *Joseph's decision (vv. 24–25).* Joseph obeys God's direction to take Mary as his wife without objection or complaint; his faith is shown by his obedience. By virtue of his action, Joseph gives Jesus' birth valid legal status. The importance of Jesus being a legitimate "son of David" through Joseph's family line may be seen in Matthew's preceding genealogy (especially 1:16) and in the angel's address to Joseph as "son of David" (v. 20). The quiet but faithful obedience of Joseph offers a model for our response to God's word during this Christmas season. When the pace of our activities causes us to lose perspective on the meaning of the celebration, let us stop and reflect upon the faith of Joseph, the carpenter, and the miracle of Christmas may be reborn in our hearts.—Charles J. Scalise

Illustrations

NAME. Harry L. Hopkins was special assistant to President Franklin D. Roosevelt and traveled with him to the famous Yalta conference in 1945. During the historical event when the leaders of the three most powerful nations in the world met, Hopkins obtained the signatures of Winston Churchill, Joseph Stalin, and Franklin D. Roosevelt on a ruble note with an exchange rate of ten dollars at that time. Hopkins got the autographs for his teenage son.

In 1981 the ruble bank note was auctioned for five thousand dollars to a private collector from Minnesota. It is a rare twentieth-century autograph and believed to be the only document bearing the signatures of the three dignitaries.

The combined power of these three world leaders changed the course of history. Even today their names have value. There is another name that has far greater value, and his power has influenced the course of human history for two thousand years. The angel announced to Joseph, "Thou shalt call his name Jesus: for he shall save his people from their sins" (Matt. 1:21). He has been given all power in heaven and in earth (Matt. 28:18), and it has not diminished or been passed on to another.— Jack Gulledge

OBEDIENCE TO GOD'S CALL.   In 1943, in the Plaza Hotel in Chicago, I spent almost half an hour with the great evangelist Gypsy Smith, who had crossed the Atlantic five times, knocking on the door of America for revival. Those were the days before Billy Graham's ministry had come to prominence. I asked Gypsy Smith why revival had not come to America. His answer is still significant. "Revival has not come to America," he said, "because when the Holy Spirit puts his hand upon some young life in this land for a consecrated and dedicated work, the average young person tends to say, like the demon-possessed man in the Gospels, 'Let me alone; what have I do to with thee, thou Jesus of Nazareth?' "—Carl F. H. Henry

Sermon Suggestions

THE HOUSE THAT YAHWEH BUILT. TEXT: 2 Sam. 7:8–16. (1) The dynasty (house) of David was not permanent historically. (2) However, Jesus Christ, "Son of David," was given the throne of David to rule in a greater sense (Luke 1:32–33; Phil. 2:9–ll).

GOD FOREVER!   TEXT: Rom. 16:25–27. (1) Because prophets spoke and wrote about the good news of the coming Messiah. (2) Because the good news is for all nations. (3) Because this good news can give us strength for whatever God gives us to bear or to do.

Worship Aids

CALL TO WORSHIP.   "Jesus answered and said unto him, 'If a man love me, he will keep my words; and my Father will love him, and we will come unto him, and make our abode with him' " (John 14:23).

INVOCATION.   Almighty God, by your hand you have established the throne of your servant David; with foundations laid before ever the earth was, made flesh in our Lord Jesus Christ, raised from ruins on the third day, and brought home to our hearts by the Spirit.

Consecrate anew, we pray, in the hearts of all who love you, the coming of the seed of Jesse, David's house, vouchsafe in sun, moon, and stars, in the oceans' tides, and upon the incoming and outgoing seas of hope. For your arm is not shortened that it cannot save, and in the palm of your hand even the oceans know their shore and rest secure.— Peter Fribley

OFFERTORY SENTENCE.   "Each one, as a good manager of God's different gifts, must use for the good of others the special gift he has received from God" (1 Pet. 4:10, TEV).

OFFERTORY PRAYER.   Show us, O God, how we may use for the good of others the different gifts we have received from you and, having shown us your will, give us love and grace to do what we know to be right.

PRAYER.   Let not the disappointments of life dominate us and embitter us, Father, we pray. From the ashes of failure build cathedrals of hope and fulfillment. Out of the agony of defeat lead us to better understanding of life's ongoing purpose. From the mistakes of yesterday turn our minds to the possibilities of the future. Remind us anew that our ambitions and plans have longlasting meaning only as they reflect and follow your will and purpose for us.

In this special Christmas season we ponder anew "what the Almighty can do when with his love he befriends us." That pondering inevitably leads to praise, and praise leads to joy, which by its very presence in life declares that the Lord is come. So take us again in Spirit and heart to Bethlehem, that we, like humble shepherds, may see this thing which has come to pass, which the Lord has made known unto us. And having seen God's greatest gift to mankind, may we not like wise men of another time vanish into obscurity, failing to be continuing instruments of Christ's presence and power. Rather, may we with all power go tell it on every mountain that Jesus Christ is born—born to save and to make whole every broken heart, every shattered dream, every disappointed life, every miserable failure, every sinful soul in all the world. Call us to you this morning, Father, and mold us into instruments of your grace and peace, that through us the world may be blessed.—Henry Fields

LECTIONARY MESSAGE

Topic: According to Your Word

Text: Luke 1:26–38

What a lady Mary must have been! Chosen above the ruling families of her day, this humble peasant girl would give birth to the Son of God. While many of us are not comfortable in elevating Mary to the high level of preeminence given by others, we surely are aware that her quality of character and her response of submission to God reflect the best in noble living. Luke, the Gospel writer, can be thanked for giving us this brief yet important insight into Mary and for holding her up as a model of what it means to be Christian.

I. Look initially to the character of Mary. The mingling of divine and human activity cannot go unnoticed here. Luke is clear to detail the events. The Son of the Most High would not just appear out of heaven untouched by human flesh. He would be divine, to be sure, but like all human life he would come by way of birth. When the angel Gabriel, "hero of God," appeared to Mary with such

earth-shattering news, unsettling her life, her first response was fear heightened by confusion. That kind of fear we can well understand. It is what we feel, that sense of overpowering awe, when the divine touches our own humanity and interrupts our ordinary lives. Such news as Mary's "chosenness," that she would conceive and bear God's unique Son, would be unsettling for anyone. Her reply, "How can this be?" was the honest response of a heart that did not understand. Again, Mary is one of us. The angel's burst of poetic response, "The Holy Spirit will come upon you, and the power of the Most High will overshadow you," is not to be minimized but neither is the prosaic example of Elizabeth's conception in her old age, reminding us of Abraham and Sarah's predicament, nor the summary statement of the angel: "With God nothing will be impossible!" And, with that said, Mary stepped forth in faith to live out her calling.

II. Mary's response is one of the most moving confessions of faith to be found in Scripture: "Behold, I am the handmaid of the Lord. Let it be to me according to your word." In placing herself into God's hands, she fulfilled the highest work of faith: obedience. Little could she have known then what it meant for her to be "chosen of God." In but a few months there would be the long and weary road to Bethlehem, the night in the stable, the birthing of her son on straw and placing him in a feeding trough. When he grew to be a man, she would see abuse hurled his way by skeptical and fickle crowds that did not understand. Finally, she would see him bear his cross on the road to Calvary and there to die an unseemly death. This is what it means to be "chosen of God"? For Mary and for each of us the answer is yes. The road that leads to the abundant life seems always to go by way of the cross. Mary is an example of faith validated, not by questions of what might have been, but by obedience: "Let it be to me according to your word."

This week, as the events of Advent draw near to Christmas Day, our attention will be focused in many ways. Families will gather, gifts will be given and received, meals will be eaten, and good memories will be built for future recollection. This is as it should be. May I ask one other thing? Will you, this week, draw aside for a while from the bustle of activity to be alone with God? And there say along with Mary, "Lord, whatever you will for me, let it be according to your word." Well, will you?—Lee McGlone

SUNDAY: DECEMBER TWENTY-SIXTH

SERVICE OF WORSHIP

Sermon: Christmas Is God's Answer

TEXT: John 1:14

Christmas is God's answer to man's need for life and truth. We want and do not want that answer. We cannot stand the man with all the answers and usually with good reason. Can we stand God's answer even if we were sure that it was his? If there is anything we do not want today it is to know the answers. Skepticism has always been endemic to academic life, but now skepticism is epidemic not only in our universities but throughout the entire intellectual community. We have spoken of how revelation grasps us; what grasps us *now* with all the intangible powers of our age is agnosticism. Once we admired honest and constructive faith; our ideal today is the honesty of the doubter and destroyer of faith, particularly if he can deny the content of faith in the name of faith.

But there are moods when we are more receptive to faith's findings. Christmas offers us peculiarly the mood of faith. It is no time for the argumentative mood any more than for the spirit of credulity. But it can give us the chance for honest openness beyond our ordinary routine of critical thinking. Within this unusual setting of openness, I want simply to suggest God's answer to our need for life and truth, within the kind of simplicity, in fact, that leaves both sincerity and sophistication behind.

I. In the fullness of time God answered man's quest for truth by a kind of life. Man's most meaningful truth is neither of thought nor of fact but is a way of living. The deepest understanding comes not at the end of an argument but through the beginning of a new relationship.

(a) Harvard's motto is *Veritas pro Christo et Ecclesia*. Modern man, embarrassed by piety, generally makes use of the first word only. But the motto is right in its deepest insistence that truth is for a kind of life and a kind of community, for the community of the kind of faith where peace comes through goodwill. "Glory to God in the highest, and on earth peace, good will toward men" is a most needed truth especially in this our dangerous day. The tragedy of Christmas is the obvious fact that we theologians and the church in general have failed to make real and relevant the high truth of Christmas.

(b)God's answer to our quest for truth is a kind of life. Life cannot be compressed into a formula. It cannot be tested in a laboratory. We cannot establish controlled conditions for measuring life. Therefore God's truth cannot be externally controlled. But it can be tried. Jesus called truth a way and a life. He knew it from within himself. He asked us to become as children to know it, to shed our pretense, to rid ourselves of artificiality, to let go of our sophistication, and to enter into the way of concern and growth, of mature integrity, into the simplest yea and nay, intro trusting acceptance beyond anxiety.

II. God also answered man's deepest need by showing him his love. When we think of man's needs we often become guilty of defining them basically in animal terms. Man's basic needs, we say, are food, clothes, and shelter. And certainly man has need of these. But man is also more than an animal. He needs bread, but even more he needs every word that proceeds from the mouth of God. That word is love. Man in the dimension of man lives basically by love. He lives at his deepest by meaning. He lives by the Word.

(a) Such is the nature of our text. In the beginning was the Word and the Word was made flesh. And we beheld his glory as of the only begotten Son. Law came through Moses, but grace and truth came through Jesus Christ. The word of truth that became flesh was God's eternal Word of love. This is the meaning of Christmas. This is the mystery of Christmas. A little child gazing at the living candles of the Christmastide has become wrapped up in the mysterious light of the Christmas story. The meaning can be put into words, but the mystery knows only the numinous silence that flickers in the darkness. Man's deepest need is to know the meaning of love, first in the circle of the bright light of a life of love, but also in the flickering mystery of the receding darkness.

(b) Christmas is a pagan holiday if it celebrates only the turning of the day toward the natural light. The light of Christmas is the light of love which illumines the darkness of man's ignorance and sin. It is a light to lead us into the paths of peace. The Christmas symbol is built on no sign of language but on the life of love, fragile and frail amidst the world's darkness of evil. The bright meaning at the center thins out as the rays stray searchingly into the darkness of men's hearts.

(c) What characterized the life of Jesus was his self-giving. He gave of himself to people. He walked with those who were shut out by society. His best gifts were of his presence and of his power. Christmas never becomes alive in its true meaning until we see the child in the light of the cross. Concern for man beyond custom and convention, beyond orthodoxy and nationalism, led Jesus to the final self-giving. We celebrate Christmas as God's self-giving. That self-giving cannot be seen in its full meaning and mystery until we see the lonely, struggling man on the cross. The joy of Christmas is not the joy of animal spirits nor of nature's turning, nor of any child mysticism. It is the joy of

love's triumph in tragedy. Christmas was born not in Bethlehem but on Calvary. The star of Bethlehem shines only by the light from Golgotha.

III. God answered man's deepest quest for truth by a kind of life and man's deepest need of life by showing his love. He also answered man's cry for salvation by coming himself.

(a) How differently God comes to us from those who are the world's great. He comes to us because he loves us. But he comes in utmost simplicity. He comes in breath-taking humility. He comes to us because he loves us. His coming is no paradox. It expresses his very nature. He waits for the right time to show us his full heart, a heart we can trust for doing right and far more than right for all form the beginning to the end. Here is the Source present in the process. Here are the Ground and Goal present in the temporal struggle. Here is the All-Holy somehow present with man in all his sinfulness. God came to us and comes to us because he loves us. But he comes in us because he respect us.

(b) This is the mystery of Incarnation. Jesus was as human as anyone else. He was no God walking on earth and no demigod entering history. He was man. God became man. The Word became flesh. The humble, holy God touched a life fulfillingly by his Spirit in such a living way that when we see this life, when we see this love, we see conclusively clarified the central nature and purpose of God. God never forces his presence. He never coerces his children. He comes. One received him so fully that we call Christmas the fullness of time. Most men to whom he came received him not. But rather than longing to punish and kill the resister, Jesus suffered and died that the full quality of that life and that love might be made clear and become power by which we, too, can become the sons of God.

(c) Life, love, and salvation root not in human effort but in divine reality. Unless man can look and long beyond himself and find beyond himself the sources of his life, love, and salvation, our hopes are meager and fugitive. Man has a hard time to do with God but even a harder time to do without him. Even those who shout God's meaninglessness keep shouting about him. More and more I know the depth of the mystery and stand awed before it, but less and less do I trust human ingenuity and goodness to save us. Beyond our puny might and poor wisdom with regard to ultimate matters lies the endless ocean of God's mystery and might, seen both simply and yet also unsearchably. Jesus Christ, "the Son of his love." Somehow in that self-revelation of life and love God has given his answer.

IV. God came into a dark world with a strange light. The world is still dark and that light is still strange. But those who receive it even today receive the power to become sons of God, who understand the light in the darkness as they are born not of blood nor of the will of the flesh, nor of the will of man, but of God. As inner love gives newness of life, the Christmas light trembles with the fairest radiance life affords, and out of the darkness there still come voices in the night, singing,

"Glory to God in the highest, and on earth peace, good will toward men." "For unto you is born this day a Savior, which is Christ the Lord."—Nels F. S. Ferré

Illustrations

GOD AND MAN. "Very God and very man." If we consider this basic Christian truth first in the light of "conceived by the Holy Spirit," the truth is clear that the man Jesus Christ has his origin simply in God, that is, he owes his beginning in history to the fact that God in person became man. That means that Jesus Christ is indeed man, true man, but he is not just a man, not just an extraordinarily gifted or specially guided man, let alone a superman; but, while being a man, he is God himself. God is one with him. His existence begins with God's special action; as a man he is founded in God, he is true God. The subject of the story of Jesus Christ is therefore God himself, as truly as a man lives and suffers and acts there. And as surely as human initiative is involved in this life, so

surely this human initiative has its foundation in the fact that in him and through him God has taken the initiative. From this standpoint we cannot avoid saying that Jesus Christ's Incarnation is an analogue of creation. Once more God acts as the Creator, but now not as the Creator out of nothing; rather, God enters the field and creates within creation a new beginning, a new beginning in history and moreover in the history of Israel. In the continuity of human history a point becomes visible at which God himself hastens to the creature's aid and becomes one with him. God becomes man.—Karl Barth

HOW CHRIST CAME. Kierkegaard told a parable about a prince who fell in love with a peasant maid. He had noticed her passing by on the street and was instantly infatuated. He knew that if he went to her as the prince and told of his love, she would certainly accept. That would be the loyal thing to do. But he wanted her to have a genuine love for him.

So he abandoned all of his royal finery and came to live as a peasant in her community. He shared her life with her, and in that sharing, she fell in love with him. When he came to a part of her world, she developed a deep and abiding love.

It is because of Christ that we are able to love God. Since God, in Christ, came to be a part of our world, we are enabled to know God as he really is, and to love him with all of our hearts.—J. Michael Shannon and Robert C. Shannon

Sermon Suggestions

A NEW NAME. TEXT: Isa. 61:10–62:3. (1) God's people may suffer humiliation for a time. (2) God, however, will take pleasure and be glorified in those he at last vindicates.

THE WHYS AND WHEREFORES OF JESUS CHRIST. TEXT: Gal. 4:4–7, NRSV. (1) When he came: in the fullness of time. (2) How he came: born of a woman. (3) Why he came: to redeem us and make us children of God. (4) What is the result of all this? (a) the experience of the Spirit of

Jesus in our hearts, (b) the rewards of being an heir of God.

Worship Aids

CALL TO WORSHIP.   'I am Alpha and Omega, the beginning and the ending, saith the Lord, which is, and which was, and which is to come, the Almighty" (Rev. 1:8).

INVOCATION.   We thank thee, O God, for the light that shines in the darkness, for the Christ who came into our world and who uses us to be instruments of his glory and love. As we rejoice at Christmas, without forgetting the sadness and the sorrow that is all abroad in the world, we remember that light which the darkness cannot put out and which, if we will let it, will shine in us.—Theodore Parker Ferris

OFFERTORY SENTENCE.   "The poor shall never cease out of the land: Therefore I command thee, saying, thou shalt open thine hand wide unto thy brother, to thy poor, and to thy needy, in thy land" (Deut. 15:11).

OFFERTORY PRAYER.   O God, as we remember the visit thou didst once make to this wayside planet, open our eyes that we may see thy presence everywhere. Quicken our minds that we may think more alertly and acutely about the places in the world where we can serve most usefully, and open our hearts that thou mayest come into our lives and make them new. Then use us in the ministry of thy Son, Jesus Christ, to tell other people about thy visit.—Theodore Parker Ferris

PRAYER.   O Giver of every good and perfect gift, we thank you for the gift of Christmas—its beauty, your glory, its meaning: the Word becoming flesh, its rapture; the joy of your presence; its peace, order out of chaos, its hope: your love from which nothing can separate us.

We thank you that in this season we have been able to share in so many different ways. As you invaded the darkness of the night on that first Christmas, so you are present in the light of your love in the dark night of every soul. That you are with the human family in all the pain and tragedy of these days is the hope of Christmas—Emmanuel, God with us. "The people who walked in darkness have seen a great light; those who dwell in a land of deep darkness, on them has light shined."

As there were those on that first Christmas who were left wondering at that which had come to pass, so may we be left wondering so that there will be room for the mystery of your coming in our every day.

O you who sent your only Son among us that your Word become flesh, bless with your grace and encourage us in our high calling to "flesh out" your love in this time and place—that we may be truly the Body of Christ.—John M. Thompson

LECTIONARY MESSAGE

Topic: A Man Called Simeon

TEXT: Luke 2:22–40

What might a person desire most in life before he or she dies? Security, prosperity, fame? Maybe so—but would it not be even more grand to come to the end of our days with the ability to say, looking back on the years, "It was good. I have no regrets. Life has been full and complete. Lord, let now your servant depart in peace, according to your word." Simeon was that sort of man.

I. Even a casual glance at the text tells us that Simeon was a man of spiritual sensitivity. His faith ran deep; he was "just and devout"; "a man of hope"; "waiting for the consolation of Israel"; intimate with the God of his fathers; and "the Holy Spirit was upon him." He was waiting for the Lord's Christ to be born. All of life was an Advent for him! Then into the Temple walked that day a young couple to perform the rite purification and bringing with them a baby boy, about two months old, just old enough to be keeping them up at night. When the aged Simeon saw the child, there arose within his heart a bubble of gladness that would have burst had he held it in. The promise of old was being fulfilled. A Savior had come, one who would be the glory of Israel and a light to all the world. How Simeon knew that Mary's baby was the promise fulfilled is not clear. No one said a word. No introductions were given. Maybe it was intuition. I would rather call it spiritual sensitivity. Simeon saw something others did not see.

II. Simeon was a man who had found his place. He discovered, perhaps early in life, where he was to fit into the scheme of things. He had found his niche. For him it meant a life of searching for intimacy with God, worship both public and private, an earnest conviction that God's way would be his, and the willingness to remain unmoved in his beliefs. We admire a man like Simeon. How unhappy, discouraged, and discouraging are those persons who have gone through life and never found his or her place. The world, as well as the church, is filled with many unhappy people who have never sensed the accomplishment of an intended purpose. How very sad! Such a sad dilemma, though, need not be the end result for all of us. There is an alternative and Simeon shows us the way. It is the way of faith. Because he had found his place, he could come to the end of his days and declare his readiness to depart. "Let now your servant depart in peace."

III. It may be that contentment is the best word of Simeon. He was one of those fortunate few who have come to the end of the way convinced that life could not have been more rewarding or fulfilling. Yet the single event that fulfilled his dreams was the event of God in Christ he recognized in the baby Jesus. Seeing and holding the Lord's Christ was the highpoint of his life. He had scaled the highest mountain and stood there with God. The Lord's salvation had become a personal acquaintance. He held God's Deliverer, the Prince of Peace, in his arms. This same Christ is our own personal, intimate, caring and living Savior. Because of him, our days can never be the same.

It is no wonder we celebrate the Incarnation as we do. Our Advent waiting and worships are every year a renewal of the drama that occurred that day in the Temple. We wait, we anticipate, we festively celebrate, we give and receive—and our waiting is never in vain. Each year the drama is completed on Christmas morning. The Christ child and the kingdom for which he was born are again the center of the world's attention. And if, just possibly, we fail to see the return of another Advent season, hopefully we will be able to say along with Simeon, "Lord, life is full and complete. Let your servant depart in peace."—Lee McGlone

SECTION III.
Messages for Communion Services

SERMON SUGGESTIONS

Topic: The Power of a Great Example
TEXT: John 13:1–17

Walk for a few moments with Jesus and his disciples along the streets of Jerusalem. The time is Passover week and the town has swelled with people—tourists, pilgrims, celebrants, local citizens–all gathered in the holy city for the great religious feast of the year. Passover was the time when all faithful Jews celebrated the deliverance of the Israelites from Egyptian bondage. It commemorated the sparing of Jewish lives even as the angel of death was snuffing out the lives of the pride of Egypt, her firstborn sons. More than any other feast, Passover set the Jews apart as a people.

The deeds of the past are very much on the minds of the people as they scurry about town, but these are not the thoughts of the disciples of Jesus. Their minds are on the future. The kingdom of God is near; it is about to burst in on them. The Master has told them so. How can one think of feasts when something as important as this is about to take place? Their interest is in the kingdom and, most important, their place in it. Their thoughts run something like this: "I wonder just where I'll fit into Jesus' plan. Surely by now he has recognized my leadership ability, my outstanding personal qualities. I am sure that I would make a great general. It is easy to see that I am as good as any of these others, if not better."

And as these self-serving egotistical thoughts run through the mind of each member of the little band, it suddenly dawns on him that the others are probably thinking the same thing. "Just watch them," he thinks. "They'll be trying to get on Jesus' good side. I can't let them get ahead of me." And so as Jesus walks on ahead they begin to push and shove to get closer to him. Their patience with each other is getting mighty thin. They are tired, and as they move on down the road their shuffling feet raise a cloud of dust that covers them to the knees and makes them choke.

Jesus knows his disciples. He sees what is happening. The small group of devoted men that he has been training for three years has disintegrated into a pack of testy, spiteful, self-serving children. Can they not see what they are doing to each other and to him? They are destroying everything that he has tried to do for them and through them. In the mind of Jesus the situation is critical because he realizes how little time he has left to be with them. There are so many things that he hasn't been able to tell them yet, and time is running out.

Finally the group makes its way to a small inn where the Master has made plans for their supper, not just a Passover meal, but a going-away party given by the one who should have been the guest of honor, a parting gift to the men whom he loved so well. However, no one feels much like having a party. Their bickering and jockeying for position has spoiled the mood, ruined the occasion. This is no time for his final teachings. None of them can hear him. They are too busy thinking about their own positions.

It is a sullen, quiet group that climbs the stairs to that little room on the second floor where the simple meal has been laid out. Without saying a single word they all decide to depart from their usual routine. Always before when they had come in from a long walk, one of the disciples would go over and pick up the basin of water and the towel and would kneel in front of the others and wash the sweat and grime of the road off the feet of his companions. Usually the lot fell to whomever was the first in the room. They had no slaves to do it for them, so they voluntarily did it for one another. But not this time. To their way of thinking, if they stooped to perform this menial task it would be to admit somehow that they were lower or less worthy than the others. "You won't catch me lowering myself before men who are at best my equals," is their collective thought.

So the meal starts with the dust of the road still on the disciples' feet. And Jesus is sick, sick in his heart because these are the men that he loves and trusts and needs to carry on the work after he is gone. He sees their shortcomings, their human frailties, but all they can see is how faithful they have been to him. They feel that they already have everything that they need for the days ahead, but Jesus knows that they have to be made to see how wrong they are. They have to be made to see what he has been telling them all along—that the first places in the kingdom are reserved not for those who are served but for those who serve. They have to be made to see that not one of them is perfect, that each still needs the Master's cleansing. So the master teacher, who has used parables to their fullest advantage all during his ministry, decides to act out a parable with this twofold message of renewal and self-sacrificial service.

In the middle of supper he rises from his place and lays aside his robe, just as he is later to lay aside his life for mankind, and he kneels down beside the men

who all along have called him teacher, and he begins to wash the filth from their feet. The room is silent. The tension is so thick that you could cut it with a knife. As Jesus demonstrates his willingness to serve them, the men realize how petty, how selfish they have been. Yet they sit there, red-faced, as he continues to wash the dust from their feet. The water in the basin just gets dirtier and dirtier, and the men feel lower and lower.

Finally, after a little discussion with Peter about whether or not he is going to let Jesus wash his feet at all, Jesus completes the task, and the men sit down to supper. The synoptic Gospels—Matthew, Mark, and Luke—tell us at this point that this is the time when Jesus institutes the ritual supper that we are going to celebrate again in a few moments. John, however, makes no mention of the fact. It is enough for him that Jesus washed the disciples' feet, because no ritual, no matter how important, can supplant the power of a great example.

That is as true today as it was then. We can talk it, we can preach it, we can become educated about it, we can even sing it, but until we model servanthood through our own example we can have no impact on the world. When we are content to let others serve us and take no steps to serve others, we have not learned from the example of Christ.

Albert Schweitzer said that only those are happy who learn to serve. We serve by caring and helping to meet human needs, most especially the need everyone has for a relationship with God.

Missionary Parkes Marler served in South Korea working among 550 lepers. When he first went to this assignment he was afraid of these diseased people. Many had lost their fingers, hands, ears, and noses. They were all disfigured by the leprosy. However, he soon came to love them dearly. As he preached to them, a number became believers and were baptized. Missionary Marler told about hearing a Korean leper lady sing the gospel song "Where He Leads Me I Will Follow." Because part of her lips were gone the words sounded as if she were singing "Where He Needs Me I Will

Follow." That is the Christian's role and calling.

The Lord's Supper serves as our reminder to follow the example of Christ through serving. Will we follow?—James M. King

Topic: Generosity in the Vineyard

Texts: Isa. 55:6–9; Phil. 1:20–24, 27; Matt. 20:1–16

While driving home I have occasionally seen arbors of grapes on side lawns or in backyards. None of the vines seem extensive enough to need any help aside from the families that live there and who on pleasant days relax under the shade of the lattice work. If we were in the Finger Lakes region or California, or had a semester for backpacking in Italy or France, we might be able to visualize ourselves standing in the village plaza, hoping, especially if our funds were running out, that some owner or steward would hire us to gather and sort the bunches.

We may be lacking in experience as workers in a vineyard, but we all have instances like the parable from our family life. How many here are the oldest of the family? How many of us are middle offspring? Who are the youngest? If we are the oldest, have we ever grumbled that the youngest "get away" with much more than we did at their age? If we are the middle child, do we note that there are more photos and videos of the oldest than there are of us? When we are the youngest, do we recall that the older ones were expected to protect us, to yield to us, sometimes even take the blame for our doings?

Fathers and mothers or other relatives of students may also be at this liturgy. They may understand more easily than we why the owner of the vineyard paid the last comer the same just wage as the first one hired. We don't like to think of the time when we will be interested in the contents of our parents' wills, but how much more common is it for the inheritance to be divided equally than for the oldest child to receive the most, the youngest the least?

We have reason to rejoice in the generous attitude of parents who love each of their children in a unique way, whether there be one, three, six, twelve in the family. They may not think they are like the owner of the vineyard, yet they have indeed adopted the ways and thoughts of God.

This semester I decided to have lunch after the one o'clock class instead of the noon hour. Since serving begins at 11:30, I anticipated that those of us who came last, at 2:00 p.m., would have no choices. As I expected, one of the trays behind the entree I preferred was empty. Then to my greater surprise a pleasant helper said, "Wait a minute, we're bringing out a fresh serving." And she did. Then I found a clean table, for students had removed their trays. Coming at the late hour I did enjoy being treated the same as those who arrived first.

The college formed a committee for the five hundredth anniversary of the discovery of America by Christopher Columbus. Featured in 1992 were the contributions of the various cultures that have enriched our nation, beginning with the Native American Indians, the Italians, the Portuguese, the Spanish, the Scandinavians, the Africans, the French, the English, then on to those who came later—the Irish, the Canadians, the Slavic peoples, Russians, Chinese, Japanese, those from India, on to the most recent immigrants from Latin America, Arab nations, parts of Asia. Surely we can celebrate the newest arrivals as joyfully as we remember the first explorers.

Generosity—we have experienced that; we have exhibited that trait. What about forgiveness? Isaiah reminded the Israelites that God is rich in forgiveness. We recall Jesus teaching the disciples that there is no limit to forgiveness of others. The outstanding sign of a Christian, the chief characteristic of a follower of Christ, is that of forgiveness.

Generosity, forgiveness—how easy it is to see how they are related. How difficult it is at times to realize we, like God, do personalize these traits. If we take a moment, each of us can think of a time that we were generous, that we did forgive. At such moments we were Christ-like. We can also remember a time that another was generous to us, that someone we offended forgave us. That other also was fulfilling God's mandate. We cannot honestly say that only God can be generous, merciful, compassionate. We have been gifted with the power to think such thoughts, the grace to act in such a way.

I trust it is too early in our lives to think we have been generous enough, that we have forgiven abundantly, that we should receive our reward now. Paul in his dreary prison was tempted to think he had preached enough, accepted more than his share of rebuffs, endured trials sufficiently, forgiven too many persecutors. He had been called at the noon hour of his life; must he continue to the last hour? Why should he not cease striving to live and just be united through death with Christ? Then he thought of the Philippians, the Colossians, the Ephesians, the Romans, the Thessalonians, the Galatians, the Corinthians, who expected his continued guidance as they formed Christian communities. Despite his miserable surroundings Paul determined that, as God had called him to a missionary life, so he, Paul, would leave the time for his reward in God's hands.

We do not know yet what people are awaiting our creativity and our service, what kind of family we will form, what way of life will be ours. But we can, like Paul, work in our present and entrust our future to God.

Instead of assembling in a vineyard at the end of the day, we have come together for the Eucharist. With the bread and the wine, we will offer ourselves, years, our days, our hours of faithfulness to our baptismal covenant. In our sacramental worship we will receive the sign that God loves us all, forgives each of us, wishes to reward us equally. Each of us, uniquely loved by God, will be offered the saving grace, the body and blood of Christ.

Certainly, in our thanksgiving there will be no room for grumbling that all have been invited, all have received, all will be sent forth to be generous, to forgive, to love and serve one another. The thoughts and ways of God can be ours. — Grace Donovan

Topic: Realize Christ's Presence

In Matt. 18:20 we have a magnificent promise from Jesus: "Where two or three come together in my name, I am there with them" (GNB).

Christ promises to be in our midst. He is in our corporate worship, prayer, and observance of the Lord's Supper. This text is not a consolation for a poor turnout. The term *two or three* is an idiom for a group of any size, large or small. The important truth in this verse is not the size of the crowd but the presence of the Christ.

We can be sure this promise from the Master was a comfort to the first-century church. They were a tiny island of believers in a sea of paganism. Christ is present in our prayer meetings and Bible study groups as surely as he is present in the church sanctuary or coliseum crusade.

This lovely text reminds us that Christ is present in our family worship. "Where two [a man and his wife] or three [along with their child] come together in my name, I am there with them." Christ is Lord of the dinner table in our homes as surely as he is Lord of the communion table at church.

Remember that "little is much when God is in it." God opened the wall of China to diplomatic relations with a ping-pong ball. Many times he accomplishes great purposes with small means.

Christ is present in our private prayer and public worship. Once in Russia a government agent attended a worship service and took down the names of all in attendance. One worshiper said to him, "There is one Person present whose name you do not have."

"No," protested the Soviet agent. "I have the name of everyone here."

"Jesus Christ is here!" said the believer.

I. God is universally present in the world. Ps. 19:1 sings, "The heavens declare the glory of God, and the firmament sheweth his handiwork" (KJV). There is no place in Creation where God is not present. I served on an ordination council for a man who had tried to escape the call of God to ministry. He had joined the navy but found that the Almighty was on the other side of the world as well as at home.

God's presence in the world is inescapable. Listen to the compelling poetry of Ps. 139:7–12:

> Whither shall I go from thy Spirit?
> Or whither shall I flee from thy
> presence?
> If I ascend to heaven, thou art there!
> If I make my bed in Sheol, thou
> art there!
> If I take the wings of the morning
> and dwell in the uttermost parts of
> the sea,
> even there thy hand shall lead me,
> and thy right hand shall hold me.
> If I say, "Let only darkness cover me,
> and the light about me be night,"
> even the darkness is not dark to thee,
> the night is bright as the day;
> for darkness is as light with thee.

This passage inspired poet Francis Thompson to write about the Hound of Heaven.

II. God is particularly present in his world. At specific times and places his Presence has been obvious and transforming. In Old Testament times, God called Moses at the burning bush. He called Abraham to leave his homeland and go on a pilgrimage of faith—he knew not where. God was present in the temple worship and called young Isaiah to be his prophet. God was also present in great events, such as the Exodus and the Israelite's return from exile.

In New Testament times, the divine Presence was not in doubt. "In Christ God was reconciling the world to himself" (2 Cor. 5:19). Jesus was God incarnate—"The Word became flesh and dwelt among us" (John 1:14).

God is particularly present today in our worship: prayer and praise, the preaching of the Word, the drama of baptism, and the Lord's Supper.

If you will be confessional, you may acknowledge that God has been present in your life. It may have been in a time of danger when you cried, "O God! Help me!" and he did. I recall experiencing such a moment while driving across an ice-covered bridge in north Georgia and losing control of the car.

God may have been present in your experience at some point of temptation. You asked for his help, and he provided a way out.

The divine Presence may well have been yours in a time of trouble or grief. In the midst of great loss or disappointment, you felt comfort as you sensed his Presence with you.

God can be with us in our daily walk. We learn to practice the Presence of the Lord. Begin your prayer times by acknowledging that he is with you. "He walks with me, and he talks with me / And he tells me I am his own."

Is Christ real in your experience? Are you consciously aware of the divine Presence? Luther declared, "God is here." He also expressed an even more significant thought: "God is here for you. Can you acknowledge that and rejoice in it? None are so blind as those who refuse to see.

The observance of the Lord's Supper invites us into God's Presence to worship and have fellowship with him. Jesus said, "Do this in remembrance of me" (Luke 22:19). The observance then sends us back to our responsibilities in the world with new freedom and joy. It constitutes a call to worship and a call to serve. In the Lord's Supper, we experience the Presence of Christ cognito—in fact.

> As we come to the table,
> may Christ enter our minds, that
> we
> may think his thoughts;
> may Christ flood our emotions,
> that
> we may feel his love;
> may Christ captivate our wills,
> that we may follow where he leads;
> may Christ fill our bodies to heal
> and to bless.
>
> —Alton McEachern

Topic: When Should We Sit at the Lord's Table?

TEXT: 1 Cor. 11:23–29

The story of King Arthur and his round table has been an inspiration to many people through the years. Legend has it that Arthur became king through an extraordinary demonstration of power—the kind of power that pulls swords out of stones. As king, Arthur realized that true power was not in might but in right. Out of that belief he conceived the notion of a round table. At this unique table no one would sit at the foot, no one would sit at the head, but all would sit in equal distinction. The Lord's table is a round table. No one can claim superiority over another there. All are sinners, and all are invited to the feast.

There are, however, certain prerequisites to this table. Paul urged the pagan-tainted Christians of Corinth to examine themselves prior to sharing the Lord's table. Whenever we sit at the table of the Lord, we should ask ourselves some important questions. When should we sit at the Lord's table?

I. *When we confess our faith in Jesus Christ (Rom. 10:9–10).* We observe Communion when we place our lives in the hand of God. As a child I was a member of a very exclusive club, the "no girls" club. There were two abiding rules. One was that only boys apply for membership. The other was that a secret password be mentioned upon entering the place we met. The club of Jesus is not at all exclusive. All are welcome. Jesus said that whoever will may come. But to sit in the fellowship of his table, the appropriate password must be used. That password is "Jesus is Lord." We only come to his table as an expression of our faith in him. No other reason is important.

During World War II, a chaplain visited a jungle in New Guinea. As his jeep pulled up, the natives of a nearby village pressed in around him. They were impressed by his uniform and the sound of his jeep horn. The chaplain was uneasy until an elderly man approached him and gently touched the gold cross on his lapel. In broken English the man said, "Me a Jesus man, too." That is the key to the Lord's table. When we come, we come as Jesus' people.

II. *When we obey the will of God.* Jesus said in John 4:34, "My food is to do the will of him who sent me" (RSV). That which nourished Jesus was his unswerv-ing commitment to do the will of his Father. What nourishes us? In John 5:30 Jesus also said, "I can do nothing on my own authority" (RSV). Actually, his example lends to us the example of one who lived a selfless life. He sought to do God's will, not his own. In Communion we seek to tune our lives to his frequency and to receive his signal without static or interference.

At Harvard University is a house dedicated to the great preacher Phillips Brooks. Beneath a bronze bust of Brooks are inscribed these words: "This house is dedicated to piety, charity, and hospitality." A new sign now hangs beneath the original one. It reads: "No trespassing: unauthorized persons not allowed in this building." Many of us hang similar signs on our lives. It does us no good to pray, "Thy will be done," when we hang no-trespassing signs on our lives for God. Many of us are determined to keep God away from the premises of our lives. But when we sit at his round table, we are saying that we have purposed in our hearts to do the will of God. The spiritual food nourishes us and reminds us to always do God's will.

III. *When we join our hearts and our hands with others in service to God.* One of the overlooked symbols of the Lord's table is the symbol of community. In Baptist circles the elements of the table are passed from one brother or sister in Christ to another. Each shares the common meal and then plays a part in serving a companion in Christ. It is a community rite. We must be together to share its full expression of grace.

The round table of the Lord reminds us of a common heritage we all share. Like Arthur's round table, there is no place for squabbling or efforts of superiority. Service to God and service to others matter at this table. Together God's people journey by faith. The path is dark, the way often rough; but God's people journey together. We need each other. Our need creates community with others. True community occurs in Christian fellowship. Thus when God's children unite in their stand for him and others, the great power of the church is unleashed in this world. Our lives are blessed when we forget self and get on with our service to God.

In a small community a little girl strayed away from her home. Her father was a farmer. He looked but could not find her. He called for help. The townspeople came and joined the search but could not find the girl either. The only area unsearched by the party was a wide open field near the girl's home. A search party formed, and they all joined hands so as not to miss any ground in the field. With hands and hearts united they marched across the field. In a matter of minutes the girl was found. She was dead. The heartbroken father fell to his knees beside the body of the little one and cried to the heavens, "In God's name, why didn't we join hands before?" That is the question at the Lord's table. In God's name, why don't we join hands and hearts in service to him?

IV. *When we need the assurance of his love.* We all need affirmation and love. Built into the framework of all of us is the need to be loved by someone. At the Lord's table we are reminded that we are unconditionally loved and accepted by God. Paul observed that even while we were still in our sin Christ died for us. We find at the Lord's table One who not only spoke of love but also One who demonstrated that love. That love invites us to a simple meal. There unlovely sinners meet a lovely Savior. Insecurity and darkness are met with love and light.

All of us arrive at the Lord's table with our sin, guilt, and shame-faced Christianity. Christ, our host, greets us with warmth, compassion, and grace. He says to all of his children, "You are loved; you are forgiven."

Once a young girl with a bad reputation went to church when the Lord's Supper was observed. When the elements came her way, the guilt of her life gave ways to tears. A nearby saint leaned over and whispered to her, "Take it, dear; it is for sinners." At this round table of love, the table of our Lord, our hatred is met by love, our hurt by healing, and our sin by forgiveness. The table is round, and it is large. It is the Lord's table, and he invites us to join him there.—Danny M. West

OTHER WORSHIP RESOURCES FOR COMMUNION

BY JOHN THOMPSON

Communion Meditation: ". . . not by bread alone but by every Word . . ." (Lent).

As we come to the Lord's Supper on this first Sunday in Lent, let us think on these things: The two antecedents usually given for the origin of Lent are the forty years of wandering of the children of Israel in the wilderness until they were prepared and disciplined for entering the Promised Land and the forty days Jesus spent in the wilderness tested in preparation for his ministry. Out of these two wilderness experiences, there is spoken a word that has meaning for us in our wilderness experience—that wrestling with ourselves to discover who we really are and our true destiny.

Moses declared to the congregation of Israel: "Man does not live by bread alone but by everything that proceeds out of the mouth of God." When Jesus is tempted to turn from his true calling and cater to the desires of men, he meets the test with the same words: "Man shall not live by bread alone but by every word that comes from the mouth of God." The Word that comes from the Father is Jesus—Christ is what God has to say to man in every generation. And Jesus is saying to us, "I am the living bread which came down from heaven; if anyone eats of this bread, he will live forever, and the bread which I shall give for the world is my flesh." In this context he extends the invitation to would-be-disciples: "Except you eat the flesh of the Son of man and drink his blood, you have not life in you." Through faith we partake of Christ as the Bread of Life—this experience is to be as real as our eating physically of the bread and drinking of the cup at this table.

The bread which we bless is it not the Communion of the BODY of Christ. The cup which we bless is it not the Communion of the BLOOD of Christ.

Prayer of Consecration. O Father, for your love that identifies with us in our deepest need so fully manifest in your self-giving as you suffer our contradictions and the contradictions of all, we give you thanks. For the meanings of these simple elements and for mystery with which your Presence is veiled in them, we are grateful. Stir up faith in us that we may come boldly, knowing that we are your sons and daughters received, forgiven, made new by the abundant grace of your love and mercy. Consecrate now the bread and the cup to that holy purpose which Christ ordained for them—communion with thee as Father and every other as brother or sister.

Prayer of Thanksgiving. Father, it is good for us to have been here. For the gift of Word and sacrament we give you thanks. Having eaten of the bread which is bread indeed and having drunk of the cup which is drink indeed, send us on our way rejoicing. May the discipline of Lent temper us for our Gethsemane and cross-bearing.

Benediction. And now may the grace of our Lord Jesus Christ, the love of God, and the communion of the Holy Spirit be with us all.

Communion Meditation: Pentecost

Nowhere is God's presence more real to us than at his table! Why is this? Is it not that here we are reminded of the deed—the deeds—through which God's grace is most fully expressed: the bread, the body broken; the cup, the blood poured out, the life given? It is in the death and Resurrection of Christ that God's grace is most fully manifest. It is this same grace that is present in our dying and being raised to new life. So the Apostle Paul declares in his teaching concerning the sacrament of baptism when he asks, "Do you not know that all of us who have been baptized into Christ Jesus were baptized into his death? We were buried therefore with him by baptism into death, so that as Christ was raised from the dead by the glory of the Father, we too might walk in newness of life."

This experience Pentecost declares and manifests. It intimates that the church, the believer, can live in perennial springtime, a continual renewal by God's living Spirit. This renewing Presence that we claim here in the sacrament of Communion this morning, we can celebrate in all of life. For God as the Divine Host spreads a table for us everywhere—even in the presence of our enemies—that we may eat and drink and live by grace, by his grace, by the grace of our Lord Jesus Christ.

With these meanings (and others that you may bring) let us prepare mind and heart to celebrate the sacrament.

Prayer of Consecration. O Father, for the meaning and mystery that these simple elements hold, we give you thanks—there is the meaning and mystery of your presence in all of life—there is the meaning and mystery of death and resurrection out of which new life comes, for "except the grain of wheat falls to the ground it abides alone, but when it dies a new plant springs forth bearing much fruit"—there is the meaning and mystery of your love broken that we may be whole.

That a small piece of bread and a meager cup should be the occasion of a rich spiritual feast is an intimation of your abundant grace. Consecrate now the bread and the cup that they may become for us the Communion of the body and the blood of Christ that we may eat and drink and live.

Prayer of Thanksgiving. We praise you, O Father, that in your house there is bread enough and to spare—that it is the divine hospitality to hand to us a cup that is not only full but running over. Such is your grace by which life is created, sustained, and renewed. For a perennial springtime of Pentecostal power available to those intent on your mission, we are grateful. As we respond to the call to be your witnesses here and beyond, we are recipients of a power from on high that encourages, sustains, and empowers, even as you have promised. Thanks be to you for you give us the victory through our Lord Jesus Christ.

Benediction. And now, may the grace of our Lord Jesus Christ, the love of the Father, and the communion of the Holy Spirit be with us all.

Communion Meditation: World Communion Sunday

"The field is the world." "God so loved the world that he gave his only Son." Although on this World Communion Sunday we do not have the spatial vantage point of the astronauts, through the window of the imagination we do see a table stretching round the world where Christians have gathered, are gathering, will gather today to celebrate a world communion in the sacrament of the Lord's Supper.

On this occasion we celebrate the Father's world-embracing love. We are called and recalled to the world dimension of God's purpose. The love we claim for ourselves we must not deny to any other human being, for we are all children of the one Father.

Who has expressed this solidarity as appropriately as has the Apostle Paul in writing to the church at Ephesus in the first century and in turn to the church in every time and place when he pens: "There is one Lord, one faith, one baptism, one God and Father of us all, who is above all and through all and in all." In the unity of this spirit, and in the bonds of peace, let us keep the feast. Let us pray in consecration.

Prayer of Consecration. That your good work begun in us may continue and come to fruition, we seek this respite at your table. May our weary spirits be renewed by your Word in Christ, at work to make all things new. That these simple elements should proclaim to us your mighty work in Christ for our salvation and the healing of the nations is an amazing grace. As gifts of your providence, we return, now, the bread and the cup to you for your consecration to that holy purpose which Christ intends.

Prayer of Thanksgiving. That as pilgrims of the Way, we have had this opportunity to unite with brothers and sisters the world over in celebration of the sacrament, we give you thanks. That we have been entrusted with the gospel of reconciliation, we are grateful. Of these privileges we can never be worthy, they are of your abounding grace. With renewed faith in the power of your love, may we go forth into all the world and all the worlds of persons proclaiming in word and deed the gospel, the good news, that you are at work in Christ reconciling the world unto yourself—even as we proclaim his presence in these moments teaching us to pray together, Our Father. . . .

Benediction. And now may your grace who Christ is, your love as Father of us all, and the communion of your perennial Spirit be with us today and tomorrow and in all life's tomorrows.

ILLUSTRATIONS FOR COMMUNION

by Robert C. Shannon

MEMORIALS. Hawthorne said, "No man who needs a monument ever ought to have one." It's true, isn't it? If persons and deeds are not remembered for some other reason, then there is no need for a memorial of stone or bronze. We do not have the memorial of the Lord's Supper because Christ needs it. His name, his deeds, are written everywhere in the very fabric of life itself. It is we who need the memorial of the Lord's Supper. We need to be reminded of the great price paid for our redemption. It will keep us from taking sin lightly. It will keep us from taking forgiveness lightly. We need to be reminded of the great love God had for us. It will make it easier for us to love one another, to love ourselves, and to love lost men and women.

THE MOST HOLY PLACE.   When God designed the Temple for the Jews he directed them to make a most holy place. In that inner room were placed the tablets of stone from Sinai, Aaron's staff, and a pot of manna. Eventually all three items were lost. In Jesus' day the most holy place was an empty room! This communion time is our most holy place. God forbid that it should ever be empty!

THE RIGHT APPROACH.   The way into ancient temples was always gradual, through forecourts, approaches, terraces until finally the holiest chamber was reached. So we must not come suddenly here—to our most holy place. The outer court is the song. Then the meditation. Then the prayers. Each a courtyard, a terrace, an approach. Each helps prepare us for the supreme moment—the breaking of the bread and the breaking of our hearts in this our Holy of Holies.

EXAMINATION.   Since Judas "kept the bag" as the Bible says and was thus the treasurer for Jesus and the Twelve. He likely purchased the very bread and wine of the Last Supper. It did not spoil the supper for Jesus, nor did it spoil the supper for the Twelve. So no distraction need spoil the supper for us. We do not come to examine the person who bought the bread, the person who poured the wine, the person who said the prayer. We come to examine ourselves.

PERSPECTIVE.   The largest single sculpture in the world is at Stone Mountain, Georgia. It is, as you might expect, a memorial. Figures have been carved into the side of a gigantic mountain of limestone. But the mountain is so large, and the distance from which the figures are viewed is so great, that one loses a sense of perspective. The figures seem small. How great is the distance from which we view the upper room, Gethsemane, Golgotha. We must not lose our perspective. The Supper, rightly understood, is large enough to dominate our lives!

SECTION IV.
Messages for Funeral Services: Preaching a Funeral Meditation

BY ALBERT J. D. WALSH

Thank God we are not all alike! This is true, in particular, for those of us in this gathering of saintly sinners we call the Body of Christ. Christ-like graces are channeled through unique individuals; each person in this community of faith enacts his or her own personal part in the unfolding drama of salvation. And yet we are more than the sum total of atomistic personalities! Mere actors on a stage! We are an empowered and empowering community—the Body of Christ—and therefore dependent on one another in trial and triumph. As Christians, we do not live in isolation and most certainly do not die in isolation!

Then perhaps it only stands to reason. When preaching to mourners, something of the deceased person's individual and unique character and contribution(s) should be celebrated. God chose and used this particular person, with all his or her burdens and beauty, to help the church carry out her ministry in the name of Christ. However, place the emphasis on what God has accomplished in and through this life, in and through the community called the church. Because even though that individual expressed his or her faithfulness in a somewhat unique fashion, he or she shared such faith with the family of God's own people. In this way, we celebrate what God has made possible in both the individual and the church.

The funeral meditation will begin to take shape in the heart and mind of the pastor as he or she attends to the dying and/or the bereaved. These hours of sharing and caring will reveal much about the person facing death and those who have loved and befriended him or her. The pastor who tends to this ministry with sensitive awareness will come to know both the dying person and his or her family in ways that life-situations might never have made possible. Sometimes faith discovers its clearest voice in the whispers of the dying and the sighs of the bereaved. We pastors can listen and learn!

Finally, let us be honest with death! We are a people with a proclamation, but that proclamation has a blood-stained cross at its very heart! In the funeral meditation, death should be faced boldly, without mincing words. Stoic pride is not merely alien to faith, it distorts faith. But let us never leave people who mourn standing at the foot of Calvary, with mouths gaping in horror! Because we also proclaim that death, any death, can never be the final word on our existence. The final Word belongs to God! And God has spoken with clarity and authority—"Awake, O sleeper, and rise from the dead, and Christ will give you light."

I. The Apostle Peter said, "Even the angels long to look into these things" (1 Pet. 1:12b, NIV). He is referring to the mysteries surrounding the suffering and glorification of Christ, yet the same is true regarding the suffering and glory of being human. The angels will never have the advantage of looking into the mysteries that encompass what it means to be human. We are the privileged ones—those created in the "image of God." Death is not the privilege, but to be human is. And to be human is to be bound by time and finiteness. Time is not the enemy of our lives, rather it is the divinely created medium of our existence—even the time to die. No wonder the psalmist could write "precious in the sight of the LORD is the death of His saints." And no wonder an elderly Christian could tell me from her death bed, "I would rather be a saint for a day, than an angel for eternity!"

II. "Be still and know that I am God." Be still and know! The knowledge which is the prerequisite for accepting the reality of death as the boundary of finiteness will come from inner stillness. This is the easing of all anxious thoughts and feelings, the full recognition that God is the God of the living, lending credence to our faithful and trusting posture when we face death. Karl Barth has somewhere written that the goal of life is (because of what God has accomplished in Jesus Christ) no longer death but resurrection. God has in Christ Jesus created a broader horizon for human life and all Creation. This particular horizon transcends and far exceeds the "valley of the shadow of death." Death is the termination of life here and now, but it is not the amputation of the human spirit from its creative source. "Even though I walk through the valley of the shadow of death, I fear no evil; for thou art with me; thy rod and thy staff, they comfort me" (Ps. 23:4, RSV). This prayer of the psalmist is a manifestation of the spirit of the "heroic few." (from Albert J. D. Walsh's book *Reflections on Death and Grief*)

III. Resurrection does not imply a continuance of life after death nor simply a "return" from the grave. It is the powerful symbol of a new God-created order of life beyond death and decay. In the promised general resurrection we stand in the light of God's faithfulness to the covenant, to creature, and to Creation. This, then, must be the essence of Christian hope in the company of death and sorrow. Those embraced by the covenant of Christ are not lost to God in death: "If we live, we live to the Lord, and if we die, we die to the Lord; so then, whether we live or whether we die, we are the Lord's" (Rom. 14:8). As long as it is true that the dead in Christ are not lost to God, we must refrain from believing in something so nebulous as the "hereafter." Christians should make every endeavor to recover the gospel of the crucified and resurrected Christ. The cross of Jesus will not allow the Christian to side-step the reality and finality of death as the end to human life. Neither will the Resurrection of Jesus Christ, as God's final Word on human existence, permit a trade-off for the notion—regardless of how well intentioned—of a "hereafter."

IV. "Jesus wept." If this were the description of a superman, it would say that Jesus was brashly indifferent. If the sentence spoke of one who was spiritually and emotionally aloof, it would attest to his detachment and disinterest! The precise miracle is this: Jesus, the Son of God, "wept." Death and sorrow impressed the heart of Jesus—and the heart of God! As the tears of Jesus touched the dry, cracked soils of human misery and anguish, the empathic-love and compassion of God saturated the ground of human discouragement. In this the love and compassion of God for all who lament was revealed. In this weeping of Jesus, the generations of those who would suffer a similar anguish—including yourselves—were freed to express sorrow over the loss of a loved one to death. This bears no feeble encouragement! Too often we feel that our tears must be withheld and our sorrow concealed; for we think that faith—true faith—demands that our eyes remain dry and our hearts bright. True, as Christians, we must not mourn as others do who "have no hope." But, "Jesus wept" and freed us to mourn our most painful losses, knowing that God has and will share our pain.

V. The fulfillment of human existence (in Christ) is that which we anticipate in the future and experience, proleptically, in the present. The implications of this conviction and faithful posture bear decisively on the question of the meaning and purpose of human existence. We faithfully confess that the fulfillment of our individual lives embodies a transcendent characteristic, promised in a time beyond time. Such a faithful attitude enables one to live with all the ambiguities and perplexities of human, finite existence. This side of the general resurrection and the fulfillment of human existence in the kingdom of our God, life must be embraced, even though inconclusive. If Christian existence holds within it the guarantee of a future fulfillment, then death brings "this life only" to a close. Notwithstanding, for the Christian death is no longer the definitive word on human existence and fulfillment. Human life, even though ambiguous and inconclusive, bears the dimension of transcendent fulfillment beyond death and the grave. In the Resurrection of Jesus Christ from the dead we acquire both proclamation and assurance that the "aim" which God intends for creature and Creation is not death but eternal life.

Topic: A Modern Day Job

TEXTS: Job 2; 1 Pet. 3:8–18a

Family, friends, associates, and colleagues of J. S., we gather today to express our thanksgiving to God for the life that J. lived among us. We are saddened by his death, so untimely and so seemingly unfair, but we rejoice over his life and his presence now with the holy Father in the kingdom.

In moments such as these we often ask, Why? Why does such a good man suffer as J. suffered? Why does one who would not harm a fly undergo the trauma and trials J. faced in his life? When we turn to Holy Scripture we discover that the first book ever written of this word was the Book of Job, and it deals directly with the subject of why evil comes to the good. Ever since humankind was formed from the dust of the earth we have wrestled with this question.

Job asked why and dared to confront God with his question. Job's friends came and shared the wisdom of the day, which was not too wise, whey they said that his sin, probably hideous and unknown, had brought this upon Job and his family.

Job, however, knew God better than they and refused to accept this answer.

Job's wife was more to the point: "Curse God and die," she said. Just get it over with; there's no use in living if this is to be life. So the entire Book of Job plays out this wonderful drama of challenge and rebuttal as to the reasons for Job's calamity.

Finally, God steps in and speaks for himself. He has heard enough, and now he comes to answer Job. But the truth is that Job is never given an answer; he never knows why he suffers. Rather, Job is told quite bluntly, "You're not smart enough to comprehend the ways of God." God simply tells Job that what Job is involved in is far bigger than he will ever realize, and he cannot comprehend it. Finite human beings cannot comprehend the infinite God. As Cowper put it:

God moves in a mysterious way
His wonder to perform;
He plants his footsteps in the sea
And rides upon the storm.
You fearful saints, fresh courage take:
the clouds you so much dread
Are big with mercy, and shall break
In blessings on your head.
Judge not the Lord by feeble sense,
But trust him for his grace;
Behind a frowning providence
He hides a smiling face.
Blind unbelief is sure to err
And scan his work in vain;
God is his own interpreter,
And he will make it plain.

J. S. was a modern-day Job. Despite all the challenges of life that came to him, he continued unwavering and diligent in his faith. He was a Christian from the inside out, all the way through. In an age when the greedy and domineering seem to move ahead quickly, J. was a classic gentleman. In an age of taunting and jeering in athletic contests, J. was a sportsman through and through. He had a class about him that rose above the attitudes and actions of others. He was compassionate, caring, considerate to a fault, and one of the most humble men I have ever known. He never talked about his exploits or accomplishments in life, and they were considerable. During all the time we spent together in recent months, J. never hinted of these achievements. He only spoke of others. He was humble.

J. loved his family deeply. You were special to J., and you knew it. What a tremendous legacy to carry forward, a heritage to uphold. This man did put his family needs before his own. That's not easy to do. Treasure that love, let it reside deep within you, and covenant with yourself to honor that love by loving others in the same way.

When I began to think of Scripture passages that would relate to the life that J. lived, the figure of Job and also the passage from 1 Peter came to mind. J. decided early on what type of person he wanted to be, what type of character he wanted to have, and then lived in that way. So often we hear people talk about discovering who they are. What if it is not that we discover who we are but decide who we are and then fashion our character accordingly? J. took the principles of his home and faith, both grounded deep within, and lived those out in a day-by-day life that could look back with no regrets.

One of the reasons death held no fear for J. was that he had lived life as he felt that it should be lived, in accordance with the biblical principles and his faith in Christ Jesus his Lord. In the words of 1 Peter, he had in his "heart set apart Christ as Lord." The character that J. possessed was no accident but was the result of a covenant made first between his parents and the Lord, and then between J. himself and the Lord. He could say with Paul, "I know whom I have believed and am persuaded that he is able to keep that which I have committed unto him against that day." He could face death squarely, and though he did not want to leave you, he had no fear. J. could "give the reason for the hope that he had."

Death is never easy to face, either as the one dying or as the family and friends. We mask the pain by saying that all die, and though that may be true the truth is also that deaths are painful for us all. "Funerals are pretty, but death not always" is how Tennessee Williams put it in *A Streetcar Named Desire*. Your pain is real and valid, and please do not let anyone tell you it is not. You hurt for the loss, I hurt for the loss, we all hurt for the loss of J. from this life, even though we would not have him back embattled by that treacherous disease.

So we have come today to share our sorrow, to do our grieving together as we should, but also to celebrate life, real life, eternal life. This is what family and friends are for, to share our lives together, the joy and the pain, the laughter and the tears. We come to the realization that "every exit is also an entrance." J. is more alive today than ever before and has left this life so that he might enter into the kingdom where "[God] will wipe every tear from their eyes. There will be no more death or mourning or crying or pain, for the old order of things has passed away" (Rev. 21:4). The pain we all feel will be replaced by the joy of the Holy Spirit as we experience afresh and anew his graceful presence in our lives.

Rabbi Edward Paul Cohn reminds us that inside the violins made from the trees of the Black Forest, violins which are renowned for their sound, these words are engraved in Italian:

I was alive in the forest before
   God.
Yet here in death I made sweet
   sounds.

Sweet sounds. Those are the memories that come flooding back to us of J. No matter how painful they may be, we know that we really wouldn't have it any other way.

Several years ago my father's only sister died of cancer. I was sitting on the front row at the funeral home before the casket with the family during a private visitation. My cousin's son was sitting with me. He went up and looked into the casket and then came back to sit beside me. He then said to me, "You know what I told Grandma?" "No," I replied. "I told her that she could stay up there with Jesus. We'll be all right down here."

J., stay up there with Jesus. We'll be all right down here.—Robert U. Ferguson

Topic: Our School on Earth

A missionary sends home his children to be educated. They cannot be taught ... where he dwells, and so some sister receives the precious charge and endeavors to supply to them the place of father and mother. They are very ignorant when they arrive, but they are trained and watched over with assiduous care. Teachers are provided for them; they are cultivated and developed on every side, and grow up to maturity, full of knowledge and loveliness and virtue. The time draws near when the parent shall come to claim them, and how anxious is their loving guardian lest he should be disappointed. Her constant thought is, How shall I present these children acceptably to their father?

As the ship that bears him approaches the land, the longing father can scarcely wait to clasp his dear ones in his arms. He makes haste to go on shore; he finds his sister's house, and when the first warm greetings are over, she leads him in with trembling joy and says, "Here are your children!" and the son whom he left, a fair-haired boy, comes forward, dark-haired, deep-eyed, and taller than his father; and the daughter, who when he saw her last could do little but smile and cry, advances timidly, with blushing cheek and all the grace of early womanhood. If they have been wayward and intractable, his love in that hour can overlook it all. If they have been docile and obedient, how gladly does he embrace them. But if more than this, they have striven to improve every advantage and to make themselves worthy of their father and of the kind friend who has guided them, with what rapture does he fold them to his heart!

Christians are God's children whom he has sent to school upon earth, and Christ is their guide and teacher, who desires to present them to him "faultless," "without spot, or wrinkle, or any such thing." When through death, the Father comes to take them home, how is Christ's heart grieved to present those who have been wayward and worldly; but they are children still, and the Father's love overlooks it, and they are "saved so as by fire." With subdued joy he presents those who have made no great attainments but have yet been teachable and obedient, and they are welcomed to the heavenly inheritance. And then with radiant face he brings those shining bands who have been the true disciples, following gladly in the footsteps of the Master; pressing forward through toil and suffering to the prize, and the Father makes haste to greet them, and saying, "Come, ye blessed," folds them with rapture to his bosom!

The entering into heaven will reveal many things unknown on earth. Some whom the world thought saintlike will barely gain admittance there, and others who went all their lives in doubt and dread will have angelic welcome and an abundant entrance into the heavenly kingdom. "The first shall be last, and the last shall be first."

What do the flowers say to the night? They wave their bells and exhale their choicest odors, as if they would bribe it to bestow upon them some new charm. In the tender twilight they look wistfully at each other and say, "Do you see any thing on me?" and when the answer is "I see nothing," they hang their heads and wait sorrowfully for the morning, fearing that they shall bring no beauty to it. Though there is no voice nor sound, yet the night hears them, and silently through the sill air the dews drop down from the sky and settle on every stem and bud and blossom, and when day dawns, at the first rosy glance that the sun sends athwart the fields, ten million jewels glitter and sparkle and quiver on the notched edges of every leaf and along each beaded blade and spire of grass and spray, and the happy flowers, stirred by the wind, nod and beckon and smile to each other, more resplendent in their dewy gems than any dream of the night had imagined. So many Christians who in the darkness of this life have longed and labored for graces, yet sad and fearing, will find themselves covered with glory when the eternal morning dawns and the light of God's countenance strikes through their earth-gained jewels!— Henry Ward Beecher

ILLUSTRATIONS

BY ROBERT C. SHANNON

LIFE.   When the bombing was at its worst in London in World War II, Leslie Weatherhead said that there had been no loss of life among the Christians in London. Many Christians had been killed, but there was no loss of life. We can never say of a Christian "he lost his life." Christians have eternal life here and now. Death for them is merely the transferring of that life from here to there, from now to forever.

THE CITY OF GOD.   There is a village in Austria, along the Danube River, that is called Gottsdorf—God's village. However noble the sentiments of those who named it, the city of God is not on this earth. And it is no small village. It is a city foursquare, a city that has foundations, a city big enough for a multitude no man can number. We often say that the place where we grew up is "God's country," but we really know that God's country, the city of God, Gottsdorf, is in heaven and not on earth, is future not present, is eternal not temporal.

A FAIR VIEW.   There are sixty-six towns in the United States named Fairview, one or more in thirty-one of the fifty states. In many of them the view is not very fair.

Perhaps it once was, but time and change and decay have changed things. However, we can always sing with absolute confidence, "There's a land that is fairer than day. And by faith we can see it afar."

AN ETERNAL CITY.   Catherine the Great ruled Russia two hundred years ago. She imagined grand new cities that she would build. Once when the Austrian emperor Joseph II was visiting she asked him to participate in laying two corner stones for a grand metropolis she envisioned. Joseph II was not optimistic about the plan. He said, "She laid the first stone, and I laid the last." He was correct. The city was never built. In fact today we do not even know the proposed site of this grand city. How comforting it is to read in Hebrew chapter 11 that there is a city that has foundations whose builder and maker is God. How comforting to hear someone sing of "the new Jerusalem that shall not pass away."

NEW JERUSALEM.   The earthly city of Jerusalem has been fought over for centuries and captured no less than thirty-seven times! Not so the new Jerusalem. It will live up to its name as a city of peace. It will conquer always, everywhere. It will never be besieged. It will never be invaded. It will never even be threatened. What peace, what comfort, what stability it brings to our hearts when we can see with the Apostle John "the New Jerusalem coming down from God out of heaven."

SECTION V.
Lenten and Easter Preaching

SERMON SUGGESTIONS

Topic: Between the Lines

TEXTS: John 12:20–27; Heb. 5:1–10

We have a penchant for summarizing and condensing. Life moves too fast to get bogged down in description—just tell me how it turned out. We live in a world of capsule reports, abridged novels, computer printouts, and *Cliff's Notes*. Without realizing it we suffer from an acute case of "synopsis." This need to abbreviate causes us to miss the real fabric of life: hopes and fears, failures and successes not always noted in the condensed version.

In our modern mania for "boiling things down," getting to the bottom line, we lose what comes between *A* and *B*. So as not to lose the texture of life, an ability to read between the lines is essential. Otherwise there is a tendency to condense life stories so they sound, well, more suitable. Like those of us who hurriedly shorten bedtime stories for our children so we can get them in bed, now! The stories come out sounding like "Once upon a happily ever after."

We all know of Abraham Lincoln, who rose from obscurity to become one of our greatest presidents, but how? How many times was he defeated in public elections before he was elected? How did he react to ridicule and rejection? What of the loss of the people he loved most? Unfortunately, we remember others in the same way. Moses from refugee to liberator; shepherd boy to mighty King David. *A* to

B. *A* to *B*. But what has been expurgated? What seems too human to be remembered?

Perhaps we can now sense the danger of leaping too quickly from a Jesus whose soul is deeply troubled to one who has confidently come "for this purpose." If we, like the Greeks in this story, are to see Jesus and see him in such a way that we are never the same again, it will mean looking between the lines. What John intended was a glimpse at a Savior who was fully human and who struggled painfully with his own doubts, fears, and the call to glorify God.

Therefore seeing Jesus in his full humanity may be helpful in our own attempt to live our lives out fully, even "between the lines." What do I mean by that phrase?

I. First of all, I mean those hidden, even guarded moments when we are engaged in deep personal struggle. Battling inner demons, we are grasping for what is above the mean-spirited and the compromised. If it is too much to say that most men and women live lives of "quiet desperation," can we not say that all know some such moments?

We must be careful at just this point, for it is possible to be a detached observer of another's struggles. "Voyeurs of crisis" may be a live option in this day of the soap opera's extreme popularity. A guide book to the Holy Land described the headquarters of a tour of Jerusalem as "a hotel with picture windows in three sides." It was aptly named the Panorama

245

Hotel and is four hundred yards from and overlooking the Garden of Gethsemane! But if we are to see our Savior in all his humanity, guidebooks must be left at home; it is no tourist attraction or soap opera. The pain and distress is not acted out; it is real, and we cannot easily "look on."

The Fourth Gospel gives us no garden, only strange, arresting words about his soul being troubled or distressed. Lest we interpret these words to mean a temporary or minor disturbance, the writer of Hebrews reveals what is really between the lines. For Jesus expresses himself in loud cries and tears. At the very least, a Savior of humanity who cries out, who hurts, gives us permission to live a life before God of emotional honesty. Even more, it means the Mediator between us and God is in every way fully human.

That is why it is a damnable pity to expurgate from the record Jesus' struggle with what lay before him. For in between the lines is the story of no easy salvation for him or us. "Now my soul is in turmoil." How can we fully enter into the wrestling with God, the rejection by his most intimate friends? Here is a stark reminder that Jesus was no plastic saint, much less an immune God. As the Book of Hebrews reminds us, our heavenly High Priest, the Son of God, is also fully human. How else could he be the *Mediator* (the one who brings us to God and God to us)?

II. To live life between the lines is to know the intensity of *prayerful struggle*. For Jesus' prayer was not a pious rehearsal. It was that honest, "no-holds-barred" communication with a God who at times seemed distant. This is epitomized in the cry from the cross. "Why hast thou forsaken me?" It is not so much reflected in our stately well-formed prayers as in the raspy throated "Why?" that seeks a God obscured by the fog of pain and uncertainty. If we see Jesus from that vantage point, what is hard to believe is not the humanness of his prayer but the assurance given here: He was heard!

Was death avoided or even postponed? He prayed the cup would pass from him,

but in his sacrifice of love he downed the cup of suffering—all of it. How was he heard? Our difficulty in believing he was heard is compounded by our understanding of prayer as linked always to a clear final answer. "Take this burden from me." "Give me success." When the final tabulation is in we know whether prayer works or not. Could it be that Jesus' prayer—intense, personal (between the lines)—was answered daily in the courage to face "the way" God had given him? The answer was not absence of fear or the avoidance of struggle but the strength to face what must be faced and to do what must be done.

III. Isn't that the key to living life between the lines? To glorify the name (essence) of God is to act wholly in character with God's nature. We see that nature supremely in self-giving love. Glorifying God is not simply how things come out in the end. It is the *process*, the pilgrimage of faith, much of it involving personal struggle and intense prayer hidden from the public gaze.

Think of those in your life who reflect, even if imperfectly, this self-giving love. The pictures that come to mind are often of moments of triumph. I see a woman overwhelmed with adversity crossing a graduation platform at age sixty. There is a vision of a mother who, abandoned by her husband, keeps a family not only fed but vibrant with faith and self-esteem. I see a teenager in an iron lung speaking a good word for Jesus Christ and that word coming to life in friends who first come out of sympathy, then stay to experience the power at work in their good friend. Now try to imagine where that perseverance, courage, and faith are forged. Yes, it is between the lines. It is not in the moment of a public triumph but is in the wintry seasons of the heart that the real victory is won. The night she wants to quit, the day "God" seems an echo of a distant reality, the moment the pain seems a cruel mockery. Here is the miracle hidden from public view, the life of obedience hidden between the lines.

For Jesus the response of obedience to God was not primarily in his call and baptism or even in his death on the cross. The costly obedience of the human Jesus giving himself up to be the Christ was in his daily, often unnoticed, dying into life. The cross was the culmination of Jesus' obedience to the self-giving nature of God. It was not an isolated crisis in Jesus' life. He was being prepared for that battle with and triumph over the very forces that nailed him to the cross by the intense prayerful struggle "between the lines." His dying into life then was not one event but the journey of One who was tempted to seek an easier way out. Yet he continually opened himself to the resources of God to endure and overcome.

If we, like the Greeks of this story, would not hear a sermon but "see" Jesus, it will mean surrender to him as he surrendered to the will of his Father. That's still the stumbling block; we don't want to surrender to anyone. Yet surrender to this self-giving love is still the way to life. For when the One who struggled with loud cries and tears between the lines is lifted up on the object of defeat, death is defeated. He will draw all men and women to himself; then will God's name be fully glorified.—Gary D. Stratman

Topic: As the Curtain Is Torn in Twain

Text: Matt. 27:45–54

The people of Israel took a major step from primitive idol worship when they are realized, first of all, that there was only one God and then a further step when they saw that he could not be represented in any way by anything made by men. Though from time to time they reverted to old ways, they recognized the sin of idolatry and followed the commandment "Thou shalt have no other gods before me." That did not keep them, however, from wanting to keep God boxed in, and the Temple in Jerusalem was an apt symbol for that desire.

I. The Temple, first built by Solomon and later added to by others, including Herod, was an architectural wonder. Thirty thousand slaves were required to build the original Temple over a seven-year period. Inside it measured approximately thirty meters by ten meters and

was fifteen meters high. On the front was a large entrance hall ten meters wide, set off by two huge brass columns. The walls were nine feet thick. The interior was done all in fine wood, mainly cedar and cypress, inlaid with gold.

The Holy of Holies, the inner sanctum where the Ark of the Covenant was kept, contained two huge cherubim of gold-trimmed olive wood, each fifteen feet high and with a fifteen foot wingspan. Beneath these wings the Ark, containing the tablets of the Ten Commandments, a vessel containing manna, and the rod of Aaron, reposed. All the wainscotted walls were filled with carved figures of gourds, cherubim, palm trees, and flowers. Leading to the Holy of Holies there was a double door of olive wood decorated in the same way as the walls.

A later addition to the Temple was the veil that covered the area in front of the Ark. It was figured with cherubim on blue, purple, and scarlet material and fine-twined linen and was hung by clasps from four pillars of acacia wood. All of these beautiful buildings and furnishings were constructed with the best of intentions. Beginning with King David himself, the people realized that it was not right for them to live in fancy houses and for the house of the Lord to be a dilapidated tent. They wanted to communicate to the world that they worshiped the Lord God of Abraham, Isaac, and Jacob supremely, and therefore they built an edifice that sent that message clearly with the magnificent Temple.

This did not prevent them, however, from attempting to keep God in a box. You see, by far the single most important spot in all of Israel from a religious, cultural, and national point of view was behind that veil in the Temple, where the Ark of the Covenant was kept. Once a year, on the Day of Atonement, the high priest would step behind the curtain, stand before the mercy seat, and utter the name of God. With elaborate ceremony that involved a week of personal purification and an all-night vigil, the priest would enter the Holy of Holies four separate times to offer blood sacrifices for the priests and then the people.

Then he would consecrate a goat known as the scapegoat. On it he would symbolically place the sins of the people and then send it out into the wilderness, finally uttering the words from Psalm 103: "As far as the east is from the west, so far does he remove our transgressions from us."

It was a deeply moving and highly significant ceremony, demonstrating the Israelites' understanding of their absolute dependence on God and their need for repentance and forgiveness. It was nonetheless yet another attempt to keep God in a box, albeit a much fancier one. Though they certainly believed that God was at work in the world, if you had asked any good Jew where God might be found, he would unhesitatingly have replied, In the Temple.

II. An event happened in A.D. 33, however, that brought this entire notion of a God who could be kept in a box into question. On a dark and troubling day in that year, during the Passover season the veil of the Temple was torn in two, all the way from the top to the bottom. The top of the curtain was so high and the tear so complete that it was impossible for anyone to see how a human hand could have done it. Later the writers of the New Testament made a significant correlation. They noted that the tearing of the temple veil took place at the precise moment that Jesus of Nazareth was being crucified. Although Matthew, Mark, and Luke state this simply and without commentary, it is obvious that they believed that the two events were profoundly related, that the Crucifixion was the cause of the rending of the veil.

III. The theological implications of this are tremendous. By the death of Jesus Christ the partition between God and man has been broken down forever. No longer does one make sacrifices of animals to obtain God's forgiveness of sins. No longer does a priest mediate between God and ourselves. In Christ we have the perfect priest who makes intercession on our behalf with the Father so our sins are forgiven immediately upon their confession and not on a single annual Day of Atonement. In a complete way Jesus

Christ destroyed our notion of a God in the box who could be hemmed into a particular place and only approached in a certain way by a few individuals. The message of the death of Christ is that we all have a way to the Father.

This understanding became God's revelation to us through the author of the Book of Hebrews. In the ninth chapter he explained the Hebrew sacrificial system.

The author of Hebrews, as the spokesman for God, was telling us not only that Christ was allowing everyone of us into the Holy of Holies, the place where the Israelites felt that they met God. He was also letting God out and into their lives where he had always belonged.

IV. We must still remind ourselves that God cannot be placed in a box, no matter how beautiful that box may be. Like the earliest human beings we can continue to construct for ourselves idols, and this building can become one of them. If we want to have the best or the most beautiful of everything so that we can brag that we have more than other churches, that is idolatry. If we think of our salvation in terms of our attendance in this building, rather than through our faith in God, that is idolatry. If in any way our membership in this church becomes a substitute for our membership in the larger family of God, and if we cannot see beyond our own church family to the greater interest that God has in all mankind, that is idolatry.

Please do not hear me saying that we should not try to make this building as attractive as possible. On the contrary, because the appearance of this place makes a strong statement about our seriousness in offering the best that we have to God, we must do everything we can to ensure that our impression to the community is the best that we can make.

Certainly most of us have matured beyond the point where we have thought of the church as what we served. Though we serve *through* the church we serve the Lord. We know that salvation is not based on a place but on a relationship with a person, God himself through Jesus Christ. That does not prevent us, however, from still trying to keep God in a box.

If our attendance at worship and our membership in the church makes no difference in the way we lead our lives every day we are still trying to keep God in this beautiful box that he has allowed us to create here for ourselves. And we have missed the single most important point in the single most important event in the history of the world.—James M. King

Topic: The Wonder of Christ's Resurrection

TEXT: 1 Cor. 15:20–28

The Seven Wonders of the World are notable objects in the world. This list began in ancient times when Greeks and Romans compiled lists of memorable things travelers should see. The first list was called the Seven Ancient Wonders of the World and included the pyramids of Egypt; the hanging gardens of Babylon; the temple of Artemis at Ephesus; the statue of Zeus at Olympia, Greece; the mausoleum at Halicarnassus in present-day Turkey; the Colossus of Rhodes, and the lighthouse of Alexandria, Egypt. Since the time of the original listing of seven ancient wonders, two additional lists have been created: (1) the seven natural wonders and (2) the seven modern wonders.

Christ's Resurrection from the dead is the wonder of the Christian faith. Nowhere in the Bible can we find a more complete explanation of Christ's Resurrection than in 1 Corinthians 15. This chapter makes clear the connection between the Resurrection of Jesus and the resurrection of believers. This connection is reason for wonder. What makes Christ's Resurrection the wonder of Christian faith?

I. Because Jesus was resurrected, we will be resurrected (v. 20). The reference to "firstfruits" reminds us of the Jewish practice of offering the first bundles of grain to God as a token of the entire crop. This act showed faith that God would bless the land with a full harvest. Just as giving the firstfruits was proof of a fuller harvest to come, so Christ's Res-

urrection is proof of the believer's resurrection.

Other people had been raised from the dead (Lazarus and the son of the widow of Nain). But Jesus was uniquely the first to come forth from a tomb, permanently and eternally, a foretaste of what was one day to be the experience of every believer. We who trust in him will have a resurrection like his.

II. Because Jesus was resurrected, we will not die in our sins (vv. 21–22). The two references to "man" in these verses point out the contrast between Adam and Christ. In Adam, all persons sinned, therefore, in Adam, all persons must die. Though death came by Adam, life came by Jesus Christ. Death entered the world through Adam, but resurrection from the dead came through Jesus Christ.

These verses do not mean that all persons will be saved. Universal salvation is not implied. But all persons who place their faith in Jesus, the resurrected One, die knowing they will not die with their sins charged against them.

III. Because Jesus was resurrected, we will share in his dominion (vv. 23–28). The word *coming* (v. 23) is the Greek world *parousia*, the New Testament word for Christ's return. At his coming, Christ will resurrect believers (v. 23), deliver his kingdom to God (v. 24), put down all evil (vv. 24–25), destroy death (v. 26), and surrender his divine reign to God (vv. 27–28).

The words of verses 23–28 call for reverence and awe rather than rhetoric and argument. Paul did not explain fully all that we would like to know. But verses 23–28 do give us hope. We will have a share in that experience in which Christ will have dominion over all. How do we know this? Jesus is "the firstfruits of them that slept" (v. 20). The dominion we share with him in this life is only a foretaste of that which is to come at the resurrection.—Gary Hardin

Topic: It's Easter ... Can You Believe It?

TEXT: 1 Cor. 15:47–58

In spite of the flowers and the springtime, in spite of the music and the celebration, in spite of the Bible and the tradition, it's not all that easy to believe in Easter.

In fact, there are a lot of reasons not to believe it. Our world looks a lot more like a Good Friday place than an Easter Sunday place. Crucifixions always seem more numerous than resurrections. We—like Pilate—hear the words "You're not Caesar's friend," and our principles get quickly compromised, our hands washed. Like the crowd that watched him die and then walked away beating their breasts, we may beat our breasts or wring our hands over injustice—but guilt doesn't necessarily lead to action.

Indeed, there are so many reasons not to believe that Easter makes any real difference. Brute strength seems always to prevail over weakness. Reality seems stronger than mystery. Hard facts turn dreams into dust.

And yet (those are the church's two words on Easter; they're synonymous with "despite appearances"), in that strange interplay between the crucifying power of Rome and the naked vulnerability of the one crucified (and after two thousand years), we now know Pontius Pilate only because of the man whom he sent to the cross. We mark time, not by the caesars, but by the Christ. And ancient Israel holds a single tomb more renowned than all its temples and the Herods who built them—and that tomb is empty. There's a lesson in that about history, about reality, and about where real power comes from.

I. Indeed Jesus' death, which looked like the end of everything, was not the end of anything; it was the beginning of something coming into focus, namely, a love which is strong enough to forgive us and save us.

It's coming into focus, but it's always been here—because God is, always was, and shall ever be love. That love is described in the Hebrew Scriptures. It's described and defined and acknowledged. But it is in the cross that that love is laid out so blatantly bare; it is there, on the tree, that the steadfast love of God really starts coming into focus. It would be pretty hard to trust—or even believe—in a God who didn't know something about pain and grief and loneliness. Where's the love in cool detachment? Where's the caring in being removed from it all?

But, you see, among the things which Jesus brought out of the grave with him were scars in his side and his hands and his feet. "Thomas, put your fingers here, reach out your hand. Stop doubting and believe." Believe what? That the Lord is alive, yes, but believe what those scars tell you—you can trust in this love. For all the sin that is in you, there is more grace in God, God who is acquainted with our kind of grief and sorrow.

And so as Donald Baillie said (in the finest book on the Incarnation I've ever read), the most remarkable fact in the history of religious thought is that when the earliest believers looked back and pondered the cross, that dreadful thing made them think of the love of God—not simply the love of Jesus, but the love of God![1]

How desperately he must love us! How deeply he must yearn for us to turn toward home and forgiveness and salvation!

You can believe that now. It's Easter! It's true! The cross is all changed—from a killing stake to a tree of new life. And the difference between Judas and Simon Peter is that one settled for a Good Friday world, while the other caught on to Easter. Here is Judas turning Jesus over to the authorities. His great failure is not in his betrayal but in not coming back to ask for forgiveness. He's paralyzed by his guilt, stuck in his sin, clutching his mistake like it's the most precious thing in the world. So he cashes in his life.

Simon failed Jesus badly, too, with that courtyard cowardice about not knowing him at all. But what Simon did know, which Judas didn't, is that the sinfulness which is in us does not run as deeply as God's love for us. So later, in an Easter world, he let go of his guilt and accepted forgiveness. The cross has that sort of

[1]*God Was in Christ* (New York: Charles Scribner's Sons, 1948), 184f.

power, if you will trust the God who loves you there.

Jesus Christ alive changes crosses! Can you believe it?

II. Some other things started coming into focus on Easter morning as well, beliefs which had been around since the beginning of the human race, convictions voiced by the poets and the prophets of Israel. But now, since that cross and empty tomb, they're clearer and stronger.

(a) For instance, evil is not the most powerful force in the world. I don't live by faith in Jesus Christ just so I can run and hide from brutal reality. Faith has to be tough-skinned and clear-headed in a world like this. But Easter faith is that when evil took its best shot—the crucifying of God's best—evil over-reached itself. In that moment, evil fell into the trap of an overcoming love and was conquered. The last word was not evil's on Friday afternoon; it was God's on Easter morning!

And so the direction of history was set, despite the tragedy and inhumanity which still befall us. In the referendum of good versus evil, the Resurrection of Christ says it's going to turn out all right. That comes clear on Easter morning. Can you believe it?

(b) Also, this comes into focus: We do not travel alone. Now, it's no accident that the Holy Spirit quickly became the glue which bonded the believers in Christ together. Their Lord was alive and among them. The familiar face hasn't been with us for centuries, but the familiar presence has never left.

Resurrection means a people to journey with and One at our side in struggle and in service and in celebration. We're not alone! And that gives us staying power and strength for the journey. Can you believe it?

(c) Then, of course, there's this: Death is not the end of life. "Death has been swallowed up in victory," writes Paul to the Corinthians—not because of the logic of human life or any proofs for immortality but because God "gives us the victory through our Lord Jesus Christ." Life imperishable is ours by faith in a risen Christ. As Dr. Fosdick used to say, this sea upon which we sail has another shore. Christ has sailed there and touched it and now beckons us to take heart as we follow: "I go to prepare a place for you. And when I go . . . I will come again and will take you to myself, that where I am you may be also" (John 14:2b–3).

Faith in a risen Christ does not cancel death—it just conquers it. Can you believe it?

(d) One other thing: Hope is an honest way to live. Hope's pretty hard to come by sometime. French philosopher Gabriel Marcel said that the great curse of modern society is our absence of hoping, as if the very possibility of hoping has been blunted by life's random hurts.

So how can we live out of hope, and how honest can that be? We can't do it on desire or human optimism; those get disappointed as often as they get rewarded. Hope can't feed on the thinness of wishful thinking.

Is there anything more solid to base it on? I believe so. How about Christ alive, conquering evil and smashing death and ending isolation?

That's where Paul comes out in our text for this morning. After nearly fifty verses on the Resurrection—after arguing the case that Christ alive gives power over death, he says, "Live right now!"

"Therefore, my dear brothers, stand firm. Let nothing move you. Always give yourselves fully to the work of the Lord, because you know that your labor in the Lord is not in vain" (v. 58). "Your life is anchored in Christ, so live in hope! Your existence is not useless—the risen Christ calls you to join him in his work of ministry and witness."

Hope is believing that that's truth. In the shifting sands and changing fortunes of life, Jesus Christ alive tells me that God can be counted on.—William L. Turner

Topic: A Revolutionary Truth: The Lordship of Christ

Text: Phil. 2:5–11

Would you believe it if I told you that there is a truth that can change your life?

If you get hold of this truth your life will be different. Of course, you may not look different. You will still be short or tall; your skin will be the same color; you will have the same quality in your voice. Yet you will be different—as different as what the Apostle Paul wrote about: a new creation. Old things gone; the new present.

The apostle wrote to a church where the need for change was urgent. The church at Philippi was about to be torn apart because two women leaders in the congregation were involved in a dispute that was known by everyone. No doubt, church members had chosen sides. "Euodia is right, and I'm behind her." "No, she is wrong; I'm behind Syntyche." And so it went. Paul addressed these two women by name and pleaded with them to get together, to compose their differences.

But note this! Paul pleaded with them on the basis of the most powerful motivation possible for Christians to do the right thing in a bad situation. He quoted a hymn that these Christians may have sung every Sunday. The hymn held a key that could turn the bickering congregation, following the lead of two prominent women, into a group of people who truly loved one another.

Could it be that the truth that Paul held out to Christians so long ago is what will make our lives new and vibrant and useful? Could it be that it is this truth which could change us into the kind of persons that we ought to be, that deep in our heart we want to be?

The transforming truth is the lordship of Jesus Christ—nothing more, nothing less. It is so simple that we could miss its power to change us, redirect our lives, and usher us into a new era of joy and fulfillment.

I. What is the lordship of Christ?

(a) The Sermon on the Mount ends with this observation: "When Jesus had finished saying these things, the crowds were amazed at his teaching, because he taught as one who had authority, and not as their teachers of the law" (Matt. 7:28–29, NIV). The scribes of Jesus' time gave their opinion of what Moses meant when he said things. What Jesus said was not mere opinion or human interpretation—it was the Word of God. Jesus even challenged the most ancient authority when he said, " 'You have heard it said . . . but I tell you . . . ' " (Matt. 5:38–39, NIV). When I was in high school, I heard John R. Sampey, then president of the Southern Baptist Theological Seminary, saying about this text, "I'll take Jesus to Moses anytime."

What Jesus taught cut across the grain so much that people did, and therefore appeared to be unrealistic or sentimental. But the centuries have proved him right. Even Bertrand Russell, a self-professed agnostic, said in so many words that what this world needs is a good dose of the Christian religion.

(b) Look at Jesus' miracles. These signs point to his lordship. Jesus and his disciples were in a boat on the Sea of Galilee when a fierce storm blew up, and the lives of all were at risk. Jesus was asleep in the stern, and it seemed to the disciples that he did not care what happened to them. The disciples roused him up, and he spoke to the wind and the sea, and a great calm settled on the water. All were safe. The disciples were awestruck and said to one another, "Even the wind and the sea obey him."

Did this not show Jesus' lordship over nature—that God was in complete control over his universe? But why was this story reported in the Gospels? Surely not just to be of comfort to people traveling on the seas, though it was no doubt important for precisely that reason. But not exclusively! This story also meant that Jesus' followers of whatever age could count on the Lord of the universe to speak to any kind of storm, a storm of persecution or suffering, and bring a great calm—peace in the heart if nowhere else.

(c) Yes, we see the lordship of Christ in the authority of his teaching and in his signs and wonders. But we see it also in his Resurrection—especially there. "If Christ has not been raised, your faith is futile; you are still in your sins," wrote Paul (1 Cor. 15:17, NIV). In other words, Jesus' teaching would come to nothing and his miracles would have no meaning without his Resurrection from the dead. Once more, Paul wrote that Jesus "through the Spirit of holiness was declared with power to be the Son of God by his Resurrection from the dead" (Rom. 1:3–4, NIV).

(d) Jesus' lordship is grounded in something God did: Jesus did not raise himself, nor did his disciples resuscitate him. God raised him from the dead. We have some beautiful symbols that we use at Easter to point to Jesus' Resurrection and emphasize the triumph of life over death. They perhaps help us to understand some things about Easter, but no symbol or comparison quite does the job. The butterfly emerging from the chrysalis and the cocoon into majestic and colorful life suggests to us that there is a higher form of life into which one may pass after this life. The coming of springtime also suggests that after the suffering and death of winter, life is victorious and that a kind of Resurrection happens over and over again.

The Resurrection of Jesus Christ is of such cosmic proportions, and the Book of Revelation sings of him, "Worthy is the Lamb, who was slain, to receive power and wealth and wisdom and strength and honor and glory and praise!" (Rev. 5:12, NIV). The hymn in our text puts it this way:

"Who, being in very nature God, did not consider equality with God something to be grasped, but made himself nothing, taking the very nature of a servant, being made in human likeness. And being found in appearance as a man, he humbled himself and became obedient to death—even death on a cross! Therefore God exalted him to the highest place and gave him the name that is above every name, that at the name of Jesus every knee should bow, in heaven and on earth and under the earth, and every tongue confess that Jesus Christ is Lord, to the glory of God the Father" (Phil. 2:6–11, NIV).

II. What does lordship do in our lives?

So we have the lordship of Christ. Now what does it mean in practical terms? Such questions do not trivialize so mighty

a truth. The practical question was the apostle's reason for quoting the hymn in the first place.

(a) The lordship of Christ puts us right with God the Father. Because Jesus Christ is Lord, we have access to the Father. He clears the way through all our sins and weaknesses and opens the way to the Father's heart. One of the most moving sermons I ever heard was a portrayal by a friend of a sermon he heard by a preacher in Wales, his native land. It was a courtroom scene: God the Father was judge. A sinner stood before him, guilty because he had broken God's law. But one stood with the guilty sinner as his advocate, his attorney—Jesus Christ, God's own Son. And Jesus pleaded that the man be forgiven because Jesus himself had paid the debt required by the law. So the Father, the judge, pronounced the sinner forgiven and free, for God's own Son had paid the price with his own blood.

What a wonderful truth: Jesus Christ sets us free from the law of sin and death. Our Lord Jesus Christ is the means by whom we become reconciled to God. Thanks be to God, we can be and are put right with God because Jesus Christ is Lord and thus is able to bring our salvation to pass.

(b) The lordship of Christ puts us right with one another. You and I need some reason outside ourselves to get along with one another. We are born selfish and grasping, and rivalry is a part of our lives. This competitiveness may be deeply buried, but it is always there. It can be controlled and trained; it can become healthy and creative, but it is always there.

As we have seen, the women, leaders in the church at Philippi, were involved in a dispute that threatened to tear the church apart. The conflict at Philippi must have been extremely serious, otherwise Paul would not have singled out the contenders, calling them by name. "I plead with Euodia and I plead with Syntyche to agree with each other in the Lord" (Phil. 4:2, NIV).

"In the Lord"! What a remarkable phrase! That was the one hope that everything would be made right between two Christian women and that others drawn by them into the dispute might become friends again. It would not only mean that they themselves would be spared distress and heartache and sleepless nights, but it would also mean that people could get back to the central concerns of true Christians: to love, care for, and serve one another, and work together toward a common goal. I can imagine that those two women somewhere along the way remembered this hymn that Paul pointed them toward, and they agreed, "If Jesus Christ is Lord, then we are going about this business in the wrong way. Each of us is trying to prove that she is better than the other, more deserving, and ought to be followed more closely than the other. If Jesus Christ is Lord, then we ought, both of us, to be following him, even if it is painful sometimes to admit that we are wrong. If we agree together, perhaps we can get others who are not speaking to agree with one another also."

After all, he said to his first disciples: "A new commandment I give you: Love one another" (John 13:34, NIV). And because he is Lord, that means us, too.

(c) Furthermore, recognizing this lordship of Jesus Christ will put us right toward life. When I believe in my heart that Jesus Christ is Lord, my outlook toward everything will take on a new tone. That may be long in coming. It may happen gradually, but come it will. When I was a teenager, I heard a man say, "There are some things in that Bible that I wish were not in there." When the pressure of temptation is strong upon us and we want to do a particular thing, we too might wish certain commandments in the Bible were not there. But how foolish! To think like that is like thinking that the guard rails on a winding mountain road should be removed; that the brakes on the family car should be removed; that all stop signs and traffic signals should be removed. The lordship of Jesus Christ, however, changes such thinking. We begin to think God's way about everything. Our work, our recreation, our politics— everything will be affected. As someone

put it a long time ago: "He will be Lord of all, or he will not be Lord at all."

There is everything to gain when Christ is Lord. Every loss is gain. Look at Jesus. He did not lay claim to equality with God but made himself nothing, assuming the form of a slave. Yet by walking the path of humiliation and the cross, Jesus gained the name above all names.

What is in it for you and me if we take to heart what we find in Christ Jesus, in his lordship? if we model his example? It will mean the approval of God. Just as God the Father approved Jesus, saying, in a way, "Well done, my good and faithful Son," so he will say to us, "Well done, my good and faithful child."

God's approval alone ought to be enough, I suppose, but following the example of our Lord should bring us the joy of the respect and love of others. The thought of the selfless service of such persons as Albert Schweitzer and Mother Teresa wells up in our hearts as a flood of gratitude and affection. Yet even if our deeds are small and unspectacular, they will not go unnoticed.

There is a price to pay for God's approval and for the joy of doing those things that bless our neighbors. The Lord who pleased God, his Father, and was the name above all names had to be willing to go to the cross to bring it to pass. This same Lord says to you and me, "If anyone would come after me, he must deny himself and take up his cross and follow me" (Mark 8:34, NIV). There is really no other way.—James W. Cox

ILLUSTRATIONS

BY ROBERT C. SHANNON

GOOD AND LASTING GRACE.   Once there was a superstition, in some parts of Europe that bread baked on Good Friday would stay fresh all year long! No one knows what gave rise to the superstition but what is needed is for the faith of Good Friday to stay fresh all year long! We need to keep the sense of gratitude, the sense of being loved, the sense of grace that comes to us on Good Friday. If we do, then the Bread of Life will stay fresh all year long!

THE VICTORIOUS CHRIST.   The lamb carrying a flag or banner has long been a symbol of the victorious Christ. Some used to say that if you took smoked glass and looked at the sun on Easter Sunday morning you could see that very symbol, the lamb and the flag of victory. Not true, of course. Besides looking at the sun is bad for your eyes, even with sunglasses on. No, on Easter Sunday morning let us look at the Son, S-o-n, and revel once again in his victory.

LIFE BEFORE AND AFTER DEATH.   Scattered around the United States are several bodies, lying frozen in nitrogen. The families of these dead hope that science will find a way to cure the disease that took their loved one's life. Then the bodies will be thawed out, the new procedures performed, and there will be life after death. It is called the science of cryobiology. Christians await no new discoveries and depend on no scientific measures but believe that life after death is a present reality. They are convinced by the Resurrection of Jesus Christ!

OUR LORD'S CROWN.   During World War II the Allies captured some Hungarian army officers and discovered that they had in their possession the symbol of Hungarian nationhood, the crown of St. Stephen. It was given to Stephen I, Hungary's first king, by Pope Sylvester II in the year 1000. The Americans brought it to the United States and kept it at Fort Knox, Kentucky. Finally, under President Jimmy Carter's administration, it was returned to Hungary. On earth our Lord wore no crown except the crown of thorns. But when Calvary was finished, the Resurrection had taken place, and Jesus had ascended, he received back again the crown that had eternally been his.

SECTION VI.
Advent and Christmas Preaching

SERMON SUGGESTIONS

Topic: Advent Meditation
TEXT: Josh. 10:15–27, reading *Joshua* as *Yeshua*

We leap forward more than twelve centuries to the circumcision ceremony of a certain baby named John, son of Zechariah. Later history will come to know him as John the Baptist. We are told that at this occasion John's father, the old priest Zechariah "was filled with the Holy Spirit" (read Luke 1:67–74).

We move forward thirty more years. It is the feast of the Pentecost. The streets of Jerusalem are jammed with pilgrims, pilgrims who came to celebrate an old festival but who will return home having heard the first sermon to be preached by a follower of Jesus (in the Hebrew, Yeshua). We listen in on the end of that sermon: Acts 2:32–36, reading *Jesus* as *Yeshua*.

And finally, twenty years after that, the Apostle Paul writes concerning this Yeshua: 1 Cor. 15:25–26.

I. Think about Zechariah, father of John the Baptist, for a few moments with me. As I reflect on this prophecy of victory—a hymn really about liberation, the raising up of a mighty savior named Yeshua, and the salvation of Israel from her enemies—as I reflect on his words I can't help but wonder what he meant. I mean, what did he really think was going to happen?

Did Zechariah understand his talk about liberation from enemies at the hand of this Yeshua to come in ways similar to the liberation offered Israel by the Yeshua of old? Did Zechariah have visions of a Yeshua who would pursue the enemies of his nation, place his foot triumphantly upon their necks, kill them, hang them from trees for all to see, and then seal them up in a cave?

Or did this old priest who was, we are told, filled with the Holy Spirit have enough of a filling to understand that the Yeshua about whom he sang praises would be very different from the Yeshua of old? In the life of this Yeshua of new, there would be a killing; there would be a hanging from a tree; there would be a sealing in a cave. But it would be so different from the killing, the hanging, and the sealing involving the Yeshua of old. Now, it is true that the Yeshua of old and the Yeshua of new would have *one* thing very much in common besides their names. Each would place his enemies under his feet. But then, once again, we quickly see that new wine will not go into the old skins. For the enemies of the Yeshua to come would not be the kings who oppressed Israel. It would not be the Herods or the Pilates or the Caesars who would feel the heel of Yeshua against their necks.

Yeshua, Son of God, identified his real enemies when, as a grown man, John, son of Zechariah, asked Jesus from the damp cell of Herod where he sat rotting awaiting his execution, "Are you the one who is to come, or should we look for someone else? Are you the one my father

256

sang so joyfully about? Are you the one who has come to conquer our enemies, or aren't you?" Luke tells us that "Yeshua, had just then cured many people of diseases, plagues, and evil spirits and had given sight to many who were blind." Luke then narrates that, in response to John's inquiry, Jesus said simply, "The blind receive their sight, the lame walk, the lepers are cleansed, the deaf hear, the dead are raised, the poor have good news brought to them."

II. The words of the old priest Zechariah ring in our ears: "We shall be saved from our enemies and from the hand of all who hate us!" But as he stood at the crossroads of the ages, that hinge of time separating the old covenant from the new, which way was he looking? Was he looking back to the victories of the Yeshua of old and hoping for more of the same? Or did he dare to wonder if the Yeshua of new might take a different course? Did he understand that, as vile and unjust as those kings were who oppressed Israel, the Yeshua who was to come had even bigger enemies to conquer—the enemies of the demonic, disease, and death? Did he recognize that these were the real enemies of God?

In the context of sacred time offered by the liturgical calendar, we stand once again at the crossroads of history, at that hinge of time separating the old from the new. We stand with Zechariah singing of the victory over our enemies, which God has promised. And as we stand at this juncture of sacred history we cannot ignore the events taking place at the juncture of profane history where we now also stand. And at this threatening juncture we hear talk of an enemy, another Herod, some have even said another Hitler. The threats of this enemy are real; we do not help the cause of justice to ignore them. But as we stand on the hinge of history with Zechariah praising God for his promised victory over the enemies, which way are we looking? From which Yeshua do we take our cue? Whom do we understand the real enemies of God to be? Do we look for the defeat of God's enemies in the grinding of our heels into the neck of this other

Herod? Or will we dare to look for God's most audacious power over his enemies in those unnoticed efforts of the little ones who, after the Lord has come again once again, will labor in the cities; who will work and serve the people of Jamaica; who will construct a clinic in Haiti; who will build a home in Guatemala; who will give the cup of cold water to the thirsty, the coat to the naked, the word of comfort to the bereaved? It is in those forces which oppress and deprive that we come face-to-face with the enemies of God. And it is against these that the Yeshua of new leads the charge.

And so it is fitting that we should pray with Zechariah, "God of Abraham, grant us rescue from the hands of our enemies." But we should pray also, "Grant us vision to recognize your enemies. Grant us faith to pursue them in the manner of the Yeshua of new, who called us to take up the cross and to follow him. Even so, Lord Jesus, come again once again. Amen."—Brad Chance

Topic: For Us and For Our Salvation
Text: Luke 2:10–11
"For us men and for our salvation, he came down from heaven . . . and was made man" (Nicene Creed).

The story of Christmas, as you have just read to you from the Gospel according to Luke, is simple and clear and well known to us all. Its author was divinely inspired, so it is also the Word of God. And as if all that were not enough, it is in fact our only source of information about the birth of Christ.

That being so, what can we add to the Bible account? What can we say that has not already been said, either by the inspired writer or by Christian saints and thinkers down through the ages? Is it possible for any homilist to say anything new this Christmas Day? Or even something old presented in a new way?

Nevertheless, I should like to invite you to ask yourselves two short questions. One about the mystery we celebrate today and the other about its meaning in your life and mine.

I. *The Why? of the Incarnation and of*

Christmas. The first question attempts to get behind the well-known narrative of Christ's birth as a Son of man. Assuming that you already know what happened and that your Christian faith assures you that he is indeed the Son of God, born on earth of a human mother, let's ask ourselves, Why?

Why? is a good question, after all. Children ask it all the time. A wise man of old once wrote that all philosophy begins with wonder. All philosophy and all science—and all theology, too. Any process that makes human beings think begins with wondering why something happens. Why Christmas? Why the Incarnation? Why did the Word become flesh and dwell among us?

It must be admitted that there could be several answers. God willed it so; and "for this reason, when he (Christ) came into the world, he said . . . Behold, I come to do your will, O God" (Heb. 10:5–7). Moreover, "God so loved the world that he gave his only Son" (John 3:16). These are good answers and true ones. But we might find another answer or another way of putting it in the age-old words of the Nicene Creed: "For us men [that is, for us human beings] and for our salvation he came down from heaven and was made man."

For our salvation! That was the will of God which Christ came to accomplish. Salvation! That was the gift of God's love in giving the world his Son. Salvation! That was the content of the "good news of great joy for all people"; namely, that "a Savior had been born" (Luke 2:10–11). It is indeed good news to know that we will live forever in happiness with God our Father, that "we are even now children of God" (1 John 3:1). Salvation is good news, and the gospel, the "good news" par excellence, is this: that now there is salvation available to us all.

II. *The meaning of Christmas for our lives.* The second question I'd like to ask you to ask yourselves today is about the meaning of Christmas for your own lives, the consequences that will follow from knowing and believing and understanding that Christ came to bring salvation to our world. If you want to frame that query

very shortly, in another of those monosyllabic questions that children make frequent use of, I would suggest "So???" A *so* delivered with that certain inflection that implies a "So what?" or "What kind of inference do you want to draw from what you just said?"

To begin with, if our salvation is so important to God that for it he gave his only begotten Son; if it is so important that for it the Son of God took on our humanity with all its consequences, then salvation ought to be a high priority in our own personal lives as well. The highest! Eternal salvation, the endless happiness of sharing God's life in heaven and even now on earth, must be something far more valuable and far more important than most people rate it among their goals and reasons for living.

Furthermore, if salvation is a gift of God, bought so dearly, we ought to take the trouble of reaching out to accept that gift. God reaches out to us—that is the plain message of Christmas, of the Incarnation, of the coming of Christ to earth as man. Now you have to reach out to God. If you don't take the trouble, the gift will never be yours. God offers you salvation, in Christ. He isn't going to twist your arm and make you take it.

How do you reach out and take it? By faith, motivated by love. Christ is God's supreme and ultimate revelation. Revelation is God's action, God reaching out to us. Faith is our human response, reaching out to meet God's outstretched hand. Reach out, then, and touch Someone. Touch the hand of God, touch Christ, with your faith. A faith that believes in salvation and accepts it. A faith that accepts Christ as your Savior and is glad.

Perhaps a comparison would help here, a little parable from life in our modern world. A person may have a fortune made over to them and on deposit for them in a bank or some other financial institution. That person will have the possibility, say, of living like a millionaire. But that same person could live in poverty and die in destitution if he or she fails to go to the bank and draw out money from that account and make use of his or her riches.

This is what actually happened to an elderly relative of some friends of mine. The relative in question was an old woman who had lived on welfare, just barely getting by in her poor and barren little flat. When she died, back in the late 1940s, they found among her effects some papers which she had never understood. They were stocks and bonds that made her, on paper at least, a millionairess. They dated back some twenty years, before the great stock market crash of 1929, and for a number of years afterward they had seemed worthless. However, with the upturn in the nation's economy at the time of World War II and after, these companies or entities had recovered their financial status and would have paid off handsomely on those securities to any owner who knew how to clip the coupons and draw the dividends that were his or hers by rights. The little old woman on welfare did not know how to do that; her husband, who had died meanwhile, had never bothered to explain such matters to his wife. It was a generation in which *men* did things like that. Women were supposed to tend to their children and their housework and leave money matters in the hands of their spouses. But whatever the reason why she did not draw on her unsuspected wealth, the fact was that this particular woman could have lived like a millionairess and didn't. All that fortune did her no good at all because she never took the proper steps to draw on it and to draw it into her daily life.

To spell out in practical terms the application of this modern parable to our own circumstances: How can you draw on the wealth of salvation now made over to you, now on deposit, so to speak, with God and his church? How does your faith, in the sense of knowledge and belief, turn into faith in the sense of reaching out to draw on your salvation, which God is offering to you in Christ, reaching out to draw it into your personal life and make use of it?

You have heard the answer already. Many answers or many forms of the same answer. Love God and keep his commandments. Read the Epistle of James and its comments on the kind of faith that is sterile, that just says, "Yes, I believe," and does nothing about it, never translates that belief into a Christian style of living.

And among the many facets, the many components, of a Christian style of living, there is one that is of special importance. That is a regular attendance at Sunday Mass. You get to know a person by spending time with him or her. You get to know Christ by spending time with him. By meeting him here present in his Word and in his sacrament. Here, in your church, you will find the same Christ whom the shepherds found at Bethlehem. Through the message of an angel, God revealed to them the birth of his Son, but they had to take the trouble of going over themselves and having a look. Some of the shepherds did, at least some of them on the testimony of Luke. What he doesn't tell us is whether they all went to Bethlehem to make contact with the infant Christ. Did some of them merely believe the words of the angel without acting on them, without going to Christ in his manger? Did some of the shepherds say they had to work or that it was too far or that they didn't have time?

What would you have said and done if you could have been one of that little band of shepherds to whom the good news was proclaimed that first Christmas night?

What are you going to do about it on this Christmas Day, as the good news of a Savior's birth is proclaimed to you again?

The answer lies within your power. Christ has been born into the world to offer you salvation. What are you to do? My advice to you is simply this: Reach out and take it, while yet there is time.— Vincent Fecher

Topic: The Emotions of Christmas
TEXT: Luke 2

If you had to select one word to most accurately describe the atmosphere of Christmas, what word would you choose? The word that comes to my mind is *emotional*. During the Christmas season, perhaps more so than at any other time of year, our emotions are stirred in some special ways. The incomparable grandeur of the Christmas story, the tinsel and Christmas tree lights, the cards of greeting from our friends, the echoing refrains of Christmas carols, the gifts, the kaleidoscope of colors, the array of Christmas goodies, and the excitement dancing in the eyes of our children. All of these ingredients combine to make Christmas the most emotional time of the year.

What are the emotions of Christmas?

I. *Wonder.* One of the emotions of Christmas is wonder. In our text, Luke attempts to describe the emotions that came bubbling to the surface in the characters of that first Christmas drama. With quick brush strokes, Luke paints a picture of a baby being born, angels filling the heavens, and shepherds kneeling in stunned amazement, listening to the heavenly chorus. Then in verse 18 he says, "And all who heard it wondered at the things which were told them by the shepherds" (NASB).

Their wonder should be no surprise because their silent night had been split with the glorious presence of God. The world of man had been invaded by the Word of God. All the hopes of all the ages had been fulfilled in this one spectacular night, yet it happened so differently from what man had expected.

When we think, for instance, of the love of Mary and Joseph, we wonder. It is easy for us to miss the incredible dimension of their love. The first Christmas event presented their love with an awesome challenge. Their marriage had not been consummated when Mary conceived her son. Pregnancy before marriage is not so uncommon today, but for two pious Hebrews in the first century this was a crisis of unbelievable magnitude. Imagine the questions, the doubts, the misgivings, and the confusion that engulfed both of them, especially Joseph. It would have been the natural thing for Joseph to break his engagement with Mary, for he was sure of one thing—the baby she was carrying was not his.

But because of his love for Mary he turned his back on the wagging tongues of the community, he swallowed his pride, and he accepted the incredible announcement of the angel that this was a special child given by God. And when we think of Joseph's love, we wonder.

When we think of the love of Mary for her son, we wonder. Verse 19 says, "Mary kept all these things and pondered them in her heart." Here we have an insight into the strain which from beginning to end was placed on the love of this mother. She pondered these things in her heart, but how little she understood what they really meant. How perplexed she must have been by the happenings which revolved around her son.

Before her son was ten days old, shepherds came, claiming that they had been told of him by special messengers from God.

Wise men came from afar, worshiping her son as the newborn king.

Two old saints in the Temple—Simon and Anna—told Mary they could die in peace now because in the face of her infant they had seen the hopes and fears of all the years.

At the age of twelve her son was already a match for the scholars of Israel.

At the age of thirty her son became one of the most popular figures in the land.

At the age of thirty-three her son was nailed to a cross as a criminal between two thieves, and she was there to watch him—suspended between the earth and the sky and left in the scorching sun to die.

What an incredible strain was put on that mother's love. Yet through it all—from the spectacular beginning to the uncertainty of his ministry to the crushing cross to the final victory—Mary loved her son dearly. She never gave him up. When we see her love, we wonder.

When we think of the love of God for us, we wonder. Even greater than Joseph's love for Mary, even greater than Mary's love for her son, is the love God had for us when he sent his only begotten Son.

We have become so accustomed to the Christmas story, so dulled to its incredible message. But as we catch again the full panorama of splendor which the

Christmas story presents, the emotion of wonder will once more come bubbling to the surface.

II. *Love.* A second emotion of Christmas is love. Matthew in his Gospel tells of a happening at the birth of Jesus that Luke omits: the visit of the magi bearing gifts for the newborn king.

One little boy told his Sunday school teacher that the wise men brought "gold, Frankenstein, and mermaids." Though inaccurate in the details, this little boy caught the spirit of what they did—they brought gifts expressing their love for the newborn king. The gifts were given as an expression of love.

At no other season of the year do we feel warmer toward our fellowman, are we more kind in our relationships, are we more sympathetic toward other's needs, are we more expressive of our love than in the Christmas season.

That is good because if there is anything the world needs, it is love. Love might not make the world go round, but it makes the ride worthwhile, and we need more of it.

Dwight L. Moody, the evangelist, said a long time ago, "I tell you there is one thing that draws above everything else in the world and that is love."

More recently, Karl Menninger said, "Love is the medicine for the sickness of the world."

One of the reasons Christmas is so special is that it calls forth from all of us that love which helps make life easier to bear.

III. *Joy.* Another emotion of Christmas is joy. "Joy to the world, the Lord has come." How vividly that song expresses our emotions at Christmas. I am not talking about the hollow smiles that some paste on their faces to hide the emptiness of their lives or the artificial happiness produced by stimulants. I am talking about the joy that is rooted in a living, personal relationship with Jesus Christ.

Mary felt joy over Jesus. Pervading her whole life was a deep sense of joy which came from her awareness of the part God was allowing her to play in the redemption of the world. Her joy was expressed in song in Luke 1.

The angels felt joy over Jesus. "We bring you good news of great joy," they said. Why? Because this One whose birth they heralded was to become the Savior of the world.

Simeon and Anna in the Temple felt joy over Jesus. Why? Because of the hope which the promised child brought to them in the midst of their problems.

When we realize again the significance of what happened on that special night long ago, we, too, should feel joy. To realize that God loves us enough to come all the way down to where we are—that brings joy. To realize that God loves us enough to become what we are so we can become what he is—that brings joy. To realize that this Jesus whose birth we celebrate is One who can meet every need and provide solutions for every problem and satisfy every longing of our soul—that brings joy.

IV. *Sadness.* Another emotion of Christmas is sadness. This is not a contradiction of what I have just said but a recognition of the fact that, in the midst of all the joy, there are some who find Christmas a depressing time.

Psychologists say that for many people Christmas is the most depressing time of the year. Sometimes the sadness comes because of the demands of the season. To others the sadness comes because they recognize more clearly than at other times the emptiness within. They see another year completed, yet no more has been accomplished in their lives. Most often the sadness of the Christmas season is caused by the awareness that the future will never be exactly like the past. Those who have to face Christmas without a loved one they lost during the year experience a certain degree of sadness in the midst of the Christmas revelry.

Some of the sadness is inevitable. The demands of the season are depressing at times. There are some people whose lives are empty. The facing of Christmas alone does hurt. Some of this sadness is inevitable.

But a rediscovery of the true meaning of Christmas will dispel much of it. For if Christmas means anything, it means hope, fulfillment, and peace. Peace comes because we do not march to the drumbeat of the world but to the drumbeat of the King of kings. Fulfillment comes not from the delicacies on the world's table but from the One who is the Bread of Life. Hope comes not from a denial of death but from the realization that not even death can eternally separate us from those we love in Christ Jesus.

In 1659, the Puritans of Massachusetts passed a "blue law" which levied a fine of four shillings on anyone caught celebrating Christmas, a law which lasted for twenty-two years. I'm glad the law was repealed because we need the stirring of our emotions which the celebration of Christmas provides.—Brian Harbour

Topic: Refugee Child

TEXT: Matt. 2:13–15, 19–23

We often let our reverence for Jesus place a sentimental haze over the harsh human circumstances of his early childhood. Shortly after his birth Jesus was a refugee child. Luther reminds us that, if we really love the baby Jesus, we will serve Christ in our needy neighbor. What have we done for the refugee children in our world?

I. *The warning (v. 13).* Joseph was directed in a dream to take Mary as his wife (1:20). Now like the magi (v. 12) he is warned in another dream about the evil intentions of Herod. The child who will serve others must now flee for his life. The angel's promise to reappear to Joseph when it is time to return from exile is kept, in verse 19.

II. *The flight (vv. 14–15).* Besides its prophetic significance, Egypt was the logical place for the holy family's flight, both for geographical (seventy-five miles to the border) and ethnic reasons. When Alexander the Great founded his new city of Alexandria, Jews were given equal privileges with the Macedonians. Consequently, over the centuries Egypt became the home of many Jewish emigres and deportees.

Matthew quotes Hosea 11:1b as a prophecy fulfilled in this flight. Hosea's prophecy originally referred to the calling out of Israel as a nation from Egypt. Israel is also described as God's Son in

Exod. 4:22 (cf. in addition Jer. 31:9 and the striking parallel in Wisd. of Sol. 18:13). Matthew applies this prophecy typologically to Jesus, who fulfills the mission of Israel on a more universal level. As Tasker comments, "as Moses was called to go to Egypt and rescue Israel, God's son, his firstborn . . . from physical bondage, so Jesus was called out of Egypt in his infancy . . . to save [hu]mankind from the bondage of sin."

III. *The resettlement (vv. 19–23).* Herod's death took place in the Year of Rome 750 (4 B.C.). Joseph is told in a dream to return to Israel (v. 19) and then is warned in yet another dream (v. 22) not to settle in his native province of Judea but to resettle in Galilee. Josephus confirms the validity of the warning about Archelaus being such a bad ruler. In C.E. 6 such damaging complaints were made against Archelaus in Rome that he was deposed and banished to Vienna in Gaul (*Antiquities* 17, 13, 2). In contrast to Archelaus's brief and bitter reign, Herod Antipas ruled in Galilee and Perea until C.E. 39.

The phrase "he will be called a Nazarene" (v. 23) is not a direct quotation of any one Old Testament text. Rather this derisive phrase (cf. John 1:46) represents a way of giving the substance of various prophetic predictions ("what had been spoken through the prophets") regarding the despising of the Messiah (e.g., Isaiah. 53).

As a refugee and as a despised Nazarene, Jesus experienced hardship and prejudice in his childhood. The babe born in a manger experienced the suffering of humanity throughout his life on earth and not just in his death on the cross. The next time we see a refugee child, we are called to remember our Lord who had "nowhere to lay his head" (8:20).—Charles J. Scalise

ILLUSTRATIONS

BY ROBERT C. SHANNON

TINSEL REQUIRED. Writing a few years ago in the *Los Angeles Times,* Zan Thompson said that Christmas is not just for children. "Having outgrown Santa Claus, and after that our parents' tutelage, we grownups see the world with the shine rubbed off, and so a little tinsel is all the more welcome. How else, in the face of ridiculous odds, can we decide to hang in there?"

CHRISTMAS YET. In Scotland and Wales it used to be the custom to take down all the Christmas greenery on January 6, which was known as old Christmas day. It was thought that to fail to remove the decorations by that day would bring bad luck. Our difficulty, of course, is not in getting rid of Christmas promptly but in keeping some of it permanently. When the halls are no longer decked with holly and the Christmas bills come in, we must still hear "Joy to the World" ringing in our hearts.

THE KING. Our Christmas falls in the midst of the old Roman holiday of Saturnalia, which ran from November 30 until February 2. During this time slaves changed places with their masters and even elected a mock king to rule over the festival. Of course, when it was all over they all went back to being slaves again. Is Jesus just king for a day—temporarily

king over a pagan festival? Or is he king of my life? "He rules the world with truth and grace," we sing on Christmas Day. Is it a temporary rule or a permanent one?

THE GIFT OF SPEECH. One English tradition said that at midnight on Christmas Eve cattle and other animals knelt before the Christ child and received the gift of speech. Christmas is a good time for us humans, who have always had the gift of speech, to use it wisely. What better gift could you give yourself or another than to speak a word of kindness, of peace, or reconciliation? What a time to use our tongues for gratitude to others and to God, for prayer and worship and confession and praise.

CHRISTMAS EXORCISM. When the Puritans came to power in England in 1644 they abolished many of the old Christmas customs, some of which certainly had pagan roots. One was that all the doors of the house should be opened at midnight on Christmas Eve to let out the evil spirits. Certainly it cannot be accomplished that easily, but Christmas is a good time to open the doors of the heart, let out the evil, and let in the good.

SECTION VII
Evangelism and World Missions

Topic: Vision of Going
TEXT: Acts 10:19–23

The vision of going always starts with God. It is God's very nature for many reasons. First, he is God of all the peoples of all the earth. Also, he is a loving God whose heart yearns for the redemption and salvation of every human being. He is a God who has created us in his own image and desires to use us in the process of reaching all the world. Therefore, it is inevitable that God is the source of the vision for going.

I. *God gives it.* Scripture reveals this truth starting in Gen. 12:3, where, as he promised to bless Abraham and his descendants, God declares that it is for the purpose that his blessings may be shared with all the nations of the earth. The children of Abraham wanted to accept the blessings without sharing them and ended up in exile in a foreign land.

But beginning then and throughout time until now, God has continued to give his vision. It was his vision to Isaiah that caused him to respond, "Here am I, send me." It was God's vision to Jonah that ultimately forced him to preach the gospel to the great city of Nineveh. It was at God's initiative that Paul saw Jesus, and the whole thrust of the early missionary movement was forged in the white heat of a vision.

And now we have Peter with his vision. It is difficult to overemphasize the signif-

icance of this event, not just in the life of Peter but in the history of Christianity. For until that time, we have little record that any of the early Christians understood Christ's call to the whole world.

I am convinced that God has to burst forth in dramatic expression of his presence, because there is a constant tension between the human nature to get, stay, and hold to ourselves and the divine nature to go, send, and reach out to the ends of the earth. We as human beings tend to identify our security with the comfortable and familiar, with what we call home. However, from a divine standpoint, that security and comfort cannot be geographically limited, because we are seeking a heavenly city. The spiritual kingdom is eternal, worldwide, and heaven high, and our security has to be found there. Our home ought to be in our hearts rather than in the soil of our native state or land.

I think it is this struggle that causes so many to resist going. Why else do students go to seminary and talk about being called anywhere as long as it is in their state? Why is it that every time missionaries are appointed some say, "My parents, though devout Baptists, have resisted my going"? I am convinced it is because we have lost our vision of a God who always commands us to go.

II. *People need it.* A Christian traveling in our world must be overwhelmed with the fact that peoples of every kind in every place desperately need a vision of

God and the redemption that Jesus alone gives. A young Frenchman on a plane claims to be Roman Catholic, but the acknowledges that he knows nothing about God or the Bible and has given himself to trying to provide security and financial support for his wife and young child. He does not understand how much he needs the Lord. In Ethiopia, a government official claims to be a member of the Orthodox church and the Communist party, giving no indication of spiritual awareness. A young Muslim man can quote the Bible and knows the Koran, but he knows absolutely nothing of spiritual resources.

The people of the earth need the Lord more than we are able to understand, and this is the reason God continues to give the vision of going to those who respond as missionaries and volunteers. Almost 70 percent of the world's masses make no claim to being remotely connected to Christ. And to reach them, God is calling not just Baptists, not just Methodists, but all Christians to go.

The vision of going comes from God because of French salesmen and Ethiopian bureaucrats and people from Georgia who need Jesus Christ as Savior. These lost, desperate people need more of us to gaze at the Holy God, high and lifted up, until we get the vision of going.

III. *God's people need it.* Certainly the vision of going comes from God. It is God's nature and God's desire. Lost people all over the earth need this vision of going. However, we who are God's people need this vision of going. Leslie Newbigin says this story is not only the conversion of Cornelius, but it is also the conversion of Peter and the church. He goes on to say, "Missions changes not only the world but also the church . . . [it] is not just church extension. It is something more costly and more revolutionary. . . . Mission is not essentially an action by which the church puts forth its own power and wisdom to conquer the world around it; it is rather an action of God putting forth the power of His spirit to bring the universal work of Christ for the salvation of the world nearer to its completion."[1] The

Acts account we have just read goes on to Acts 11:18. Nebigin adds, "The church itself became a kind of society different from what it was before Peter and Cornelius met. It has been a society enclosed within the cultural world of Israel: it became something radically different—a society which spanned the enormous gulf between Jew and pagan and was open to embrace all the nations which had been outside the covenant by which Israel lived."[2] This was the beginning of a great struggle which came to a climax in Acts 15 about the nature of the *ecclesia* and how one became a Christian. It was there, when Peter reported this experience and adamantly testified that the Holy Spirit was given to the Gentiles, that the church was silenced in its objection. Between these events, the persecution-scattered followers were first identified as Christians—not another Jewish group, but a significantly different kind of people. I suggest that the true nature of the church is found only if and when we catch a vision of the going which God gives, the need of the world to receive Jesus Christ, and the need we have to be open to the fullest meaning of what it is to follow Jesus as Savior.

Genuine conversion raises us above the restrictions that culture, language, and nationalities place on us. We suddenly find our identity, our security, our purpose, and our meaning, not in the fact that we are Americans, not in the fact that we come from Texas or Georgia, but in the fact that we are a new creature and a new race. Our identity is now Christian. The limits of the kingdom to which we belong are heaven high, humanity wide, hell deep, and eternity long. The vision of going causes us to become citizens of the kingdom of God and changes our whole approach to life. Going is not optional; it is commanded. It is not peripheral; it is central. It is not secondary; it is

---

[1]Leslie Newbigin, *The Open Secret* (Grand Rapids: William B. Eerdmans, 1978), 66.
[2]Ibid.

primary. It is not institutional; it is personal.

We must have this vision of going if we are to be a people of God.—R. Keith Parks

Topic: I Believe in Jesus Christ

TEXTS: Phil. 2:5–11; Col. 1:13–20, 2:9–10a

The late Bishop Pike said the Muslims are winning because they offer one God and three wives while Christianity offers three Gods and one wife. It is startling to note that there are more Muslims in the United States than many mainline Christians realize. Of course Bishop Pike was wrong—Christians worship one God, not three, and Muslims are allowed four wives.

"I believe in Jesus Christ his only Son and our Lord." Who is Jesus? That is not a new question. Jesus asked his disciples that at Caesarea Philippi and the church dealt with it in the Council of Chalcedon in A.D. 451. The question is current. A couple of years ago Jesus made the cover of *Time* magazine (for the sixteenth time). The article concluded that no one will follow an uninteresting Jesus. Some liberals have trouble accepting the deity of Christ, while some fundamentalists do not actually believe Jesus was fully human. Of course he was *both* fully human and fully divine. Jesus was as human as we are and as divine as God. This is a great mystery and truth.

The Apostles' Creed has been recited as a summary of the faith in Christian worship since around A.D. 100. However, the earliest creed consisted of only three words: Jesus Christ Lord.

I. *Jesus* is his common name and speaks of his humanity. Jewish historian Josephus identified twenty prominent men named Jesus—ten of them were the Lord's contemporaries. Two other men in the New Testament bore this name: Jesus Justus and Ben Jesus.

To call the Master Jesus is to speak of his humanity. He was a man who knew what it was to be hungry, thirsty, and weary. He felt emotions such as anger, amazement, and disappointment. Jesus worked as a carpenter or cabinetmaker, he walked the roads of Palestine and sailed its inland sea. He was tempted as we are, prayed to his Father, bled and died. Jesus carried our humanity into the Godhead. Therefore, heaven understands what we endure and can comfort us.

The earliest heresy was the denial of Jesus' humanity. One of the early church fathers delighted to say, "Jesus went through the wall of Mary's womb as he went through the wall of Joseph's tomb." Actually, he did neither. Jesus was conceived by the Virgin Mary, but his birth was perfectly natural, and the stone was rolled away from the entrance to his tomb. Jesus was fully man, born of woman like all humankind. He was a man of courage and incredible spiritual insight, the greatest of men.

II. *Christ* is Jesus' title. It means Messiah or Anointed One in Hebrew. In the Old Testament it was first believed that the nation would live in obedience to the commandments of God. When they failed they were carried away into Babylonian captivity. Then the hope of salvation rested in the remnant. They, too, failed to be obedient, so hope was fixed in a coming messiah who would establish the kingdom of God on earth. Suddenly there was the voice of one crying in the wilderness, "Prepare the way of the Lord!" John the Baptist was herald to the long awaited king. He baptized Jesus in the River Jordan and recognized him as the Messiah. Jesus is the Messiah who came at Bethlehem, who comes to us in our need and in our joys, and who is coming again at the end of time.

III. *Lord* is the name of the divine Son of God. Lord occurs six hundred times in the New Testament. In the Greek-speaking world *Lord* was a term of respect like *sir* or *mister*. It is also used to describe the owner, as in the lord of the vineyard. The term was also used of one who was master, due absolute obedience. When the Old Testament was translated into Greek, the word of God was *kurios,* or Lord. Therefore *Lord* is the name of the deity and describes Jesus as the divine Son of God.

Note the action verbs in the Apostles' Creed:

He was *conceived* by the power of the Holy Spirit,
Born of the Virgin Mary.
Suffered under Pontius Pilate (a historic faith),
He was *crucified, died* and was *buried,*
He *descended* to the place of the dead (really dead)
On the third day he *rose* again,
He *ascended* into heaven at the Father's right hand,
From there he shall *come* to *judge* the living and the dead

Jesus came incarnate, as God in human flesh. He came to show us the Father in his love. He came to save us from our sins, providing forgiveness by his death on the cross. He sent the Holy Spirit to empower us for our spiritual witness and worship. One day he is coming again in glory at the end of time.

Jesus did not say, "Discuss me." He said, "Come *follow me.*" Is Jesus Christ the Lord of your heart, life, and home? Remember, the earliest Christian creed was simply "Jesus Christ Lord."—Alton H. McEachern

Topic: For the Mood of Skepticism
Text: Hab. 1:1–24

Should we condemn ourselves when the mood of skepticism settles in upon us? Should we feel guilty, as if we had committed some sort of unpardonable sin?

Before we are too hard on ourselves, before we place ourselves in the company of Voltaire, Paine, and Ingersoll, we ought to face one undeniable fact: The Bible itself is not only a book of faith, it is also a book of skepticism. The Bible is too honest to cover up the weaknesses and faults even of its best men and women. Though the heroes of the Bible scaled great heights of courage and daring and demonstrated amazing faith in God, these same heroes sometimes fell into chilling depths of doubt and hopelessness.

Listen to the plaint of the psalmist:

Will the Lord spurn for ever,
and never again be favorable?
Has his steadfast love for ever ceased?
Are his promises at an end for all time?
Has God forgotten to be gracious?
Has he in anger shut up his compassion? (Ps. 77:7–9, rsv).

Listen to Job in his suffering lamenting:

Oh, that I knew where I might find him,
that I might come even to his seat! (Job 23:3, rsv).

Listen to Habakkuk:

O Lord, how long shall I cry for help, and thou wilt not hear?
Or cry to thee "Violence!"
and thou wilt not save?
(Hab. 1:2, rsv).

Listen to John the Baptist, inquiring from prison of Jesus: "Are you he who is to come, or shall we look for another?" (Luke 7:20, rsv)

Listen to the disciple Thomas, saying of the risen Lord, "Unless I see in his hands the print of the nails, and place my finger in the mark of the nails, and place my hand in his side, I will not believe" (John 20:25, rsv).

Here are statements and questions that, except for the ancient setting and poetic style, might come from a recent discussion in a philosophy class on a university campus.

These are facts that we cannot hide in a closet. And we shouldn't want to. These facts are recorded for our encouragement.

If the Bible is a book of skepticism, it is also a book of faith. Faith is the more important thing. Doubt is but a shadow sometimes cast by faith. Yet true faith is often born in the throes of unbelief, despair, or doubt and refined and purified by them. Job said with throbbing confidence:

Behold, I go forward, but he is not there; and backward, but I cannot perceive him;
on the left hand I seek him, but I cannot behold him;
I turn to the right hand, but I

cannot see him.

But he knows the way that I take;
when he has tried me, I shall
come forth as gold (Job 23:8–10,
RSV).

Some have assumed that because the world has "come of age" we can get along quite well without faith. Many are saying that science can give us everything religion once promised and more. God belongs to our hierarchy of Western values as does Santa Claus. But can we survive as a world, as a nation, as families, or as individuals without faith? An old fable tells of a spider that slid down a single filament of web from the high rafters of a barn to a lower level where he established himself. He spread his web, caught flies, prospered, and grew sleek and fat. One Sunday afternoon as he wandered about, he looked at the single filament that stretched up into the dark and said, "How useless!" He snapped the thread, but his whole web came tumbling down and was trampled underfoot. This kind of thing can happen to us if we cut the cord of faith. Everything that makes life meaningful for us will collapse without faith in God and in his revelation of himself.

This fact makes our skepticism a matter of urgent concern. Doubt is only a step away from unbelief. What, then, can we do about our doubts and skepticisms? Can we overcome them?

I. For one thing, we can wait hopefully for the answer to our plight. This may be hard to do, for we are impatient. We want an answer now! But sooner or later we have to agree with George Meredith who said,

Ah, what a dusty answer gets the soul
When hot for certainties in this
   our life.

The trouble is, we may want God to answer in our own way, not his. We sometimes imagine that because the astronauts can go around the earth in the time it took our grandfathers to go across town and back, God ought to keep up-to-date and solve our difficulties with the speed of an electronic computer. But

have we forgotten that some important things take just about as much time as they ever did? Recovery from a coronary thrombosis, the knitting of a broken bone, the birth of a child—all still take as long as they ever did.

Some of our modern, hammer-and-saw evangelism does not take this truth into account. A friend told me of a revival meeting he attended in a village church. At the close of the service a young man just back from the military service was set upon by some tactless believers. He had made the mistake of telling them that he thought he was an atheist. They were determined to make a believer out of him whether God had anything to do with or not. The air was blue with threats. If my friend had not rescued the young man, the poor fellow not only would have continued to think he was an atheist, he would have soon been sure of it and rejoiced. Don't forget that George Mueller prayed for two men for nearly sixty years that they might become committed followers of Christ. One of them, we are told, was converted in the last service Mueller conducted and the other within six months after Mueller died.

Yet, should the fact that God takes his time in working out our doubts be any reason for a doubter to be blas- or for any of us concerned about doubters to leave everything to God and do nothing ourselves? Pascal had it right when he said that there are only two kinds of people who are intelligent: those who serve God because they have found him, and those who are busy seeking him because they have not found him.

If you are plagued with doubts, wait patiently and hopefully for God to help you but take care not to lose your concern.

II. In the second place, if we have doubts and skepticism, we can trust the experience of others and be encouraged by their faith.

I thank God again and again for the men and women of faith I have known. I can't imagine where I would be today if it had not been for them. When I was weak, they were strong, and I leaned on their strength. When I had misgivings, they were confident, and I trusted their wisdom. They were, of course, as human as I was, with problems of their own, but they had character and faith and were like a tower of defense to me. I am not ashamed to acknowledge my debt to them.

At the same time, I am aware that I did not accept all of their beliefs simply because I accepted some of them, nor would they agree with all of mine. Even so, they helped me to believe what I believe, and I am grateful.

What was it that gripped Moses when God spoke to him at the back of the desert? Wasn't it God's identifying himself with Abraham, Isaac, and Jacob? The names of those men of faith awakened faith and awe in the heart of Moses. He saw himself as a part of that stream of history. Through them he was caught up into the purpose of God. He was full of doubts and fears, but one by one they fell away as the God of his fathers became more real to him, as he saw that this God about whom he had heard as a child was his God, too. Many men and women believe today because of the faith of Martin Luther, John Wanamaker, Dorothy Sayers, Harry Emerson Fosdick, or T. S. Eliot.

There is a sense in which decision about God is a highly individual matter. This is what the existentialist philosophers and theologians keep telling us. There is no authentic being where there is no personal responsibility of decision. Yet we must not overlook that our decisions are never made in a vacuum. We are never completely alone when we make our agonizing decisions about God. It is as if unknown and unseen by us and surrounding us like the atmosphere are the friendly and encouraging voices and lives of thousands of others of all ages, speaking to our subconscious minds at a frequency where their presence and power are not obvious.

The Letter to the Hebrews puts it well: "Therefore, since we are surrounded by so great a cloud of witnesses, let us also lay aside every weight, and sin which clings so closely, and let us run with perseverance the race that is set before us, looking to Jesus the pioneer and perfecter of our faith, who for the joy that was set before him endured the cross, despising the shame, and is seated at the right hand of the throne of God. "Consider him who endured from sinners such hostility against himself, so that you may not grow weary, or fainthearted" (12:1–3, RSV).

Who are these kind hearts that have been like guardian angels to us? We could begin with the first man or woman who worshiped God and passed that heritage down to us. We would have to include all those Hebrew prophets and people who saw God's hand in their life and celebrated his power and mercy with their witness. We would have to include Jesus Christ, the Word of God made flesh; the disciples who walked with him; and the plain people who welcomed his words of grace. We would have to include the apostolic fathers of the church, the Reformers, the evangelists, the pastors, and again the ordinary folk who believed what these persons said and proved it true in their own lives. We would have to include also our own fathers and mothers or those persons who brought God closest to us.

Remember, when you are overwhelmed with doubt, the total responsibility for discovering truth is not yours alone. You don't have to begin all over again and figure everything from scratch. Thousands upon thousands of friendly voices are trying to help us find the way, though our pride and our rebellion sometimes drown out their chorus of encouragement. These voices are all about us, and we are never alone.

III. Now in the third place, we can obey even when we cannot fully believe. As Dr. George Buttrick put it, "What we need is a strategy rather than a proof, a strategy and a certain valor of the spirit."

Wasn't this what Habakkuk had to come to? He wanted God to give him a satisfying answer to the evil he saw in the world, some justification of God in the face of man's inhumanity to man. Habakkuk was hot and angry about it all. He demanded that God give him an answer, and he climbed up on a watchtower in a vineyard and waited. The sun beat down on his brazen face, and he waited. The wind whipped about the heap of stones where he stood and sat and knelt and stood again and waited. But the answer he had looked for until his eyes were red and strained and his spirit crushed did not come as he had hoped for it. But it came. It came, and how astonished he must have been at what it was!

It was no philosophy of good and evil that he got. It was a word that had the force of a command: "Behold, he whose soul is not upright in him shall fail, but the righteous shall live by his faith" (2:4, RSV).

We must not read the doctrine of justification by faith into these words prematurely, for this said to him, "Habakkuk, you ought to be concerned about one thing: your faithfulness to what you know to be right just now. God will take care of the problem of the wicked man in his own way. See to it that you are not one whose soul is not upright. You will live, you will survive the sifting of the good and the bad by your faithfulness, your loyalty to me even when you get no answer for your hectoring doubts. You may still be a skeptic, but you will have to be an obedient skeptic if you make it."

I read somewhere an old Latin saying: *solvitur ambulando* (some things get solved just by going along with them). Obey God today, and tomorrow you lose a fear; obey God tomorrow, and the next day you lose a doubt. You will remember that Jesus said, "If any man's will is to do his will, he shall know whether the teaching is from God or whether I am speaking on my own authority" (John 7:17, RSV).

Here is a mother who has haunting misgivings, but she is determined not to let her own misgivings keep her children from Christ. She obeys what God tells her is right in that situation, and she puts her little ones into the arms of Jesus Christ and finds her own faith strengthened as their faith grows and flowers. Or there is a businessman who finds his faith a matter of some amusement among his associates and sometimes wonders if they

are right and he is wrong. He tries to bring what he feels to be the purpose of Christ into the tensions and the ambiguities of the business world, and his faith grows in proportion to his commitment. Or here is a minister who takes Peter Boehler's advise to John Wesley: "Live *by* faith till you *have* faith." He doesn't surrender the possibility of certitude because he happens not to have it at the moment but believes it is even for him, and at last he finds it.

Jesus Christ has baffled the minds of men and women through the ages. They have continued to ask, "What manner of man is this?" Some have fled from the mystery of his person and sought refuge in their doubts and fears. Others, just as skeptical at first, have said to him, "Lord to whom shall we go? You have the words of eternal life." The same God confronts us in Christ today. As Albert Schweitzer put it, "He comes to us as One unknown, without a name, as of old, by the lakeside, He came to those men who knew Him not. . . . And to those who obey Him, . . . he will reveal Himself in the toils, the conflicts, the sufferings which they shall pass through in His fellowship, and as an ineffable mystery, they shall learn in their own experience Who He is."—James W. Cox

Topic: Jesus and the Outsider
TEXT: Mark 7:24–30

For some memorable years I taught in a New York school on the borderline of Spanish Harlem. In taking registration for first graders, we scrupulously arranged the cards according to the time the parent appeared. Then we placed the expected acceptances and waiting list candidates in the order of "First registered, first accepted." That evening the principal informed us that our pastor had rearranged the cards with preference given to the ethnicity of the last name. "We take care of our own" was his explanation.

Of course, we were indignant, wished to tell him so, then to take the next train back to New England, etc. Our principal did explain our reaction (without relaying the threat of our departure without our wherewithal for subway fare, never mind train fare). His further explanation was that there was a chapel, a semi-parish for the Hispanics; our school, church, expenses were provided by the first generation Irish who then formed 99 percent of the parishioners (they were now 1 percent in the same parish).

How I wish we could have been as witty as the woman in the Gospel, that we could have challenged the pastor with the parable from Mark. That non-Jewish mother in gentile territory could understand Jesus' concern for his own people, but she also knew his love was not exclusive, that he could and would include other peoples in his healing of spirit and body.

I find there is a special bond among us who gather each morning to begin our day together in prayer. I know, too, how we will welcome those who will join us in Lenten days, how we include all peoples in our intercessions and thanksgiving. We have experienced the love of the Lord, the forgiveness of the Lord. We know the Lord's healing reaches out to our loved ones at home and elsewhere. May we "go off" after worship, with faith in the outreach of Jesus Christ.—Grace Donovan

ILLUSTRATIONS

BY ROBERT C. SHANNON

FAITH BY HEARING.   A mission in Haiti distributes Gideon Bibles. In the beginning they gave them only to people who could read. They changed that plan. Now they give them to people who cannot read. When that person meets someone who can, he gets the other person to read the Bible to him. Two people get the message instead of one. Sometimes others will gather around the one who is reading aloud and ten or fifteen people hear the word. They hear it the way it was intended. The New Testament was written in a time when few people were literate. It was written to be read aloud (Col. 4:16) and to be received by hearing.

SERENDIPITY.   Some years ago a boy in Decatur, Illinois, ordered a book on photography. By mistake he was sent a book on ventriloquism. Rather than return it, he kept it and read it. His name was Edgar Bergen, a name synonymous with ventriloquism! He used an unexpected opportunity. Jesus planned evangelistic tours, but he also used unplanned opportunities that came along. We, too, must do both. We must plan for evangelism, but we must also be alert to unexpected opportunities.

GOD DISPOSES.   If you visit the Ferentari Baptist Church in Bucharest, Romania, you will see across the street a little building that was once the neighborhood headquarters of the Communist party. Today the church rents it for Sunday School rooms!

ISLAM.   What is the most common name in the world? It is not Fred Smith or John Jones. It is Mohammed. Nearly every family in the world of Islam has a child named Mohammed. To bring it closer home, if Islam keeps growing at its present rate it will surpass Judaism by the year 2000 and become the second largest religion in the United States!

NEEDED—MANHUNT.   He was an intense-looking older man handing out posters. Each displayed a picture of a handsome couple and offered a $40,000 reward for information leading to the arrest and conviction of their murderer. That man was looking for the person who murdered his son. He wanted to bring that person to justice. God is looking for the person who murdered his Son—not to bring that person to justice but to bring that person to mercy, to grace, to salvation. We need to join the search.

SECTION VIII.
Preaching on the Sermon on the Mount

BY WILLIAM POWELL TUCK

The Sermon on the Mount is considered by many to be the greatest sermon ever delivered. Some believe that the Sermon on the Mount was delivered as a sermon on one particular occasion, while other scholars surmise that Matthew brought together these teachings of Jesus from lessons that Jesus taught over a long period of time. The latter is more likely true. The subjects and themes are so vast and seem to be disconnected sometimes with what went before or after them. In this section, Matthew has collected the major teachings of Jesus under various headings. This "sermon" presents a summary of the teachings of Jesus to his disciples.

The sermon was addressed to the disciples of Jesus—the Twelve and other disciples who were a part of the kingdom of God. The Sermon on the Mount was presented here like a charge to the disciples as they were preparing to go out and fulfill the ministry to which they had been called.

This sermon contains some of the greatest of all the teachings from Jesus—the Beatitudes, the Lord's Prayer, the Golden Rule, and many of the most penetrating sayings of our Lord. Whole sermon series can be built on different parts of this great sermon. One could preach for years out of the Sermon on the Mount.

The emphasis in the Sermon on the Mount began with a focus not on what a person does but on who one is as a child of God. In this first section, the characteristics of the kingdom disciple are humility, grief over one's sins, gentleness, righteousness, a merciful nature, purity of thought, waging peace, and the willingness to suffer in the cause of righteousness.

Following the Beatitude declaration, there is a shift in the emphasis from the inner person to the external life. Now a new direction is asserted. If a disciple has these inner characteristics, how will he or she live? The focus falls now on their action. The religion of the heart needs to find expression in daily living. What is within a person must be expressed outwardly. The idea must take on form and shape in one's life. What will be the effect that the disciples will have on the world because they have been changed internally?

The timeless teachings of the Sermon on the Mount offer a rich mine from which the preacher can gather valuable gems for preaching.

Topic: The Church as the Salt of the Earth

TEXT: Matt. 5:13

In the ancient world, salt had much more value than it seems to have in our society today. Salt is so common and ordinary today. In some parts of the ancient world a bag of salt was considered more valuable than a man's life. In the Roman world, soldiers were often paid in salt. This practice became the root for the word *salary*. There is a statement in the Jewish Talmud that salt symbolizes the Torah. "Just as the world cannot exist without salt, so the world cannot exist without the Torah." Homer has referred to salt as "divine." Jesus drew on rich images about salt when he told his disciples, "You are to be salt to the world."

I. This was a commission, an announcement of the mission of the disciples. "This is what your influence or your impact is to be on the world. You are to be salt."

(a) As salt, you will make an impact. If you have a cut and get salt in it, you know how that wound bites or stings from the contact with the salt. When Jesus comes into our lives, sometimes there is a biting or stinging influence because of our hurts, wounds, or sins. Often there is no healing without some pain.

(b) Salt also has a characteristic of making us thirsty. If we create that kind of thirst, Jesus stands ready to be the one to quench that thirst and lead all persons to God.

II. Jesus may be using a figure in the image of salt that indicates the gradual, quiet, and inconspicuous way the kingdom has its effect in the world. When salt is put in food, you really don't want to notice the salt when you eat the food. You just want to notice the difference that it makes in the taste of the food.

(a) The importance of the minute is obscured by a pseudoemphasis on bigness. Some of the most powerful forces in the world are small and inconspicuous. I think of the power of the microscopic atom. The lowly earthworm ever so gradually and quietly does its work in decomposition of soil. Bacteria carries out its duty inconspicuously.

(b) The small group of disciples seemed to have such an unlikely possibility of making any real difference in the world of the first century. Yet this small band of believers, gathering in homes in Jerusalem, and other disciples in Thessalonica, Ephesus, Corinth, Rome, and in other places became the spark that ignited the fire of Christ that would sweep around the world. Fishermen, tax collectors, slaves, and other people became the salt that gave the church its start.

III. Salt in the ancient world was sometimes a symbol for purity. In the Beatitudes, Jesus had declared that "the pure in heart shall see God." You are to be those "holy" persons in society who can make a radical difference for good. We are to live righteous lives like our Lord. Others will know by our living that we are the disciples of Jesus.

IV. Salt is also used to give seasoning or flavor to our food. In Job we read, "Can there be any taste in the white of an egg?" We know how bland the white of an egg can be. Christians should be the force in society that influences it for good. Christians should give a seasoning of encouragement, zest, peace, trust, love, and worship.

V. The basic thing that Jesus was saying about the disciples as salt denotes that the Christian should be the preservative force in society. Christians should be the element that preserves the world from decay. There was no refrigeration in that day. Without refrigeration, it was necessary to salt meat to preserve it. Jesus is saying to his disciples, "You are to be like salt in society, to preserve it from corruption."

(a) Christians cannot preserve society by living apart from the world, any more than salt can preserve meat if it stays in the salt shaker or box. Salt has to be put on food to make a difference. If you and I are going to make a difference in the world, we must come in contact with the world.

(b) Christians are to be salt to the world. They are not to be salt merely inside a church building and not be concerned about the world. You are to be salt in your work, play, at home, or wherever you are.

VI. Jesus reminds us that if salt loses its salty nature, it is good for nothing but to be trodden under the feet of people. In the first century, however, pure salt did not exist. Salt was often mixed with residue along the Dead Sea or other places where it was gathered. Sometimes the real salt would be washed out of the composite and only the residue would remain.

What does it mean today for us not to be salty as Christians?

(a) We have lost the sense of joy in Christ.

(b) A second sign is indifference. Some have begun their pilgrimage with Christ and then have fallen away.

(c) Others are willing to settle for a distorted image of the Christian. They accept the residue as salt. They are surrounded with the outward appearances of religion, but there is nothing within that is genuine. When the church becomes so identified with the world and its culture, it is no longer salt. It has become good for nothing! The subtle danger for the church is to be corrupted by and conformed to the world's image instead of being salt to the world and transforming the world into Christ's likeness.

Topic: The Jot and Tittle of Religion

TEXT: Matt. 5:17–21

I. There is an eternal validity to the moral laws of God. Jesus was not attempting to invalidate the moral laws of God. He didn't hesitate to break the traditions, customs, ceremonial or judiciary laws of the scribes and Pharisees. These laws were not seen by Jesus as the moral laws of God. The moral laws are seen in the Ten Commandments, for example. There is a moral law within the universe that abides no matter how much change there is around us. These moral laws remain absolute.

Although we may be Christians and live under grace, this does not mean that the moral laws have been set aside and we are free to do anything we desire.

II. Jesus wanted us to learn that the best way to keep a commandment was to see the purpose behind the moral laws. Jesus did not hesitate to break some of the ceremonial or scribal traditions. He didn't consider these rules a part of God's eternal laws. Even the fourth commandment about keeping the Sabbath day holy had to be understood in light of the purpose behind the commandment.

The real purpose behind all the moral laws of God is that we might reverence God, reverence his name, and show reverence for the Sabbath. We are to respect other people, their rights, their reputation, their prerogatives, and their property. Jesus is not attempting to abolish all of the abiding moral laws but is calling us to learn how to live and respond to the God who is behind these laws.

III. Jesus states that the keeping of the Law begins with the right motive within a person's heart. Any overt action stems first from a thought from within. Out of the heart comes the issue of life. In Matt. 5:21–48, Jesus gives six illustrations about the motive behind our actions. He begins with murder. He says, "Murder is not confined to killing somebody physically. Murder first begins in an attitude of hatred within one's mind. Adultery is not limited to the physical act. Adultery begins with lust in a person's mind or heart." Jesus also speaks about oath-taking, overcoming evil with good, and loving your enemy as illustrations or examples that focus on the motive behind such action.

IV. Jesus said that he came to fulfill the Law, not to abolish it. If Jesus had come to destroy the Law, he would have been a revolutionary. But Jesus said, "I have not come to set aside the Law, the moral law of God, I have come to make its meaning full or complete." Rather than destroying the Law, Jesus extends it further. Jesus did indeed fulfill the Law and the Prophets. The New Testament affirms this truth on almost all its pages.

V. The Law, through Jesus' interpretation, calls us to a higher righteousness as we are obedient to him. He says that our righteousness should go beyond the righteousness of the scribes and Pharisees. This shows how seriously Jesus takes moral living. You can't say you are a Christian and live any way you want.

Jesus is not trying to teach a works righteousness. He is not telling us that, though the Pharisees fail by their attempt to fulfill the Law, you and I have to fulfill it in another way. We are still saved by grace. But as James says, "Faith without works is dead." Jesus is saying that any person who is his disciple will be shown by his or her fruits. People will see that we are disciples of Jesus by the way we live.

Topic: The Hand That Offends You

TEXT: Matt. 5:29–30

I do not believe that we are supposed to take this text literally. Jesus is telling us clearly in this text, as he does in so many others, that to follow him is a radical demand. "You must be willing to make any sacrifice to follow me," Jesus says. This demand is absolute and unconditional.

Jesus knew that the seat of our sinfulness resided deep within—in our mind or heart. Our eyes, hands, feet, or any other part of our body sins because its original motivation for sin comes from within. But the eye, the hand, or the feet are instruments in carrying out our sinfulness. Jesus states that sometimes radical surgery is necessary to cut out our sinful behavior.

If you and I are going to find life, there are certain things we need to cut away, root out, or extract.

I. To do what Jesus is talking about in our text today requires, first of all, *courage*. It takes unbelievable courage to stand up for your Christian convictions when you go through life—in the workplace, on the playground, or at home. When you stand up for Christ, you may be misunderstood, criticized, ridiculed, or ostracized.

II. To follow Christ takes courage, but it also takes *discipline*. Nothing worthwhile in life ever comes about without some kind of discipline. If you are going to be educated, it requires discipline. If you are going to be an attorney, a doctor, a dentist, a musician, or an athlete, it takes discipline. No one reaches a high goal by just saying, "I want to do that thing," and you are automatically there.

III. The radical discipleship of Christ requires faith.

(a) This step begins with *faith in yourself*. You are modeled after God, and you need to be true to that high self that reflects the image of the God who made you. Let your conscience be modeled after Christ who can strengthen you within to withstand those who criticize or challenge your convictions.

(b) Have *faith in others*. It is so easy to see the faults in others, but we can't see the faults in ourselves. When you read the New Testament, notice how Jesus responded to sinners. Rather than focusing on their sin or weaknesses, Jesus could see the potential good within them. Jesus would forgive them their sins and encourage them.

(c) We need *faith in God*. We can never have enough strength within our own resources to meet all of life's challenges and difficulties. We have to lean on God for supportive strength.

If we would genuinely follow Jesus' radical call to discipleship as set forth in our text, we will hear our Lord's call that the "life" he offers is worth any sacrifice. If we are going to make that kind of sacrifice, this will require courage, discipline, and faith.

Topic: Turning the Other Cheek

TEXT: Matt. 5:38–42

Jesus gave a new vision of resistance that was revolutionary and startling to his hearers. Too often we miss Jesus' message by getting caught up in the literal act of someone hitting us. Jesus was dealing here primarily with a person being insulted.

I. How do people usually respond to these teachings today?

(a) Some react by saying that these teachings are an idealistic or impractical philosophy. Jesus is talking about personal relationships and not about violent attacks on someone's personal life. The reference to a slap on the face is an image of personal insult and not about the possible injury by somebody attempting to rape you, rob you, or kill you. Of course, you should defend yourself in these matters.

(b) There are others who take this teaching literally. The Mennonites and Quakers in our own country have taken this passage literally. They have refused to participate in any kind of war.

II. Is it possible to understand these difficult sayings of Jesus?

(a) Let me begin by saying that we need to understand clearly that Jesus is offering his followers a picture here that is radical in his call to a higher way of responding to personal resistance. He called his followers to a higher way that demanded a radical response to the abrasive actions of others.

(b) The key fact that needs to be understood here, is that these teachings are not for the world at large. These are not teachings which any person can apply. These are the radical demands for one who is Jesus' disciple.

III. Let's see now if we can understand what Jesus is trying to tell us here.

(a) Before you can go the second mile, before you can give somebody your overcoat, or before you can turn the other cheek, you first have to take the blow on one side of your face, you have to go the first mile and give away your first coat. We can't leap to the second mile before we go the first mile.

(1) What is the first mile? The first mile is the mile of obligation, responsibility, and duty.

(2) This demand is answered by the willingness to go further than is legally required.

(3) The way of "turning the other cheek" and "the second mile" is undertaken voluntarily. You turn the other cheek because you feel that in doing so you can overcome evil with good.

I remember a story that I read about a young priest who went to a leper colony on the Island of Molokai. The first day he was there he stood up and greeted the lepers in the colony by saying, "Friends, I come today to greet you in the name of Jesus Christ." Several years later after he had contracted leprosy himself, he stood up to preach and said, "Fellow lepers, I greet you in the name of Jesus Christ." No one could have made him go to that leper colony. Nobody could force him to work there, but out of a sense of grace and love he voluntarily went there to minister to these people in the name of Christ.

(b) The way of the second mile or turning the other cheek is more than anybody will ever expect. Many expect you to retaliate in the same way they acted toward you. This higher way is the plane on which Christ has called us to live.

(1) We learn from Jesus Christ that our lives will constantly be interrupted. The way of a Christian is to respond in grace and love.

(2) These were not meant to be impractical or idealistic teachings. They were meant to bring reconciliation in the lives of people.

(3) We reach out with the love of Christ in our life and transform evil and hatred with love. We overcome evil with good.

Topic: How Do I Love My Enemy?
Text: Matt. 5:43–44

The statement by Jesus that we are to love our enemies seems not only difficult but, if we are honest, impossible to put into practice. But this teaching also sounded difficult in the day when Jesus first uttered it. When Jesus said, "Forgive your enemies," he was talking to a people who were at that very moment enslaved by the Romans. The tax collectors, their fellow Jews, were working in cahoots with the Roman government to collect taxes from them. The Jewish religious leaders often set up restrictions of the Law that were so binding that no person who had any kind of ordinary job could possibly follow their rigid regulations. What in the world then are we going to do with this strange teaching from Jesus? Let's ask some questions.

I. Who are your enemies? Enemies are easy to define in wartime, aren't they? We can see them easily then. But let's put wartime, terrorists, murderers, and rapists aside for a moment and bring our enemies closer to home. Who is your enemy? Your enemy and my enemy is anybody who hates us or who wishes us harm or injury through word or deed. An enemy is somebody who has smeared your name or hurt your reputation through gossip or slander. An enemy is anyone who makes fun of you, puts you down, or ridicules you. Some of these enemies may seem near and others farther away.

II. But the more basic question seems to be, *Why* should I love my enemy? Why should we try to love somebody who wants to hurt us, hates us, or wants to cause us harm?

(a) I would suggest this hatred is a self-destructive attitude. If you respond to people who dislike you or hate you with the same attitude they are directing toward you, you will soon find that your life is poisoned within.

(b) We need to make a distinction between hating things and hating people. A hard lesson to learn is that instead of hating persons we ought to focus our hate on murder, prostitution, war, injury, oppression, prejudice, slums, and economic or political exploitation.

III. Why should we love our enemy?

(a) We love our enemy because love is the only power which can change our enemy. Jesus was not interested in condemning persons but in saving them, making them whole. An enemy is not changed by treating him as an enemy. Love is the power which can convert an enemy into a friend. When a person is your friend, he or she is no longer your enemy.

(b) Why do we want to love? Because it is only in forgiving others that we are really forgiven ourselves. This is what Jesus taught us in the Lord's Prayer. "Forgive us our trespasses as we forgive those who have trespassed against us."

IV. How is it possible to love your enemy?

(a) We begin to love our enemy by realizing that we don't always have to like our enemy.

(b) It is possible to love our enemy by not identifying persons with their sins. I make a distinction between my *real* self and what I do. I need to do the same for others.

(c) This is what God does for us. We can learn to forgive our enemies when we begin to realize how often people do not really understand their own actions.

V. Jesus told his disciples that if they learned to forgive their enemies they would be children of the most high (Luke 6:35). This kind of love reveals that we are like our Father.

(a) God doesn't like our sinning, but he continues to love us and tries to draw us to himself.

(b) Forgiveness is never easy. Jesus didn't say his way was easy. This talk about loving our enemies is difficult and hard to accept. But it is at the heart of

our faith. This difficult teaching from our Lord reminds us to reach out to those closest at hand or farthest away and seek to love them even as our Lord has loved us.

Topic: Ah, Who Can Be Perfect?
TEXT: Matt. 5:47–48

I. As Christians, we are called to a higher way, a way modeled after God. We are to imitate God. Paul, writing to the Ephesians, says, "You have been created in Christ Jesus for good works" (Eph. 2:10). We are to live a new life-style that we have seen in the life of Jesus Christ.

II. The teaching from Jesus also calls us to reach forward for our greatest growth, development, and potential and not to be content with where we are.

(a) Christ calls each of us to reach for the highest within ourselves. The word for *perfect* in our text is a word in Greek that can mean end, aim, or goal. The perfection that it describes is functional. This perfection doesn't mean flawless. The aim is to fulfill the purpose for which something was created.

One can have a perfect saw when that saw fulfills its function to cut wood properly. One has a perfect piano when the piano is able to fulfill its purpose and serve as an instrument on which a good melody, hymn, or song can be played. Our lives can be perfect when they fulfill what God has created us to be.

(b) The challenge to be perfect is a constant reminder that we cannot be content with where we have arrived in our spiritual journey. The call to perfection constantly pulls us forward.

III. Jesus reminds us that we live by this standard by the grace of God. The new birth experience has opened the door to an authentic relationship to God. Jesus said, "Be perfect as your Father is perfect." Here is the key. Our link is God. Like father like son! Like father like daughter! We are able to find strength to live this kind of life because we are linked to God the Father.

IV. We are called by our text to a higher vision of what we can be as per sons. Hang on to the vision that God holds before you. Do not be content with less. We are challenged to reach toward what God wants us to be. He calls us to be perfect. Perfection is always an ever receding goal. When we reach toward God to grow spiritually, we realize how much greater God is and how sinful we are. But we continually model our lives after God and strive to be nurtured by God's grace and love. We may never arrive, but we continue to reach for the goal.

Jesus has lifted before us a goal that seems to be impossible. But our Lord is beside us to guide us, undergird us, and help us live the Christ-like life. God grant that we will seek to continue to follow, no matter how hard or difficult the way is.

Topic: The Lord's Prayer—Our Daily Bread

TEXT: Matt. 6:9

When Jesus taught his disciples to pray for daily bread, he was speaking to a nation of people who knew hunger. Many of the people of Israel lived at the edge of starvation most of their lives. Most families baked their own bread each day. Many of them ate meat only once a week.

I. This petition begins, I think, with a reminder of our absolute dependence on God. "Give us our daily bread." *Give.* Ultimately all that we have comes to us as a gift from God. It doesn't make any difference whether we are rich or poor, educated or uneducated, we are all ultimately dependent on God. The soil and the seeds we plant in that soil are gifts from God. This petition recognizes the source of our bread. Only God in the final analysis can supply our basic needs.

II. We can go a step further into the petition and note that it calls us to a simplicity of life. We pray for *bread.* "Give us this day our daily bread." It is a prayer of moderation. We are not to ask for cake or pie but for bread—the necessity of life. Luther insisted that daily bread symbolized the necessities that a person had to have for the support and comfort of existence, such as food, shelter, clothing, and the like. This petition does not focus on luxuries. This petition reminds us of

our need for modesty in our request before God.

III. But go a step further and notice that this petition reminds us that we are to trust God. "Give us *this day* our *daily* bread." Or as Luke expresses it, "Give us day by day our daily bread." The Greek word *epiousios* literally means "belonging to tomorrow." Its central focus is a childlike trust. We lean in trust upon God from day to day. We cast our worries and anxieties on him. We trust the One who alone can provide for us.

Our prayer for bread *this day* indicates our awareness of our dependence ultimately upon God who provides for our basic needs. Walk by faith in the day you have before you. Trust God. Lean upon him as a child relies upon a parent.

IV. Take another step with me into the meaning of this petition and hear its call to our involvement with others. The Lord's Prayer can never be prayed selfishly. We do not pray, "Give me" or "*I* want this" or "Meet *my.* . . ." We always pray, "*Our* Father," "Give *us,*" "Lead *us,*" "Forgive *us.*" "Give *us* this day *our* daily bread." When we pray *Our* Father we have to remember others. Our prayer for daily bread reminds us of our brothers and sisters throughout the world who are hungry. The bread question is the question of all times and countries. Your prayer and my prayer for daily bread is directed to *our* Father, and we ask that he give *us our* daily bread. Our lives are intertwined with our fellow men and women around the world.

V. We cannot think long about our need for physical bread without seeing that bread pointing us to the Bread of Life. In fact, some New Testament scholars believe that the request for "our bread for tomorrow" directs the Christian toward the ultimate banquet feast where Christ the Messiah will feed all humanity with the Bread of Life—the "heavenly manna."

When we break our ordinary daily bread, let it remind us of the One who is the Bread of Life. We can and should pray for our physical needs, but let us always remember to acknowledge that we never live by bread alone.

Topic: Jesus' Teaching on Divorce
TEXT: Matt. 5:31–32

The Gospels of Matthew, Mark, and Luke tell about an experience that Jesus had when he was questioned one day by some lawyers. These Pharisees raised a trick question to him. "Now Moses gave a bill of divorcement. We want to know if you think there are grounds for divorce." The Pharisees raised the question about divorce, hoping to entrap Jesus. They knew that wherever he landed, on one side or the other of this argument, he would anger some.

I. Jesus is holding before his listeners the ideal of marriage. Jesus' appeal is not to the Law but to Creation. He reaches behind the Law and goes all the way back to Creation, when God created man and woman. Divorce, he says, is grounded in the Law, but marriage is grounded in Creation.

(a) In this passage, Jesus, as he did on other occasions, championed the cause of women. Women often suffered injustices at the hands of their husbands. Jesus declared that a woman, if she gets a divorce, is just as guilty as a man who divorces his wife. Jesus is stating that both, likewise, have the necessity for keeping their covenant. Jesus lifts marriage out of the mire of the commonplace to a lofty plain of radical demand.

(b) Jesus holds before us an absolute ideal for all persons, and he finds his reason for this in God's Creation. The Jewish word for marriage means consecration. In their covenant together, a man and a woman consecrate themselves completely to each other. Each is exclusively the possession of the other as an offering that is exclusively dedicated to God. A permanent union was God's intention from Creation. This union is more than just a sexual bonding. It is a unity in which each strives to help develop the other's personality.

II. But there is a note of pain in the words of Jesus. Although the ideal for marriage is stated here by Jesus, he knows that many fall far short of that ideal and divorce does take place. The divine intention in marriage, unfortunately, does not always occur.

III. Are there never any grounds for divorce? The ideal is not always realized, even for persons who are Christians. Jesus was not a Pharisee. He fought their narrowness at every corner. What stance then should the church take regarding divorce and remarriage in the light of Jesus' teachings?

(a) I think the church needs to teach and preach clearly the ideal of marriage. We proclaim that from Creation God has desired that one man and one woman be bonded in a covenant with one another until death do them part. This is the Christian ideal.

(b) When persons fail in their marriages, rather than rejecting them, heaping guilt and scorn upon them, and increasing their pain, the church needs to reach out to these persons with love, care, acceptance, and grace. A person who is divorced can experience forgiveness and grace from God and the opportunity to begin a new life.

(c) The church also needs to provide counseling and divorce- support groups to help guide and support persons during this difficult period. As a church family, we want to say to persons going through a divorce or already divorced that we still see you as a person, one of God's children, with special needs such as all of us have.

(d) The church also needs to remind all persons of the inclusive nature of God's love and the church's acceptance of all persons. No matter who you are, male or female, married or single, the church still reaches out its arms to you with a message of Christ's love and invites you to be a part of its fellowship. You are not rejected because you are single, divorced, or married.

(e) We also want to listen more and respond to the needs, hurts, and pain of people who are divorced, in blended families, in the midst of a divorce, struggling as a single parent, or whatever the circumstances are. Through our teaching and programs, we want divorced persons and children of divorced parents to know we care and want to help them.

In one hand the church boldly and unapologetically lifts up the torch of the ideal of marriage where one man and one woman make a commitment to each other until death parts them. This indissoluble union was ordained by God in Creation. Facing the pain of the reality of how many people are divorced, we lift up with the other hand a torch that reaches out to divorced persons to minister, to care for, and love them, even as our Lord showed his love to all persons when he was on the earth.

Topic: How Can I Keep from Judging Others?

TEXT: Matt. 7:1–5

If we are honest, this statement from Jesus is troublesome, isn't it? We make judgments all the time. We can't avoid them completely. By his commandment against judgment, Jesus did not mean that we are not to have any discrimination at all. The Greek word for *judge* is the root for our word *critic*. The word *judge* really means "do not censor another with unjust criticism."

I. Why are our judgments often so wrong?

(a) We simply never have all the facts. No one can possibly know everything about every situation. Too often we listen to rumor, innuendo, half-truth, and jump to conclusions. We make decisions on inadequate or false information.

(b) We are also not impartial in our judgments. Every person has some prejudice. Prejudice may blind us to truth about another person.

II. Be aware that your judging may have a way of returning to judge you.

(a) Criticism of others is sometimes self-judgment. Psychologists tell us that often the things we detest most in other people may really be a response to the weaknesses we see within ourselves. As the old saying goes, "It takes one to know one."

(b) What we despise in others may be a reflection on what we see buried deep with us. Jesus said, "The standard of judgment that you use to measure other people will be the one by which your own life is measured." Sometimes the persons who are always complaining about some-

one else gossiping or cheating may reveal something about themselves.

With a log protruding out of his eye, someone may complain about the tiny sawdust speck he sees in somebody else's eye. Jesus says, "Old log-eye, you quit worrying about somebody else's eye. You get busy taking out the log that is in your own eye." Look at the faults within ourselves.

III. Try to see with clear eyes. This is one of the significant points in this text. The "log" or "speck" is a "foreign object" in the eye and needs to be removed so a person can see clearly. When some people look at another person, they may see the "speck" or "splinter" in another's eye. They can't see the real person for the "speck." Jesus looked at a person and saw the real individual when the evil was exorcised from them.

(a) Remember that we all are sisters and brothers in Christ. Learn to look upon other people as real persons, and do not see others primarily in terms of their function.

(b) When we see other people as our brothers and sisters, then we begin to be concerned not to hurt or insult them, but we want to do what we can to love and help them.

IV. Here are three simple questions you might ask yourself before you attempt to reach conclusions about anybody else's actions. First, is it true? Second, is it necessary? Third, is it kind?

Jesus said that the judgment we use to judge other people is the means by which we ourselves will be judged. Don't be concerned about the tiny speck or fault or weakness that you see in somebody else, but look at the big lob—the huge weakness—in your own life. And get busy trying to change your own fault.

Topic: Is It Possible to Live by the Golden Rule?

TEXT: Matt. 7:12

Many New Testament scholars have described Jesus' words called the Golden Rule—"Treat others as you would have them treat you"—as the epitome of his teachings. Other have seen this rule as the key or summary of his teachings, while others called it the capstone or Mount Everest of Jesus' ethical thought. In some sense all of this may be true.

I. To try to understand this teaching from Jesus, let's begin with a negative note. Unfortunately, the Golden Rule has been used in a way that reveals deficiencies and abuses.

(a) To begin with, let's acknowledge that this saying from Jesus does not contain the full essence of one's relationship to God. The Golden Rule is not a summary of all the teachings of Jesus. This teaching says nothing about our personal relationship to God. It does not address worship, prayer, or spiritual growth. It says nothing about the cross, the many other teachings of Jesus, nothing about his death, Resurrection, the Holy Spirit, or the church. It is not the whole truth about God.

(b) Secondly, there are others who use the Golden Rule as a kind of disguise for selfish, inferior, or even evil behavior. How can that be done? An example might be "I get my highs from alcohol, so it is OK for others to drink to excess, too." "I don't forgive other people, therefore, why should I want anybody to forgive me?" Sometimes people base their attitude toward others on a bad premise and try to twist the Golden Rule into whatever they want to make it.

(c) The Golden Rule is used by some as a sort of a reward technique. They declare, "I will do good for you. By doing something for you, you will in turn do something good for me." They do what they do not for an unselfish reason. They are seeking to gain something from their action. They assume that "it pays to serve Jesus."

(d) Others say this teaching is primarily a lesson about morality. It is an ethical precept and has nothing to do with religion. If we can live in harmony, that is all one needs to know about life.

II. Let us begin by acknowledging that Jesus is providing us a guide for relating to other people.

(a) The Golden Rule is a challenge to put ourselves in somebody else's place. The challenge is to look at somebody else

before you act and ask yourself, "Would I want this done to me if I were in that person's place?"

(b) If we are going to practice the Golden Rule in our lives, this teaching has to be related to the Teacher. The resources for living this teaching are realized in one's allegiance to Christ, the Teacher.

III. If you and I are really going to try to live out the Golden Rule, we have to realize that this teaching is meant to be very practical. It was not meant simply to be admired or praised. We are to practice it in our lives daily. The focus is not on what to know but on what to do.

(a) Genuine religion leads to action. We are called to live out this teaching in our daily life. The Good Samaritan is lifted up later by Jesus as an example of authentic religion because the Good Samaritan demonstrated genuine religion by showing mercy to one in need.

(b) Jesus has reminded us that our service to others is rendered unto him. "When you have done it unto the least of these, you do it unto me." Matthew 25 quotes Jesus as affirming that, when we visit a person in prison or give a cup of cold water or clothe the naked or feed the hungry, we are ministering to him.

(c) The Golden Rule is a practical way of living out the words of Jesus: "A new commandment I give unto you, that you love one another as I have loved you" (John 13:34). We are challenged to get inside the head and skin of other persons and to understand them and their needs.

This maxim rests on our desire to love God with all of our heart, soul, mind, and spirit. To follow the Golden Rule is not easy. That is the reason we seldom really see it lived out in life.

Topic: Built on a Foundation That Lasts

TEXT: Matt. 7:24–27

Jesus knew a great deal about the necessity of strong foundations. He had been a carpenter. Certain characteristics about the two houses built on different foundations are recorded both in the Gospel of Matthew and the Gospel of Luke. The house that did not survive was the one built on sand. It was most probably built in a riverbed or right by it on the sandy soil. If you happened to build your house in a creek bed, you would have to suffer the consequences if a raging torrent came. You may have picked that spot because it was an easy place to build; it was accessible to water, seemed to be very convenient for other needs, and it also gave you some security from the wind. When the river rose too high, however, your house was likely to be destroyed by the stream.

I. Jesus himself is the foundation on which life is built. Jesus concluded the Sermon on the Mount with a parable. He had presented his chief teachings, and then he declared that the foundation that undergirded life was his teachings and his way of life. Jesus was declaring, "I am the foundation upon which life is built."

II. A second lesson we can draw from this parable is the necessity for action. Jesus stated before he gave this parable and even ended it with the same basic thrust: Following him is not merely hearing what he has to say but doing it. His teachings need to take on flesh in our lives each and every day.

(a) Some of us like to admire Jesus.

(b) Others want simply to delay following Christ's teachings.

III. Each of us is always building his or her house. We are laying the foundation. Early in life we begin putting in the planks that form our character. Some of them may be twisted or marred. We begin to nail in impressions and directions. Soon we begin to form the structure. The

actions we do or do not do and those lessons we learn or do not learn from the mistakes we make form a part of our house of life.

IV. We have to live in the house we build and on the foundation we have made for ourselves. Jesus gives us that freedom. He allows us to build on a rock that will withstand the storms when they come, or he lets us build on the sand in the pathway of a raging storm.

V. Remember that the storms will come. Storms will beat upon the house that we build, and it will be tested by the raging storms of life. Jesus spoke about the great fall of the one which was not built on a proper foundation. God has never promised us that storms would not come in life. Storms do come. It rains on the just and the unjust. The rains come, and they beat down upon our lives, and we need to anticipate them.

VI. The ultimate foundation that Jesus is talking about is not visible. It is something internal. It is constructed inside of us, so that when the raging storms of life come upon us, whether they are illness, grief, failure, criticism, frustration, or something else, you and I can withstand them because we have a force and power within us to confront them.

It is Jesus Christ who is Lord of life. The foundation has been built by his presence in our life and by our surrender and commitment to him. Our life is built by seeking to forge our life on his teachings and on his way of life. Inner security comes from knowing him as Lord of our life.

SECTION IX.
Preaching on Difficult Problems

BY RICHARD B. CUNNINGHAM

Every preacher routinely faces the need to preach on the tough questions that arise out of the difficult problems of peoples' lives. They are usually "why" questions that probe one's sense of God's silence or inactivity in relation to life's crises and needs. "Why did God take my little girl?" "Can God heal my mother's cancer?" "Why can't God provide food for the people of Ethiopia or Bangladesh?" "We prayed for rain, so why are our crops dying from drought?" "Why do people have to die?" "Why doesn't God stop a Hitler or a Saddam Hussein from committing human atrocities?"

Questions like these have both a personal, pastoral care dimension and an apologetic, theological dimension. They touch both the heart and the mind. They are usually intensely personal questions that arise out of human perplexity, doubt, pain, anguish, suffering, and hurt. They grow out of different experiences in which people would like a decisive divine action to alleviate a particular problem. These hoped-for actions, when they do not occur, can produce negative reactions or serious doubt about the goodness or power of God or, at worst, even the existence of God. In wrestling with life's fundamental perplexities, people ask questions like, "Why does God let some things happen?" "What can we legitimately pray for or hope for or expect?" "What can we ask of God?" They are often a cry for practical help in coping with the press of daily problems or the stress of life's crises.

Such personal, practical questions also pose serious apologetic and theological problems about the nature of God and God's ways with the world—as to whether God is loving enough or powerful enough or available enough to have any involvement in human affairs. They probe highly complex theological issues related to divine power, goodness, omniscience, immanence, transcendence, providence, the character of the divine activity, and restraint in relation to Creation and human freedom. Preachers should address difficult problems in a pastoral way, but they also should be treated apologetically as our best minds speak to the minds of our congregation. My own intention in this section is to focus on an apologetic approach to selected difficult problems, with a hope that pastors will add pastoral-care insights appropriate to their own particular parish contexts.

The most formidable problems relate to questions about miracles, petitionary prayer, evil and suffering, death, and providential activity in history. The seeming diversity of such topics veils the large amount of common theological ground that they in fact occupy. Consequently, preaching answers to any one of these problems will often be applicable to several others. Any preaching effort to deal apologetically with these theological problems or the personal experiences relating to them will presume a certain doctrine of God and God's relation to the world.

I must be straightforward about the understanding of God that shapes the approach to difficult problems in the suggested sermons. It is a broad biblical style of theism. God is personal, holy, loving, omnipotent, omniscient, transcendent, and immanent. As the only eternal reality, God freely creates the universe out of nothing. God did not make the world out of some preexisting material or out of his own divine being. The universe is neither divine nor inherently evil. God calls the original Creation a finite good.

The universe is paradoxically both absolutely dependent upon God for its total existence and yet in a sense semi-independent from God in its detailed working within its general natural processes. Without God, the universe would not have come to be nor could it continue in existence. On the other hand, God gives a limited freedom to nature's development by building into the universe natural operational principles and regularities that humans sometimes refer to as "laws." God generally upholds and respects his own regular processes within the universe, even when they produce harm and suffering to species living in the world. Nevertheless, as transcendent, God is free to act outside the normal patterns of the universe if he chooses. God also creates humans with free will and responsibility for their lives on this planet. He respects human freedom, even when it is misused, and holds people accountable for the choices that they make. These theological ideas are basic in addressing life's difficult problems.

Preaching on the difficult problems of miracles, petitionary prayer, evil, and death presents several demands on the preacher. The first is to think through one's theology. A preacher's overall theology not only heavily shapes one's general approach to life's difficult problems but also impacts, consciously or unconsciously, what texts the preacher uses and how one interprets a particular text.

A second demand is to find images and preaching structures that faithfully translate intricate and interlocking theological concepts into the language and thought forms of average people in the pew. Most

parishioners have neither the theological training nor critical skills to handle sticky or technical theological issues.

A third demand is to determine what sermonic type will best facilitate the dual purpose of speaking both practically and theologically to life's difficult problems. In the following suggested sermons, we will use a topical rather than an expository approach. Expository sermons that work out of a single text, while valuable for most kinds of preaching, will often not allow a preacher the flexibility to range as widely or thoroughly as demanded by an apologetic treatment of difficult problems. Topical sermons enable the preacher to provide a more balanced and comprehensive scriptural and theological approach to these difficult problems.

The following sermons develop an interlocking understanding of God and God's activity in the world that provide help for other problems than the one focused in a particular sermon. My hope is that individual preachers may utilize the sermon ideas in ways appropriate to their particular congregation. Many of the ideas can be adapted and translated into simpler form in some congregations. Any one of the suggested sermons might be broken into several individual sermons and the ideas expanded. The sermons that follow might best be preached in a series that unfolds a comprehensive understanding of who God is and what God might be reasonably expected to do in particular crisis situations of life.

Topic: Miracles

TEXT: Mark 4:35–41

The Bible is full of miracle stories. One of the best known is how Jesus saved his disciples from drowning by instantly stilling the storm on the Sea of Galilee. Amazed, the disciples asked, "Who then is this, that even wind and sea obey him" (Mark 4:41)? Miracles often accompanied the saving activity of God at the great turning points of Israel's history and in the ministry of Jesus. When asked by John's disciples whether he was the Messiah, Jesus replied, "Go and tell John what you have seen and heard: the blind receive their sight, the lame walk, lepers are cleansed, and the deaf hear, the dead are raised up. . . ." (Luke 7:22).

The Bible is packed with miracle stories. Everyone knows of God's miracles in Israel's history—of his delivering Israel from Egypt, water flowing from a rock, manna appearing in the desert, the River Jordan drying up, Jericho's walls falling down, Elijah's calling fire from heaven, the blinding of the Syrian army, and the destruction of Sennacherib's army. Jesus' ministry was filled with miracles of healing the blind, deaf, cripples, lepers, and people with other physical afflictions. He exorcised demons. He overcame nature in raising the dead, feeding crowds, stilling the storm, and walking on water. The preaching of the apostles was frequently accompanied by miraculous signs and wonders.

What about miracles today? Should modern Christians still expect miracles from God? In fact, some contemporary preachers spotlight miracles in their advocacy of the gospel. They encourage people "to expect a miracle." If so many miracles happened in biblical times, why shouldn't they happen in modern times? Three extreme viewpoints are found in the contemporary era. Some Christians expect miracles on frequent occasions. Others think that miracles, if they ever actually happened, were confined to biblical times. Others conclude that miracle stories are simply the product of human imagination and interpretation and that miracles are impossible. What then are we to conclude about miracles? Are miracles possible?

I. *A definition of miracles.* We first need to define miracle. Two frequent modern understandings of miracle are out of touch with the biblical view. One attempts to avoid the problem of miracle by viewing everything within Creation as a miracle, so that any particular miracle story takes away from the whole miraculous character of the universe. But if everything is a miracle, then nothing is a miracle. To speak of miracle, in this view, is simply a way of expressing our awe and wonder at the mystery and beauty of Creation. Another misunderstanding, one espoused by many advocates of miracles and by virtually all skeptics about miracles, holds that a miracle is a violation of a law of nature. While that understanding fits some biblical miracles, it does not encompass the biblical understanding or the full range of miracles in the Bible.

The biblical view of God's relationship to the world is strikingly different from our modern understanding. The Bible views the eternal God as the creator of a world that is distinguished from himself and has its own semi-independent existence. God gives order to all that he has created by willing regularities by which nature operates. The reliability and predictability of nature are an expression of the creative activity and faithfulness of God. Thus God is immanent and active in all the creative processes of the world. In order to act within nature, God does not have to intervene from the outside. God can work within the normal processes of the world. At the same time, God is creator of the universe and is not bound by the regularities that he has established. Thus God is free over nature and can act outside of normal patterns if he chooses.

Consequently, the biblical words translated or regarded as miracle refer to a wide range of God's activity. They point to God's manifestation of his presence and power in both ordinary and extraordinary events, in both normal and abnormal happenings, as he acts to redeem his people. Whether the miracle breaks or uses normal regularities, the unique factor in a biblical miracle is that it peculiarly discloses God's presence and activity. Some biblical miracles may embody rather normal natural processes involved in psychosomatic illnesses or in nature itself. Others would appear to defy any current understanding of how nature operates. The real problem that puzzles us is whether miracles are possible that occur outside of any known pattern of nature. Can the dead be raised, a leprous limb restored, or a physically blind person made to see?

II. *The possibility of miracles.* Let us-

heighten the problem of miracles by confining our reflection to the types of miracles that appear to defy any normal pattern that we have ever observed in nature. Can such a miracle occur? We might get at that problem by asking a negative question. What would prevent such an extraordinary event from happening? Does our current scientific understanding of the universe or our understanding of God preclude it? One is a scientific, the other a theological question.

First, the scientific question. Many people conclude that our scientific understanding of nature rules out the possibility of miracle. That view basically reflects either a naturalistic philosophical assumption disguised as a scientific view or an outmoded understanding of science. Philosophical naturalism sometimes is wrongly assumed to be a scientific view. Naturalism is a philosophical worldview that the universe is a closed system, that no supernatural reality like God exists, and that nothing can occur outside the normal processes of nature itself. If nature is all there is, then no miracle can occur. Here the naturalist makes an assumption that cannot be proved, even if it were true. The only way one could sufficiently demonstrate that nature is a closed system would be to stand outside of nature and view it from beginning to end in all its awesome detail. Standing within nature, one could never do more than argue that our observation of nature would statistically lead us to conclude that nature normally conforms to highly predictable patterns.

Others rule out the possibility of miracle on the basis of their scientifically outmoded Newtonian view that the universe is something like a machine that operates by rigid laws of cause and effect, so that everything is determined by an observable chain of causal events. In our current scientific understanding of the universe growing out of quantum physics and relativity theory, scientists have been abandoned any view that the universe is like a machine. An element of indeterminacy or chance exists at the very heart of the atom. There appears to be no causal

explanation for the behavior of individual atomic particles. Scientists no longer view nature as a neat interlocking and perfectly explainable causal order. While there is a broad predictable order in nature, randomness and chance are now also seen as integral components of the natural process itself. Nature is a mixture of regularity and chance. Science cannot automatically rule out an alleged miracle simply because it is unique and unrepeatable.

Nor does theology rule out the possibility of miracle. In fact, traditional Christian theism requires it. Miracles are a testimony to the transcendence and freedom of God. As the absolute creator of the universe, God transcends nature. Because God is faithful, he normally operates within nature's regular patterns. Yet nature's so-called "laws" are *God's* created regularities, and God is subject to them only as he chooses to respect what he has established. God is free in relation to his own Creation and may manifest himself however he wills, in both regularities and extraordinary events. In either case, God, as immanent, does not have to intervene from "up there." He always acts from within the natural process, at times utilizing natural processes and at times acting in ways that do not conform to our scientific understanding of how nature works.

People wonder how God as Spirit can cause physical events in nature. We are all familiar with how our human mind often is the cause of some physical event as I will my body to do certain actions in the physical world. It is no less difficult to think of God as Spirit influencing the course of his own created universe.

Miracles are never merely oddities for the curious or impressionable. Revelation and redemption are always central in a miracle. Biblical miracles are manifestations of God. The critical element is never whether the miracle involves ordinary or extraordinary natural events. Miracles are linked up with God's saving purposes. In the New Testament, miracles are evidence of the powers of the kingdom of God at work and normally involve faith in the recipients.

Can miracles occur? The best evidence for the possibility of miracle is the occurrence of the grand miracle—the Incarnation of God in Jesus Christ. If the infinite God can become embodied in a particular finite human individual, then no other miracle could be greater. Miracles are possible. The question then becomes whether in fact other miracles have actually occurred. And that is a historical question.

III. *The historical question.* Did a particular alleged miracle actually occur? One of the problems Christians face is that miracles are not peculiar to the Christian faith. Human history and most religions are filled with stories of miraculous happenings, often as events in which a particular god manifests himself. It is one thing to argue that miracles can happen but another to argue that any particular miracle took place.

The universal occurrence of miracle stories forces Christians to examine carefully the historical credentials of any alleged miracle. In terms of the Bible, a historical judgment involves various kinds of critical methods and questions. Not all Christians will reach the same conclusion about every biblical miracle. Many healing miracles are easier for modern people to understand than are the nature miracles. Some Christians may conclude that certain miracle stories involve an instant cure of a psychosomatic illness or a heightened interpretation of the event or a parable designed to teach spiritual truth. Such judgments should be made on a historical basis, without either spiritual naiveté or a closed naturalistic view. A key principle is whether the event has revelatory and redemptive significance.

IV. *The contemporary question.* Can I expect a miracle in my life? Some Christians conclude that miracles ended with the apostolic age. Others think miracles are a common occurrence today. Are miracles still possible and, if so, what kind could a Christian reasonably expect?

We might conclude that if miracles happened in biblical times, they might be expected to occur in similar circumstances in modern times. Based on the biblical pattern, they would happen rarely and, when they do, they would have some saving or revelatory significance. As in the Bible, many miracles would occur within the normal processes of life today. Healing miracles might be expected to occur most often—and today that would likely be in conjunction with the best utilization of modern medicine. The extraordinary healing miracles of restoring the flesh of lepers or the sight of people born blind might have been tied to the initial inbreak of the kingdom of God into human history. In established areas of Christianity, they would not have the same purpose today.

Nature miracles could be similarly understood. If they occur today, they would not be designed to dazzle people into belief but would be tied to some major action of God in human history, perhaps in ways that might be difficult to discern. After two thousand years of preaching the gospel, people who live in the older established areas of Christendom do not need them in the same way as those who heard the first preaching of the gospel in the apostolic era. It may be that those kinds of miracles are more confined to the frontiers of the missionary preaching of the gospel, if some stories from certain mission fields are credible.

For most of us, it might be proper to pray for the miracle of healing from a serious illness or to recover from the imminent threat of death or to have provided our minimal economic needs. God does care about our daily needs and is creatively at work in all aspects of our lives. But any miracle must be consistent with the values of the kingdom of God and with God's overall will for our individual lives. Our hope and expectation must always be tempered by the knowledge that Jesus did not heal every sick or handicapped person, restore mental stability to every demoniac, or raise every dead person from the grave—even when miracles were evidence of the kingdom at work in his own historical life. Nor will God miraculously act in every circumstance today. But it does not dishonor God to pray for and expect a miracle, within the will of God, when we have the proper motivation and purpose in mind. God is a God of miracle!

Topic: Petitionary Prayer

TEXT: Matt. 7:7; 21:22

Many Christians are at times perplexed about petitionary prayer. Prayer takes various forms—praise, adoration, thanksgiving, confession, submission, communion—that never create problems for faith. Petitionary prayer is another matter. The Bible mandates that we are to place our petitions before God. Jesus invites, "Ask, and it will be given you" (Matt. 7:7). Or he promises, "And whatever you ask in prayer, you will receive, if you have faith" (Matt. 21:22). The Lord's Prayer, Jesus' suggested role model, alone contains five specific petitions. Petitions take many forms. Some merely petition God to what God will do anyway—like the coming of his kingdom or his will being done on earth. The real difficulty comes with petitions that ask God to cooperate with our desires, some of which God might do without the prayer and others that might alter God's intention for our individual lives or human affairs.

Jesus' extravagant promises about God answering petitionary prayers trigger varied responses—a kind of reckless abandon about what we may properly ask for, gratitude for apparent answers to requests, and frequent disappointment in unanswered prayers. As thoughtful people reflect about the logic of petitionary prayer, they may be puzzled about why a loving God would want humans to request something that a good God ought naturally to provide. That includes petitions for our daily bread. Then there are the many times when God does not seem to deliver on the promises of Jesus. Any Christian can relate numerous occasions when one has petitioned God in a specific way, with faith that God would respond, and yet the request has gone unanswered.

Devout Christians often develop coping mechanisms for these situations when petitions appear to fail. One way is to think of reasons why God did not respond. "I just didn't have enough faith. If I had, God would have moved a moun-

tain." "I asked for something that would have been bad for me, and God knew better." Yet deep down beneath the surface reasoning, one might be thinking, "God really didn't answer my prayer." Another coping method is for Christians to build an escape clause into their petitions by praying in such a general way that no specific request is ever made or in such a submissive way that their prayer is nothing more than an alignment of their will with whatever might happen.

Yet Jesus generously invites us, "Ask, and it will be given you." So let us think through this multifaceted problem of petitionary prayer. The apologetic problem is not merely with petitions that seem to go unanswered. It focuses on why a loving, powerful God would invite us to make petitions, how those petitions can be understood in relation to God's creative and redemptive purposes, the limits and proper kinds of petitionary prayer, and the value of petitionary prayer.

I. *The theological problem with petitionary prayer.* Petitionary prayer creates several theological dilemmas for reflective Christians. One is similar to that posed by the problem of evil for the omnipotence and goodness of God. How can we reconcile petitionary prayer with what we believe about a loving, all-powerful, all-knowing God? Many people have wondered, "If God is loving and wills what is best for me, and powerful enough to do what he wills, why wouldn't God provide what I request without insisting that I ask?"

Another dilemma concerns the omniscience of God. If people believe, as many do, that God knows every future event of their lives in minor detail, then they face the problem that whatever God knows about the future is already determined. Otherwise God could not know it. Therefore the future could not be altered by God's response to a petitionary prayer for anything other than what will happen anyway. In short, God's foreknowledge makes petitionary prayer for a change in the future impossible.

Reflective people might stumble onto another dilemma about whether prayer actually makes any difference in what God would do. If God's answer to my prayer would make life better for me, would not a loving God provide that good thing anyway? If the answer to my prayer would make life worse for me, would not a loving God refuse to do other than the best for me? Either way, petitionary prayer is irrelevant in the relationship of a human being to a loving god. Let us reflect theologically upon some of those questions.

II. *God's nature and the possibility of petitionary prayer.* It is difficult to make real sense of petitionary prayer if our understanding of God is that of a grand author who foreknows, predetermines, and forcefully brings about every minor detail of Creation from start to finish. Simply put, if a petitionary prayer should alter what God has foreknown and predetermined, then God's knowledge would have been wrong from the beginning. Since God cannot be wrong in his knowledge, petitionary prayer that would change God's action in the future is ruled out.

Petitionary prayer can make better sense when we understand God in a more dynamic way. Christians have historically affirmed that God is omnipotent, omniscient, and good. If God has less than these qualities, he would not be the biblical God. But Christians have understood these attributes in different ways, not always consistently. Most Christians have always believed that God limited his own power when he created the universe, so that he built predictable regularities into the universe that he upholds. God does not capriciously intervene except on rare occasions. Might God, in a similar way, have limited his detailed knowledge about future events within the universe for the sake of human freedom? Or is it even possible that future events cannot be known until they occur, even by an omniscient God who knows everything that has actually taken place?

It is possible that God knows the general course of the universe, history, and our individual lives but not the specific details in the dynamic openendedness of the future universe. God might be thought of as a master chessman playing against a much weaker opponent. The master may know with certainty that he will make the final move and win the game and yet not know exactly how the game will unfold or how he will respond to the other player's strategy within the game. God is like that in relation to his Creation. The long developmental process of the universe and the freedom of human beings introduce factors that God has not determined or specifically willed. Both a relatively independent universe and the freedom of human beings require that the future not be predetermined. God can know the final outcome of Creation and redemption without determining all the details of future events. The script of the future is written by many different kinds of causes, including that of petitionary prayer—if God chooses to take some petitions into account in determining his own responses and initiatives in relation to human beings. If much of the future is openended, then God is free, as he chooses, to respond to the requests of humans in relation to his long-term goals for history and individual people.

The God of Jesus Christ is a personal God who enters into relations with free human persons. God takes an interest in our individual lives. Communication is at the heart of personal relationships. In communication with God, we expose our needs, our hopes, our desires. The Bible indicates that God cares about what we think. God listens as well as speaks to his human creatures. When we pray for God's will to be done, our petitions are one of the elements God takes into account in determining his will. For that reason, Jesus invites us to make known our requests to God.

III. *The limits of petitionary prayer.* Part of the maturing process within the Christian life is to learn what requests are proper to make of a loving God. Petitions vary, and the type of petition will shape the nature of the divine response. For example, I may ask for God's help in enduring pain or adjusting to life after a loved one's death. I might ask God to cure a terminal illness and save me from death. I might ask God to help me submit to his will for my life. Or I might ask God instantly to feed all the starving people of the world, melt the North and South Poles, or turn the Sahara Desert into a tropical rain forest. I might ask God to kill my enemy. All of these are petitions that might appear to fall within Jesus' promise that we will receive *whatever* we ask in prayer. Yet they quite clearly involve very different aspects of God's relation to the universe, his general will for life on this planet, and his specific will for individual lives. The probabilities that God will answer these different types of petitions vary from zero to high possibility.

Because God is God, he will not answer every type of petition. God will not answer petitions that run counter to his own nature or to his general will and purposes in nature. That would include such things as permanent alteration of patterns in the universe or on the planet related to geography, weather patterns, life processes, or the mortality of all created beings. Life giving and life destroying conditions are all built into the natural processes within the universe. God will not answer petitions that would harm other people or the one who prays, since God wills the best for all people. God will not answer trivial petitions. He likely is not concerned with who wins the Super Bowl or the Illinois lottery.

Even when petitionary prayer falls within proper limits, God may not honor our request. In Gethsemane, Jesus asked for the cup of his death to pass from him (Matt. 26:39). Paul repeatedly pled for his thorn in the flesh to be removed (2 Cor. 12:09). Neither request was granted because it was not God's better will. Often our requests will not be granted, perhaps for different reasons. At times we are ignorant in our asking, so that if God honors the form of our request, he would deny the substance. A man wanting a happy marriage might pray to marry a particular woman, one with whom God knows he would have a disastrous marriage. God could not grant both of his desires. At times petitionary prayer becomes a substitute for intelligence and hard work. One might pray to

win a lottery when what God wills is intelligent vocational choices and hard work as a path to economic security. At times we request gifts we are not yet prepared to receive, which might require more discipline on our part or persistence in prayer itself. Petitionary prayers occur in the dynamics of a personal relationship with a God who loves us more than we love ourselves and wills for us the best gifts within the limits of our personal lives. Thus even when God may say no to a request, it might be for our own good or for reasons that are beyond our power to grasp.

Petitionary prayer is a gift to us from God. Through petitioning God for a specific response, God may be able to open up people to relations with himself and also to educate people in the art of responsible living and proper requesting in relation to divinely willed values for human life. Jesus invites us, "Ask, and you will receive." God surely knows what is best for us. A part of the divine humility in helping us to grow into maturity as the children of God is to take into account what we humans think and wish at a given stage of our own pilgrimage. The longer we live and develop as Christians, the more God will guide our asking into ways that are consistent with his purposes for life and with values that last eternally. Along the way, we must always condition our earnest petitions and expectations with "Thy will be done."

Topic: Evil
Text: Luke 13:1–5

All human beings wrestle with the problem of evil in the world. Everyone thinks that the world would be a better place if some things were not in it. Evil is those things that make the world a worse place than we can imagine it to be. For people who do not believe in God, evil may be just another fact of life that we have to deal with, one that we must either combat or resign ourselves to. For Christians, the presence of large amounts of evil in the world is not only a practical fact of life, but it raises serious questions about the nature or even the existence of God. The problem is how we can justify what we believe about God in relation to the evil in the world.

We live in a world where bad things happen to all kinds of people. Most people think of two kinds of evil, one found in nature, the other as the result of human moral choices. Natural evil includes such phenomena as floods, droughts, hurricanes, earthquakes, volcanoes, or insect devastations. It grows out of the nature of life on earth, where animals eat other animals, animals routinely experience pain, and organisms are born, degenerate, and die. It includes all the malfunctions in the biological process— genetic aberrations that produce physical deformities, mental deterioration or retardation, disease, and ultimately death. Moral evil results from the misuse of human will. It produces killing, rape, brutality, war, ecological mismanagement, the spread of disease, and the massive injustices that afflict the human family. Moral evil often intensifies the impact of natural evil.

Both types of evil are highlighted in Luke 13:1–5. In discussing the judgment of God upon all sinners, Jesus rejects a false, simplistic view that moral and natural evil are God's judgment upon particularly bad people. He challenges Jews who thought that Pilate killed some Galileans because they were worse sinners than other people around them. He makes the same point about natural evil, rejecting the view that the Tower of Siloam fell on especially bad people who deserved it. Both moral and natural evil fall indiscriminately on both good and bad people. That may help guide us away from one misunderstanding of evil, but it does not explain why God allows so much evil in the world.

The great amount of human suffering produced by evil creates both a practical and a theological problem. People must deal in a very practical way with the evil they experience in life. The theological problem for Christians is how to maintain faith in a loving, all-powerful God in the face of the excessive amount of evil in the world. The theological problem can be stated very simply. Either God wills to remove evil and is unable, or God is able but does not will to remove it. Therefore, God is either not omnipotent or not good. In either case, if such a God exists, God is not worthy of our worship. Can we make an adequate apology for a theistic God in the face of evil?

I. *A theological understanding of God.* If we are to justify God in relation to evil, it is important to get clear what kind of God we are trying to justify. Evil is an even greater theological problem for some badly defined views of God. If God's omnipotence means that God can do anything, then God determines everything by his power and is directly responsible for every evil there is. Or if God is all-loving by our finite human standards, which might mean he is something like a doting old grandfather, then he will only dispense candy and never medicine to his human children. Either view is difficult to square with the fact of evil.

God's nature must be carefully defined, not in philosophical abstraction, but in light of God's relationship to and his purposes in the world. God is the creator of the world that he calls good. Nothing exists that God did not originally will into existence (Genesis 1). If God created everything good, then every evil thing can only be an original good that has gone bad. In creating the world over against himself, God limited himself in relation to the world, so that God will generally be faithful to the natural processes at work on the planet—even when they produce evil.

Our understanding of God's omnipotence and goodness must be qualified by his purposes on this planet. When we say that God is all-powerful, we do not mean that God can do *anything*. There are limits on God's power. God cannot do anything that violates his own nature. If he could, he would not be God. Nor can God do anything that is logically contradictory. Even God cannot make a rock so heavy he could not lift it or make square circles. Those are not real possibilities, and so they represent no real limits on God. They are just things that cannot be done. But God's omnipotence is limited also by his design and purposes for Creation.

Our understanding of God's goodness must also be qualified. Some people want to measure God by some sentimental, saccharine view of human love. God's love vastly transcends our broken human understanding of love. God wills the best for all his creatures. What is best is determined by God's purposes in Creation and redemption. God's goodness is directed to his final goal of bringing all human beings into the maturity of the children of God, in which we freely choose to live joyfully and creatively to the glory and honor of God. All created goods are measured by their relationship to God's final purposes. With these qualifications in mind, let us think through both natural evil and moral evil in relation to the nature of God.

II. *Natural evil.* If God wills the maximum stage for his drama of Creation and redemption, then it follows that this is the best of all possible natural worlds for what God intends to accomplish. God's creative will is at work in all the forces of nature—at some level. When any natural process produces evil, it can only occur in so far as God wills the natural part of the event, and yet he does not will the evil it produces. God's active will is reflected in every natural thing that occurs—in so far as it is natural—and his permissive will—in so far as it may produce evil.

Any finite created world will contain conditions and characteristics that will not be equally good in all circumstances. Water, volcanoes, shifting tectonic plates, and atmospheric currents are essential to the development of this planet on which human life has emerged. Earthquakes, floods, and tornados are morally neutral unless biological organisms happen to live in the vicinity. It is hard to imagine any kind of world in which neutral factors might not produce evil in relation to intelligent life under some circumstances. In our kind of ecological system, many life forms survive by consuming other life forms. Our ecological system sets the limit for the kinds of organisms that can emerge within it. The only alternative on this planet would be not to have life. Much of what we call natural evil is simply a way of describing evil results from

neutral natural conditions for life on earth.

It is also the case that life requires a stable, reliable environment. No stable environment will not be equally agreeable to everyone on every occasion. The same gravity that we rely on in going about our daily business without fear of floating off into space will kill us if we jump off a tall building. The same inertia that makes auto or air travel possible will kill us in a collision. If God suspended natural processes every time they start to do harm to people, life would become chaotic.

Chance factors within the natural world also have a destructive impact on all organisms, including humans. The Ecclesiastes writer observes that time and chance happen to the best of people (Eccles. 9:11). God apparently wills that random elements operate unpredictably at all levels of nature, from the subatomic to larger natural and historical events. A skier just happens to be in the path of an avalanche, a driver at an exact instant in the middle of an intersection, a child in a space where she breathes in a deadly virus, or a chromosome where radiation alters its structure. God did not will it. No one intended it. Some things just happen! That is the price we pay for living in a dynamic universe filled with powerful natural forces and complex life forms.

It is also possible that God may have other purposes than only those connected with human life. Some events that may be unfortunate for humans may be beneficial for other living species or even for the ecological well-being of future generations of human beings.

God may have designed the complex world of nature to force humans to make responsible choices. God intends for the world to be a training ground for the children of God, not a paradise for pleasure seekers. The world's dangers may help people to develop a sense of responsibility for life in this world and to learn how to function properly within the world of nature. In this sense, even some suffering that results from natural evil may be educative and redemptive for certain people. Too much can be made of this, but it is the case that some good qualities can only be achieved through suffering. Yet natural evil can never be more than a qualified instrumental good. Ultimately, as pictured in the Christian hope for heaven, God will rectify all the evil produced by natural processes on earth. In the meantime, God wills that people participate in God's own creative activity in overcoming the disordered aspects of Creation, as mandated in Genesis 1:26.

III. *Moral evil.* Moral evil is the direct result of the free choices of intelligent human beings. The vast majority of evil and suffering humans experience comes from moral choices and the complication of natural evil they produce. The only adequate defense of God in light of this kind of evil is that God is willing to pay the price of the massive amount of suffering from moral causes in order to have the possibility of a personal relationship with finite, free creatures made in his own image. Moral evil results from God's grand experiment of transforming human creatures into the children of God.

A powerful logic is at work in this free-will defense. Freedom lies at the heart of personal life. A personal God freely creates human beings as persons made in his own image who can freely enter into a loving relationship with the creator. God could not have a personal relationship with robots or programmed humans. Personal relationships require genuine free choice. They can never be coerced. Love is something that must be offered from the inside of each partner in a relationship.

Free will opens the possibility that humans or other intelligent beings will misuse their freedom to rebel against God, choose sin, and harm other persons. In fact, the conditions of human finitude are such that sin was almost inevitable with the first humans and today is inescapable. Our free moral choices create the vast majority of evil in our world today.

Some critics of Christian theism contend that God could have created free human beings who are not programmed robots but who would always freely choose to do what is right. Yet it is difficult to see how God could assure that they would always do what is right without himself *determining* that they always make the right free choices. No, genuine freedom demands the *real* possibility that it can be misused. The value of personal life is so great that God was willing to take that chance, even when he knew that humans would use freedom to commit moral evil.

So in a sense, God is responsible for moral evil. God did not have to create humans free. Yet for the sake of personal life, God was willing to take that chance and to bear the burden of his own choice to create free persons who would choose evil. Although humans are directly responsible for moral evil, God creates the conditions—the existence of humans and their freedom—that make it possible. In his own continuing creative activity, God wills the continued existence of human persons as they do their evil deeds. God concurs in the natural acts they commit but not the evil the acts produce. He allows a human to live and to pull the trigger of a gun, but he does not will the death of a husband by a bullet. Yet even though God does not will, he must in some sense permit the evil.

This complex dilemma of being involved in natural events but not willing their evil must cause God great suffering. That is a price God pays for the Creation of free beings. Human freedom is not something that God can have both ways. He cannot at the same time allow and not allow human freedom, so that only good and never bad results from free choices. Freedom is a mere fiction *if* God overrules a person's will each time one chooses evil. Our human guilt is a monument to our responsibility for our own sin and to the fact that God does not will moral evil as a path to virtue.

We can never fully understand why there is so much evil in a universe created good by an omnipotent and benevolent God. We do know that God enters into human suffering and takes the world's evil upon himself. The cross of Jesus remains the enduring symbol of how God transforms our sin and suffering through his resurrection power into his higher purposes for the universe. Our ultimate hope offers Christians the promise that "in everything God works for good with those who love him, who are called according to his purpose" (Rom. 8:28). For now we will continue to see evil through a mirror dimly until we see God face-to-face (1 Cor. 13:12).

Topic: Death
TEXT: John 11:1–46

Death is a universal human experience. Death is one of the natural elements of life. It is inevitable and unpredictable. We will die, and we do not know when. Death can be a terror, a threat, a slow excruciating process, a tragedy, a release, an enigma, a puzzle, a mystery, a curse, a blessing. As the final cancellation of life's possibilities, death is a point of reference from which we must define our lives.

Every human culture develops elaborate explanations and rituals related to death. All reflective persons ask similar questions. "Why do people die?" "What is death?" "Is there anything beyond death?" Job posed the universal question, "If a man die, shall he live again" (Job 14:14)? Religious people often ask, "Why would a good and loving God allow people to go through the pain and tragedy of death? Could not God have made a universe in which death does not occur?"

I. *Mortality as a part of nature.* The first thing to note is that Christians believe that humans are mortals and live in a mortal universe that has a beginning and an end. The in-between is an ongoing process in which things come to be and pass away. Stars are born and die; the earth takes shape and will become uninhabitable with the death of our sun; and living organisms are created, develop, birth new offspring, degenerate, and die. The death of existing organisms makes room on the planet for other organisms. Imagine what planetary life would be like if creatures were not mortal and all the organisms that have been born on earth had never died. Think of amoebas, star fish, whales, brontosauruses, pre-humans, and humans—all attempting to

feed themselves with the limited resources of our very small planet, stacked in skyscrapers rearing from both land and sea to accommodate the billions upon billions of organisms created and procreated by the life process. That would be impossible! And even if possible, it would not be a desirable quality of life.

No, God intended for life to be a transitional delight, not a final good, an experience that would give way to a heavenly kind of life lived eternally in the immediacy of God's own presence. So God created a mortal universe. Death is one step in the rich productivity of the universe that has led to the dazzling variety of species on earth. The universe itself, according to the second law of thermodynamics, will ultimately die a heat death sometime in the distant future. Humans, like all other living organisms, are mortal. The Bible states that we come from dust and return to dust (Gen. 3:19). Every generation is a link between its foreparents and its posterity. Death is a natural part of life. It is one price paid for the privilege of living. In the original Creation, death might be seen as a blessing.

Some Christians believe that death is the result of the sin of the first humans and is the curse upon a fallen humanity. Some scriptures can be interpreted that way. Yet we are aware that all creatures that existed before humans on earth have been mortal. From simple-celled creatures to fish to dinosaurs to apes, everything that has existed has died. The fossil remains of creatures stretching back several billion years impregnate rock strata all over the world. Humans die like other species. And yet not like other species! As far as we know, only humans puzzle over the fact of death or reflect on the inevitable yet undetermined point of their individual deaths. Death is the natural termination of natural life.

II. *The paradox of death.* Death is natural, and yet most humans struggle with the fact of death. For many, it is a curse. How can that be? How can death be natural if God is the creator of life? We might conjecture several helpful ideas.

Death is a natural fact that sin transforms into a terror. Paul is clear that death is a necessary door into eternal life. He asserts that flesh and blood cannot enter into the heavenly kind of life (1 Cor. 15:51–55).

Imagine what death might be in an unfallen world! Humans would live in an intimate, free, responsible relationship with the creator. Life would be filled with a consciousness of the glory, holiness, love, and presence of the eternal God. Humans would trust God in all the minor details of every new day, knowing that a providential God would provide our every need. The day of death, like every other day, would be engulfed with an intimate awareness of God's nearness. We would know that on the other side of death would be God and all the good things God has created as an environment for eternal life. In this kind of paradisal existence, we would know without argument that nothing created by God can finally cease to be. Death would simply be one more of the facts that characterize our lives before God, a point of transition to eternal life.

Yet humans rarely view death this way because we do not view life this way. If we do not live daily out of the divine resources in conscious awareness of our lives before God, then we could never view death as one of God's creatively willed elements in our earthly life. Our problem is that we are fallen sinners in a fallen world. Death takes on new dimensions. We find it difficult to see death as a transitional point between time and eternity as we continue to live in the presence of God. Death then becomes a puzzle, an enigma, a threat to the living.

The New Testament pictures sin as the cause of our terror of death. In Paul's words, "The sting of death is sin" (1 Cor. 15:56). Hebrews heightens the terror for fallen people: "And just as it is appointed for men to die once, and after that comes judgment. . . ." (Heb. 9:27). Depending upon their relationship to God, humans may view death as a deliverance or a threat. For believers, death is a deliverance from the power of sin in a fallen world. For unbelievers, it is an entry way

into the hall of final judgment. Beyond death, we will face God again and give an account of our earthly lives in relation to him (Rom. 14:10).

III. *The reality beyond death.* Christians both agree and disagree about what lies beyond death. The New Testament is clear on one thing: Beyond death is God. Some people might hope that death leads to extinction. We cannot escape God even by the simple convenience of dying. We may meet God as redeemer or as judge, as eternal comfort or as eternal terror, but beyond death we will face God.

Christians also agree that following the general resurrection and final judgment, believers will be with God in heaven for eternity. They do not agree on what happens immediately at death. Christians have appealed to Scripture for several different views of the state immediately beyond death. Some believe that death is annihilation. In this view, we die as whole persons, body and spirit, and if we live again, it will require the radical re-creation of individuals by God. Some believe that at death we enter into an intermediate state in which we are either maintained in a low level existence or are perfected until a resurrection day sometime in the future. Some believe that we are resurrected individually at death into the heavenly presence of God. In all these views, despite their differences, the Christians in the next moment of consciousness after death will find oneself, in some sense, in the presence of God. With that belief, Paul can confidently anticipate death as a departure into the presence of God: "My desire is to depart and be with Christ, for that is far better" (Phil. 1:23).

IV. *Living life in view of death.* Philosopher Martin Heidegger says that humans are creatures headed toward death. If we do not understand that, we have not yet begun to know how to live. One of death's blessings is that it heightens the significance of this life. A basic question for people is then, How should I live in light of the fact that I am going to die and I don't know when? John Donne posed the classic question: "What if this present were the world's last night?" How would I live or what would I do if I really understand that I am going to die? I would certainly pursue the most important things in life. I would prioritize my commitments. I would make each day count as though it might be my last. One will be!

The question about living life in light of death can be asked in one of two ways. The first is a more general human way of putting the question. In light of the fact I am going to die, how shall I live? But it is possible for one merely to prioritize each day within the span of life itself, so that each day's meaning would merely reflect our overall view that this life is the only reality. If we think that this life is all there is, then we would pursue the goods that we think most characterize the best thing in life. That might be to live in loving relationships with our family and friends. It might mean to help needy people. It might mean drinking our fill of pleasure—of wealth, bodily appetites, sex, power, and many other earthly values people choose to live for. There is no guarantee that we will choose to live for anything more than transcient values.

Perhaps the question needs to be asked another way. If I should live again after death, how then should I live today? That is the critical question forced upon us by the Christian faith. Death terminates our earthly life, but it is not the end. Beyond death there is God! As finite creatures, we bear an "eternal weight of glory" (2 Cor. 4:17). Our decisions in life carry eternal consequences. If I am to meet *God* there, how then should I live? That way of putting the question should alter our scale of values. If we are to give an account of our lives to him, then we want to know what God wills for life on earth, what he calls good, and what he says is worth living for.

Jesus underlines the importance of this understanding of death and life in relation to God. He teaches, "Do not lay up for yourselves treasures on earth . . . but lay up for yourselves treasures in heaven where neither moth nor rust consume and where thieves do not break in and steal" (Matt. 6:19–20). To the rich farmer

building bigger barns and neglecting more important issues in life, he says, "Fool! This night your soul is required of you, and the things you have prepared, whose will they be?" (Luke 12:20) Because of the judgment of God, every person rightly should be concerned with what lies beyond death. The life-beyond-death will largely determine our proper understanding of both life and death.

V. *The transformation of death.* For sinners in a fallen world, death is properly a terror, even though it is natural. Beyond death we must give an account of our lives to God. But a loving God has acted on our behalf in Jesus Christ to take the sting out of death. The Resurrection of Jesus is our best picture, even if in broken terms, of God's promise that death is not the final word to people who love God and have been redeemed in Jesus Christ. Easter is a sneak preview of the grand eternal picture of the resurrection of the redeemed into eternal life—a future of transformed spiritual bodies in a transformed heavenly environment in which we see God face-to-face and live in the consuming awareness of his glory, holiness, and love (1 Corinthians 15).

Faith in Jesus Christ gives Christians a hope. The Lazarus story in John 11 is an unforgettable story underlining the power of Jesus' death and Resurrection. Jesus' self-interpretation is our promise: "I am the Resurrection and the Life; he who believes in me, though he die, yet shall he live, and whoever lives and believes in me shall never die" (John 11:26).

The mystery of the Christian's death is that we die and yet do not die. We will go through the experience of physical death. All mortal things do. Although Jesus' Resurrection is our hope for eternity, it does not relieve the agony of suffering, the debilitating experience of a lingering death, the possible loss of our physical or mental capacities, the anguish of leaving or losing loved ones in the experience, the jarring experience of having to restructure life in the face of death, or the decomposition of one's physical body. All of those elements are there in the Lazarus story. Jesus himself weeps at Lazarus's death. Even our hope does not save us, or him, from the stark characteristics of death's intrusion into the course of life.

God does not exempt us from the possible agony and suffering involved in dying, but he can deliver us from the fear. The resurrected Christ promises that death is not God's final word, that those who love God and live according to his promises will be resurrected into eternal life. It is a venture into the unknown but a venture in which God will be our companion and God will be on the other side awaiting us with open arms and an eternal embrace.

Ultimately, the resurrected, reigning Lord, Jesus Christ, will abolish death. In the final abode of the redeemed, God "will wipe away every tear from their eyes, and death shall be no more, neither shall there be mourning nor crying nor pain anymore, for the former things have passed" (Rev. 21:4). No wonder the Scripture is so effusive in promising us that the eye has not seen, nor the ear heard, what God has for those who love him and live for his glory (1 Cor. 2:9).

SECTION X.
Children's Sermons and Stories

Children's Sermons: Should We or Shouldn't We?

The use of children's sermons in public worship is a matter of some debate among ministers of various denominations. Some utilize them every Sunday, convinced that they help children feel "at home" in worship services and provide a time when they are affirmed within the worshiping congregation. Others use them periodically as part of special emphases or festival seasons. Still other ministers eschew children's sermons all together, believing that they are often disruptive, paternalistic, or manipulative.

Whatever one's opinion, churches would do well to consider children's sermons within the whole context of the nurture and instruction of children within the community of faith. They do not exist in a vacuum but reflect one facet of the church's response to children at worship. Some ministers deal with worship and children in the following ways:

1. If children's sermons are to be used, select the topic and the "preacher" carefully. Some ministers prefer to do all the children's sermons, others select certain members of the church staff, while others use laity. Some utilize all those approaches.

2. Topics may be coordinated with the Scripture texts for the day or centered on the theme of the entire service. Some ministers preach the sermon of the day to the children in an abbreviated form.

Be careful in doing that; the adults may decide they have already heard the sermon once!

3. Some churches substitute the "children's moment" or the "children's time" for a children's sermon. That makes for more variety and allows for diversity of approaches.

4. Attention should also be given to the age of the children invited to the children's sermons. Most churches seem to focus on kindergarten or primary years, those who may then be taken to "children's church," a special service for children only. The age of the children determines the content of the sermon.

5. Another alternative to the children's sermons is the use of children within the worship service itself. A church where I have been a member frequently uses children to read scripture, carry banners, or provide special participation in worship.

6. Children's sermons, if used, should be addressed to children, not to adults. Every effort should be made to provide brief object lessons, narratives, or affirmations in terms which the specific age group can understand. — Bill J. Leonard

CHILDREN'S SERMONS: SUGGESTED TOPICS

The following suggestions represent general topics for children's sermons which might be adapted to particular ages and occasions.

SELECTED CHILDREN'S SERMONS: GOD'S WORLD NEEDS OUR HELP

This series of sermons focuses on the importance of loving God's world and helping to protect it.

January 3. Naming the Animals

"So God formed of the ground all the wild animals and all the birds of heaven. He brought them to the man to see what he would call them, and whatever the man called each living creature, that was its name" (Gen. 2:19, NEB). Adam named all the animals. He looked at them and decided what to call them. Naming is a very important task for us. We learn to name animals, too. [*Give examples, you might even use a book which teaches animal names.*] Something is happening in our world. Many of the animals we name are disappearing. We call these endangered species. We, like Adam and Eve, have a responsibility for naming and protecting the animals God created. Names like the spotted owl, the gray whale, and the black rhino are on the endangered species list. We must learn to take care of them so they will not vanish. We learn their names, and we help protect them. Adam named the animals. We have to help keep them in God's good world.— Bill J. Leonard

January 10. Protecting the Animals

And God said to Noah, "And you shall bring living creatures of every kind into the ark to keep them alive with you, two of each kind, a male and a female; two of every kind of bird, beast, and reptile, shall come to you to be kept alive" (Gen. 6:19–20). Remember Noah? Noah built a big boat we call an ark. And Noah put two of every kind of animal on board the ark so that they would stay alive when the great floods came. Noah kept the animals alive so that they would survive the Flood and fill the earth. Today we are like Noah. Our world is an ark of sorts, and we must protect the animals, or they will not survive. We must keep them from dying off because of pollution, killing, or changes in the environment. We must learn to get along with the animals. We have a responsibility as great as Noah. We can be God's helpers in taking care of the earth and the animals who live here.— Bill J. Leonard

January 17. God Loves the World—All of It

"The earth is the Lord's and all that is in it, the world and those who dwell therein" (Ps. 24:1). We have been talking these days about taking care of the earth. Today we want to remember that the earth and everything in it belongs to God. God loves the earth. God made the earth. God made everything on the earth. God loves people, true enough. But God also loves the animals and plants, the rivers and oceans, which God created. Today we sing a song of God's love for Creation. It is called "All Creatures of Our God and King." It comes from a poem written by St. Francis of Assisi, a man who lived in the thirteenth century (a long time ago). Francis reminded all of us that wind, water, earth, sky, and creatures show us how much God loves and cares for the world and everything in it. If God loves the world that much, we should also. Help us sing that song today.— Bill J. Leonard

January 24. Feeding and Caring

"Look at the birds of the air; they do not sow and reap and store in barns, yet your heavenly Father feeds them" (Matt. 6:26). This is the last Sunday in our conversation about God's Creation. Today we remember Jesus' words about God's love and care for all living things. Jesus reminded his listeners that if they wanted to know how much God loved them they had only to look at the "birds of the air." If God takes care of birds, Jesus said, won't God also take care of human beings? When we think about taking care of God's Creation, we should also remember that we belong to that Creation and that God cares for us.— Bill J. Leonard

January 31. Brand New Bodies

TEXT: Romans 7

Object: A picture of someone getting rescued.

See this picture? This person is in trouble, isn't he? How would you feel if that happened to you? I would be scared and would want someone to rescue me. Would you?

There are lots of people who rescue others. Let's name some. [Firemen, policemen, etc.] We need people who will rescue us when we are in danger. God knows this, and he sends the people we need to rescue us.

Prayer: Dear God, thank you for sending people to rescue us when we are in trouble. Please take care of them, and thank you for taking care of us.—Michael Lanway

February 7. Will You Do Something for Me?

TEXT: Isaiah 6:8

Occasion: Deacon/ordination/church worker installment.

[*The purpose of this sermon is to generate enthusiasm in the children when they are asked to do something. The minister will leave something near his seat (a Bible, glass of water, etc.) and ask someone to get it for him or her.*]

I need someone to do something for me. I left my Bible over there. Who wants to get it for me? Raise your hand. [*Allow the enthusiasm to build by repeating the question several times. Then pick someone to get the object.*]

Thank you very much. And thanks to all of you for wanting to help me. It makes me feel good inside that you wanted to help me and did the thing I needed.

Do you feel good inside when people help you? How do you think God feels when we help him? Let's help each other feel good by helping each other and help God feel good by helping him whenever he asks.

Prayer: Thank you, God, for making us feel good inside by having others help us. Help us to make others feel good by helping them whenever they need our help.—Michael Lanway

February 14. I Love You!

Boys and girls, do you know what to-

day is? That's right! It's Valentine's Day. For a long, long time—almost two thousand years—this has been a very special time.

What is special about this day? We exchange Valentine cards with our friends, people we like very much. Sometimes these Valentines are a way of telling special people that we love them. Did you give or receive a Valentine this year? I want to give each of you a Valentine. [*This can be a card the leader made, a simple card with a message of love or friendship.*]

God has done something for us to show us that he loves us, that he loves us more than anyone in the whole world could love us, that we are very special people to him. What did God do to show us that he loves us? That's right! He gave his only Son Jesus, who is our Lord and Savior.

The Bible tells us that God is love and that he gave his only Son so that everyone who believes in him, everyone who trusts in him, may have eternal life. That means that because of God's love for us we will live with him forever.

Let us thank God for sending Jesus to tell us how much God loves us.—James W. Cox

February 21. The Lesson from a Shell

Have any of you even been to Florida? One of the things people like to do in Florida is to walk the beach and look for shells. There are all kinds of shells to be found every day on the beaches, and they come in all kinds of shapes. [*Show actual shells or pictures of shells.*]

The shell is the protective covering on different kinds of creatures who live in the sea. Each day new shells are washed up on the beaches of the oceans. The little creature who lived in the shell is gone, but the shell remains.

We do not live in shells, but there is a lesson for us here in the shell. Each day, we leave something of ourself behind, for good or bad. When we are kind to others and try to make other people happy, we leave a good memory behind that adds beauty to life. Once the day is over, we cannot change that memory. It is like the shell; what we have done is set. But with each new day, we have a new chance for good things.

[*If you have a number of shells, you might give each child one as a reminder of your time together.*]—Kenneth Mortonson

RETELLING THE BIBLICAL STORY: JACOB

This series of children's sermons focuses on the story of Jacob. Three brief sermons tell different aspects of Jacob's story.

February 28. Twins!

How many of you have a brother or sister? Do you know any twins? Today I want to tell you about two brothers named Jacob and Esau. They were brothers, they were twins, and they were always fighting. In fact, their mother said that they wrestled each other even before they were born. When they were born, Jacob was first, and Jacob held on to his heel. Esau was rough and tough. He loved to hunt and fish. Jacob liked to stay home and think about things. He was always thinking of ways to cheat his older brother. He was very good at it. Indeed, he cheated his brother out of some of his most valuable possessions. It took Jacob a long time to realize that mistreating his brother got him nowhere. Jacob and Esau were very different people, but they were also brothers, and they wasted a lot of time and energy fighting each other. Brothers and sisters, friends and neighbors do not always get along with each other. But the lesson of Jacob and Esau is a reminder that it is better to help than hurt each other. It is better to be kind to others than to cheat them. Let's learn to enjoy and help our brothers and sisters and friends.—Bill J. Leonard

March 7. All Alone

Remember last week we talked about Jacob and his brother Esau? We said that Jacob sometimes cheated his brother? Once Jacob even pretended to be Esau and tricked their father into giving him something that belonged only to his brother. Esau was furious and threatened to kill Jacob. So Jacob had to run for his life. He ran away from home and was heading for his uncle's house when night came, and he had to rest. He had run a long way and was out in the middle of nowhere all alone. There he was a long way from home, all by himself, having cheated his father and his brother. And Jacob was afraid. He went to sleep out in the desert all alone, but he dreamed he saw a ladder going up to the sky and angels climbing up and down the ladder. Jacob woke up and decided that he was not alone after all but God was with him. Jacob learned that even when he had behaved badly, when he had cheated people, when he was all alone, God could find him, even way out in the desert. That is the good news for us today. God always finds us. We are never alone. God knows who we are, and God stays with us, even when we think no one is around. God surprised Jacob. God can find you, too. God is always there. God never leaves us.—Bill J. Leonard

March 14. Coming Back Home

Remember Jacob? We have talked about him a lot lately. Remember how he cheated his brother Esau and was forced to leave home because he was afraid his brother would kill him? Well, Jacob, lived away from home for many years. Then he decided it was time to come back home. It was time to get back to his home and his family again. But Jacob was still afraid. He was afraid his brother Esau would kill him as he promised he would years before. Anyway, he started home, and when he got close to home he waited, alone, for his brother to find him. But in the morning his brother showed up and, the Bible says, he "fell on him and kissed him." Esau forgave Jacob for cheating him years before. Jacob received Esau's forgiveness and the two brothers were friends again. Can you do that? Can you ask forgiveness—say "I'm sorry" to someone who has hurt your feelings or cheated you or treated you in a bad way? If Esau could forgive Jacob after all he had done, you and I can learn to forgive people and to ask forgiveness from friends, family, parents when we need it. We can even find forgiveness from God,

who made us and loves us every one.—
Bill J. Leonard

March 21. Setting Things Right

When someone says you have made a mistake, what do they mean by that? [*They are saying you did something wrong.*] And what do you do when you make a mistake? [*You say you are sorry, and if you can, you try to set things right.*]

Now what do you think you should do if you find that someone else has made a mistake? Suppose you went home after church and found that someone had knocked over all the chairs around your kitchen table. What would you do? [*Set them right so that you could sit on them to eat.*]

Suppose you saw someone sitting on a curb, holding his head, and his head was bleeding. What would you do? [*Call for help so that someone could set things right for that person.*]

Jesus called such a person a Good Samaritan, for he told a story about a man who found an injured person and helped him, even though he did not know him.

Whenever we see someone who needs help, even if they have been hurt by making a mistake, we can set things right for that person by offering to help if we can. When we or someone else makes a mistake, the results of that mistake need to be corrected. Because we care, we should do whatever we can do to set things right. That is an important lesson for every Christian to remember. Thank you for coming up here this morning.—Kenneth Mortonson

March 28. Mistakes and Erasers

TEXT: Romans 9–11

Objects: Pencils with erasers.

Tell me what I have in my hand. Which end is the one that writes? What is this thing on the other end [*point to eraser*]? That's right.

We use erasers when we make a mistake in writing. [*Take a sheet of paper and let some children erase some markings.*] It's nice to have erasers to help us with our mistakes.

We don't have erasers for other kinds of mistakes, do we? If we say or do something in a way that isn't quite right, there isn't an eraser than can wipe it away. But that's OK. God knows that we aren't perfect and that we can't do everything just right.

God knows we will make mistakes, and he will help us when we make them. He won't get mad at us if we don't get things perfect. So don't get too upset when you make a mistake. Just say, "I'm sorry for that mistake, God. Help me make things better."

Prayer: Dear God, thanks for understanding when we make mistakes. Help us not to worry about the mistakes we make and help us to make things better.—Michael Lanway

April 4. God is Good

TEXT: Rom. 8:28–39

Objects: A "special" nickel or penny for every child.

I have something that God wants me to give you. You know what it is? Let me show you. This is a "special" nickel, and I have a special nickel for each of you. [*Pass them out.*]

You can't buy very much with a nickel, can you? So don't try to spend the nickel; I want you to keep it in your pocket or on your dresser at home. Every time you see that nickel, I want you to say, "This is my special nickel that God gave me." Let your special nickel remind you that God is good to you and loves you very much.

Prayer: Thank you for all you give us, God. We love you very much. Thanks for loving us.—Michael Lanway

April 11. A Baptism Service

Object: A baby book (use the book of a person familiar to the children or of the person being baptized. As you deliver the sermon you may want to give a few examples from the book; i.e., first word, etc.).

Have you ever seen one of these? This is a baby book. You've probably had fun looking through one of your own. There are usually baby pictures in these books. Isn't it hard to believe there was a time you were so little or so fuzzy-headed? You usually write down a baby's first words or favorite things to do in these books. Can you believe there was a time when you couldn't talk? Baby books keep records of all the growth a person goes through on the way to growing up. It records all these important steps that make you who you are. It's important to remember those steps. They remind us that we're growing and that we need to keep growing.

Today our church celebrates a baptism. Today we're celebrating an event in this new Christian life. From now on, [name] will be able to look back and remember that this was an important day when [she/he] said to the church that [she/he] would be a Christian and be part of this church. And today is a day when our church says that this means we have a new member in our family, which brings us lots of joy. In the years ahead, [name] will grow stronger as a Christian and learn more, but this day will always be important, just like that first step you took when you learned to walk or the first words you said were important. Let's thank God for _____'s life and for the step [she/he] is taking today.—Carol Younger

April 18. Surprise!

Have you ever had a nice surprise? What is a nice surprise? We have surprises happening all the time, every day. When someone gives you a smile and says hello to you, that is a nice surprise. Do you know what you will have for dinner today? It will be a nice surprise. When you watch television, you do not know what will happen in the story you are watching. That is a surprise. Each day is filled with nice surprises, and therefore we should look forward to each day and be happy with all the nice, new things that happen to us.

One of the things that makes each day special is the surprising things that happen to us. Long ago a person who had faith in God discovered that each day was filled with many wonders and surprises, and he wrote, "This is the day which the Lord has made; let us rejoice and be glad in it" (Ps. 118:24).

Now I have a surprise for each one of you, but I want you to wait until you get home to open it. And have a nice surprise-filled day. [Your surprise can be anything from a picture to color to a treat to a sticker to whatever is available to you in an amount to cover the number of children present.]—Kenneth Mortonson

April 25. Taking Care of the Earth
TEXT: Ps. 24:1

Have any of you heard the old expression "Well, you learn something new every day?" It really means that nobody knows it all, and everybody needs to keep learning all through life. I am sorry to say that Christians are just beginning to learn something that we should have known for a long, long time. Do you have any ideas what that could be?

We are learning that the earth really is the Lord's and not ours! All of you live in a house with a little bit of yard, don't you? I bet you have said to one of your friends, "Come over to my yard and play." Here at the church we say, "The grounds here are outside the building are our property." That's natural. It wouldn't make much sense to your friends if you said, "Come over and play in the yard that I call mine but which really belongs to the Lord."

The problem is that we forget who really owns it, and we think it is all right do whatever we want with our property. Dad may think it is all right to pour dirty motor oil into the ground, when really that is damaging the Lord's ground. Somebody else owns a thousand acres of forest and saws it all down to sell, maybe causing damage to the soil, but doesn't really think that God cares about the soil and the animals who need homes.

What are some things that we do to the land or water or air that we wouldn't do if we remembered that it all belongs to God, who loves it?—Stuart G. Collier

May 2. We All Need Help
Object: A hearing aid.

This morning I have something I want to show you that you may not have seen before. Does anyone know what this is? [*A hearing aid.*] And what is it used for? [*To help a person hear better.*] Some people are not able to hear as well as you do, so they have to wear a hearing aid that magnifies the sounds so that they can hear better. Isn't that wonderful? It's just like these glasses. Some people wear glasses so that they can see better.

Now, what would you think of a person who needed a hearing aid or glasses, and they could afford to buy them but did not? That's not very smart, is it? And what about a boy or girl who wants to learn how to ride a bike, who does not know how and also will not let anyone help? That's not very smart either.

The point I want you to remember is that there are times when we all need help, and wise is the person who will ask for help when it is needed.

Now, who would like to help me get up? Thank you.—Kenneth Mortonson

May 9. The Control Center

Object: Television remote control.

This morning I have an interesting little gadget that I think some of you have probably seen or even used. Do you know what this is? It is called a remote control. And do you know what it is used for? With a remote control, you can make things happen by just pushing a button.

So, let's see what happens when I push the "on" button. Nothing happened. Why? Because there has to be something around that can be turned on or off by this remote control.

I can push this button, and it will send out a signal, but nothing happens because there is no television here to receive that signal.

The lesson of this is simple: What is sent must be received, or nothing will happen. And the lesson applies to many things. God sent his love to us in Jesus, but if we do not receive it, nothing happens.

Your parents send you a message of what they want you to do, but if you do not receive it, if you fail to remember what they said, nothing will happen in the way your parents want it to happen. When you talk to a friend, if they do not really listen to you, nothing will change because of what you said.

So we all need to listen when people speak to us, and we want others to listen

to us when we speak. This is an important lesson for your parents as well as for you. Thank you.—Kenneth Mortonson

May 16. Remembering the Fun of It

What if you were inside one afternoon working on your homework and your mom said, "Before you do your homework, go outside and play on your swing set for two hours. When I look out that swing better be going back and forth. It better be way up high. Don't even think of trying to sneak back into this house to do school work." You would probably stare at your mom for a moment and then run outside before she came to her senses.

What if at dinner that night your father said, "Put that broccoli away. The broccoli goes back on the stove, because you are not going to get another bite until you finish three pieces of chocolate cake. I better see you eating cake. Don't even think of trying to sneak over to the oven and eating broccoli." You would probably stare at your dad for a moment and then go for the chocolate cake before he came to his senses.

It seems like it would be fun if our parents only made us do the things we already wanted to do, but it isn't true. If our parents made us play outside and eat chocolate cake, after a while, it wouldn't be as much fun to play outside and eat chocolate cake. If you think somebody is making you do things, they don't seem as much fun.

There are a lot of good things which would be more fun if we didn't think we had to do them, if we would just remember how much fun they are. Playing with your sisters and brothers is like that. It is more fun to play with them if you just remember how much fun it is to play with your sisters and brothers. Going to school is like that. If someone asked you if you would like to spend the day with twenty children your age, you would probably say yes, but because you have to go to school, you can forget how much fun it is. Going to church is like that. Meeting with your friends, singing, and learning about Jesus is a lot of fun, if you just remember how much fun it is.

Most of what Jesus asks us to do is a lot of fun, if we will just remember that it is fun. Caring for other people, sharing what we have, being a friend are all fun things which Jesus invites us to enjoy.—Brett Younger

May 23. The Gift of Smell

TEXT: Rom. 12:1

Objects: Things that smell good (perfume, etc.).

What is this thing in the middle of my face? My nose! Everyone, touch your nose. What do we do with our noses? We smell things.

Smell these perfumes and tell if they smell good or bad. [*Let each child smell it and comment.*]

There are lots of things that smell good. Let's name some. [*Flowers, cookies, bread baking in the oven, etc.*]

To be able to smell these nice things is a gift that God gives us. Let's thank him for this gift.

Prayer: Thank you, God, for giving us the ability to smell good things.—Michael Lanway

May 30 (Pentecost). United We Stand/ The Strength of Togetherness

This morning I would like to do a little experiment with you. I would like each one of you to take a piece of paper and see if you can tear it in half. Now, let me have the two pieces of paper and put them all together. Can anyone tear them all in half? [*Repeat, if needed.*]

Soon we get to the place where all the paper together is too strong and nobody can tear it. Plywood is another example of this truth. This is a piece of plywood, and as you can see, it has three layers, which makes it stronger than each layer alone.

This is an important lesson for life. People together can do many things which people alone could not do. But for that to happen, people need to be close to one another and to share life together if they are to strengthen each other. And the more people who are willing to work together, the better.

This applies to the home as well as to the church. So once again we see how im-

portant you are, for you are, part of our togetherness.—Kenneth Mortonson

June 6. A Holy Place

Instructions: This children's sermon takes a little preparation. Take three-by-five cards to a group of children before the Sunday morning worship service. Ask them to write "a good rule to follow in the church sanctuary." Follow the same procedure with a group of adults, instructing them to write "a rule which will help us be reverent in the sanctuary." Both groups should be invited to give answers both serious and not so serious. Encourage creativity. Each answer should be signed. You should tell everyone that they are helping you with the children's sermon. Go through your stack of answers and choose the best ones to share in the worship service. You may want to share the humorous ones you have chosen first and then move on to the more serious answers. You can also move from negative prohibitions of unacceptable behavior to positive affirmations of how to worship. Duplications should be skipped. The larger your sampling the more selective you can be in which answers you will present. After having explained the question you have asked and shared the answers you have chosen, close with a reminder of the importance of reverence.

This sanctuary is a special place. We should treat it as special. We come here to remember God and his place in our lives. It is not that God is here and not everywhere else. It is that we come here and listen. We are still and quiet and know that God is here. Then we remember that God is everywhere else, too.—Brett Younger

June 13. Being Happy and Being Sad

TEXT: Rom. 3:9–31

Objects: Newspaper pictures of people showing emotion.

I want to show you some pictures of people in this newspaper. Tell me if you think the people are happy or sad. [*Show three or four pictures, one at a time, and allow the children to label the emotion.*] What do you think happened to make this person happy (sad)?

Which do you like better: feeling happy or feeling sad? When we are sad, do you think God wants to help us feel better? Yes, he does.

The Bible tells us that there are a lot of people who feel sad, and that God sent Jesus to help them feel better and be happy. Let's thank God for helping us to feel better.

Prayer: God, thank you for helping us feel better when we are sad. Thank you for sending Jesus so that we can be happy.—Michael Lanway

June 20. Following the Leader

TEXT: Rom. 4:13–25

Let's all stand up and get in one line. We are going to play follow-the-leader, so you have to do everything I do. Let's go.

[*The minister will go to three or four people in the congregation and do one of the following: shake hands; give a hug; say, "You're special"; say, "Jesus loves you and I do, too."*]

[*Back where you began*]. Stay in line and look at me. The things we just did are things Jesus wants to do. Jesus wants us to help people feel good by hugging and shaking hands. Jesus wants us to tell others they are special and that we love them. When we do these things, we are following Jesus, our leader.

Prayer: Dear God, help us to do the things Jesus wants us to do, and to always follow him.—Michael Lanway

June 27. Hands

This morning I want you to think for a few moments about things you all have. In fact, you have two of them. They are out in the open where everyone can see them. You used them this morning to get dressed and to eat your breakfast and to brush your teeth. How many of you think you know what I am thinking about?

We are told that the movement of our hand is governed by thirty different joints and more than fifty muscles. Every day we use these hands to perform nearly a thousand different functions. Our hands are a precision of movement and are perfectly coordinated with the eye and mind. Our hands are indeed a most wonderful part of our body.

It is important for us to remember that, because we can use our hands in so many ways for good or bad. You can be greedy with your hands, hold onto things, or you can share with your hands. You can use your hand to hurt someone, or you can use your hand to be a friend.

So today I want you to remember how important your hands are and to try to use your hands for good things so that by your hands the people around you will know what a good person you are.

Now, as you go back to your places, I would like each one of you to shake hands with the other boys and girls and with me.—Kenneth Mortonson

July 4. Christians Are Patriots, Too

Object: American flag.

I looked up the word *patriotism* today. One of Webster's dictionaries defines it, "love for or devotion to one's country." Boys and girls, I want you to be the best patriots you can possibly be. I want you to love this flag. Maybe even get a lump in your throat when you hear "The Star Spangled Banner." Go to Fourth of July parades and have a great time celebrating the birth of this country. Get excited about what the United States stands for in the world.

But I want to tell you to be careful. Sometimes being a Christian patriot is unpopular. Sometimes it is dangerous. When I was young, I thought it meant glorious things like winning wars or being the most powerful country on earth or making other countries do what Americans wanted them to do. I was proud of everything about the country.

Then I began to think of what a Christian would be proud of in a country, and my views changed. The things I am proudest of are things like making sure all Americans have equal rights and freedoms or a president's insistence that we support basic human rights for all people around the world or American leadership in the struggle for peace, for the end to world hunger, for new medicines, for protection of the world's environment and resources, for things that are good for all people at home and around the world.

Where the United States is wrong, I want to try to change it or help others who can change things. Supporting the good, opposing the bad—that is Christian patriotism.—Stuart G. Collier

July 11. Getting Stronger

TEXT: Rom. 5:1–11

Objects: Dumbbells/weights of five pounds, ten pounds, fifteen pounds.

See these things? These are weights, and people use these to get stronger and make their muscles bigger. Let's see your arm muscles. Wow! Want to see mine? [*Show them.*] Our muscles are pretty big, aren't they?

God gave us muscles to help us lift heavy things like people, bags of groceries, etc. We can make our muscles bigger and stronger by lifting heavy things, like these weights. Do you want to try to lift them? [*Let them try.*]

It's good that God made our muscles be able to get stronger and bigger so that we can lift and carry the things we need. Let's thank God for making us that way.

Prayer: Dear God, thank you for our muscles. Help us to keep getting stronger.—Michael Lanway

July 18. Kindness

TEXT: Gal. 5:22–23

At my house we have a dog and a cat. They are both adults, but sometimes the stresses of life get too much for them, and they revert to their childhood behavior. They play together. (Other adults should take a lesson from them!)

Their favorite game goes like this. Smudge, our black cat, innocently walks across the yard, which belongs to Lady, our black-and-white dog. Lady (who has no tail) rushes up to Smudge and enviously bites his tail, whereupon Smudge somersaults, yowls, and tries to claw the dog's face. A royal battle for the cat's tail follows. Warfare continues throughout the yard until the two are worn out or distracted.

The dog and cat are about the same size, and each has teeth, claws, and strength that could hurt the other one badly. But each animal is careful not to hurt the other. There is an essential rule of kindness in their relationship.

The Bible tells us that when the Spirit of God lives within us and has control of our lives, one of the characteristics of our personalities will be kindness. We can hurt each other so easily. Remember that God is working within you to produce a kind spirit that will not hurt another person. Or yourself, either: Be kind to yourself, always. And while we are at it, why don't we expand our kindness to animals and all of Creation? The well-being of all Creation depends on our kindness.—Stuart G. Collier

July 25. A Cool Drink of Water

This morning I wanted to do something nice for you. Since it is so hot, I wanted to give you a nice drink of cold water. But I had a problem. If I brought a cup of water in here for each one of you and then let it sit for a while before you came up here, the water would get warm. So I had what I thought was a good idea. I could freeze the water in some styrofoam cups and then let them warm up so that the ice would melt and the water would still be nice and cold.

But I forgot something that I learned a long time ago. Do you know what happens to water when it freezes? [*It expands.*] And do you know what happens to a styrofoam cup when water expands with it? [*It cracks.*] So by the time the ice is melted, all I would have is an empty cup. The water would all run out.

Let me read a passage from the Bible, Eph. 5:15–17. Paul is advising us to be careful about what we do in life. That means that just wanting to do something good for someone is not enough. You also have to think about what you are doing and what might happen. We really have to be careful in life.

So I am not able to give you a cool drink of water this morning because I was not careful; but I do have a cool drink for you. And please be careful with it. [*Give each child a small fruit drink in a container with a straw.*]—Kenneth Mortonson

August 1. Our Gardens and God's Garden

TEXT: Rom. 1:19–20

Objects: Fruits and vegetables grown by members, if possible.

I have some special things in my bag today. I need you to tell me what they are. [*Pull each item out and let them identify it. Also ask who likes to eat it and give it to them.*]

Do you know where these things come from? They come from gardens. How do things grow in a garden? Do things just pop up out of the ground, or do people have to plant them? People who plant gardens are called gardeners.

Did you know this whole world is one big garden? It is. Who is the gardener of the world? God is. God grows all the trees and bushes and mountains and everything.

Let's thank God for our gardens and for God's great big garden called the world.

Prayer: Thank you, God, for our gardens and the food they grow. Thank you for making this world your garden and for taking care of us.—Michael Lanway

August 8. The Ministry of Interruptions

TEXT: Mark 5:21–34

[*This children's sermon will require the preparation of several people.*]

Pastor: Good morning, girls and boys. I would like to talk to you about . . . , excuse me for just a second. [*The pastor notices a child's untied shoe and stops to tie it.*] Your shoe is untied. I would hate to see you fall and get hurt. This will only take a minute. I am sorry about the interruption, I would like to talk about . . .

Music director (interrupting): Pastor, if I could have just a minute?

Pastor (surprised): This is not the best time I could imagine, but what can I do for you?

Music director: I am worried about the next song. I'm just not sure it is going to go well. Do you think we should change hymns?

Pastor: I think it will be fine. You do a good job of picking the hymns. Let's go ahead with it. It will be okay. [*The pastor*

turns back to the children.] As I was saying, I would like to talk about . . .

Pianist (interrupting): Pastor, if I could have just a minute? I know this is not a good time, but it won't take long.

Pastor: That's fine. How can I help you?

Pianist: I feel so bad about the last song I played. Don't you think I did a terrible job?

Pastor: I don't think that at all. You are a wonderful pianist. You need to stop being so hard on yourself. You do a great job. [*The pastor turns again to the children.*] As I started to say, I would like to talk about . . . [*The pastor sees a mother who is visibly upset.*] I am sorry. I will be back in just a minute. [*The pastor's attention is given to the woman.*] Are you okay?

Mother: I am sorry. I did not mean to interrupt the children's sermon. I was just looking at the children, and I realized that my children are getting older. They will be leaving home in a few years.

Pastor: I can certainly understand why you are upset, but your children will always be your children. They will grow up, but you will never stop being their mother.

Mother: That's right. That makes me feel better. Thank you for your help. I will be fine. You can go back to the children's sermon.

Pastor: Children, I am sorry, but we are out of time. I wanted to talk about interruptions and how important they can be. Jesus was often interrupted by someone in need. Many times Jesus stopped what he was doing to take care of someone. Sometimes just when we are busiest, a friend will need a kind word, a compliment, or our help. We need to remember the example of Jesus. We need to remember that sometimes interruptions are very important.—Brett Younger

August 15. Is It Okay to Get Mad?

TEXT: Eph. 4:26

When I was a boy I wasn't allowed to show it when I got mad. I couldn't even slam the back door. And I didn't know how to deal with my anger in any better way. Do you know what happens when you get angry and can't do anything about it? You go off and feel sorry for yourself and feel down in the dumps. Maybe you cry or maybe you hit somebody or say mean things.

In the Bible, Paul wrote to his Christian friends something you need to understand, so that when you get angry you will know what to do. Paul says, first of all, to go ahead and be angry, if somebody was feeling angry. He said it is all right to be angry. When somebody hurts you or threatens to hurt you, you do get angry, and your anger helps you make that person stop doing that. When someone is unfair to you, you feel angry. It is normal. When you see someone hurting someone else, you need to get angry about it and help to stop that, too.

Then Paul warned his friends not to let their anger cause them to sin. He knew that we want to lash out and hurt people when we are angry, and that is not the right way to deal with our anger.

What do you think is a better way? The best thing usually is to talk about it. You can say, "Bobby, I'm mad about your taking my football without asking. I don't want you to do it again." Or you may need to say to your parents, "I'm mad at you." They will ask you why, and you can say, "Because I don't think you are being fair." Then you can talk it out and feel better, and maybe you can get things changed. That's the best way to act when you get angry.—Stuart G. Collier

August 22. A Lesson from a Mirror

[*Before your time with the children, stick a piece of paper to your face.*]

Most people use a mirror like this every day. They will look into it to see if their face is clean or their hair looks all right or maybe to check out a sore on their face.

You see, we cannot see our face like we can see our hand or feet. Now, when you look at my face what do you see?

Well, thank you for telling me. That looks silly; I better take it off. I saw it when I looked in the mirror, but then we were busy talking, and I forgot what I saw. That was not very smart of me.

So sometimes we need other people to

help us see things and to set them right. I hope you will remember that when someone at home or school tries to help you. Thank you for helping me this morning.—Kenneth Mortonson

August 29. What Bugs Can Teach Us

TEXT: Romans 6

Objects: Locust body shells (or snake skins or cocoon, etc.).

See these bugs? Well, they are only shells, but locusts used to live in them. You know what happened? The locusts got new bodies, and they didn't need these old ones anymore.

Do you know how that happened? I don't either. That's just the way God works. In the Bible, God tells us that when we get to heaven, we'll have new bodies there.

Prayer: Thank you, God, for our bodies. Thank you for the new bodies you promise us.—Michael Lanway

September 5. What Are People For? (The Question)

TEXT: Matt. 22:23–40

A man [*Wendell Berry*] I admire wrote a book with a weird title. The title of his book was *What Are People For?* Have you ever thought about that question? I bet not many people have. But it really is an important question, because God made all the people for some reason or other.

It's a tough question, isn't it? Especially because God made everybody so different—different colors, different shapes, different abilities, interests, living places, life-styles, languages. And so many of us—billions of us! Einstein and Hulk Hogan, Wilt Chamberlain and Willie Shoemaker, Billy Graham and Adolf Hitler, Eskimos and aborigines, university professors and shrimp fishers and spies and senators and dentists—what a bunch of characters!

What do you think people are for? Don't answer right now. When you get into the car after church, I want you to ask your mom or dad what they think, too. Ask your friends. Next week, I'm going to ask for your answers.—Stuart G. Collier

September 12. What Are People For? (The Answer)

TEXT: Matt. 22:23–40

Do you remember last week's question: What are people for? Now I want to hear your answers.

Do you know what I think? It is all part of one word. What is that word? *Love!* One day Jesus was teaching the people, and somebody asked him to name the greatest commandment of all. He answered with two commandments. The first was to love God in every way you can—with your thoughts and mental gifts, with your feelings, and with your actions. The second commandment was to love other people just as much as you love yourself, and Jesus wanted that to be a lot. Then Jesus said that every other commandment would be taken care of if we really loved God, our neighbors, and ourselves.

Doesn't it seem like God created us for love? I think God made us to have someone to love. God made us for himself! One of the psalms [100] says that God made us for himself; we are his, and his love endures forever. And because God loves our neighbor, we love our neighbor, too. We love people.

Now, the fact people are for God to love and to love God means something very important for us. It means that we are not to mistreat any of God's people or to use them just to make money for us or to ignore them when they need help or to live our lives in a way that makes life hard for other people.

It also means that we can all be happy. Very happy. Because God loves us very much, enough to send his Son Jesus Christ to us.—Stuart G. Collier

September 19. What Is a Lie?

What is a lie? A lie is something that is stated as being true when it is not true. Why do you think it is wrong to tell a lie? Because it can hurt people.

Let me show you what I mean. If I invited you to a party and told you that it would be held tomorrow at 3:00 P.M. when I knew it was going to be held this afternoon at 3:00 P.M., how would you feel if you came to my house tomorrow and no one was home?

Suppose you are playing baseball and you hit the ball and break a window, and the owner of the house comes out and asks who broke the window. What happens if no one tells the truth? The owner has to buy a new window, and he is hurt because he does not know the truth. He has to pay for something for which he was not to blame.

You see, it is very important for people to have the truth in life if they are to avoid being hurt by something that was not their fault. Sometimes telling the truth may cause you to have to face the consequences of what you did, and that may hurt you. But if you lie to save yourself some pain, you will probably hurt someone else. If we love one another we cannot do that.—Kenneth Mortonson

September 26. Feeding People

TEXT: Mark 6:30–44

Objects: Cans of food, different shapes and sizes.

Occasion: World Hunger Day or food drive.

I have some things in this bag I want to show you. You tell me what each thing is by looking at the picture. [*The minister will take out one can at a time and let the children see the picture and shout out what it contains. Do this until all the cans are seen.*]

What do each of these have in common? [*They're all round, all metal, all have paper on them, all are foods.*] That's right. People eat these foods that are in the cans.

Do you have cans of food in your home? Did you know that there are some people who do not have any cans of food in their homes?

Today you and I can help the people who have nothing to eat. We can bring cans of food to church and then give them to hungry people. We can give money to help buy food for hungry people. Let's ask God to have everyone here do that.

Prayer: Dear God, thank you for all the cans of food in our homes and for all the food we eat. Let everyone of us help feed the hungry people who have nothing to eat.—Michael Lanway

October 3. Forgiveness

TEXT: Matt. 18:21–22

Object: Pocket calculator.

Boys and girls, what is this? [*Calculator.*] Many of you use them in school, don't you? Are they very accurate? Do they remember what you put into them? I don't know, but I bet the disciple Peter would have been good with a calculator. Do you know why? Because he liked to keep score, at least until Jesus taught him better.

One day Jesus was teaching about how to get along with people. To do that, you always have to be forgiving people for all kinds of things that they sometimes mean to do and sometimes don't mean to do to hurt you. You probably know that when you don't forget somebody, pretty soon you notice that you don't like that person anymore. Before long you notice that you don't have any friends at all, because everybody has failed you somehow, and you just don't like anybody, and nobody likes you because you are mad at everybody.

The disciple Peter knew to forgive people, but he wanted to know how long he had to go on forgiving the same person. So he asked Jesus if seven times was enough. That sounds generous, doesn't it? It was, back then. But Jesus said, "No, Peter, not seven times, but seventy times seven!" Peter would need a calculator to keep up with that much forgiving, wouldn't he? But what Jesus was really saying was this: "Don't ever stop forgiving as long as anybody needs it. Throw your calculator away, Peter." Let's do that, too.—Stuart G. Collier

October 10. A String to Remember

Object: A piece of string or ribbon.

Do you ever have a hard time remembering things? I sure do! Sometimes I'm supposed to do something or be somewhere at a particular time, and I just completely forget! And forgetting can get us in trouble, can't it?

Did you know this string can help you remember? Hard to believe, isn't it?

There's an old-fashioned custom that said to tie a string around your finger to help you remember something. The idea is that you will notice that string on your finger, and it will remind you that there is something you need to do or somewhere you need to go. Sounds simple, doesn't it?

That's a little bit like the way we are with the Bible, God's Word. God has given us the Bible as a reminder of who he is and how much he loves us. It has all kinds of wonderful stories that remind us of how God can help us when we get into trouble or have a problem.

But it doesn't help us if we don't look at it! Unless we take a few minutes every day to look at God's Word—or maybe have someone read some Bible stories to us—then we sometimes forget all that God wants for us.

A string is a good reminder, but your Bible is an even better reminder. Let's don't forget to look at it.—J. Michael Duduit

October 17. Finding the Lost

TEXT: Luke 5:12–15

One of my favorite games is hide-and-seek. Have you ever played that game? I like the part where I get to hide and let others try to find me. That's really fun! Do you like that part, too? But do you know when I don't like that game? When no one can find me. When no one can find me, it is not fun anymore because then I am all by myself.

In the Bible, Jesus tells us that there are other people who feel sad like that, because they feel all alone. They don't know that Jesus loves them, that God loves them, that we love them. So they are sad.

Do you want to help them feel happy? Jesus does, too! Here is how we can help. Whenever we see someone in school or down the street or anywhere, we can tell them that Jesus loves them, that God loves them, and that you love them, too. Then you can invite them to church so they can be here with us. Then they will know that they don't have to be sad anymore. Let's tell God to help people feel happy and tell them that they are loved.—Michael Lanway

October 24. No Beginning or End

TEXT: 1 Cor. 12:27–13:13.

Object: A faded piece of wallpaper.

Good morning, boys and girls. I'd like you to sit in a circle today. [*Help them arrange themselves into a circle.*] I'm going to pass around this piece of paper, and I'd like you to tell me something about it as goes by you. [*Pass around the faded wallpaper and elicit responses as each child sees it.*] It's wallpaper. It's faded. It's brittle. It looks like it peeled off a wall. It probably used to have clear colors. You can't really tell what the colors were. You can hardly see the original pattern. Do you think this wallpaper was very pretty once? [*Let them respond.*] Yes, I think it was very pretty when it was new. Then the sun shone on it, and it faded, and now it looks like it's falling apart. It was probably on someone's wall once a long time ago. Oh well, nothing lasts forever. Everything gets old and dies or falls apart.

Our lesson says that most things will not last, but it tells us that one thing will last forever. Do you know what it is? [*Let them answer.*] Our verse says that love never ends. Everything else does, but not love. Does anyone have any idea why we are sitting in a circle? [*Let them respond.*] A circle is a shape that has no beginning and no end. Some people call it a perfect shape. A circle is the shape of a ring. A gold band, the kind that men and women sometimes give each other at their weddings are in the shape of a circle. In the wedding the bride and groom promise that they will each love the other one forever and always. The wedding ring is supposed to remind them of their promise that their love will never end. But do all couples love each other always? [*Let them respond.*] No, sometimes they stop loving each other, and they don't always stay married.

So if our lesson says that love never ends, whose love is it talking about? [*Let them respond.*] God's love for us never ends. It's always there forever and ever, just like a ring with no beginning and no ending. Sometimes when someone very special dies, we keep on loving that person the rest of our life. That's another kind of love that never ends. Have you ever known anyone who has been married for seventy-five years? [*Let them respond.*] That's a very long time! I think love like that never ends either. When we love someone, we should try to make it last forever. But even if our love fades like this wallpaper, it's nice to know that God's love never ends. It has no beginning and no end—just like a ring or our circle. Love never ends!—*Children's Sermon Service Plus!*

October 31. A Lesson from Leaves

When you see colored leaves like these, what do you think of? [*Fall.*] I did not expect to see very much color in the leaves this fall, because it has been so dry during the summer. But I was wrong, and the color has been beautiful. Now, if I had followed my expectations, I would not have bothered to even look at the trees. And I would have missed a beautiful sight.

We sometimes do this in life. I have some children [*or grandchildren*] who are like that sometimes in regard to new foods. They make up their minds that they will not like the food, even before they try it, and they will not eat it. That is too bad, for they miss many good things that way.

Some boys and girls even come to church with the idea that they will not like what happens here, and so they ignore what is going on, and they spend all their time talking to a friend and never even hear the music or what is said. That is too bad, because they might learn something if they listen.

Today I would like to suggest that you try to find some pretty leaves and put them between two pieces of paper and then put a heavy book on top, and after a few days they will be nice and flat and dry, and you can keep them to remind you of the beautiful colors of fall. Thank you for coming up here today.—Kenneth Mortonson

November 7. All of Us Are Different and All of Us Are Special

TEXT: Romans 14 and 15.

Let's see how we are the same and how are we different. Stand up and let's look at each other.

We all have eyes. We all have mouths and noses. Everyone have legs? How about hands and arms? See, we are the same in some ways.

But we are different, too. Who has blue eyes? Who has brown eyes? Who has the longest hair? The biggest hands? The biggest feet? Who's the tallest?

We are all different; we have different hair, eyes, sizes, and everything. But we are all the same, too. God says that each of us is special.

Each of us is special to God. Each of us is special to each other. It doesn't matter how we are different. What matters is that God loves us all the same.

Prayer: Dear God, thank you for making each of us special and for how we are the same and for how we are different. Help us to love each other for who we are, no matter how different. — Michael Lanway

November 14. Loving the Unlovely

TEXT: Matt. 25:36

Have you ever seen a prison? Did it look like a nice place to live, if you had a choice? They are not nice places to be. The people there often are dangerous, and nobody really loves them.

I used to visit people in prison. Jesus said to do that. He wanted us to visit and express our care. Why would Jesus command us to do that?

Let me tell you what I think. I think Jesus knew that people in prison need love just as much and probably much, much more than we do out here. More than that, Jesus knew that everybody — you and me, your parents and your friends — has failed God and other people in many, many ways. So in God's sight, we all depend on and receive God's love in spite of ourselves. We call it grace. It means love that we don't really deserve, but love that is great and good and free, in spite of everything.

One day I hope some of you will visit people in prison. Even now, you could have a class project to make Christmas cards or Easter cards for people in the county jail. When people experience grace — real love that they don't expect or deserve — lots of times they experience God in it. They turn to God when they feel loved; they love other people, too. Then, all the angels in heaven rejoice over a lost sheep the shepherd has found. — Stuart G. Collier

November 21. Being Thankful

Boys and girls, when I was in school studying to be a minister I wrote a long paper, called a dissertation, about a man named Karl Barth. You would complain very loudly if you had to write a paper that long.

Karl Barth was a minister and a teacher. He has taught me many wonderful things about what it means to be a Christian. One thing he wrote comes to my mind very often, and I want to share it with you.

First, I want you to know that he wrote many books — enough to fill a wheelbarrow — so when he says something, you know he has thought about it a great deal, and he is worth listening to. Well, he said that the basic response of a Christian to God is thankfulness.

Does that sound impressive to you? Be thankful? Probably not. We may think our response ought to be active, doing something great for God. But Barth said gratitude is our first response to the love of God for us in Jesus Christ. We realize what God has done, how much God loves us, how wonderful it is that God wants us to be in heaven with him, and we melt in thankfulness. All our arrogant pride, independence, meanness — all that isn't lovely just melts away before the love of God. Because we are so thankful and so overcome with love for God, we want to do great things in return. But first and last, above and below all else, even when we don't have all the things of life we could have, we are still full of thankfulness. — Stuart G. Collier

November 28. Being at Peace with One Another

Objects: Two jars and two candles. Fasten one candle to a piece of wood so that it can float in the jar. You will also need a way to add water to both jars. A baster will work.

I have a special situation here in these two jars that I want you to look at this morning. In each jar is a candle that is burning. Now, what do you think will happen if I add water to the jar? Let's see.

Well, that one went out because fire and water cannot exist together in the same place. But this one is still burning, for there is something else in this jar. The candle is on a piece of wood, and the wood floats on the water, and that keeps the water away from the fire and so both can exist together in the jar.

This reminds us of something we all need to remember as we live with other people. There are times when we have to add something special to prevent a problem. That something special that we can add is to be a peacemaker. That means, we will do what we can to keep a friend.

What do you do if someone hits you? Hitting back is one thing you can do; or you can be a peacemaker and not hit back. You can do a lot of things to keep a friend as a friend. You can do it because you have something special that we call love. I hope you will keep this in mind as you live and play with others.—Kenneth Mortonson

December 5. A Book of Instructions

Some books are not written just to be read. Just reading some things is not nearly enough. For instance, a cookbook is not written just to be read. You can read over and over how to bake a cake. It might be nice to know how to make a cake, but until you get out the ingredients and put them together, you do not have a cake. A telephone book is not written just to be read. People do not get out the phone book just to read very often. There are not many people who read the phone book just to learn the numbers. The phone book is helpful only when you need to call somebody. The instructions for a model airplane are not written just to be read. It is not much fun just to read the instructions. You have to put the plane together, or it is a waste of time.

The Bible is like that. It is not enough just to read it. You have to do something about it. For instance, the Bible says we should forgive people. That is a good thing to know. It becomes important when someone does something wrong and we have to decide if we will forgive them. The Bible tells us to pray. It is a good thing to know, but it only helps us to know that if we pray. It is not enough just to read the Bible. We need to do what the Bible says.—Brett Younger

December 12. Make a Prayer List

TEXT: Phil. 4:4–7

Object: A Christmas catalog.

Good morning, boys and girls. It's getting closer to Christmas so I thought I'd make out my Christmas list. Why do we make Christmas lists? [*Let them respond.*] It lets people who want to give us gifts know what we want. How many of you have made a Christmas list already? [*Wait for show of hands.*] Let's go around our group and each of you tell us one thing that's on your Christmas list. [*Go around the group and give them each a turn.*] There are a lot of things on your Christmas lists. How many things do you have on your lists? [*Let them respond.*] Some of you have ten things on your lists and some of you probably have twenty-five things on your list. When I look through a catalog, I see things I wouldn't even think of that would be nice to have for Christmas. While I'm looking at the Christmas catalog, my list gets longer and longer. Let's look at some of the things on my list. [*Have several pages marked in the catalog with things from your list. Show them the pages and pictures.*] Are your lists exactly like mine? [*Let them respond.*] No, usually kids have lots more toys on their lists than grown-ups do. Our ages are different so we want different things. When I was your age, I had lots of toys on my list, too. When you are older, you'll probably have lots of grown-up things on your list. This is a pretty big list. Do you think I'll get all these things? [*Let them respond.*] No, I might get some of them, and I might get other things that aren't on my list. Some of them I'll like, and some I won't! Do you always get everything on your lists? [*Let them respond.*] No, of course you don't!

Our lesson today is about a special list. It's not a Christmas present list. But it's kind of like it because we don't always get everything on it. It's a prayer list. Our verse says we should let God know what we want. It means that through prayers we can go to God and ask for anything we want or need or wish for. It might be some things on our Christmas list, or it might be prayers for someone who is sick or sad or lonely. Can you each think of something to put on a list to God? [*Let them take turns.*] That's a big prayer list. Will we each get everything on our prayer list? [*Let them respond.*] No, we probably won't. We need to keep on asking for everything we want. That's what prayer is!—*Children's Sermon Service Plus!*

December 19. The Son of God

TEXT: John 1:14

Object: An iron.

Sometimes when I am preaching I wonder how much you understand of what I am saying. Let me tell you right away that none of us understands all about God. The Bible says God's thoughts are too complicated for us to understand fully, and God's ways of acting in the world are beyond our finding out completely.

One of those mysteries concerns Jesus. When you are old enough, God will come to you, and in some way you will find yourself wanting to give your life to Christ. You will be making a decision about Jesus—was this Jesus you hear about really the Son of God?

The faith of the Christian has always been that Jesus was both God and man. Jesus was fully divine—but he was fully human, just like you and me. We wonder how that can be. Some people will tell you that it is impossible.

But it is possible. Look at this iron [*unplugged*]. The flat part of it is just metal, isn't it. It is cold, too. But what would happen if I plugged it in and turned it on? Something invisible would flow through the metal. It comes from electricity, and we call it heat. But the iron itself is still absolutely the same iron. We can think of Jesus the same way. He was still fully a man, but he was filled with something invisible that made him also divine. We say in faith that God came to earth and took the form of flesh, and that flesh was Jesus. That is what we celebrate on Christmas Day.—Stuart G. Collier

December 26. Someone to Count On

Some things cannot be counted on. If you get here right on time for Sunday school, you cannot count on everyone already being here. You cannot count on the weather when you are going to school. It might rain, snow, or be sunny. You cannot count on your favorite baseball team. They might win, but they might lose.

Some things you can almost always count on. If you come to the Sunday worship service, you can count on an opportunity to give an offering. You can count on the weather when you are going on a picnic. It will probably rain. You can count on my favorite baseball team—the Cleveland Indians. They will almost always lose.

The Bible tells us the one we can always count on is God. When you are frightened, you can be certain God is with you. When you do something wrong, you can know that God will forgive you. When you pray, you can be sure that God is listening.

With so many things you cannot count on, we should be most thankful that we can always count on God to be with us, always loving us.—Brett Younger

SECTION XI.
A Little Treasury of Sermon Illustrations

BY ROBERT C. SHANNON

AGE.   We should never worry about getting older. Someone has said that when you are over the hill you pick up speed! Another reminds us that the best tunes are played on the old violins! Never worry about getting older. Some never have the privilege.

AGE.   Anyone who has tried to understand temperature in Celsius as well as Fahrenheit will appreciate the quip of the man who said that while some said he was eighty, he was really only twenty-seven Celsius!

AGE.   Pirate's Alley in New Orleans is lined with sidewalk artists ready to paint portraits of visitors to the French Quarter. One enterprising artist put up a sign: "Under forty, Likeness Guaranteed. Over forty, Likeness Avoided!"

ALCOHOL.   Some misguided cynic put a bumper sticker on the back of his car that read, "Booze Is the Only Answer." You don't have to be very observant to know that booze is never the answer, that it may be the problem but is never the solution. What a warped view of life that person had to suggest that life is so bad you can only get through it if you are under the influence of alcohol!

ANGER.   In Bud Blake's *Tiger* comic strip little Hugo is very angry. His friend says, "You oughta control yourself when things go wrong, Hugo. Sometimes it's a good idea to bottle it up for a day." Hugo answers, "This is some from yesterday's bottle I'm letting out to make room in it for what went wrong today!"

ATTITUDES.   Andy Capp, the scamp in the comic strip, is coming home in the small hours of the morning to an infuriated wife. She growls, "Get to bed!" He says, "Think, woman, every minute you spend being angry is sixty seconds in which you could have had a good time."

ATTITUDES.   George Bernard Shaw wrote, "People are always blaming circumstances for what they are. I don't believe in circumstances. The people who get on in the world are the people who get up and look for the circumstances they want, and if they can't find them, make them."

BIBLE.   Last year the weekly tabloid of the Yugoslav Communist Party *Kommunist* carried a full-page advertisement for the Bible Society of Yugoslavia, including a response coupon for those who wanted more information or who wanted to order a Bible! Incongruously the front page carried a picture of Karl Marx. But already the Bible is overturning communism, and soon Karl Marx will be on the back page and the Bible on the front!

BIBLE.   1991 marked the bicentennial of the death of Mozart. At Lincoln Center in New York, musicians performed every one of the more than six hundred compositions of Mozart. A few people have undertaken to memorize vast portions of Scripture (and it is good to memorize Scripture), but the significant thing is not how much Scripture we know but how much Scripture we practice.

BIBLE.   Dorothy L. Sayers, referring to the lack of information about the twelve apostles in the New Testament wrote, "The gospel must be a narrative of fact; nobody inventing a story could be so vague and slipshod about the *dramatis personae!*"

BIBLE.   Some years ago the National College of Education in Evanston, Illinois, surveyed a large number of CEOs and college presidents. They cited the Bible as the most influential book. Charles Dickens' *A Tale of Two Cities* came in second.

BIBLE.   In *The Romance of the Last Crusade* Major Vivian Gilbert told how his British troops took Mickmash during World War I. They read in the Bible in 1 Samuel 13 and 14 about the way Saul and Jonathan took it and moved successfully through the same rocky pass those two had used thousands of years before!

BLOOD.   The city of Zagreb, Croatia, was once two towns known as Kaptol and Gradec. Then there was a stream that divided them, though it is now covered over. Across the stream was a bridge (now a street) called Krvavi most: the bridge of blood! The only thing that could span the gulf between us sinners and a holy God was a bridge of blood!

BLOOD.   Garnets can be found on the gray boulders of the Scottish Highlands, beautiful wine-colored fragments. Legend says that at death the souls of fighting men are caught up in the air. There they are cast backward and forward for years, unable to make peace until they make expiation for their sons on earth. Sometimes on windy nights you can hear them fighting high up in the clouds. The next morning you find these rocks spotted with their blood.

CHRISTIANS.   There is a small group of men and women who are called Noachides. Many are disillusioned Christians. They follow many Jewish practices but have not converted to Judaism. They identify with the ethical monotheism of Judiasm and uphold the laws of Noah against idolatry, blasphemy, bloodshed, sexual sins, and theft. They regard Jesus as only a great teacher. They are called the children of Noah. John wrote, "Consider the incredible love that the Father has shown us in allowing us to be called children of God!" (1 John 3:1, Phillips).

CHRIST THE KING.   Every king in Saudi Arabia builds his own palace. He never lives in a palace built by the previous king. But Christ, the King of kings, is quite willing to occupy a throne once occupied by another. Take self off the throne of your life, and Christ the King will come there and reign there.

CHRIST-LIKE.   When Francis I of France got a scar on his chin, he decided to grow a beard to hide it. Since he did not want to look out of place, he ordered the entire male population of France to follow his example. Of course, it is in a very different way that we are asked to emulate Christ. It is not his dress. It is not the way he wore his beard or hair. It is the character of our king that we must emulate.

CHRISTMAS.   A man sent his friend a cryptic Christmas card. It said: A B C D E F G H I J K M N O P Q R S T U V W X Y Z. The recipient puzzled over it for weeks, finally gave up and wrote asking for an explanation. In July he received the explanation on a postcard: "No L."

CHURCH.   For years nothing in Cologne, Germany, stood higher than the spire of the city's magnificent cathedral. Finally, however, the skyline changed, and one structure rises higher than that spire. It is a television tower! No matter. The *church* in its truest sense, the church in its nonmaterial sense, will always tower above anything man can make, do, or even think!

COMMITMENT.   There is a town in Walton County Georgia named Between. If people ask you where you live you say, "I live in Between." It's only a little place but thousands live *in between*. They are not ready to abandon Christ for the world, nor are they ready to abandon the world for Christ. They want to live where really no one *can* live—in between!

COMMUNION.   The oldest synagogue in the Western hemisphere is on the island of Curacao in the Caribbean sea. Daily they spread sand on the floor as a reminder of the journey their forefathers made across the wilderness to the Promised Land. The Lord's Supper is a little like that. It reminds us of the journey Jesus made to and through the spiritual wilderness of this world so that we, following him, might come to an eternal Promised Land.

COMMUNION.   The Christ of the Andes is a memorial on the border between Argentina and Chile. The Christ of Communion guards the border between the past and the future. It is a token that says the sacrifice of Christ must never be forgotten. It is a token that says our forgiven sins *are* forgotten. Looking the other way—into the future—the Christ of Communion reassures us that he is coming again, that our labor is not in vain, and that we must resolve to live better tomorrow than we did yesterday.

CONFESSION.   The Orthodox church has never been large in the United States, but there is a Russian Orthodox monastery in Jordanville, New York. Each monk lives in a tiny room. Each day he is awakened by a bell. Each day begins in exactly the same way. Each monk makes the sign of the cross and begins the day with this simple prayer in Russian: "Lord Jesus Christ, Son of God, have mercy on me, a sinner."

CONSISTENCY.   A tourist from Florida was visiting Hungary. He was explaining to his Hungarian host the peculiar flora and fauna of Florida. He went into a detailed explanation of the chameleon, that little lizard that changes color to match whatever he lights upon. "We don't have them in Hungary," said his host. "But we have people like that!"

CONSISTENCY.   In *Alice in Wonderland* the Duchess said, "Be what you would seem to be, or if you'd like it put more simply, Never imagine yourself not to be otherwise than what it might appear to others that what you were or might have been was not otherwise than what you had been would have appeared to them otherwise."

CONSUMERISM.   Malcolm Forbes's seventieth birthday party was called the bash of the century. He chartered a DC-8 *and* a 747 and a Concorde to fly six hundred guests from New York City to Morocco. Food, drinks, tents, and entertainment came to nearly one million dollars. But only a few months afterward Forbes was dead—remembered not for some philanthropic gift that fed the hungry or clothed the naked but rather remembered for an unconscionable waste to feed one man's hungry ego.

COURAGE.   Antigonius was a great Greek warrior. He had an ailment so painful he fought to forget it. He really did not care if he were killed, so he plunged into battle. His general was so impressed with his courage he had him cured. Then he would no longer fight!

CROSS.   Several people sued the Marine Corps because there was a sixty-five-foot cross at the Camp Holland M. Smith Marine Corps base in Honolulu. Supporters of the cross defended it as a "nonsectarian symbol." They said it was a "nonsectarian symbol of our national resolve to obtain a full accounting of American servicemen still missing or unaccounted for in Southeast Asia." Surely we'd like to see the cross remain. Surely we'd hate to see it stripped of its meaning and made something other than a symbol of Christ and the Christian religion.

CROSS.   Someone noted that Christ said take up your cross, not take up your cudgel. He did not say take up your flag and follow me. (What fun that would be!) He did not say take up your torch and follow me, take up your banner and follow me, or take up your club and follow me. He said take up your cross and follow me.

CROSS.   It is common to see shrines along the roadsides in Austria. One modest one sits alongside a quiet country lane by a bench. There is a nice view of pastures and forest. The verse beneath the simple shrine says, "Here you can see in the beautiful temple of Nature the footprints of a great God. But if you would like to see something greater, stand beside the cross."

CROSS.   The island of Sicily will soon be linked with the mainland of Italy by a suspension bridge, built in a joint effort by the Italians and the Japanese. It will extend 6,560 feet, and it will be the longest suspension bridge in the world. In a spiritual sense the longest bridge was at Calvary where Jesus' cross bridged the gulf between sinful man and holy God.

DEATH.   Stephen Leacock, the famous American humorist, said, "I detest life insurance agents. They always argue that I shall someday die, which is not so!"

DEATH.   In C. S. Lewis's book *The Last Battle* (one of the Chronicles of Narnia) are these words: "Then Aslan turned to them and said, ". . . you are—as you used to call it in the Shadowlands—dead. The term is over: the holidays begun. The dream is ended: this is the morning." Lewis went on to say, "All their life in this world and all their adventures in Narnia had only been the cover and the title page: now at last they were beginning Chapter One of the Great Story which no one on earth has read: which goes on forever: in which every chapter is better than the one before."

DEATH.   Mark Twain once said, "Whoever has lived long enough to find out what life is, knows how deep a debt of gratitude we owe to Adam, the first ben-efactor of our race. He brought death into the world."

DEATH.   As the rays of the sun slant in a different direction in the autumn they block the chlorophyll that keeps the leaves on the trees green. As the leaves begin to die the lovely fall colors become visible. They were there all along, but they were not visible until death came. So, often, it is only at death that we learn of hidden greatness, unseen nobility, unnoticed goodness.

DEPRESSION.

> If you keep your nose to the grindstone rough
> And you keep it down there long enough,
> In time you'll say there's no such thing
> As brooks that babble and birds that sing.
> These three will all your world compose:
> Just you, the stone, and your poor old nose.
>
> —Anon.

DISAPPOINTMENT.   The name *Goodyear* is synonymous with tires, but Charles Goodyear who discovered the process of vulcanization that began the rubber tire industry died penniless. Infringements on his patent rights plus legal and financial problems robbed him of the due reward of his genius.

DISAPPOINTMENT.   In April 1986 a Chicago television station planned a spectacular live program. Before the television cameras they would unseal Al Capone's secret vault beneath Chicago's Lexington Hotel. It was thought to contain money, diamonds, and other riches. Geraldo Rivera hosted the two-hour show. Tension mounted as experts blasted through the walls. The IRS was there claiming Capone still owed $80,000 in back taxes. The police were there. Finally the vault was opened. All it contained was two empty gin bottles.

EASTER. The funeral of the Chinese emperor Xi Chun lasted one whole year. The body was carried by hand from Peking to Kashgar, a distance of 2,300 miles! The funeral procession lasted from January 1, 1912, to January 1, 1913! By contrast the burial of Jesus was accomplished hastily and without ceremony. That didn't matter. Within three days he was back on earth again, alive forevermore!

EASTER. Most bees can only sting you once. The stinger is left in your flesh and the bee cannot grow another. The sting of death was removed when Jesus died on the cross (1 Cor. 15:55,56; Heb. 9:22). Now the stinger is gone. Death is still present, and we shall all die, but for the believer the pain is gone, the poison is gone. The sting is gone.

EASTER. There used to be a theory that the wind that blows on Easter Eve will be the prevailing wind throughout the rest of the year. How grand it would be if that were true, for on Easter there is a fresh breeze of renewed faith and hope and worship. How wonderful it would be if that remained as the prevailing wind through the rest of the year!

EVANGELISM. Most of the rivers in Siberia flow north into the Arctic Ocean, leaving very little water for irrigation. A few have talked seriously about the engineering possibilities of reversing the flow so that the water can be used, making those rivers flow south into the Caspian Sea. Evangelism turns around the stream of life and makes its currents run in the opposite direction, bringing refreshment to the soul, growth, life!

FAITH. We believe the sun is in the sky at noon, not because we can see *it*, but rather because we see others things more clearly. We do not believe in God because we can see him. We believe in God for this reason: Because of him we can see other things more clearly.

FAITH. "Many a man has lost faith in God because he first lost faith in man,

and many a one has regained his faith in God because he met a man who took the bitterness out of his heart."—Cardinal Faulhaber

FAME. Remember the seven wonders of the ancient world. Only one of them had any real use. It is far, far better to be useful than to be famous.

FAME. Edwin Booth, the actor, was the brother of John Wilkes Booth, who killed Abraham Lincoln. In a curious coincidence, Edwin Booth had saved the life of Lincoln's son, Robert. Waiting for a train in Jersey City, New Jersey, Robert was pushed off the platform by a surging crowd just as a locomotive began to move. Booth, a bystander, pulled the young Lincoln to safety. Edwin Booth was not a Confederate sympathizer and admired President Lincoln. He was regarded at the time as the greatest American actor to ever play Hamlet, but things were never the same for Booth after his brother assassinated the president.

FEAR. There is an old Russian proverb that says, "Fear has big eyes." It's true. It may or may not be true that love is blind, but it is certainly true that fear is not blind. Fear even magnifies what it sees—and often sees what is not even there!

FORGETFULNESS. On July 20, 1979, a gunman burst into a grocery store in Wandsworth, England. "Give me the money or I will shoot!" demanded the robber. The grocer, Mohammed Razaq, had always prided himself on his eye for details. "Where is your gun?" he asked. The robber had forgotten to bring it!

FRUIT OF THE SPIRIT. No doubt it was with the best of intentions that a deeply religious man named the little shopping center he developed the Maranatha Shopping Center. No one can quarrel with his desire to express his faith in the Second Coming, even in such an unusual way. The disturbing part was the fruit and vegetable market in the center, named "Fruits of the Spirit." Surely he knew, as we all must know, that the fruits of the spirit are not apples, peaches, and pears but love, joy, peace, longsuffering, kindness, and gentleness.

FUTURE.   The place mat in the Chinese restaurant depicted the Chinese zodiac and explained the belief that one's personality and one's future success are determined by the year in which you were born. He checked his own. He was born in the year of the horse, and the paper said such people were popular and attractive. "It's right," he said, "that's me." Then he read another year, the year of the dog. It said, "Loyal and honest," He read them all and found that all twelve could be said of him! He decided that either the Chinese zodiac was a hoax or else he was a very well-rounded man.

GIVING.   Ships full of gold were brought from the New World by Columbus, but the *first* load was used to decorate a church in Rome! You can still see it today. Do Christ and the church have first call on *your* gold?

GOD.   Some years ago a heavy rain undermined the sidewalk in the city of Fort Lauderdale, Florida. A man fell on the broken sidewalk and sued the city. He lost. The courts ruled that the accident was caused by "an act of God." Upon hearing that, the man filed a second lawsuit. He sued God. The judge threw that case out, too. He said he lacked jurisdiction!

GOD.   Andy Rooney, the columnist, once wrote a piece about slush, the ugly, black stuff that runs in the gutters when the snow melts. He said it should be arranged so that lovely, white snow should not turn into ugly, black slush. He thought it would be better if snow fell black and gradually turned white! It's something to think about, but surely we all agree that God "doeth all things well."

GOD.   No one can fault the artistic genius of Michelangelo, and the Sistine chapel ceiling is certainly a masterpiece. One can, however, demur with regard to his theology as well as his knowledge of Scripture. The famous painting shows God touching with his finger the finger of Adam. We know that, in fact, God breathed into his nostrils the breath of life. When we perform artificial resuscitation to restore life, we do what God did to create life. And, of course, we know that a figure of an old bearded man is not adequate for the ageless God who is spirit, not flesh, and whom no man has seen. But then any image of God, whether painted or simply held in the imagination, is bound to be incorrect and insufficient.

GOOD FRIDAY.   It was on June 17, 1940, that General Charles de Gaulle fled Nazi-occupied France for England to begin the Free French movement. On the eighteenth of June he began a series of radio broadcasts from England beamed into France to rally the resistance and to keep the French from losing hope. Because the first broadcast was on that day, he came to be known as "the man of the eighteenth of June." Since it was on a Friday that Jesus Christ died for our sins, we might well call him "the man of Good Friday" or, better yet, "the man of Easter Sunday!"

HEART.   We always describe deep emotion by referring to a part of the body that is only a pump—the heart. We are heartsick, heartbroken, downhearted, or heavy-hearted. When we use the word *discouraged* the Latin word for *heart* is in the word (*cor*). In Shakespeare's day it was the custom for a young man to attach to his sleeve a gift for his sweetheart. Sometimes he'd have her name embroidered on his sleeve. So Shakespeare gave us the expression "wearing his heart on his sleeve." Certainly, we ought to display in conduct and in conversation our love for Jesus Christ so that all may know our heart belongs to him.

HEAVEN.   S. Y. Agnon won the Nobel prize for literature in 1966. He said, "I was born in one of the cities of the exile, but I always regarded myself as one who was born in Jerusalem." Paul wrote to the Philippians that "our citizenship is in heaven." Wherever we were born, our native land is the New Jerusalem that comes down from God.

HOLINESS.   G. K. Chesterton wrote, "It is impossible to be an artist and not care for laws and limitations. Art is limitation; the essence of every picture is the frame. . . . You may, if you like, free a tiger from his bars, but do not free him from his stripes. Do not free a camel of the burden of his hump; you may be freeing him from being a camel." Chesterton's point was this: "Thou shalt not" is only one of the necessary corollaries of "I will."

HOLY LAND.   In the year 200, fifty-three ships brought soil from Palestine to Pisan to the Campo Santo so that men could be buried there in holy ground. But we believe no ground is holy, and no land is holy. It is only people made in the likeness of God, people with a free will to do good or evil that can be holy *or* sinful.

HONESTY.   Wedding Nurseries in St. Petersburg, Florida, is an old, established firm. Over the years they have often had plants stolen. One incident is remarkable. A young man was saved. He returned *three truckloads* of interior and exterior plants he had stolen from Wedding. He even brought back plants he himself had raised from the original stolen plants!

IMMORTALITY.   The world's largest radio telescope is at Arecibo, Puerto Rico. It is owned by Cornell University. It is dedicated to searching for signals from intelligent life in outer space. Dr. Frank Drake is the director. He said, "I fear we have been making a dreadful mistake by not focusing all our searches . . . on the detection of signals of the immortals. For it is the immortals we will most likely discover." The headline for a newspaper article about the project ran like this: SCIENTIST THEORIZES EXISTENCE OF IMMORTAL BEINGS. There *are* immortal beings. That scientist is sur-

rounded by immortal beings. He *is* one! So are you and so am I.

INFINITY.   Thoreau said of Walden Pond, "I am thankful that this pond was made deep and pure for a symbol. While men believe in the infinite, some ponds will be thought to be bottomless."

INFINITY.   George Grella wrote an article on baseball in 1977. He pointed out that no other game opens rather than encloses space. All other games are limited by a defined field; but if you removed the outfield bleachers "the game could continue its space across the land, widening ever outward." He added, "Baseball not only extends space to infinity but also suspends and dissolves time." In baseball there are no clocks and, theoretically, the game could go on forever. It's hard to find illustrations for infinity and eternity. Baseball supplies one.

INFLATION.   You think inflation is bad. You think prices keep going up and never come down. But in Atlanta, Georgia, in 1864, a pair of women's shoes cost $500 and a woolen shawl $600. Between 1861 and 1863 flour went from $6.25 a barrel to $110.00 a barrel. You probably haven't priced a barrel of flour lately, but this really is not the worst of times.

IRONY.   In 1974, the Consumer Product Safety Commission brought out eighty thousand buttons to promote its campaign for safe toys. The buttons read "For Kid's Sake, Think Toy Safety." All eighty thousand buttons had to be recalled. It was found that they were unsafe! They had sharp edges and dangerous lead paint.

JESUS CHRIST.   James Vernon operates an inner city mission in Atlanta, Georgia, called "Jesus' Place." At one time, the mission had been forced to vacate the building it had been using and had no other. Vernon gave a ride to a homeless man in his battered van with "Jesus' Place" painted on the side. "Where is this Jesus' Place?" asked the man. "You're sitting in it," said Vernon. "Oh," said the man, "then Jesus is homeless, too!"

JESUS CHRIST.   We can measure the speed of light—186,284 miles per second. We can measure the intensity of light with our light meters, marking it in foot candles. We can never measure the Light of the World.

JESUS CHRIST.   Some years ago the holder of the light-weight boxing crown was a Puerto Rican named Esteban de Jesus. When he faced another contender the newspaper wrote a headline: "DE JESUS DEFENDS CROWN TODAY." The Lord Jesus Christ will never need to defend his crown. He did that long ago and proved that there are no real contenders.

JESUS CHRIST.   Patrick Henry is remembered more for his words than for his deeds. His speech "Give me liberty or give me death" was powerful when it was spoken and is powerful yet today. A colleague said, "He spoke as man was never known to speak before." Henry, however, barely passed his bar exam and had no great legal mind. Though he was twice governor of Virginia, he was not a great administrator. He is remembered for his words. Jesus is remembered both for his words and for his deeds.

KINDNESS.   Lee Atwater led the first election campaign for President George Bush. Later he died from brain cancer. He was known during the campaign as a very tough guy who played hardball politics. As illness overtook him, he said, "I used to say that the president might be kinder and gentler, but I wasn't going to be. How wrong I was. There is nothing more important in life than human beings and nothing sweeter than the human touch . . . . My illness helped me to see that what was missing in society is what was missing in me—a little heart and a lot of brotherhood."

LIFE.   Life involves taking certain risks. The risk of failure is taken by all

who succeed. But surely life is better for those who take such risks and do not opt for the safe and bland life described in verse by the Earl of Rochester:

Here lies a great and mighty king
Whose promise none relies on;
He never said a foolish thing,
Nor ever did a wise one.

LIFE.   The Edmonton (Canada) *Journal* published a cartoon by Uluschak showing a couple in front of the television set. She is saying to her husband, "Let's turn it off. He just said, 'And now the news' and began to cry."

LIFE AND DEATH.   In a historic cathedral in Jamaica there is a tomb with this epitaph: "Life teaches us how to die; death teaches us how to live." They are both good teachers. Unfortunately, we are such slow learners.

LUCK.   Don Marquis, who died in 1937, had a habit of writing his verse without punctuation and without capital letters but with a lot of insight and wisdom. Once he wrote the following:

now and then
there is a person born
who is so unlucky
that he runs into accidents
which started out to happen
to someone else

MONEY.   Some cynic said, "Remember the Golden Rule. Whoever has the gold makes the rules."

MONEY.   Silver was often connected with the pagan gods, and it was said that an enchantment could never be put on silver. It was said that it could be used as a talisman to increase the power of its object but had no power of its own. The silver bullet has become a proverb. If you believe silver has no power of its own, you have never carefully observed the tenacity of greed.

MONEY.   In Brickman's "The Small Society" comic strip, one character says,-

"Did you see the prices of new compacts?" The other replies, "Well, if you want economy you've got to pay for it."

MONEY.   Who was it said that only kisses and money could be so full of germs and still be so popular.

NATURE.   Richard Reeves wrote, "When I first saw Santa Barbara twenty-five years ago I thought it was what God would have done if he had the money." He went on to say that perhaps the Creator never intended for man to live along the Pacific coast, where they have to pipe the water in and can't pipe the bad air out, where threats of forest fires, mud slides, and earthquakes are commonplace. It is certainly true that sometimes man's work enhances nature. It is also true that often man ruins it.

NATURE.   Some of our best scientists have been trying for years to figure out a way to predict earthquakes. Now it appears that the lowly cockroach is able to do what we cannot. A study indicates that roaches become restless before an earthquake, but no one knows why. Perhaps such lowly creatures have sensing devices we do not understand and cannot duplicate.

THE NEW YEAR.   The date of January 1 for the beginning of a new year is comparatively modern. In ancient Egypt the new year was tied to the annual flooding of the Nile River. For the Jews it was a moveable feast, the date varying. In Babylon it was celebrated in March/April. Even in England the new year began in March until 1752. Whenever we celebrate the new year we must remember "every day is a new beginning, every morn is a world made new."

PARENTS.   In Billingsley's comic strip "Curtis" a little friend asks Curtis how the battle is going between him and his parents over music. Curtis says, "Dad and I came to an agreement. I agreed not to play my stereo loudly, and Dad has agreed not to put me up for adoption."

PAUL.   It is claimed that boxer Bruce Strauss has been knocked out more times than anybody else in the sport. He has been knocked out thirty-one times! Someone has translated Paul's little autobiography in Corinthians like this: "I am often knocked down but never knocked out!"

PEACE OF MIND.   How would you like to live in Happy, Texas? Yes, there is a town with such a name. What about Tranquility, New Jersey? Or maybe you'd like Pleasureville, Kentucky. Do you think the people in Happy, Texas, are really happier than those who live anywhere else? Do you think the people in Tranquility are really tranquil? Surely, peace of mind is not a city and state but a state of mind—and heart!

PERSEVERANCE.   Charles de Gaulle once said, "Difficulty attracts the man of character because it is in embracing it that he realizes himself."

PERSEVERANCE.   Sequoyah was a brilliant Cherokee Indian who devised an alphabet and a written language for the Cherokee. While he was doing this, his wife worked the fields. Weary of that, she burned their house down and destroyed all his work. Sequoyah had to begin all over again—and did. And on February 21, 1828, in New Echota, Georgia, the first Indian newspaper was published.

PESSIMISM.   Jeff MacNelly's "Shoe" comic strip often hits dead center the frustrations of life. Two men are sitting at a lunch counter. One says, "Here comes something we've all been expecting: the all-purpose warning label." And a man walks in carrying a sign: "The Surgeon General has determined we are all doomed."

PESSIMISM.   Two old friends met and fell to discussing the health of their wives. "And how is your wife getting along?" asked one. "Oh," said the other, "she complains of feeling better."

PESSIMISM.   Two men were discussing a third, an acquaintance of theirs. "He's not the man he used to be," said one. "No," said the other, "he never was."

PESSIMISM.   Andrei Gromyko was Soviet foreign minister for many years and negotiated with nine different U.S. secretaries of state. Often he would say, "There's an old Russian proverb." One of them was this: "Life is unbearable, but death is not so pleasant either."

PESSIMISM.   You miss a lot of wisdom if you don't read the funny papers. In "Animal Crackers," two characters are looking up at the stars. One asks, "Do you think there is intelligent life somewhere out there?" The other answers, "I don't ponder those questions. I'm having enough trouble convincing myself that we've got it here!"

POVERTY.   A few years ago, Robert Regent won the title of World's Champion Liar with this entry: "Folks think they have it tough these days, but we were so poor in our youth our parents couldn't afford to go window shopping."

PRAYER.   It's hard to believe, but it really is true. In Douglasville, Georgia, the First Baptist Church is on the corner of Church Street and Pray Street! Of course, every church, no matter its location, must be situated on Pray Street.

PRAYER.   Recently, police in a major U.S. city discovered 115 keys in the possession of a seventeen-year-old youth. He had keys to apartments, keys to stores, keys to vending machines. He didn't have the keys to the kingdom! And there are not 115 of them. We sing about one of them: "Prayer is the key that open's heaven's door."

PRAYER.   A scroll, has been found older than the Dead Sea scrolls. It is a tiny, silver scroll, and it contains a prayer—a prayer from the Bible. It's what might be called the Lord's Prayer of the Old Testament. "The Lord bless thee and keep thee; the Lord make his face shine upon thee and be gracious unto thee; the Lord lift up his countenance upon thee and give thee peace." Isn't it interesting that the oldest fragment of the Bible that we have contains a prayer!

PRAYER.   An epiphyte is an air plant. It needs no soil. It is sustained by the nourishment it receives from air, rainfall, and sunlight. The best known of such plants is the orchid, though there are many others. The vine is not among them. It was the vine Jesus chose to illustrate our relationship to him. Cut a branch off a vine, and it will die. If we forget to pray, if we cut ourselves off from God, we cut off the very source of spiritual nourishment and life.

PROCRASTINATION.   Shoe, the comic character, said, "I try to set aside one day each week and devote it entirely to my work." His friend remarks, "That's a good idea. What day of the week is that for you?" Shoe answers, "Tomorrow!"

RESURRECTION.   There is a legend which says that Thomas, still doubting the Resurrection of Christ, caused the tomb to be opened and found a bank of lilies and roses blooming where Christ's body had lain. Of course, we put no stock in such things, but we do say that a rose bloomed in our hearts when we came to believe in Christ's Resurrection.

RESURRECTION.   Paul Theroux went to visit the royal tombs in Vietnam. Old women hobbled from exhibit to exhibit, lighting candles to show the objects. When the guests left, they blew them out and remained in the darkness of the tombs where they lived and ate and slept. While Christianity is associated with a tomb, it is an empty tomb and an open tomb into which light streams. And Christians never saw themselves as living in the tomb but rather as going forth from the tomb to tell the good news.

SALT.   For centuries salt was the only thing with which to preserve meat, and so it was highly valued. Roman soldiers received part of their pay in an allowance with which to buy salt. And so we gained the expression "worth his salt." When Jesus said we were the salt of the earth, did he exaggerate? Are we, in that far different sense, worth our salt?

SATAN.   There used to be a superstition in some parts of Europe which held that the sign of the cross should always be made over bread left to rise. This will protect it from Satan's influence. We always do well to remember the cross, but protection from Satan's influence comes from cherishing the truth Jesus taught and not from some simple, physical gesture, however symbolic or meaningful.

SECOND COMING.   Some folk in Seattle are sure the end of the earth will come in the year 2000. Earthquakes, floods, wars, and tornadoes will devastate the earth, they say, by the year 2001. They plan to build an airship so that they can escape. Whatever of good or ill lies ahead, we need not worry about some human device to rescue us. In his own good time "the Lord shall descend from heaven with a shout" and "we which are alive shall be caught up to meet him in the air." We have nothing to fear, and the only preparation we need to make is to stay close to the Lord Jesus and keep our lives pure.

SELF-CENTERED.   Have you ever been to Center of the World, Ohio? It's at the intersection of State Route 82 and State Route 5. The town got its name in 1840 when a merchant put a sign over his store: "Center of the World." Of course, many are convinced that *their* home town is the center of the world. Such civic pride is harmless. It is when we think that *we* are the center of the world that there is trouble ahead.

SELF-CENTERED.   The popular dog Snoopy, in "Peanuts," is answering a question: "What do you mean, what good are dogs? Dogs are the best things ever invented! We're the highest form of life on this earth! The world revolves around

us! . . . Doesn't it?" We may act as if we think the world revolves around us—but in our hearts we have the same reservations as Snoopy.

SENSITIVITY.   Russell Baker wrote a column in which he characterized ours as the Numb Generation. Is it true? Is it true of Christians? Have we heard so much and seen so much that human suffering no longer pains us? If so, we are in great danger.

SIN.   In *Alice in Wonderland,* Alice meets a new word—uglification. "I never heard of 'uglification,' " Alice ventured to say. "What is it?" The Gryphon lifted up both its paws in surprise. "What! Never heard of uglifying! You know what to beautify is, I suppose? . . . Well then, if you don't know what to uglify is, you must be a simpleton.' " Of course, we all know what uglification is. It is what sin does to our lovely world, to our fair lives.

SIN.   One of the wise folk sayings of the Russian people is this: "Make peace with men, and make war with your sins." Unfortunately, we usually do just the opposite!

SIN.   If you took half a million viruses and laid them end to end, they would make a line no longer than the word *virus* itself. Three thousand million billion of them would weigh an ounce. But how much misery they bring to us. Sometimes they destroy us. Sin is like that. We view a sin as a little thing. We don't realize that little sin can cause enormous pain—and has the potential to destroy us.

SIN.   The cavalier attitude some take toward sin is reflected in a line from *Punch* magazine, written in 1876. "It's worse than wicked, my dear. It's vulgar." There are, indeed, those who regard a breach of etiquette as far more serious than a breach of ethics.

SIN.   Some of the strands of a spider's web are sticky and some are not. The sticky ones catch the insects, but the spider knows which strands can be walked on safely. Still, he must be careful. He can get stuck in his own web! Many a person has done the same!

SOUL. Why do we say "God bless you" when someone sneezes? Some say it comes from an ancient belief that we were getting rid of demons when we sneezed. Others say the ancients believed the soul leaves the body when we sneeze and only a blessing can bring it back!

SUFFERING. Napoleon Bonaparte once said, "It requires more courage to suffer than to die." If that's true, each of us has known some courageous souls, people who fulfilled the words of Romans 12 and were "patient in suffering."

THOUGHTS. One of Britain's oldest and most prestigious societies is the "Order of the Garter," dating from the fourteenth century when knighthood was in flower. Their motto is a good one for us all. The Latin words, translated, are "Evil to him who thinks evil."

TIME. In Browne's comic strip "Hi and Lois," the father is explaining to his son that there are twenty-four hours in a day and sixty minutes in an hour. Then he asks, "Do you know how long a minute is?" His son answers, "It depends. Do you mean a regular minute or WAIT a minute?"

TIME. Laurence G. Broadmoore of Tivoli, New York, decided a few years ago that he would live in the past. He heats his shop with a coal stove. He parts his hair in the middle and wears antique suits. His work is repairing player pianos. His home does have electricity, reluctantly; but he burns candles for light, hand pumps his water from a well, and the toilet facilities are in a little house in the back. Few people literally live in the past. But many mentally live in the past, while some live in the future. The wise ones live in the present.

TIME. Dennis the Menace was looking out the window on a rainy day and said, "Boy, I wish we could fast forward this day." It's a wish we all have sometimes made.

TIME. Lori Lynn Martin wrote these words: "There must be something wrong with my clocks because they don't seem to keep the same speed throughout the day. The hands move much too quickly if I have a deadline to meet, and they creep far too slowly when I am worrying!"

TIME. Someone said that leap year was badly mismanaged. Why prolong the already endless month of February. If we have to add an extra day, why not July 32?

TITHING. After the stock market fell on the Black Monday a few years ago, a man said to his pastor, "You've convinced me about tithing. I'll be by the office next week, and you can write me a check for $2,600. That's one tenth of what I lost in the stock market."

TRUST. The words *In God We Trust* have been on U.S. coins continuously since 1864 except for one interval. President Theodore Roosevelt had the motto eliminated. He said, "It seems to me eminently unwise to use it on coins, just as it would be to cheapen it to use on postage stamps and advertisements."

TRUTH. Sixty years ago, Miami was a boom town, and thousands rushed to Florida to invest their money. William Jennings Bryan said that Miami was the only city in the world where you can tell a lie at breakfast that will come true by evening.

TRUTH. Many have read the stories of the fictional detective Hercule Poirot. In one of Agatha Christie's stories someone says, "Oh, Mr. Poirot, if I could only believe you were on our side." Poirot answered, "I do not take sides. I am on the side only of the truth."

WORD OF GOD. The finance committee of the U.S. Senate printed 4,500 copies of a 452-page document with every single word crossed out! They had rejected a

House bill, but law requires that such a bill be printed to show that every word of it was rejected. So they printed *HR 3838 As Reported in the Senate, Part I,* and sold the copies for $17 each! Sometimes we'd like to cross out a word or two, even a verse or two, in the Bible. But we dare not!

WORSHIP.   The third most sacred city in Islam is Jerusalem, surpassed only by Mecca and Medina. It is said that one act of worship there is like a thousand acts of worship anywhere else. But we believe that worship depends upon the person, not the place; upon what he does, not where he does it.

WORSHIP.   Carlyle said, "The man who cannot wonder, who does not habitually wonder and worship . . . is but a pair of spectacles behind which there is no eye."

WORSHIP.   Isaac Watts wrote fifty-two books, twenty-nine of them on theology. But he is best remembered for his hymns. He wrote more than seven hundred, and even today the average modern hymnal will have twenty or more of his songs—276 years after they were written. When he died, he was reciting one of his favorites: "I'll Praise My Maker While I Breathe."

ACKNOWLEDGMENTS

Acknowledgment and gratitude are hereby expressed to the following for kind permission to reprint material from the books and periodicals listed below:

HARPERCOLLINS PUBLISHERS, INC.: Excerpts from Arnold H. Lowe, *When God Moves In,* © 1952, Harper & Brothers; Excerpts from Frederick Keller Stamm, *Seeing the Multitudes,* © 1943, Harper & Brothers; Excerpts from William Sloane Coffin, *Living the Truth in a World of Illusions,* © 1985, Harper & Row; Excerpts from Arnold H. Lowe, *Power for Life's Living,* © 1954, Harper & Brothers; Excerpts from Karl Barth, *Deliverance to the Captives,* © 1961, Harper & Brothers; Excerpts from Harry Emerson Fosdick, *Riverside Sermons,* © 1958, Harper & Brothers; Excerpts from Paul Scherer, *The Word God Sent,* © 1965, Harper & Row; Excerpts from Harold A. Bosley, *Sermons on the Psalms,* © 1956, Harper & Brothers; Excerpts from Paul Scherer, *The Place Where Thou Standest,* © 1942, Harper & Brothers; Frederick Keller Stamm, *The Conversations of Jesus,* © 1939, Harper & Brothers; Excerpts from Harold A. Bosley, *He Spoke to Them in Parables,* © 1963, Harper & Row; Excerpts from Robert E. Luccock, *If God Be for Us,* © 1954, Harper & Brothers; Excerpts from Halford E. Luccock, *Marching Off the Map,* © 1952, Harper & Brothers; Excerpts from Edgar DeWitt Jones, *Sermons I Love to Preach,* © 1953, Harper & Brothers; Excerpts from Nels F. S. Ferré, *God's New Age,* © 1962, Harper & Brothers; Excerpts from Samuel H. Miller, *Prayers for Daily Use,* © 1957, Harper & Brothers.

SUNDAY SCHOOL BOARD OF THE SOUTHERN BAPTIST CONVENTION: Excerpts from Don M. Aycock, "A Time for Rainbows," in *Proclaim,* January-March, 1988, pp. 20–21, © 1987, The Sunday School Board of the Southern Baptist Convention; Excerpts from Stephen Shoemaker, *Strength in Weakness,* pp. 126–137, © 1989, Broadman Press; Excerpts from David Chancey, "Reasons to Rejoice," in *Proclaim,* October-December, 1991, pp. 21–22, © 1991, The Sunday School Board of the Southern Baptist Convention; Excerpts from Alton H. McEachern, *The Lord's Presence,* pp. 9–13, © 1986, Broadman Press; Excerpts from Danny M. West, "When Should We Sit at the Lord's Table," in *Proclaim,* April-June, 1988, pp. 29–30, © 1988, The Sunday School Board of the Southern Baptist Convention; Excerpts from Gary Hardin, "The Wonder of Christ's Resurrection," in *Proclaim,* January-March, 1990, p. 31, © 1989, The Sunday School Board of the Southern Baptist Convention; Excerpts from James W. Cox, "A Revolutionary Truth," in *Discipleship Training,* February, 1991, pp. 34–35, © 1990, The Sunday School Board of the Southern Baptist Convention; Excerpts from Brian Harbour, "The Emotions of Christmas," in *Proclaim,* October-December, 1991, pp. 6–7, © 1991, The Sunday School Board of the Southern Baptist Convention; Excerpts from R. Keith Parks, "Vision of Going," in *Proclaim,* April-June, 1988, pp. 28–29, © 1988, The Sunday School Board of the Southern Baptist Convention; Excerpts from James W. Cox, *Surprised by God,* pp. 94–102, © 1979, Broadman Press.

C.S.S. PUBLISHING COMPANY: Selections from *Children's Sermon Service, Plus!,* "Make a Prayer List," for Dec. 15, 1991; "No Beginning or End," for Feb. 2, 1992.

ABINGDON PRESS: Excerpts from Mark Trotter, "Wait and See", in *What Are You Waiting For,* © 1992, Abingdon Press.

INDEX OF CONTRIBUTORS

SERMON TITLE INDEX

(Children's stories and sermons are identified as **cs***; sermon suggestions as* **ss***)*

SCRIPTURAL INDEX

INDEX OF PRAYERS

INDEX OF MATERIALS USEFUL AS CHILDREN'S STORIES AND SERMONS NOT INCLUDED IN SECTION X

INDEX OF MATERIALS USEFUL FOR SMALL GROUPS

TOPICAL INDEX